Teach...
Inspire...
Lead...

MW01044737

Research & Education Association

The Best Teachers' Test Preparation for the

TExES
Mathematics
(Field 135)
8–12 Test

Mel Friedman, M.S.

For updates to the test or this book visit: www.REA.com/TExES/Math135/NS.htm

Research & Education Association

61 Ethel Road West
Piscataway, New Jersey 08854
E-mail: info@rea.com

Texas TExES Mathematics 8–12 (135) Test

Published 2011 by Research & Education Association, Inc.

Copyright © 2010 by Research & Education Association, Inc.
All rights reserved. No part of this book may be reproduced
in any form without permission of the publisher.

Printed in the United States of America

Library of Congress Control Number 2009933879

ISBN-13: 978-0-7386-0646-0
ISBN-10: 0-7386-0646-4

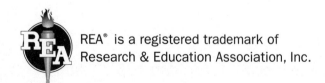

REA® is a registered trademark of
Research & Education Association, Inc.

About Research & Education Association

Founded in 1959, Research & Education Association is dedicated to publishing the finest and most effective educational materials—including software, study guides, and test preps—for students in middle school, high school, college, graduate school, and beyond.

REA's Test Preparation series includes books and software for all academic levels in almost all disciplines. Research & Education Association publishes test preps for students who have not yet entered high school, as well as for high school students preparing to enter college. Students from countries around the world seeking to attend college in the United States will find the assistance they need in REA's publications. For college students seeking advanced degrees, REA publishes test preps for many major graduate school admission examinations in a wide variety of disciplines, including engineering, law, and medicine. Students at every level, in every field, with every ambition can find what they are looking for among REA's publications.

REA's practice tests are always based upon the most recently administered exams and include every type of question that you can expect on the actual exams.

REA's publications and educational materials are highly regarded and continually receive an unprecedented amount of praise from professionals, instructors, librarians, parents, and students. Our authors are as diverse as the fields represented in the books we publish. They are well-known in their respective disciplines and serve on the faculties of prestigious high schools, colleges, and universities throughout the United States and Canada.

Today, REA's wide-ranging catalog is a leading resource for teachers, students, and professionals.

We invite you to visit us at *www.rea.com* to find out how REA is making the world smarter.

Acknowledgments

We would like to thank REA's Pam Weston, Publisher, for setting the quality standards for production integrity and managing the publication to completion; Larry Kling, Vice President, Editorial, for his editorial direction; Kathleen Casey, Senior Editor, for project management and preflight editorial review; Diane Goldschmidt, Senior Editor, for post-production quality assurance; Christine Saul, Senior Graphic Artist, for cover design; and Maureen Mulligan, Graphic Artist, for typesetting revisions.

We also gratefully acknowledge the team at Macmillan Publishing Solutions for typesetting, Anne McGowan for copyediting, and Stephanie Reymann for indexing the manuscript.

About the Author

Author Mel Friedman, M.S., is a former classroom teacher at the high school and university levels. He has also worked as a test-item writer for Educational Testing Service and ACT, Inc.

Contributing Authors

Stephen Reiss, M.B.A., is the founder and owner of the Math Magician and the Reiss SAT Seminars. He also tutors students in the math portions of the SAT, SAT II and the ACT. Reiss serves as a consultant to San Diego area high schools, teaching his SAT seminars on campus.

Adel Arshaghi, M.S., has taught mathematics at both the high school and college level. He has been a frequent contributor to mathematics books.

CONTENTS

INTRODUCTION

CHAPTER 1

CHAPTER 2

CHAPTER 3

CHAPTER 4

CHAPTER 5

CHAPTER 6

CHAPTER 7

CHAPTER 8

CHAPTER 9

CHAPTER 10

DIFFERENTIAL AND INTEGRAL CALCULUS 129

CHAPTER 11

MEASUREMENT IN GEOMETRY 163

CHAPTER 12

AXIOMS, PROPERTIES, AND THEOREMS OF EUCLIDEAN GEOMETRY 179

CHAPTER 13

APPLICATIONS OF EUCLIDEAN GEOMETRY TO CIRCLES AND COMPOSITE FIGURES 201

CHAPTER 14

CHAPTER 15

CHAPTER 16

CHAPTER 17

CHAPTER 18

CHAPTER 19

CHAPTER 20

PRACTICE TEST 1   357

PRACTICE TEST 2   389

INDEX   423

TExES

Mathematics Test

Introduction

Introduction

About This Book

REA's *The Best Teachers' Test Preparation for the TExES 135 Mathematics 8-12 Test* is a comprehensive guide designed to assist you in preparing to take this TExES test, the purpose of which is to ensure that you have the prerequisite content and professional knowledge necessary for an entry-level position in Texas public schools.

To help you to succeed in this important step toward your teaching career in Texas schools, this test guide features:

- An accurate and complete overview of the *TExES 135 Mathematics 8-12* Test

- The information you need to know about the exam

- A targeted review of each domain

- Tips and strategies for successfully completing standardized tests

- Diagnostic tools to identify areas of strength and weakness

- Two full-length, true-to-format practice tests based on the most recently administered *TExES 135 Mathematics 8-12* Test

- Detailed explanations for each answer on the practice tests. These allow you to identify correct answers and understand not only why they are correct but also why the other answer choices are incorrect.

When creating this test prep, the authors and editors considered the most recent test administrations and professional standards. They also researched information from the Texas Department of Education, professional journals, textbooks, and educators. The result is the best TExES test preparation materials based on the latest information available.

About the TExES 135 Mathematics 8-12 Test

The purpose of the TExES 135 Mathematics 8-12 Test is to assess the knowledge and skills of prospective Texas teachers in the areas of mathematics. The Mathematics 8–12 test will contain 80 scorable multiple-choice items and approximately 10 nonscorable items. Your final scaled score will be based only on scorable items. The nonscorable multiple-choice items are included for the purpose of pilot-testing of proposed new questions. These pilot questions do not count toward your score. However, they are not identified on the test either.

There will be four answer choices for each multiple-choice question. Answers will be marked on a separate answer sheet.

A Definitions/Formula Page will be provided for you.

Calculators. If you wish to use a calculator you must bring your own to the test site. However, it is very important that you bring a calculator that is listed with the brands and models seen on the TExES registration bulletin. The approved list of calculator brands and models could change. The test administration promises that you will be notified if such a change occurs. All of the calculators on the approved list are graphing calculators, which perform all the operations of typical scientific calculators. As some test questions are designed to be solved with a graphing calculator, it makes good sense to bring a graphing calculator with you to the test site. However, you will not be allowed to share calculators. If there is a change in the approved calculator brands and models, the test administrator website promises to notify you of that change.

The testing staff will clear your calculator's memory both before and after the test.

What Does the Test Cover?

The following table lists the domains and competencies used as the basis for the TExES 135 Mathematics 8-12 Test and the approximate percentage of questions in each domain. A thorough review of all the specific germane skills is the focus of this book.

Test Framework

Domain	Topic	Competencies	% of test
I	Number Concepts	001-003	14%
II	Patterns & Algebra	004-010	33%
III	Geometry & Measurement	0011-014	19%
IV	Probability & Statistics	015-019	14%
V	Mathematical Processes & Perspectives	018-019	10%
VI	Mathematical Learning Instruction, and Assessment	020-021	10%

Who Administers the Test?

The Texas Education Agency has contracted with Educational Testing Service (ETS) to assist in the development and administration of the TExES.

For additional information you can contact:
ETS-Texas Educator Certification Program
PO Box 6001
Princeton, NJ 08541-6001
Telephone: 1-800-205-2626 (U.S., U.S. Territories, and Canada)
1-609-771-7393 (all other locations)
Hours: Monday-Friday 8:00 a.m.-5:00 p.m. Central time
Fax: 1-973-735-0156 or 1-866-484-5860
E-mail: texes-excet_inquiries@ets.org

Test Administration

The TExES tests are administered six times during the testing year. Each test date has morning and afternoon test sessions. Each session is five hours long.

Do I Pay a Registration Fee?

To take the TExES, you must pay a registration fee. For information about the fees, log on to http://www.texes.ets.org/texes/AboutTheTest/.

How Is the TExES 135 Mathematics 8-12 Test Scored?

Test results are reported as **scaled scores** in a range from 100 to 300. Your **total** scaled score shows how you performed on the test as a whole and whether you passed the test. The scale score allows comparison among any version of the same test. The raw scores cannot be compared from one version of a test to another. You receive one point for each correct response and no points for each incorrect response. Most tests will also include nonscorable questions. Therefore the total number of questions reported on your score report is usually less than the total number of questions that you saw on the test. The nonscorable questions will not be used in the calculation of your score.

When Will I Receive My Score Report, and What Will It Look Like?

Approximately four weeks after the test, you will receive a score report in the mail. The report will say if you have passed the test and will include:

- a total test scaled score that is reported on a scale of 100–300. The minimum passing score is a scaled score of 240. This score represents the minimum level of competency required to be an entry-level educator in this field in Texas public schools.
- your performance in the major content domains of the test and in the specific content competencies of the test. Be aware that this information may be less reliable because it may be based on fewer test questions.

Unofficial test scores will be posted on the Internet on the score report mailing date of each test administration. You can find information about receiving your unofficial scores, your score scale, and other score report topics on the SBEC Web site at www.sbec.state.tx.us.

Can I Retake the Test?

Retaking a Test. If you wish to retake the paper-based test, you may do so at any subsequent paper-based test administration. You must wait 60 days to retake the test online. Please consult the TExES Website at http://texes.ets.org/texes/ for information about test registration. The TExES website also includes information regarding test retakes and score reports.

When Should I Start Studying?

It is never too early to start studying for the TExES 135 Mathematics 8-12 Test. The earlier you begin, the more time you will have to sharpen your skills. Do not procrastinate! Cramming is not an effective way to study because it does not allow you the time you need to think about the content, review the domains, and take the practice tests.

What Do the Review Sections Cover?

The targeted review in this book is designed to help you sharpen the mathematical skills you need to approach the TExES 135 Mathematics 8-12 Test, as well as provide strategies for attacking the questions.

Each competency area included in the TExES 135 Mathematics 8-12 test is examined in a separate chapter. The skills required for all domains are extensively discussed to optimize your understanding of what the examination covers.

Your schooling has taught you most of the information you need to answer the questions on the test. The review sections in this book are designed to help you fit the information you have acquired into the domains and competencies specified on the TExES. Going over your class notes and textbooks together with the reviews provided here will give you an excellent springboard for passing the examination.

Studying for the TExES 135 Mathematics 8-12 Test

Choose the time and place for studying that works best for you. Some people set aside a certain number of hours every morning to study, while others prefer to study at night before going to sleep. Other people study off and on during the day—for instance, while waiting for a bus or during a lunch break. Only you can determine when and where your study time will be most effective. Be consistent and use your time efficiently. Work out a study routine and stick to it.

When you take the practice tests, simulate the conditions of the actual test as closely as possible. Turn off your television and radio, and sit down at a table in a quiet room, free from distraction. On completing a practice test, score it and thoroughly review the explanations to the questions you answered incorrectly; however, do not review too much at any one time. Concentrate on one problem area at a time by reviewing the question and explanation, and by studying the review in this guide until you are confident that you have mastered the material.

Keep track of your scores so you can gauge your progress and discover general weaknesses in particular sections. Give extra attention to the reviews that cover your areas of difficulty, so you can build your skills in those areas. Many have found the use of study or note cards very helpful for this review.

How Can I Use My Study Time Efficiently?

The following study schedule allows for thorough preparation for the TExES 135 Mathematics 8-12 Test. The course of study presented here is seven weeks, but you can condense or expand the timeline to suit your personal schedule. It is vital that you adhere to a structured plan and set aside ample time each day to study. The more time you devote to studying, the more prepared and confident you will be on the day of the test. Don't wait until the last minute to begin your studying!

Study Schedule

Week 1	After reading this first chapter to understand the format and content of this exam, take the first practice test. The scores will indicate your strengths and weaknesses. Make sure you simulate real exam conditions when you take the test. Afterward, score it and review the explanations, especially for questions you answered incorrectly. Review the explanations for the questions you missed, and begin to review the appropriate chapter sections.
Week 2	Continue your review of the explanations for the questions you missed, and review the appropriate chapter sections. Useful study techniques include highlighting key terms and information, taking notes as you review each section, and putting new terms and information on note cards to help retain the information.
Weeks 3 and 4	Reread all your note cards, refresh your understanding of the competencies and skills included in the exam, review your college textbooks, review the appropriate chapters in this book, and read over notes you took in your college classes. This is also the time to consider any other supplementary materials that your counselor or the TExES Department of Education suggests. Review the department's Website at **www.texes.ets.org.**
Week 5	Begin to condense your notes and findings. A structured list of important skills and concepts, based on your note cards and the TExES 135 Mathematics 8-12 domains and competencies, will help you thoroughly review for the test. Review the answers and explanations for any questions you missed.
Week 6	Have someone quiz you using the note cards you created. Take the second practice test, adhering to the time limits and simulated test day conditions. Again review the explanations for any questions that you missed along with the related material in the book that is related to them.
Week 7	Using all your study materials, continue to review areas of weakness revealed by your score on the second practice test.

Test-Taking Tips

Although you may not be familiar with tests like the TExES, this book will acquaint you with this type of exam and help alleviate your test-taking anxieties. By following the seven suggestions listed here, you can become more relaxed about taking the TExES, as well as other tests.

Tip 1. Become comfortable with the format of the TExES. When you are practicing, stay calm and pace yourself. After simulating the test only once, you will boost your chances of doing well, and you will be able to sit down for the actual TExES with much more confidence.

Tip 2. Read all the possible answers. Just because you think you have found the correct response, do not automatically assume that it is the best answer. Read through each choice to be sure that you are not making a mistake by jumping to conclusions.

Tip 3. Use the process of elimination. Go through each answer to a question and eliminate as many of the answer choices as possible. If you can eliminate two answer choices, you have given yourself a better chance of getting the item correct, because only two choices are left from which to make your guess. Do not leave an answer blank; it is better to guess than not to answer a question on the TExES test because you will not be penalized for incorrect answers.

Tip 4. Place a question mark in your answer booklet next to the answers you guessed, and then recheck them later if you have time.

Tip 5. Work quickly and steadily. You will have a total of five hours to complete the test. Taking the practice tests in this book will help you learn to budget your time.

Tip 6. Learn the directions and format of the test. This will not only save time but also will help you avoid anxiety (and the mistakes caused by being anxious).

Tip 7. When taking the multiple-choice portion of the test, be sure that the answer oval you fill in corresponds to the number of the question in the test booklet. The multiple-choice test is graded by machine, and marking one wrong answer can throw off your answer key and your score. Be extremely careful.

The Day of the Test

Before the Test

On the morning of the test, be sure to dress comfortably so you are not distracted by being too hot or too cold while taking the test. Plan to arrive at the test center early. This will allow you to collect your thoughts and relax before the test and will also spare you the anguish that comes with rushing. You should check your TExES Registration Bulletin to find out what time to arrive at the center.

What to Bring

Before you leave for the test center, make sure that you have your admission ticket. Your admission ticket lists your test selection, test site, test date, and reporting time. See the Test Selection *http: www.texes.ets.org/faq.*

You must also bring personal identification that includes one piece of current, government-issued identification, in the name in which you registered, bearing a recent photograph and signature and one additional piece of identification (with or without a photograph). If the name on your identification differs from the name in which you are registered, you must bring official verification of the change (e.g., marriage certificate, court order). Be sure to check the TExES website for any updates or changes in the identification policy.

You must bring several sharpened No. 2 pencils with erasers, because none will be provided at the test center. No mechanical pencils or mechanical erasers may be used. If you like, you can wear a watch to the test center. However, you cannot wear one that makes noise, because it might disturb the other test takers. Dictionaries, textbooks, notebooks, cell phones, beepers, PDAs, scratch paper, listening and recording devices, briefcases, or packages are not permitted. Drinking, smoking, and eating during the test are prohibited. Very especially, remember that cell phones are not allowed in the test center. Using or having a cell phone in your possession in the test center may be grounds for dismissal.

Security Measures

As part of the identity verification process, your thumbprint, or your photograph or videotape may be taken at the test site. A refusal to participate would lead to dismissal with no refund of test fees. This is in addition to the requirement that you must present acceptable and valid identification. It is important that you visit the testing website for the latest updates and security requirements and updates at http://texes.ets. org/texes/dayOfTheTest/#idreqiden.

Late Arrival Policy

You must report to the test site by the time stipulated. If you are late for a test session you will not be admitted.

During the Test

Any time that you take for restroom breaks is considered part of the available testing time, and additional testing time will not be granted. Procedures will be followed to maintain test security. Once you enter the test center, follow all the rules and instructions given by the test supervisor. If you do not, you risk being dismissed from the test and having your score canceled.

Once the test begins, mark only one answer per question, completely erase unwanted answers and marks, and fill in answers darkly and neatly.

After the Test

When you finish your test, hand in your materials and you will be dismissed. Then, go home and relax—you deserve it!

Chapter 1

The Real Number System

Welcome to Chapter 1. In this chapter, we will review the following topics for real numbers:

(a) Categories
(b) Properties
(c) Equivalent representations
(d) Algebraic models

Number Categories

Natural numbers, which we will designate as N, consist of the set of counting numbers.

Thus, N consists of 1, 2, 3, 4, ..., commonly written as $N = \{1, 2, 3, 4, ...\}$.

Whole numbers, designated as W, consist of all the natural numbers, plus the number zero. Thus, $W = \{0, 1, 2, 3, ...\}$

The set of numbers that consists of all the numbers in W, plus all the negatives of the counting numbers, are called the **integers**. Thus, $I = \{....-3, -2, -1, 0, 1, 2, 3, ...\}$.

A rational number, designated as Q, is defined as a quotient of two integers $\dfrac{a}{b}$, in which b is not zero.

Examples of rational numbers are $\dfrac{1}{3}$, $-\dfrac{2}{5}$, and $\dfrac{12}{7}$. So we know that any fraction qualifies as a rational number. A mixed fraction would also be rational, since we can write it as an improper fraction.

Percents, terminating decimals, and repeating decimals are also rational numbers because they can be written as fractions. As examples, $0.3\% = \dfrac{0.3}{100} = \dfrac{3}{1000}$, $0.55 = \dfrac{55}{100}$ or $\dfrac{11}{20}$, and $0.\overline{45} = \dfrac{5}{11}$.

Note that any integer is also a rational number, since we can simply write it as a fraction with a 1 in the denominator. As examples, $13 = \dfrac{13}{1}$, $-4 = \dfrac{-4}{1}$, and $0 = \dfrac{0}{1}$.

Some square roots and cube roots are also rational. Since $\sqrt{25} = 5$, $-\sqrt[3]{8} = -2$, and $\sqrt{\dfrac{4}{49}} = \dfrac{2}{7}$, each of $\sqrt{25}$, $-\sqrt[3]{8}$, and $\sqrt{\dfrac{4}{49}}$ are rational.

Irrational numbers, designated as S, are real numbers that cannot be written as a quotient of two integers. Examples of such numbers are $-\sqrt{5}, \sqrt[3]{12}, \pi$, and $1.04004000400004,\dots$.

Note that even though there is a pattern for $1.04004000400004,\dots$, it is not a <u>repeating</u> pattern.

All real numbers can be classified as either rational or irrational. Letting R represent the set of real numbers, $R = Q \cup S$. Real numbers can be assigned positions on the number line, as shown below. All numbers to the right of zero are positive, while all numbers to the left of zero are negative. *Zero is neither positive nor negative.* Figure 1.1 illustrates a number line.

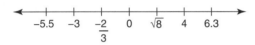

Figure 1.1

EXAMPLE 1

Which of the following ten numbers are irrational?

$$0, 10, \pi, -\sqrt{80}, 11\%, 2.\overline{5}, 0.616616661\dots, \frac{20}{3},$$

$$-9.345, \text{ and } \sqrt[3]{\frac{1}{27}}$$

SOLUTION

The irrational numbers are $\pi, -\sqrt{80}$ and $0.616616661\dots$. These numbers cannot be written as a quotient of two integers.

EXAMPLE 2

Which of the following six numbers are integers?

$$-7, 0.8\%, \frac{15}{5}, \frac{11}{4}, -\sqrt{100}, \text{ and } 2.001$$

SOLUTION

$-7, \frac{15}{5}$, and $-\sqrt{100}$ are integers, since they can be written as a fraction with 1 as a denominator. Note that $\frac{15}{5} = \frac{3}{1}$.

Number Properties

Here are the most common properties that govern real numbers:

(a) For any two numbers x and y, $x + y = y + x$. This is called the **Commutative Property of Addition**. For example, $6 + 8 = 8 + 6$.

(b) For any two numbers x and y, $x \bullet y = y \bullet x$. This is called the **Commutative Property of Multiplication**. For example, $4 \bullet 8 = 8 \bullet 4$

(c) For any three numbers x, y, and z, $x + (y + z) = (x + y) + z$. This is called the **Associative Property of Addition**. For example, $5 + (2 + 9) = (5 + 2) + 9$.

(d) For any three numbers x, y, and z, $x \bullet (y \bullet z) = (x \bullet y) \bullet z$. This is called the **Associative Property of Multiplication**. For example, $3 \bullet (10 \bullet 2) = (3 \bullet 10) \bullet 2$.

(e) For any three numbers x, y, and z, $x \bullet (y + z) = x \bullet y + x \bullet z$. This is called the **Distributive Property of Multiplication over Addition**. For example, $6 \bullet (8 + 12) = 6 \bullet 8 + 6 \bullet 12$.

Equivalent Representations

Decimals, fractions, and percents are common equivalent ways to represent rational numbers. As examples, $\frac{3}{4} = 0.75 = 75\%$, $\frac{7}{5} = 1.4 = 140\%$, and $\frac{1}{3} = 0.\overline{3} = 33.\overline{3}\%$. However, we recognize that this process also applies to integers. For example, $3 = \frac{3}{1} = 3.0 = 300\%$. To change from a fraction (or integer) to a decimal number, divide the denominator into the numerator. To change the decimal number to a percent, move the decimal point two places to the right, adding zeros if necessary, then add the percent sign.

The four basic operations of addition, subtraction, multiplication, and division apply to all real numbers, with the exception of division by zero. Another commonly used operation is **exponentiation**, which represents repeated multiplication. Thus, $5 \times 5 \times 5$ can be written as 5^3, and $\frac{1}{2} \cdot \frac{1}{2}$ can be written as $\left(\frac{1}{2}\right)^2$. Exponentiation also applies to negative numbers, so that $\left(\frac{2}{3}\right)^{-2} = \frac{1}{\left(\frac{2}{3}\right)^2}$ and $(-3)^5 = (-3)(-3)(-3)(-3)(-3)$.

EXAMPLE 3

Which property of numbers is illustrated by $(-5 + 6) + 13 = -5 + (6 + 13)$?

SOLUTION

This is the Associative Property of Addition, in which $x = -5$, $y = 6$, and $z = 13$. The numbers -5, 6, and 13 appear in the same order; however they are grouped differently.

EXAMPLE 4

Which two properties of numbers are illustrated by the following sequence?

$(9 \bullet 2) \bullet 5 = 9 \bullet (2 \bullet 5) = 9 \bullet (5 \bullet 2)$

SOLUTION

The statement $(9 \bullet 2) \bullet 5 = 9 \bullet (2 \bullet 5)$ illustrates the Associative Law of Multiplication. The numbers 9, 2, and 5 appear in the same order but are grouped differently. The statement $9 \bullet (2 \bullet 5) = 9 \bullet (5 \bullet 2)$ illustrates the Commutative Law of Multiplication. The numbers 2 and 5 switch positions.

EXAMPLE 5

What is the value of $2^{-2} + \left(-\frac{1}{3}\right)^3$?

SOLUTION

$2^{-2} = \frac{1}{2^2} = \frac{1}{4}$ and $\left(-\frac{1}{3}\right)^3 = -\frac{1}{27}$. Their sum is $\frac{23}{108}$.

Scientific Notation

Scientific notation is an equivalent way to write a number. It is commonly used to write very small or very large numbers, but may be used for any integer or decimal number. This notation uses a number between 1 and 10, multiplied by an integer power of 10. For example 56,000,000 is written as 5.6×10^7. Likewise, 0.000821 is written as 8.21×10^{-4}.

EXAMPLE 6

What is the scientific notation for the number 0.046?

SOLUTION

First move the decimal point so that it is positioned between 4 and 6. The number now reads as 4.6. The next and final step is to multiply 4.6 by a power of 10 so that the value becomes 0.046. Since we must move the decimal point two places to the left when going from 4.6 to 0.046, the power of 10 needed is -2. The final answer is 4.6×10^{-2}.

EXAMPLE 7

What is the scientific notation for the decimal equivalent of $\frac{8}{3}$?

SOLUTION

Change $\frac{8}{3}$ to its decimal equivalent of $2.\overline{6}$. This number lies between 1 and 10, so its scientific notation is $2.\overline{6} \times 10^0$. Remember that when a nonzero number is raised to the zero power, it has a value of 1.

Algebraic Models

In algebra, the letters that are often used to replace numbers are called **variables.**

The most commonly used variables are $w, x, y,$ and z. Let's consider the basic number operations as they apply to variables.

The sum of x and y is written as $x + y$ or $y + x$.

The difference of two numbers represents a subtraction. The expressions "w subtracted from x", "x less w", "x subtracted by w", and "x minus w" are all written as $x - w$.

The product of y and z means to multiply these two variables. This is written as yz or zy. The quotient of w and y means to divide w by y. This is written as $w \div y$ or $\dfrac{w}{y}$.

Variables may also be raised to a power. Thus the "square of y" is written as y^2 and the "cube of z" is written as z^3. If the power is a fraction, then we are seeking a root of the number. Thus, "w raised to the $\dfrac{1}{2}$ power" is equivalent to the "square root of w" and is written as $\sqrt{w}$. Likewise, "x raised to the $\dfrac{1}{3}$ power" is equivalent to the "cube root of x" and is written as $\sqrt[3]{x}$.

Quiz for Chapter 1

1. The following three steps are applied to a number x. *a.* It is squared. *b.* The result of part *a* is subtracted from 100. *c.* The result of part *b* is raised to the power of $\dfrac{1}{2}$. How does this number appear after step *c*?

    (A) $\sqrt{x^2 + 100}$ (C) $\sqrt{100 - x^2}$

    (B) $100 - \sqrt{x^2}$ (D) $\sqrt{(100 - x)^2}$

2. What is the scientific notation for the number $\dfrac{31}{2}$?

    (A) 1.55×10^1 (C) 0.155×10^2

    (B) 15.5×10^0 (D) 155×10^{-1}

3. Which one of the following is an integer, but is not a natural number?

    (A) $\dfrac{1}{4}$ (C) 12

    (B) -8 (D) -0.52

4. Roberta needed to multiply 12 by 4, then multiply that answer by 2. She decided to first multiply 4 by 2 to get 8. Then she multiplied 12 by 8 to get 96. Which one of the following conclusions is valid concerning the steps that Roberta took to solve this problem?

    (A) Her answer is wrong because she should have first multiplied 12 by 4.

    (B) Her answer is wrong but she did follow a correct sequence of steps.

    (C) Her answer is right and she used the Associative Property of Multiplication.

    (D) Her answer is right and she used the Commutative Property of Multiplication.

5. Marty claimed that all negative numbers are less than -1. Which one of the following responses is most appropriate?

    (A) His claim is completely correct.

    (B) His claim is wrong because some numbers less than -1 are irrational.

(C) His claim is wrong because there are negative fractions between -1 and 0.

(D) His claim is wrong because a negative number always lies to the right of 0 on the number line.

6. Which one of the following is undefined?

(A) 12×0 (C) $0 + 12$

(B) $0 \div 12$ (D) $12 \div 0$

7. How is the expression "the product of w and x subtracted by y" written algebraically?

(A) $wx - y$ (C) $(w - y)(x)$

(B) $y - wx$ (D) $(w)(x - y)$

8. Tommy is about to evaluate the expression $(-4)(6 + 9)$. He decides to use the Distributive Property of Multiplication over Addition? Which one of the following illustrates this approach.

(A) $(-4)(15)$ (C) $(-4)(6) + 9$

(B) $(-4)(9 + 6)$ (D) $(-4)(6) + (-4)(9)$

9. Sherry is asked to simplify the expression $\left(-\dfrac{2}{5}\right)^{-3}$.

She wants to first change the expression so that it has a positive exponent. Which one of the following expressions should she evaluate in order to arrive at the correct answer?

(A) $\left(-\dfrac{2}{5}\right)^{3}$ (C) $\dfrac{1}{\left(\dfrac{2}{5}\right)^{3}}$

(B) $\dfrac{1}{\left(-\dfrac{2}{5}\right)^{3}}$ (D) $\dfrac{1}{\left(-\dfrac{5}{2}\right)^{3}}$

10. Consider the following list of six numbers. $-\dfrac{3}{19}$, $\sqrt[3]{64}$, $0.51515151....$, $-0.34344344434444....$, 1.732, and $\sqrt{\dfrac{16}{9}}$. How many of these are rational?

(A) 2   (C) 4

(B) 3   (D) 5

Quiz for Chapter 1
SOLUTIONS

1. **(C)**

By squaring x, it becomes x^2. Subtracting x^2 from 100 becomes $100 - x^2$. Then, raising this expression to the $\dfrac{1}{2}$ power becomes $(100 - x^2)^{1/2}$, which is equivalent to $\sqrt{100 - x^2}$.

2. **(A)**

Change $\dfrac{31}{2}$ to 15.5. In order to change 15.5 to scientific notation, move the decimal point between the 1 and 5 to get 1.55. Since the decimal point will be moved one place to the right in order to go from 1.55 to 15.5, the power of 10 needed is 1. The correct answer is 1.55×10^{1}.

3. (B)

Any negative integer, such as -8, is not a natural number.

4. (C)

Roberta is using the Associative Property of Multiplication in which $(12 \bullet 4) \bullet 2 = 12 \bullet (4 \bullet 2)$.

5. (C)

Marty is incorrect because there are numbers such as $-\dfrac{2}{3}$ which are greater than -1.

6. (D)

Division in which the denominator is zero is undefined.

7. (A)

The product of w and x is written as wx. This product is subtracted <u>by</u> y, so the answer becomes $wx - y$.

8. (D)

In order to use the Distributive Property of Multiplication over Addition, Tommy should multiply -4 by 6, then multiply -4 by 9, then add these two products.

9. (B)

The result of any number raised to a negative exponent is equivalent to 1 divided by that same number raised to the positive value of that exponent. Sherry should evaluate $\dfrac{1}{\left(-\dfrac{2}{5}\right)^{3}}$.

10. (D)

The only <u>irrational</u> number in this group is $-0.34344344434444\ldots$. Note that $\sqrt[3]{64} = 4$ and $\sqrt{\dfrac{16}{9}} = \dfrac{4}{3}$. Both of these numbers are rational.

The Complex Number System

Welcome to Chapter 2. In this chapter, we will review the following topics for complex numbers:

(a) Arithmetic operations

(b) Solutions to quadratic equations

(c) Equivalent representations

(d) Powers and roots

(e) Vectors

Arithmetic Operations

A **complex number** is one that can be written in the form $a + bi$. Each of a and b represents a real number and $i = \sqrt{-1}$. Remember that real numbers include both rational and irrational numbers. Also, either a or b or both may be zero. Here are five examples of complex numbers.

$4 + 2i, -1 + \dfrac{1}{2}i, 1.5 - \sqrt{2}i, 18, 6i$. Note that 18 may be written as $18 + 0i$, and that $6i$ may be written as $0 + 6i$.

Categories of Complex Numbers

Recall that the set of real numbers has been designated as R. Let C represent the set of complex numbers.

Since any real number can be written in complex number form we conclude that R is a subset of C. Here is a tree diagram that summarizes the various categories of numbers that we have discussed to this point.

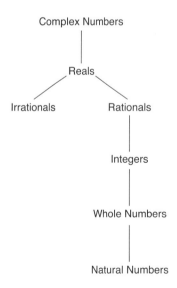

We can determine three identities that are directly related to i.

(a) $i^2 = (\sqrt{-1})^2 = -1$, (b) $i^3 = (i^2)(i) = -1i = -i$, (c) $i^4 = (i^2)(i^2) = (-1)(-1) = 1$.

pattern repeats in a cycle of 4, so that $i = i^5 = i^9 = i^{13} = \ldots$, $i^2 = i^6 = i^{10} = i^{14} = \ldots$, $i^3 = i^7 = i^{11} = i^{15} = \ldots$, and $i^4 = i^8 = i^{12} = i^{16} = \ldots$.

EXAMPLE 1

What is the simplified expression for $-5i^3 - 3(6 + i)$?

SOLUTION

We can use the Distributive Property of Multiplication over Addition to $-5i^3 - 3(6 + i) = (-5)(-i) - 18 - 3i = -18 + 2i$

EXAMPLE 2

What is the simplified expression for $(4 + i)(-3 + 7i)$?

SOLUTION

Multiply these binomials just as you would with real numbers. $(4 + i)(-3 + 7i) = -12 + 28i - 3i + 7i^2 = -19 + 25i$. Note that $7i^2 = (7)(-1)$.

 A **conjugate** is a representation of a complex number the sign of whose imaginary part has been switched. (The conjugate of $-2 + 3i$, denoted as $\overline{-2 + 3i}$. is written as $-2 - 3i$.) For example, the conjugate of a complex number $a + bi$, denoted as $\overline{a + bi}$, is defined as $a - bi$.

 Conjugates are used to perform a division between two complex numbers.

EXAMPLE 3

What is the simplified expression for $(5 + 2i) \div (1 - 3i)$?

SOLUTION

Rewrite the example as $\dfrac{5 + 2i}{1 - 3i}$. Now multiply both numerator and denominator by the conjugate of $1 - 3i$, which is $1 + 3i$. Then $\dfrac{5 + 2i}{1 - 3i} \bullet \dfrac{1 + 3i}{1 + 3i} = \dfrac{5 + 15i + 2i + 6i^2}{1 - 9i^2}$

$= \dfrac{-1 + 17i}{10}$ The final answer can also be written as $-\dfrac{1}{10} + \dfrac{17}{10}i$.

Solutions to Quadratic Equations

In some quadratic equations containing a single variable, there are no solutions in the real number system. However, there will be complex number solutions.

EXAMPLE 4

What are the values of x in the equation $2x^2 - 3x + 6 = 0$?

SOLUTION

Using the quadratic formula, $x = \dfrac{3 \pm \sqrt{9 - (4)(2)(6)}}{4}$

$= \dfrac{3 \pm i\sqrt{39}}{4}$.

Equivalent Representations

Each complex number of the form $a + bi$ consists of two parts. The number a is called the real part and the number bi is called the imaginary part. Most complex numbers have nonzero values for *a* and *b*, but we have seen examples in which one of *a* or *b* is zero. As examples, $18 = 18 + 0i$ and $6i = 0 + 6i$.

Graphing Complex Numbers

Complex numbers can be illustrated using the *xy*-coordinate plane. In this setting, the *x*-axis represents the real part of the complex number, while the *y*-axis represents the imaginary part. Let *A*, *B*, *C*, *D*, *E*, and *F* represent the following complex numbers: $A = 3 + 0i = 3$, $B = 4 + 2i$, $C = -2 + 5i$, $D = -3 - i$, $E = 0 - 4i = -4i$, and $F = 5 - 6i$.

Figure 2.1 shows how these complex numbers are plotted in the *xy*-coordinate plane. (This is called the complex plane when complex numbers are used.)

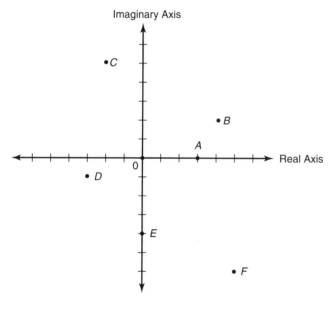

Figure 2.1

Similar to the plotting of points in the real *xy*-coordinate plane, we can also write the coordinates of points in the complex plane. This is accomplished by just writing the ordered pair using only the real number values of the complex number. For example, since $A = 3 + 0i$, we can write the coordinates of *A* as $(3, 0)$. Likewise, since $C = -2 + 5i$, we can write the coordinates of *C* as $(-2, 5)$.

NOTE:

The **magnitude of a complex number** is defined as the distance between its corresponding point on the complex plane and $(0, 0)$, which is the origin. For any complex number $a + bi$, its magnitude is calculated as $\sqrt{a^2 + b^2}$. Symbolically, the magnitude of $a + bi$ is represented as $|a + bi|$. For example, the magnitude of $5 - 6i$ is $\sqrt{5^2 + (-6)^2} = \sqrt{61}$. Likewise, the magnitude of $-3 - i$, represented as $|-3 - i|$, is $\sqrt{(-3)^2 + (-1)^2} = \sqrt{10}$. As a special case, note that the magnitude of $0 + 9i$ is $\sqrt{0^2 + 9^2} = 9$. This is certainly no surprise!

Any complex number written as $a + bi$ is considered to be in rectangular form. (Another name for rectangular is *Cartesian*.) Another popular form for expressing a complex number is called its *polar form*. Suppose the complex number $Z = a + bi$ is graphed, as shown below in Figure 2.2

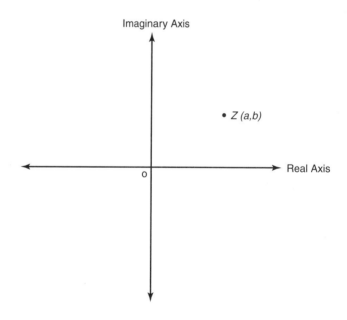

Figure 2.2

Let's now connect the origin to the point associated with the complex number Z. Then we complete a right triangle by drawing a perpendicular segment from (a, b) to the real axis. Use θ as the angle formed by the hypotenuse of this triangle and the segment along the real axis. The hypotenuse, labeled as r, represents the magnitude of Z, since $r = \sqrt{a^2 + b^2}$. Figure 2.3 illustrates the concepts of this paragraph.

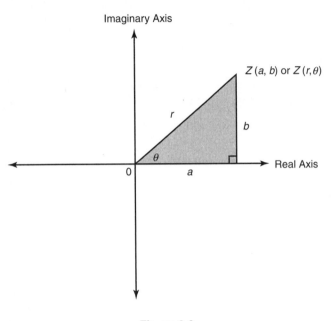

Figure 2.3

Then a represents the horizontal segment, and b represents the vertical segment. From your study of trigonometry, you recall that $\cos\theta = \dfrac{a}{r}$ and that $\sin\theta = \dfrac{b}{r}$. This implies that $a = r\cos\theta$ and that $b = r\sin\theta$. Thus, we can write $Z = r\cos\theta + (r\sin\theta)i = r(\cos\theta + i\sin\theta)$. This is called the polar form of the complex number Z. Also, the angle represented by θ is called the argument.

Notice that the point associated with the complex number Z can be labeled using its rectangular coordinates (a, b) or its polar coordinates (r, θ).

Polar coordinates are simply defined as the magnitude of the complex number (hypotenuse) and the angle associated with the right triangle formed by the real axis and the perpendicular segment from the point affiliated with the complex number. Let's discuss the situations in which $\theta > 90°$.

If $90° < \theta < 180°$, then $\sin\theta$ is positive and $\cos\theta$ is negative.

If $180° < \theta < 270°$, then $\sin\theta$ and $\cos\theta$ are both negative.

If $270° < \theta < 360°$, then $\sin\theta$ is negative and $\cos\theta$ is positive.

EXAMPLE 5

What is the polar form of the complex number $Z = -2 + 4i$?

SOLUTION

We will use a diagram, as shown below. Note that for brevity, we have labeled the imaginary and real axes as simply yi and x. Henceforth, we will use these abbreviations.

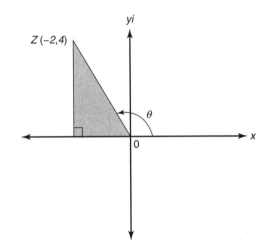

We calculate r (the hypotenuse) using $r = \sqrt{(-2)^2 + 4^2} = \sqrt{20} = 2\sqrt{5}$. Also, $\theta = \tan^{-1}\left(\dfrac{4}{-2}\right) \approx 117°$. Note that another value for $\tan^{-1}\left(\dfrac{4}{-2}\right)$ is approximately 297°: however, since our answer is confined to the second quadrant, we can only use the value of 117°. The final answer is $Z = 2\sqrt{5}(\cos 117° + i\sin 117°)$.

EXAMPLE 6

Referring back to Example 5, what are the polar coordinates for Z?

SOLUTION

The polar coordinates are in the form (r, θ), which become $(2\sqrt{5}, 117°)$.

Two comments are needed at this point.

1. The value of θ may also be expressed in radians. For this book, all angles will be expressed in degrees. In order to convert to radian measure, you would multiply the answer in degrees by $\dfrac{\pi}{180°}$. For example, $60° = (60°)\left(\dfrac{\pi}{180°}\right) = \dfrac{\pi}{3}$ radians.

2. In Example 5, we found the value of θ by using the inverse tangent function. The value of θ can also be determined by using either the inverse cosine function or the inverse sine function. In Example 5,
$$\cos\theta = \frac{-2}{2\sqrt{5}} = -\frac{1}{\sqrt{5}} \quad \text{and} \quad \sin\theta = \frac{4}{2\sqrt{5}} = \frac{2}{\sqrt{5}}.$$
Then $\theta = \cos^{-1}\left(-\dfrac{1}{\sqrt{5}}\right) = \sin^{-1}\left(\dfrac{2}{\sqrt{5}}\right) \approx 117°$.

EXAMPLE 7

> What are the polar form and the polar coordinates of the number $Z = \sqrt{3} - 3i$?

SOLUTION

Let's use a diagram, in which Z is located in the fourth quadrant.

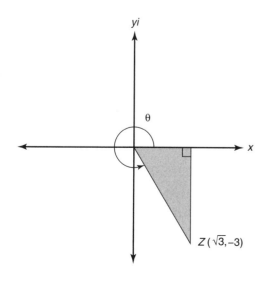

$Z(\sqrt{3}, -3)$

First determine r, which is $\sqrt{(\sqrt{3})^2 + (3)^2} = \sqrt{12} = 2\sqrt{3}$. Using the cosine ratio, $\theta = \cos^{-1}\left(\dfrac{\sqrt{3}}{2\sqrt{3}}\right) = \cos^{-1}\left(\dfrac{1}{2}\right) = 300°$. The answer becomes $Z = 2\sqrt{3}(\cos 300° + i\sin 300°)$. Once again, you must be careful to only use the fourth quadrant angle when finding the value of $\cos^{-1}\left(\dfrac{1}{2}\right)$. The polar coordinates are $(2\sqrt{3}, 300°)$.

EXAMPLE 8

> What is the polar form of the number $Z = -1 - 2.5i$?

SOLUTION

In this example, Z is located in the third quadrant, as illustrated in the following diagram.

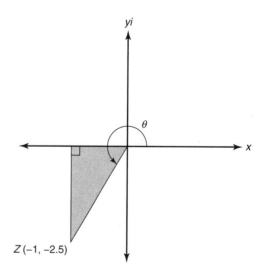

$Z(-1, -2.5)$

We determine that $r = \sqrt{(-1)^2 + (-2.5)^2} = \sqrt{7.25}$. Using the tangent ratio, $\theta = \tan^{-1}\left(\dfrac{-2.5}{-1}\right) \approx 248°$. The answer is $\sqrt{7.25}(\cos 248° + i\sin 248°)$.

EXAMPLE 9

What is the rectangular form of the complex number whose polar form is given as $Z = 5(\cos 200° + i\sin 200°)$?

SOLUTION

For this example, Z is located in the third quadrant, as shown below.

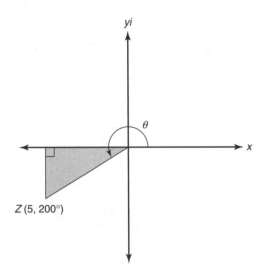

Z (5, 200°)

We need to determine the values of a and b in the rectangular form of $Z = a + bi$. We know that $a = r\cos\theta$ and $b = r\sin\theta$. By substitution, $a = (5)(\cos 200°) \approx -4.70$ and $b = (5)(\sin 200°) \approx -1.71$. Our answer is $Z = -4.70 - 1.71i$.

Notice that in Example 8, each of a and b is negative; this is expected because Z is located in the third quadrant. Also, note that we rounded off a and b to the nearest hundredth.

EXAMPLE 10

What is the rectangular form for the complex number $Z = \sqrt{10}(\cos 35° + i\sin 35°)$?

SOLUTION

Let's do this example without the diagram. Th value of a is given by $\sqrt{10}\cos 35° \approx 2.59$ and the valu of b is given by $\sqrt{10}\sin 35° \approx 1.81$. The answer i $Z = 2.59 + 1.81$.

Now you realize that we could have also solve Example 8 without a diagram. Whenever we are con verting from polar form to rectangular form, we jus perform the required arithmetic steps. However, a dia gram is recommended when converting from rectangu lar form to polar form. The only exception to this las statement would be if the rectangular form contained zero value for either a or b, as explained in the next tw examples.

EXAMPLE 11

What is the polar form of the number $Z = 0 + 12i$?

SOLUTION

The point associated with this Z value lies on th positive yi axis. This means that $\theta = 90°$. Instantly, w know that $r = 12$, since $\sqrt{0^2 + 12^2} = 12$. The answer i $Z = 12(\cos 90° + i\sin 90°)$.

EXAMPLE 12

What is the polar form of the number $Z = -5 + 0i$?

SOLUTION

The corresponding point for Z lies on the negativ x axis, so $\theta = 180°$. Also, $r = \sqrt{(-5)^2 + 0^2} = 5$. Th answer is $Z = 5(\cos 180° + i\sin 180°)$.

Arithmetic Operations with Complex Numbers

Just as with the rectangular form of complex number the operations of addition, subtraction, multiplication and division can be applied to complex numbers that are expressed in polar form. Surprisingly, the addition and subtraction of complex numbers in polar form is more complicated (and beyond the scope of this book) than these arithmetic operations for complex numbers in rectangular form. However, the multiplication and division operations are very compact for complex numbers in polar form.

Let $Z_1 = r_1(\cos\theta_1 + i\sin\theta_1)$ and $Z_2 = r_2(\cos\theta_2 + i\sin\theta_2)$ represent two complex numbers in polar form. Then the product of Z_1 and Z_2, namely $(Z_1)(Z_2)$, equals $(r_1)(r_2)[\cos(\theta_1 + \theta_2) + i\sin(\theta_1 + \theta_2)]$. Similarly, the quotient of Z_1 and Z_2, namely $\dfrac{Z_1}{Z_2}$, equals

$$\frac{r_1}{r_2}[\cos(\theta_1 - \theta_2) + i\sin(\theta_1 - \theta_2)].$$

EXAMPLE 13

What is the simplest polar form for $4(\cos 27° + i\sin 27°) \cdot 13(\cos 100° + i\sin 100°)$?

SOLUTION

We just multiply the r values and add the θ values. The answer is $52(\cos 127° + i\sin 127°)$.

EXAMPLE 14

What is the simplest polar form for $44(\cos 250° + i\sin 250°) \div 8(\cos 170° + i\sin 170°)$?

SOLUTION

Just divide the r values and subtract the θ values. The answer is $5.5(\cos 80° + i\sin 80°)$.

Powers and Roots

One of the most important benefits in the use of the polar form of a complex number is the ability to calculate a power of a complex number in simplest form. If $Z = r(\cos\theta + i\sin\theta)$, then $Z^n = r^n(\cos n\theta + i\sin n\theta)$. This means that given a complex number in polar form, there is a quick method for evaluating a power of that number. This rule is called **DeMoivre's Theorem**. It states that in order to take a power of a complex number in polar form, raise r to that power and multiply that power by the angle measure.

EXAMPLE 15

What is the simplest polar form for $[3(\cos 40° + i\sin 40°)]^6$?

SOLUTION

By DeMoivre's Theorem, the answer is $3^6(\cos 240° + i\sin 240°)$.

In Example 15, we could have written 729 in place of 3^6. If you are determining the value of the power of a complex number given in rectangular form, first change the number to polar form. Then apply DeMoivre's Theorem in order to calculate the answer in either polar or rectangular form.

EXAMPLE 16

What is the simplest polar form for $(3 - 2i)^6$?

SOLUTION

Using polar form, the value of r is $\sqrt{(3)^2 + (-2)^2} = \sqrt{13}$. The value of θ is $\tan^{-1}\dfrac{-2}{3} \approx 326°$. Since $(\sqrt{13})^6 = 2197$, the answer is $2197(\cos 1956° + i\sin 1956°) = 2197(\cos 158° + i\sin 158°)$.

If we had to provide the rectangular form for the answer to Example 16, the final step would have been approximately $-2035 + 828i$.

Roots of Complex Numbers

A variation of DeMoivre's Theorem is applied when we are seeking roots of a complex number. There are n distinct nth roots of any complex number. This means that there are two square roots, three cube roots, four fourth roots, etc.

Let $Z = r(\cos\theta + i\,\sin\theta)$. Then the n distinct nth roots can be found by the formula $Z_k = (\sqrt[n]{r})\left[\cos\left(\dfrac{\theta}{n} + \dfrac{360°k}{n}\right) + i\sin\left(\dfrac{\theta}{n} + \dfrac{360°k}{n}\right)\right]$, in which $k = 0, 1, 2, 3, \ldots, n-1$.

EXAMPLE 17

> What are the three cube roots of $(10)(\cos 165° + i\sin 165°)$?

SOLUTION

The three cube roots are in the form $\sqrt[3]{10}$, $\left[\cos\left(\dfrac{165°}{3} + \dfrac{360°k}{3}\right) + i\sin\left(\dfrac{165°}{3} + \dfrac{360°k}{3}\right)\right]$ with $k = 0, 1, 2$. This simplifies to $\sqrt[3]{10}(\cos 55° + i\sin 55°)$, $\sqrt[3]{10}(\cos 175° + i\sin 175°)$, and $\sqrt[3]{10}(\cos 295° + i\sin 295°)$.

EXAMPLE 18

> What are the five fifth roots of $2\sqrt{3} + 2i$?

SOLUTION

In polar form, we find that $r^2 = (2\sqrt{3})^2 + 2^2 = 16$, so $r = 4$ and $\theta = \tan^{-1}\left(\dfrac{2}{2\sqrt{3}}\right) = 30°$. The five roots are in the form $\sqrt[5]{4}\left[\cos\left(\dfrac{30°}{5} + \dfrac{360°k}{5}\right) + i\sin\left(\dfrac{30°}{5} + \dfrac{360°k}{5}\right)\right]$, with $k = 0, 1, 2, 3, 4$. This simplifies to $\sqrt[5]{4}(\cos 6°$

$+ i\sin 6°)$, $\sqrt[5]{4}(\cos 78° + i\sin 78°)$, $\sqrt[5]{4}(\cos 150° + i\sin 150°)$, $\sqrt[5]{4}(\cos 222° + i\sin 222°)$, and $\sqrt[5]{4}(\cos 294° + i\sin 294°)$.

EXAMPLE 19

> What are the four fourth roots of 12?

SOLUTION

In polar form, this number is represented as $12(\cos 0° + i\sin 0°)$. The four fourth roots are in the form $\sqrt[4]{12}\left[\cos\left(\dfrac{0°}{4} + \dfrac{360°k}{4}\right) + i\sin\left(\dfrac{0°}{4} + \dfrac{360°k}{4}\right)\right]$, with $k = 0, 1, 2, 3$. This simplifies to $\sqrt[4]{12}(\cos 0° + i\sin 0°)$, $\sqrt[4]{12}(\cos 90° + i\sin 90°)$, $\sqrt[4]{12}(\cos 180° + i\sin 180°)$, and $\sqrt[4]{12}(\cos 270° + i\sin 270°)$.

Vectors

We now return to the xy-coordinate plane of real numbers for our discussion of vectors. A **vector** is a line segment with direction. It has an initial point and a terminal point and its length is the distance between these two points. The length of any vector is called its **magnitude**.

Geometrically, a vector appears the same as a **ray**, but you recall that a ray has an initial point and direction. (no finite length). Thus, vector $\overrightarrow{AB}$ has an initial point at A and a terminal point at B. The symbol $\overrightarrow{AB}$ is used regardless of the actual direction of the vector. *Two vectors are equivalent if they have the same direction and the same magnitude.* This means that equivalent vectors must be parallel to each other.

Figure 2.4 shows three equivalent representations of the vector $\overrightarrow{AB}$.

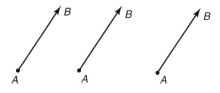

Figure 2.4

Two vectors are opposite if they have the same magnitude, are parallel, but face in opposite directions. Figure 2.5 shows a pair of opposite vectors, $\overrightarrow{CD}$ and $\overrightarrow{DC}$.

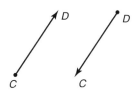

Figure 2.5

In the xy-coordinate plane, the standard position of a vector is such that the initial point is the origin. Figure 2.6 shows vectors $\overrightarrow{EF}$ and $\overrightarrow{GH}$ in standard position.

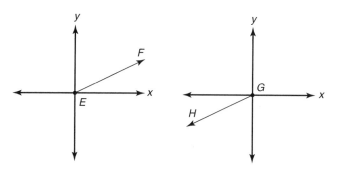

Figure 2.6

Unit Vectors

The *unit vector* **i** is a vector of magnitude 1 in the direction of the *x*-axis. The *unit vector* **j** is a vector of magnitude 1 in the direction of the *y*-axis. Figure 2.7 shows both of these unit vectors. Note that **i** is in standard position, whereas **j** is not in standard position.

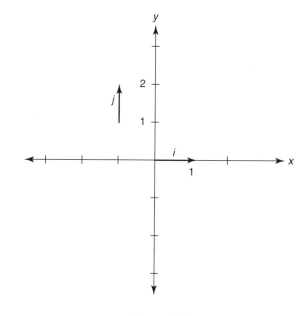

Figure 2.7

If vector $\overrightarrow{AB}$ has its initial point at (x_1, y_1) and its terminal point at (x_2, y_2), then it can be expressed as $a\mathbf{i} + b\mathbf{j}$, where $a = x_2 - x_1$ and $b = y_2 - y_1$. Furthermore, the magnitude of $\overrightarrow{AB}$, written as $|\overrightarrow{AB}|$, is the value of $\sqrt{a^2 + b^2}$. If the vector $\overrightarrow{AB}$ is in standard position, then $(x_1, y_1) = (0,0)$. In this case, we can represent $\overrightarrow{AB}$ as $x_2\mathbf{i} + y_2\mathbf{j}$.

EXAMPLE 20

For vector $\overrightarrow{KL}$, point K is located at $(-2, 3)$ and point L is located at $(1, 4)$. How is $\overrightarrow{KL}$ represented using the form $a\mathbf{i} + b\mathbf{j}$?

SOLUTION

$a = 1 - (-2) = 3$ and $b = 4 - 3 = 1$. Thus $\overrightarrow{KL} = 3\mathbf{i} + \mathbf{j}$

EXAMPLE 21

In Example 20, what is the value of $|\overrightarrow{KL}|$?

SOLUTION

$|\overrightarrow{KL}| = \sqrt{(1-(-2))^2 + (4-3)^2} = \sqrt{10}$.

EXAMPLE 22

Vector $\overrightarrow{MN} = 4\mathbf{i} + 2\mathbf{j}$, with its initial point at (0, 0). If vector $\overrightarrow{PQ} = c\mathbf{i} + d\mathbf{j}$, has its initial point at (0, 0), and is opposite to vector $\overrightarrow{MN}$ what are the values of c and d?

SOLUTION

Simply take the opposites of the values of a and b. Then $\overrightarrow{PQ} = -4\mathbf{i} - 2\mathbf{j}$.

EXAMPLE 23

Vector $\overrightarrow{RS}$ is equivalent to vector $\overrightarrow{MN}$ in Example 22. If the terminal point of $\overrightarrow{RS}$ is (1, −5), what is its initial point?

SOLUTION

Let (x, y) represent the initial point of $\overrightarrow{RS}$. Then $1 - x = 4$ and $-5 - y = 2$. So, $x = -3$ and $y = -7$. The initial point of $\overrightarrow{RS}$ is $(-3, -7)$.

The rules for adding or subtracting vectors are very straightforward. If $\overrightarrow{AB} = a\mathbf{i} + b\mathbf{j}$ and $\overrightarrow{CD} = c\mathbf{i} + d\mathbf{j}$, then $\overrightarrow{AB} \pm \overrightarrow{CD} = (a \pm c)\mathbf{i} + (b \pm d)\mathbf{j}$.

In the world of vectors, numbers are often called **scalars**. If $\overrightarrow{EF} = ka\mathbf{i} + kb\mathbf{j}$, for some number k, then $\overrightarrow{EF}$ is called a scalar multiple of $\overrightarrow{AB}$. Whenever one

vector is a scalar multiple of the other, the vectors must be parallel. As an example, if $\overrightarrow{AB} = 2\mathbf{i} - 5\mathbf{j}$ and $\overrightarrow{EF} = 6\mathbf{i} - 15\mathbf{j}$, then $k = 3$, so these are parallel vectors. Note that k need not be an integer. If k is negative, then these vectors are still parallel but they face in opposite directions. As an example, the vector $-4\mathbf{i} + 10\mathbf{j}$ is parallel to $\overrightarrow{AB}$, but faces in the opposite direction. (However, it is <u>not</u> an opposite vector).

EXAMPLE 24

What is the sum of $-\mathbf{i} + 6\mathbf{j}$ and $-7\mathbf{i} + 2\mathbf{j}$?

SOLUTION

The answer is $(-1 - 7)\mathbf{i} + (6 + 2)\mathbf{j} = -8\mathbf{i} + 8\mathbf{j}$.

A graphical representation of the sum of the two vectors from Example 24 is shown in Figure 2.8 below. The resulting vector is the diagonal of a parallelogram in which the two given vectors represent adjacent sides.

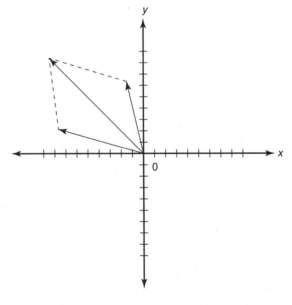

Figure 2.8

EXAMPLE 25

Given the vector $\overrightarrow{KL} = 8\mathbf{i} - 14\mathbf{j}$, write the vector that is parallel to $\overrightarrow{KL}$, faces in the opposite direction, and has a magnitude of 2.5 times that of $\overrightarrow{KL}$.

SOLUTION

Simply multiply each scalar (number) part of $\overrightarrow{KL}$ by -2.5. The answer is $-20\mathbf{i} + 35\mathbf{j}$.

Dot Product of Vectors

The multiplication of $\overrightarrow{AB}$ and $\overrightarrow{CD}$ is called the **dot product** of these vectors, and is represented as $\overrightarrow{AB} \infty \overrightarrow{CD}$. Its value is expressed as $ac + bd$. Note that this product is a scalar, <u>not</u> a vector.

If θ is the angle between vectors $\overrightarrow{AB}$ and $\overrightarrow{CD}$,

then $\cos\theta = \dfrac{\overrightarrow{AB} \bullet \overrightarrow{CD}}{|\overrightarrow{AB}| \bullet |\overrightarrow{CD}|} = \dfrac{ac + bd}{|\overrightarrow{AB}| \bullet |\overrightarrow{CD}|}$

Figure 2.9 shows vectors $\overrightarrow{AB}$ and $\overrightarrow{CD}$, with the angle θ between them. Note that it is always possible to move one or both vectors in order that they share a common initial point. (Refer back to equivalent vectors.)

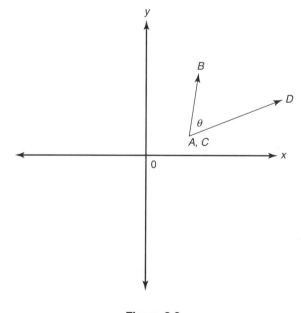

Figure 2.9

Projection Vectors

The projection of vector $\overrightarrow{AB}$ onto vector $\overrightarrow{CD}$ is found as follows. Move $\overrightarrow{AB}$ so that $\overrightarrow{AB}$ and $\overrightarrow{CD}$ share a common initial point. Drop a perpendicular segment from point B onto $\overrightarrow{CD}$. Label the intersection point E. The segment $\overrightarrow{AE}$, which is the same as $\overrightarrow{CE}$, is the projection. Also, the length of this projection, commonly named as $\mathsf{Proj}_{\overrightarrow{CD}}\,\overrightarrow{AB}$, is equal to $|\overrightarrow{AB}| \bullet \cos\theta$

$= \dfrac{\overrightarrow{AB} \bullet \overrightarrow{CD}}{|\overrightarrow{CD}|} = \dfrac{ac + bd}{\sqrt{c^2 + d^2}}$. If point E lies beyond $\overrightarrow{CD}$, simply extend $\overrightarrow{CD}$ until point E lies on this vector. Also, if θ is an obtuse angle, $\mathsf{Proj}_B\,\overrightarrow{A}$ will be negative. Figure 2.10 illustrates the projection of vector $\overrightarrow{AB}$ onto vector $\overrightarrow{CD}$.

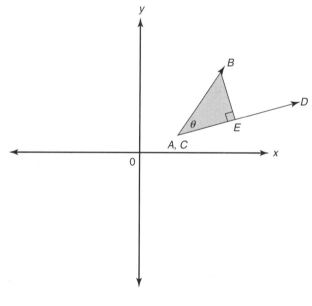

Figure 2.10

EXAMPLE 26

What is the value of $(-2\mathbf{i} + 3\mathbf{j}) \bullet (7\mathbf{i} - 5\mathbf{j})$?

SOLUTION

This is the dot product of the vectors. Its value is $(-2)(7) + (3)(-5) = -29$.

EXAMPLE 27

Referring to Example 26, what is the value in degrees of the angle between these vectors?

SOLUTION

$|-2\mathbf{i} + 3\mathbf{j}| = \sqrt{13}$ and $|7\mathbf{i} - 5\mathbf{j}| = \sqrt{74}$. Then $\cos\theta = \dfrac{-29}{(\sqrt{13})(\sqrt{74})} \approx -0.9350$. Thus, $\theta \approx 159°$. Note that if $\cos\theta$ is negative, then θ lies in the second quadrant.

A graphical representation of the vectors from Examples 26 and 27 is shown below in Figure 2.11.

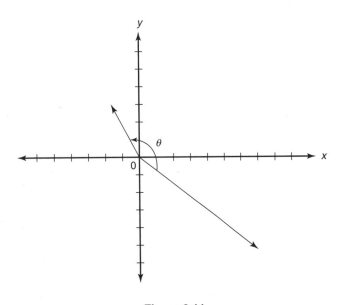

Figure 2.11

EXAMPLE 28

Referring to the results of Examples 26 and 27, what is the value of the projection of $-2\mathbf{i} + 3\mathbf{j}$ onto $7\mathbf{i} - 5\mathbf{j}$?

SOLUTION

The value of the projection is $|-2\mathbf{i} + 3\mathbf{j}| \bullet \cos\theta = (\sqrt{13})(-0.9350) \approx -3.37$.

EXAMPLE 29

What is the value of the projection of $7\mathbf{i} - 5\mathbf{j}$ onto $-2\mathbf{i} + 3\mathbf{j}$?

SOLUTION

The answer is $|7\mathbf{i} - 5\mathbf{j}| \bullet \cos\theta = (\sqrt{74})(-0.9350) \approx -8.04$

Relationship between a Vector and Its Unit Vector Representation

The last concept to discuss concerning vectors is the representation of a unit vector in the direction of a given vector $\overrightarrow{AB}$. We have already seen that a unit vector parallel to the *x*-axis is written as $\mathbf{i} = 1\mathbf{i}$. Similarly, $\mathbf{j} = 1\mathbf{j}$ represents a unit vector parallel to the *y*-axis. If $\overrightarrow{AB} = a\mathbf{i} + b\mathbf{j}$, then a unit vector in the direction of $\overrightarrow{AB}$

is $\dfrac{a\mathbf{i} + b\mathbf{j}}{|\overrightarrow{AB}|} = \dfrac{a\mathbf{i} + b\mathbf{j}}{\sqrt{a^2 + b^2}}$.

EXAMPLE 30

Express in simplest form a unit vector in the direction of $-8\mathbf{i} - \mathbf{j}$?

SOLUTION

Since $|-8\mathbf{i} - \mathbf{j}| = \sqrt{65}$, the answer is $-\dfrac{8}{\sqrt{65}}\mathbf{i}$ $-\dfrac{1}{\sqrt{65}}\mathbf{j}$. An equally acceptable answer is $\dfrac{-8\mathbf{i} - \mathbf{j}}{\sqrt{65}}$.

Quiz for Chapter 2

1. What is the simplified expression for $(1 + 5i) \div (-2 + 7i)$?

    (A) $\dfrac{33}{53} + \dfrac{17}{53}i$ (C) $\dfrac{11}{15} + \dfrac{17}{45}i$

    (B) $\dfrac{33}{53} - \dfrac{17}{53}i$ (D) $\dfrac{11}{15} - \dfrac{17}{45}i$

2. Which one of the following is equal to $-i^{35}$?

    (A) i (C) 1

    (B) $-i$ (D) -1

3. Which one of the following complex numbers is located on the positive imaginary axis?

    (A) -4 (C) 4

    (B) $2i$ (D) $-2i$

4. Which one of the following complex numbers has a magnitude of $\sqrt{106}$?

    (A) $100 + 6i$ (C) $10 + 36i$

    (B) $53 + 2i$ (D) $9 + 5i$

5. The polar coordinates of a complex number are given by $(8, 210°)$. What are the rectangular coordinates? (nearest hundredth)

    (A) $(-4, -6.93)$ (C) $(-3, -7.42)$

    (B) $(-6.93, -4)$ (D) $(-7.42, -3)$

6. What is the polar form of the complex number $6 - 4i$?

    (A) $2\sqrt{13}(\cos 214° + i\sin 214°)$

    (B) $4\sqrt{13}(\cos 295° + i\sin 295°)$

    (C) $2\sqrt{13}(\cos 326° + i\sin 326°)$

    (D) $4\sqrt{13}(\cos 245° + i\sin 245°)$

7. What is the simplest polar form for the value of $50(\cos 200° + i\sin 200°)$ divided by $10(\cos 20° + i\sin 20°)$

    (A) $40(\cos 180° + i\sin 180°)$

    (B) $40(\cos 10° + i\sin 10°)$

    (C) $5(\cos 180° + i\sin 180°)$

    (D) $5(\cos 10° + i\sin 10°)$

8. What is the simplest polar form for the expression $\left[4(\cos 15° + i\sin 15°)\right]^5$?

    (A) $1024(\cos 75° + i\sin 75°)$

    (B) $1024(\cos 20° + i\sin 20°)$

    (C) $20(\cos 75° + i\sin 75°)$

    (D) $20(\cos 20° + i\sin 20°)$

9. What is the rectangular form for $(-2 + i)^8$? (nearest integers)

    (A) $557 - 284i$ (C) $455 - 450i$

    (B) $-506 + 367i$ (D) $404 + 533i$

10. Which one of the following is not a fourth root of $16(\cos 128° + i\sin 128°)$?

    (A) $2(\cos 302° + i\sin 302°)$

    (B) $2(\cos 212° + i\sin 212°)$

    (C) $2(\cos 112° + i\sin 112°)$

    (D) $2(\cos 32° + i\sin 32°)$

11. In polar form, which one of the following is a cube root of -8 ?

    (A) $2(\cos 90° + i \sin 90°)$

    (B) $2(\cos 150° + i \sin 150°)$

    (C) $2(\cos 210° + i \sin 210°)$

    (D) $2(\cos 300° + i \sin 300°)$

12. For vector $\overrightarrow{MN}$, point M is located at $(7, -2)$ and point N is located at $(2, 10)$. Which one of the following statements is <u>completely</u> correct?

    (A) $\overrightarrow{MN} = 9\mathbf{i} + 8\mathbf{j}$ and $\left|\overrightarrow{MN}\right| = \sqrt{145}$.

    (B) $\overrightarrow{MN} = -9\mathbf{i} - 8\mathbf{j}$ and $\left|\overrightarrow{MN}\right| = \sqrt{145}$.

    (C) $\overrightarrow{MN} = -5\mathbf{i} + 12\mathbf{j}$ and $\left|\overrightarrow{MN}\right| = 13$.

    (D) $\overrightarrow{MN} = 5\mathbf{i} - 12\mathbf{j}$ and $\left|\overrightarrow{MN}\right| = 13$.

13. Which one of the following represents a pair of parallel vectors?

    (A) $4\mathbf{i} - 14\mathbf{j}$ and $-6\mathbf{i} + 21\mathbf{j}$

    (B) $4\mathbf{i} - 14\mathbf{j}$ and $8\mathbf{i} + 28\mathbf{j}$

    (C) $-6\mathbf{i} + 21\mathbf{j}$ and $-9\mathbf{i} + 24\mathbf{j}$

    (D) $-6\mathbf{i} + 21\mathbf{j}$ and $-21\mathbf{i} + 6\mathbf{j}$

14. What is the measure of the angle between the vectors $\mathbf{i} + 3\mathbf{j}$ and $4\mathbf{i} + 3\mathbf{j}$? (nearest degree)

    (A) $29°$ (C) $41°$

    (B) $35°$ (D) $47°$

15. What is the value of the projection of the vector $\mathbf{i} - \mathbf{j}$ onto the vector $-2\mathbf{i} + 3\mathbf{j}$?

    (A) $\dfrac{5}{\sqrt{2}}$ (C) $\dfrac{-5}{\sqrt{2}}$

    (B) $\dfrac{5}{\sqrt{13}}$ (D) $\dfrac{-5}{\sqrt{13}}$

16. Which one of the following represents a unit vector in the direction of $10\mathbf{i} - \mathbf{j}$?

    (A) $\dfrac{10\mathbf{i} + \mathbf{j}}{\sqrt{99}}$ (C) $\dfrac{10\mathbf{i} + \mathbf{j}}{\sqrt{101}}$

    (B) $\dfrac{10\mathbf{i} - \mathbf{j}}{\sqrt{99}}$ (D) $\dfrac{10\mathbf{i} - \mathbf{j}}{\sqrt{101}}$

Quiz for Chapter 2
SOLUTIONS

1. **(B)**

    Multiply by the conjugate of $-2 + 7i$, which is $-2 - 7i$. Then $\dfrac{1 + 5i}{-2 + 7i} \cdot \dfrac{-2 - 7i}{-2 - 7i} = \dfrac{-2 - 17i - 35i^2}{4 - 49i^2}$

    $= \dfrac{33 - 17i}{53}$.

2. **(A)**

    $-i^{35} = -(i^{32})(i^3) = -(1)(-i) = i$

3. **(B)**

    Any number on the positive imaginary axis is of the form $0 + bi$, where b is positive.

4. (D)

The magnitude of $9 + 5i$ is $\sqrt{9^2 + 5^2} = \sqrt{106}$.

5. (B)

In rectangular form (a, b), $a = r\cos\theta = (8)$ $(\cos 210°) \approx -6.93$ and $b = r\sin\theta = (8)(\sin 210°)$ $= -4$.

6. (C)

$r = \sqrt{6^2 + (-4)^2} = \sqrt{52} = 2\sqrt{13}$. Also, in the fourth quadrant, $\theta = \tan^{-1}(-\dfrac{4}{6}) \approx 326°$.

7. (C)

When dividing two complex numbers in polar form, divide the r values and subtract the θ values.

8. (A)

Using DeMoivre's Theorem, the r value is found by calculating 4^5 and the θ value is $(15°)(5)$.

9. (B)

The value of r is $\sqrt{5}$ and $\theta = \tan^{-1}(-\dfrac{1}{2}) \approx 153°$. Then $[\sqrt{5}(\cos(153° + i\sin 153°)]^8 = 625(\cos 1224° + i\sin 1224°) \approx -506 + 367i$.

10. (C)

The fourth roots of $16(\cos 128° + i\sin 128°)$ are $2(\cos 32° + i\sin 32°)$, $2(\cos 122° + i\sin 122°)$, $2(\cos 212° + i\sin 212°)$, and $2(\cos 302° + i\sin 302°)$.

11. (D)

$-8 = 8(\cos 180° + i\sin 180°)$, so its three cube roots are $2(\cos 60° + i\sin 60°)$, $2(\cos 180° + i\sin 180°)$, and $2(\cos 300° + i\sin 300°)$.

12. (C)

For $\overrightarrow{MN}$, the coefficient of **i** is $2 - 7$ and the coefficient of **j** is $10 - (-2)$. Its magnitude is $\sqrt{(2-7)^2 + (10-(-2)^2} = 13$.

13. (A)

Two vectors are parallel if one is a scalar multiple of the other. $-6\mathbf{i} + 21\mathbf{j} = (1.5)(4\mathbf{i} - 14\mathbf{j})$.

14. (B)

$(\mathbf{i} + 3\mathbf{j}) \bullet (4\mathbf{i} + 3\mathbf{j}) = 13$, $|\mathbf{i} + 3\mathbf{j}| = \sqrt{10}$, and $|4\mathbf{i} + 3\mathbf{j}| = 5$.

$\cos\theta = \dfrac{13}{\sqrt{10} \bullet 5} \approx 0.8222$, so $\theta \approx 35°$.

15. (D)

The value of the projection of $\mathbf{i} - \mathbf{j}$ onto $-2\mathbf{i} + 3\mathbf{j}$ is given by $\dfrac{(1)(-2) + (-1)(3)}{\sqrt{(-2)^2 + (3)^2}} = \dfrac{-5}{\sqrt{13}}$.

16. (D)

A unit vector is calculated by dividing the given vector by its magnitude. In this case, the unit vector is $\dfrac{10\mathbf{i} - \mathbf{j}}{\sqrt{10^2 + 1^2}}$.

Number Theory

Welcome to Chapter 3. In this chapter, we will review the following topics for real numbers:

(a) Prime numbers and factorization
(b) Greatest common factors and least common multiples
(c) Congruence classes and modular arithmetic
(d) Properties of vectors and matrices

Prime Numbers and Factorization

A **prime number** is any positive integer that has only two integer factors, namely itself and 1. The list of primes is 2, 3, 5, 7, 11, 13, ….

A **composite number** is any integer that has at least three positive integer factors. The list of composites is 4, 6, 8, 9, 10, 12, …. Note that the number 1 is <u>neither</u> prime nor composite.

The **Fundamental Theorem of Arithmetic** states that any integer greater than 1 is either (a) prime, or (b) uniquely factorable as a product of primes. In part (b), the "uniqueness" characteristic does not include the order of the factors. This method is called the **prime factorization of numbers**.

For example, $30 = 2 \times 3 \times 5$, which can also be written as $2 \times 5 \times 3$. Likewise, $40 = 2^3 \times 5$, but it can also be written as $2 \times 5 \times 2 \times 2$. Our approach will be to write the prime factorization of the bases in ascending order, with the appropriate exponents. Thus, we will write the prime factorization of 60 as $2^2 \times 3 \times 5$ and 525 will be prime factored as $3 \times 5^2 \times 7$. *The prime factorization of a prime number is simply itself.* Thus, 17 is the prime factorization of 17. A technique for determining the prime factorization of any number involves the creation of a **factor tree**, by which a number is continually subdivided into products of smaller numbers. It is assumed that you are familiar with the divisibility rules for most integers up through 11.

Figure 3.1 shows a possible factor tree for the number 2574.

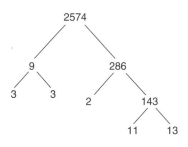

Figure 3.1

Thus, $2574 = 2 \times 3^2 \times 11 \times 13$.

Greatest Common Factor

The **greatest common factor** of two or more numbers, abbreviated as the GCF, is the largest number that is a factor of each of the given numbers. For example, the greatest common factor of 4 and 6 is 2. A shortcut way to express this statement is GCF (4, 6) = 2. Similarly, the greatest common factor of 15 and 5 is 5. Thus, GCF (15, 5) = 5. An equivalent word for *factor* is *divisor*.

When the numbers are considerably larger and/or when there are three given numbers, it is best to apply the prime factorization method in order to find the GCF.

EXAMPLE 1

What is the GCF of the numbers 99 and 330?

SOLUTION

In prime factorization form, $99 = 3^2 \times 11$ and $330 = 2 \times 3 \times 5 \times 11$.

We now identify the lowest exponent of each common base. The common bases are 3 and 11. The lowest common exponent for each of these bases is 1. Thus, the greatest common factor is (3)(11) = 33.

EXAMPLE 2

What is the GCF of the numbers 728 and 140?

SOLUTION

$728 = 2^3 \times 7 \times 13$ and $140 = 2^2 \times 5 \times 7$. The common bases are 2 and 7. The lowest common exponent for the base 2 is 2, and the lowest common exponent for the base 7 is 1. Thus the greatest common factor is $(2^2)(7) = 28$.

EXAMPLE 3

What is the GCF of the numbers 63, 42, and 476?

SOLUTION

$63 = 3^2 \times 7$, $42 = 2 \times 3 \times 7$, and $476 = 2^2 \times 7 \times 17$. The only base that is common to all three numbers is 7. Since the lowest common exponent of this base is 1, the greatest common factor is 7.

If there is no common base among the given numbers, then the greatest common factor becomes 1. As an example, the GCF of 12 and 35 is 1.

Least Common Multiple

The **least common multiple of two or more numbers**, abbreviated as the LCM, is the smallest number that is divisible by each of the given numbers. For example, the least common multiple of 6 and 8 is 24. Likewise, the least common multiple of 15 and 20 is 60. These statements can be written as LCM (6, 8) = 24 and LCM (15, 20) = 60, respectively.

Just as we suggested with the greatest common factor of a group of numbers, we can use prime factorization to facilitate our search for the least common multiple.

EXAMPLE 4

What is the LCM of the numbers 99 and 330?

SOLUTION

We already know that $99 = 3^2 \times 11$ and $330 = 2 \times 3 \times 5 \times 11$. The least multiple will be the product of each different base found in either number, along with the highest exponent for any base. The bases we need to use are 2, 3, 5, and 11. Note that the highest exponent for the base 3 is 2. Thus, the least common multiple is $2 \times 3^2 \times 5 \times 11 = 990$.

EXAMPLE 5

What is the LCM of the numbers 56, 539, and 165?

SOLUTION

$56 = 2^3 \times 7$, $539 = 7^2 \times 11$, and $165 = 3 \times 5 \times 11$. We need to use all five bases of 2, 3, 5, 7, and 11. The highest exponent found for the base 2 is 3, and the highest exponent found for the base 7 is 2. Thus, the least common multiple is $2^3 \times 3 \times 5 \times 7^2 \times 11 = 64,680$.

NOTE:

> If a group of numbers has no common bases, then the least common multiple is simply the product of the numbers. For example, LCM $(12, 35) = (12)(35) = 420$.

There is an interesting connection between any two given numbers, their greatest common divisor, and their least common multiple. The product of the GCF and LCM equals the product of the numbers. For example, given the numbers 6 and 8, their GCF is 2 and their LCM is 24. Note that $(6)(8) = (2)(24)$. As another example, given the numbers 99 and 330, we found that the GCF is 33 and the LCM is 990. Sure enough, $(99)(330) = (33)(990)$. Incidentally, this rule does <u>not</u> apply to three numbers.

EXAMPLE 6

> The greatest common factor of two given numbers is 24 and their least common multiple is 104,880. If one of the given numbers is 912, what is the other number?

SOLUTION

Let x represent the unknown number. Then $912x = (24)(104,880) = 2,517,120$. Thus, $x = 2,517,120 \div 912 = 2760$.

Congruence Classes

A **congruence class** consists of all numbers that are equivalent to each other under a given numbering system.

Consider the following three statements.

(a) $(16 - 4)$ is divisible by 6, (b) $(22 - 7)$ is divisible by 5, and (c) $(-3 - 11)$ is divisible by 2.

For statement (a), suppose our numbering system only had the numbers 0, 1, 2, 3, 4, and 5. Then the number 6 would be counted as 0, the number 7 would be counted as 1, and the number 8 would be counted as 2. The numbering system would appear as follows:

0, 1, 2, 3, 4, 5, 0, 1, 2, 3, 4, 5, 0, 1, 2, 3, 4, 5, ...

The number 16 would be counted as 4. This implies that the difference of 16 and 4 is divisible by 6, which is true since 12 is divisible by 6. The notation used to describe this situation is $16 \equiv 4 (\mod 6)$. This statement is read as "16 is congruent to 4 modulo 6." The number 6 is called the modulus of the congruence.

For statement (b), we suppose our numbering system only had the numbers 0, 1, 2, 3 and 4. Then the number 5 would be counted as 0, the number 6 would be counted as 1, and the number 7 would be counted as 2. Here is how this numbering system would appear:

0, 1, 2, 3, 4, 0, 1, 2, 3, 4, 0, 1, 2, 3, 4, ...

Each of the numbers 7 and 22 would correspond to the number 2. This implies that their difference is divisible by 5. Sure enough, $22 - 7 = 15$ is divisible by 5. We can write $22 \equiv 7 (\mod 5)$, which is read as "22 is congruent to 7 modulo 5."

For statement (c), we suppose that our numbering system only had the numbers 0 and 1. This numbering system would appear as 0, 1, 0, 1, 0, 1, 0, 1,... Counting backwards from 0, -1 would correspond to 1, -2 would correspond to 0, -3 would correspond to 1, etc. Each odd negative integer, (including -3 and -11), would correspond to 1 and each even negative integer would correspond to 0. It is easy to verify that their difference is divisible by 2. We can write $-3 \equiv -11 (\mod 2)$, which is read as "-3 is congruent to -11 modulo 2."

In general, if x, y, and m are integers, with $m > 0$, the statement $x \equiv y (\mod m)$ is read as "x is congruent to y modulo m" and implies that both $(x - y)$ and $(y - x)$ are divisible by m. The number m is called the modulus of the congruence.

Suppose that $x \equiv y (\mod 3)$. When any integer is divided by 3, the only possible remainders are 0, 1, or 2.

Using the modulus 3, let [0] represent all numbers congruent to 0 modulo 3, let [1] represent all numbers congruent to 1 modulo 3, and let [2] represent all numbers congruent to 2 modulo 3.

Then $[0] = \{ ...., -9, -6, -3, 0, 3, 6, 9, ... \}$, $[1] = \{ ...., -8, -5, -2, 1, 4, 7, ... \}$, and $[2] = \{ ..., -7, -4, -1, 2, 5, 8, ... \}$. Each of [0], [1], and [2] is called a congruence class.

In [0], each number is of the form $3n$, where n represents any integer (n may be negative, zero, or positive). Likewise, in [1], each number is of the form $3n + 1$, and in [2], each number is of the form $3n + 2$.

Using modulo 3, [0] is equal to the congruence class of any other number contained within [0]. So we can write [0] = [6] = [−9]. In the same way we can write [1] = [−8] = [4], and [2] = [5] = [−7].

EXAMPLE 7

Given $27 \equiv x(\bmod 5)$, which one of the following numbers could represent x?

$-9, -23, 8, 18.$

SOLUTION

Evaluating $27 - x$ for each potential x value yields 36, 50, 19, and 9, respectively. Of these four numbers, only 50 is divisible by 5. Thus, the correct answer is −23.

EXAMPLE 8

Given $-15 \equiv 13(\bmod m)$, which of the following numbers could <u>not</u> represent m?

$4, 7, 14, 21.$

SOLUTION

$-15 - 13 = -28$, which is divisible by each of 4, 7, and 14, but is not divisible by 21. The correct answer is 21.

EXAMPLE 9

Suppose $x \equiv 2(\bmod 8)$. Which one of the following could represent $x - 3$?

$102, 103, 107, 112$

SOLUTION

By substituting each of these four numbers for $x - 3$, the four values of x are 105, 106, 110, and 115,

respectively. Since $106 \equiv 2(\bmod 8)$, the correct answer is 103.

EXAMPLE 10

Using modulo 7, which one of the following is <u>not</u> a member of [4] ?

$-31, -10, 20, 32$

SOLUTION

Any member of [4] must be in the form $7n + 4$ for some integer n. Of these four numbers, only the number 20 does not fit this description. Thus, 20 is the correct answer. Note that the solution to $7n + 4 = 20$ is not an integer.

Properties of Vectors and Matrices

For the real number system, there are four basic properties that exist for the addition and multiplication operations, namely:

(a) Associative

(b) Commutative

(c) Distributive

(d) Inverse

Let's show an example of each.

(a) For addition: $3 + (7 + 6) = (3 + 7) + 6$; for multiplication: $(3)[(7)(6)] = [(3)(7)](6)$

(b) For addition: $2 + 8 = 8 + 2$; for multiplication: $(2)(8) = (8)(2)$

(c) $(4)(9 + 5) = (4)(9) + (4)(5)$

(d) For addition: $(5) + (-5) = 0$; for multiplication: $(5)\left(\dfrac{1}{5}\right) = 1$

Properties of Vectors

We will now investigate whether these properties exist for vectors. From Chapter 2, you recall that the multiplication of two vectors has been defined as the dot product.

Let's use $\overrightarrow{AB} = 4\mathbf{i} - \mathbf{j}$, $\overrightarrow{CD} = 2\mathbf{i} + \mathbf{j}$, and $\overrightarrow{EF} = -3\mathbf{i} + 2\mathbf{j}$.

(a) For addition, $(4\mathbf{i} - \mathbf{j}) + [(2\mathbf{i} + \mathbf{j} + (-3\mathbf{i} + 2\mathbf{j})] = [(4\mathbf{i} - \mathbf{j}) + (2\mathbf{i} + \mathbf{j})] + (-3\mathbf{i} + 2\mathbf{j}) = 3\mathbf{i} + 2\mathbf{j}$. However, for multiplication, we have $(4\mathbf{i} - \mathbf{j}) \bullet [(2\mathbf{i} + \mathbf{j}) \bullet (-3\mathbf{i} + 2\mathbf{j})] \neq [(4\mathbf{i} - \mathbf{j}) \bullet (2\mathbf{i} + \mathbf{j})] \bullet (-3\mathbf{i} + 2\mathbf{j})$. The left side of this inequality simplifies to $-16\mathbf{i} + 4\mathbf{j}$, whereas the right side simplifies to $-21\mathbf{i} + 14\mathbf{j}$.

(b) For addition, using vectors $\overrightarrow{CD}$ and $\overrightarrow{EF}$, $(2\mathbf{i} + \mathbf{j}) + (-3\mathbf{i} + 2\mathbf{j}) = (-3\mathbf{i} + 2\mathbf{j}) + (2\mathbf{i} + \mathbf{j}) = -\mathbf{i} + 3\mathbf{j}$. For multiplication, using these same vectors, $(2\mathbf{i} + \mathbf{j}) \bullet (-3\mathbf{i} + 2\mathbf{j}) = (-3\mathbf{i} + 2\mathbf{j}) \bullet (2\mathbf{i} + \mathbf{j}) = -4$.

(c) $(4\mathbf{i} - \mathbf{j}) \bullet [(2\mathbf{i} + \mathbf{j}) + (-3\mathbf{i} + 2\mathbf{j})] = (4\mathbf{i} - \mathbf{j}) \bullet (2\mathbf{i} + \mathbf{j}) + (4\mathbf{i} - \mathbf{j}) \bullet (-3\mathbf{i} + 2\mathbf{j})$. Each side of this equation has a value of -7.

(d) Using vector $\overrightarrow{AB} = 4\mathbf{i} - \mathbf{j}$, there is a unique vector $-4\mathbf{i} + \mathbf{j}$ such that $(4\mathbf{i} - \mathbf{j}) + -4\mathbf{i} + \mathbf{j} = 0\mathbf{i} + 0\mathbf{j}$. This is called the zero vector.

However, multiplicative inverses for vectors do not exist.

Summary

These are the number properties that exist among vectors:

For **addition of vectors**, the properties of *associativity, commutativity*, and *inverses* apply.

For the **multiplication of vectors**, the property of *commutativity* applies. However, the property of *associativity* does not apply, and there does not exist a multiplicative inverse. The *Distributive property involving multiplication over addition* applies.

Properties of Matrices

We will now investigate whether these four basic properties apply to matrices.

In order to check the properties as they apply to addition, we must select two matrices that have an equal number of rows and an equal number of columns.

Let $\mathbf{A} = \begin{bmatrix} 3 & -1 & 2 \\ 4 & 1 & 0 \end{bmatrix}$ $\mathbf{B} = \begin{bmatrix} 5 & -2 & 3 \\ -4 & 2 & 1 \end{bmatrix}$ and $\mathbf{C} = \begin{bmatrix} -3 & 1 & -5 \\ 2 & 0 & 4 \end{bmatrix}$

We will now check the basic properties of numbers that only involve addition.

(a) $\mathbf{A} + (\mathbf{B} + \mathbf{C})$

$= \begin{bmatrix} 3 & -1 & 2 \\ 4 & 1 & 0 \end{bmatrix} + \left\{ \begin{bmatrix} 5 & -2 & 3 \\ -4 & 2 & 1 \end{bmatrix} + \begin{bmatrix} -3 & 1 & -5 \\ 2 & 0 & 4 \end{bmatrix} \right\}$

$= \begin{bmatrix} 3 & -1 & 2 \\ 4 & 1 & 0 \end{bmatrix} + \begin{bmatrix} 2 & -1 & -2 \\ -2 & 2 & 5 \end{bmatrix} = \begin{bmatrix} 5 & -2 & 0 \\ 2 & 3 & 5 \end{bmatrix}$

$(\mathbf{A} + \mathbf{B}) + \mathbf{C}$

$= \left\{ \begin{bmatrix} 3 & -1 & 2 \\ 4 & 1 & 0 \end{bmatrix} + \begin{bmatrix} 5 & -2 & 3 \\ -4 & 2 & 1 \end{bmatrix} \right\} + \begin{bmatrix} -3 & 1 & -5 \\ 2 & 0 & 4 \end{bmatrix}$

$= \begin{bmatrix} 8 & -3 & 5 \\ 0 & 3 & 1 \end{bmatrix} + \begin{bmatrix} -3 & 1 & -5 \\ 2 & 0 & 4 \end{bmatrix} = \begin{bmatrix} 5 & -2 & 0 \\ 2 & 3 & 5 \end{bmatrix}$

Thus, the Associativity property of addition does apply to matrices.

(b) Using matrices $\mathbf{A}$ and $\mathbf{B}$,

$\begin{bmatrix} 3 & -1 & 2 \\ 4 & 1 & 0 \end{bmatrix} + \begin{bmatrix} 5 & -2 & 3 \\ -4 & 2 & 1 \end{bmatrix} = \begin{bmatrix} 8 & -3 & 5 \\ 0 & 3 & 1 \end{bmatrix}$

and this matrix sum is exactly the sum of $\mathbf{B} + \mathbf{A}$.

Thus, the Commutative property of addition does apply to matrices.

For the operation of multiplication to apply to two matrices, the number of columns of the first matrix must match the number of rows of the second matrix.

As a review, suppose $\mathbf{W} = \begin{bmatrix} -1 & 0 & 7 \\ 5 & 2 & 6 \end{bmatrix}$, $\mathbf{Y} = \begin{bmatrix} -4 & -2 \\ -1 & 2 \\ 3 & 1 \end{bmatrix}$ and $\mathbf{Z} = \mathbf{W} \times \mathbf{Y}$.

Then

$\mathbf{Z} = \begin{bmatrix} (-1)(-4)+(0)(-1)+(7)(3) & (-1)(-2)+(0)(2)+(7)(1) \\ (5)(-4)+(2)(-1)+(6)(3) & (5)(-2)+(2)(2)+(6)(1) \end{bmatrix}$

$= \begin{bmatrix} 25 & 9 \\ -4 & 0 \end{bmatrix}$

NOTE:

> The conventional symbol for multiplication with matrices is $\times$ in place of $\bullet$

Returning to our original discussion of the properties of numbers as they apply to matrices, let

$$\mathbf{A} = \begin{bmatrix} 3 & -1 & 2 \\ 4 & 1 & 0 \end{bmatrix} \quad \mathbf{D} = \begin{bmatrix} -2 & 1 \\ 3 & -3 \\ 2 & 3 \end{bmatrix} \quad \text{and } \mathbf{E} = \begin{bmatrix} -4 \\ 1 \end{bmatrix}$$

(a) $\mathbf{A} \times (\mathbf{D} \times \mathbf{E}) = \begin{bmatrix} 3 & -1 & 2 \\ 4 & 1 & 0 \end{bmatrix} \times \left\{ \begin{bmatrix} -2 & 1 \\ 3 & -3 \\ 2 & 3 \end{bmatrix} \times \begin{bmatrix} -4 \\ 1 \end{bmatrix} \right\}$

$$= \begin{bmatrix} 3 & -1 & 2 \\ 4 & 1 & 0 \end{bmatrix} \times \begin{bmatrix} 9 \\ -15 \\ -5 \end{bmatrix} = \begin{bmatrix} 32 \\ 21 \end{bmatrix}$$

$(\mathbf{A} \times \mathbf{D}) \times \mathbf{E} = \left\{ \begin{bmatrix} 3 & -1 & 2 \\ 4 & 1 & 0 \end{bmatrix} \times \begin{bmatrix} -2 & 1 \\ 3 & -3 \\ 2 & 3 \end{bmatrix} \right\} \times \begin{bmatrix} -4 \\ 1 \end{bmatrix}$

$$= \begin{bmatrix} -5 & 12 \\ -5 & 1 \end{bmatrix} \times \begin{bmatrix} -4 \\ 1 \end{bmatrix} = \begin{bmatrix} 32 \\ 21 \end{bmatrix}$$

Thus, the Associative property of multiplication applies to matrices, provided that the given matrices can be multiplied. The number of columns of the first matrix must match the number of rows of the second matrix; furthermore, the number of columns of the second matrix must match the number of rows of the third matrix.

In order to check the Commutative property of multiplication, we need either two square matrices or a situation in which the number of rows and columns of one matrix is the reverse of the number of rows and columns of the second matrix.

Let $\mathbf{F} = \begin{bmatrix} 1 & 3 \\ -4 & 2 \end{bmatrix}$ and $\mathbf{G} = \begin{bmatrix} -2 & -1 \\ 5 & 4 \end{bmatrix}$

(b) Then $\mathbf{F} \times \mathbf{G} = \begin{bmatrix} 1 & 3 \\ -4 & 2 \end{bmatrix} \times \begin{bmatrix} -2 & -1 \\ 5 & 4 \end{bmatrix} = \begin{bmatrix} 13 & 11 \\ 18 & 12 \end{bmatrix}$

However,

$$\mathbf{G} \times \mathbf{F} = \begin{bmatrix} -2 & -1 \\ 5 & 4 \end{bmatrix} \times \begin{bmatrix} 1 & 3 \\ -4 & 2 \end{bmatrix} = \begin{bmatrix} 2 & -8 \\ -11 & 23 \end{bmatrix}$$

It is evident that $\mathbf{F} \times \mathbf{G} \neq \mathbf{G} \times \mathbf{F}$ for two square matrices. Let's consider two non-square matrices. Suppose matrix $\mathbf{H}$ has m rows and n columns, and matrix $\mathbf{J}$ has n rows and m columns. Then $\mathbf{H} \times \mathbf{J}$ is a square matrix with m rows and m columns; however, $\mathbf{J} \times \mathbf{H}$ is a square matrix with n rows and n columns. *This implies that $\mathbf{H} \times \mathbf{J} \neq \mathbf{J} \times \mathbf{H}$, so the Commutative property of multiplication does not apply to matrices.*

Let's check for the Distributive property of multiplication over addition, using new matrices $\mathbf{K}$, $\mathbf{L}$, and $\mathbf{M}$. We want to know if $\mathbf{K} \times (\mathbf{L} + \mathbf{M})$ $= \mathbf{K} \times \mathbf{L} + \mathbf{K} \times \mathbf{M}$. In order to use a numerical example, matrices $\mathbf{L}$ and $\mathbf{M}$ must match in rows and columns. In addition, the number of columns in $\mathbf{K}$ must match the number of rows in $\mathbf{L}$ (which matches the number of rows in $\mathbf{M}$).

Let $\mathbf{K} = \begin{bmatrix} 2 & 0 & 5 \\ -1 & 4 & 3 \end{bmatrix}$, $\mathbf{L} = \begin{bmatrix} -2 \\ 1 \\ -3 \end{bmatrix}$ and $\mathbf{M} = \begin{bmatrix} 3 \\ -5 \\ 2 \end{bmatrix}$

(c) Then $\mathbf{K} \times (\mathbf{L} + \mathbf{M}) = \begin{bmatrix} 2 & 0 & 5 \\ -1 & 4 & 3 \end{bmatrix} \times \left\{ \begin{bmatrix} -2 \\ 1 \\ -3 \end{bmatrix} + \begin{bmatrix} 3 \\ -5 \\ 2 \end{bmatrix} \right\}$

$$= \begin{bmatrix} 2 & 0 & 5 \\ -1 & 4 & 3 \end{bmatrix} \times \begin{bmatrix} 1 \\ -4 \\ -1 \end{bmatrix} = \begin{bmatrix} -3 \\ -20 \end{bmatrix}$$

$\mathbf{K} \times \mathbf{L} + \mathbf{K} \times \mathbf{M}$

$$= \begin{bmatrix} 2 & 0 & 5 \\ -1 & 4 & 3 \end{bmatrix} \times \begin{bmatrix} -2 \\ 1 \\ -3 \end{bmatrix} + \begin{bmatrix} 2 & 0 & 5 \\ -1 & 4 & 3 \end{bmatrix} \times \begin{bmatrix} 3 \\ -5 \\ 2 \end{bmatrix}$$

$$= \begin{bmatrix} -19 \\ -3 \end{bmatrix} + \begin{bmatrix} 16 \\ -17 \end{bmatrix} = \begin{bmatrix} -3 \\ -20 \end{bmatrix}$$

This implies that the Distributive property of multiplication over addition applies to matrices. The only provision is that the operations of multiplication and addition can actually be performed.

With respect to inverses, we first consider the inverse of a matrix under addition. The identity matrix for addition is any matrix with all zeros. Given any matrix **A**, its additive inverse is represented as −**A**. The actual numbers (elements) in −**A** are simply the additive inverses of the elements in **A.** For example, if

$$A = \begin{bmatrix} 2 & 3 \\ -1 & 5 \\ 7 & -4 \end{bmatrix}, \text{ then } -A = \begin{bmatrix} -2 & -3 \\ 1 & -5 \\ -7 & 4 \end{bmatrix}$$

Before we explore multiplicative inverses for matrices, we need to define the identity matrix for multiplication. This matrix must be square and consists of all 1's on its main diagonal and 0's everywhere else. As examples,

$$\text{each of} \begin{bmatrix} 1 & 0 \\ 0 & 1 \end{bmatrix} \text{ and } \begin{bmatrix} 1 & 0 & 0 \\ 0 & 1 & 0 \\ 0 & 0 & 1 \end{bmatrix}$$

is an identity matrix. Identity matrices are denoted as *I*.

If *B* is any square matrix with *m* rows and *m* columns, its multiplicative inverse, if it exists, is denoted as B^{-1} and will also contain *m* rows and *m* columns.

Then $B \times B^{-1} = B^{-1} \times B = I$. For example if

$$B = \begin{bmatrix} 3 & 5 \\ 1 & 2 \end{bmatrix}, \text{ then } B^{-1} = \begin{bmatrix} 2 & -5 \\ -1 & 3 \end{bmatrix}.$$

You can check that the product of B and is the matrix $\begin{bmatrix} 1 & 0 \\ 0 & 1 \end{bmatrix}$.

The actual technique for finding B^{-1} will be shown in Example 14.

NOTE:

The Commutative property of multiplication does apply to a matrix and its multiplicative inverse. Non-square matrices do not have multiplicative inverses. Furthermore, not every square matrix has a multiplicative inverse. The requirement for the existence of a multiplicative inverse is that the determinant of the given matrix is not zero.

Given the matrix $\mathbf{X} = \begin{bmatrix} a & b \\ c & d \end{bmatrix}$, the determinant of **X**, written as det **X** is defined as the value of ad − bc. Note that the determinant of a matrix is a scalar, not a matrix.

EXAMPLE 11

What is the determinant of the matrix $Y = \begin{bmatrix} -2 & 6 \\ 4 & 1 \end{bmatrix}$?

SOLUTION

The determinant equals $(-2)(1) - (6)(4) = -26$.

EXAMPLE 12

If the matrix $\begin{bmatrix} 5 & x \\ -2 & 3 \end{bmatrix}$ does not have a multiplicative inverse, what is the value of *x*?

SOLUTION

In order that the multiplicative inverse does not exist, $(5)(3) - (-2)(x) = 0$. Then $x = -7\frac{1}{2}$. (Elements of matrices need not be integers.)

The Multiplicative Inverse Matrix of a Given Matrix

Let's confine our discussion to square matrices that have 2 rows and 2 columns. As a quick review of a rule involving scalars (numbers) and matrices, when a scalar is multiplied by a matrix, simply multiply each element of the matrix by that scalar.

EXAMPLE 13

What is the product $5 \times \begin{bmatrix} 3 & 7 \\ -\frac{1}{3} & -2 \end{bmatrix}$?

SOLUTION

Just multiply 5 by each element. The answer is

$$\begin{bmatrix} 15 & 35 \\ -\dfrac{5}{3} & -10 \end{bmatrix}$$

Given a square matrix $\boldsymbol{B} = \begin{bmatrix} a & b \\ c & d \end{bmatrix}$ for which $ad - bc \neq 0$, the multiplicative inverse B^{-1} is given by the matrix that results from the product $\left(\dfrac{1}{ad - bc}\right) \times$

$$\begin{bmatrix} d & -b \\ -c & a \end{bmatrix}$$

EXAMPLE 14

What is the multiplicative inverse matrix for

$$A = \begin{bmatrix} -3 & 2 \\ 4 & -6 \end{bmatrix}?$$

SOLUTION

First calculate $(-3)(-6) - (4)(2) = 10$.

The multiplicative inverse is given by $\left(\dfrac{1}{10}\right) \times$

$$\begin{bmatrix} -6 & -2 \\ -4 & -3 \end{bmatrix} = \begin{bmatrix} -\dfrac{3}{5} & -\dfrac{1}{5} \\ -\dfrac{2}{5} & -\dfrac{3}{10} \end{bmatrix}$$

To check this answer, $\begin{bmatrix} -3 & 2 \\ 4 & -6 \end{bmatrix} \times \begin{bmatrix} -\dfrac{3}{5} & -\dfrac{1}{5} \\ -\dfrac{2}{5} & -\dfrac{3}{10} \end{bmatrix}$

must equal $\begin{bmatrix} 1 & 0 \\ 0 & 1 \end{bmatrix}$, and it does!

The procedure for finding the multiplicative inverse of a matrix with 3 rows and 3 columns is beyond the scope of this book. (It is also beyond the scope of the TexES Math $8 - 12$ exam). However, for further practice in matrix multiplication, if $M = \begin{bmatrix} 3 & 3 & -1 \\ -2 & -2 & 1 \\ -4 & -5 & 2 \end{bmatrix}$ then

$$M^{-1} = \begin{bmatrix} 1 & -1 & 1 \\ 0 & 2 & -1 \\ 2 & 3 & 0 \end{bmatrix}$$

The product of these two matrices is the identity matrix for 3 rows and 3 columns.

Quiz for Chapter 3

1. What is the least common multiple of the numbers 24, 75, and 112?

   (A) 560   (C) 8400

   (B) 2800   (D) 25,200

2. The greatest common factor of 36 and a number n is 1. What is a valid conclusion concerning the value of n?

   (A) It has no common prime factors with the number 36.

   (B) It must be greater than 36.

   (C) It must be less than 36.

   (D) It must be a prime number.

3. If $41 \equiv 6 (\bmod\ x)$, which one of the following could represent a value of x?

   (A) 10   (C) 8

   (B) 9   (D) 7

4. Using modulo 9, which one of the following is <u>not</u> a member of [2]?

   (A) -25 (C) 20

   (B) -18 (D) 38

5. If $x \equiv 5(\bmod 11)$, which one of the following could represent the value of $2x$?

   (A) 54   (C) -16

   (B) 16   (D) -54

6. Which one of the following properties does <u>not</u> apply to vectors?

(A) Commutativity for addition

(B) Commutativity for multiplication, using the dot product

(C) Associativity for addition

(D) Associativity for multiplication, using the dot product

7. Which one of the following properties does <u>not</u> apply to matrices?

(A) Associativity for addition

(B) Commutativity for multiplication

(C) Associativity for multiplication

(D) Additive inverse

8. For which one of the following conditions does **M** × **N** exist for matrices **M** and **N** ?

(A) **M** has 4 rows and 5 columns; **N** has 5 rows and 6 columns.

(B) **M** has 3 rows and 2 columns; **N** has 3 rows and 4 columns.

(C) **M** has 5 rows and 5 columns; **N** has 4 rows and 4 columns.

(D) **M** has 2 rows and 8 columns; **N** has 6 rows and 2 columns.

9. If $\mathbf{C} = \begin{bmatrix} 3 & -4 \\ -6 & 10 \end{bmatrix}$, then which one of the following represents C^{-1}?

(A) $\begin{bmatrix} \frac{5}{3} & \frac{1}{2} \\ \frac{2}{3} & 1 \end{bmatrix}$

(B) $\begin{bmatrix} \frac{1}{2} & -1 \\ -\frac{2}{3} & \frac{5}{3} \end{bmatrix}$

(C) $\begin{bmatrix} \frac{5}{3} & \frac{2}{3} \\ 1 & \frac{1}{2} \end{bmatrix}$

(D) $\begin{bmatrix} -\frac{1}{2} & 1 \\ \frac{2}{3} & -\frac{5}{3} \end{bmatrix}$

10. If the multiplicative inverse of $\begin{bmatrix} -10 & 4 \\ x & 6 \end{bmatrix}$ does not exist, what is the value of x?

(A) 15

(B) 12

(C) −12

(D) −15

Quiz for Chapter 3
SOLUTIONS

1. (C)

$24 = 2^3 \times 3$, $75 = 3 \times 5^2$, and $112 = 2^4 \times 7$. The least common multiple is $2^4 \times 3 \times 5^2 \times 7 = 8400$.

2. (A)

The number n must not have any factors that are common to 36. Two such numbers will have a greatest common factor of 1. Note that a possible value of n is 169, which is 13^2. This means that n may not necessarily be a prime number.

3. (D)

$41 - 6 = 35$ must be divisible by x, and 35 is divisible by 7.

4. (B)

A member of [2], using modulo 9, must be of the form $9n + 2$, for some integer n. Among the given choices, the equation $9n + 2 = -18$ does not have an integer solution.

5. (A)

If $2x = 54$, then $x = 27$. Also, $27 \equiv 5(\mathrm{mod}11)$.

6. (D)

Using the dot product, associativity for multiplication does not apply to vectors.

For example, $(\mathbf{i} + \mathbf{j}) \bullet [(2\mathbf{i} + \mathbf{j}) \bullet (\mathbf{i} - 3\mathbf{j})]$
$\neq [(\mathbf{i} + \mathbf{j}) \bullet (2\mathbf{i} + \mathbf{j})] \bullet (\mathbf{i} - 3\mathbf{j})$.

The left side of this inequality simplifies to $-\mathbf{i} - \mathbf{j}$, whereas the right side simplifies to $3\mathbf{i} - 9\mathbf{j}$.

7. (B)

The commutative property for multiplication does not apply to matrices.

For example, $\begin{bmatrix} 1 & 2 \\ 4 & 3 \end{bmatrix} \times \begin{bmatrix} 5 & 8 \\ 6 & 7 \end{bmatrix} = \begin{bmatrix} 17 & 22 \\ 38 & 53 \end{bmatrix}$

However, $\begin{bmatrix} 5 & 8 \\ 6 & 7 \end{bmatrix} \times \begin{bmatrix} 1 & 2 \\ 4 & 3 \end{bmatrix} = \begin{bmatrix} 37 & 34 \\ 34 & 33 \end{bmatrix}$

8. (A)

In order for $\mathbf{M} \times \mathbf{N}$ to exist, the number of columns of $\mathbf{M}$ must equal the number of rows of $\mathbf{N}$.

9. (C)

The determinant of C is $(10)(3) - (-6)(-4) = 6$. Thus, the multiplicative inverse of $\mathbf{C}$ is

$$\frac{1}{6} \times \begin{bmatrix} 10 & 4 \\ 6 & 3 \end{bmatrix} = \begin{bmatrix} \frac{5}{3} & \frac{2}{3} \\ 1 & \frac{1}{2} \end{bmatrix}$$

10. (D)

The multiplicative inverse does not exist for a square matrix whenever the determinant is zero. So, $(-10)(6) - (4)(x) = 0$. Thus, $x = -15$.

Sequences and Series

Welcome to Chapter 4. In this chapter, we will review the following algebraic topics:

(a) Patterns and properties of sequences

(b) Patterns and properties of series

(c) Applications of sequences and series to the mathematics of finance

An **arithmetic sequence** is an infinite list of numbers for which there is a common difference. Let a_1, a_2, a_3, ... a_n, ... represent an arithmetic sequence.

This means that $a_2 - a_1 = a_3 - a_2 = ... = a_n - a_{n-1} = ...$ If we call this common difference d, then $a_n = a_{n-1} + d$ for all n >1.

Here are four examples of an arithmetic sequence.

(a) 2, 6, 10, 14, ...

(b) 5, 2, –1, –4, ...

(c) $\frac{1}{2}, \frac{3}{4}, 1, \frac{5}{4}, ...$

(d) $15, 13\frac{2}{3}, 12\frac{1}{3}, 11, ...$

The common difference, d, for these examples are $4, -3, \frac{1}{4},$ and $-1\frac{1}{3}$, respectively.

NOTE:

Besides integers, fractions (and decimals) may be used for this type of sequence. Usually, the first four numbers will be provided, followed by four dots. This will indicate that the sequence is infinite.

The formula for finding the nth term of an arithmetic sequence is given by $a_n = a_1 + (n - 1)(d)$.

EXAMPLE 1

What is the 90th term of the sequence 2, 6, 10, 14, ... ?

SOLUTION

$a_{90} = 2 + (89)(4) = 358.$

EXAMPLE 2

What is the 25th term of the sequence $15, 13\frac{2}{3}, 12\frac{1}{3}, 11, ...$?

SOLUTION:

$$a_{25} = 15 + (24)\left(-1\tfrac{1}{3}\right) = -17$$

EXAMPLE 3

In a certain arithmetic sequence, the first term is –23 and the 19th term is 5.8. What is the value of the common difference?

SOLUTION

$5.8 = -23 + (19 - 1)(d)$. Simplifying, we get $28.8 = 18d$. Thus, $d = 1.6$

EXAMPLE 4

In a certain arithmetic sequence, the 7th term is 43 and the 22nd term is 31.

What is the value of the first term?

SOLUTION

We need to use two equations for the unknowns a_1 and d. Since 43 represents the seventh term, we can write $43 = a_1 + 6d$. In similar fashion, we can express the information that 31 is the 22nd term with the equation $31 = a_1 + 21d$. By subtracting the second equation from the first, $12 = -15d$. Then $d = -\dfrac{12}{15} = -\dfrac{4}{5}$. Using the first equation, $43 = a_1 + (6)\left(-\dfrac{4}{5}\right)$. Thus, $a_1 = 47\dfrac{4}{5}$.

NOTE:

We could have used the known d value to find a_1 in the second equation.

Geometric Sequence

Another popular type of sequence is called a **geometric sequence**, which is an infinite list of numbers

for which there is a common ratio. Let $a_1, a_2, a_3, \ldots. a_n, \ldots.$ represent a geometric sequence. This means that $\dfrac{a_2}{a_1} = \dfrac{a_3}{a_2} = \ldots. = \dfrac{a_n}{a_{n-1}} = \ldots.$ If we call this common ratio r, then $a_n = (r)(a_{n-1})$ for all n > 1.

Here are four examples of a geometric sequence.

(a) 2, 8, 32, 128, ….

(b) 1, −5, 25, −125,….

(c) 90, 45, 22.5, 11.25, ….

(d) $\dfrac{1}{4}, \dfrac{1}{6}, \dfrac{1}{9}, \dfrac{2}{27}, \ldots.$

NOTE:

The value of r may be integer or fraction, negative or positive.

Also, to check that (d) represents a geometric ratio, you can verify that $\dfrac{1}{6} \div \dfrac{1}{4} = \dfrac{1}{9} \div \dfrac{1}{6} = \dfrac{2}{27} \div \dfrac{1}{9} = \dfrac{2}{3}.$

The formula for finding the nth term of a geometric sequence is given by $a_n = (a_1)(r)^{n-1}$. When the actual values of a_n become either very large or very small, it is acceptable to use scientific notation.

EXAMPLE 5

What is the tenth term of the sequence 2, 8, 32, 128, ….?

SOLUTION

$$a_{10} = (2)(4)^9 = 524,288$$

EXAMPLE 6

What is the 30th term of the sequence 90, 45, 22.5, 11.25, ….?

SOLUTION

$$a_{30} = (90)\left(\dfrac{1}{2}\right)^{29} \approx 1.68 \times 10^{-7}.$$

EXAMPLE 7

In a certain geometric sequence, the eighth term is 2624.4 and the common ratio is −3. What is the value of the first term?

SOLUTION

$2624.4 = (a_1)(-3)^7$, which simplifies to $2624.4 = -2187a_1$. Thus, $a_1 = -1.2$.

EXAMPLE 8

In a certain geometric sequence, the third term is $\frac{8}{3}$ and the sixth term is $\frac{512}{81}$. What is the value of the common ratio?

SOLUTION

We need to use two equations for the unknowns a_1 and r. Since $\frac{8}{3}$ represents the third term, we can write $\frac{8}{3} = (a_1)(r)^2$. Similarly, $\frac{512}{81}$ represents the sixth term, so $\frac{512}{81} = (a_1)(r)^5$. Dividing the second equation by the first equation will cancel out a_1, and will yield $\frac{64}{27} = r^3$. This means that $r = \sqrt[3]{\frac{64}{27}} = \frac{4}{3}$.

CAUTION!

If the ratio is unknown and we are solving an equation such as $\frac{64}{25} = r^2$, then there are <u>two</u> correct values of r, namely $\pm\frac{8}{5}$. Furthermore, if the value of a_1 is also unknown, then each of $\frac{8}{5}$ and $-\frac{8}{5}$ must be used to find the two answers of a_1.

EXAMPLE 9

In a certain geometric sequence, the fourth term is 48.6 and the sixth term is 437.4. What is the value of the first term?

SOLUTION

Similar to Example 8, we'll use two equations, namely $48.6 = (a_1)(r)^3$ and $437.4 = (a_1)(r)^5$. Dividing the second equation by the first equation yields $9 = r^2$. So, $r = \pm3$. When $r = -3$, $48.6 = (a_1)(-3)^3 = -27a_1$. So, one answer is $a_1 = -1.8$. When $r = 3$, $48.6 = (a_1)(3)^3 = 27a_1$. Thus, a second answer is $a_1 = 1.8$.

Recursive Sequence

A **recursive sequence** is a list of numbers in which each number depends on the values of previous numbers. In this type of sequence, the value of the first term is given. For each successive term, a formula is given that depends on the value of the previous term. In some cases, the values of the first two terms are given. For each successive term, a formula is given that depends on the values of the two previous terms. These sequences are also infinite and can be labeled as $a_1, a_2, a_3, \ldots a_n, \ldots$.

EXAMPLE 10

Given a sequence in which $a_1 = 5$ and $a_n = 4a_{n-1} + 7$ for $n > 1$, what are the values of the second, third, and fourth terms?

SOLUTION

$a_2 = 4a_1 + 7 = (4)(5) + 7 = 27$;
$a_3 = 4a_2 + 7 = (4)(27) + 7 = 115$;
$a_4 = 4a_3 + 7 = (4)(115) + 7 = 467$.

EXAMPLE 11

Given a sequence in which $a_1 = -12$ and $a_n = \frac{1}{2}a_{n-1} + 1$ for $n > 1$, what are the values of the second, third, and fourth terms?

SOLUTION

$$a_2 = \frac{1}{2}a_1 + 1 = \left(\frac{1}{2}\right)(-12) + 1 = -5;$$

$$a_3 = \frac{1}{2}a_2 + 1 = \left(\frac{1}{2}\right)(-5) + 1 = -\frac{3}{2};$$

$$a_4 = \frac{1}{2}a_3 + 1 = \left(\frac{1}{2}\right)\left(-\frac{3}{2}\right) + 1 = \frac{1}{4}.$$

EXAMPLE 12

Given a sequence in which $a_1 = 0.6$, $a_2 = 2$, and $a_n = 3a_{n-1} - 5a_{n-2}$ for $n > 2$, what are the values of the third and fourth terms?

SOLUTION

$$a_3 = 3a_2 - 5a_1 = (3)(2) - (5)(0.6) = 3;$$
$$a_4 = 3a_3 - 5a_2 = (3)(3) - (5)(2) = -1$$

A very famous sequence in mathematics is known as the **Fibonacci sequence**. For this sequence, $a_1 = 1$, $a_2 = 1$, and $a_n = a_{n-1} + a_{n-2}$ for $n > 2$. The first ten terms of this sequence are 1, 1, 2, 3, 5, 8, 13, 21, 34, and 55.

Patterns and Properties of Series

An **arithmetic series** is a list of numbers that represent the partial sums of an arithmetic sequence. If $a_1, a_2, a_3, ..., a_n$ represents a finite arithmetic sequence, let $s_1 = a_1$, $s_2 = a_1 + a_2$, $s_3 = a_1 + a_2 + a_3$. This pattern continues up through $s_n = a_1 + a_2 + a_3 + ... + a_n$. Then each of $s_1, s_2, s_3, ..., s_n$ is a finite arithmetic series.

The formulas for finding the nth term of an arithmetic series are given by $s_n = \frac{n}{2}[2a_1 + (n-1)(d)]$ *and* $s_n = \frac{n}{2}(a_1 + a_n).$

EXAMPLE 13

What is the sum of the first 18 terms of the arithmetic sequence 2, 6, 10, 14, ...?

SOLUTION

$a_1 = 2$, $d = 4$, and $n = 18$. Then $s_{18} = \frac{18}{2}[(2)(2) + (17)(4)] = 648.$

EXAMPLE 14

What is the sum of the first 81 terms of the arithmetic sequence $\frac{1}{2}, \frac{3}{4}, 1, \frac{5}{4}, ...$?

SOLUTION

$$a_1 = \frac{1}{2}, d = \frac{1}{4}, \text{and} n = 81. \text{Then} = s_{81} = \frac{81}{2}\left[(2)\left(\frac{1}{2}\right) + (80)\left(\frac{1}{4}\right)\right] = 850\frac{1}{2}.$$

EXAMPLE 15

What is the sum of the first 32 terms of the arithmetic sequence in which $a_1 = 26.4$ and $a_{32} = 43.8$?

SOLUTION

$$a_1 = -6.4, a_{32} = 43.8, \text{and} n = 32. \text{Then} = s_{32} = \left(\frac{32}{2}\right)(-6.4 + 43.8) = 598.4.$$

Geometric Series

A **geometric series** is a list of numbers that represents the partial sums of a geometric sequence. If $a_1, a_2, a_3, ..., a_n$ represents a finite geometric sequence, let $s_1 = a_1$, $s_2 = a_1 + a_2$, $s_3 = a_1 + a_2 + a_3$. This pattern continues up through $s_n = a_1 + a_2 + a_3 + ... + a_n$. Then each of $s_1, s_2, s_3, ..., s_n$ is a finite geometric series.

The formula for finding the nth term of a geometric series is given by $s_n = \dfrac{a_1 - (a_1)(r^n)}{1-r}$ with $r \neq 1$. (If $r = 1$, then $s_n = (n)(a_1)$ because all terms of the corresponding sequence are the same).

EXAMPLE 16

What is the sum of the first 24 terms of the geometric sequence 2, 8, 32, 128,….? (Leave your answer in scientific notation.)

SOLUTION

$a_1 = 2$, $r = 4$, and $n = 24$. Then $s_{24} = \dfrac{2 - (2)(4^{24})}{1-4}$ $\approx 1.88 \times 10^{14}$.

EXAMPLE 17

What is the sum of the first 15 terms of the geometric sequence 90, -30, 10, $-\dfrac{10}{3}$, ….?

SOLUTION

$a_1 = 90$, $r = -\dfrac{1}{3}$, and $n = 15$.

Then $s_{15} = \dfrac{90 - (90)\left(-\dfrac{1}{3}\right)^{15}}{1-\left(-\dfrac{1}{3}\right)} \approx 67.5$.

Consider the following infinite geometric sequence: 3, 6, 12, 24, …. The value of $r = 2$ and each term of the sequence increases in size. There would be no numerical value for the sum of this sequence. Thus, there is no value for s_∞.

However, if $|r| < 1$ for a geometric sequence, then the infinite geometric series has a numerical value, given by the formula $s_\infty = \dfrac{a_1}{1-r}$.

EXAMPLE 18

What is the sum of all the terms of the infinite sequence 60, 15, $\dfrac{15}{4}$, $\dfrac{15}{16}$, ….?

SOLUTION

$a_1 = 60$ and $r = \dfrac{1}{4}$. Then $s_\infty = \dfrac{60}{1-\dfrac{1}{4}} = 80$.

EXAMPLE 19

The sum of all the terms of an infinite geometric sequence is $-\dfrac{4}{9}$. If the common ratio is $-\dfrac{1}{2}$, what is the value of the first term?

SOLUTION

$s_\infty = -\dfrac{4}{9}$ and $r = -\dfrac{1}{2}$.

Then $-\dfrac{4}{9} = \dfrac{a_1}{1-\left(-\dfrac{1}{2}\right)} = \dfrac{a_1}{\dfrac{3}{2}}$.

Thus, $a_1 = \left(-\dfrac{4}{9}\right)\left(\dfrac{3}{2}\right) = -\dfrac{2}{3}$.

NOTE:

An infinite arithmetic series cannot have a sum, regardless of the values of a_1 or d.

Application of Sequences and Series to Finance

Application of Arithmetic Sequence

An application of an arithmetic sequence in the world of finance is *simple interest*. Suppose P = the original principal, r = annual interest rate, t = time in years, and A = amount. Then $A = P + Prt$. The corresponding values of the amount for 1 year, 2 years, 3 years, 4 years, ... are given by $P + Pr$, $P + 2Pr$, $P + 3Pr$, $P + 4Pr$, ... This is an arithmetic sequence in which the first term is $P + Pr$ and the common difference is Pr.

EXAMPLE 20

If $200 is deposited into a bank in which the annual simple interest rate is 4.5%, what is the amount after 9 years?

SOLUTION

$A = \$200 + (\$200)(0.045)(9) = \$281$.

EXAMPLE 21

$350 is deposited into a bank in which the amount becomes $402.50 after $2\frac{1}{2}$ years. What is the annual simple interest rate?

SOLUTION

$\$402.50 = \$350 + (\$350)(r)(2.5) = \$350 + \$875r$.
Then $r = \dfrac{\$52.50}{\$875} = 0.06$, which is 6%.

Application of Geometric Sequence

Now let's look at an application of a geometric sequence as it relates to the mathematics of finance. In particular, consider the topic of *compound interest*. Suppose that P_0 = original principal, r = annual interest rate, n = number of compounding periods per year, t = total number of years, and $P(t)$ = amount after t years.

Then $P(t) = P_0\left(1 + \dfrac{r}{n}\right)^{nt}$. The corresponding values of the amount for 1 year, 2 years, 3 years, 4 years, ...

are given by $P_0\left(1 + \dfrac{r}{n}\right)^{n}$, $P_0\left(1 + \dfrac{r}{n}\right)^{2n}$, $P_0\left(1 + \dfrac{r}{n}\right)^{3n}$,

$P_0\left(1 + \dfrac{r}{n}\right)^{4n}$, ...

This is a geometric sequence in which the first term is $P_0\left(1 + \dfrac{r}{n}\right)^{n}$ and the common ratio is $\left(1 + \dfrac{r}{n}\right)^{n}$.

EXAMPLE 22

If $600 is deposited into a bank in which the interest rate is 8% compounded quarterly, what is the amount after 5 years?

SOLUTION

There are four compounding periods per year and a total of $(5)(4) = 20$ compounding periods.

$$P(5) = (\$600)\left(1 + \frac{0.08}{4}\right)^{20} \approx \$891.57.$$

EXAMPLE 23

A person will need $5000 in 3 years to help pay off a car loan. How much money should be deposited into a bank in which the interest rate is 10% compounded monthly? (nearest dollar)

SOLUTION

There are twelve compounding periods per year and a total of $(12)(3) = 36$ compounding periods.

Then $\$5000 = P_0 \left(1 + \dfrac{0.10}{12}\right)^{36} \approx 1.3482 P_0.$ Thus,

$P_0 \approx \$3709.$

If the number of compounding periods per year gets increasingly larger, the value of n approaches infinity. This concept is called *continuous compounding* and would be appropriate in examples dealing with inflation. *The formula for continuous compounding is*

$P(t) = P_0 e^{rt}$, *where* $e = \lim\limits_{n \to \infty}\left(1 + \dfrac{1}{n}\right)^{n} \approx 2.7183$.

EXAMPLE 24

If the annual rate of inflation is 4.4 %, and the annual rate of interest is compounded continuously, what will be the value of $2000 in 12 years? (nearest dollar)

SOLUTION:

$P(12) = (\$2000)(e^{(0.044)(12)}) = (\$2000)(e^{0.528}) \approx \$3391.$

EXAMPLE 25

If the annual rate of inflation is 3%, and the annual rate of interest is compounded continuously, in how many years will $1500 grow to $4500? (nearest tenth of a year)

SOLUTION

$\$4500 = (\$1500)(e^{0.03t})$, which simplifies to $3 = e^{0.03t}$. Taking the natural logarithm of each side, $\ln 3 = (0.03t)$

$(\ln e) = 0.03t$. Thus, $t = \dfrac{\ln 3}{0.03} \approx 36.6$ years.

EXAMPLE 26

Assuming that the annual rate of interest is compounded continuously, at what interest rate will $900 grow to $3800 in a period of 20 years? (nearest tenth of one percent)

SOLUTION

$\$3800 = (\$900)(e^{20r})$, which simplifies to $4.\overline{2} = e^{20r}$.

Then $\ln 4.\overline{2} = (20r)(\ln e) = 20r$. Thus, $r = \dfrac{\ln 4.\overline{2}}{20} \approx$

$0.072 = 7.2\%$.

Quiz for Chapter 4

1. What is the 52nd term of the sequence 27, 13, −1, −15,....?

   (A) −687   (C) −714

   (B) −701   (D) −727

2. In a certain arithmetic sequence, the fifth term is 20.4 and the 12th term is 36.5. What is the value of the first term?

   (A) 8.6   (C) 11.2

   (B) 9.9   (D) 12.5

3. In a certain geometric sequence, the seventh term is 14,745.6 and the common ratio is –4. What is the value of the first term?

   (A) 3.6   (C) 3.4

   (B) 3.5   (D) 3.3

4. Which one of the following sequences is neither arithmetic nor geometric?

   (A) 19.4, 20.1, 20.8, 21.5,….

   (B) $-\dfrac{1}{4}, -\dfrac{3}{8}, -\dfrac{9}{16}, -\dfrac{27}{32},\ldots$

   (C) 100, 40, 16, 6.4,….

   (D) 1.1, 2.02, 3.003, 4.004, ….

5. In a certain geometric sequence, the fifth term is 3232 and the eighth term is 50.5. What are the possible values of the common ratio?

   (A) Only $\dfrac{1}{4}$ (C) Only $\dfrac{1}{8}$

   (B) Both $\dfrac{1}{4}$ and $-\dfrac{1}{4}$ (D) Both $\dfrac{1}{8}$ and $-\dfrac{1}{8}$

6. What is the sum of the first 20 terms of the sequence 21, 26.5, 32, 37.5, ….?

   (A) 1410   (C) 1520

   (B) 1465   (D) 1575

7. The first term of an infinite geometric sequence is 21. If the sum of all the terms is 30, what is the value of the common ratio?

   (A) 0.7   (C) 0.3

   (B) 0.6   (D) 0.2

8. What is the approximate sum of the first 16 terms of the sequence $\dfrac{5}{3}$, 10, 60, 360,….?

   (A) 9.40×10^{11} (C) 4.18×10^{11}

   (B) 6.79×10^{11} (D) 1.57×10^{11}

9. Given a sequence in which $a_1 = 8$ and $a_n = 1.8a_{n-1} - 3$ for $n > 1$, what is the value of the third term?

   (A) 11.40   (C) 15.48

   (B) 13.44   (D) 17.52

10. Suppose $1200 is deposited into a bank in which the annual simple interest rate is 8.5%. After how many years will this amount grow to $2730?

    (A) 14   (C) 16

    (B) 15   (D) 17

11. If $2150 is deposited into a bank in which the interest rate is 9% compounded semi-annually, what is the amount after 7 years? (nearest dollar)

    (A) $3982   (C) $3837

    (B) $3930   (D) $3805

12. A person will need $8000 in 4 years to help pay off a car loan. How much money should be deposited into a bank in which the interest rate is 10% compounded quarterly? (nearest dollar)

    (A) $5415   (C) $5389

    (B) $5403   (D) $5371

13. If the annual rate of inflation is 4%, and the annual rate of interest is compounded continuously, in how many years will $5500 grow to $11,000? (nearest tenth of a year)

    (A) 21.2   (C) 18.6

    (B) 19.9   (D) 17.3

14. If the annual rate of inflation is 2.8%, and the annual rate of interest is compounded continuously, what will be the value of $36,000 in 6 years? (nearest dollar)

    (A) $42,390   (C) $42,586

    (B) $42,488   (D) $42,684

Quiz for Chapter 4
SOLUTIONS

1. (A)

This sequence is arithmetic. The 52nd term is $(27) + (51)(-14) = -687$.

2. (C)

$20.4 = a + 4d$ and $36.5 = a + 11d$. By subtraction, $16.1 = 7d$. Then $d = 2.3$. Substitute this value into the first equation to get $20.4 = a + (4)(2.3)$. Thus, $a = 11.2$.

3. (A)

$14,745.6 = (a_1)(-4)^6$. Thus, $a_1 = \dfrac{14,745.6}{4096} = 3.6$.

4. (D)

To check that this sequence is not arithmetic, note that $2.02 - 1.1 \neq 3.003 - 2.02$. Also, this sequence is not geometric since $\dfrac{2.02}{1.1} \neq \dfrac{3.003}{2.02}$.

5. (A)

$3232 = a_1 r^4$ and $50.5 = a_1 r^7$. Dividing the second equation by the first equation, $\dfrac{1}{64} = r^3$. Thus, $r = \sqrt[3]{\dfrac{1}{64}} = \dfrac{1}{4}$.

6. (B)

In this arithmetic sequence, $s_{20} = \dfrac{20}{2}\big[(2)(21) + (19)(5.5)\big] = 1465$.

7. (B)

$30 = \dfrac{21}{1 - r}$, which simplifies to $30 - 30r = 21$. Thus, $r = \dfrac{-9}{-30} = 0.3$.

8. (A)

In this geometric sequence, $s_{16} = \dfrac{\dfrac{5}{3} - \left(\dfrac{5}{3}\right)(6)^{16}}{1 - 6} \approx 9.40 \times 10^{11}$.

9. (D)

$a_2 = (1.8)(8) - 3 = 11.4$. Then $a_3 = (1.8)(11.4) - 3 = 17.52$.

10. (B)

$\$2730 = \$1200 + (\$1200)(0.085)(t) = \$1200 + \$102t$. Then $t = \dfrac{\$1530}{\$102} = 15$ years.

11. (A)

$P(7) = (\$2150)\left(1 + \dfrac{0.09}{2}\right)^{14} \approx \$3982$.

12. (C)

$\$8000 = P\left(1 + \dfrac{0.10}{4}\right)^{16} \approx 1.4845P$. Thus, $P \approx \$5389$.

13. (D)

$\$11,000 = \$5500e^{0.04t}$, which simplifies to $e^{0.04t} = 2$. Then $0.04t = \ln 2 \approx 0.6931$. Thus, $t \approx 17.3$ years.

14. (C)

$P(6) = (\$36,000)(e^{(0.028)(6)}) = (\$36,000)(e^{0.168}) \approx \$42,586$

Functions

Welcome to Chapter 5. In this chapter, we will review the following algebraic topics:

(a) Relations
(b) Domain and range of functions
(c) Categories of functions
(d) Transformations of functions
(e) Operations on functions

Relations

A **relation** is a set (collection) of members that are ordered pairs. Each ordered pair is called an element. The set is indicated by braces and is normally assigned a capital letter.

Here are a few examples of relations:

$A = \{(5, 7), (9, 1)\}$. The two elements of set A are $(5, 7)$ and $(9, 1)$.

$B = \{(\text{tree, w}), (6, 6), (\text{math, tree}), \left(-3, \frac{1}{2}\right)\}$. Set B has four elements.

The number 6 appears in both the first and second parts of the element $(6, 6)$; also, the word "tree" appears as the first part of (tree, w) but as the second part of (math, tree).

$C = \{(\text{a}, 10), (\text{b}, 10), (\text{c}, 10), (\text{d}, 10), (\text{e}, 10), (\text{f}, 10)\}$. Set C has six elements.

The number 10 appears as the second part of each element.

$D = \{(\text{shoe}, 3), (-2, 5), (\text{shoe}, 7), (\text{c}, 0), (\text{b}, 10)\}$. Set D has five elements.

The word "shoe" appears as the first part of two different elements.

Also, we have used the element (b, 10) in both this set and in set C.

In any relation, some elements may have shared "parts," but there is no repetition of elements. Thus, if a set contained the element $(-3, 4)$, it could also include the element $(-3, 5)$ or even $(4, -3)$, but we would not repeat $(-3, 4)$ as an additional element.

Domain and Range of Functions

For each ordered pair of a relation, the set of all first parts is called the domain; the set of all second parts is called the **range**. For set A, the domain is $\{5, 9\}$ and the range is {7,1}. For set *B*, the domain is {tree, 6, math, -3} and the range is {w, 6, tree, $\frac{1}{2}$}.

For set *C*, the domain is {a, b, c, d, e, f} and the range is {10}. Finally, for set *D*, the domain is {shoe, -2, c, b} and the range is {3, 5, 7, 0, 10}.

Recall that the members of a set may be listed in any order. Thus, we could have stated the domain of set B as {6, -3, math, tree}.

A **function** is a special type of relation in which for each different element in the domain, there is exactly one element in the range that is assigned to it. Sets *A*, *B*, and *C* shown above are all functions, since this rule is followed. Notice that there is repetition of the range element in set *C*. This does not violate the definition of functions, because each of the six elements of the domain, (namely a, b, c, d, e, f) is assigned to exactly one range element. (namely 10).

In order for a relation to not qualify as a function, we need to use two elements in which the domain value is the same but the range value is different. Set *D* shown above is such an example. There are two elements, (shoe, 3) and (shoe, 7), in which the domain value "shoe" is paired with both 3 and 7. This means that *D* is not a function.

EXAMPLE 1

Given the set $E = \{(-5, 4), (b, 2), (\_, 6)\}$, fill in the blank so that *E* is not a function.

SOLUTION

The two possibilities are -5 and b. If the third element of *E* were either $(-5, 6)$ or $(b, 6)$, set *E* would not be a function.

EXAMPLE 2

Given the set $F = \{(4, \text{hat}), (\text{hat}, -8), (9, \text{z}), (\_, \text{z})\}$. If *F* is a function with four elements, what are the restrictions in filling in the blank?

SOLUTION

The blank may not be filled in with any of 4, hat, or 9. Each of 4 and hat is already paired with a range value. The reason that 9 cannot be used is that (9, z) is already an element of *F*. If this same element were to be repeated, then *F* would really have only three elements, not four elements.

Some functions may be described with *equations*. For example, suppose the domain of a function is {0, 2, 4, 6} and the range is described by $f(x) = x - 5$. This means that for each *x* value in the domain, the range value is found by the expression $x - 5$. Thus, $f(0) = 0 - 5 = -5$, $f(2) = 2 - 5 = -3$, $f(4) = 4 - 5 = -1$, and $f(6) = 6 - 5 = 1$. This function can now be written as $\{(0, -5), (2, -3), (4, -1), (6, 1)\}$.

Another example of a function that is described by an equation is $\{(x,y) \mid y = 3x^2, \text{ for } x = -1, 3, 5\}$. When $x = -1$, $y = 3(-1)^2 = 3$; when $x = 3$, $y = 3(3)^2 = 27$; when $x = 5$, $y = 3(5)^2 = 75$. This function may be written as $\{(-1, 3), (3, 27), (5, 75)\}$.

A vertical line test can be used to check if a given relation is a function. Any vertical line may intersect the graph of a function <u>at</u> <u>most</u> <u>once</u>. In Figure 5.1 shown below, $f(x)$ is a function, but $g(x)$ is not a function.

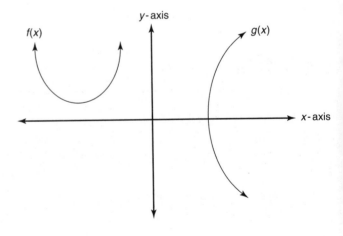

Figure 5.1

Categories of Functions

Two special categories of functions are called *even functions* and *odd functions*.

Even Functions

A function $f(x)$ is called <u>even</u> if for each x in the domain, $f(x) = f(-x)$. In this notation, each element of the function is in the form $(x, f(x))$. As ordered pairs, for a specific x (domain) value, each of x and $-x$ must be paired with the same range value.

Here are some examples:

$G = \{(-5, 1), (7, 9), (5, 1), (-7, 9)\}$. Notice that if the domain value is 5 or -5, the range value is 1. Similarly, when the domain value is 7 or -7, the range value is 9.

$H = \{(x, f(x)) \mid f(x) = -x^2$, for $x = 0, -1, 1 -4, 4, -10, 10\}$. The range values are given by $f(0) = 0$, $f(-1) = -1, f(1) = -1, f(-4) = -16, f(4) = -16$, $f(-10) = -100$, and $f(10) = -100$.

$J = \{(x, |x|)\}$, for all real numbers x. The domain is all real numbers and the range is all non-negative numbers. Since the value of $|x|$ is the non-negative value of x, this function must be even. Set J has an infinite number of elements; some of its elements are $(0, 0)$, $(6, 6)$, $(-6, 6)$, $(1.4, 1.4)$, and $(-1.4, 1.4)$.

Graphically, every even function is symmetric about the y-axis. In Figure 5.2 shown below, each of $h(x)$ and $k(x)$ is an even function.

Odd Functions

A function $f(x)$ is called odd if for each x in the domain, $f(x) = -f(-x)$. In notation form, each element of the function is still shown as $(x, f(x))$. For a specific x value, the range values of x and $-x$ must be additive inverses. Here are two examples:

$K = \{(3, 7), (-3, -7), (0, 0), (8, -1), (-8, 1)\}$. Notice that $f(3) = -f(-3)$ and $f(8) = -f(-8)$. Of course $0 = -0$, so $f(0) = -f(-0) = 0$.

$L = \{(x,y) \mid y = x^3$, for all real values of $x\}$. The domain is all real numbers and the range is also all real numbers. As examples of elements of L, if $x = 2$, $y = 2^3 = 8$; if $x = -2$, then $y = (-2)^3 = -8$; if $x = 0.3$, then $y = (0.3)^3 = 0.027$; and if $x = -0.3$, $y = (-0.3)^3 = -0.027$.

Graphically, every odd function is symmetric about the origin. In Figures 5.3 and 5.4 shown below, each of $m(x)$ and $n(x)$ is an odd function.

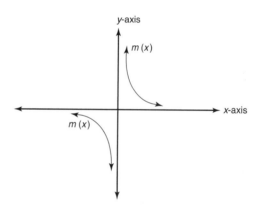

Figure 5.3

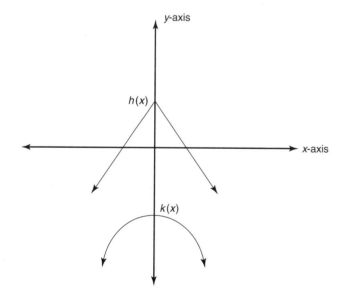

Figure 5.2

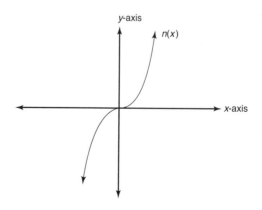

Figure 5.4

Neither Odd nor Even Functions

There are many functions that are neither odd nor even. Three such examples are $f(x) = 9 - 4x$, $f(x) = x^2 - x + 3$, and $f(x) = |x| + x$. Letting $x = 2$, the three corresponding $f(x)$ values are 1, 5, and 4. Letting $x = -2$, the three corresponding $f(x)$ values are 17, 9, and 0. Note that $f(x) \neq f(-x)$ and $f(x) \neq -f(-x)$.

One-to-One Function

A one-to-one function satisfies the condition that for each range value, there is exactly one domain value. Mathematically, if $f(x_1) = f(x_2)$, then $x_1 = x_2$. Let's look at a few examples of functions to see if they are one-to-one.

EXAMPLE 3

$N = \{(x,y)|\ y = 4x^2$ for all real values of $x\}$. Is N a one-to-one function?

SOLUTION

Let $y = 16$. Then $16 = 4x^2$, from which $x = \pm\sqrt{4} = \pm 2$. Thus, N is not a one-to-one function. Both $(2, 4)$ and $(-2, 4)$ are elements of N.

EXAMPLE 4

$P = \{(0, 5), (-2, 9), (10, -1)\}$. Is P a one-to-one function?

SOLUTION

For each of the different range values of P, namely 5, 9, and -1, there is exactly one domain value. Thus, P is a one-to-one function.

EXAMPLE 5

$Q = \{x,y)|\ y = 6 + x^3$ for $x \geq 0\}$. Is Q a one-to-one function?

SOLUTION

Let $y = 10$ represent a particular range value. Then $10 = x^3 + 6$, which simplifies to $4 = x^3$. Thus, $x = \sqrt[3]{4} \approx 1.59$, which is the only domain value for this particular range value. By substituting any other allowable range value, we find that there is only one corresponding domain value.

Thus, Q is a one-to-one function.

EXAMPLE 6

$R = \{(8, 6), (2, 5), (-2, -4), (5, 1), (3, 6)\}$. Is R a one-to-one function?

SOLUTION

Looking at the two elements, $(8, 6)$ and $(3, 6)$, we can conclude that R is not a one-to-one function. For the given range value of 6, there are two different corresponding domain values, namely 8 and 3.

Graphically, a one-to-one function must obey both the *vertical line* test and the *horizontal line* test. As mentioned earlier, a vertical line may intersect the graph of a function at most once. Additionally, if a horizontal line intersects the graph of a function at most once, then that function is one-to-one. In Figure 5.5 shown below, $p(x)$ is a one-to-one function. Notice that $q(x)$ is a function, but it is not one-to-one.

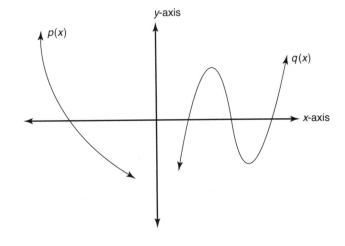

Figure 5.5

Remember many different small letters may precede (x) to indicate a function. We are not required to always use $f(x)$ or $g(x)$. These other notations are particularly useful when dealing with two or more functions in the same problem.

For <u>Examples 7, 8, and 9,</u> we'll use the following information:

$S = \{(0, 4), (3, 7), (6, -2), (3, -1), (10, -5)\}$

$T = \{(x, y)|\, y = 3x - 9$, for all non-positive values of $x\}$

$U = \{(1, 3), (-2, 4), (3, -3), (9, 4)\}$

$V = \{(x, g(x))|\, g(x) = 1 - x^2$, for all real values of $x\}$

$W = \{(x,y)|\, x^2 + y^2 = 9$, for all x values between -3 and 3, inclusive$\}$

$X = \{(x, h(x))|\, h(x) = 5x^3$, for $x = 1, 2, 3, 4, 5\}$

$Y = \{(1, 2), (2, 1), (3, 4), (4, 3), (5, 6), (6, 5)\, \}$

EXAMPLE 7

Which ones are not functions?

SOLUTION

Both S and W are not functions. For S, the presence of $(3, 7)$ and $(3, -1)$ means that the same domain value is matched up with two different range values. For W, let $x = 1$. Then $1^2 + y^2 = 9$, which simplifies to $y^2 = 8$. Thus, $y = \pm\sqrt{8}$, which again matches up two range values for the same domain value.

EXAMPLE 8

Which ones are functions, but not one-to-one?

SOLUTION

Both U and V are functions, but not one-to-one. For each of these two relations, any allowable domain value leads to exactly one range value. For U, the presence of $(-2, 4)$ and $(9, 4)$ indicates that the range value of 4 is paired with two different domain values. For V, let $x = -4$ and 4. In each case, $g(x) = -15$. Thus the

range value of -15 is paired with two different domain values.

EXAMPLE 9

Which one is a one-to-one function in which the domain values are the same as the range values?

SOLUTION

Y is a one-to-one function for which the $\{1, 2, 3, 4, 5, 6\}$ represents the range and the domain. The graph of this function is just six points, through which any vertical or horizontal line passes at most once.

Note that T and X are also one-to-one functions, but their domains and ranges are different. For T, the domain is non-negative numbers and the range is all numbers less than or equal to -9. For X, the domain is 1, 2, 3, 4, and 5; the range is 5, 40, 135, 320, and 625. The domains and ranges of any of these relations can be verified by their graphs.

Sometimes, we are interested in determining the domain of a function in a strictly algebraic manner. In these instances, the dependent variable (y or $f(x)$) is given explicitly in terms of the independent variable (x). One common type is a rational function that contains a denominator that contains the independent variable.

A second common type is function involving a square root that contains the independent variable.

EXAMPLE 10

What is the domain of the function $f(x) = \dfrac{3}{x + 7}$?

SOLUTION

When dealing with a fraction, the denominator cannot be zero. This means that $x + 7 \neq 0$, which becomes $x \neq -7$. The domain is all numbers except -7.

EXAMPLE 11

> What is the domain of the function
> $$g(x) = \frac{2-x}{x^2 - 25}?$$

SOLUTION

Similar to Example 10, we write $x^2 - 25 \neq 0$, which becomes $(x-5)(x+5) \neq 0$. This leads to $x \neq 5$ and $x \neq -5$. The domain is all numbers except 5 and -5.

EXAMPLE 12

> What is the domain of the function
> $$h(x) = \frac{6x}{2x^2 + 7x - 4}?$$

SOLUTION

First write $2x^2 + 7x - 4 \neq 0$, which factors as $(2x-1)(x+4) \neq 0$. If $2x - 1 \neq 0$, then $x \neq \frac{1}{2}$. If $x + 4 \neq 0$, then $x \neq -4$. The domain is all numbers except $\frac{1}{2}$ and -4.

EXAMPLE 13

> What is the domain of the function
> $$w(x) = \sqrt{3x + 15}?$$

SOLUTION

Even though $f(x), g(x),$ and $h(x)$ are most often used for function notation, other letters may also be used. In the world of real numbers, quantities within a square root symbol must be non-negative. This means that $3x + 15 \geq 0$. Solving, we get $x \geq -5$. The domain is all numbers greater than or equal to -5.

EXAMPLE 14

> What is the domain of the function
> $$v(x) = \sqrt{20 - 6x}?$$

SOLUTION

Similar to Example 13, we write $20 - 6x \geq 0$. Then $x \leq \frac{20}{6} = \frac{10}{3}$. The domain is all numbers less than or equal to $\frac{10}{3}$.

Parent Function

Parent functions are basic functions from which more complicated (but similar) functions can be evaluated. For example, $f(x) = x$ is a parent function for all linear functions in the form $f(x) = ax + b$, where a and b are constants. A second example would be $f(x) = \frac{1}{x}$, which is a parent function for all reciprocal functions in the form $f(x) = \dfrac{c}{a_0 + a_1 x + a_2 x^2 + ... + a_n x^n}$, where $c, a_0, a_1, ..., a_n$ are constants.

Family of Functions

A **family of functions** includes the parent function and all related functions, of which there are an infinite number. For example, given the parent function $f(x) = x$, the associated family of functions would include $f(x) = 3x, f(x) = x - 7,$ and $f(x) = 4x + 11$. In a similar fashion, given the parent function $f(x) = \frac{1}{x}$, the associated family of functions would include $f(x) = \dfrac{5}{x + 9}$, $f(x) = \dfrac{-2}{x^2 + 8x - 1}$, and $f(x) = \dfrac{12}{7x^3 + 3}$.

Transformations of Functions

The process by which we discover the members of a family of functions for a particular parent function is called a **transformation**. The number of existing transformations is virtually uncountable, but we will discuss four basic transformations.

Four Basic Transformations

1. Given the parent function in the form $f(x)$, the function $f(x) + k$, where k is a constant.

   As an example, using the parent function $f(x) = x$, a member of this family would be $g(x) = x + 5$. So, $g(x) = f(x) + 5$. For each specific x value, $g(x)$ is five units larger than $f(x)$. Then the graph of $g(x)$ can be drawn by shifting the graph of $f(x)$ five units upward. This is easy to check. Consider the points $(-1, -1)$, $(2, 2)$, and $(5, 5)$ that belong to the graph of $f(x)$. Now, by adding five units to the second member of each ordered pair, we get $(-1, 4)$, $(2, 7)$, and $(5, 10)$. These points belong to the graph of $g(x)$. The graphs of $f(x)$ and $g(x)$ are shown below in Figures 5.6 and 5.7 .

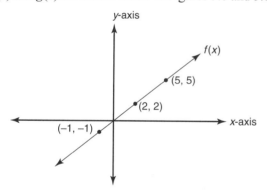

Figure 5.6

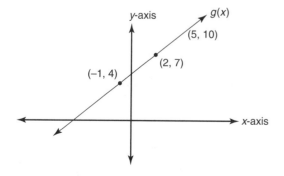

Figure 5.7

As a second example, let $f(x) = x^3$ represent the parent function and let $g(x) = x^3 - 2$. For each specific value of x, the value of $g(x)$ is two units less than $f(x)$. Thus, given the graph of $f(x)$, we can draw the graph of $g(x)$ by shifting the graph of $f(x)$ two units downward. Using the points $(0, 0)$, $(2, 8)$, and $(-1, -1)$ that belong to the graph of $f(x)$, we can check that $(0, -2)$, $(2, 6)$ and $(-1, -3)$ belong to the graph of $g(x)$. The graphs of $f(x)$ and $g(x)$ are shown below in Figures 5.8 and 5.9 .

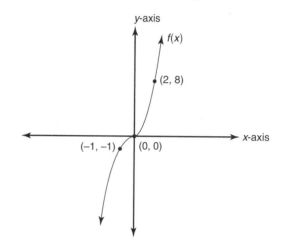

Figure 5.8

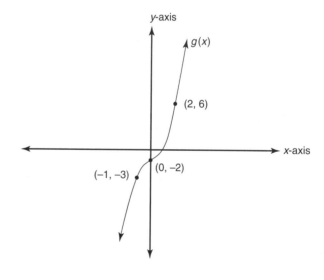

Figure 5.9

2. Our second transformation for consideration is the comparison of the parent function $f(x)$ with (k) $(f(x))$, where k is a constant.

   As an example, using the parent function $f(x) = x^2$, let $g(x) = 3x^2$. Consider the points $(-3, 9)$, $(1, 1)$, and

(2, 4) that belong to the graph of $f(x)$. Using the same x values, we note that the points $(-3, 27)$, $(1, 3)$, and $(2, 12)$ belong to the graph of $g(x)$. This indicates that by multiplying the second member of each ordered pair of $f(x)$ by three, we get the graph of $g(x)$. Notice also that the graph of $g(x)$ is narrower than that of $f(x)$. The graphs of $f(x)$ and $g(x)$ are shown below in Figures 5.10 and 5.11.

of $f(x)$. Using the same x values, and multiplying the second member of each ordered pair by -5, we find the points $\left(-2, \frac{5}{2}\right)$, $\left(3, -\frac{5}{3}\right)$, and $\left(4, -\frac{5}{4}\right)$ belong to the graph of $g(x)$. The graphs of $f(x)$ and $g(x)$ are shown below in Figures 5.12 and 5.13.

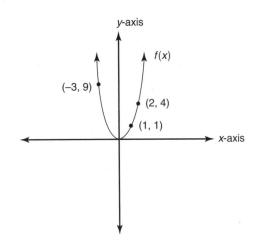

Figure 5.10

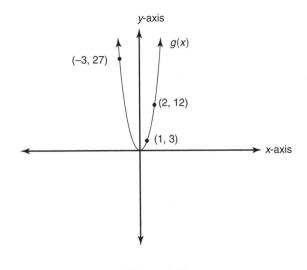

Figure 5.11

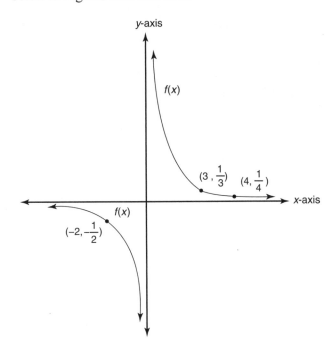

Figure 5.12

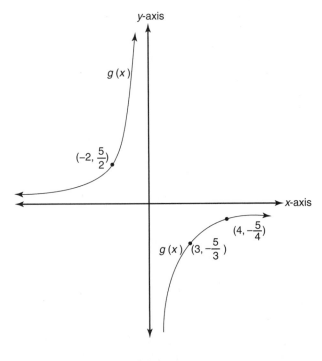

Figure 5.13

As a second example, let $f(x) = \frac{1}{x}$ represent the parent function and let $g(x) = \frac{-5}{x}$. Consider the points $\left(-2, -\frac{1}{2}\right)$, $\left(3, \frac{1}{3}\right)$, and $\left(4, \frac{1}{4}\right)$ that belong to the graph

3. The third comparison is of the parent function $f(x)$ with $f(x+k)$, where k is a constant.

As an example, using the parent function $f(x) = x^4$, let $g(x) = (x+1)^4$. Let's use the points $(0, 0)$, $(-2, 16)$, and $(3, 81)$ that belong to the graph of $f(x)$. Instead of using the same x values for $g(x)$, we will use the x values that represent one unit less than each of these x values, namely -1, -3, and 2. By substitution, the points we identify on the graph of $g(x)$ are $(-1, 0)$, $(-3, 16)$, and $(2, 81)$. This means that by subtracting one unit from each x value of $f(x)$, the second member values (y) of each ordered pair of $f(x)$ and $g(x)$ will match. Basically, we need to shift the graph of $f(x)$ one unit to the left in order to create the graph of $g(x)$. The graphs of $f(x)$ and $g(x)$ are shown below in Figures 5.14 and 5.15.

As a second example, let $f(x) = \sqrt{x}$ represent the parent function and let $g(x) = \sqrt{x-3}$. We will restrict our selections of x to values greater than or equal to 3; in this way, each of $f(x)$ and $g(x)$ will be defined for the selected x values. We'll use the points $\left(3, \sqrt{3}\right)$, $(4, 2)$, and $(9, 3)$ that belong to the graph of $f(x)$. The x values to be chosen for $g(x)$ will be three units higher than the ones we used for $f(x)$, namely 6, 7, and 12. By substitution, we find the points $\left(6, \sqrt{3}\right)$, $(7, 2)$ and $(12, 3)$ belong to the graph of $g(x)$. Basically, we need to shift the graph of $f(x)$ three units to the right to draw the graph of $g(x)$. The graphs of $f(x)$ and $g(x)$ are shown below in Figures 5.16 and 5.17.

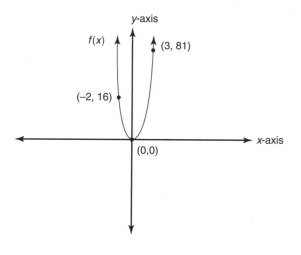

Figure 5.14

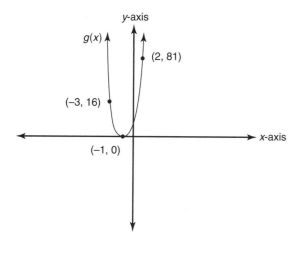

Figure 5.15

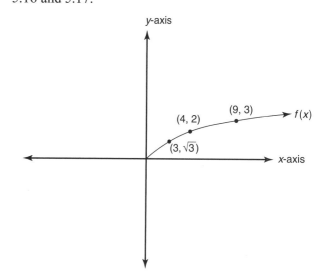

Figure 5.16

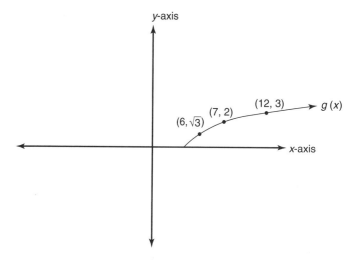

Figure 5.17

4. The final comparison is of the parent function $f(x)$ with $f(kx)$, where k is a constant.

CAUTION!

Be sure that you do NOT confuse $f(kx)$ with $(k)(f(x))$.

As an example, using the parent function, $f(x) = x^2$ let $g(x) = (2x)^2 = 4x^2$. We'll use the x values of -1, 2, and 5 for identifying three points for the graph of each of $f(x)$ and $g(x)$. Then $(-1, 1)$, $(2, 4)$, and $(5, 25)$ belong to the graph of $f(x)$; the points $(-1, 4)$, $(2, 16)$, and $(5, 100)$ belong to the graph of $g(x)$. We note that each of $f(x)$ and $g(x)$ is a quadratic function. By using the same x values for each quadratic function, the corresponding y values of $g(x)$ are $2^2 = 4$ times those of $f(x)$. The graphs for these two functions are shown below in Figures 5.18 and 5.19. Note that the graph of $f(x)$ is wider than the graph of $g(x)$.

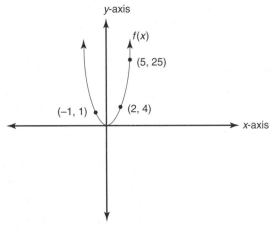

Figure 5.18

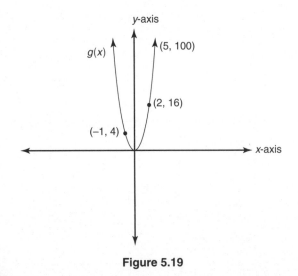

Figure 5.19

As a second example, let $f(x) = x^3$ represent the parent function and let $g(x) = \left(\dfrac{1}{2}x\right)^3 = \dfrac{1}{8}x^3$. We'll use the x values of -1, 2, and 4 for each of these functions. Then the graph of $f(x)$ will contain the points $(-1, -1)$, $(2, 8)$, and $(4, 64)$. The graph of $g(x)$ will contain the points $\left(-1, -\dfrac{1}{8}\right)$, $(2,1)$, and $(4, 8)$. We note that each of $f(x)$ and $g(x)$ is a cubic function. By using the same x values for each cubic function, the corresponding y values of $g(x)$ are $\left(\dfrac{1}{2}\right)^3 = \dfrac{1}{8}$ as large as those of $f(x)$.

The graphs for these two functions are shown below in Figures 5.20 and 5.21.

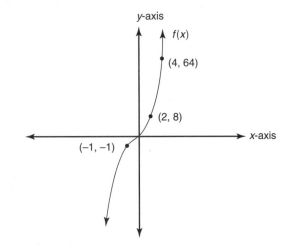

Figure 5.20

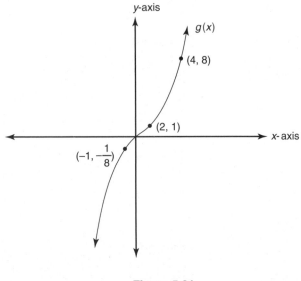

Figure 5.21

Summary

Here are the conclusions we have reached regarding the various transformations of a parent function $f(x)$. In each instance, k is a constant.

1. The graph of $f(x) + k$ lies k units above $f(x)$ if $k < 0$, and lies k units below $f(x)$ if $k < 0$.

2. For a given set of x values, the y values of $(k)(f(x))$ are k times those of $f(x)$. When $k > 1$, the graph of $(k)(f(x))$ is narrower than that of $f(x)$. For $k < 1$, the graph of $(k)(f(x))$ is wider than that of $f(x)$. This can be verified by comparing the graph of $f(x) = x^2$ and the graph of $h(x) = \frac{1}{2}x^2$.

3. The graph of $f(x + k)$ lies k units to the left of $f(x)$ if $k > 0$, and lies k units to the right of $f(x)$ if $k < 0$.

4. For a given set of x values, the y values of $f(kx)$ equal the product of those of $f(x)$ and k raised to the power of $f(x)$. For example, if $f(x)$ is quadratic, then the y values of $f(kx)$ equal those of $f(x)$ times the square of k.

EXAMPLE 15

> Write the equation of a function whose graph lies seven units to the right of the graph of $f(x) = x^6$.

SOLUTION

Using item #3 of our summary, the answer is $g(x) = (x - 7)^6$.

EXAMPLE 16

> Write the equation of a function whose graph lies eight units below the graph of $f(x) = \sqrt{x}$.

SOLUTION

Using item #1 of our summary, the answer is $g(x) = \sqrt{x} - 8$.

EXAMPLE 17

> If $f(x) = x^2$, write the equation of a function in the form $g(x) = f(kx)$ whose y values are $\frac{1}{25}$ as large as the y values of $f(x)$ for a given set of x values.

SOLUTION

Using item #4 of our summary $k^2 = \frac{1}{25}$, so $k = \frac{1}{5}$.

The answer is $g(x) = f\left(\frac{1}{5}x\right)$.

Composite Functions

A **composite function** is one whose values are found from two given functions. We know that a function represents a procedure for creating an output value for an input value of x. For example, if the input value of x is 2 and $f(x) = 3x - 1$, then the output value is given by $f(2) = 3(2) - 1 = 5$.

A composite function uses two (usually different) functions in which the output of a first function becomes the input of the second function. The final answer is the output of the second function. Suppose we are given two functions $f(x)$ and $g(x)$, in which $f(x)$ is the second function and $g(x)$ is the first function. The notation for the composite function is written as either $(f \circ g)(x)$ or $f[g(x)]$. We will use the latter notation.

EXAMPLE 18

> Given $f(x) = x^2$ and $g(x) = 4x - 1$, express in simplest terms $f[g(x)]$.

SOLUTION

First replace $g(x)$ by $4x - 1$, so that we have $f[4x - 1]$. We can think of $f(x) = x^2$ as follows: For any input, the function $f(x)$ creates the output of the square of the input. In this case the input is $4x - 1$. Thus, $f[4x - 1] = (4x - 1)^2 = 16x^2 - 8x + 1$.

EXAMPLE 19

> Returning to the given functions in Example 18, express in simplest terms the composite function $g[f(x)]$.

SOLUTION

If you suspect that the answer is different than the one we obtained in Example 18, your suspicion is correct. First replace $f(x)$ by x^2 so that we have $g[x^2]$. The function rule for $g(x)$ is to multiply the input by 4, then subtract 1. Thus, $g[x^2] = 4x^2 - 1$.

EXAMPLE 20

> Given $h(x) = \sqrt{8-x}$ and $k(x) = -5x$, express $h[k(x)]$ in simplest form.

SOLUTION

$$h[k(x)] = h[-5x] = \sqrt{8-(-5x)} = \sqrt{8+5x}.$$

EXAMPLE 21

> Return to the functions of Example 20. Express $k[h(x)]$ in simplest form.

SOLUTION

$k[h(x)] = k\left[\sqrt{8-x}\right] = -5\sqrt{8-x}$. Notice that $h[k(x)] \neq k[h(x)]$.

EXAMPLE 22

> If $f(x) = x^3 + 6$ and $h(x) = \frac{2}{3}x + 4$, what is the value of $f[h(-3)]$?

SOLUTION

First evaluate $h(-3) = \left(\frac{2}{3}\right)(-3) + 4 = 2$.

Then $f(2) = 2^3 + 6 = 14$.

EXAMPLE 23

> If $g(x) = \frac{3}{2}x - 5$ and $k(x) = -x^2 + x$, what is the value of $g[k(5)]$?

SOLUTION

First evaluate $k(5) = -5^2 + 5 = -20$. Then $g(-20) = \left(\frac{3}{2}\right)(-20) - 5 = -35$.

Inverse Functions

Two **functions** $f(x)$ and $g(x)$ are **inverses** of each other if they are one-to-one and $f(g(x)) = g(f(x)) = x$. The inverse of a function $f(x)$ is commonly denoted as $f^{-1}(x)$.

NOTE:

> Only one-to-one functions have inverses. In addition, the domain of $f(x)$ equals the range of $f^{-1}(x)$ and the range of $f(x)$ equals the domain of $f^{-1}(x)$.

EXAMPLE 24

> What is the inverse function of $f(x) = \{(2, 4), (-3, 7), (0, 5), (7, -1)\}$?

SOLUTION

We simply reverse the domain and range of $f(x)$. Thus, we get $f^{-1}(x) = \{(4, 2), (7, -3), (5, 0), (-1, 7)\}$.

If $f(x)$ is described by an equation, we can determine the equation for $f^{-1}(x)$ by first replacing $f(x)$ by y, then interchanging each x and y. The "new" expression, written explicitly in terms of x, becomes $f^{-1}(x)$.

EXAMPLE 25

What is the inverse of $f(x) = 4x + 10$?

SOLUTION

Rewrite as $y = 4x + 10$. Interchange the variables to get $x = 4y + 10$. Solving for y, $x - 10 = 4y$. Thus, $y = \dfrac{x - 10}{4}$ (or $y = \dfrac{1}{4}x - \dfrac{5}{2}$). We can state that $f^{-1}(x) = \dfrac{x - 10}{4}$.

Two solid ways to check that this answer is correct are:

1. Find points that lie on the graph of $f(x)$, then interchange the first and second members. These new points should lie on the graph of $f^{-1}(x)$.

2. Verify that $f(g(x)) = g(f(x)) = x$.

Let's use these two methods to verify the solution to Example 25. For $f(x) = 4x + 10$, we'll use x values of 1 and 4. By substitution, the points (1, 14) and (4, 26) must lie on the graph of $f(x)$. Interchanging the members of each ordered pair yields the points (14, 1) and (26, 4). By substitution, we can see that each of these points satisfies the equation $f^{-1}(x) = \dfrac{x - 10}{4}$.

As another check, we'll use $g(x)$ in place of $f^{-1}(x)$. Then $f(g(x)) = f\left(\dfrac{x - 10}{4}\right) = (4)\left(\dfrac{x - 10}{4}\right) + 10 = x$. Furthermore, $g(f(x)) = g(4x + 10) = \dfrac{(4x + 10) - 10}{4}$ $= x$.

EXAMPLE 26

What is the inverse of $f(x) = \sqrt{2x - 1}$?

SOLUTION

We start with $y = \sqrt{2x - 1}$. By interchanging the variables, we get $x = \sqrt{2y - 1}$. By squaring both sides, $x^2 = 2y - 1$. By adding 1 and dividing by 2, we arrive at $y = \dfrac{x^2 + 1}{2}$. Thus, $f^{-1}(x) = \dfrac{x^2 + 1}{2}$.

EXAMPLE 27

What is the inverse of $f(x) = 7e^x$?

SOLUTION

Rewrite as $y = 7e^x$. By interchanging the variables, $x = 7e^y$. This leads to $\ln x = \ln(7e^y) = \ln 7 + \ln e^y$. Since $\ln e^y = y$, we have $y = \ln x - \ln 7 = \ln\left(\dfrac{x}{7}\right)$. Thus, $f^{-1}(x) = \ln\left(\dfrac{x}{7}\right)$.

As a check for the solutions to Examples 26 and 27, let's first show that in Example 26, $f(g(x)) = g(f(x))$. Remember that in this context, $g(x) = f^{-1}(x)$.

Then $f(g(x)) = f\left(\dfrac{x^2 + 1}{2}\right) = \sqrt{(2)\left(\dfrac{x^2 + 1}{2}\right) - 1}$ $= \sqrt{x^2 + 1 - 1} = x$. Also, $g(f(x)) = g\left(\sqrt{2x - 1}\right) =$ $\dfrac{\left(\sqrt{2x - 1}\right)^2 + 1}{2} = \dfrac{2x - 1 + 1}{2} = x$.

In Example 27, let $x = 2$. Then $f(2) = 7e^2 \approx 51.7234$, so the point (2, 51.7234) lies on the graph of $f(x)$. We must check that (51.7234, 2) satisfies the equation $g(x) = \ln\left(\dfrac{x}{7}\right)$.

By substitution, $g(51.7234) = \ln\left(\dfrac{51.7234}{7}\right)$ $\approx \ln 7.389 \approx 2$. Any "error" in this computation is due only to rounding off.

With respect to the graphs of $f(x)$ and $f^{-1}(x)$, we know that if (a, b) belongs to the graph of $f(x)$, then (b, a) must belong to the graph of $f^{-1}(x)$. Notice that the points (a, b) and (b, a) are symmetric about the line $y = x$. This means that the graph of $f^{-1}(x)$ is a reflection of the graph of $f(x)$ about the line $y = x$. Figure 5.22, as shown below, is an example of the comparison of the graphs of $f(x)$ and $f^{-1}(x)$.

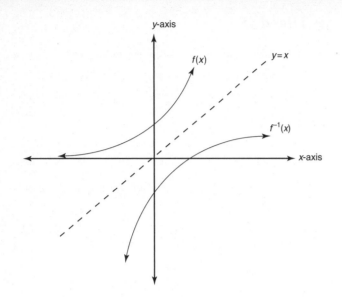

Figure 5.22

Quiz for Chapter 5

1. Set $H = \{(6, 2), (1, -3), (9, 4), \_\_\_\}$. Which one of the following ordered pairs, when used to fill in the blank, would guarantee that H is not a function?

   (A) $(2, 6)$　　　　(C) $(1, 5)$

   (B) $(-3, 4)$　　　　(D) $(4, 4)$

2. Which one of the following statements applies to an even function?

   (A) Its graph is symmetric about the y-axis.

   (B) Its graph is symmetric about the x-axis.

   (C) It must be a one-to-one function.

   (D) Each element must contain even integers.

3. The graph of an odd function is known to contain the point $(7, -2)$. Which one of the following points must also lie on this graph?

   (A) $(-2, 7)$　　　　(C) $(-7, -2)$

   (B) $(2, 7)$　　　　(D) $(-7, 2)$

4. Which one of the following represents a one-to-one function?

   (A) $\{(x, g(x)) \mid g(x) = -2x^3,\ \text{for } x = 1, 2, 3, 4\}$

   (B) $\{(4, 8), (0, -3), (2, 8), (6, -1)\}$

   (C) $\{(x, y) \mid x^2 - y^2 = 9,\ \text{for } x \ge 10\}$

   (D) $\{(6, 3), (-6, 3), (0, 0)\}$

5. What is the domain of the function $f(x) = \dfrac{x + 4}{x^2 + 2x - 15}$?

   (A) All numbers except -4

   (B) All numbers except -1 and 15

   (C) All numbers except -3 and 5

   (D) All numbers except -5 and 3

6. For which one of the following functions is the domain all numbers greater than or equal to 1?

   (A) $h(x) = \dfrac{7x}{x-1}$

   (B) $k(x) = \dfrac{x+1}{x^2-4}$

   (C) $v(x) = \sqrt{x+1}$

   (D) $w(x) = \sqrt{x-1}$

7. You are given that $g(x) = x^3$ and that $h(x) = (k)(g(x))$, where k is a constant. Which one of the following could represent two points, both of which lie on the graph of $h(x)$?

   (A) $(4, 128)$ and $\left(-\dfrac{1}{2}, -2\right)$

   (B) $\left(\dfrac{1}{2}, \dfrac{1}{64}\right)$ and $(-4, -8)$

   (C) $(3, 9)$ and $(-5, -25)$

   (D) $\left(\dfrac{1}{4}, \dfrac{1}{16}\right)$ and $\left(-\dfrac{1}{3}, -\dfrac{4}{27}\right)$

8. You are given the parent function $w(x) = x^5$. The graph of the function $z(x)$ lies four units to the left of the graph of $w(x)$. Which one of the following represents the expression for $z(x)$?

   (A) $x^5 - 4$ (C) $x^5 + 4$

   (B) $(x+4)^5$ (D) $(x-4)^5$

9. It is known that $g(x) = x^3$. If $h(x) = g(2x)$, then which one of the following points must lie on the graph of $h(x)$?

   (A) $(3, 54)$ (C) $(3, 216)$

   (B) $(3, 81)$ (D) $(3, 243)$

10. Given $f(x) = x^2 - 4$ and $g(x) = 5x + 8$, which one of the following represents $f(g(x))$?

   (A) $25x^2 + 80x + 60$

   (B) $5x^3 + 8x^2 - 20x - 32$

   (C) $5x^2 - 12$

   (D) $25x^2 - 32$

11. If $h(x) = \sqrt{5+2x}$ and $k(x) = 2x^2$, which one of the following represents $k(h(x))$?

   (A) $10 + 2x$ (C) $\sqrt{5+2x^2}$

   (B) $10 + 4x$ (D) $\sqrt{5+4x^2}$

12. If $f(x) = \sqrt{6x+4}$, which one of the following represents the inverse function $f^{-1}(x)$?

   (A) $\dfrac{1}{\sqrt{6x+4}}$ (C) $\dfrac{x^2-4}{6}$

   (B) $(6x+4)^2$ (D) $\dfrac{x^2-6}{4}$

13. If $g(x) = \dfrac{5-x}{8}$, which one of the following represents the inverse function $g^{-1}(x)$?

   (A) $\dfrac{8-x}{5}$ (C) $5 - 8x$

   (B) $\dfrac{8}{5-x}$ (D) $8 - 5x$

14. The point $(-7, 4)$ lies on the graph of $f(x)$. Which one of the following points must lie on the graph of $f^{-1}(x)$?

   (A) $(7, -4)$ (C) $(7, 4)$

   (B) $(4, 7)$ (D) $(4, -7)$

Quiz for Chapter 5
SOLUTIONS

1. (C)

The addition of the ordered pair $(1, 5)$ would mean that the domain value of 1 is paired with both -3 and 5. Then H would not be a function.

2. (A)

By definition, if (a, b) satisfies the equation of an even function, then $(-a, b)$ also satisfies this equation. These points are symmetric about the y-axis.

3. (D)

For any odd function, $f(x) = -f(-x)$. Let $x = 7$. Since $f(7) = -2$, it must also be true that $f(-7) = -(-2) = 2$. This means that the point $(-7, 2)$ must lie on the graph.

4. (A)

$g(x)$ qualifies as a function, since each x value corresponds to a single $g(x)$ value. In addition, by selecting a particular $g(x)$ value, there is only one corresponding x value. Furthermore, the graph of $g(x)$ passes the vertical and horizontal line tests. Notice that for answer choices (B) and (D), it is possible to find two domain values for some particular range value. Answer choice (C) is not a function; for example $(5, 4)$ and $(5, -4)$ both satisfy the given relation.

5. (D)

The denominator factors as $(x + 5)(x - 3)$. Then $(x + 5)(x - 3) \neq 0$, which means that the excluded numbers of the domain are -5 and 3.

6. (D)

The domain of $w(x) = \sqrt{x - 1}$ is found by the equation $x - 1 \geq 0$, which leads to $x \geq 1$.

7. (B)

We must find a k value that works for both points within any one answer choice. For (B), substituting $\left(\dfrac{1}{2}, \dfrac{1}{64}\right)$ into $h(x) = (k)(x^3)$, we get $\dfrac{1}{64} = (k)\left(\dfrac{1}{2}\right)^3 = \dfrac{1}{8}k$. Then $k = \dfrac{1}{8}$, which implies that $h(x) = \dfrac{1}{8}x^3$. However, we must check that the point $(-4, -8)$ also satisfies this function. By substitution, $-8 = \dfrac{1}{8}(-4)^3$ is a correct statement. This process will not work for the other answer choices.

8. (B)

$z(x)$ represents the form $w(x + k)$. Since $z(x)$ lies to the right of $w(x)$, this means that $k < 0$. Thus, $z(x) = (x + 4)^5$.

9. (C)

$h(x) = g(2x)$ and $g(x)$ is a cubic parent function. This means that for a given x value, the corresponding $h(x)$ value is $2^3 = 8$ times the $g(x)$ value. The point $(3, 27)$ lies on the graph of $g(x)$. Since $(27)(8) = 216$, the corresponding point on the graph of $h(x)$ is $(3, 216)$.

10. (A)

$$f(g(x)) = f(5x + 8) = (5x + 8)^2 - 4$$
$$= 25x^2 + 80x + 60.$$

11. (B)

$$k(h(x)) = k\left(\sqrt{5 + 2x}\right) = (2)\left(\sqrt{5 + 2x}\right)^2$$
$$= 10 + 4x.$$

12. (C)

Rewrite as $y = \sqrt{6x + 4}$. Interchanging variables leads to $x = \sqrt{6y + 4}$. Then $x^2 = 6y + 4$. Thus, $y = \dfrac{x^2 - 4}{6}$.

13. (C)

Rewrite as $y = \dfrac{5 - x}{8}$. Interchange the variables so that the equation becomes $x = \dfrac{5 - y}{8}$. Then $8x = 5 - y$. Thus, $y = 5 - 8x$.

14. (D)

Whenever the point (a, b) lies on the graph of $f(x)$, the point (b, a) must lie on the graph of $f^{-1}(x)$. In this case, $a = -7$ and $b = 4$. Thus, $(4, -7)$ must lie on the graph of $f^{-1}(x)$.

Chapter 6

Linear and Quadratic Functions

Welcome to Chapter 6. In this chapter, we will review the following algebraic topics:

(a) Properties of lines and their equations
(b) Systems of linear equations
(c) Quadratic functions
(d) Applications of linear and quadratic equations to word problems

Properties of Lines and Their Equations

The Slope of a Line

In the Cartesian coordinate system, the **slope of a line** is measured by its angle of inclination with respect to the x-axis. If this angle is acute when measured against the positive portion of the x-axis, the slope has a positive value. If this angle is acute when measured against the negative portion of the x-axis, the slope has a negative value. All horizontal lines, including the x-axis, have a slope of zero. All vertical lines, including the y-axis, have an undefined slope.

Figure 6.1 shows these four possibilities, using lines $l_1, l_2, l_3,$ and l_4.

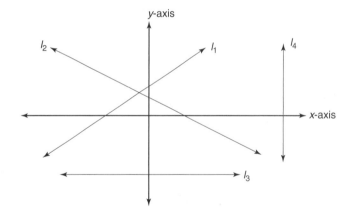

Figure 6.1

Line l_1 has a positive slope, l_2 has a negative slope, l_3 has a zero slope, and l_4 has an undefined slope. Note that "undefined slope" may also be considered as "no slope." The numerical value of a slope, denoted as m, can be determined by the expression $\dfrac{y_2 - y_1}{x_2 - x_1}$, where (x_1, y_1) and (x_2, y_2) represent two points on the line. For example, suppose $(-3, -1)$ and $(1, 2)$ lie on l_1. Then the slope of $l_1 = \dfrac{2 - (-1)}{1 - (-3)} = \dfrac{3}{4}$. As a second example, suppose $(6, -3)$ and $(-2, 0)$ lie on l_2. Then the slope of $l_2 = \dfrac{0 - (-3)}{-2 - 6} = -\dfrac{3}{8}$.

We can easily check that the slope of l_3 is zero, since any two of its points must have identical y values. Similarly, the slope of l_4 must be undefined, since any two of its points must have identical x values. Note that for any line, either point may be designated as (x_1, y_1) and that the slope can be determined by $\dfrac{y_1 - y_2}{x_1 - x_2}$.

The **slope-intercept form** of an equation of a line is $y = mx + b$, where m represents the slope and b represents the y-intercept. The only exception is for vertical lines. The equation for a vertical line is of the form $x = k$, where k is a constant.

EXAMPLE 1

What is the slope-intercept form of the equation of the line that contains the points (8, 4) and (−2, 8)?

SOLUTION

The slope is $\dfrac{8-4}{-2-8} = -\dfrac{2}{5}$. Thus far, the equation is $y = -\dfrac{2}{5}x + b$. Now select either point to substitute into this equation. By selecting the first point, $4 = (-\dfrac{2}{5})(8) + b$. Then $b = \dfrac{36}{5}$. Thus, the answer is $y = -\dfrac{2}{5}x + \dfrac{36}{5}$.

EXAMPLE 2

What is the slope-intercept form of the equation of the line that contains the point (9, −1) and has a y-intercept of −4?

SOLUTION

Since $b = -4$, the equation reads $y = mx - 4$. By substitution of the point (9, −1), we get $-1 = 9m - 4$. Then $m = \dfrac{3}{9} = \dfrac{1}{3}$. Thus, the answer is $y = \dfrac{1}{3}x - 4$.

EXAMPLE 3

What is the slope-intercept form of the equation of the line that contains the point (6, 7) and has a slope of –2 ?

SOLUTION

We start with $y = -2x + b$. Substituting (6, 7) into this equation leads to $7 = (-2)(6) + b$, so $b = 19$. The answer is $y = -2x + 19$.

Systems of Linear Equations

A system of two linear equations, using the variables x and y, can be solved both algebraically and geometrically. We will use the algebraic approach because it provides for greater accuracy. (This is especially true if the answers are fractions.) Any one of three possibilities can occur.

1. Exactly one set of answers for x and y. This means that the associated lines intersect (at one point).

2. No answers for x and y. This means that the associated lines are parallel to each other.

3. An infinite number of pairs of answers for x and y. This means that both equations refer to the same line.

EXAMPLE 4

Write an equation of a line that is parallel to the line represented by $2x - 5y = 12$.

SOLUTION

By solving the given equation for y, we can determine that the slope of the associated line is $\dfrac{2}{5}$. (The equation in slope-intercept form is $y = \frac{2}{5}x - \frac{12}{5}$.) All that needs to change is the y-intercept. If we change the y-intercept to 6, the answer becomes $y = \frac{2}{5}x + 6$. Of course, the answer may also be written as $2x - 5y = -30$.

EXAMPLE 5

> The equations $ax + 4y = 1$ and $-3x + by = 5$ are graphed by the same line. What are the values of a and b?

SOLUTION

In order for both equations to refer to the same line, either equation must be a multiple of the other. In this case, $\frac{5}{1} = 5$, so the coefficients of the second equation must be five times those of the first equation. Then $-3 = 5a$ and $b = (5)(4)$. The answers are $a = -\frac{3}{5}$ and $b = 20$.

A linear equation written as $Ax + By = C$ is considered to be in standard form. Each of A, B, and C must be integers, at most two of which may be zero. One method of solving a system of two linear equations in two unknowns written in standard form involves the use of an augmented matrix This matrix is formed by using the coefficients of the variables of each equation and the constant on the right side of each equation. A vertical bar is used to separate the coefficients of the variables from the single constant.

EXAMPLE 6

> What is the augmented matrix for the following system of equations?
> $$5x - y = 14$$
> $$3x + 2y = -2$$

SOLUTION

Using only the numbers, the answer is $\begin{bmatrix} 5 & -1 & | & 14 \\ 3 & 2 & | & -2 \end{bmatrix}$

In order to solve an augmented matrix for the values of the variables, row operations are used to transform the original matrix into one that appears as $\begin{bmatrix} 1 & 0 & | & a \\ 0 & 1 & | & b \end{bmatrix}$ where a and b are numbers. The solution will be $x = a$ and $y = b$.

EXAMPLE 7

> Using the augmented matrix of Example 6, solve for x and y.

SOLUTION

First, to get a 1 in the first row, first column, multiply the first row by $\frac{1}{5}$ to get the matrix $\begin{bmatrix} 1 & -\frac{1}{5} & | & \frac{14}{5} \\ 3 & 2 & | & -2 \end{bmatrix}$

Second, to get a zero in the second row, first column, change the second row by multiplying the first row by -3 and adding the entries of the second row. This is often abbreviated as $R_2 \rightarrow (-3)(R_1) + R_2$, resulting in the matrix $\begin{bmatrix} 1 & -\frac{1}{5} & | & \frac{14}{5} \\ 0 & \frac{13}{5} & | & -\frac{52}{5} \end{bmatrix}$

Third, to get a 1 in the second row, second column, divide the second row by $\frac{13}{5}$ to get the matrix $\begin{bmatrix} 1 & -\frac{1}{5} & | & \frac{14}{5} \\ 0 & 1 & | & -4 \end{bmatrix}$

Finally, to get a zero in the first row, second column, change the first row by multiplying the second row by $\frac{1}{5}$ and adding the entries of the first row. This is abbreviated as $R_1 \rightarrow \left(\dfrac{1}{5}\right)(R_2) + R_1$,

resulting in the matrix $\begin{bmatrix} 1 & 0 & | & 2 \\ 0 & 1 & | & -4 \end{bmatrix}$

The original augmented matrix has now been transformed into the desired form so that the answers are $x = 2$ and $y = -4$.

There are cases in which it will be impossible to create the second row as 0 1 n, where n is any number. If the second row appears as 0 0 0, then the two equations represent the same line. This means that there are an infinite number of paired solutions. If the second row appears as 0 0 n, where n is any nonzero number, then the equations represent parallel lines. This means that there are <u>no</u> solutions.

EXAMPLE 8

Using an augmented matrix, what is the solution to the following system of equations?
$$x - 5y = 7$$
$$-4x + 20y = -28$$

SOLUTION

We start with the augmented matrix $\begin{bmatrix} 1 & -5 & | & 7 \\ -4 & 20 & | & -28 \end{bmatrix}$

The first row, first column already has the entry 1. To get a zero in the second row, first column, change the second row by multiplying the first row by 4 and adding the entries of the second row. The matrix becomes

$\begin{bmatrix} 1 & -5 & | & 7 \\ 0 & 0 & | & 0 \end{bmatrix}$

This example came to a quick ending! Our conclusion is that there are an infinite number of paired answers for x and y.

EXAMPLE 9

Using an augmented matrix, what is the solution to the following system of equations?
$$3x + 5y = 10$$
$$6x + 10y = 17$$

SOLUTION

We start with the augmented matrix $\begin{bmatrix} 3 & 5 & | & 10 \\ 6 & 10 & | & 17 \end{bmatrix}$

Multiply the first row by $\dfrac{1}{3}$ to get the matrix

$\begin{bmatrix} 1 & \frac{5}{3} & | & \frac{10}{3} \\ 6 & 10 & | & 17 \end{bmatrix}$

To get a zero in the second row, first column, change the second row by multiplying the first row by –6 and adding the entries of the second row.

The matrix now becomes $\begin{bmatrix} 1 & \frac{5}{3} & | & \frac{10}{3} \\ 0 & 0 & | & -3 \end{bmatrix}$

Our conclusion is that there is no solution.

A good way to remember these two special cases as shown in Examples 8 and 9 is as follows: When the second row of an augmented matrix reads as 0 0 0, you can think of this as $0x + 0y = 0$. Any values of x and y will satisfy this equation, so this translates to an infinite number of pairs of answers. Likewise, when the second row reads as 0 0 n, where $n \neq 0$, you can write this as $0x + 0y = n$. If $n \neq 0$, then there is no possible solution.

Quadratic Functions

A **quadratic function**, using the variables x and y, is an equation that can be written in the form $y = ax^2 + bx + c$, where a, b, c are constants and $a \neq 0$. Another useful form for a quadratic function is $y = a(x - h)^2 + k$, where a, h, k are constants and $a \neq 0$.

The graph of a quadratic function is a parabola. Figures 6.2, 6.3, 6.4 and 6.5, as shown below, illustrate the shape and direction of four parabolas and their associated equations. A selection of three points for each parabola is also shown on the graphs.

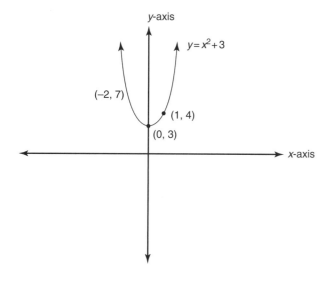

Figure 6.2

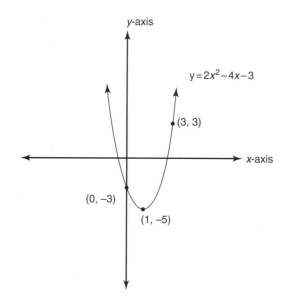

Figure 6.3

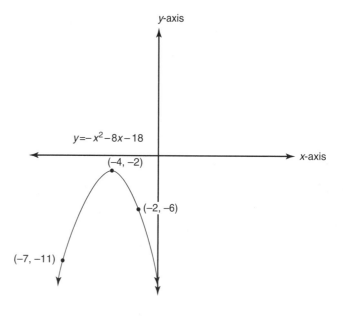

Figure 6.4

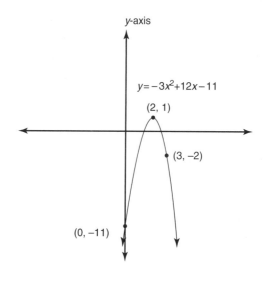

Figure 6.5

Each of the parabolas in Figures 6.2 and 6.3 has a lowest point, whereas each of the parabolas in Figures 6.4 and 6.5 has a highest point. This particular point of any parabola is called the vertex. In looking at any of these parabolas, except perhaps for Figure 6.2, it would be difficult to state a relationship between the vertex numbers and the coefficients of the associated equation. Let's change each equation into the form $y = a(x - h)^2 + k$. For Figure 6.2, it is easy to rewrite the equation as $y = 1(x - 0)^2 + 3$.

For Figure 6.3, start by just factoring the number 2 from the first two terms to get $y = 2(x^2 - 2x + \_) - 3$. To create a perfect trinomial square, replace the blank with 1. Since we will be actually adding $(2)(1) = 2$ to the right side, we will also need to subtract 2 on the right side. Now the equation appears as $y = 2(x^2 - 2x + 1) - 3 - 2$. In simplified form, this equation becomes $y = 2(x - 1)^2 - 5$.

For Figure 6.4, factor the number -1 from the first two terms to get $y = -1(x^2 + 8x + \_) - 18$. Now we will replace the blank by 16 to create a perfect trinomial square. The right side has now changed by $(-1)(16) = -16$, so we must also add 16 to the right side to "balance" the equation. The equation will now appear as $y = -1(x^2 + 8x + 16) - 18 + 16$. In simplified form, we get $y = -1(x + 4)^2 - 2$.

For Figure 6.5, factor the number -3 from the first two terms to get $y = -3(x^2 - 4x + \_) - 11$. The "magic" number to create a perfect trinomial square is 4, so this number replaces the blank. Since we have added $(-3)(4) = -12$ to the right side, we must also add $+12$ to this side. The equation will now appear as $y = -3(x^2 - 4x + 4) - 11 + 12$. In simplified form, we get $y = -3(x - 2)^2 + 1$. Each of the equations for Figures 6.2, 6.3, 6.4, and 6.5 has now been converted to the form $y = a(x - h)^2 + k$. We can conclude the following:

1. The vertex is given by (h, k).

2. The graph has a lowest point when $a > 0$, and has a highest point when $a < 0$.

In addition, each parabola has an axis of symmetry. This is the vertical line that passes through the vertex. Figures 6.7 and 6.8 illustrate how the axis of symmetry would appear from Figures 6.3 and 6.4, respectively.

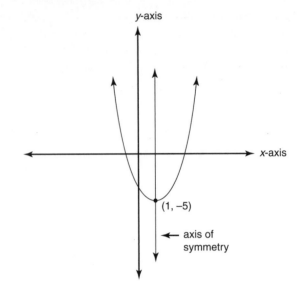

Figure 6.7

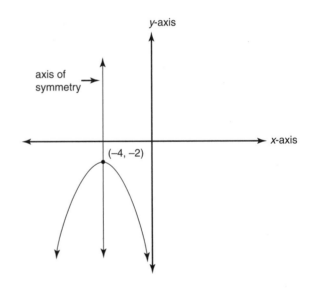

Figure 6.8

The equations of these axes of symmetry are $x = 1$ and $x = -4$, respectively. In general, the axis of symmetry for the graph of $y = a(x - h)^2 + k$ is $x = h$. This can be easily verified for Figures 6.2 and 6.5.

EXAMPLE 10

What is the equation of the axis of symmetry for the graph of $y = 5(x + 6)^2 - 4$?

SOLUTION

If you write the equation as $y = 5(x - (-6))^2 - 4$, you can see that $h = -6$. The desired equation is $x = -6$.

EXAMPLE 11

What is the vertex of the graph of the quadratic function $y = -2(x - 3)^2$?

SOLUTION

The function can be written as $y = -2(x - 3)^2 + 0$, so the vertex is $(3, 0)$.

EXAMPLE 12

What is the vertex of the graph of the quadratic function $y = -2x^2 + 20x - 49$?

SOLUTION

The steps to convert this function into $y = a(x - h)^2 + k$ are as follows: $y = -2(x^2 - 10x + \_) - 49$, $y = -2(x^2 - 10x + 25) - 49 + 50$, and finally $y = -2(x - 5)^2 + 1$. The vertex is $(5, 1)$.

It should be noted that the x value of the vertex can also be found using the expression $-b/2a$. In Example 12, $-b/2a = -20/-4 = 5$. Then we calculate the y value by direct substitution. Note that the value of a is unchanged no matter whether the function is in the form $y = ax^2 + bx + c$ or $y = a(x - h)^2 + k$.

EXAMPLE 13

The graph of which one(s) of the following four functions has (have) a maximum value at the vertex? $y = 7x^2 + 3$, $y = (x + 13)^2 - 9$, $y = 5(x - 8)^2 - 2$, $y = -4(x + 4)^2 - 1$

SOLUTION

In order for the graph to have a maximum value (which must occur at the vertex of a quadratic function), the value of a must be negative. The answer is $y = -4(x + 4)^2 - 1$.

Zeros of a Function

If $y = f(x)$ is any function, then the zeros of this function are the values of x for which $y = 0$. When graphing this function, the **zeros** represent the intersection points of the x-axis and the function. In the case of a quadratic function, the number of zeros is either 0, 1, or 2. Each of Figures 6.2 and 6.4 has no zeros, whereas each of Figures 6.3 and 6.5 has two zeros.

The quadratic formula is used to find the actual values of the zeros. For the quadratic function $y = ax^2 + bx + c$, we replace y by 0. The solution(s) to this equation are given by $x = \dfrac{-b \pm \sqrt{b^2 - 4ac}}{2a}$.

If $b^2 - 4ac > 0$, then there are two real zeros. If $b^2 - 4ac = 0$, then there is one real zero. If $b^2 - 4ac < 0$, then there are two complex zeros. Incidentally, the word "roots" can be used in place of "zeros". Also, the expression $b^2 - 4ac$ is called the discriminant.

EXAMPLE 14

What are the zeros for the function described in Figure 6.3? (Nearest hundredth)

SOLUTION

We need to solve $0 = 2x^2 - 4x - 3$. Then $x = \dfrac{-(-4) \pm \sqrt{(-4)^2 - (4)(2)(-3)}}{(2)(2)}$ This simplifies to $x = \dfrac{4 \pm \sqrt{40}}{4}$, so the answers are approximately -0.58 and 2.58. Notice that these numbers also correspond to the x-intercepts of $(-0.58, 0)$ and $(2.58, 0)$

EXAMPLE 15

What are the zeros for the function described in Figure 6.5?

SOLUTION

We need to solve $0 = -3x^2 + 12x - 11$. Then $x = \dfrac{-12 \pm \sqrt{(12)^2 - (4)(-3)(-11)}}{(2)(-3)}$. This simplifies to $x = \dfrac{-12 \pm \sqrt{12}}{-6}$, so the answers are approximately 1.42 and 2.58.

EXAMPLE 16

What are the roots (zeros) for the function described in Figure 6.4?

SOLUTION

The equation to solve is $0 = -x^2 - 8x - 18$. In order to avoid an unnecessary number of negative signs, let's rewrite the equation as $0 = x^2 + 8x + 18$. Then $x = \dfrac{-8 \pm \sqrt{(8)^2 - (4)(1)(18)}}{2}$. This simplifies to $x = \dfrac{-8 \pm \sqrt{-8}}{2}$, so the two answers are complex numbers. There are no real answers, as evidenced by the fact that the graph of this function does not intersect the x-axis.

For the graph in Figure 6.2, it is clear that there are no zeros. The appropriate equation to solve would be $0 = x^2 + 3$. We could use the quadratic formula, but this equation is equivalent to $-3 = x^2$, which has only complex roots.

The use of the quadratic formula is not necessary in solving all second-degree equations; some equations may be solved by factoring.

EXAMPLE 17

What are the zeros of the graph for the function $y = 2x^2 + 9x$?

SOLUTION

In solving $0 = 2x^2 + 9x$, it is much quicker to use factoring than to use the quadratic formula. Then $0 = x(2x + 9)$, which means that $x = 0$ or $2x + 9 = 0$. The two zeros are 0 and $-\dfrac{9}{2}$.

EXAMPLE 18

What are the zeros of the graph for the function $y = 3x^2 - x - 2$?

SOLUTION

In solving $0 = 3x^2 - x - 2$, we'll factor the right side so that it reads as $0 = (3x + 2)(x - 1)$. Then $3x + 2 = 0$ or $x - 1 = 0$. The two zeros are $-\dfrac{2}{3}$ and 1.

Another interesting feature of the quadratic function $y = ax^2 + bx + c$ is that when there are real zeros, their sum equals $-\dfrac{b}{a}$ and their product equals $\dfrac{c}{a}$. In checking Examples 17 and 18, we can verify this information. For Example 17, the sum of the zeros is $-\dfrac{9}{2}$, which is the same as $-\dfrac{b}{a}$. The product of the zeros is 0, and since $c = 0$, $\frac{c}{a} = 0$. Likewise, in Example 18, the sum of the zeros is $\frac{1}{3}$, and this matches $-\frac{b}{a}$. The product of the zeros is $-\frac{2}{3}$, and this equals $\frac{c}{a}$.

When the zeros are approximate answers, this check still applies, but a small error may appear. In Example 15, the sum of the zeros should be $-\frac{12}{-3} = 4$, and this answer matches exactly the sum of 1.42 and 2.58. The product of the zeros should be $\frac{11}{3}$, which is very close to $(1.42)(2.58)$.

EXAMPLE 19

> The zeros of $y = 4x^2 + bx + c$ are $\frac{1}{2}$ and -4.
>
> What are the values of b and c?

SOLUTION

The sum of these zeros is $-\frac{7}{2}$, so $-\frac{b}{4} = -\frac{7}{2}$. Then $b = 14$. Likewise, the product of the zeros is -2, so $\frac{c}{4} = -2$. Then $c = -8$.

EXAMPLE 20

> The zeros of $y = ax^2 - 16x + c$ are $\frac{6}{5}$ and 2.
>
> What are the values of a and c?

SOLUTION

Since the sum of the zeros is $\frac{16}{5}$, we can write $\frac{16}{a} = \frac{16}{5}$. Then $a = 5$. The product of the zeros is $\frac{12}{5}$, so $\frac{c}{a} = \frac{c}{5} = \frac{12}{5}$. Then $c = 12$.

The Application of Quadratic Equations in One Variable to Verbal Problems

Although there are an endless number of real-life examples in which a quadratic equation can be used, we will discuss only the ones that deal with either distance, work, or geometric figures. When answers are not exact, they will be rounded off to the nearest hundredth. Also, only positive answers need be considered.

EXAMPLE 21

> A boat takes 2 hours longer to travel a distance of 40 miles when traveling upstream than the time it takes to travel downstream. If the rate of the current is 3 miles per hour, what is the rate of the boat in still water?

SOLUTION

If x is the rate in still water, then $x + 3$ and $x - 3$ are the respective rates when traveling downstream and upstream. Time equals distance divided by rate, and since the upstream time is 2 hours longer than the downstream time, $\frac{40}{x - 3} - \frac{40}{x + 3} = 2$. After multiplying this equation by $(x - 3)(x + 3)$ and simplifying, we get $0 = 2x^2 - 258$. We can avoid using the quadratic formula by adding 258, dividing by 2, and taking the positive square root. The (positive) answer is $\sqrt{129} \approx 11.36$ miles per hour.

EXAMPLE 22

> From a given location, Karen walks north at a constant speed. At the same time, Ron walks east at a constant speed. After 3 hours, they are 17 miles apart. If Ron's speed is one mile per hour faster than Karen's speed, what is Karen's <u>distance</u>?

SOLUTION

Let x represent Karen's speed and let $x + 1$ represent Ron's speed. Here is an appropriate diagram.

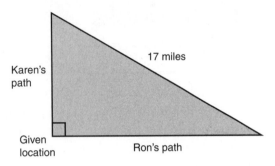

Karen's distance is represented by $3x$ and Ron's distance is $3(x + 1)$. By the Pythagorean theorem, $(3x)^2 + (3x + 3)^2 = 17^2$. Simplifying this equation, we get $9x^2 + 9x - 140 = 0$. Using the quadratic formula, the positive answer for x becomes $\dfrac{-9 + \sqrt{5121}}{18} \approx 3.48$. This is Karen's speed in miles per hour, so her distance is approximately $(3)(3.48) = 10.44$ miles.

EXAMPLE 23

Working alone, Laura can mow a lawn in 3 hours. Working alone, Tim can mow this same lawn in 4 hours. If Laura and Tim work together, in how many hours can they mow this lawn? Assume that they start at the same time and stop when the entire lawn is mowed.

SOLUTION

Let x represent the hours needed when Laura and Tim work together. The sum of the fractions that represent the amount of work done by each person must add up to 1. Then $\dfrac{x}{3} + \dfrac{x}{4} = 1$. This leads to $7x = 12$, so $x = 1\dfrac{5}{7}$ hours.

NOTE:

If the question asked what <u>fraction</u> of the work Laura has completed, the answer would be $1\dfrac{5}{7} \div 3 = \dfrac{4}{7}$. In a similar fashion, we would discover that the fraction of work that Tim will have completed is $1\dfrac{5}{7} \div 4 = \dfrac{3}{7}$.

EXAMPLE 24

Two computers are processing the payroll for a company. Working alone the first computer requires 20 minutes to complete this task. Working with a second computer, the payroll can be processed in 15 minutes. How many minutes would the second computer require if it were working alone? Assume that both computers start processing the payroll at the same time.

SOLUTION

Let x represent the number of minutes required by the second computer working alone. The fraction of work completed by each computer is the time working together divided by the time required alone. Then $\dfrac{15}{20} + \dfrac{15}{x} = 1$. This leads to $15x + 300 = 20x$. Thus, $x = 60$ minutes.

EXAMPLE 25

The 3 sides of a rectangular fence are being built in a small backyard, as shown in the diagram below.

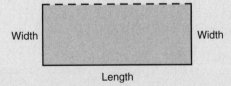

The area to be fenced in is 80 square feet. If the length is five feet greater than the width, what is the size of the width, in feet? (Nearest hundredth)

SOLUTION

Let x represent the width and $x + 5$ represent the length. The above diagram shows two widths, but the area only uses one width and one length. So, $x(x + 5) = 80$, which leads to $x^2 + 5x - 80 = 0$. Using the quadratic formula for the positive x value,

$$x = \frac{-5 + \sqrt{345}}{2} \approx 6.79 \text{ feet.}$$

EXAMPLE 26

In the diagram shown below ΔABC is inscribed in the circle with center D.

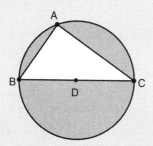

The area of the circle is 64π and $\overline{AC}$ is 6 units larger than $\overline{AB}$. What is the length of $\overline{AC}$?

SOLUTION

Let x represent the length of $\overline{AB}$ and $x + 6$ represent the length of $\overline{AC}$. Since $\overline{BC}$ passes through the center of the circle, it must be a diameter. Also, ΔABC must have a right angle at A. The area of the circle is 64π, which means that the diameter is 16. Then $x^2 + (x + 6)^2 = 16^2$. This simplifies to $x^2 + 6x - 110 = 0$. The positive answer of this equation is given by $x = \dfrac{-6 + \sqrt{476}}{2} \approx 7.91$. Thus, the length of $\overline{AC}$ is approximately 13.91 units.

Quiz for Chapter 6

1. What is the y-intercept of the line that contains the points $(4,0)$ and $(-3, -14)$?

   (A) -4 (C) -8

   (B) -6 (D) -10

2. A line contains the point $(-2, 4)$. If this line has no slope, which one of the following points lies on this line?

   (A) $(4, -2)$ (C) $(2, 4)$

   (B) $(-2, -4)$ (D) $(-4, 2)$

3. Which one of the following equations represents a line that is parallel to the graph of $5x - 4y = 9$ and contains the point $(-3, 3)$?

   (A) $y = \dfrac{5}{4}x + \dfrac{27}{4}$ (C) $y = \dfrac{5}{4}x + \dfrac{3}{4}$

   (B) $y = -\dfrac{5}{4}x - \dfrac{3}{4}$ (D) $y = -\dfrac{5}{4}x - \dfrac{27}{4}$

4. A system of linear equations is in the form $ax + by = c$ and $dx + ey = f$, where a, b, c, d, e, and f are constants. If the answers are $x = 5$

and $y = -3$, which one of the following is the augmented matrix that reveals this solution?

(A) $\begin{bmatrix} 0 & 1 & | & 5 \\ 1 & 0 & | & -3 \end{bmatrix}$ (C) $\begin{bmatrix} 1 & 0 & | & 5 \\ 0 & 1 & | & -3 \end{bmatrix}$

(B) $\begin{bmatrix} 0 & 1 & | & -3 \\ 1 & 0 & | & 5 \end{bmatrix}$ (D) $\begin{bmatrix} 1 & 0 & | & -3 \\ 0 & 1 & | & 5 \end{bmatrix}$

5. For a system of linear equations in the form $ax + by = c$ and $dx + ey = f$, where a, b, c, d, e, and f are constants, suppose the final augmented matrix is $\begin{bmatrix} 1 & -2 & | & 3 \\ 0 & 0 & | & 1 \end{bmatrix}$ What is the solution for x and y?

(A) An infinite number of paired answers

(B) $x = 3$ and $y = 1$

(C) No solution

(D) $x = -2$ and $y = 3$

6. The graph of which one of the following equations has a highest point at $(-7, 8)$?

(A) $y = 2(x - 7)^2 + 8$ (C) $y = -4(x - 7)^2 + 8$

(B) $y = 4(x + 7)^2 + 8$ (D) $y = -2(x + 7)^2 + 8$

7. Which one of the following statements is correct concerning the graph of $y = 6x^2 + 48x + 29$?

(A) Its lowest point is $(-4, -67)$

(B) Its lowest point is $(4, 317)$

(C) Its highest point is $(-4, -67)$

(D) Its highest point is $(4, 317)$

8. If $0 = ax^2 - 11x + 4$ has no real zeros, what are the restricted values of a?

(A) $a < \dfrac{121}{16}$ (C) $a > \dfrac{121}{16}$

(B) $a < -\dfrac{121}{16}$ (D) $a > -\dfrac{121}{16}$

9. The zeros of $y = 6x^2 + bx + c$ are 2 and $-\dfrac{7}{6}$. What is the value of c?

(A) $-\dfrac{7}{3}$ (C) -7

(B) $-\dfrac{7}{12}$ (D) -14

10. The two roots of $0 = ax^2 + bx + c$ are $\dfrac{1}{2}$ and $-\dfrac{1}{5}$. Which one of the following provides a possible set of values for a and b?

(A) $a = 3$ and $b = -10$

(B) $a = 10$ and $b = -3$

(C) $a = 1$ and $b = -10$

(D) $a = 10$ and $b = -1$

11. From a given location, Ted drives north at a constant speed. At the same time, Christine drives west at a constant speed. After two hours, they are 80 miles apart. If Christine's speed is seven miles per hour faster than Ted's speed, what is Ted's speed? (Nearest hundredth of a mile per hour)

(A) 24.57   (C) 31.57

(B) 26.37   (D) 33.37

12. Working alone, Peter can paint a fence in five hours. Working with Mary, the two of them can paint this fence in two hours. If Mary were working alone, how many hours would she need to paint this fence?

(A) $3\dfrac{2}{3}$ (C) $2\dfrac{3}{4}$

(B) $3\dfrac{1}{3}$ (D) $2\dfrac{1}{2}$

13. The length of a rectangle is 3 inches longer than twice its width. If the area is 25 square inches, what is the length of this rectangle? (Nearest hundredth of an inch)

(A) 2.86 in.   (C) 6.76 in.

(B) 4.82 in.   (D) 8.72 in.

14. A triangle has the same area as a square with a side of 10. The base of the triangle is 6 units longer than its height. How many units is the height of the triangle? (Nearest hundredth)

(A) 11.46   (C) 8.78

(B) 10.12   (D) 7.44

Quiz for Chapter 6
SOLUTIONS

1. (C)

The slope equals $\dfrac{-14-0}{-3-4} = 2$. The equation now reads as $y = 2x + b$. Substitution of (4, 0) yields the value of b as -8.

2. (B)

For a line with no slope, each point must have the same x-coordinate. Thus, $(-2, -4)$ must lie on this line.

3. (A)

The original equation can be written as $y = \dfrac{5}{4}x - \dfrac{9}{4}$, so the line that is parallel must have a slope of $\dfrac{5}{4}$. The equation becomes $y = \dfrac{5}{4}x + b$. Substitution of $(-3, 3)$ yields the value of b as $\dfrac{27}{4}$.

4. (C)

The augmented matrix that is associated with the solution must contain the identity matrix $\begin{bmatrix} 1 & 0 \\ 0 & 1 \end{bmatrix}$ followed by the column of values for x and y, where the x value is in the first row and the y value is in the second row.

5. (C)

In an augmented matrix, when the first row, first column element is 1 and the second row reads 0 0 n, where $n \neq 0$, there is no solution for the variables.

6. (D)

In the form $y = a(x - h)^2 + k$, the corresponding graph will have a highest point if $a < 0$. The coordinates of the highest point are (h, k). For this answer choice, $h = -7$ and $k = 8$.

7. (A)

$y = 6x^2 + 48x + 29$ becomes $y = 6(x^2 + 8x + 16) + 29 - 96$, which becomes $y = 6(x + 4)^2 - 67$. This means that its lowest point is $(-4, -67)$.

8. (C)

If $0 = ax^2 - 11x + 4$, then $11^2 - (4)(a)(4) < 0$. The solution to this inequality is $a > \dfrac{121}{16}$.

9. (D)

Since the product of the zeros is $-\dfrac{7}{3}$, we can write $\dfrac{c}{6} = -\dfrac{7}{3}$. Thus, $c = -14$.

10. (B)

The sum of the roots is $\dfrac{3}{10}$, which must be equal to $-\dfrac{b}{a}$. One possible combination is $a = 10$ and $b = -3$.

11. (A)

Let x represent Ted's speed in miles per hour and let $x + 7$ represent Christine's speed in miles per hour. Then $2x$ and $2x + 14$ represent Ted's distance and Christine's distance in miles after two hours, respectively. Then $(2x)^2 + (2x + 14)^2 = 80^2$. This equation simplifies to $2x^2 + 14x - 1551 = 0$. The positive x value is given by $x = \dfrac{-14 + \sqrt{12{,}604}}{4} \approx 24.57$ miles per hour.

12. (B)

Let x represent Mary's time working alone. Then $\dfrac{2}{5} + \dfrac{2}{x} = 1$. Simplified, this equation becomes $2x + 10 = 5x$, thus $x = 3\dfrac{1}{3}$ hours.

13. (D)

Let x and $2x + 3$ represent the width and length, respectively. Then $(x)(2x + 3) = 25$, which simplifies to $2x^2 + 3x - 25 = 0$. The positive answer for x is $\dfrac{-3 + \sqrt{209}}{4} \approx 2.86$, which is the width. Thus, the length is approximately 8.72 inches.

14. (A)

Let x and $x + 6$ represent the triangle's height and base, respectively. Since the area of the square is 100 sq. units, the equation becomes $\left(\dfrac{1}{2}\right)(x)(x + 6) = 100$. This simplifies to $x^2 + 6x - 200 = 0$. Thus, $x = \dfrac{-6 + \sqrt{836}}{2} \approx 11.46$.

Rational and Radical Functions

Welcome to Chapter 7. In this chapter, we will review the following algebraic topics:

(a) Special functions: polynomial, rational, absolute value, and piecewise functions

(b) Domains and ranges

(c) Significant points, such as zeros, minimum, and maximum values

(d) Types of asymptotes

(e) Equations and inequalities

Special Functions

Polynomial Functions

A **polynomial function** of degree n is an expression of the form $a_n x^n + a_{n-1} x^{n-1} + a_{n-2} x^{n-2} + ... + a_1 x + a_0$. The stipulations are that all a_i are real numbers and that $a_n \neq 0$. The associated polynomial function, $f(x)$, is normally expressed as $f(x) = a_n x^n + a_{n-1} x^{n-1} + a_{n-2} x^{n-2} + ... + a_1 x + a_0$.

Domain and Range

For second-degree functions, namely $f(x) = a_2 x^2 + a_1 x + a_0$, the **domain** is all real numbers and the **range** is determined by the location of the vertex.

EXAMPLE 1

What is the range of the function $f(x) = 5(x - 2)^2 + 1$?

SOLUTION

The vertex is located at $(2, 1)$, and since $5 > 0$, the vertex represents a minimum (lowest) point on the graph. Thus, the range is all numbers greater than or equal to 1. The graph of $f(x)$ is shown below.

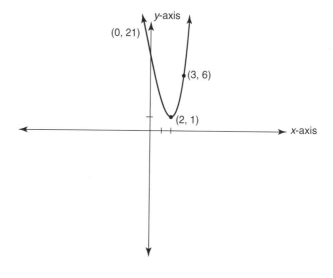

NOTE:

> The minimum (or maximum) value refers to the value of *f(x)*, which is *y*. For second-degree (also called "quadratic") functions, there is always either one minimum point or one maximum point.

EXAMPLE 2

> What is the range of the function $g(x) = -(x + 4)^2 + 10$?

SOLUTION

The vertex is located at $(-4, 10)$, and since $-1 < 0$, this vertex is the highest point of the graph. Thus, the range is all numbers less than or equal to 10. The graph of *g(x)* is shown below.

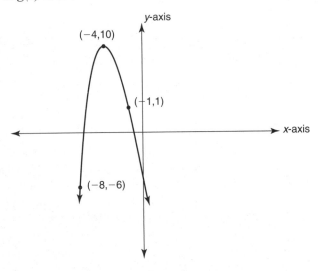

In general, for any function $f(x) = a_n x^n + a_{n-1} x^{n-1} + a_{n-2} x^{n-2} + ... + a_1 x + a_0$, the graph will appear as one of the following four prototypes:

1. If *n* is even and $a_n > 0$ 2. If *n* is even and $a_n < 0$

3. If *n* is odd and $a_n > 0$ 4. If *n* is odd and $a_n < 0$

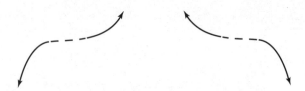

In each instance, the dotted line portion of the graph is not determined by the prototype shown. Thus, within the dotted line portion, the graph may increase, decrease, or both. The conclusions that we can draw are as follows:

For Prototype 1: As $x \to \infty$ or as $x \to -\infty$, the function value approaches ∞.

For Prototype 2: As $x \to \infty$ or as $x \to -\infty$, the function value approaches $-\infty$.

For Prototype 3: As $x \to \infty$, the function value approaches ∞.; as $x \to -\infty$, the function value approaches $-\infty$.

For Prototype 4: As $x \to \infty$, the function value approaches $-\infty$; as $x \to -\infty$, the function approaches ∞.

Thus, for the graph of $f(x) = 3x^3 + x^2 - 2$, as *x* approaches negative infinity, *f(x)* approaches negative infinity. As another example, for the graph of $g(x) = -4x^2 + 5x + 9$, as *x* approaches infinity, $g(x)$ approaches negative infinity.

As mentioned in Chapter 6, the real zeros of any function are the *x* values of the points where the function intersects the *x*-axis. Basically, we are looking for *x* values for which $f(x) = 0$. A polynomial function of degree *n* has at most *n* distinct zeros. If there are complex zeros for a given function, they will occur in pairs such that if $a + bi$ is a zero, then $a - bi$ is also a zero. However, a function need not have any complex zeros.

CAUTION!

> Complex zeros do <u>not</u> appear in the graph of a polynomial function; thus, they <u>cannot</u> be *x*-intercepts of any polynomial function.

Suppose that *a*, *b*, *c*, and *d* are the (distinct) zeros of a fourth-degree function *f(x)*. Then we can write an example of the actual function as $f(x) = k[(x - a)$

$(x - b)(x - c)(x - d)]$, where k is a constant. (Usually, we will let $k = 1$.) Likewise, if a fifth-degree function $g(x)$ has only distinct zeros m, n, and p, one possible function is $g(x) = (x - m)^2(x - n)^2(x - p)$. In some textbooks, each of m and n is called a double *zero* or a double *root*. However, note that when the right side of this function is expanded, the highest exponent of x will be 5. Another equally correct answer for *g(x)* would be $g(x) = (x - m)(x - n)(x - p)^3$. Here, p would be called a triple zero.

EXAMPLE 3

> A polynomial function of degree 5 has at least one complex zero. What is the maximum number of distinct real zeros for this function?

SOLUTION

Complex zeros come in pairs, so there are really at least two complex zeros. Then the maximum number of distinct real zeros must be three.

EXAMPLE 4

> A polynomial function of sixth-degree has five distinct real zeros. What is the maximum number of complex zeros for this function?

SOLUTION

The answer is none! It would be impossible for there to exist only one complex zero. One of these five distinct zeros must be a double zero.

EXAMPLE 5

> $h(x)$ is a fourth-degree polynomial function with distinct zeros q and r. If each of these is a double zero, write an expression for *h(x)*.

SOLUTION

One possible answer is $h(x) = (x - q)^2(x - r)^2$. Any multiple of the right side, such as $5(x - q)^2(x - r)^2$, would also be a correct answer.

EXAMPLE 6

> *f(x)* is a third-degree polynomial function with a real zero of t and a complex zero of $a + b$i. Write an expression for *f(x)*.

SOLUTION

It should be noted that if the given zeros include complex numbers, an appropriate polynomial function can still be written using the factored form shown in Example 5. Noting that $a - bi$ must also be a zero, one acceptable answer is $f(x) = (x - [a + bi])(x - [a - bi])(x - t)$.

Rational Functions

A **rational function** is the quotient of two polynomials, in which the denominator is not the zero polynomial. Each of $f(x) = \dfrac{2x^2 - 1}{x}$, $g(x) = \dfrac{-3}{x^4 + x}$, and $h(x) = \dfrac{x^5 + 4x^2 - 7}{6x^3 + 8}$ is an example of a rational function.

Technically, an example such as $p(x) = \dfrac{9x^3 - 6x + 10}{2}$ can be considered a rational function, but this expression can be written as a simpler polynomial function $p(x) = \dfrac{9}{2}x^3 - 3x + 5$. In fact, since each polynomial function can be written as itself divided by 1, all polynomial functions are rational functions.

Domain and Zeros

For any rational function $f(x) = \dfrac{p(x)}{q(x)}$, the domain is governed by the restrictions for the denominator. If there are no restrictions for $q(x)$, then the domain for

$f(x)$ is all real numbers. The zeros of $f(x) = \dfrac{p(x)}{q(x)}$ are governed by the numerator. If $p(x)$ has no zeros, then there are no zeros for $f(x)$.

EXAMPLE 7

> What is the domain for the function $f(x) = \dfrac{x^2 + 6x + 5}{3x - 2}$?

SOLUTION

Solving $3x - 2 = 0$, $x = \dfrac{2}{3}$. The domain is all real numbers except $\dfrac{2}{3}$.

EXAMPLE 8

> What is the domain for the function $h(x) = \dfrac{x^2 + 11x - 7}{3x^2 - 2x - 8}$?

SOLUTION

$3x^2 - 2x - 8 = 0$ becomes $(3x + 4)(x - 2) = 0$. The domain is all real numbers except $-\dfrac{4}{3}$ and 2.

EXAMPLE 9

> What are the zeros of the function $g(x) = \dfrac{x^2 - x - 90}{x + 11}$?

SOLUTION

$x^2 - x - 90 = 0$ becomes $(x - 10)(x + 9) = 0$. The zeros are 10 and -9.

EXAMPLE 10

> What are the zeros of the function $h(x) = \dfrac{(x)(x + 3)^3(2x + 11)}{(8)(x + 5)}$?

SOLUTION

The zeros are found by the equations $x = 0$, $x + 3 = 0$ and $2x + 11 = 0$. The three (distinct) zeros are 0, -3, and $-\dfrac{11}{2}$. (Note that -3 is a triple zero)

Remember that complex numbers can also be zeros of functions; however, since they do not appear on the graphs of functions, they cannot qualify as x-intercepts. Thus, if a second-degree function has two complex zeros, there would be no x-intercepts.

Similarly, if a fifth-degree function has four complex zeros and one real zero, the only x-intercept would correspond to the real zero. The number x-intercepts for a rational function correspond to the number of distinct real zeros. These comments apply to any rational functions, which include polynomial functions.

EXAMPLE 11

> Given the rational function $f(x) = \dfrac{(2x)(x^2 + 4)}{x - 6}$, how many distinct zeros and how many x-intercepts are there?

SOLUTION

The zeros are found from $2x = 0$ and $x^2 + 4 = 0$. The first equation leads to the real zero of 0 and the second equation leads to two complex numbers, namely $2i$ and $-2i$. Thus, there are three distinct zeros but only one x-intercept.

EXAMPLE 12

Given the function $g(x) = \dfrac{(9 - x)(3x - 10)^4(x^2 + x + 1)}{5 - x}$, how many distinct zeros and how many x-intercepts are there?

SOLUTION

For $9 - x = 0$, the zero is 9. For $(3x - 10)^4 = 0$, the one zero is $\dfrac{10}{3}$. For $x^2 + x + 1 = 0$, the two complex zeros are $\dfrac{-1 \pm i\sqrt{3}}{2}$. Thus, there are four distinct zeros but only two x-intercepts.

Vertical Asymptotes

In graphing rational functions, there may be one or more vertical lines that the function approaches but does not intersect. These are called **vertical asymptotes**. In Figure 7.1, shown below, $f(x)$ has one vertical asymptote and $g(x)$ has two vertical asymptotes.

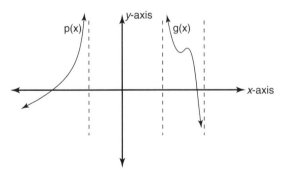

Figure 7.1

In order to locate the vertical asymptote(s) for a rational function, given by $f(x) = \dfrac{p(x)}{q(x)}$, we find all real zeros for $q(x)$. If c is a zero for $q(x)$, then $x = c$ is the equation of the vertical asymptote. If $q(x)$ has no real zeros, even though it may have complex zeros,

then there are no vertical asymptotes. We actually looking for the values of $f(x)$ that are <u>not</u> in its domain.

EXAMPLE 13

What are the vertical asymptotes of $f(x) = \dfrac{x^2 + 6x + 5}{3x - 2}$?

SOLUTION

You have seen this function in Example 7. The zero of the denominator is $\dfrac{2}{3}$. Thus, the vertical asymptote is $x = \dfrac{2}{3}$.

EXAMPLE 14

What are the vertical asymptotes of $g(x) = \dfrac{x^2 - 4}{(5x)(x^2 + 4)(3x + 7)}$?

SOLUTION

If $5x = 0$, then $x = 0$. If $3x + 7 = 0$, then $x = -\dfrac{7}{3}$. We need not be concerned about the middle factor of the denominator because the solutions to $x^2 + 4 = 0$ are two complex numbers, which <u>cannot</u> be asymptotes. Thus, the two vertical asymptotes are $x = 0$ (y-axis) and $x = -\dfrac{7}{3}$.

Horizontal Asymptote

In graphing rational functions, there may be one horizontal line that the function approaches either as $x \to \infty$ or as $x \to -\infty$. It is also possible that the function intersects this horizontal line for some x values(s). This is called a **horizontal asymptote**.

There are two key issues to emphasize regarding the comparison of a vertical asymptote with a horizontal asymptote.

1. A function cannot cross a vertical asymptote, but may cross a horizontal asymptote.

2. There may be more than one vertical asymptotes for a function, but there can only exist at most one horizontal asymptote.

In Figure 7.2, shown below, *f(x)* has a horizontal asymptote, but *f(x)* does not intersect it. The function *g(x)* also has a horizontal asymptote, but does intersect it once.

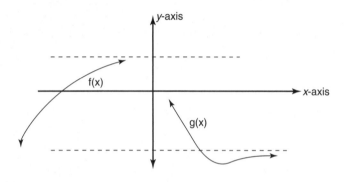

Figure 7.2

As with the situation for vertical asymptotes, there is a direct method for finding the horizontal asymptote, if it exists, of a rational function $f(x) = \dfrac{p(x)}{q(x)}$. For any polynomial function in the form $a_n x^n + a_{n-1} x^{n-1} + a_{n-2} x^{n-2} + ... + a_1 x + a_0$, as x approaches either infinity or negative infinity, the value of the function is most influenced by the leading term $a_n x^n$. There are three different cases to consider to determine the equation of the horizontal asymptote for $f(x) = \dfrac{p(x)}{q(x)}$. Suppose that

$p(x) = a_n x^n + a_{n-1} x^{n-1} + a_{n-2} x^{n-2} + ... + a_1 x + a_0$

and that $q(x) = b_m x^m + b_{m-1} x^{m-1} + b_{m-2} x^{m-2} + ...$ $+ b_1 x + b_0$. Of course, $a_n \neq 0$ and $b_m \neq 0$.

1. If $p(x)$ and $q(x)$ have the same degree, ($m = n$), then the equation of the horizontal asymptote is given by $y = \dfrac{a_n}{b_m}$. This is simply the ratio of the leading coefficients of $p(x)$ and $q(x)$.

2. If the degree of $p(x)$ is less than the degree of $q(x)$, ($n < m$), then the equation of the horizontal asymptote is given by $y = 0$ (*x*-axis). This is really a special instance of case 1. We can always add the term $0x^m$ to the function $p(x)$ without changing its degree. Notice that the ratio of the terms $0x^m$ to $b_m x^m$ is zero.

3. If the degree of $p(x)$ is greater than the degree of $q(x)$, ($n > m$), then there is no horizontal asymptote. Even this is a special instance of case 1. We simply add the term $0x^n$ to the function $q(x)$, without changing its degree. Notice that the ratio of the terms $a_n x^n$ to $0x^n$ is undefined.

EXAMPLE 15

What is the horizontal asymptote of $h(x) = \dfrac{x^2 + 11x - 7}{3x^2 - 2x - 8}$?

SOLUTION

You have seen this function is Example 8. The numerator and denominator are each of degree 2. Then just using the ratio of the leading coefficients, the horizontal asymptote is $y = \dfrac{1}{3}$.

EXAMPLE 16

What is the horizontal asymptote of $g(x) = \dfrac{2x^4 - x^3 + 1}{x^5 + 7x^3 + 10x + 5}$?

SOLUTION

We only need to compare the leading coefficients. However, since the degree of the numerator is less than the degree of the denominator, the horizontal asymptote is $y = 0$.

EXAMPLE 17

What is the horizontal asymptote of $r(x) = \dfrac{x^6 + x^2 - 3x - 5}{4x^3 - 9x}$.

SOLUTION

The degree of the numerator is higher than the degree of the denominator. Our conclusion is that there is no horizontal asymptote.

EXAMPLE 18

What is the horizontal asymptote of $f(x) = \dfrac{(2x - 3)(x + 7)(3x + 2)}{(x^2 + 8)(2x + 11)}$?

SOLUTION

By inspection, we can determine that the leading term of the numerator is $6x^3$ and the leading term of the denominator is $2x^3$. Since the top and bottom of this fraction have the same degree, the horizontal asymptote is $y = \dfrac{6}{2}$, which simplifies to $y = 3$.

NOTE:

The existence (or non-existence) of a horizontal asymptote has no bearing on the existence (or non-existence) of a vertical asymptote for a given function. It is important to remember that the existence of either of these asymptotes means that the function must get closer to the asymptote as $x \to \infty$ or as $x \to -\infty$. The function may cross only the horizontal asymptote.

Slant Asymptote

The last type of asymptote to consider is the slant asymptote, also called the oblique asymptote. This represents any linear asymptote that is neither vertical nor horizontal. As with a horizontal asymptote, the function may intersect a slant asymptote. For any function, there is a maximum of one slant asymptote.

CAUTION!

There cannot exist both a horizontal and slant asymptote for a given function.

In Figure 7.3 shown below, each of $f(x)$ and $g(x)$ has a slant asymptote. Notice that $f(x)$ does not intersect its slant asymptote, but $g(x)$ does intersect its slant asymptote.

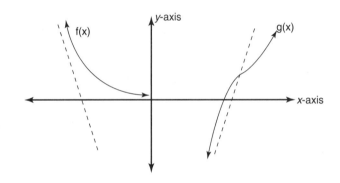

Figure 7.3

In order to find the slant asymptote, if it exists, of the rational function $r(x) = \dfrac{p(x)}{q(x)}$, there are two conditions that must be met.

1. The degree of the numerator must be 1 greater than the degree of the denominator.
2. When $p(x)$ is divided by $q(x)$, there must be a non-zero remainder.

The quotient becomes the equation of the slant asymptote.

EXAMPLE 19

What is the equation of the slant asymptote of $f(x) = \dfrac{4x^2 + x - 4}{x - 1}$?

SOLUTION

Using the technique of either long division or synthetic division, $\dfrac{4x^2 + x - 4}{x - 1} = 4x + 5 + \dfrac{1}{x - 1}$. Thus, the slant asymptote is $y = 4x + 5$.

EXAMPLE 20

What is the equation of the slant asymptote of
$$g(x) = \frac{-3x^3 + 2x^2 + x - 6}{x^2 - 2}?$$

SOLUTION

By long division, we find that $\dfrac{-3x^3 + 2x^2 + x - 6}{x^2 - 2}$
$= -3x + 2 + \dfrac{-5x - 2}{x^2 - 2}$. Thus, the slant asymptote is $y = -3x + 2$.

EXAMPLE 21

What is the equation of the slant asymptote of
$$h(x) = \frac{10x^2 + 9x - 7}{2x - 1}?$$

SOLUTION

By long division or by factoring, we get $\dfrac{10x^2 + 9x - 7}{2x - 1} = 5x + 7$. Since there is no remainder, there is no slant asymptote.

Referring to this last example, the graph of $h(x) = \dfrac{10x^2 + 9x - 7}{2x - 1}$ would be identical to the graph of $y = 5x + 7$, except for the point $\left(\dfrac{1}{2}, \dfrac{19}{2}\right)$. This point does not exist on the graph of $h(x)$ because the domain excludes the number $\dfrac{1}{2}$.

Piecewise Function

A **piecewise function** uses a different formula for each of different non-overlapping parts of its domain. In contrast to our earlier functions, some of these functions are discontinuous. In general, a single piecewise function is defined differently for different domain values. It must still obey the key rule of all functions; namely, for each value in the domain, there can be only one range value.

EXAMPLE 22

Let a function be defined as follows:
$$f(x) = \begin{cases} 1, \text{ if } x \le 0 \\ 2x + 1, \text{ if } x > 0 \end{cases}$$
Draw the graph of $f(x)$ for $-3 \le x \le 5$

SOLUTION

When $-3 \le x \le 0$, $f(x) = 1$. When $0 < x \le 5$, $f(x) = 2x + 1$. Here is the graph of $f(x)$ for the given domain values. The coordinates for a few points are also identified.

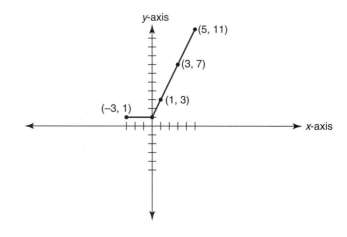

In Example 22, the graph shows that the function is continuous at $(0, 1)$. The range of $f(x)$ is all numbers between 1 and 11, inclusive.

EXAMPLE 23

Let a function be defined as follows:

$$g(x) = \begin{cases} -x, \text{ if } -2 \le x < 1 \\ x^2, \text{ if } x \ge 1 \end{cases}$$

Draw the graph of $g(x)$ and identify the range.

SOLUTION

The appropriate graph, with the coordinates of a few points, appears below.

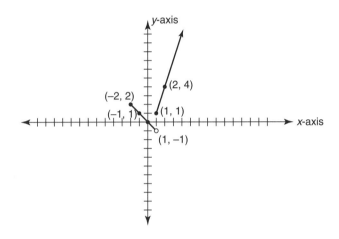

Notice that there is a discontinuity at $x = 1$. A circle is drawn around the point $(1, -1)$ because it is not included as part of the graph of $g(x)$. The range of g(x) is all numbers greater than -1.

The easiest way to verify the range is to take a ruler and slide it upwards from the point $(1, -1)$. You will see that for any y value above -1, there is at least one corresponding x value. In fact, for any y value such that, $1 \le y \le 2$ there are two corresponding x values.

Let's look at two examples that show the application of piecewise functions.

EXAMPLE 24

A car rental agency charges $0.30 per mile for each mile up to 100 miles. For any mileage in excess of 100 miles, the rate is $0.20 per mile.

(a) Describe this piecewise function algebraically and graphically.

(b) Find the cost if a person drives a car for 150 miles.

(c) Find the number of miles driven if the total cost is $102.80

SOLUTION

(a) If $g(x)$ represents the function, then

$$g(x) = \begin{cases} \$0.30x, \text{ if } 0 \le x \le 100 \\ \$30 + (\$0.20)(x-100), \text{ if } x > 100 \end{cases}$$

Notice that the cost of the mileage above 100 miles is represented as the total cost for the first 100 miles, which is $(100)(\$0.30) = \$30$, plus each additional mile at a cost of $0.20 per mile. The graph below shows $g(x)$, along with three selected points. (Since both x and $g(x)$ cannot be negative, only the first quadrant needs to be shown.)

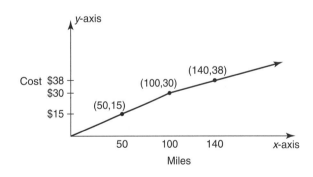

(b) The cost of driving 150 miles is $30 + (\$0.20)(150 - 100) = \$40.00$.

(c) $\$102.80 = \$30 + (\$0.20)(x - 100)$. This equation simplifies to $\$102.80 = \$30 + \$0.20x - \$20$. Thus, $x = \$92.80 \div \$0.20 = 464$ miles.

EXAMPLE 25

At the Tarryville Post Office, the cost of mailing a package is as follows: If the package weighs no more than 3 pounds, the cost is a flat rate of $2.00. For packages that weigh more than 3 pounds but not exceeding 10 pounds, the cost is $0.80 per pound. For packages in excess of 10 pounds, the cost is $1.20 per pound. The weight of each package is rounded off to the nearest pound.

(a) Describe this piecewise function algebraically and graphically.

(b) Find the cost of mailing a package that weighs 9 pounds.

(c) Find the number of pounds of a package that costs $17.20.

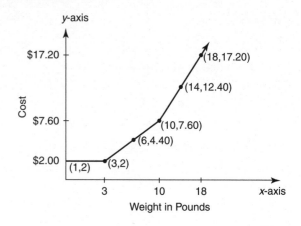

(b) The cost of a 9-pound package is $2.00 + ($0.80)(9 − 3) = $6.80.

(c) $17.20 = $7.60 + ($1.20)(x − 10). This equation simplifies to $17.20 = $7.60 + $1.20x − $12. Thus, x = $21.60 ÷ $1.20 = 18 pounds.

Greatest Integer Function

A specific type of piecewise function that has applications in calculus is the **greatest integer function**, written as $f(x) = [[x]]$. For each x value $f(x)$ is defined as the greatest integer less than or equal to x. As examples, $f(10) = 10$, $f(4.3) = 4$, $f(-1.8) = -2$, and $f(-6) = -6$. Here is a graph of $f(x) = [[x]]$, shown in Figure 7.4.

SOLUTION

(a) Let $h(x)$ represent the function. If the weight is at most 3 pounds, then $h(x) = 2.00. A package that weighs more than 3 pounds but at most 10 pounds, will cost an extra $0.80 per pound; so for a package in this weight class, the cost is $2.00 + ($0.80)(x − 3). Note that a package that weighs 10 pounds, the cost is $2.00 + ($0.80)(7) = $7.60. Finally, for a package that weighs more than 10 pounds, the cost will be $1.20 per pound; so the cost of a package in this weight class is $7.60 + ($1.20)(x − 10). Thus,

$$h(x) = \begin{cases} \$2.00, \text{ if } 0 \le x \le 3 \\ \$2.00 + (\$0.80)(x - 3) \text{ if } 3 < x \le 10 \\ \$7.60 + (\$1.20)(x - 10) \text{ if } x > 10 \end{cases}$$

The graph below, restricted to the first quadrant, shows $h(x)$, along with a few selected points.

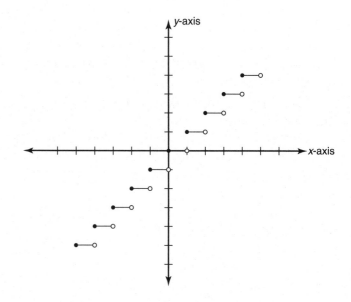

Figure 7.4

Notice that the domain is all real numbers, but the range is all integers.

Absolute Value Function

The **absolute value function** is denoted as $f(x) = |x|$. This is really a subcategory of piecewise step functions, since we can also write

$$\begin{cases} f(x) = x, \text{ if } x \geq 0 \\ -x, \text{ if } x < 0 \end{cases}$$

The graph of $f(x)$ is shown below, with selected points.(Fig. 7.5)

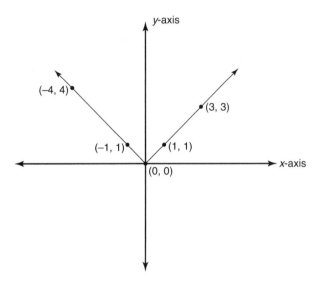

Figure 7.5

In Chapter 5, we discussed transformations of parent functions. Let $f(x) = |x|$ represent a parent function. Consider the function $g(x) = |x| - 4$. The graph of $g(x)$, as shown below, can be drawn by subtracting 4 units from each value of $f(x)$. (Figure 7.6)

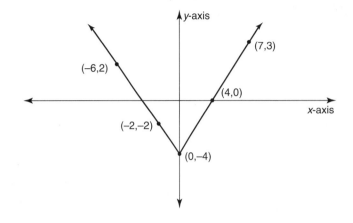

Figure 7.6

A second type of transformation can be obtained with the function $k(x) = (-2)|x|$. This function can be drawn by multiplying each value of $f(x)$ by -2. The graph of $k(x)$ is shown below, with selected points. (Figure 7.7)

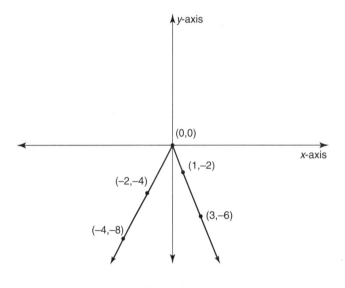

Figure 7.7

Now let's consider the graph of $h(x) = |x + 3|$. This graph can be drawn by subtracting 3 units from each x value of $f(x)$. The graph of $h(x)$, with selected points, is shown below in Figure 7.8.

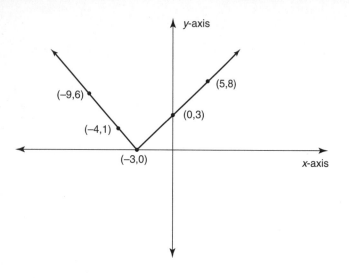

Figure 7.8

Polynomial Inequalities

Earlier in this chapter, we discussed the zeros of a polynomial function. We now investigate polynomial inequalities; specifically, we will look at only the polynomial functions that are factorable. You recall that each factor reveals the zeros of the function. At this time, our interest is focused on determining the values of x for which the function is either less than zero or greater than zero. Graphically, these are x values for which the function lies either below or above the x-axis.

EXAMPLE 26

Given $f(x) = (3x - 4)(x + 1)$, for which values of x is f(x) < 0 ?

SOLUTION

We first locate the zeros of $f(x)$, which result from $3x - 4 = 0$ and $x + 1 = 0$. So the zeros are $\frac{4}{3}$ and -1. These two values divide the domain into three sections, namely x values less than -1, x values between -1 and $\frac{4}{3}$, and x values greater than $\frac{4}{3}$. We just need to select

one value from each of these sections in order to determine whether $f(x) < 0$ or $f(x) > 0$ for that entire section of x values. We also do not need to evaluate $f(x)$ for any specific x value. All that is required is to determine the sign of each factor.

Let's begin with $x = -3$. For this x value, we can determine that $3x - 4$ and $x + 1$ are negative. Their product is positive, whenever $x < -1, f(x) > 0$.

Now choose $x = 0$. For this x value, $3x - 4$ is negative and $x + 1$ is positive, so their product is negative. Thus, whenever, $-1 < x < \frac{4}{3}, f(x) < 0$.

Finally, we will choose a number greater than $\frac{4}{3}$. Suppose we select $x = 2$. For this x value, $3x - 4$ is positive and $x + 1$ is positive. Their product is positive, which means that $f(x) > 0$. The answer to our original question is that whenever $-1 < x < \frac{4}{3}, f(x)$ is negative.

This approach works equally well in higher degree polynomial functions, even when there are double or triple zeros.

EXAMPLE 27

Given, $g(x) = (x)(2x - 1)^2(x - 5)^3$ for which x values is $g(x) > 0$?

SOLUTION

Setting each of x, $2x - 1$, and $x - 5$ equal to zero, the three zeros are 0, $\frac{1}{2}$, and 5. Notice that $g(x)$ is a sixth-degree function with a double zero of $\frac{1}{2}$ and a triple zero of 5. The four regions are (a) numbers less than 0, (b) numbers between 0 and $\frac{1}{2}$, (c) numbers between $\frac{1}{2}$ and 5, and (d) numbers greater than 5.

We'll begin with $x = -2$. For this value, x is negative, $(2x - 1)^2$ is positive, and $(x - 5)^3$ is negative. Their product is positive, so $g(x) > 0$. Next, consider $x = 0.4$. For this value, x is positive, $(2x - 1)^2$ is positive, and $(x - 5)^3$ is negative. Their product is negative, so $g(x) < 0$.

Now let's check $x = 1$. For this x value, x is positive, $(2x - 1)^2$ is positive, and $(x - 5)^3$ is negative. Their product is negative, so $g(x) < 0$.

Finally, to check a value of x greater than 5, we'll select $x = 6$. For this x value, x is positive, $(2x - 1)^2$ is positive, and $(x - 5)^3$ is positive. Their product is positive, so $g(x) > 0$.

Thus, the values of x for which $g(x) > 0$ are $x < 0$ or $x > 5$. Another way to express this answer is all numbers that are not between 0 and 5, inclusive.

CAUTION!

Be sure that when checking each factor of the function, you also include the associated powers of these factors. Thus, for Example 27, we did not simply check $2x - 1$ for positive or negative value; we checked $(2x - 1)^2$. In a similar fashion, note that we checked the entire factor $(x - 5)^3$, not just $(x - 5)$.

EXAMPLE 28

Given $h(x) = (6 - x)^2 (7x + 1)^6$, for which x values is $h(x) > 0$?

SOLUTION

This will be real quick! Normally, we first find the zeros of 6 and $-\dfrac{1}{7}$, then subdivide the domain into three sections. But for this example, notice that the factors are raised to even powers. This forces the value of each factor to be at least zero. Neither of $(6 - x)^2$ or $(7x + 1)^6$ can ever be negative. Our answer is all values of x except 6 and $-\dfrac{1}{7}$.

NOTE:

If the question in Example 28 had asked for values of x for which $h(x) < 0$, the answer would have been no solution.

Radical Equations

A **radical equation** is one in which there is at least one expression under a radical symbol, usually a square root. In this discussion we will confine the radical signs to square roots. Checking all answers for this type of equation is a necessity, not a luxury. In some cases, there may be no solution. Even when there appears to be two solutions, one (or both) may be extraneous. The maximum number of solutions will be two.

EXAMPLE 29

Given $\sqrt{3x - 7} = 6$, what are the values of x?

SOLUTION

By squaring each side, we can remove the radical sign. This leads to $3x - 7 = 36$. Thus, $x = \dfrac{43}{3}$. This answer will check since, by substitution, we get $\sqrt{36} = 6$.

EXAMPLE 30

Given $\sqrt{12 - 3x} = x - 4$, what are the values of x?

SOLUTION

Similar to Example 29, just square both sides to get $12 - 3x = x^2 - 8x + 16$. Be sure that you performed $(x - 4)^2$ on the right side. Then $x^2 - 5x + 4 = 0$. This equation factors as $(x - 4)(x - 1) = 0$. The two potential answers are 4 and 1. The answer of 4 will check, since by substitution, we get $\sqrt{0} = 0$. However, when we substitute the value of 1, the equation reads $\sqrt{9} = -3$, which is false. The only answer is 4.

EXAMPLE 31

Given $\sqrt{x^2 - 12x} = 8$, what are the values of x?

SOLUTION

Squaring both sides and simplifying leads to $x^2 - 12x - 64 = 0$. Then $(x - 16)(x + 4) = 0$, so the potential answers are 16 and -4. Both are actual answers, since they check the original equation.

EXAMPLE 32

Given $\sqrt{3x^2 - 7x + 23} = x - 5$, what are the values of x?

SOLUTION

Squaring both sides leads to $3x^2 - 7x + 23 = x^2 - 10x + 25$, which simplifies to $2x^2 + 3x - 2 = 0$. By factoring, we get $(2x - 1)(x + 2) = 0$. The two potential answers are $\frac{1}{2}$ and -2. However, when either one of these numbers is substituted into the original equation, the right side becomes negative. Thus, neither number is an actual answer. Our conclusion is that there is no solution.

Quiz for Chapter 7

1. If $f(x) = a_6 x^6 + a_5 x^5 + ... + a_1 x + a_0$ is of degree six, which one of the following must be true?

    (A) $a_0 \neq 0$ (C) $a_6 \neq 0$

    (B) $f(x)$ has 7 terms   (D) $f(x)$ has fewer than 7 terms

2. What is the range of the function $g(x) = -4(x + 8)^2 - 7$?

    (A) All numbers less than or equal to -8

    (B) All numbers less than or equal to -7

    (C) All numbers greater than or equal to -8

    (D) All numbers greater than or equal to -7

3. Which one of the following is completely correct concerning the graph of $h(x) = 5x^7 - 10x^6 - 25x - 31$?

    (A) As $x \to \infty$, $h(x) \to \infty$. Also, as $x \to -\infty$, $h(x) \to \infty$.

    (B) As $x \to \infty$, $h(x) \to -\infty$. Also, as $x \to -\infty$, $h(x) \to -\infty$.

    (C) As $x \to \infty$, $h(x) \to -\infty$. Also, as $x \to -\infty$, $h(x) \to \infty$.

    (D) As $x \to \infty$, $h(x) \to \infty$. Also, as $x \to -\infty$, $h(x) \to -\infty$.

4. Which one of the following has a single zero at $-\dfrac{1}{2}$ and a double zero at 9?

(A) $p(x) = (2x + 1)^2(x - 9)$

(B) $q(x) = (2x + 1)(x - 9)^2$

(C) $r(x) = (2x - 1)(x + 9)^2$

(D) $s(x) = (2x - 1)^2(x + 9)$

5. Which one of the following circumstances is <u>impossible</u> for the nature of the zeros of a polynomial function?

(A) Two distinct real zeros and six complex zeros.

(B) One triple real zero and no complex zeros.

(C) Five distinct real zeros, including a double zero, and three complex zeros.

(D) Four double real zeros and four complex zeros.

6. $h(x)$ is a fourth-degree polynomial whose only zeros are $2 + 3i$ and $2 - 3i$. Which one of the following could represent $h(x)$?

(A) $-2(x - 2 - 3i)(x - 2 + 3i)^3$

(B) $-3(x - 2 - 3i)^2(x - 2 + 3i)^2$

(C) $2(x + 2 - 3i)(x + 2 + 3i)^3$

(D) $3(x - 2 - 3i)(x - 2 + 3i)$

7. Which one of the following rational functions has both two distinct real zeros and a domain of all real numbers?

(A) $f(x) = \dfrac{(3x + 5)(-x + 2)}{x^2 + 16}$

(B) $g(x) = \dfrac{(3x + 2)(-x + 5)}{x^2 - 49}$

(C) $h(x) = \dfrac{(3x + 4)^2}{x^2 + x}$

(D) $k(x) = \dfrac{6x}{x^2 + x + 1}$

8. The graph of a polynomial function $g(x)$ has four distinct zeros but only two x-intercepts. Which one of the following could represent $g(x)$?

(A) $(x - 3)(x + 6)(2x + 1)(2x - 5)$

(B) $(x + 1)^2(x - 3 - i)(x - 3 + i)$

(C) $(x - 5)(x + 5)(x + 3 - i)^2$

(D) $(x - 1)(x + 1)(x + 3 - 4i)(x + 3 + 4i)$

9. The function $g(x)$ has two vertical asymptotes. Which one of the following could represent $g(x)$?

(A) $\dfrac{5x - 9}{x^2 - x - 90}$

(C) $\dfrac{(x)(3x - 8)}{x^2 - 10x + 25}$

(B) $\dfrac{(2x - 9)(x + 4)}{x^2 + x + 2}$

(D) $\dfrac{x^2 + 16}{(x - 10)(x^2 + 9)}$

10. The function $f(x) = \dfrac{9x^3 + 7x^2 - 3}{bx^3 - 2x + 1}$ has a horizontal asymptote with the equation $y = -\dfrac{2}{3}$. What is the value of b?

(A) $\dfrac{27}{2}$

(C) -6

(B) 6

(D) $-\dfrac{27}{2}$

11. The function $k(x) = \dfrac{3x^m + 8x - 6}{12x^6 + 3x - 1}$ has no horizontal asymptote. What are the restrictions on the value of m?

(A) $m > 6$

(C) $m < 6$

(B) $m > 1$

(D) No restrictions

12. What is the equation of the slant asymptote for $g(x) = \dfrac{4x^3 - x^2 + 8}{x^2 - 2}$?

(A) $y = 4x + 4$

(C) $y = 4x - 1$

(B) $y = 4x + 1$

(D) $y = 4x - 4$

13. Let $h(x) = \begin{cases} 5x, \text{ if } -5 \le x \le 0 \\ x^2 + 2, \text{ if } x > 0 \end{cases}$

What is the range of $h(x)$?

(A) All numbers greater than or equal to -25, except numbers between 0 and 2

(B) All numbers greater than or equal to -25, except zero.

(C) All numbers greater than or equal to -5, except numbers between 0 and 2.

(D) All numbers greater than or equal to -5, except zero

14. In a certain company, the cost of mailing a package depends on its weight. The cost is $0.25 for each pound up to 10 pounds. The cost is $0.20 for each pound above 10 pounds up to 30 pounds. The cost is $0.15 per pound for each pound in excess of 30 pounds. If the cost of mailing a package is $8.30, what is its weight?

(A) 48 pounds   (C) 44 pounds

(B) 46 pounds   (D) 42 pounds

15. What is the equation of the function $g(x)$ whose graph lies 8 units to the right of $f(x) = |x|$?

(A) $g(x) = |x| + 8$ (C) $g(x) = |x| - 8$

(B) $g(x) = |x - 8|$ (D) $g(x) = |x + 8|$

16. Given $f(x) = (2x - 5)(x - 4)$, for which values of x is $f(x) > 0$?

(A) All numbers between -4 and $-\dfrac{5}{2}$

(B) All numbers less than -4 or greater than $-\dfrac{5}{2}$

(C) All numbers between $\dfrac{5}{2}$ and 4

(D) All numbers less than $\dfrac{5}{2}$ or greater than 4

17. Given $h(x) = (x + 2)(4x + 13)^2 (x - 3)$, which one of the following is correct?

(A) $h(-1) > 0$ (C) $h(-3) < 0$

(B) $h(-4) > 0$ (D) $h(-6) < 0$

18. What are the values of x in the equation $\sqrt{3x^2 - 2x} = 4$?

(A) $\dfrac{8}{3}$ and -2 (C) $-\dfrac{2}{3}$ and 2

(B) Only $\dfrac{8}{3}$ (D) Only 2

19. What are the values of x in the equation $\sqrt{2x - 10} = 5 - x$?

(A) 5 and 7   (C) Only 5

(B) Only 7   (D) No solution

20. Let $g(x) = [[x]]$. What is the value of $g(3.2) - g(-3.2)$?

(A) 8   (C) 6

(B) 7   (D) 0

Quiz for Chapter 7
SOLUTIONS

1. (C)

For any polynomial function, the leading coefficient must not equal zero.

2. (B)

The vertex is located at $(-8, -7)$. Since the coefficient of x^2 is negative, the graph reaches its highest point at the y value of the vertex, which is -7.

3. (D)

The leading coefficient of the polynomial function is positive and the degree of the function is odd. Thus, when x approaches infinity, so does the function approach infinity. In addition, when x approaches negative infinity, the function also approaches negative infinity.

4. (B)

A zero of $-\dfrac{1}{2}$ can be derived from a factor of $2x + 1$. A zero of 9 can be derived from a factor of $x - 9$. Since the double zero is located at 9, the factor $x - 9$ must be squared.

5. (C)

When they occur, complex zeros of a polynomial function must exist in pairs.

6. (B)

If $2 + 3i$ and $2 - 3i$ are the only zeros of a fourth-degree polynomial, then each of them must be a double zero. Only answer choice (B) shows a double zero for each complex number.

7. (A)

The only two answer choices with two distinct zeros are (A) and (B). Of these two, only answer choice (A) has a domain of all real numbers.

8. (D)

The function $g(x)$ must have two distinct real zeros (that correspond to the x-intercepts), and two distinct complex zeros. The zeros for answer choice (D) are 1, -1, $-3 + 4i$, and $-3 - 4i$.

9. (A)

The denominator factors as $(x - 10)(x + 9)$, so that the vertical asymptotes are $x = 10$ and $x = -9$.

10. (D)

The equation of the horizontal asymptote is
$$y = \frac{9}{b} = -\frac{2}{3}, \text{ so } b = -\frac{27}{2}.$$

11. (A)

If a rational function has no horizontal asymptote, the degree of the numerator must be higher than the degree of the denominator.

12. (C)

Using long division, $\dfrac{4x^3 - x^2 + 8}{x^2 - 2} =$ $4x - 1 + \dfrac{8x + 6}{x^2 - 2}$. The equation of the asymptote only uses the quotient of $4x - 1$, not the remainder of $8x + 6$.

13. (A)

When $-5 \le x \le 0$, the values of y are $-25 \le y \le 0$. When $x > 0$, the values of y are $y > 2$. Thus, the range of y can be described as $y \ge -25$, but-excluding all values between 0 and 2.

14. (D)

If the package weighed 10 pounds, the cost would be $(\$0.25)(10) = \$2.50$ If the package weighed 30 pounds, the cost would be $(\$2.50 + (\$0.20)(20) = \$6.50$. Let x represent the number of pounds in excess of 30. Then $\$8.30 = \$6.50 + \$0.15x$. Then $x = 12$, so the weight of the package is 42 pounds.

15. (B)

In the equation of $f(x)$, just replace x with $x - 8$ to express $g(x)$.

16. (D)

The zeros of $f(x)$ are $\dfrac{5}{2}$ and 4, so there are three regions to consider. In selecting any number less than $\dfrac{5}{2}$, $f(x) > 0$. In selecting any number between $\dfrac{5}{2}$ and 4, $f(x) < 0$. In selecting any number greater than 4, $f(x) > 0$.

17. (B)

The four regions are (a) numbers less than $-\dfrac{13}{4}$, (b) numbers between $-\dfrac{13}{4}$ and -2, (c) numbers between -2 and 3, and (d) numbers greater than 3. By selecting one number from each region, we find the following:

(a) When $x < -\dfrac{13}{4}$, $h(x) > 0$.

(b) When $-\dfrac{13}{4} < x < -2$, $h(x) > 0$.

(c) When $-2 < x < 3$, $h(x) < 0$

(d) When $x > 3$, $h(x) > 0$. Thus, the statement $h(-4) > 0$ is correct.

18. (A)

Squaring both sides and simplifying leads to $3x^2 - 2x - 16 = 0$. Then $(3x - 8)(x + 2) = 0$, which yields the answers $\dfrac{8}{3}$ and -2. Both answers check the original equation.

19. (C)

Squaring both sides and simplifying leads to $x^2 - 12x + 35 = 0$. Then since $(x - 7)(x - 5) = 0$, the potential answers are 5 and 7. The number 5 checks the equation; however, the number 7 does not because $\sqrt{4} \ne -2$.

20. (B)

$g(x)$ represents the greatest integer function. Then $g(3.2) = 3$ and $g(-3.2) = -4$. The computation becomes $3 - (-4) = 7$.

Chapter 8

Exponential and Logarithmic Functions

Welcome to Chapter 8. In this chapter, we will review the following algebraic topics concerning these two functions:

(a) Algebraic properties

(b) Equations

(c) Graphical features, including domain, range, and inverses

(d) Exponential growth, exponential decay, compound interest, and proportion problems

Logarithm is really another word for exponent. The statement $2^3 = 8$ can be written equivalently as $3 = \log_2 8$, which is read as follows: "3 is the logarithm of the number 8 for the base 2." Thus, using the base 2, we can write the equation $y = 2^x$ explicitly for x as $x = \log_2 y$. This equation states that x is the exponent (logarithm) for the base 2 that produces the value of y. In general, if $y = a^x$, then $x = \log_a y$. The restrictions on a are as follows: $a > 0$ and $a \neq 1$. The two most popular values of a are 10 and e. You recall that

$$e = \lim_{x \to \infty} \left(1 + \frac{1}{x}\right)^x \approx 2.71828.$$

When the expression $x = \log y$ is written without the base number, it is understood to be 10. For example, since $10^4 = 10,000$, we can write $4 = \log 10,000$. Keep in mind that negative exponents are allowed.

Thus, $-2 = \log 0.01$, since $10^{-2} = 0.01$. When base 10 is used, the expression $\log y$ is called a **common logarithm**.

The expression $x = \ln y$ is written when it is understood that the base number is e. So, $\ln y$ is equivalent to $\log_e y$. Using your calculator, you can verify that $\ln 7 \approx 1.9459$. This would imply that $e^{1.9459} \approx 7$. As another example, since $\ln 0.5 \approx -0.6931$, we can write $e^{-0.6931} \approx 0.5$. When base e is used, the expression $\ln y$ is called a **natural logarithm**.

Algebraic Properties

Rules of Logarithms

There are several **rules of logarithms**. For brevity, we will assume that we are using base 10. However, these rules apply to any base, provided the base remains constant. For all these rules, $M, N > 0$ and x may be any real number.

Rule 1: $\log 1 = 0$.

Rule 2: $\log (MN) = \log M + \log N$

Rule 3: $\log \left(\dfrac{M}{N}\right) = \log M - \log N$

Rule 4: $\log M^x = (x)(\log M)$

Rule 5:   If $\log (M) = \log (N)$, then $M = N$

EXAMPLE 1

How is the expression $3^{-4} = \dfrac{1}{81}$ written in logarithmic form?

SOLUTION

The equivalent expression is $log_3\left(\dfrac{1}{81}\right) = -4$

EXAMPLE 2

If $\log Q = y$ and $\log R = z$, write an expression in y and z that represents $\log\left(\dfrac{Q^2}{R}\right)$.

SOLUTION

$\log\left(\dfrac{Q^2}{R}\right) = \log(Q^2) - \log(R) = (2)(\log Q) - \log (R) = 2y - z$.

CAUTION: Be aware of the following inequalities

1. $\log (M + N) \neq \log M + \log N$
2. $\log (M - N) \neq \log M - \log N$
3. $\left(\log M\right)^x \neq \log (M^x)$

We can use one or more of the above five rules to solve equations involving logarithms and exponents. Assume that each logarithm is using base 10.

Equations

EXAMPLE 3

What is the value of x in the equation $\log (x + 6) = (3)(\log 2)$?

SOLUTION

Rewrite as $\log (x + 6) = \log(2^3) = \log 8$. Then $x + 6 = 8$, so $x = 2$.

EXAMPLE 4

What is the value of x in the equation $(2)(\log x) = \log 4 + \log (x + 3)$?

SOLUTION

Rewrite as $\log(x^2) = \log[(4)(x + 3)] = \log(4x + 12)$. Then $x^2 - 4x - 12 = 0$. So, $(x - 6)(x + 2) = 0$. The possible answers are 6 and -2. However, if we substitute $x = -2$, we recognize that $\log (-2)$ has no meaning. Thus, $x = 6$ is the only answer.

EXAMPLE 5

What is the value of x in the equation $\log 5 + \log x - \log(x - 7) = \log 8$?

SOLUTION

Rewrite as $\log\left(\dfrac{5x}{x - 7}\right) = \log 8$. Then $\dfrac{5x}{x - 7} = 8$, which becomes $5x = 8x - 56$. Thus, $x = 18\dfrac{2}{3}$.

EXAMPLE 6

What is the value of x in the equation $\log x + \log(x - 15) = 2$?

SOLUTION

Rewrite just the left side as $\log(x^2 - 15x)$. Inserting the "invisible" base 10, the equation now appears as $\log_{10}(x^2 - 15x) = 2$. The simplest way to complete this example is to use the exponential form of this last equation, namely $x^2 - 15x = 10^2 = 100$. Then $(x - 20)(x + 5) = 0$. Of the two potential answers, only $x = 20$ is an actual solution.

NOTE:

> In Example 6, if you were able to spot that since $10^2 = 100$, then you could have written the right side as log 100. At this point, your equation would still be $x^2 - 15x = 100$.

EXAMPLE 7

> What is the value of x in the equation $6^x = 3$?

SOLUTION

Take the logarithm of each side so that $\log 6^x = \log 3$, which becomes $(x)(\log 6) = \log 3$. Thus, $x = \dfrac{\log 3}{\log 6} \approx 0.6131$

EXAMPLE 8

> What is the value of x in the equation $7^{x+2} = 0.5$?

SOLUTION

Rewrite as $\log(7^{x+2}) = (x+2)(\log 7) = \log 0.5$. Then $x + 2 = \dfrac{\log 0.5}{\log 7} \approx -0.3562$. Thus, $x \approx -2.3562$.

EXAMPLE 9

> What is the value of x in the equation $e^{3x+1} = 10$?

SOLUTION

Take the logarithm of each side, but use a base of e instead of a base of 10.

Then $\ln e^{3x+1} = 3x + 1 = \ln 10$. Thus, $x = \dfrac{\ln 10 - 1}{3} \approx 0.4342$.

NOTE:

> We used the fact that for any exponent p, $\ln e^p = p$. The justification for this statement is as follows: By Rule 4, $\ln e^p = p \ln e$. Furthermore, $\ln e = 1$.

EXAMPLE 10

> What is the value of x in the equation $6^{8-x} = \dfrac{1}{216}$?

SOLUTION

Instead of taking logarithms of both sides, note that $\dfrac{1}{216} = \dfrac{1}{6^3} = 6^{-3}$. Then $8 - x = -3$. Thus, $x = 11$.

Graphic Features of Logarithmic and Exponential Functions

Consider $y = 3^x$, which is equivalent to $x = \log_3 y$. Here are some selected points which we can use for graphing this function. For convenience, we'll round off decimals to the nearest hundredth. Using x values of -2, -1, 0, 1, and 2, the points are $(-2, 0.11)$, $(-1, 0.33)$, $(0, 1)$, $(1, 3)$, and $(2, 9)$.

As a second example, we'll consider $y = \left(\dfrac{1}{2}\right)^x$, which is equivalent to $x = \log_{\frac{1}{2}} y$. Using the same x values of -2, -1, 0, 1, and 2, the five points we get are $(-2, 4)$, $(-1, 2)$, $(0, 1)$, $(1, 0.5)$, and $(2, 0.25)$. The graphs of $y = 3^x$ and $y = \left(\dfrac{1}{2}\right)^x$ are shown below in Figure 8.1.

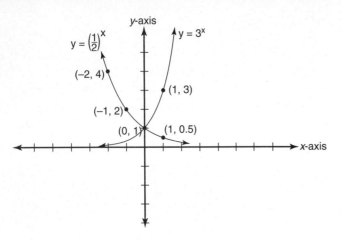

Figure 8.1

you check the points we used for $f(x)$, you will notice that $g(x)$ shows the switch in the numbers used in some of the points. For examples $(1, 3)$ and $(2, 9)$ belong to the graph of $f(x)$. Sure enough, the points $(3, 1)$ and $(9, 2)$ belong to the graph of $g(x)$. This is not a shocking surprise, since we expect the domain of either function to match the range of its inverse function. The graphs of $f(x) = 3^x$ and $g(x) = \log_3 x$ are shown below in Figure 8.2. You will note that inverse functions represent reflections across the line $y = x$. Also, note that for $f(x)$, the horizontal asymptote is the x-axis. For $g(x)$, the vertical asymptote is the y-axis.

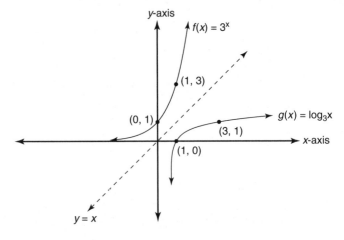

Figure 8.2

Domain and Range

By inspection, you can see that for each of these examples, the domain is all real numbers and the range is all non-negative numbers. Remember we mentioned that for $y = a^x$, $a > 0$ and $a \neq 1$. This implies that $y > 0$. In general, for the graph of $y = a^x$, the domain is all real numbers and the range is all non-negative numbers.

Inverses

In Chapter 5, we discussed the concept of inverse functions. You recall that one of the features of inverse functions that we discovered is the following: If $f(x)$ and $g(x)$ are inverse functions, then the domain of $f(x)$ matches the range of $g(x)$. Also the range of $f(x)$ matches the domain of $g(x)$.

Let $f(x) = 3^x$. To write $g(x)$ in an explicit fashion, start with $y = 3^x$ and interchange the variables. This leads to $x = 3^y$, which is equivalent to $y = \log_3 x$. This means that $g(x) = \log_3 x$ is the explicit representation of the inverse function of $f(x)$. We can draw the graph of $g(x)$ by selecting some (positive) values of x. Any decimal values will be rounded off to the nearest hundredth. In order to use our calculator for values of $\log_3 x$, we will use the formula $\log_3 x = \dfrac{\log_{10} x}{\log_{10} 3}$.

For example, $\log_3 20 = \dfrac{\log_{10} 20}{\log_{10} 3} \approx 2.73$.

Using x values of 1, 3, 9, 18, and 30, the points are $(1, 0)$, $(3, 1)$, $(9, 2)$, $(18, 2.63)$, and $(30, 3.10)$. If

For completeness in our discussion, let's also do a similar comparison with $h(x) = \left(\dfrac{1}{2}\right)^x$. To find the inverse function, call it $k(x)$, start with $y = \left(\dfrac{1}{2}\right)^x$ and interchange the variables. Then $x = \left(\dfrac{1}{2}\right)^y$, which is equivalent to $y = \log_{\frac{1}{2}} x$. So, $k(x) = \log_{\frac{1}{2}} x$ is the inverse function.

We'll use the formula $\log_{\frac{1}{2}} x = \dfrac{\log_{10} x}{\log_{10} \frac{1}{2}}$ in determining $k(x)$ values. Let's use x values of 0.5, 1, 2, 6, and 10. Then these x values lead to the following five points on the graph of $k(x)$: $(0.5, 1)$, $(1, 0)$, $(2, -1)$, $(6, -2.58)$, and $(10, -3.32)$.

If you check the points we used for $h(x)$ in the graph of Figure 8.1, you will notice that $k(x)$ shows a switch in the numbers used for some of the points. For examples, $(-1, 2)$ and $(1, 0.5)$ belong to the graph of $h(x) = \left(\frac{1}{2}\right)^x$.

Now notice that $(2, -1)$ and $(0.5, 1)$ belong to the graph of $k(x) = \log_{\frac{1}{2}} x$. The graphs of h(x) and k(x) are shown below in Figure 8.3. As expected, the domain of one function matches the range of its inverse. Note that each function is a reflection of the other across the line $y = x$.

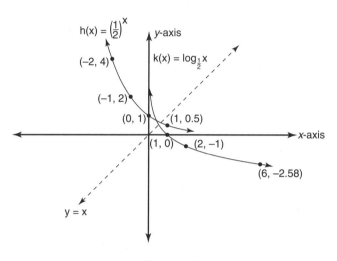

Figure 8.3

Exponential Growth, Exponential Decay, Proportions

Logarithmic and Exponential Functions in Real-life Scientific Situations

In the field of science that deals with sound, the level of sound is measured in units called decibels. The formula is $D = (10)\left(\log \frac{I}{I_0}\right)$, where D = number of decibels, I = the intensity of the sound being measured, and I_0 = the intensity of the least audible sound that can be heard by an average healthy individual. The unit

of measurement for I and I_0 is watts per square meter. The standard acceptable value of I_0 is 10^{-12} watts per square meter.

EXAMPLE 11

If the number of decibels associated with a normal conversation is 65.05, what is its sound intensity?

SOLUTION

By substitution, $65.05 = (10)\left(\log \frac{I}{10^{-12}}\right)$. Then $6.505 = \log \frac{I}{10^{-12}}$, which leads to $\frac{I}{10^{-12}} = 10^{6.505}$. Thus, $I = 10^{-5.495} \approx 3.20 \times 10^{-6}$ watts per square meter.

The **Richter scale** is used to measure the magnitude of earthquakes. The formula is $M = \left(\frac{2}{3}\right)\left(\log \frac{E}{E_0}\right)$, where M = magnitude, E = amount of energy released by the actual earthquake, and E_0 = amount of energy released by a small reference earthquake. The values of E and E_0 are measured in *joules*. The standard acceptable value of E_0 is $10^{4.40}$ joules. Small earthquakes have a magnitude of less than 4.5 on the Richter scale, whereas a very large earthquake has a magnitude of more than 7.5. The 1906 San Francisco earthquake had a magnitude of 8.25.

EXAMPLE 12

Suppose that the energy released by a second earthquake is 100 times the amount of energy released by a first earthquake. How much larger is the Richter scale reading (magnitude) of the second earthquake compared to the first earthquake?

SOLUTION

For simplicity, let's select 10^5 joules to represent the value of the energy released by the first earthquake. We must select a value greater than $10^{4.40}$, since $10^{4.40}$ represents the lowest acceptable reading. So, the magnitude of the first earthquake is $\left(\frac{2}{3}\right)\left(\log\frac{10^5}{10^{4.40}}\right) =$ $\left(\frac{2}{3}\right)(\log 10^{0.6}) = 0.4$. Now, the second earthquake has an energy value of $(10^5)(100) = 10^7$ joules. So, the magnitude of the second earthquake is $\left(\frac{2}{3}\right)\left(\log\frac{10^7}{10^{4.40}}\right) =$ $\left(\frac{2}{3}\right)(\log 10^{2.6}) = 1.7\overline{3}$. Thus, the second earthquake's magnitude is $1.\overline{3}$ larger than that of the first earthquake.

Population growth, whether it deals with people, animals, or even bacteria can be modeled with the function $P(t) = P_0 e^{rt}$, where P_0 = initial population, r = exponential rate of growth, t = time (usually in years), and $P(t)$ = population after a period of t.

In Chapter 4, we have seen this formula as it relates to a geometric series.

EXAMPLE 13

Currently, the population of the town of Peo-plefine is 5,400. If this population grows at the exponential rate of 2.5%, what will be the population in seven years? (Nearest integer)

SOLUTION

$P(7) = (5,400)(e^{(0.025)(7)}) \approx 6433$

EXAMPLE 14

Using the information given in Example 13, in how many years will the current population triple? (Nearest hundredth)

SOLUTION

The new population, $P(t)$, will be $(5,400)(3) = 16,200$. Then $16,200 = (5,400)(e^{(0.025)(t)})$. After simplifying this equation to $3 = e^{(0.025)(t)}$, we can write

$\ln 3 = 0.025t(\ln e) = 0.025t$. Thus, $t = \frac{\ln 3}{0.025} \approx 43.9$ years.

Another application of exponential equations, **radioactive decay, is the spontaneous change of one element into another element.** Radioactive substances are useful in the field of medicine. Most problems involving radioactive decay are connected to the half-life of the substance. Half-life refers to the time required in order for half of the substance to decay. The formula to be used is $A(t) = (A_0)\left(\frac{1}{2}\right)^{t/h}$, where $A(t)$ = amount left after time t, A_0 = initial amount, t = time, and h = half-life.

EXAMPLE 15

A radioactive substance has a half-life of 10 hours. Initially, there are 50 grams of this substance. How many grams remain after 15 hours?

SOLUTION

By substitution, $A(15) = (50)\left(\frac{1}{2}\right)^{15/10} \approx 17.68$ grams.

(Note that if the problem had asked for the number of grams that had <u>decayed</u>, our answer would have been approximately 32.32 grams.)

EXAMPLE 16

Initially, there are 180 milligrams of a radioactive isotope. After four days, 30% of this isotope has decayed. What is its half-life? (Nearest hundredth)

SOLUTION

First, we must remember that $A(t)$ is always the amount <u>remaining</u> after a time period of t. For this example, $A(4) = (180)(0.70) = 126$. Then $126 = (180)\left(\frac{1}{2}\right)^{4/h}$. After dividing 126 by 180 to get 0.70, take the common logarithm of each side to get $\log 0.70 = \left(\dfrac{4}{h}\right)\left(\log \dfrac{1}{2}\right)$.

Thus, $h = \dfrac{(4)\left(\log \dfrac{1}{2}\right)}{\log 0.70} \approx 7.77$ days.

EXAMPLE 17

> The half-life of an active ingredient in a certain chemical is six hours. What percent of this ingredient has decayed after two hours? (Nearest tenth of a percent)

SOLUTION

For this example, $A(2) = (A_0)\left(\dfrac{1}{2}\right)^{2/6} \approx 0.794(A_0)$.

This means that approximately 79.4% of this ingredient remains after two hours. Thus, $100\% - 79.4\% = 20.6\%$ of this ingredient has decayed. (It is not necessary to know the initial amount of this ingredient.)

Applications to Calculus

The final application of the use of exponential equations will be one that is directly related to calculus. Suppose that we are given any exponential function, $f(x) = a^x$, where a is a constant. The first derivative of $f(x)$, denoted as $f'(x)$, can be shown to be

$(a^x)(\ln a) = f(x)(\ln a)$. This implies that $f'(x)$ is directly proportional to $f(x)$, where $\ln a$ is the constant of proportionality.

EXAMPLE 18

> For a given function $f(x)$, its derivative is directly proportional to $f(x)$. If $f(4) = 12$, write an explicit expression for $f(x)$.

SOLUTION

Since $f(x) = a^x$, we can write $f(4) = 12 = a^4$. Then $a = \sqrt[4]{12} \approx 1.86$. Thus, $f(x) = 1.86^x$.

EXAMPLE 19

> Given a function $g(x)$ such that $g'(x) = (3)$ $(g(x))$, write an explicit expression for $g(x)$.

SOLUTION

We know that $g(x) = a^x$ and that $g'(x) = (a^x)(\ln a)$. By substitution, we can write $g'(x) = (3)(g(x)) = (3)(a^x) = (a^x)(\ln a)$. Then $3 = \ln a$, so $a \approx 20.09$. Thus, $g(x) = 20.09^x$.

Quiz for Chapter 8

1. Which one of the following is equivalent to x?

(A) $\log_{10} x^{10}$ (C) $10^{\log_{10} x}$

(B) $\log_x 10^x$ (D) $10^{\log_x 10}$

2. If $A = \log_b R$ and $C = \log_b T$, then which one of the following is equivalent to $A + 3C$?

(A) $(\log_b R)(\log_b T^3)$ (C) $\log_b(RT^3)$

(B) $\log_b R + \log_b T^3$ (D) $\log_b(RT)^3$

3. Assuming base 10 is used, what is the value of x in the equation $\log 4 - \log x + \log(x + 2) = \log 7$?

   (A) $\dfrac{2}{3}$ (C) 2

   (B) $\dfrac{4}{3}$ (D) $\dfrac{8}{3}$

4. What is the value of x in the equation $\log_3 x + \log_3(2x + 3) = 2$?

   (A) $\dfrac{2}{3}$ (C) 2

   (B) $\dfrac{3}{2}$ (D) 3

5. What is the value of x in the equation $9^{x+4} = 12.5$? (Nearest hundredth)

   (A) 1.15 (C) -2.85

   (B) 0.29 (D) -5.15

6. What is the value of x in the equation $4^{4-x} = \dfrac{1}{256}$?

   (A) 8 (C) 4

   (B) 6 (D) 2

7. Which one of the following statements is correct regarding the graph of $y = a^x$? $(a > 0, a \ne 1)$

   (A) The domain and range are all real numbers.

   (B) The domain is all real numbers and the range is all non-negative numbers.

   (C) The domain and range are all non-negative numbers.

   (D) The domain is all non-negative numbers and the range is all real numbers.

8. Given $f(x) = \log_5 x$ and that $g(x)$ represents the reflection of $f(x)$ across the line $y = x$, which one of the following is the explicit representation of $g(x)$?

   (A) 5^x (C) x^5

   (B) $\log_x 5$ (D) $\log_5 e^x$

9. The energy released by a certain earthquake is 10^8 joules. What is its measurement on the Richter scale? Use $10^{4.40}$ as the value of E_0.

   (A) 2.4 (C) 3.2

   (B) 2.8 (D) 3.6

10. If the number of decibels associated with heavy vehicular traffic is 89.3, what is its sound intensity, in watts per square meter? Use 10^{-12} as the value of I_0.

    (A) 6.5×10^{-1} (C) 8.5×10^{-3}

    (B) 6.5×10^{-2} (D) 8.5×10^{-4}

11. Currently, the population of Appleville is 3,800. It is expected that the population growth will be exponential, and that the population will be 8,550 in six years. What is the exponential rate of growth? (Nearest tenth of a percent)

    (A) 17.8% (C) 9.8%

    (B) 13.5% (D) 6.5%

12. The half-life of an ingredient in a certain chemical is 15 hours. What percent of this ingredient has decayed after seven hours? (Nearest tenth of a percent)

    (A) 27.6% (C) 69.1%

    (B) 30.9% (D) 72.4%

13. Initially, there are 60 grams of a radioactive isotope. After nine days, only 20% of this isotope remains. What is the half-life of this isotope, in days? (Nearest hundredth)

    (A) 3.58 (C) 4.18

    (B) 3.88 (D) 4.48

14. The function $h(x)$ is directly proportional to its first derivative. If $h(10) = 5$, what is the explicit expression for $h(x)$?

    (A) 2^x (C) 1.33^x

    (B) 1.58^x (D) 1.17^x

15. The ratio of the function $k(x)$ to $k'(x)$ equals $\dfrac{2}{5}$. What is the explicit expression for $k(x)$?

    (A) 1.49^x (C) 12.18^x

    (B) 2.5^x (D) 16.2^x

Quiz for Chapter 8
SOLUTIONS

1. (C)

Let $Q = 10^{\log_{10} x}$. Then $\log_{10} Q = (\log_{10} x)(\log_{10} 10) = \log_{10} x$. Thus, $Q = x$.

2. (C)

$A + 3C = \log_b R + (3)(\log_b T) = \log_b R + \log_b T^3 = \log_b RT^3$.

3. (D)

Rewrite the equation as $\log\left[\left(\dfrac{4}{x}\right)(x + 2)\right] = \log 7$. Then $\dfrac{4x + 8}{x} = 7$, which leads to $4x + 8 = 7x$. Thus, $x = \dfrac{8}{3}$.

4. (B)

Rewrite the equation as $\log_3(2x^2 + 3x) = 2$. Then $2x^2 + 3x - 9 = 0$, which factors as $(2x - 3)(x + 3) = 0$. Thus, $x = \dfrac{3}{2}$ is the only allowable answer.

5. (C)

Rewrite as $(x + 4)(\log 9) = \log 12.5$. Thus, $x = \dfrac{\log 12.5}{\log 9} - 4 \approx -2.85$.

6. (A)

Since $\dfrac{1}{256} = 4^{-4}$, we get $4 - x = -4$. Thus, $x = 8$.

7. (B)

In the graph of $y = a^x$, the domain is all real numbers and the range is all non-negative numbers.

8. (A)

Since $g(x)$ is the reflection of $f(x)$ across the line $y = x$, $g(x)$ is the inverse function of $f(x)$. Thus, $g(x) = 5^x$.

9. (A)

The measurement on the Richter scale is $\left[\dfrac{2}{3}\right]\left[\log\left(\dfrac{10^8}{10^{4.40}}\right)\right] = \left(\dfrac{2}{3}\right)(\log 10^{3.6}) = \left(\dfrac{2}{3}\right)(3.6) = 2.4$.

10. (D)

Let I represent the sound intensity. Then $89.3 = (10)\left(\log \dfrac{I}{10^{-12}}\right)$. Simplifying, we get $8.93 = \log I - \log 10^{-12} = \log I + 12$. Thus, $I = 10^{-3.07} \approx 8.5 \times 10^{-4}$.

11. (B)

Let r = rate of growth. Then $P(6) = 8,550 = (3,800)(e^{6r})$. This equation simplifies to $2.25 = e^{6r}$. Then $6r = \ln 2.25 \approx 0.81$. Thus, $r \approx 0.135 = 13.5\%$.

12. (A)

$A(7) = (A_0)\left(\dfrac{1}{2}\right)^{\frac{7}{15}} \approx 0.724 A_0$. This means that 72.4% of this ingredient remains after seven hours. Thus, $100\% - 72.4\% = 27.6\%$ has decayed.

13. (B)

$A(9) = (60)(0.20) = 12$ grams. Letting $h =$ half

life, $12 = (60)\left(\dfrac{1}{2}\right)^{\frac{9}{h}}$. Then $\log 0.20 = \left(\dfrac{9}{h}\right)\left(\log \dfrac{1}{2}\right)$. Thus,

$h = \dfrac{(9)\left(\log \dfrac{1}{2}\right)}{\log 0.20} \approx 3.88$ days.

14. (D)

$h(x) = a^x$. Then $h(10) = 5 = a^{10}$. Thus, $a = \sqrt[10]{5}$
≈ 1.17.

15. (C)

We are given that $\dfrac{k(x)}{k'(x)} = \dfrac{2}{5}$. Since $k(x) = a^x$

and $k'(x) = (a^x)(\ln a)$, $\dfrac{k(x)}{k'(x)} = \dfrac{1}{\ln a}$. Then $\dfrac{2}{5} = \dfrac{1}{\ln a}$,

which means that $\ln a = \dfrac{5}{2}$. Thus, $a = e^{\frac{5}{2}} \approx 12.18$.

Chapter 9

Trigonometric and Circular Functions

Welcome to Chapter 9. In this chapter, we will review the following topics:

(a) The Cartesian coordinate system
(b) Basic trigonometric functions using right triangles
(c) Special angles
(d) Inverse trigonometric functions
(e) Right triangle trigonometry
(f) Graphical features of trigonometric functions
(g) Trigonometric identities and equations
(h) The unit circle

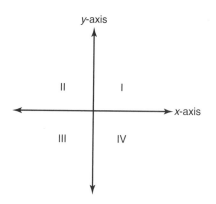

Figure 9.1

The Cartesian Coordinate System

The **Cartesian coordinate system**, also known as the **rectangular coordinate system**, consists of a vertical axis (y-axis), a horizontal axis (x-axis), and four sections called **quadrants**. The quadrants are numbered I, II, III, and IV, as shown in Figure 9.1.

Each point in this system is identified by its corresponding x value and y value, which is written in the form (x, y). The expression (x, y) is called an ordered pair whereas each of x and y is called a **coordinate**. The point at which the two axes intersect is called the **origin** and is designated as $(0,0)$. Positive x values are located to the right of $(0,0)$ and negative x values are located to the left of $(0,0)$. Positive y values are located above $(0,0)$ and negative y values are located below $(0,0)$. Figure 9.2, shown below, illustrates the points A, B, C, and D in different quadrants.

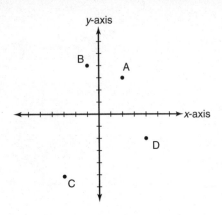

Figure 9.2

to represent angles in standard position. Figures 9.4, 9.5, 9.6, and 9.7 illustrate various angle values of θ. For convenience we'll use subscripts to represent each angle.

The labeling of each point is as follows: A is located at (2, 3), B is located at (−1, 4), C is located at (−3, −5), and D is located at (4, −2).

Points that have either an *x*-coordinate of zero or a *y*-coordinate of zero do not lie in any quadrant. Figure 9.3, shown below, illustrates the points E, F, G, and H. Notice that each of these points lies on one of the axes.

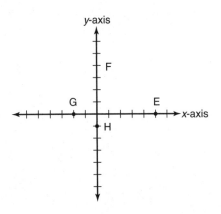

Figure 9.3

The labeling of each point is as follows: E is located at (5, 0), F is located at (0, 4), G is located at (−2, 0), and H is located at (0, −1).

Angles in Standard Position

An **angle in standard position** is an angle whose initial ray lies on the positive x-axis. Its terminal ray may lie in any quadrant or on any axis. *Angles are measured in a counterclockwise direction.* The Greek letter θ (pronounced "thay-tuh") is commonly used

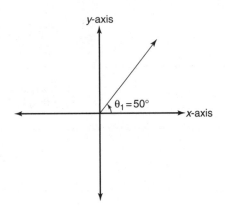

Figure 9.4

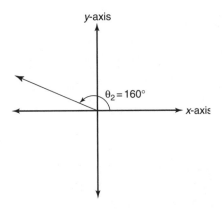

Figure 9.5

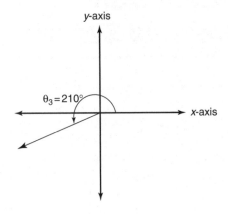

Figure 9.6

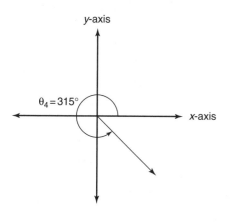

Figure 9.7

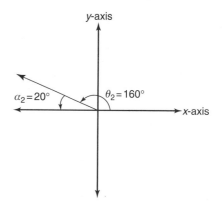

Figure 9.9

Reference Angles and Reference Triangles

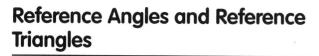

For any angle in standard position, there is a corresponding reference angle and a reference triangle. The **reference angle** is the acute angle formed by the terminal side and the x-axis. The Greek letter α (pronounced "alpha") is commonly used to represent reference angles. The method for finding the measure of a reference angle is as follows:

If $0° < \theta < 90°$, then $\alpha = \theta$; if $90° < \theta < 180°$, then $\alpha = 180° - \theta$; if $180° < \theta < 270°$, then $\alpha = \theta - 180°$; if $270° < \theta < 360°$, then $\alpha = 360° - \theta$. (We'll discuss the "special" angles 0°, 90°, 180°, and 270°, at a later time.) Figures 9.8, 9.9, 9.10, and 9.11 are re-creations of Figures 9.4, 9.5, 9.6, and 9.7, respectively. They illustrate the corresponding reference angle for a given angle in standard position.

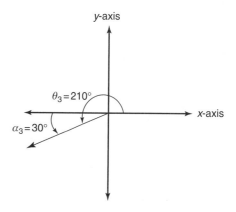

Figure 9.10

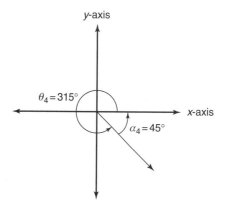

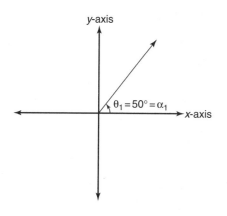

Figure 9.8

Figure 9.11

Note the use of subscripts for each reference angle in these figures. Also, note that when θ is less than 90°, the value of the reference angle equals the value of the angle in standard position.

The **reference triangle** is a right triangle formed by drawing a perpendicular segment from any point P on the terminal side to the *x*-axis. Figures 9.12, 9.13, 9.14, and 9.15 are re-creations of Figures 9.8 through 9.11, with the addition of the reference triangle. For consistency, each point P also has a subscript that matches the subscript of θ and α in the same figure. (Angle measures have been omitted to facilitate the viewing of these figures.)

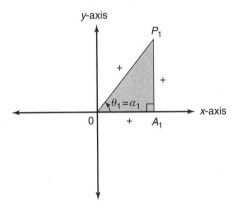

Figure 9.12

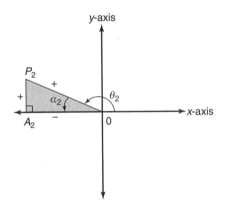

Figure 9.13

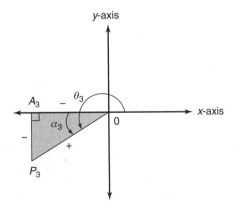

Figure 9.14

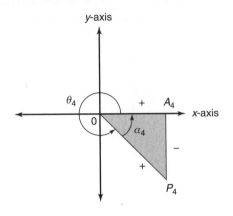

Figure 9.15

For each of the above figures, you will notice that a plus or minus sign has been assigned to each leg of the reference triangle. This is consistent with the signs of the *x* and *y* coordinates of the point P. In the first quadrant, each coordinate of P_1 is positive; thus the two legs of the reference triangle have plus signs. Likewise, in the second quadrant, the *x* coordinate of P_2 is negative but the *y* coordinate is positive; thus the leg that lies on the *x*-axis has a negative sign and the other leg has a positive sign.

The hypotenuse of each triangle is always positive, and for a good reason. We can label the horizontal leg as *h* and the vertical leg as *v*. Using the Pythagorean Theorem, the length of the hypotenuse must be $\sqrt{h^2 + v^2}$. This value must be positive, even if either or both of *h* and *v* were negative.

Basic Trigonometric Functions

Sine Function

The **sine** function is commonly called the sine ratio. To determine the sine of an angle θ, written as $\sin\theta$, we first find the associated reference angle α, (which is <u>always</u> acute), and the corresponding reference (right) triangle. For this triangle, the sine of the reference angle is the ratio of the length of the opposite side to the hypotenuse. All sides of any triangle are positive, so this ratio <u>must</u> be a positive number.

Look at Figure 9.12, in which $\theta_1 = \alpha_1$. Then $=$ $\sin\theta_1 = \sin\alpha_1 = \dfrac{A_1P_1}{OP_1}$. Since the sine of a reference angle is always positive, $\sin\theta_1$ must also be positive. You recall that the measure of θ_1 is 50°. Using your calculator, press in sequence "sin", "50", "enter". Your display will read approximately 0.7660. This can be written as $\sin 50° \approx 0.7660$. Be sure that your calculator is in "degree" mode.

Consider Figure 9.13. We know that $90° < \theta_2 < 180°$ and that $0° < \alpha_2 < 90°$. In fact, $\theta_2 + \alpha_2 = 180°$. By the definition of the sine ratio, $\sin\alpha_2$ must be positive. In order to determine whether is $\sin\theta_2$ positive, we check the signs attached to the vertical side and the hypotenuse. Both of these are positive, so their ratio is also positive. This means that $\sin\theta_2$ must be positive. Then $\sin\theta_2 = \sin\alpha_2 = \dfrac{A_2P_2}{OP_2}$. You recall that the measure of θ_2 is 160°, and with your calculator you can check that $\sin 160° \approx 0.3420$. The measure of α_2 is 20° and we can easily check that $\sin 20° \approx 0.3420 = \sin 160°$. As a general rule, if $90° < \theta < 180°$, then $\sin\theta = \sin(180° - \theta)$.

Now look at Figure 9.14, for which the measure of θ_3 is 210°. In this figure, notice that the vertical leg has a minus sign. Then the ratio of the signs for the vertical leg and the hypotenuse is negative. This means that $\sin 210°$ must be negative, so that $\sin\theta_3 = -\dfrac{A_3P_3}{OP_3} = -\sin\alpha_3$. You can check on your calculator that $\sin 210° = -0.5$. The reference angle α_3 in this figure is 30°, which is $210° - 180°$. As expected, $\sin\alpha_3$ is positive; in fact, $\sin 30° = 0.5$. We see that $\sin 210° = -\sin 30°$ As a general rule, if $180° < \theta < 270°$, then $\sin\theta = -\sin(\theta - 180°)$.

We now look at Figure 9.15, for which $\theta_4 = 315°$. Notice that the vertical leg has a minus sign. Thus the ratio of the signs for the vertical leg and the hypotenuse is negative, so that $\sin\theta_4 = -\dfrac{A_4P_4}{OP_4} = -\sin\alpha_4$. This means that when $270° < \theta < 360°$, $\sin\theta$ is negative. Using your calculator, it is easy to check that $\sin 315° \approx -0.7071$. For this figure, we recall that $\alpha_4 = 360° - \theta_4$, so that $\sin\alpha_4 = \sin 45° \approx 0.7071$. As a general rule, if $270° < \theta < 360°$, then $\sin\theta = -\sin(360° - \theta)$.

As a summary, for any angle θ in standard position whose terminal side is in the first or second quadrant,

$\sin\theta$ must be positive. If the terminal side is in the third or fourth quadrant, $\sin\theta$ is negative. Using symbols, if, $0° < \theta < 180°$ then $\sin\theta$ is positive. Likewise, if $180° < \theta < 360°$, then $\sin\theta$ is negative.

EXAMPLE 1

If $\sin\theta = \sin 25°$ and $\theta \neq 25°$, what is the value of θ?

SOLUTION

We just need to find a second quadrant angle whose reference angle is 25°. The answer is $180° - 25° = 155°$. As a check, $\sin 155° = \sin 25° \approx 0.4226$.

EXAMPLE 2

If $\sin\theta = -\sin 40°$, what is the value of θ?

SOLUTION

We seek an angle whose reference angle is 40°, but whose sign value is negative. Our answers are found in the third and fourth quadrants. In the third quadrant, $\theta = 180° + 40° = 220°$. In the fourth quadrant, $\theta = 360° - 40° = 320°$. As a check, $\sin 220° = \sin 320° \approx -0.6428 = -\sin 40°$.

EXAMPLE 3

Look at the diagram below.

If point P is located at $(-3, 4)$, what is the value of $\sin\theta$?

SOLUTION

$$OP = \sqrt{3^2 + 4^2} = 5.$$ Thus, $\sin\theta = \dfrac{AP}{OP} = \dfrac{4}{5}.$

EXAMPLE 4

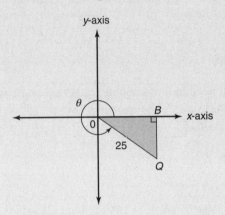

Look at the diagram below.

If $\sin\theta = -0.28$, what are the coordinates of point Q?

SOLUTION

Since $\sin\theta = -\dfrac{BQ}{25} = -0.28$, we can determine that $BQ = (25)(-0.28) = -7$. Also, $OQ = \sqrt{25^2 - (-7)^2} = 24$. Thus, the coordinates of Q are $(24, -7)$.

NOTE:

As we introduce (and review) the remaining five trigonometric ratios (which are also functions), we do not need to re-create the explanations that we used for the sine ratio. We will just use Figures 9.12, 9.13, 9.14, and 9.15. Before studying the remaining ratios, be sure you have reviewed the relationship between the angle in standard position (θ) and the reference angle (α).

Cosine Function

The **cosine** of θ, written as $\cos\theta$, is the ratio of the adjacent side to the hypotenuse of a right triangle. Just as with the sine ratio, $\cos\theta$ will have a positive or a negative value, depending on the quadrant in which θ is found. Using Figures 9.12, 9.13, 9.14, and 9.15, we get the following relationships:

$$\cos\theta_1 = \dfrac{OA_1}{OP_1}, \quad \cos\theta_2 = -\dfrac{OA_2}{OP_2}, \quad \cos\theta_3 = -\dfrac{OA_3}{OP_3}, \quad \text{and}$$

$$\cos\theta_4 = \dfrac{OA_4}{OP_4}.$$

NOTE:

The cosine ratio is positive in the first and fourth quadrants; it is negative in the second and third quadrants. Just as we showed for the sine ratio, we can establish the following equivalences for the cosine of different angles.

If $90° < \theta < 180°$, the reference angle for θ is $180° - \theta$. Then $\cos\theta = -\cos(180° - \theta)$.

If $180° < \theta < 270°$, the reference angle for θ is $\theta - 180°$. Then $\cos\theta = -\cos(\theta° - 180°)$.

If $270° < \theta < 360°$, the reference angle for θ is $360° - \theta$. Then $\cos\theta = \cos(360° - \theta)$.

EXAMPLE 5

If $\cos\theta = \cos 32°$ and $\theta \neq 32°$, what is the value of θ?

SOLUTION

We know that θ must lie in the fourth quadrant, so $\theta = 360° - 32° = 328°$.

EXAMPLE 6

If $\cos 203° = \cos\theta$ and $\theta \neq 203°$, what is the value of θ?

SOLUTION

Since 203° lies in the third quadrant, cos 203° must be negative. The corresponding reference angle is 23°. The cosine ratio is also negative in the second quadrant. We seek a second quadrant angle whose reference angle is 23°. Thus $\theta = 180° - 23° = 157°$.

EXAMPLE 7

Look at the diagram below.

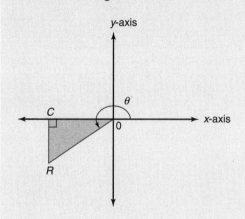

If point R is located at $(-5, -2)$, what is the value of $\cos \theta$?

SOLUTION

$OR = \sqrt{(-5)^2 + (-2)^2} = \sqrt{29}$. Thus,

$\cos \theta = -\dfrac{5}{\sqrt{29}}$. Note that this answer may also be

written as $-\dfrac{5\sqrt{29}}{29}$.

EXAMPLE 8

Look at the diagram below.

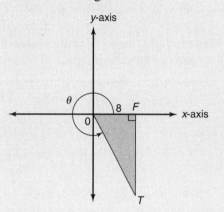

If $\cos \theta = 0.5$, what are the coordinates of point T?

SOLUTION

Since $\cos \theta = \dfrac{8}{OT} = 0.5$, we can determine that $OT = \dfrac{8}{0.5} = 16$. Also, $FT = \sqrt{16^2 - 8^2} = \sqrt{192}$. Thus, the coordinates of T are $(8, -\sqrt{192})$.

Note that we can also simplify $-\sqrt{192}$ to $-8\sqrt{3}$.

Tangent Function

Trigonometric ratio, the **tangent** of θ, written as $\tan \theta$, represents the ratio of the opposite side to the adjacent side of a right triangle. As with the previous two trigonometric ratios, we must be aware of the quadrant in which θ is found. Once again, using Figures 9.12, 9.13, 9.14, and 9.15, we get the following relationships.

$$\tan \theta_1 = \frac{A_1 P_1}{OA_1}, \tan \theta_2 = -\frac{A_2 P_2}{OA_2}, \tan \theta_3 = \frac{A_3 P_3}{OA_3}, \text{ and}$$

$$\tan \theta_4 = -\frac{A_4 P_4}{OA_4}.$$

NOTE:

> The tangent ratio is positive in the first and third quadrants; it is negative in the second and fourth quadrants. This can be verified just by inspecting the signs for each of the sides of the triangle in each of these four figures.

Here are the equivalences for the tangent of different angles.

If $90° < \theta < 180°$, then $\tan\theta = -\tan(180° - \theta)$.

If $180° < \theta < 270°$, then $\tan\theta = \tan(\theta - 180°)$.

If $270° < \theta < 360°$, then $\tan\theta = -\tan(360° - \theta)$.

EXAMPLE 9

> If $\tan\theta = -\tan 36°$, what is the value of θ?

SOLUTION

We know that θ must lie in either the second or fourth quadrants. In the second quadrant, $\theta = 180° - 36° = 144°$. In the fourth quadrant, $\theta = 360° - 36° = 324°$. Both answers are needed.

EXAMPLE 10

> If $\tan\theta = \tan 222°$, and $\theta \neq 222°$, what is the value of θ?

SOLUTION

Besides the third quadrant, the only other quadrant in which the tangent ratio is positive is the first quadrant. Since the reference angle for $222°$ is $42°$, this is the required value of θ.

EXAMPLE 11

Look at the diagram below.

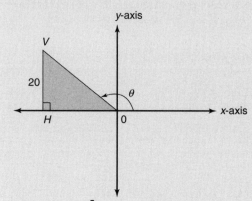

If $\tan\theta = -\dfrac{5}{7}$, what are the coordinates of point V?

SOLUTION

$$Tan\theta - \frac{20}{OH} - -\frac{5}{7}, \quad \text{so} \quad OII = -\frac{140}{5} = -28$$

Thus, the coordinates of V are $(-28, 20)$.

NOTE

> We do not need the length of the hypotenuse.

EXAMPLE 12

Look at the diagram below.

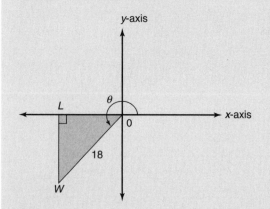

If the x-coordinate of point W is -12, what is the value of $\tan\theta$?

SOLUTION

Since $OL = 12$, $WL = \sqrt{18^2 - 12^2} = \sqrt{180}$. Thus, $\tan\theta = \dfrac{\sqrt{180}}{12}$.

This answer can be simplified to $\dfrac{\sqrt{5}}{2}$.

Figure 9.16, shown below, is a handy way to remember the quadrants in which each of the sine, cosine, and tangent ratios is positive.

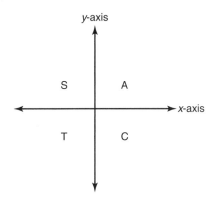

Figure 9.16

Let S = Sine, A = All, T = Tangent, and C = Cosine. As you read the letters from left to right, think of the phrase "**S**ave **A**ll **T**he **C**hildren."

Then you immediately know that in the third quadrant, the tangent ratio is positive, but both the sine ratio and cosine ratio are negative.

NOTE:

> Give any number n, where $n \neq 0$, its reciprocal is represented as $\dfrac{1}{n}$.

Let's begin with the **cosecant** of θ, written as $\csc\theta$. This represents the ratio of the hypotenuse to the opposite side of a right triangle. This ratio is the reciprocal of the sine ratio. Therefore, the cosecant ratio is positive whenever the sine ratio is positive; it is negative whenever the sine ratio is negative.

In order to calculate the value of $\csc\theta$, just take the reciprocal of $\sin\theta$. For example, $\csc 85° = \dfrac{1}{\sin 85°} \approx \dfrac{1}{0.9962} \approx 1.0038$. As a second example,

we'll chose an angle in the third quadrant. Then $\csc 200° = \dfrac{1}{\sin 200°} \approx \dfrac{1}{-0.3420} \approx -2.9238$. Note that by rounding $\sin 200°$ to the nearest ten-thousandth, $\dfrac{1}{-0.3420}$ would appear to be closer to -2.9240. However, -2.9238 is slightly more accurate since it is calculated without rounding off the value of $\sin 200°$.

Secant Function

The secant of θ, written as $\sec\theta$ represents the ratio of the hypotenuse to the adjacent side of a right triangle. This ratio is the reciprocal of the cosine ratio. Therefore, the secant ratio is positive in the first and fourth quadrants; this corresponds to the quadrants in which the cosine ratio is also positive. As expected, the secant ratio must be negative in the second and third quadrants. To calculate $\sec\theta$, take the reciprocal of $\cos\theta$. For example, $\sec 118° = \dfrac{1}{\cos 118°} \approx \dfrac{1}{-0.4695} \approx -2.1301$.

As a second example,

$$\sec 310° = \dfrac{1}{\cos 310°} \approx \dfrac{1}{0.6428} \approx 1.5557.$$

Cotangent Function

The **cotangent** of θ, written as $\cot\theta$ represents the ratio of the adjacent side to the opposite side of a right triangle. It will come as no surprise that this ratio represents the reciprocal of the tangent ratio. Thus, we can determine that the cotangent ratio is positive in the first and third quadrants; it is negative in the second and fourth quadrants. To calculate $\cot\theta$, take the reciprocal of $\tan\theta$.

For example, $\cot 70° = \dfrac{1}{\tan 70°} \approx \dfrac{1}{2.7475} \approx 0.3640$.

As a second example,

$$\cot 173° = \dfrac{1}{\tan 173°} \approx \dfrac{1}{-0.1228} \approx -8.1443.$$

(If you use the rounded value of -0.1228, your final answer would be approximately -8.1433.)

EXAMPLE 13

If $\sec\theta = \dfrac{9}{2}$, what is the value of $\cos\theta$?

SOLUTION

You won't see many problems this short! The answer is $\dfrac{1}{9/2} = \dfrac{2}{9}$.

EXAMPLE 14

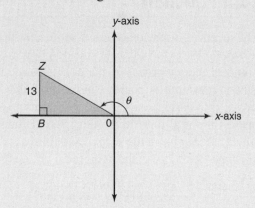

Look at the diagram below.

If $\cot\theta = -\dfrac{2}{3}$, what are the coordinates of point Z?

SOLUTION

Since $\cot\theta = -\dfrac{OB}{13} = -\dfrac{2}{3}$, we can calculate $OB = \dfrac{26}{3} = 8\dfrac{2}{3}$. Thus, the coordinates of Z are $\left(-8\dfrac{2}{3},\ 13\right)$.

EXAMPLE 15

If $\csc\theta = -\csc 65°$, what is the value of θ?

SOLUTION

The cosecant ratio is negative in the third and fourth quadrants. The angles in those two quadrants whose reference angle is $65°$ are $180° + 65° = 245°$ and $360° - 65° = 295°$.

"Special " Angles

You have probably noticed that we have not yet mentioned the trigonometric ratios in connection with angles such as $0°$ and $90°$. A **quadrantal** angle is one whose initial ray lies on the *x*-axis and whose terminal ray lies on either the *x*-axis or the *y*-axis. The four quadrantal angles on are $0°, 90°, 180°,$ and $270°$. (Technically, $360°$ would also qualify as a quadrantal angle, but it is equivalent to $0°$.) Also, if any multiple of $360°$ is added to any of these four numbers, that value would also be a quadrantal angle. However, this is beyond the scope of our book.

Let's "construct" a triangle AOB in the first quadrant with a reference angle of $0°$, as shown in Figure 9.17. In reality, there would be no triangle because $\overline{OA}$ would lie on top of $\overline{OB}$.

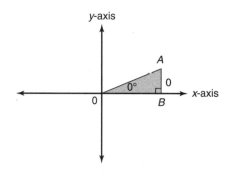

Figure 9.17

NOTE:

We have indicated that $AB = 0$. Also, OA <u>must</u> equal OB, even though we cannot draw the figure to show this equality. Let's look at the six trigonometric ratios.

$Sin0° = \dfrac{0}{OA} = 0$ $Csc0° = \dfrac{OA}{0} = $ not defined

$Cos0° = \dfrac{OB}{OA} = 1$ $Sec0° = \dfrac{OA}{OB} = 1$

$Tan0° = \dfrac{0}{OB} = 0$ $Cot0° = \dfrac{OB}{0} = $ not defined

In order to discuss the trigonometric ratios for an angle of $180°$, we construct a triangle COD in the second quadrant, for which the reference angle is $0°$. This is shown below in Figure 9.18. In reality, there would be no triangle because $\overline{OC}$ would lie on top of $\overline{OD}$.

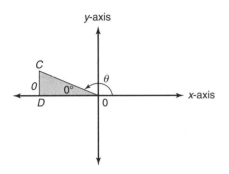

Figure 9.18

NOTE:

We have indicated that $CD = 0$. Also, OC must equal OD, even though we cannot draw the figure to show this equality.

Here are the six trigonometric ratios.

$$Sin180° = \frac{0}{OC} = 0 \quad Cos180° = -\frac{OD}{OC} = -1$$

$$Tan180° = -\frac{0}{OD} = 0$$

$$Csc180° = \frac{OC}{0} = \text{not defined} \quad Sec180° = -\frac{OC}{OD} = -1$$

$$Cot180° = -\frac{OD}{0} = \text{not defined}$$

Our last consideration for the construction of an imaginary triangle will be for an angle of 270°. In this case, triangle EOF would have a reference angle of 90°, as shown below in Figure 9.19.

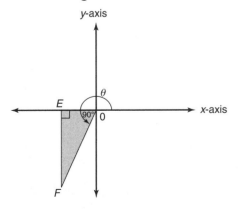

Figure 9.19

NOTE:

We have indicated that $OE = 0$. Also, EF must equal OF. We cannot actually draw the figure to reflect this equality because $\overline{EF}$ would lie on top of $\overline{OF}$.

Following are the six trigonometric ratios.

$$Sin270° = -\frac{EF}{OF} = -1 \qquad Csc270° = -\frac{OF}{EF} = -1$$

$$Cos270° = \frac{0}{OF} = 0 \qquad Sec270° = \frac{OF}{0} =$$
$$\text{not defined}$$

$$Tan270° = \frac{EF}{0} = \qquad Cot270° = -\frac{0}{EF} = 0$$
$$\text{not defined}$$

The trigonometric ratios of any of these "special" angles can be easily checked with a calculator. If you try to calculate a ratio for an angle for which the answer is *not* defined, most calculators will show the word *ERROR*.

Inverse Trigonometric Functions

An **inverse trigonometric function** is an angle whose trigonometric ratio value is known. Consider the following three equivalences that can be checked by a calculator.

(a) $Sin30° = 0.5$, (b) $Sec200° \approx -1.0642$, and (c) $Tan135° = -1$

The statement $Sin30° = 0.5$ can also be written as $\sin^{-1}(0.5) = 30°$, which is read as "the inverse sine of 0.5 is 30°." Another way to phrase "$\sin^{-1}(0.5) = 30°$" is to say "the angle whose sine value is 0.5 is 30°". The purpose of the parentheses used after "$\sin^{-1}$" is for readability. Be sure that you do *not* interpret $\sin^{-1}(0.5)$ as $\dfrac{1}{\sin 0.5}$.

Statement (b) can be written as $\sec^{-1}(-1.0642) \approx 200°$, which means that the angle whose secant value is -1.0642 is approximately $200°$. In a similar fashion, statement (c) can be written as, $\tan^{-1}(-1) = 135°$ which means that the angle whose tangent value is -1 is $135°$.

Before doing any exercises, we need to make several comments concerning the use of the calculator with respect to determining inverse trigonometric values.

Consider the statement $Sin\,30° = 0.5$. Most calculators have the inverse sine, inverse cosine, and inverse tangent buttons. These are indicated as $\sin^{-1}$, $\cos^{-1}$, and $\tan^{-1}$, respectively. If we are asked to complete the statement $\sin^{-1}(0.5) =$ _____, our calculator will provide the answer of $30°$. But, this is <u>not</u> the only answer! We know that the sine ratio is positive in both the first and second quadrants. Thus, the other answer is $150°$.

Now look at the statement $Sec\,200° \approx -1.0642$. If we were asked to fill in the blank for $\sec^{-1}(-1.0642) =$ _____, we already know that $200°$ is correct. We find the second answer by recognizing that the secant ratio is negative in both the second and third quadrants. Thus, we need the second quadrant angle of $180° - 20° = 160°$.

Notice that your calculator does not have a button marked as "$\sec^{-1}$". Since the cosine ratio is the reciprocal of the secant ratio, we change $\sec^{-1}(-1.0642)$ to

$$\cos^{-1}\left(-\frac{1}{1.0642}\right) \approx \cos^{-1}(-0.9397).$$ By following this

instruction, your calculator will give the answer of $160°$. You must then proceed to identify the second answer of $200°$.

In a similar fashion, in order to calculate an inverse cosecant value, you would need to calculate the inverse sine of the reciprocal of that value. For example, to calculate $\csc^{-1}(3)$, simply calculate $\sin^{-1}\left(\frac{1}{3}\right)$. The procedure for calculating an inverse cotangent value is to use the inverse tangent of the reciprocal of that value. For example, $\cot^{-1}(0.8) = \tan^{-1}\left(\frac{1}{0.8}\right) = \tan^{-1}(1.25)$.

Looking at statement (c) from a few pages ago, we can see that given that $\tan 135° = -1$, then $\tan^{-1}(-1) = 135°$ is certainly true. But, if we are to fill in the blank for $\tan^{-1}(-1) =$ _____, we must realize

that there is another answer besides $135°$. This second answer is found in the fourth quadrant, where the tangent ratio is also negative.

Thus, the second answer is $360° - 45° = 315°$.

When dealing with quadrantal angles, there are occasions when there is only one answer for an inverse trigonometric ratio. As examples, $\sin^{-1}(1) = 90°$ and $\cos^{-1}(-1) = 180°$.

But an expression such as $\tan^{-1}(0)$ has two answers, namely $0°$ and $180°$.

EXAMPLE 16

Which trigonometric ratios, when applied to $270°$, are not defined?

SOLUTION

Both $\tan 270°$ and $\sec 270°$ are not defined.

The best way to remember these answers is to draw the associated triangle, labeling the adjacent side (x-axis portion) as zero. Then identify the trigonometric ratios in which the adjacent side represents the denominator.

EXAMPLE 17

To the nearest degree, what are the values of $\csc^{-1}\left(-\frac{11}{10}\right)$?

SOLUTION

$Csc^{-1}\left(-\frac{11}{10}\right) = \sin^{-1}\left(-\frac{10}{11}\right)$. Since $\sin^{-1}\left(\frac{10}{11}\right) \approx 65°$, the two required angles, which lie in the third and fourth quadrants, are $245°$ and $295°$.

EXAMPLE 18

To the nearest degree, what are the values of $\cos^{-1}(0.14)$?

SOLUTION

The first answer we get from the calculator is approximately $82°$. Since we also need the fourth quadrant angle, the second answer is $278°$.

EXAMPLE 19

To the nearest degree, what are the values of $\cot^{-1}(-1.56)$?

SOLUTION

$$\mathrm{Cot}^{-1}(-1.56) = \tan^{-1}\left(-\frac{1}{1.56}\right).$$

Since $\tan^{-1}\left(\dfrac{1}{1.56}\right) \approx 33°$, the two required angles, which lie in the second and fourth quadrants, are $147°$ and $327°$.

Right Triangle Trigonometry

Let's look at the use of trigonometric ratios to solve for any side or angle of a right triangle. This would be an appropriate time to point out that we will only use degree measurements for angles. Another way to measure angles is to use radians, which will be only used in the graphing portion of this chapter.

Our model triangle is ΔABC, in which $\angle C = 90°$. Each side of this triangle can be labeled with a small letter corresponding to its opposite vertex. For example, c represents $\overline{AB}$, which lies opposite point C. Figure 9.20 shows this triangle, with all parts labeled.

We note that c is the hypotenuse, so it is the longest side of the triangle. Either a or b may be the shortest side. It is also possible that $a = b$. Each of Examples 20 − 23 refer to Figure 9.20 , and each problem is independent of the others.

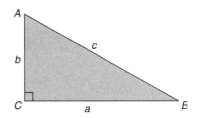

Figure 9.20

EXAMPLE 20

If $\angle A = 35°$ and $c = 24$, what is the value of a, to the nearest hundredth?

SOLUTION

Since sides a and c are used in the sine ratio for $\angle A$, we can write $\sin 35° = \dfrac{a}{24}$. Thus, $a = (24)(\sin 35°)$ ≈ 13.77 .

EXAMPLE 21

If $b = 7.5$ and $c = 40.2$, what is the measure of $\angle A$, to the nearest degree?

SOLUTION

Sides b and c are used in the cosine ratio for $\angle A$, so $\cos \angle A = \dfrac{7.5}{40.2}$. Thus, $\angle A = \cos^{-1}\left(\dfrac{7.5}{40.2}\right) \approx 79°$. Note that it is not necessary to compute the value of $\dfrac{7.5}{40.2}$ as a separate step.

EXAMPLE 22

If $a = 7$ and $c = 12$, what is the value of $\csc \angle B$, to the nearest ten-thousandth?

SOLUTION

$Csc\angle B = \dfrac{c}{b}$, so we first need to determine the value of b. By the Pythagorean Theorem, $b = \sqrt{12^2 - 7^2} = \sqrt{95} \approx 9.75$. Thus, $\csc \angle B = \dfrac{12}{9.75} \approx 1.2308$.

EXAMPLE 23

If $\tan \angle A = \dfrac{6}{5}$, what is the measure of $\angle B$, to the nearest degree?

SOLUTION

One efficient way to solve this question is to first determine the measure of $\angle A$. From the given information, $\angle A = \tan^{-1}(\dfrac{6}{5}) \approx 50°$. Thus, $\angle B = 90° - 50° = 40°$.

Let's solve two word problems associated with right triangles. The answers to any angle measures will be to the nearest degree and the answers to any sides will be to the nearest hundredth.

EXAMPLE 24

A 72-foot ladder is leaning against the vertical side of a building. If the angle of elevation is $43°$, then the bottom of the ladder is how many feet from the bottom of the building?

SOLUTION

Shown below is an appropriate diagram.

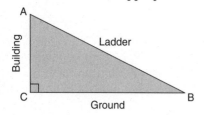

The angle of elevation is represented by $\angle B$, the angle between the ground and the ladder.

Let a = distance between the bottom of the ladder to the bottom of the building, shown as the ground. Then $\cos 43° = \dfrac{a}{72}$. Thus, $a = (72)(\cos 43°) \approx 52.66$ feet.

EXAMPLE 25

Eileen is standing at point A, which is on the top of a bridge that is 150 feet above and parallel to a lake. She is looking at a boat in the lake at point B, as shown below.

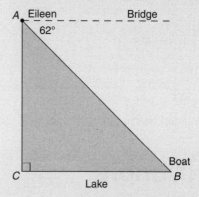

If the angle of depression is $62°$, how many feet apart are Eileen and this boat?

SOLUTION

Notice that the angle of depression is defined as the angle between the bridge and the imaginary line segment that would extend from Eileen to the boat. Then, due to the rule concerning the equality of alternate interior angles of parallel line, $\angle B = 62°$. This leads to

$$\sin 62° = \dfrac{150}{c}.$$

Thus, $c = \dfrac{150}{\sin 62°} \approx 169.89$ feet.

CAUTION!

Here are four situations in which two right triangles are presented. It is extremely important to know what "piece" is missing that will assist you in finding the answer to the question.

EXAMPLE 26

Look at the following diagram.

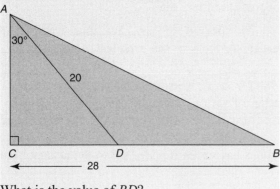

What is the value of *BD*?

SOLUTION

Using triangle ADC is the key to finding the value of BD.

We can determine the value of CD by using $\sin 30° = \dfrac{CD}{20}$. So, $CD = (20)(\sin 30°) = 10$. Then $BD = CB - CD = 18$.

EXAMPLE 27

Look at the following diagram.

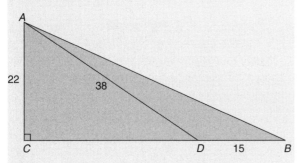

What is the measure of $\angle B$? (Nearest degree)

SOLUTION

Let's focus on $\triangle ADC$. By the Pythagorean Theorem, $CD = \sqrt{38^2 - 22^2} = \sqrt{960} \approx 30.98$. Since

$BC = CD + DB$, $BC = 45.98$. Then $\tan \angle B = \dfrac{22}{45.98}$, so $\angle B = \tan^{-1}\left(\dfrac{22}{45.98}\right) \approx 26°$.

EXAMPLE 28

Look at the following diagram.

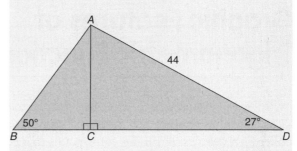

What is the value of BC, to the nearest hundredth?

SOLUTION

First, we need to find the value of AC. Using $\triangle ACD$, $\sin 27° = \dfrac{AC}{44}$. Then, $AC = (44)(\sin 27°) \approx 19.98$. Now, switching over to $\triangle ABC$, $\tan 50° = \dfrac{19.98}{BC}$. Thus, $BC = \dfrac{19.98}{\tan 50°} \approx 16.76$.

EXAMPLE 29

Look at the following diagram.

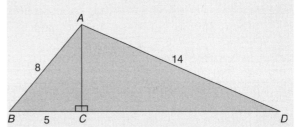

What is the value of $\angle CAD$? (Nearest degree)

SOLUTION

As in Example 28, the missing link is AC. Using $\triangle ABC$, $AC = \sqrt{8^2 - 5^2} = \sqrt{39} \approx 6.24$.

Now, using $\triangle ACD$, $\cos\angle CAD = \dfrac{6.24}{14}$.

Thus, $\angle CAD = \cos^{-1}\left(\dfrac{6.24}{14}\right) \approx 64°$.

Graphic Features of Trigonometric Functions

In most discussions of the graphical aspects of these functions, angles are measured using radians, rather than degrees. A **radian** corresponds to a central angle of a circle for which the intercepted arc length is exactly the same as the radius. In Figure 9.21 shown below, where P is the center of the circle, the measure of $\angle APB$ is one radian.

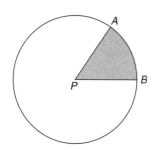

Figure 9.21

In order to compare radians with degrees, we recall that a complete circle represents $360°$, and a circumference whose length is $2\pi r$. But, by definition, AP $= r$. Then, $360°$ is equivalent to 2π radians, so 1 radian is equivalent to $\dfrac{360}{2\pi} \approx 57.3°$. Note the following equivalences of other "popular" degree measures and their radian measures. $30° = \dfrac{\pi}{6}$ radians, $45° = \dfrac{\pi}{4}$ radians, $60° = \dfrac{\pi}{3}$ radians, $90° = \dfrac{\pi}{2}$ radians, $180° = \pi$

radians, and $270° = \dfrac{3\pi}{2}$ radians. To convert radians to degrees, multiply by $\dfrac{180}{\pi}$.

The **period** of any function (whether trigonometric or not) is the smallest number p for which $f(x + p) = f(x)$. Let's look at the graph of $f(x) = \sin x$, where x is measured in radians. Here is a list of various points $(x, \sin x)$ where x is in radian measure. Be sure that your calculator is in radian mode to verify these points. For some of these angles, the sine values have been rounded off to the nearest hundredth.

$(0,0)$, $\left(\dfrac{\pi}{6}, 0.5\right)$, $\left(\dfrac{\pi}{4}, 0.71\right)$, $\left(\dfrac{\pi}{3}, 0.87\right)$, $\left(\dfrac{\pi}{2}, 1\right)$, $(\pi, 0)$,

$\left(\dfrac{7\pi}{6}, -0.5\right)$, $\left(\dfrac{3\pi}{2}, -1\right)$, $\left(\dfrac{11\pi}{6}, -0.5\right)$, $(2\pi, 0)$.

The graph appears in Figure 9.22.

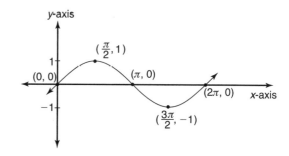

Figure 9.22

Since there are x values outside the domain between 0 and 2π, Figure 9.23 shows the graph of the sine function for values not included between 0 and 2π.

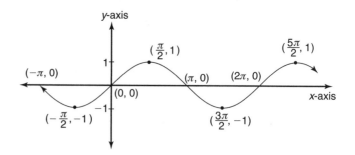

Figure 9.23

Graphs of Variations of a Sine Function

Observations concerning the graph of $f(x) = \sin x$:

1. The domain is all real numbers and the range is all real numbers between -1 and 1, inclusive.

2. The sine function is periodic, with a period of 2π. For example, $\dfrac{17\pi}{6} = 2\pi + \dfrac{5\pi}{6}$ and $\sin\dfrac{17\pi}{6} = \sin\dfrac{5\pi}{6}$.

3. The x-intercepts occur at $...,-2\pi,-\pi,0,\pi,2\pi,....,$ which means at each integral multiple of π. The only y-intercept occurs at 0.

4. The maximum value of the function is 1 and its minimum value is -1.

For each of the next few graphs that are related to $f(x) = \sin x$, we will only graph x values between 0 and 2π or between those x values that constitute one complete period, whichever is larger.

Our next graph for consideration is for the function $f(x) = 2\sin\left(x + \dfrac{\pi}{2}\right)$. For comparison reasons, we will use some of the same x values as was used for $f(x) = \sin x$. The x values we'll use are $-\dfrac{\pi}{2}, 0, \dfrac{\pi}{2},$ $\pi, \dfrac{3\pi}{2},$ and 2π. The corresponding points are $\left(-\dfrac{\pi}{2},0\right), (0,2), \left(\dfrac{\pi}{2},0\right), (\pi,-2), \left(\dfrac{3\pi}{2},0\right),$ and $(2\pi, 2)$.

These six points yield a general sketch for the graph, which appears below as Figure 9.24.

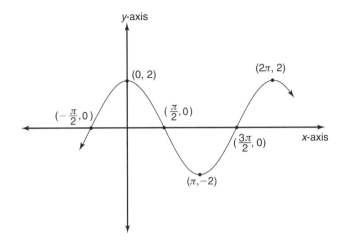

Figure 9.24

Let's make some observations concerning the graph of $f(x) = 2\sin(x + \dfrac{\pi}{2})$.

1. The domain is all real numbers and the range is all real numbers between -2 and 2, inclusive.

2. This function is periodic, with a period of 2π, same as for $f(x) = \sin x$.

3. The x-intercepts occur at $...-\dfrac{\pi}{2}, \dfrac{\pi}{2}, \dfrac{3\pi}{2},...,$ which means at each value of $\dfrac{k\pi}{2}$, where k is an odd integer. The only y-intercept occurs at 2.

4. The maximum value of the function is 2 and its minimum value is -2.

As a third example using the sine function, we will graph $f(x) = \dfrac{1}{2}\sin 4x - 1$. The x values to be used will be $0, \dfrac{\pi}{8}, \dfrac{\pi}{4}, \dfrac{3\pi}{8}, \dfrac{\pi}{2}$ and $\dfrac{5\pi}{8}$. The corresponding points are $(0,-1), \left(\dfrac{\pi}{8},-0.5\right), \left(\dfrac{\pi}{4},-1\right), \left(\dfrac{3\pi}{8},-1.5\right), \left(\dfrac{\pi}{2},-1\right)$ and $\left(\dfrac{5\pi}{8},-0.5\right)$. These six points are sufficient to illustrate the graph, as shown below in Figure 9.25.

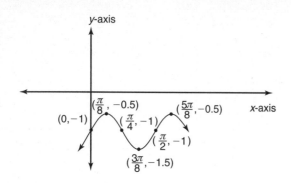

Figure 9.25

Here are our observations concerning the graph of

$$f(x) = \frac{1}{2}\sin 4x - 1.$$

1. The domain is all real numbers and the range is all real numbers between -1.5 and -0.5, inclusive.

2. The function is periodic, with a period of $\frac{2\pi}{4} = \frac{\pi}{2}$.

    This period can be checked by subtracting the x values of any two points where the graph shows the same pattern.

3. There are no x-intercepts, and the y-intercept occurs at -1.

4. The maximum value of the function is -0.5 and its minimum value is -1.5.

Generalizations Concerning Any Sine Function of the Form $y = A\sin(Bx - C) + D$

A, B, C, and D Are Real Numbers, and A > 0 and D is called the vertical shift of the graph.

1. The domain is all real numbers and the range is all numbers between $D-A$ and $D + A$, inclusive.

2. The function is periodic, with a period of $\frac{2\pi}{B}$.

3. With respect to the function $f(x) = \sin x$, the function is "moved" or shifted $\frac{C}{B}$ units horizontally. If $C > 0$, this shift is to the right; if $C < 0$, this shift is to the left. The quantity $\frac{C}{B}$ is called the **phase shift.**

4. The value of $|A|$ is called the **amplitude**. It represents one-half the difference between the lowest and highest y values.

5. The maximum value of the function is D + A and its minimum value is D − A. Figure 9.26 shows a general graph of $y = A\sin(Bx - C) + D$, in which all variables are positive.

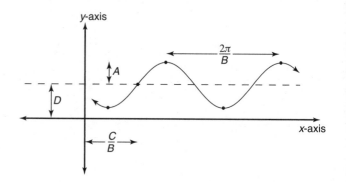

Figure 9.26

If $A < 0$, then the graph of $y = A\sin(Bx - C) + D$ is just a reflection over the x-axis of the graph of $y = A\sin(Bx - C) + D$ where $A > 0$. For example, the graph of $f(x) = -4\sin(x - \pi) - 2$ is just a reflection over the x-axis of the graph of $f(x) = 4\sin(x - \pi) - 2$. The periods, amplitudes, and phase shifts are identical for these two functions. For $A < 0$, the lowest value of the function is given by $D + A$ and the highest value of the function is given by $D - A$.

EXAMPLE 30

What are the amplitude, period, phase shift, and lowest function value for

$$f(x) = \frac{1}{3}\sin(x - \frac{\pi}{2}) + 3?$$

SOLUTION

In this example, $A = \frac{1}{3}$, $B = 1$, $C = \frac{\pi}{2}$, and $D = 3$.

The amplitude is $\left|-\frac{1}{3}\right| = \frac{1}{3}$. The period is $\frac{2\pi}{1} = 2\pi$.

Since $C > 0$, the phase shift is $\frac{\pi/2}{1} = \frac{\pi}{2}$ units to the right. The lowest function value is $3 - \frac{1}{3} = \frac{8}{3}$.

NOTE:

> The phase shift and the vertical shift for the graph of any function $y = A\sin(Bx - C) + D$ is *always* with respect to the graph of $y = \sin x$. Also, the horizontal line $y = D$ lies halfway between the lowest and highest function values.

EXAMPLE 31

> What are the amplitude, period, phase shift, and highest function value for $f(x) = -5\sin(3x + \pi) + 2$?

SOLUTION

The graph of this function is just the reflection of the graph of $f(x) = 5\sin(3x + \pi) + 2$. The amplitude is $|-5| = 5$. The period is $\dfrac{2\pi}{3}$. Since $C = -\pi$, the phase shift is $\dfrac{\pi}{3}$ units to the left. The highest function value is $2 - (-5) = 7$.

EXAMPLE 32

> If the lowest function value of $f(x) = \sin\left(\dfrac{1}{2}x + \dfrac{\pi}{4}\right) + Q$ is 6, what are the values of Q, the phase shift, and the period?

SOLUTION

Since $A = 1$, the lowest function value, which is 6, is represented by $Q - 1$. So, $Q = 7$. Now, since $C = -\dfrac{\pi}{4}$, the phase shift is $\dfrac{\pi/4}{1/2} = \dfrac{\pi}{2}$ units to the left.

Finally, the period is $\dfrac{2\pi}{1/2} = 4\pi$.

We now consider the graph of $f(x) = \cos x$, where x is measured in radians. Here is a list of various points $(x, \cos x)$, using the same x values as we did for the graph of $f(x) = \sin x$.

$$(0,1), \left(\frac{\pi}{6}, 0.87\right), \left(\frac{\pi}{4}, 0.71\right), \left(\frac{\pi}{3}, 0.5\right), \left(\frac{\pi}{2}, 0\right), (\pi, -1),$$

$$\left(\frac{7\pi}{6}, -0.87\right), \left(\frac{3\pi}{2}, 0\right)\left(\frac{11\pi}{6}, 0.87\right), (2\pi, 1)$$

The graph of $f(x) = \cos x$ appears in Figure 9.27.

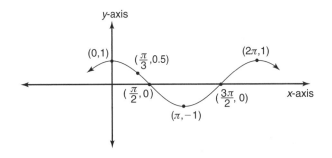

Figure 9.27

There are a considerable number of similarities between this graph and the graph of $f(x) = \sin x$. Their amplitudes and periods are exactly alike. In fact, all the statements we made concerning $f(x) = A\sin(Bx - C) + D$ also apply to $f(x) = A\cos(Bx - C) + D$.

The graph of $f(x) = \cos x$ is really just a phase shift of $\dfrac{\pi}{2}$ units (either left or right) from the graph of $f(x) = \sin x$.

EXAMPLE 33

> What are the amplitude, period, phase shift, and lowest function value for $f(x) = \dfrac{3}{4}\cos 2x - 1$?

121

SOLUTION

The amplitude is $\frac{3}{4}$ and the period is $\frac{2\pi}{2} = \pi$. Notice that we can write this function as $f(x) = \frac{3}{4}\cos(2x - 0) - 1$. Then the phase shift is $\frac{0}{2} = 0$.

The lowest function value is $-1 - \frac{3}{4} = -\frac{7}{4}$.

EXAMPLE 34

> What is the phase shift and the highest function value for $f(x) = -2\cos(x + \frac{\pi}{6}) - 4$?

SOLUTION

The coefficient of x is 1, so the phase shift is $\frac{\pi}{6}$ units to the left. The highest function value is $-4 - (-2) = -2$. Coincidentally, this number is also the value of A.

EXAMPLE 35

> If the period of $f(x) = \frac{1}{5}\cos(Cx - \pi) + D$ is 3π and the highest function value is 2, what are the values of C and D?

SOLUTION

The period is represented by $\frac{2\pi}{C}$, so $3\pi = \frac{2\pi}{C}$. Then $C = \frac{2}{3}$. Also, the highest function value is given by $D + \frac{1}{5}$, so $2 = D + \frac{1}{5}$. Then $D = \frac{9}{5}$.

Trigonometric Identities and Equations

The next part of this chapter will deal with solutions to trigonometric equations. Before you study this material, you should be very familiar with solving linear equations, as well as second degree equations in which factoring is used.

Also, there are a number of key trigonometric identities with which you must be familiar. These are in addition to the reciprocal identities that you have already mastered such as $\sec x = \frac{1}{\cos x}$. The identities will now be presented without proof.

$$\tan x = \frac{\sin x}{\cos x}, \qquad \sin^2 x + \cos^2 x = 1,$$
$$\tan^2 x + 1 = \sec^2 x, \qquad \cot^2 x + 1 = \csc^2 x,$$
$$\sin 2x = 2\sin x \cos x, \quad \text{and} \quad \cos 2x = \cos^2 x - \sin^2 x$$
$$= 2\cos^2 x - 1 = 1 - 2\sin^2 x.$$

For each of the following examples, all answers will be rounded off to the nearest degree.

EXAMPLE 36

> What are the values of x in the equation $3\tan x - 0.56 = 1.25$?

SOLUTION

Adding 0.56 to each side yields $3\tan x = 1.81$. Then $\tan x \approx 0.6033$, so $x \approx 31°$ or $211°$. (The answer is found by finding $\tan^{-1}(0.6033)$)

EXAMPLE 37

> What are the values of x in the equation $6(\csc x - 2) = 13\csc x$?

SOLUTION

Simplifying, this equation becomes $6\csc x - 12 = 13\csc x$. Then $-12 = 7\csc x$.

Thus, $x = \csc^{-1}\left(-\dfrac{12}{7}\right) \approx 216°$ or $324°$.

EXAMPLE 38

> What are the values of x in the equation $5\cot^2 x - 0.75 = 2\cot^2 x - 0.5$?

SOLUTION

By rearranging the terms, we get $3\cot^2 x = 0.25$. Then we can write $\cot x = \pm\sqrt{\dfrac{0.25}{3}} \approx \pm 0.2887$. The four answers are $74°, 106°, 254°,$ and $286°$.

EXAMPLE 39

> What are the values of x in the equation $2\cos^2 x - 5\cos x = 0$?

SOLUTION

We can factor the left side so that the equation reads as $(\cos x)(2\cos x - 5) = 0$. If $\cos x = 0$, $x = 90°$ or $270°$. If $2\cos x - 5 = 0$, $x = \cos^{-1}\left(\dfrac{5}{2}\right)$, which does not exist. The only answers are $90°$ or $270°$

EXAMPLE 40

> What are the values of x in the equation $3\sec^2 x + 2\sec x - 5 = 0$?

SOLUTION

Factoring the left side, we get $(3\sec x + 5)(\sec x - 1) = 0$. If $3\sec x + 5 = 0$, then $x = \sec^{-1}\left(-\dfrac{5}{3}\right) \approx 127°$ or $233°$. If $\sec x - 1 = 0$, then $x = \sec^{-1}(1) = 0°$.

EXAMPLE 41

> What are the values of x in the equation $\sin x - 2\tan x = 0$?

SOLUTION

Use the identity $\tan x = \dfrac{\sin x}{\cos x}$ to rewrite the equation as $\sin x - \dfrac{2\sin x}{\cos x} = 0$.

Multiply by $\cos x$ to get $(\sin x)(\cos x) - 2\sin x = 0$, which factors as $(\sin x)(\cos x - 2) = 0$. The solutions to $\sin x = 0$ are $0°$ or $180°$. The equation $\cos x - 2 = 0$ has no solution. Thus, the answers are $0°$ or $180°$.

EXAMPLE 42

> What are the values of x in the equation $\cos^2 x + 8\cos x + \sin^2 x = 0$?

SOLUTION

Hopefully, you spotted the identity $\sin^2 x + \cos^2 x = 1$. The equation can be written as $1 + 8\cos x = 0$. Then $\cos x = -\dfrac{1}{8}$, so $x = \cos^{-1}\left(-\dfrac{1}{8}\right) \approx 97°$ or $263°$.

EXAMPLE 43

> What are the values of x in the equation $5\sec^2 x + 2\tan x - 21 = 0$?

SOLUTION

The key is to use the identity $\tan^2 x + 1 = \sec^2 x$. Then we get $5(\tan^2 x + 1) + 2\tan x - 21 = 0$, which simplifies to $5\tan^2 x + 2\tan x - 16 = 0$. Factoring leads to $(5\tan x - 8)(\tan x + 2) = 0$. If $5\tan x - 8 = 0$, then $x = \tan^{-1}\left(\dfrac{8}{5}\right) \approx 58°$ or $238°$. If $\tan x + 2 = 0$, then $x = \tan^{-1}(-2) \approx 117°$ or $297°$.

EXAMPLE 44

> What are the values of x in the equation $3\cos 2x + 11\cos x + 6 = 0$?

SOLUTION

Let's use the identity $\cos 2x = 2\cos^2 x - 1$. Then the original equation becomes $3(2\cos^2 x - 1) + 11\cos x + 6 = 0$. Upon simplification, we get $6\cos^2 x + 11\cos x + 3 = 0$. Factoring leads to $(3\cos x + 1)(2\cos x + 3) = 0$. If the first factor is zero, then $x = \cos^{-1}\left(-\dfrac{1}{3}\right) \approx 109°$ or $251°$. If the second factor is zero, there is no further answer since $\cos^{-1}\left(-\dfrac{3}{2}\right)$ does not exist.

EXAMPLE 45

> What are the values of x in the equation $5\cos x - 4\sin 2x = 0$?

SOLUTION

We need to use the identity $\sin 2x = 2\sin x \cos x$ so that the equation becomes $5\cos x - (4)(2\sin x)(\cos x) = 0$. Factoring leads to $(\cos x)(5 - 8\sin x) = 0$. If $\cos x = 0$, then $x = 90°$ or $270°$. If $5 - 8\sin x = 0$, then $x = \sin^{-1}\left(\dfrac{5}{8}\right) \approx 39°$ or $141°$.

EXAMPLE 46

> What are the values of x in the equation $\cos 2x + \sin^2 x = 0.5$?

SOLUTION

Using the identity $\cos 2x = \cos^2 x - \sin^2 x$, the equation simplifies to $\cos^2 x = 0.5$. Then, $\cos x = \pm\sqrt{0.5}$. Thus, $x = 45°, 135°, 225°,$ or $315°$.

Unit Circle

The last topic of this chapter deals with the **unit circle**. This is a circle with center at $(0,0)$ and a radius of 1. Let P represent any point on this circle with coordinates (a,b) and let θ represent an angle in standard position whose terminal ray passes through (a,b), as shown below in Figure 9.28

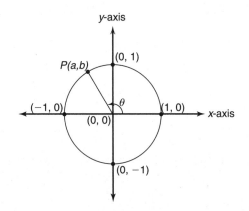

Figure 9.28

Then $\sin\theta = b$, $\cos\theta = a$, $\tan\theta = \dfrac{b}{a}$, $\csc\theta = \dfrac{1}{b}$, $\sec\theta = \dfrac{1}{a}$, and $\cot\theta = \dfrac{a}{b}$. These relationships hold regardless of the quadrant in which point P occurs. The only restrictions are: $a \neq 0$ for the tangent and secant ratios; $b \neq 0$ for the cosecant and cotangent ratios.

Quiz for Chapter 9

1. Which one of the following angles in standard position has a reference angle of $23°$?

   A) $67°$ (C) $247°$

   (B) $123°$ (D) $337°$

2. Point Q is located in a quadrant in which both the tangent ratio and cosine ratio are negative. Which one of the following could represent the coordinates of Q?

   (A) $(-2, 3)$ (C) $(-2, 0)$

   (B) $(-3, -2)$ (D) $(2, -3)$

3. If $\csc\theta = -1.2$ and θ lies in the third quadrant, what is the value of $\cot\theta$? (Nearest hundredth)

   (A) 0.66 (C) 1.51

   (B) -0.66 (D) -1.51

4. Look at the diagram below.

   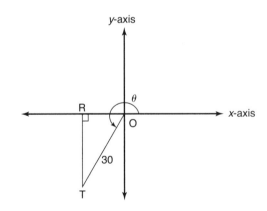

   If $\sec\theta = -7.5$, which of the following represent the coordinates of point T?

   (A) $(-8, -28.91)$ (C) $(-4, -29.73)$

   (B) $(-7.5, -29.05)$ (D) $(-3.5, -29.80)$

5. Let m, n represent positive real numbers. If $\sin^{-1}\left(\dfrac{m}{n}\right)$ is not defined, what conclusion is certain concerning the values of m and n?

   (A) $m < n$ (C) $0 < m < 1$ and $0 < n < 1$

   (B) $m > 1$ and $n > 1$ (D) $m > n$

6. A wire is connected from the top of a vertical telephone pole to a stake in the ground. The height of the telephone pole is 80 feet, and the angle of elevation of the wire is $36°$. What is the length of the wire, to the nearest hundredth of a foot?

   (A) 74.04 (C) 108.80

   (B) 98.89 (D) 136.10

7. Look at the diagram below.

   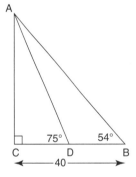

   What is the value of AD, to the nearest integer?

   (A) 54 (C) 60

   (B) 57 (D) 63

8. Look at the diagram below.

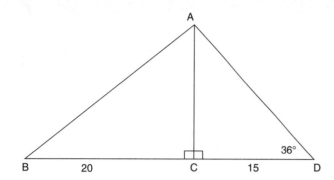

What is the measure of $\angle B$, to the nearest degree?

(A) 23°   (C) 29°

(B) 26°   (D) 32°

9. For the graph of $f(x) = \sin x$, which one of the following statements is <u>false</u>?

(A) The period is 2π.

(B) The maximum value of the function is π.

(C) The y-intercept occurs at (0, 0).

(D) The domain is all real numbers.

10. With respect to the graph of $f(x) = \sin x$, the graph of which one of the following has a phase shift of $\dfrac{\pi}{6}$ units to the right?

(A) $f(x) = \sin\left(3x - \dfrac{\pi}{2}\right) + 3$

(B) $f(x) = \sin(\pi x - 6) - 2$

(C) $f(x) = 6\sin(x - \pi) + 1$

(D) $f(x) = 3\sin(6x - 1) - \pi$

11. With respect to the graph of $f(x) = \sin x$, the graph of which one of the following has both a period of $\dfrac{\pi}{8}$ and an amplitude of 5 ?

(A) $f(x) = 5\sin(4x - \pi)$

(B) $f(x) = 8\sin(5x - \pi)$

(C) $f(x) = -5\sin(16x + \pi)$

(D) $f(x) = -8\sin(x + 5\pi)$

12. The highest function value of the graph of $f(x) = 6\cos(x - 3\pi) + R$ is -2. What is the value of R?

(A) -8 (C) 4

(B) -4 (D) 8

13. What are the values of x in the equation $4\cot x - \dfrac{\tan x}{3} = 0$?

(A) Only 74° or 254°

(B) 74°, 106°, 254°, or 286°

(C) Only 85° or 265°

(D) 85°, 95°, 265°, or 275°

14. What are the values of x in the equation $\sec^2 x - 7\sec x - 8 = 0$?

(A) 97°, 180°, or 263°

(B) 0°, 97°, or 263°

(C) 83°, 180°, or 277°

(D) 0°, 83°, or 277°

15. What are the values of x in the equation $3\cos 2x + 22\sin^2 x - 4 = 0$?

(A) Only 15° or 165°

(B) Only 4° or 176°

(C) 4°, 176°, 184°, or 356°

(D) 15°, 165°, 195°, or 345°

16. Point Q is located at (c, d) on the unit circle. If $\overline{OQ}$ represents the terminal side of the angle θ and $c, d \neq 0$, which one of the following statements is <u>false</u>?

(A) $\tan\theta = \dfrac{d}{c}$

(B) $\sec\theta = c$

(C) $\sin\theta = d$

(D) OQ = 1

Quiz for Chapter 9
SOLUTIONS

1. (D)

The reference angle is the acute angle formed by the terminal side and the *x*-axis. For a standard position angle whose measure is 337°, the reference angle is $360° - 337° = 23°$.

2. (A)

Point Q must lie in the second quadrant, if both the tangent ratio and cosine ratios are negative.

3. (C)

In the reference triangle, assign the hypotenuse 1.2 and the horizontal side -1. The vertical side is then assigned $-\sqrt{1.2^2 - 1^2} \approx -0.663$. Then $\cot\theta = \dfrac{-1}{-0.663} \approx 1.51$.

4. (C)

$\sec\theta = -\dfrac{30}{OR} = -7.5$, so OR = 4. Then $RT = \sqrt{30^2 - 4^2} = \sqrt{884} \approx 29.73$. Thus, the coordinates of T are approximately $(-4, -29.73)$.

5. (D)

If $m > n$, with both variables positive, then $\dfrac{m}{n} > 1$. Since the sine value of any angle must lie between -1 and 1, inclusive, $\sin^{-1}\left(\dfrac{m}{n}\right)$ would not exist.

6. (D)

Let *x* represent the length of the wire. Then $\sin 36° = \dfrac{80}{x}$. Thus, $x = \dfrac{80}{\sin 36°} \approx 136.10$ feet.

7. (B)

Using $\triangle ABC$, $\tan 54° = \dfrac{AC}{40}$. Then $AC = (40)(\tan 54°) \approx 55.06$. Now, in $\triangle ADC$, $\sin 75° = \dfrac{55.06}{AD}$. So, $AD = \dfrac{55.06}{\sin 75°} \approx 57$.

8. (C)

Using $\triangle ACD$, $\tan 36° = \dfrac{AC}{15}$. Then $AC = (15)(\tan 36°) \approx 10.90$. Now in $\triangle ADC$, $\tan\angle B = \dfrac{10.90}{20} = 0.545$. So, $\angle B = \tan^{-1}(0.545) \approx 29°$.

9. (B)

Answer choices (A), (C), and (D) are true. However, the maximum value of the function is 1.

10. (A)

For the graph of $f(x) = A\sin(Bx - C) + D$, the phase shift is $\dfrac{C}{B}$ units to the right. For answer choice (A), the phase shift is $\dfrac{\pi/2}{3} = \dfrac{\pi}{6}$.

11. (C)

For the graph of $f(x) = A\sin(Bx - C) + D$, the amplitude is $|A|$ and the period is $\frac{2\pi}{B}$. For answer choice (C), the amplitude is $|-5| = 5$ and the period is $\frac{2\pi}{16} = \frac{\pi}{8}$.

12. (A)

For the graph of $f(x) = A\cos(Bx - C) + D$, where $A > 0$, the highest function value is given by $D + A$. So $-2 = R + 6$. Thus, $R = -8$.

13. (B)

Rewrite the equation as $\frac{4}{\tan x} - \frac{\tan x}{3} = 0$.

Multiply by $3\tan x$ to get $12 - \tan^2 x = 0$.

Then $\tan x = \pm\sqrt{12} \approx \pm 3.4641$. Thus,

$x = \pm\tan^{-1}(3.4641) \approx 74^\circ, 106^\circ, 254^\circ, \text{ or } 286^\circ$.

14. (C)

Factor the equation as $(\sec x - 8)(\sec x + 1) = 0$. If $\sec x - 8 = 0$, then $x = \sec^{-1}(8) \approx 83^\circ$ or 277°. If $\sec x + 1 = 0$, then $x = \sec^{-1}(-1) = 180^\circ$.

15. (D)

Substitute $1 - 2\sin^2 x$ for $\cos 2x$ so that the equation reads as $3(1 - 2\sin^2 x) + 22\sin^2 x - 4 = 0$. After removing the parentheses and combining similar terms, this equation simplifies to $16\sin^2 x - 1 = 0$. Then $(4\sin x - 1)(4\sin x + 1) = 0$. Thus, $\sin x = \pm\frac{1}{4}$, which leads to the answers of $15^\circ, 165^\circ, 195^\circ,$ or 345°.

16. (B)

The correct ratio for $\sec\theta$ is $\frac{1}{c}$.

Differential and Integral Calculus

Welcome to Chapter 10. In this chapter, we will review the following topics:

(a) Limits of functions

(b) Continuity of functions

(c) Average rate of change

(d) Instantaneous rate of change

(e) Rules for finding first derivatives

(f) Rules for finding second derivatives

(g) Applications of first and second derivatives to key points of graphs

(h) Antiderivatives

(i) Definite integrals

Limits and Continuity of Functions

We begin by exploring the concept of a limit of a function, both algebraically and graphically. Consider the function $f(x) = x^2 + x - 1$. Let's construct a table of x values near 2, but not equal to 2.

x	1.96	1.97	1.98	1.99	2.01	2.02	2.03	2.04
$f(x)$	4.8016	4.8509	4.9004	4.9501	5.0501	5.1004	5.1509	5.2016

Notice that as the x value gets closer to 2, in either direction, the value of $f(x)$ gets closer to 5. In fact, $f(2) = 2^2 + 2 - 1 = 5$.

Figure 10.1, shown below, is a graph of $f(x) = x^2 + x - 1$. For easy reading, only points with integral values of x and $f(x)$ are shown.

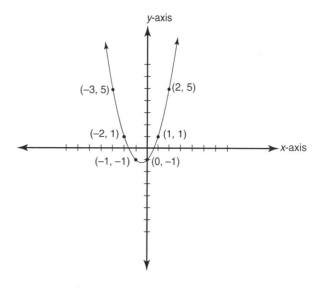

Figure 10.1

129

In general, for any polynomial function of the form $P(x) = a_0 + a_1 x + a_2 x^2 + ... + a_n x^n$, the limit of the function as x approaches a particular value c is $P(c)$. This statement also applies to other functions (such as trigonometric, exponential and logarithmic) for which their graphs can be drawn without any "gaps."

EXAMPLE 1

What is the limit of $k(x) = 9x - x^3$ as x approaches -1?

SOLUTION

Since $k(x)$ is a polynomial function, the limit is $k(-1) = 9(-1) - (-1)^3 = -8$.

EXAMPLE 2

What is the limit of $h(x) = 3\sin 2x$ as x approaches $\dfrac{\pi}{4}$? (x is given in radians).

SOLUTION

Simply substitute $\dfrac{\pi}{4}$ for x in the equation of the function. Then $h\left(\dfrac{\pi}{4}\right) = 3\sin\left[(2)\left(\dfrac{\pi}{4}\right)\right] = 3\sin\dfrac{\pi}{2} = 3$.

Rational Functions

A **rational function** is a quotient of two polynomial functions in which the denominator is not the zero function. Thus, if $R(x)$ is a rational function, then it can be expressed as $\dfrac{P(x)}{Q(x)}$, where $Q(x)$ is not the zero function. We are aware that it is possible that $R(x)$ is not defined for all x. In fact, $R(x)$ is not defined whenever $Q(x) = 0$. We are now interested in determining if a limit for a rational function can exist even as x approaches a value for which the function is not defined.

As an example, consider the function $g(x) = \dfrac{x^2 - x - 2}{x - 2}$. This function is not defined for $x = 2$, but let's construct a table of values that are very close to 2.

x	1.996	1.997	1.998	1.999	2.001	2.002	2.003	2.004
$g(x)$	2.996	2.997	2.998	2.999	3.001	3.002	3.003	3.004

As the x value gets closer to 2, in either direction, the value of $g(x)$ gets closer to 3. We can simplify $\dfrac{x^2 - x - 2}{x - 2} = \dfrac{(x - 2)(x + 1)}{x - 2} = x + 1$, provided that $x \neq 2$. Thus, the function g(x) is identical to the line $y = x + 1$, except where $x = 2$. Even though $g(x)$ is not defined for $x = 2$, we can still claim that as x approaches 2, the limit of $g(x)$ is 3. Figure 10.2, shown below, is a graph of $g(x) = \dfrac{x^2 - x - 2}{x - 2}$. Only points with integral values of x and $g(x)$ are shown. The point $(2, 3)$ is shown with a circle because it does not belong to the graph of $g(x)$.

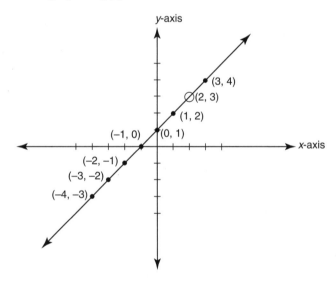

Figure 10.2

Let's check the procedure for finding a limit for this function when $x \neq 2$. If we wanted the limit of $g(x)$ as x approaches 4, we simply substitute into the given equation for $g(x)$. Since $g(4) = \dfrac{4^2 - 4 - 2}{4 - 2} = 5$, as x approaches 4, the limit of g(x) is 5.

EXAMPLE 3

If $m(x) = \dfrac{x-1}{x^2+x+3}$, what is the limit of $m(x)$ as x approaches 3?

SOLUTION

The answer is found by determining the value of $m(3)$, which is $\dfrac{3-1}{3^2+3+3} = \dfrac{2}{15}$.

EXAMPLE 4

If $n(x) = \dfrac{-3x-6}{x^3+8}$, what is the limit of $n(x)$ as x approaches -2?

SOLUTION

We cannot simply calculate $n(-2)$, since the denominator would equal zero. The correct procedure is to reduce the fraction for $x \neq -2$. Rewrite the function as $n(x) = \dfrac{-3(x+2)}{(x+2)(x^2-2x+4)} = \dfrac{-3}{x^2-2x+4}$. By substitution, $n(-2) = \dfrac{-3}{(-2)^2-2(-2)+4} = -\dfrac{1}{4}$. Thus, the limit is $-\dfrac{1}{4}$.

Notation for Limits

A specific notation is used when a limit exists for a function. Let $f(x)$ represent a function for which c is a point in the interior of its domain, and let L and M represent real numbers.

If x approaches the value of c from the left, this means that x is increasing from values slightly less than c up to (but possibly not including) c. Suppose that as x approaches this value of c from the left, $f(x)$ approaches a value of L. Then the notation we use is $lim_{x \to c^-} f(x) = L$.

If x approaches the value of c from the right, this means that x is decreasing from values slightly greater than c down to (but possibly not including) c. Suppose that as x approaches this value of c from the right, $f(x)$ approaches a value of M. Then the notation we use is $lim_{x \to c^+} f(x) = M$.

If $L = M$, then we can state that the function has a limit at the point $x = c$. This is true even if $f(c)$ does not exist. The notation becomes $lim_{x \to c} f(x) = L$. (Of course M could be substituted for L.) However, if $L \neq M$, then $lim_{x \to c} f(x)$ does not exist. Each of $lim_{x \to c^-} f(x) = L$ and $lim_{x \to c^+} f(x) = M$ is called a **one-sided** limit, whether or not $lim_{x \to c} f(x)$ actually exists. Thus, $lim_{x \to c^-} f(x) = L$ is a one-sided limit as x approaches c from the left, while $lim_{x \to c^+} f(x) = M$ is a one-sided limit as x approaches c from the right.

In each of Examples 1 through 4, the limit as x approaches the specific number from the left is equal to the limit as x approaches that same number from the right. Thus, for Example 1, we can write $lim_{x \to -1}(9x - x^3) = -8$ Likewise, for Example 3, we can write $lim_{x \to 3} \dfrac{x-1}{x^2+x+3} = \dfrac{2}{15}$. Remember that a limit can exist at a point even when the function is not defined at that point. Figure 10.2 referred to the graph of $g(x) = \dfrac{x^2-x-2}{x-2}$. Although g(x) is not defined at $x = 2$, we can still write $lim_{x \to 2} \dfrac{x^2-x-2}{x-2} = 3$.

Left-sided and Right-sided Limits

Let's look at some functions for which the left-sided limit at a specific point does not equal the right-sided limit. A graph will accompany each function.

Suppose $f(x) = \begin{cases} x-1, & x \leq 0 \\ x^2+1, & x > 0 \end{cases}$ The graph of $f(x)$ is shown below in Figure 10.3.

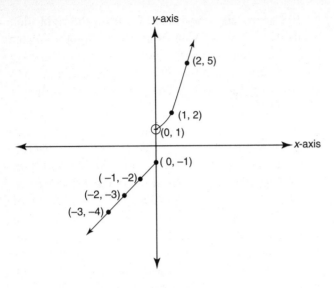

Figure 10.3

Non-existent Limits

Before we do a third example in which the limit does not exist, we must mention that <u>for a given function, a limit may not exist at one point but can certainly exist at a different point.</u> In the previous example concerning $g(x)$, we can verify both graphically and algebraically that $lim_{x \to 6^-} g(x) = lim_{x \to 6^+} g(x) = \frac{1}{3}$.

Now consider the function $h(x) = 4x^2 + 1, x \geq 0$. The graph is shown below in Figure 10.5.

From the graph, we can determine that $lim_{x \to 0^-} f(x) = -1$ and that $lim_{x \to 0^+} f(x) = 1$. Therefore, $lim_{x \to 0} f(x)$ does not exist.

Now suppose $g(x) = \begin{cases} \dfrac{1}{x-3}, & x > 3 \\ 5, & x \leq 3 \end{cases}$ The graph of $g(x)$ is shown below in Figure 10.4.

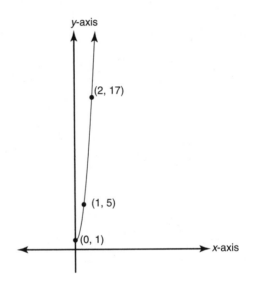

Figure 10.5

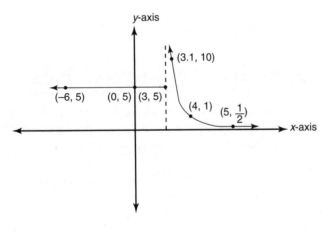

Figure 10.4

From the graph, we can determine that $lim_{x \to 3^-} g(x) = 5$, but $lim_{x \to 3^+} g(x)$ does not even exist. Therefore $lim_{x \to 3} g(x)$ does not exist. Be aware that some books will use the notation $lim_{x \to 3^+} g(x) = \infty$ to show that $lim_{x \to 3^+} g(x)$ does not exist.

It is easy to see that $lim_{x \to 0^+} h(x) = 1$, but how do we calculate $lim_{x \to 0^-} h(x)$? The answer is that since there are no domain values immediately to the left of zero, $lim_{x \to 0^-} h(x)$ does not exist. Even if $h(x)$ were defined for some particular negative x value, $lim_{x \to 0^-} h(x)$ would still be nonexistent. Thus, $lim_{x \to 0} h(x)$ does not exist. Of course, a limit would exist at any positive number. For example, $lim_{x \to 5} h(x) = (4)(5^2) + 1 = 101$.

Our next area of concern with limits deals with the situations in which x approaches positive or negative infinity. If $f(x)$ is a polynomial function, the value of the limit will be $+\infty$ or $-\infty$, depending on the leading coefficient. Thus, the limit does <u>not</u> exist.

Rules for Limits

If $f(x)$ is a rational function in the form $\dfrac{p(x)}{q(x)}$, then there are three basic rules to follow:

Rule 1: If the degree of $p(x)$ is less than that of $q(x)$, then $\lim_{x \to \infty} f(x) = 0$.

Rule 2: If the degree of $p(x)$ is equal to that of $q(x)$, then $\lim_{x \to \infty} f(x) = k$, where k is the ratio of the leading coefficients of $p(x)$ and $q(x)$.

Rule 3: If the degree of $p(x)$ is greater than that of $q(x)$, then $\lim_{x \to \infty} f(x) = \infty$. This is equivalent to stating that $\lim_{x \to \infty} f(x)$ does not exist.

EXAMPLE 5

What is the value of $\lim_{x \to \infty}(3x^5 - 10x^3 + 40)$?

SOLUTION

The leading term is $3x^5$. As x increases without bound, the value of $3x^5$ also increases without bound.

EXAMPLE 6

What is the value of $\lim_{x \to \infty} \dfrac{-3x^4 + 7x - 4}{6x^4 + 91}$?

SOLUTION

Since the degrees of the numerator and denominator are equal, the limit is the ratio of the leading coefficients, which is $-\dfrac{1}{2}$.

EXAMPLE 7

What is the value of $\lim_{x \to -\infty} \dfrac{10x^3 + 5}{8x^5 + x + 9}$?

SOLUTION

The same rules apply whether x approaches ∞ or $-\infty$. Since the degree of the numerator is smaller than that of the denominator, the answer is 0.

EXAMPLE 8

What is the value of $\lim_{x \to \infty} \dfrac{-9x^6 + 5x + 2}{10x^4 - 3x}$?

SOLUTION

The degree of the numerator is larger than that of the denominator. Thus, the limit does not exist.

There is one additional important instance in which a limit does not exist for a rational function. If $f(x) = \dfrac{p(x)}{q(x)}$ is in reduced form and $q(c) = 0$ but $p(c) \neq 0$, then $\lim_{x \to c} f(x)$ does not exist. An example of this phenomenon is $\lim_{x \to 4} \dfrac{5x - 2}{3x - 12}$. By substituting the value of 4 for x, this fraction appears as $\dfrac{18}{0}$, which has no value. The limit does not exist.

NOTE:

The concept of continuity for functions is very closely related to that of limits. In a visual sense, continuity of a function at a point means that its graph contains that point and all points within a fixed distance from it. Figures 10.6 and 10.7 shown below illustrate functions which are continuous at $x = 2$. The function $g(x)$ in figure 10.7 is not continuous at $x = -1$. Also, since the domain of $g(x)$ does not exceed 5, $g(x)$ is not continuous at $x = 5$.

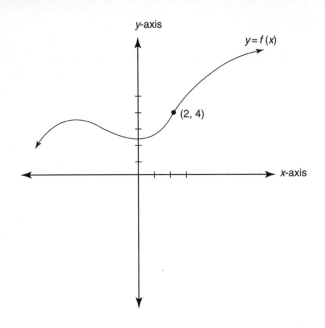

Figure 10.6

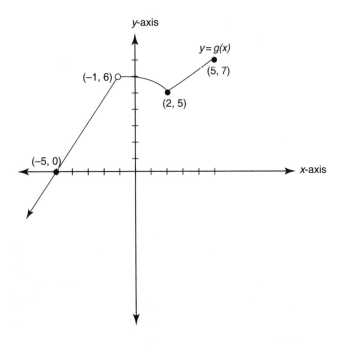

Figure 10.7

Continuity of Functions

The formal definition of **continuity** is: A function $f(x)$ is continuous at a point $x = c$ if and only if

$\lim_{x \to c} f(x) = c$. This definition is really a combination of three distinct sub-statements, namely:

1. $\lim_{x \to c} f(x)$ exists.   2. $f(c)$ exists
3. $\lim_{x \to c} f(x) = f(c)$

If any of these conditions are not met, $f(x)$ is discontinuous at point c. Remember that $x = c$ <u>cannot</u> represent an endpoint of an interval on which $f(x)$ is defined. The reason is that $\lim_{x \to c} f(x)$ would not exist.

Figure 10.8 shown below is an example of a function $t(x)$ for which the first two conditions of continuity are met, but the third condition is not met.

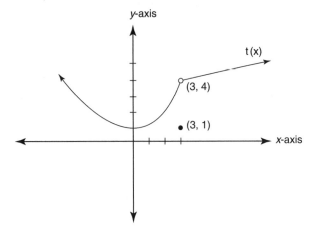

Figure 10.8

Notice that $\lim_{x \to 3} t(x) = 4$, but that $t(3) = 1$. Thus, $t(x)$ is discontinuous at $x = 3$.

Each polynomial function is continuous for the domain of all real numbers. One such example is $p(x) = -2x^5 + 3x - 4$. We observe that $p(x)$ is defined for all real numbers If we choose a specific domain value, such as -1, we can verify that $\lim_{x \to -1} p(x)$ exists, $p(-1)$ exists, and $\lim_{x \to -1} p(x) = p(-1) = -5$.

With rational functions, their discontinuities occur at points where there are vertical asymptotes. The x values of these points are the values for which the denominator of the rational function is not defined. Figure 10.9 shown below is the graph of the function $f(x) = \dfrac{2}{(x-1)(x+4)}$, along with a few selected points.

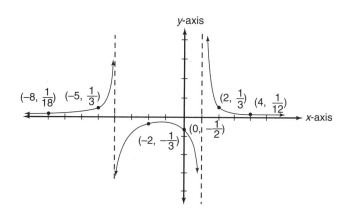

Figure 10.9

Notice that $f(1)$ and $f(-4)$ are not defined, so $f(x)$ cannot be continuous at either $x = 1$ or $x = -4$.

The Intermediate Value Theorem

One very important consequence of continuity for a function is the **Intermediate Value Theorem**. First, we must state that a function $f(x)$ is continuous on a closed interval [a, b] if it is continuous at each point of the open interval (a, b). Also, $\lim_{x \to a^+} f(x) = f(a)$ and $\lim_{x \to b^-} f(x) = f(b)$.

Now, let $f(x)$ represent a function that is continuous on a closed interval $[a,b]$. Let N represent any value between $f(a)$ and $f(b)$. The Intermediate Value Theorem states that there exists at least one value c, where $a < c < b$, such that $f(c) = N$. Translated into straight English, this theorem is claiming that if a function is continuous between any two x values a and b, then the function must assume all y values between $f(a)$ and $f(b)$. Figure 10.10 shows a general continuous function with the Intermediate Value Theorem.

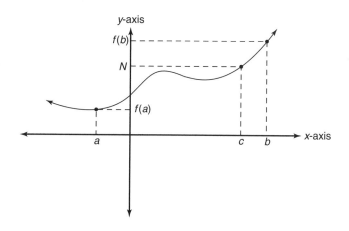

Figure 10.10

As a specific example, consider $g(x) = -x^2 + 6x + 1$, which is continuous for all x values. On the closed interval $[-1,4]$, $g(-1) = -6$ and $g(4) = 9$. Next, any number between -6 and 9 is selected. If we select 6, the Intermediate Value Theorem states that there is at least one x value between -1 and 4 for which $g(x) = 6$. In fact, we are looking for the solution(s) to $6 = -x^2 + 6x + 1$. This equation can be written as $x^2 - 6x + 5 = 0$, which is factored as $(x - 5)(x - 1) = 0$. The two solutions are 5 and 1, and note that 1 does lie in the interval $[-1,4]$.

Figure 10.11 shown below is the graph of $g(x) = -x^2 + 6x + 1$.

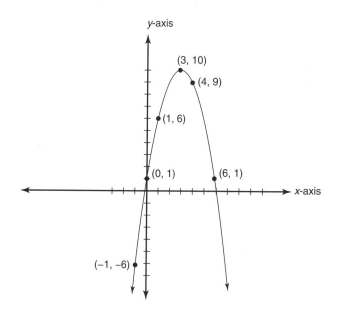

Figure 10.11

NOTE:

The Intermediate Value Theorem applies to functions that contain discontinuities. The only requirement is that given the closed interval $[a,b]$, the function must be continuous on that interval. Returning to Figure 10.9, we know that $f(x) = \dfrac{2}{(x - 1)(x + 4)}$ is discontinuous at $x = 1$ and $x = -4$. But the Intermediate Value Theorem would certainly apply in the interval $[-8,-5]$.

EXAMPLE 9

If $h(x) = \dfrac{x+4}{3x^2 + 26x - 9}$, then $h(x)$ is not continuous for which x value(s)?

SOLUTION

The x values for which $h(x)$ is not continuous are found by setting the denominator equal to zero. Then $3x^2 + 26x - 9 = 0$, which factors as $(3x - 1)(x + 9) = 0$. Thus, the two x values are $\dfrac{1}{3}$ and -9.

EXAMPLE 10

If $\lim_{x \to 2}(x^3 + kx + 8) = 6$, what is the value of k?

SOLUTION

Since we are dealing with a polynomial function, $x^3 + kx + 8$ must equal 6 when $x = 2$. By substitution, $2^3 + 2k + 8 = 6$. Simplifying, this equation becomes $2k = -10$. Thus, $k = -5$.

Average Rate of Change

Consider the function $f(x)$ that is continuous in the interval $[a, b]$.

The **average rate of change** is defined as the slope of the line segment, with endpoints $(a, f(a))$ and $(b, f(b))$. Its value is calculated as $\dfrac{f(b) - f(a)}{b - a}$. This line segment is part of the secant line through $(a, f(a))$ and $(b, f(b))$.

EXAMPLE 11

What is the average rate of change for $g(x) = -x^3 + 4$ over the interval $[1, 6]$?

SOLUTION

$g(1) = 3$ and $g(6) = -212$. Thus, the average rate of change is $\dfrac{-212 - 3}{6 - 1} = -43$.

EXAMPLE 12

What is the average rate of change for $f(x) = 2x^2 + 5$ over the interval $[2, 5]$?

SOLUTION

$f(2) = 13$ and $f(5) = 55$. Thus, the average rate of change is $\dfrac{55 - 13}{5 - 2} = 14$.

Similar to a slope, the average rate of change can be positive, negative, or zero. It may also be a non-integer.

Returning to the function in Example 12, let's change the interval to $[2, 3]$

EXAMPLE 13

What is the average rate of change for $f(x) = 2x^2 + 5$ over the interval $[2, 3]$?

SOLUTION

$f(2) = 13$ and $f(3) = 23$. This time, the average rate of change is $\dfrac{23 - 13}{3 - 2} = 10$.

EXAMPLE 14

What is the average rate of change for $f(x) = 2x^2 + 5$ over the interval $[2, 2.1]$?

SOLUTION

$f(2) = 13$ and $f(2.1) = 13.82$. Thus, the average rate of change is $\dfrac{13.82 - 13}{2.1 - 2} = 8.2$.

Notice that in Example 14, the interval was very small, compared to the intervals used for Examples 12 and 13. Figure 10.12 shown below illustrates a magnified version of the secant line for each of Examples 13 and 14.

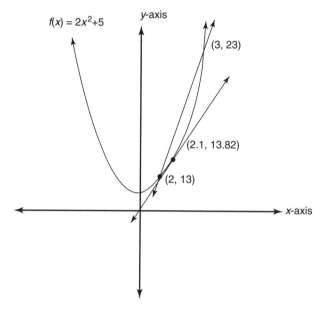

Figure 10.12

Instantaneous Rate of Change

This leads us to the concept of **instantaneous rate change**. For a specific point P of a function, this is defined as the slope of the tangent line at point P. It represents the limit of the average rate of change between P and a second point Q that belongs to the function as $Q - P$ becomes increasingly smaller.

In general, let $f(x)$ be defined and continuous at point P with coordinates $(x, f(x))$. Let point Q belong to $f(x)$ such that its coordinates are $(x + \Delta x, f(x + \Delta x))$, where Δx is a very small number. (Use your own perception of "very small"). Then the instanta-

neous rate of change of $f(x)$ at point P is given by $\lim_{\Delta x \to 0} \dfrac{f(x + \Delta x) - f(x)}{\Delta x}$.

Let's return to the function $f(x) = 2x^2 + 5$ given in Examples 12, 13, and 14, and calculate the average rate of change by using the interval $[2, 2.001]$. Since $f(2) = 13$ and $f(2.001) = 13.008002$, the average rate of change is $\dfrac{13.008002 - 13}{2.001 - 2} = 8.002$.

Let's now calculate the instantaneous rate at $(x, f(x))$ by using the limit formula shown above. Since $f(x) = 2x^2 + 5$, $f(x + \Delta x) = 2(x + \Delta x)^2 + 5 = 2x^2 + 4x\Delta x + 2(\Delta x)^2 + 5$. Then $\lim_{\Delta x \to 0} \dfrac{f(x + \Delta x) - f(x)}{\Delta x}$

$$= \lim_{\Delta x \to 0} \frac{2x^2 + 4x\Delta x + 2(\Delta x)^2 + 5 - (2x^2 + 5)}{\Delta x}$$

$$= \lim_{\Delta x \to 0} \frac{4x\Delta x + 2(\Delta x)^2}{\Delta x} = \lim_{\Delta x \to 0} 4x + 2(\Delta x) = 4x.$$

The expression $4x$ represents the instantaneous rate of change for the function $f(x) = 2x^2 + 5$ at <u>any</u> point $(x, f(x))$. As such, $4x$ represents the slope of the tangent line at any point on the graph of this function. In particular, if we want the instantaneous rate of change at the point $(2, 13)$, the answer is $(4)(2) = 8$. Notice how close this answer is to the average rate of change between $(2, 13)$ and $(2.001, 13.008002)$.

Figure 10.13 shown below illustrates the tangent line to $f(x) = 2x^2 + 5$ at the point $(2, 13)$.

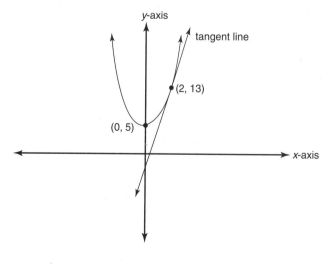

Figure 10.13

EXAMPLE 15

> For the function $f(x) = 2x^2 + 5$, what is the instantaneous rate of change at the point $(-4, 37)$?

SOLUTION

Using the expression $4x$, the answer is $(4)(-4) = -16$.

EXAMPLE 16

> For the function $f(x) = 2x^2 + 5$, what is the equation of the tangent line at $x = 2$?

SOLUTION

We already know that the slope of the tangent line is $(4)(2) = 8$. Since the tangent line contains the point $(2, 13)$, we can use the following equation for a line: $y - y_1 = m(x - x_1)$. In this equation, m represents the slope and (x_1, y_1) represents a point on the line. By substitution, $y - 13 = 8(x - 2)$, which simplifies to $y = 8x - 3$.

EXAMPLE 17

> What is the instantaneous rate of change at the point $(x, g(x))$ for the function $g(x) = -x^3 + 4$?

SOLUTION

We calculated the average rate of change for this function in Example 11. The instantaneous rate of change is $\lim_{\Delta x \to 0} \dfrac{g(x + \Delta x) - g(x)}{\Delta x}$. Then $g(x + \Delta x) = -(x + \Delta x)^3 + 4 = -x^3 - 3x^2(\Delta x) - 3x(\Delta x)^2 - (\Delta x)^3 + 4$.

So $g(x + \Delta x) - g(x) = (-x^3 - 3x^2(\Delta x) - 3x(\Delta x)^2 - (\Delta x)^3 + 4) - (-x^3 + 4)$

$= -3x^2(\Delta x) - 3x(\Delta x)^2 - (\Delta x)^3$.

Now, $\lim_{\Delta x \to 0} \dfrac{g(x + \Delta x) - g(x)}{\Delta x}$

$= \lim_{\Delta x \to 0} \dfrac{-3x^2(\Delta x) - 3x(\Delta x)^2 - (\Delta x)^3}{\Delta x}$

$= \lim_{\Delta x \to 0} -3x^2 - 3x(\Delta x) - (\Delta x)^2 = -3x^2$.

NOTE:

> This method of finding the instantaneous rate of change is called the "Δ-method," ("Δ" is pronounced "delta"). You can see that the algebraic steps require a great deal of attention to accuracy! We will develop a short cut later in this chapter.

EXAMPLE 18

> For the function $g(x) = -x^3 + 4$, what is the instantaneous rate of change at the point where $x = 0.5$?

SOLUTION

Using the expression $-3x^2$, the answer is $-3(0.5)^2 = -0.75$. Note that the corresponding y-coordinate at the point of tangency, which is 3.875, is not used to find the instantaneous rate of change.

Figure 10.14 shown below illustrates the tangent line to $g(x) = -x^3 + 4$ at the point $(0.5, 3.875)$.

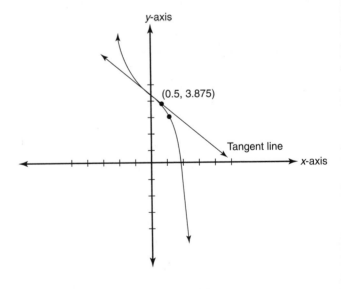

Figure 10.14

EXAMPLE 19

For the function $g(x) = -x^3 + 4$, what is the y-intercept of the tangent line at (0.5, 3.875)?

SOLUTION

From Example 18, we already know that the slope is -0.75. The equation of the tangent line can be found by using the point slope formula. Then $y - 3.875 = -0.75(x - 0.5)$, which simplifies to $y = -0.75x + 4.25$. Thus, the y-intercept is (0, 4.25).

First Derivative

The instantaneous rate of change at a point of a function is called the **first derivative** of the function at that point. Thus, the first derivative corresponds to the slope of the tangent line. Given a function $f(x)$, the notation commonly used for a first derivative is $f'(x)$, which is read as "f prime of x". If we are given that $y = f(x)$, two other notations for the first derivative are y' and $\frac{dy}{dx}$.

So, we can write $f'(x) = \lim_{\Delta x \to 0} \frac{f(x + \Delta x) - f(x)}{\Delta x}$. For a specific point where $x = c$, we can write the derivative of $f(x)$, denoted as $f'(c)$, as $\lim_{\Delta x \to 0} \frac{f(c + \Delta x) - f(c)}{\Delta x}$.

An alternative way to write $f'(c)$ is $\lim_{x \to c} \frac{f(x) - f(c)}{x - c}$. Remember that $f'(c)$ represents the slope of the tangent line to $f(x)$ at $x = c$.

You can see that the "Δ method" is quite involved algebraically in finding the first derivative. This is especially true in examples such as Example 17. This method is even more of a challenge, in the algebraic sense, for rational functions such as $f(x) = \frac{x - 3}{x^2 + x - 2}$.

Rules for Finding First Derivatives

Fortunately, there are rules that govern the derivatives for many types of functions. Let's begin with a few basic ones.

Rational Functions

Rule #	Function	First Derivative
1.	$y = k$, k a constant	$\frac{dy}{dx} = 0$
2.	$y = kx$, k a constant	$\frac{dy}{dx} = k$
3.	$y = x^k$, k a constant	$\frac{dy}{dx} = kx^{k-1}$
4.	$y = a_n x^n + a_{n-1} x^{n-1} + a_{n-2} x^{n-2} + \ldots a_1 x + a_0$	

then

$$\frac{dy}{dx} = na_n x^{n-1} + (n-1)a_{n-1} x^{n-2} + (n-2)a_{n-2} x^{n-3} + \ldots a_1$$

5.	$y = k \times f(x)$, k a constant	$\frac{dy}{dx} = (k)(f'(x))$
6.	$y = f(x) \pm g(x)$	$\frac{dy}{dx} = f'(x) \pm g'(x)$
7.	$y = f(x) \times g(x)$	

$$\frac{dy}{dx} = f(x) \times g'(x) + g(x) \times f'(x)$$

8. $y = \frac{f(x)}{g(x)}$

$$\frac{dy}{dx} = \frac{g(x) \times f'(x) - f(x) \times g'(x)}{[g(x)]^2}$$

EXAMPLE 20

If $y = 7x - 12$, what is the simplified expression for $\frac{dy}{dx}$?

SOLUTION

We can use the first two rules to get $\frac{dy}{dx} = 7 + 0 = 7$.

EXAMPLE 21

If $y = -x^4 + 5x^3 + x$, what is the simplified expression for $\frac{dy}{dx}$?

SOLUTION

We can just use the fourth rule, which is really a combination of the first three rules. Then $\frac{dy}{dx} = (4)(-1)x^3 + (3)(5)x^2 + 1 = -4x^3 + 15x^2 + 1$.

EXAMPLE 22

If $y = (x^2 - 2x + 9)(6x + 3)$, what is the value of $\frac{dy}{dx}$ at $x = 2$?

SOLUTION

We have two choices here. Let's use the seventh rule, with $f(x) = x^2 - 2x + 9$ and $g(x) = 6x + 3$. So, $f'(x) = 2x - 2$ and $g'(x) = 6$. Thus,
$$\frac{dy}{dx} = (x^2 - 2x + 9)(6) + (6x + 3)(2x - 2)$$
$$= 6x^2 - 12x + 54 + 12x^2 - 6x - 6 =$$
$18x^2 - 18x + 48$. Finally, when $x = 2$, $\frac{dy}{dx} = (18)(2^2) - (18)(2) + 48 = 84$.

Looking back at Example 22, we could have multiplied and simplified the original expression for y to get $6x^3 - 9x^2 + 48x + 27$. Then, $\frac{dy}{dx} = (3)(6)x^2 - (2)(9)x + 48 =$
$18x^2 - 18x + 48$, which matches the expression for $\frac{dy}{dx}$ we already obtained.

EXAMPLE 23

If $y = \frac{x - 3}{x^2 + x - 2}$, what is the simplified expression for $\frac{dy}{dx}$?

SOLUTION

The eighth rule should be used. Let $f(x) = x - 3$ and let $g(x) = x^2 + x - 2$. Then $f'(x) = 1$ and $g'(x) = 2x + 1$. So,
$$\frac{dy}{dx} = \frac{(x^2 + x - 2)(1) - (x - 3)(2x + 1)}{(x^2 + x - 2)^2} =$$
$$\frac{x^2 + x - 2 - (2x^2 - 5x - 3)}{(x^2 + x - 2)^2} = \frac{-x^2 + 6x + 1}{(x^2 + x - 2)^2}.$$

NOTE:

We didn't take the extra step to expand the denominator. The answer we have shown is generally accepted as the final answer. However, you should always simplify completely the numerator of a fraction. Also, if there were a common factor in both the numerator and denominator of the final answer, that factor would be divided out.

EXAMPLE 24

If $y = \frac{7}{x^2} - \frac{5}{2x^6}$, what is the value of $\frac{dy}{dx}$ at $x = -1$?

SOLUTION

We could combine the terms on the right side by using a common denominator, but it will be just as easy to rewrite this example using negative exponents. Then $y = 7x^{-2} - \frac{5}{2}x^{-6}$, so $\dfrac{dy}{dx} = (-2)(7)x^{-3} + (-6)\left(-\dfrac{5}{2}\right)x^{-7} = -\dfrac{14}{x^3} + \dfrac{15}{x^7}$

$= \dfrac{-14x^4 + 15}{x^7}$. At $x = -1$,

$\dfrac{dy}{dx} = \dfrac{(-14)(-1)^4 + 15}{(-1)^7} = -1$.

NOTE:

An alternative way to answer Example 24 is to rewrite the right side as $\dfrac{14x^4 - 5}{2x^6}$, then use the eighth rule.

Trigonometric, Logarithmic, and Power Functions

Rules 9 though 16 concerning derivatives apply to trigonometric, logarithmic, and power functions.

Rule	Function	First Derivative
9.	$y = \sin x$	$\dfrac{dy}{dx} = \cos x$
10.	$y = \cos x$	$\dfrac{dy}{dx} = -\sin x$
11.	$y = \tan x$	$\dfrac{dy}{dx} = \sec^2 x$
12.	$y = \cot x$	$\dfrac{dy}{dx} = -\csc^2 x$
13.	$y = \sec x$	$\dfrac{dy}{dx} = (\sec x)(\tan x)$
14.	$y = \csc x$	$\dfrac{dy}{dx} = -(\csc x)(\cot x)$
15.	$y = a^x$, where $a > 0$	$\dfrac{dy}{dx} = (a^x)(\ln a)$

16. $y = \log_a x$, where $a > 0$, $a \neq 1$ $\dfrac{dy}{dx} = \left(\dfrac{1}{\ln a}\right)\left(\dfrac{1}{x}\right)$

As special cases, if $y = e^x$, then $\dfrac{dy}{dx} = (e^x)(\ln e) = e^x$.

Also, if $y = \log_e x = \ln x$, then $\dfrac{dy}{dx} = \left(\dfrac{1}{\ln e}\right)\left(\dfrac{1}{x}\right) = \dfrac{1}{x}$.

EXAMPLE 25

If $y = \dfrac{\cos x}{3x^2}$, what is the simplified expression for $\dfrac{dy}{dx}$?

SOLUTION

We'll use rules 8 and 10. Then

$\dfrac{dy}{dx} = \dfrac{(3x^2)(-\sin x) - (\cos x)(6x)}{(3x^2)^2}$

$= \dfrac{-3x^2 \sin x - 6x \cos x}{9x^4} = \dfrac{-x \sin x - 2\cos x}{3x^3}$.

EXAMPLE 26

If $y = (\sec x)(4x^3)$, what is the simplified expression for $\dfrac{dy}{dx}$?

SOLUTION

Be careful that you do <u>not</u> interpret this as $y = \sec(4x^4)$!

We'll use rules 7 and 13. Then

$\dfrac{dy}{dx} = (\sec x)(12x^2) + (4x^3)(\sec x)(\tan x)$

or $(4x^2 \sec x)(3 + x \tan x)$.

EXAMPLE 27

> If $y = 3\csc x - 5^x$, what is the simplified expression for $\dfrac{dy}{dx}$?

SOLUTION

We'll use rules 6, 14, and 15. Then $\dfrac{dy}{dx} = -3(\csc x)(\cot x) - (5^x)(\ln 5)$.

EXAMPLE 28

> If $y = x(\ln x)$, what is the simplified expression for $\dfrac{dy}{dx}$?

SOLUTION

Using rule 7 and the special case that applies to rule 16, $\dfrac{dy}{dx} = (x)\left(\dfrac{1}{x}\right) + (\ln x)(1) = 1 + \ln x$.

Chain Rule

We now consider the **Chain Rule** as it applies to derivatives. The Chain rule is a method by which we can take the derivative of a composite function. Suppose $y = g(h(x))$. The function y is considered a composite function of $g(x)$ and $h(x)$. Another way to state this relationship is: $y = g(u)$ and $u = h(x)$. Rule 17 would then be : If $y = g(h(x))$, where $y = g(u)$ and $u = h(x)$, then $\dfrac{dy}{dx} = \left(\dfrac{dy}{du}\right)\left(\dfrac{du}{dx}\right)$.

A second way to determine $\dfrac{dy}{dx}$ is to use the formula $\dfrac{dy}{dx} = g'(h(x)) \times (h'(x))$. Either method should work when determining $\dfrac{dy}{dx}$.

EXAMPLE 29

> If $y = \sin 4x$, what is the simplified expression for $\dfrac{dy}{dx}$?

SOLUTION

Let $u = 4x$, so that the original function reads as $y = \sin u$. Then $\dfrac{dy}{du} = \cos u$ and $\dfrac{du}{dx} = 4$. So, $\dfrac{dy}{dx} = (\cos u)(4)$. The last step is to replace u by $4x$.

Thus, $\dfrac{dy}{dx} = 4\cos 4x$.

EXAMPLE 30

> If $y = (3x^2 - 7)^3$, what is the simplified expression for $\dfrac{dy}{dx}$?

SOLUTION

Let $u = 3x^2 - 7$, so that the original function reads as $y = u^3$. Then $\dfrac{dy}{du} = 3u^2$ and $\dfrac{du}{dx} = 6x$. Thus, $\dfrac{dy}{dx} = (3u^2)(6x) = (3)(3x^2 - 7)^2(6x) = (18x)(3x^2 - 7)^2$.

NOTE:

> Regarding the solution to example 30: For most of the questions concerning the Chain rule for derivatives, an answer such as $(18x)(3x^2 - 7)^2$ is considered simplified, since it is presented in factored form. If we expand this answer, we get $162x^5 - 756x^3 + 882x$. The only other approach to use would be to expand the original expression as $y = (3x^2 - 7)^3 = (3x^2)^3 - (3)(3x^2)^2(7) + (3)(3x^2)(7)^2 - (7)^3 = 27x^6 - 189x^4 + 441x^2 - 343$. Then $\frac{dy}{dx} = 162x^5 - 756x^3 + 882x$.
>
> For future problems of this nature, we will leave the final answer in factored form.

EXAMPLE 31

> If $y = \cot^5(5 - 3x)$, what is the simplified expression for $\frac{dy}{dx}$?

SOLUTION

This example can be written as $y = [\cot(5 - 3x)]^5$. Let $u = \cot(5 - 3x)$, so that $y = u^5$. Then, using rules 3 and 12, $\frac{dy}{du} = 5u^4$ and $\frac{du}{dx} = [-\csc^2(5 - 3x)][-3] = 3\csc^2(5 - 3x)$. So, using the Chain rule, $\frac{dy}{dx} = (5u^4)[3\csc^2(5 - 3x)]$. Now, we just need to replace u with $cot(5 - 3x)$ and simplify. Thus, $\frac{dy}{dx} = [5\cot^4(5 - 3x)][3\csc^2(5 - 3x)] = 15[\cot^4(5 - 3x)][\csc^2(5 - 3x)]$.

EXAMPLE 32

> If $y = (9x)(e^{7x^2 - 1})$, what is the simplified expression for $\frac{dy}{dx}$?

SOLUTION

We begin by letting $f(x) = 9x$ and $g(x) = e^{7x^2 - 1}$. By rule 7, $\frac{dy}{dx} = f(x) \times g'(x) + g(x) \times f'(x)$. We can easily see that $f'(x) = 9$, but to determine $g'(x)$, we need the Chain rule. To avoid using "y" twice, let $w = e^{7x^2 - 1}$ and let $u = 7x^2 - 1$. Then we can write $w = e^u$, so that $\frac{dw}{dx} = \left(\frac{dw}{du}\right)\left(\frac{du}{dx}\right) = (e^u)(14x) = (e^{7x^2 - 1})(14x)$.

This means that $g'(x) = (e^{7x^2 - 1})(14x)$. Now, we have $\frac{dy}{dx} = (9x)(e^{7x^2 - 1})(14x) + (e^{7x^2 - 1})(9) = (126x^2)(e^{7x^2 - 1}) + (9)(e^{7x^2 - 1})$. Another acceptable answer is $(9e^{7x^2 - 1})(14x^2 + 1)$.

Rules for Finding Second Derivatives

We have discovered that for a given function $y = f(x)$, the first derivative, written as $f'(x)$ or $\frac{dy}{dx}$, represents the slope of the tangent line at a general point $(x, f(x))$.

Our next concern deals with the **second derivative** of a given function $y = f(x)$. The notation for the second derivative is $f''(x)$ or $\frac{d^2y}{dx^2}$. This is defined as the instantaneous rate of change of the first derivative of the function at a general point $(x, f(x))$. We calculate the second derivative by finding the derivative of the first derivative for any function.

Graphically, $f''(x)$ examines how the slope of the tangent line is changing at any point $(x, f(x))$. Another visual explanation would be as follows: Let $y = f(x)$ and $g(x) = f'(x)$. Then the second derivative of $f(x)$ would be the slope of the tangent line at $(x, g(x))$.

Specifically, suppose $f(x) = x^3 - 2x$. Then $f'(x) = 3x^2 - 2$. Now, by differentiating (taking the derivative of) $f'(x)$, we find that $f''(x) = 6x$. Figure 10.15 shown below is the graph of $f'(x) = 3x^2 - 2$. The accompanying tangent line represents $f''(x)$ at $(x, g(x)) = (x, f'(x))$.

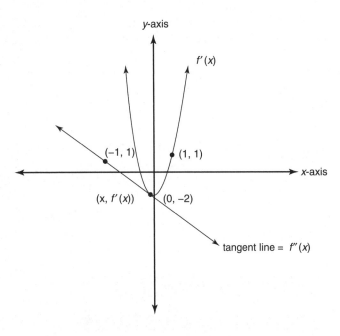

Figure 10.15

EXAMPLE 33

If $y = x^4 - 6x + 2$, what is the simplified expression for $\dfrac{d^2 y}{dx^2}$?

SOLUTION

First, $\dfrac{dy}{dx} = 4x^3 - 6$. Thus, $\dfrac{d^2 y}{dx^2} = 12x^2$.

EXAMPLE 34

If $f(x) = (x)(4^x)$, what is the simplified expression for $\dfrac{d^2 y}{dx^2}$?

SOLUTION

$f'(x) = (x)(4^x)(\ln 4) + (4^x)(1) = (4^x)(x \ln 4 + 1)$. Now we repeat the process of taking a derivative. Be aware that the derivative of $x \ln 4$ is just $\ln 4$. Using rule 7 again, we get $f''(x) = (4^x)(\ln 4) + (x \ln 4 + 1)(4^x)(\ln 4) = (4^x \ln 4)(2 + x \ln 4)$.

EXAMPLE 35

If $y = x^4 + 5x^3 + 8$, what is the value of $\dfrac{d^2 y}{dx^2}$ at $x = -2$?

SOLUTION

We find $\dfrac{dy}{dx} = 4x^3 + 15x^2$, followed by $\dfrac{d^2 y}{dx^2} = 12x^2 + 30x$. Thus, at $x = -2$,

$\dfrac{d^2 y}{dx^2} = 12(-2)^2 + 30(-2) = -12$.

EXAMPLE 36

If $f(x) = \tan 2x$, what is the value of $f''(x)$ at $x = \dfrac{\pi}{4}$ radians?

SOLUTION

First, $f'(x) = 2 \sec^2 x = 2(\sec x)^2$. Then $f''(x) = (4)(\sec x)(\sec x)(\tan x)$ or $(4)(\sec^2 x)(\tan x)$.

Thus, at $x = \dfrac{\pi}{4}$ radians, $f''\left(\dfrac{\pi}{4}\right) = (4)\left(\sec^2 \dfrac{\pi}{4}\right)\left(\tan \dfrac{\pi}{4}\right)$

$= (4)(\sqrt{2})^2(1) = 8$.

Applications of First and Second Derivatives to a Graph

Our next objective is to analyze the graphs of continuous functions, as well as their first and second derivatives. All our functions will also be continuous for all values in the domain of x.

Figure 10.16 shown below illustrates a general continuous function $y = k(x)$ over the closed interval $[a, f]$. Note that $k'(x)$ exists at every point in the open interval (a, f) except at $(d, k(d))$, since we cannot draw a single tangent line to the curve at this point. Remember, *only a one-sided limit is possible at an endpoint.*

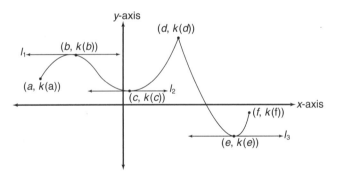

Figure 10.16

Critical Points on a Graph

We need some definitions for the six points of the graph that have been identified with coordinates, and some observations about the three horizontal lines.

The function has an **absolute maximum** value of $k(d)$, which occurs when $x = d$. The function has an **absolute minimum** value of $k(e)$, which occurs when

$x = e$. The function has a **local maximum** value of $k(b)$, which occurs when $x = b$. A local maximum value means that the point has the largest function value, but only within a specific neighborhood of this point.

The function has a **local minimum** value of $k(e)$, which occurs when $x = e$. A local minimum value means that the point has the smallest function value, but only within a specific neighborhood of this point.

A **critical point** on the graph is one that lies in the open interval (a, f) for which its derivative is either zero or undefined. Each of the four points $(b, k(b))$, $(c, k(c))$, $(d, k(d))$, and $(e, k(e))$ are critical points for this function.

The lines l_1, l_2, and l_3, each of which has **a slope of zero**, are tangent to $(b, k(b))$, $(c, k(c))$, and $(e, k(e))$, respectively. *This implies that given a point on the graph of a continuous function for which the first derivative is zero, this point represents either a **maximum** or **minimum** point.* Be careful that you do <u>not</u> accept the converse of this statement as being always true! The point $(d, k(d))$ is an absolute maximum point, but $k'(d)$ does not exist. The reason is more than one tangent line can be drawn at $(d, k(d))$.

EXAMPLE 37

What are the critical points for the graph of $f(x) = 4x^2 - 16x + 1$?

SOLUTION

We need to find $f'(x)$ and equate it to zero. So, $f'(x) = 8x - 16 = 0$. Then, $x = 2$. Thus, the critical point is $(2, f(2)) = (2, -15)$.

EXAMPLE 38

What are the critical points for the graph of $g(x) = -x^3 + x^2 + 5x$?

SOLUTION

We write $g'(x) = -3x^2 + 2x + 5 = 0$. Rewriting this equation as $3x^2 - 2x - 5 = 0$, we can factor to get $(3x - 5)(x + 1) = 0$. Then $x = \frac{5}{3}$ or $x = -1$. Thus, the critical points are $\left(\frac{5}{3}, g\left(\frac{5}{3}\right)\right) = \left(\frac{5}{3}, \frac{175}{27}\right)$ and $(-1, g(-1)) = (-1, -3)$.

NOTE:

> This procedure does not reveal whether the critical points are maximum or minimum. The physical graph of each function will definitely reveal this information. However, we will develop an algebraic method for determining whether a given critical point represents a maximum or minimum function value.

Let's redraw Figure 10.16, calling it Figure 10.17, and replace the lines l_1, l_2, and l_3, with lines, l_4, l_5, and l_6 (Some points are not identified in order to avoid congestion in the figure.)

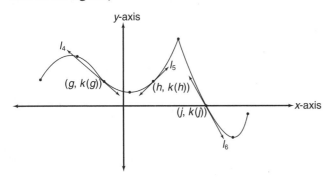

Figure 10.17

Line l_4 is tangent to the graph at $x = g$, line l_5 is tangent to the graph at $x = h$, and line l_6 is tangent to the graph at $x = j$.

We note that the point $(g, k(g))$ lies on a portion of the graph where the value of $k(x)$ is decreasing from $k(b)$ to $k(c)$. Also, the slope of l_4 is negative.

Likewise, the point $(h, k(h))$ lies on a portion of the graph where the value of $k(x)$ is increasing from $k(c)$ to $k(d)$. Thus, the slope of l_5 is positive.

In a similar fashion, $(j, k(j))$ lies on a portion of the graph where the value of $k(x)$ is decreasing from $k(d)$ to $k(e)$. Thus, the slope of l_6 is negative.

We can draw some conclusions from these observations about any continuous function $f(x)$ for which $(x_1, f(x_1))$ and $(x_2, f(x_2))$ are any two consecutive critical values in the domain, with $x_1 < x_2$.

1. If $f(x_1) < f(x_2)$ then the slope of the tangent line is positive for any point $(p, f(p))$, where $x_1 < p < x_2$. Also, $f(x_1) < f(p) < f(x_2)$.

2. $f(x_1) > f(x_2)$, then the slope of the tangent line is negative for any point $(q, f(q))$, where $x_1 < q < x_2$. Also, $f(x_1) > f(q) > f(x_2)$.

3. As the x value increases, if the slope of the tangent line changes from positive to zero to negative, the point at which the slope is zero is an absolute (or local) maximum point.

4. As the x value increases, if the slope of the tangent line changes from negative to zero to positive, the point at which the slope is zero is an absolute (or local) minimum point.

EXAMPLE 39

> Using the slopes of tangent lines for the graph for Example 37, determine if the critical point $(2, -15)$ is a maximum or minimum point.

SOLUTION

Since $(2, -15)$ is the only critical point, let's select two x values, one less than 2 and one greater than 2. Using x values of 1 and 3, we note that $f'(1) = -8$ and $f'(3) = 8$. Since the slope of the tangent line changed from negative to positive, $(2, -15)$ is a minimum point.

EXAMPLE 40

> Using the slopes of tangent lines for the graph for Example 38, determine if the critical points $\left(\frac{5}{3}, \frac{175}{27}\right)$ and $(-1, -3)$ are maximum or minimum points.

SOLUTION

We'll start with the point $\left(\dfrac{5}{3}, \dfrac{175}{27}\right)$. We select two x values, one less than $\dfrac{5}{3}$ and one greater than $\dfrac{5}{3}$. Using the values of 1 and 2, we note that $g'(1) = 4$ and $g'(2) = -3$. Since the slope of the tangent line changed from positive to negative, $\left(\dfrac{5}{3}, \dfrac{175}{27}\right)$ is a maximum point. Now for the point $(-1, -3)$, we can use x values of -2 and 0. We find that $g'(-2) = -11$ and $g'(0) = 5$. The slope of the tangent line changed from negative to positive, so $(-1, -3)$ is a minimum point.

As a quick review, the average rate of change is the slope of the line segment that connects endpoints $(a, f(a))$ and $(b, f(b))$ for a continuous function $f(x)$ on the closed interval $[a, b]$. Its value is $\dfrac{f(b) - f(a)}{b - a}$.

Mean Value Theorem

Closely related to the average rate of change is the **Mean Value Theorem**. Using a continuous function $f(x)$ on a closed interval $[a,b]$, this theorem states that there is at least one value c, where $a < c < b$, such that $f'(c) = \dfrac{f(b) - f(a)}{b - a}$. This means that there is at least one point in the open interval (a, b) for which the instantaneous rate of change (slope of the tangent line) equals the average rate of change of $f(x)$ over $[a, b]$. Figure 10.18 shown below illustrates this theorem.

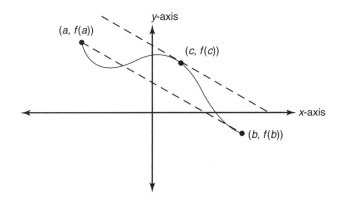

Figure 10.18

EXAMPLE 41

Returning to Example 11, determine a value of c in the open interval $(1, 6)$ for which $g'(c)$ equals the average rate of change for $g(x) = -x^3 + 4$ over the closed interval $[1, 6]$.

SOLUTION

We already know that the average rate of change is -43. Since $g'(x) = -3x^2$, we can write $g'(c) = -3c^2 = -43$. Thus, $c = \pm\sqrt{\dfrac{43}{3}} \approx \pm 3.79$, but the only answer in $(1, 6)$ is $+3.79$.

EXAMPLE 42

Returning to Example 14, determine a value of c in the open interval $(2, 2.1)$ for which $f'(c)$ equals the average rate of change for $f(x) = 2x^2 + 5$ over the closed interval $[2, 2.1]$.

SOLUTION

We found the average rate of change to be 8.2. Since $f'(x) = 4x$, we can write $f'(c) = 4c = 8.2$. Thus, c = 2.05.

EXAMPLE 43

Given $h(x) = 2x^3 + 1$ over the closed interval $[-3, 3]$, find a value of c in the open interval $(-3, 3)$ such that the slope of the tangent line at c equals the average rate of change of $h(x)$ over $[-3, 3]$.

SOLUTION

$h(3) = 55$ and $h(-3) = -53$ so the average rate of change is $\dfrac{55 - (-53)}{3 - (-3)} = 18$. Then $h'(c) = 6c^2 = 18$.

Thus $c = \pm\sqrt{3} \approx \pm 1.73$. In Example 43, there are two c values. The Mean Value Theorem only guarantees at least one value of c.

We now return to a more thorough discussion of the second derivative of a function. You recall that the second derivative of $y = f(x)$, denoted as $f''(x)$ or d^2y/dx^2, indicates the instantaneous rate of change of $f'(x)$.

Let's start with $f(x) = 3x$, which is simply the graph of a line with a slope of 3. We find that $f'(x) = 3$, which just confirms that the instantaneous rate of change at any point is 3. Now $f''(x) = 0$, which means that there is no change in the first derivative. This is no surprise because the slope of any line is constant.

Now suppose that $g(x) = x^2 - x$. If we want to determine the values of x for which the tangent line has a positive slope, we only need to solve $g'(x) = 2x - 1 > 0$. This leads to $x > \dfrac{1}{2}$, which means that the tangent line has a positive slope for all x values greater than $\dfrac{1}{2}$. With a similar argument, we can show that the tangent line has a negative slope for $x < \dfrac{1}{2}$. Also, since $g'\left(\dfrac{1}{2}\right) = 2\left(\dfrac{1}{2}\right) - 1 = 0$, we know that a critical point exists for $x = \dfrac{1}{2}$.

Figure 10.19 shown below is the graph of $g(x) = x^2 - x$.

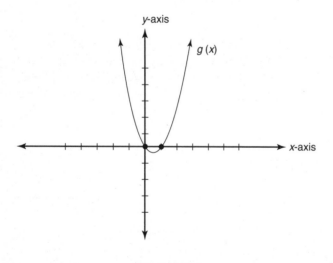

Figure 10.19

The graph immediately tells us that if we were to choose a point whose x value is less than $\dfrac{1}{2}$, the slope of the tangent line would be negative. By choosing a value of x greater than $\dfrac{1}{2}$, the tangent line has a positive slope.

To understand the second derivative, denoted as $g''(x)$, let's consider any two values of x. For $x = -3$, $g'(-3) = (2)(-3) - 1 = -7$; for $x = 0$, $g'(0) = -1$. Now bearing in mind that the second derivative measures the <u>change</u> in the first derivative, we can see that $g'(0)$ is actually greater than $g'(-3)$. So, as x increases by three units, from -3 to 0, $g'(x)$ increases six units, from -7 to -1. This implies that for $x = -3$, $g'(x)$ is actually positive. In fact, since $g'(x) = 2x - 1$, it follows that $g''(x) = 2$. This statement tells us that for $g(x) = x^2 - x$, the second derivative is always the positive number 2.

Concavity of a Function

We know that the first derivative measures the slope of a function. The second derivative measures the change in the slope, which is also known as the **concavity** of the function.

If $g''(x) > 0$ on an interval, then $g(x)$ is said to be **concave upward**.

If $g''(x) < 0$ on an interval, then $g(x)$ is said to be **concave downward**.

Graphically, Figures 10.20, 10.21, 10.22, and 10.23 show four different cases that highlight the appearance of a function when the first derivative is positive or negative, along with the second derivative being positive or negative.

In Figure 10.20, the function is increasing and is concave upward.

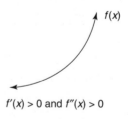

$f'(x) > 0$ and $f''(x) > 0$

Figure 10.20

In Figure 10.21, the function is increasing and is concave downward.

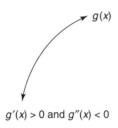

$g'(x) > 0$ and $g''(x) < 0$

Figure 10.21

In Figure 10.22, the function is decreasing and is concave upward.

$h'(x) < 0$ and $h''(x) > 0$

Figure 10.22

In Figure 10.23, the function is decreasing and is concave downward.

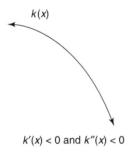

$k'(x) < 0$ and $k''(x) < 0$

Figure 10.23

NOTE:

These four cases are not dependent on whether the function itself is positive or negative. For that reason, the coordinate axes were not drawn.

Points of Inflection

If $g''(x) = 0$ on an interval, the associated points of $g(x)$ are called **points of inflection.** These are points at which the first derivative changes sign from negative to positive or positive to negative. In Figure 10.24 shown below, each of points P and Q are inflection points for the graph of $g(x)$.

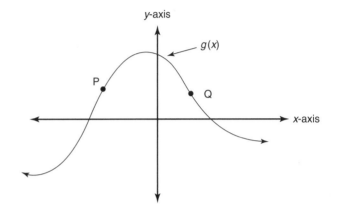

Figure 10.24

EXAMPLE 44

Given the function $f(x) = x^3 - 4x^2 + 5$, on which interval(s) is $f(x)$ concave downward?

SOLUTION

In order for $f(x)$ to be concave downward, $f''(x)$ must be negative. Now $f'(x) = 3x^2 - 8x$ and $f''(x) = 6x - 8$. Then $6x - 8 < 0$ means that $x < \dfrac{4}{3}$. Thus, the desired interval is the open interval $\left(-\infty, \dfrac{4}{3}\right)$.

By determining $f\left(\dfrac{4}{3}\right) = \left(\dfrac{4}{3}\right)^3 - 4\left(\dfrac{4}{3}\right)^2 + 5 = \dfrac{7}{27}$, we find the actual point of inflection is $\left(\dfrac{4}{3}, \dfrac{7}{27}\right)$.

The graph of $f(x) = x^3 - 4x^2 + 5$, shown below in Figure 10.25, will further clarify the concept of concavity. (Notice that for $x > \dfrac{4}{3}$, $f(x)$ is concave upward.)

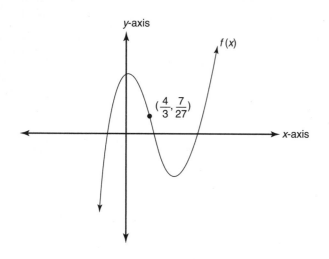

Figure 10.25

EXAMPLE 45

> Given the function $g(x) = 2x^3 - 9x^2 + 12x - 3$, on which interval(s) is $g(x)$ both decreasing and concave upward?

SOLUTION

We are looking for values of x for which $g'(x) < 0$ and $g''(x) > 0$. We find that $g'(x) = 6x^2 - 18x + 12$ and $g''(x) = 12x - 18$. To solve $6x^2 - 18x + 12 < 0$, divide by 6 and factor the left side to yield $(x - 2)(x - 1) < 0$. The solution for this inequality is $1 < x < 2$. Now we solve $12x - 18 > 0$ to get $x > \dfrac{3}{2}$. The solution to the two inequalities $1 < x < 2$ and $x > \dfrac{3}{2}$ is the single inequality $\dfrac{3}{2} < x < 2$. Thus, the desired interval is the open interval $\left[\dfrac{3}{2}, 2 \right]$.

The graph of $g(x) = 2x^3 - 9x^2 + 12x - 3$ is shown below in Figure 10.26.

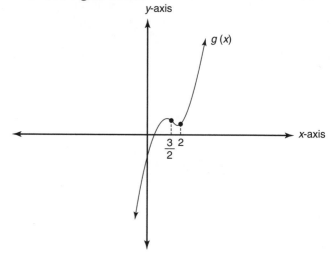

Figure 10.26

Earlier in this chapter, we learned that by solving $f'(x) = 0$, we could find the critical values of $f(x)$. To determine if a given critical value was a minimum or maximum, our best available method was to check $f'(x)$ near these critical values. This was done in Examples 38 and 39. The good news is that we can use the first and second derivatives to find out if a critical value represents a minimum or maximum point on the graph.

The Second Derivative Test

The **Second Derivative Test** for minimum and maximum values of a function is as follows. Suppose the domain of $f(x)$ is the closed interval $[a, b]$. Let $x = c$ represent a point on the open interval (a, b). These are the guidelines to follow:

If $f'(c) = 0$ and $f''(c) > 0$, then $f(c)$ represents a local minimum value.

If $f'(c) = 0$ and $f''(c) < 0$, then $f(c)$ represents a local maximum value.

If both $f'(c) = 0$ and $f''(c) = 0$, then no conclusion can be drawn.

EXAMPLE 46

> If $f(x) = x^3 - 4x^2 + 5$, what are the x-coordinates of the maximum and/or minimum points?

SOLUTION

You have already seen this function in Example 44. We set $f'(x) = 3x^2 - 8x = 0$. Then $(x)(3x - 8) = 0$, so the critical points have x-coordinates of 0 and $\frac{8}{3}$. The next step is $f''(x) = 6x - 8$. Then $f''(0) = -8$, so $x = 0$ must represent a local maximum value. Also, $f''\left(\frac{8}{3}\right) = 8$, so $x = \frac{8}{3}$ must be represent a local minimum value. (Figure 10.25 will verify these conclusions.)

EXAMPLE 47

If $g(x) = 2x^3 - 9x^2 + 12x - 3$, what are the x-coordinates of the maximum and/or minimum points?

SOLUTION

You are not imagining things! This function was presented in Example 45. We have already determined that $g'(x) = 6x^2 - 18x + 12$ and $g''(x) = 12x - 18$. To solve $6x^2 - 18x + 12 = 0$, we factor to get $(6)(x - 2)(x - 1) = 0$. Then $x = 2$ or $x = 1$. Now, $f''(2) = 6$, which means that $x = 2$ must represent a local minimum point. Similarly, $f''(1) = -6$, which means that $x = 1$ must represent a local maximum point. (Figure 10.26 will verify these conclusions.)

Word Problem Applications

Linear Motion

Linear motion is motion in a straight line. Let $x(t)$ represent the position of a particle that moves along the x-axis at a given time t. The particle is moving from time $t = a$ to time $t = b$, which may be represented as the time interval $[a, b]$. The **displacement** is then given by $\Delta x = x(b) - x(a)$. For this same time interval, the **average velocity** is given by $\frac{\Delta x}{\Delta t} = \frac{x(b) - x(a)}{b - a}$.

The **instantaneous velocity** is the limit of the average velocity. As such, the instantaneous velocity is given by $\lim_{\Delta t \to 0} \frac{\Delta x}{\Delta t} = \frac{dx}{dt}$. Furthermore, if we let $v(t)$ represent the velocity of this particle at any time t in the interval $[a, b]$, and let $\Delta v = v(b) - v(a)$ represent the corresponding change in velocity, the **average acceleration** is given by $\frac{\Delta v}{\Delta t} = \frac{v(b) - v(a)}{b - a}$. Then the **acceleration** at time t is given by $\lim_{b \to a} \frac{v(b) - v(a)}{b - a} = \lim_{\Delta t \to 0} \frac{\Delta v}{\Delta t} = \frac{dv}{dt}$.

The analogy between the concepts presented here and those for the derivatives should seem very logical. Let $v(t)$ represent the velocity of a particle at any time t and let $a(t)$ represent the acceleration of this particle at any time t. Then if $x(t)$ represents a function $f(x)$, then $v(t)$ would represent $f'(x)$ and $a(t)$ would represent $f''(x)$.

For Examples 48 − 51, use the following information.

The position of a particle moving along the x-axis is defined as follows:

$$x(t) = \frac{1}{3}t^3 + 7t^2 - 3t \text{ for } 3 \leq t \leq 9,$$

where t represents time. If necessary, use the graphing feature on your calculator in which y represents $x(t)$ and x represents t.

EXAMPLE 48

What is the average velocity over the time period from $t = 1$ to $t = 9$?

SOLUTION

Since $x(3) = 63$ and $x(9) = 783$, the average velocity is $\frac{783 - 63}{9 - 3} = 120$.

EXAMPLE 49

What is the instantaneous velocity at $t = 5$?

SOLUTION

The instantaneous velocity is $v(t) = \dfrac{dx}{dt} = t^2 + 14t - 3$, so $v(5) = 92$.

EXAMPLE 50

> What is the average acceleration between $t = 2$ and $t = 6$?

SOLUTION

Since $v(2) = 29$ and $v(6) = 117$, the average acceleration is $\dfrac{117 - 29}{6 - 2} = 22$.

EXAMPLE 51

> What is the acceleration at $t = 3$?

SOLUTION

The acceleration is given by $a(t) = \dfrac{dv}{dt} = 2t + 14$. Thus, $a(3) = 20$.

Optimization

Optimization focuses on maximizing or minimizing a particular quantity, so we will use the first derivative of an appropriate function. In doing this type of problem, sometimes a diagram is needed as an aid.

EXAMPLE 52

> Consider the triangular region bounded by the positive x-axis, the positive y-axis and the line whose equation is $y = 5 - 2x$. A rectangle will be placed inside this region so that one vertex lies at the origin and its opposite vertex lies on the line. What is the largest possible area for this rectangle?

SOLUTION

Below is a diagram that is absolutely imperative.

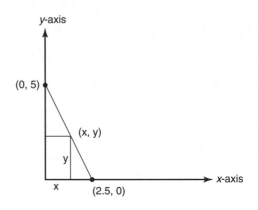

Using x as the width, y as the height, and A as the area, the formula to use is $A = xy$. Since $y = 5 - 2x$, we can write the area formula as $A = x(5 - 2x) = 5x - 2x^2$. The maximum value of A can be found by using the equation $\dfrac{dA}{dx} = 0$. So, $5 - 4x = 0$, which leads to $x = \dfrac{5}{4}$. Then $y = 5 - (2)\left[\dfrac{5}{4}\right] = \dfrac{5}{2}$. Thus, the required area is $\left[\dfrac{5}{4}\right]\left[\dfrac{5}{2}\right] = \dfrac{25}{8}$.

EXAMPLE 53

> In the ABC company, the cost (C) to manufacture x file cabinets each day is given by the equation $C = x^3 - 33x^2 + 336x + 100$. How many file cabinets per day should the ABC company manufacture in order to minimize its cost?

SOLUTION

We need to find the first derivative $\dfrac{dC}{dx}$, which is $3x^2 - 66x + 336$. Then we solve $3x^2 - 66x + 336 = 0$ by dividing each side by 3 and factoring. The equation becomes $(x - 14)(x - 8) = 0$. We have the answers of 14 and 8, but we need to check if these answers represent maximum or minimum values. Using the Second Derivative method, $\dfrac{d^2C}{dx^2} = 6x - 66$.

When $x = 14, \dfrac{d^2C}{dx^2} = 18$. Since $\dfrac{d^2C}{dx^2} > 0$, the value

of 14 represents a minimum cost. However, when $x = 8, \dfrac{d^2C}{dx^2} = -18$. Since $\dfrac{d^2C}{dx^2} < 0$, the value of 8 would represent a maximum cost. The only answer is $x = 14$.

Related Rates

Related rates utilize the Chain rule as applied to three different variables. As a general example, if z is related to y and y is related to x, then z is related to x by the following using first derivatives:

$$\frac{dz}{dx} = \left(\frac{dz}{dy}\right)\left(\frac{dy}{dx}\right).$$

EXAMPLE 54

Air is blown into a spherical balloon at the rate of 4 cubic inches per minute. At what rate is the radius changing at the instant that the radius is 3 inches? (The formula for the volume of a sphere is $V = \dfrac{4}{3}\pi r^3$.)

SOLUTION
The Chain rule allows us to use. $\dfrac{dV}{dt} = \left[\dfrac{dV}{dr}\right]\left[\dfrac{dr}{dt}\right]$

Now $\dfrac{dV}{dr} = 4\pi r^2$. So, when $r = 3$, $\dfrac{dV}{dr} = 4\pi(3)^2 = 36\pi$.

Since $\dfrac{dV}{dt} = 4$, we have $4 = (36\pi)\left[\dfrac{dr}{dt}\right]$. Thus, $\dfrac{dr}{dt}$

$= \dfrac{4}{36\pi} = \dfrac{1}{9\pi}$ inches per minute.

Antiderivatives

Consider the following three statements:

1. If $f(x) = 3x^2$, then $f'(x) = 6x$.

2. If $g(x) = 3x^2 - 10$, then $g'(x) = 6x$

3. $h(x) = 3x^2 + 4$, then $h'(x) = 6x$.

Each of the given functions differs only by a constant and their derivatives are identical. Let $k(x) = 6x$. Then each of $f(x), g(x)$, and $h(x)$ is called an **antiderivative** of $k(x)$. Thus, a general function $F(x)$ is an antiderivative of $f(x)$ if $\dfrac{dF}{dx} = f(x)$. As hinted in the three numbered statements above, all antiderivatives of any function can differ only by a constant.

As the name implies, determining an antiderivative is the reverse process of finding a derivative. The symbol for finding an antiderivative is the integral symbol $\int$ with the symbol dx following the function. Thus, using statements 1, 2, and 3 above, we could write $\int 6x\,dx = 3x^2 + C$, where C is a constant.

The Most Popular Rules for Finding the Antiderivatives of Specific Types of Non-trigonometric Functions. (For each rule, C and K are constants.)

Rational Functions

Rule 1: $\int k\,dx = kx + C$

Rule 2: $\int kx^n\,dx = \dfrac{k}{n+1}x^{n+1} + C$, provided that $n \neq -1$.

Rule 3: $\int kx^{-1}\,dx = k\ln x + C$

Rule 4: $\int ke^x\,dx = ke^x + C$

Rule 5: $\int ka^x\,dx = \dfrac{ka^x}{\ln a} + C$

Rule 6: $\int [f(x) \pm g(x)]\,dx = \int f(x)\,dx$
$$\pm \int g(x)\,dx + C$$

EXAMPLE 55

$$\int (5x + 3x^2)dx \text{ is equivalent to which function?}$$

SOLUTION

Writing $5x$ as $5x^1$ and using Rules 2 and 6, the answer is $\frac{5}{2}x^2 + x^3 + C$. Note that "C" is only needed once.

EXAMPLE 56

$$\int \left[9 - \frac{7}{x}\right] dx \text{ is equivalent to which function?}$$

SOLUTION

Writing $\frac{7}{x}$ as $7x^{-1}$ and using Rules 1, 3, and 6, the answer is $9x - 7\ln x + C$.

EXAMPLE 57

$$\int \left[8^x + \frac{3}{4}x^4\right] dx \text{ is equivalent to which function?}$$

SOLUTION

Using Rules 2, 5, and 6, the answer is $\frac{8^x}{\ln 8} + \frac{3}{20}x^5 + C$.

NOTE:

If you are a little confused about the number $\frac{3}{20}$, it was obtained by dividing $\frac{3}{4}$ by 5, which becomes $\left[\frac{3}{4}\right]\left[\frac{1}{5}\right]$.

Trigonometric Functions

Since we learned the derivatives of the six trigonometric formulas, it would be worthwhile to recognize the following antiderivatives:

<u>Rule 7:</u> $\int (k\sin x)dx = -k\cos x + C$

<u>Rule 8:</u> $\int (k\cos x)dx = k\sin x + C$

<u>Rule 9:</u> $\int (k\tan x)dx = -k\ln(\cos x) + C$

<u>Rule 10:</u> $\int (k\cot x)dx = k\ln(\sin x) + C$

There are other antiderivative formulas, both for algebraic functions and trigonometric functions, but they are beyond the scope of this book.

EXAMPLE 58

$$\int \frac{1}{2}\cos x dx \text{ is equivalent to which function?}$$

SOLUTION

Using Rule 8, the answer is $\frac{1}{2}\sin x + C$.

EXAMPLE 59

$$\int (4\cot x + \tan x)dx \text{ is equivalent to which function?}$$

SOLUTION

Using Rules 6, 9, and 10, the answer is $4\ln(sin\ x) - \ln(cos\ x) + C$.

Definite Integral

Suppose that $f(x)$ is a continuous function on the closed interval $[a, b]$. Let us subdivide [a,b] into n rectangles, each of width Δx. We'll label these subintervals as $[x_0, x_1]$, $[x_1, x_2]$, $[x_2, x_3]$,....$[x_{n-1}, x_n]$. With this notation, $\Delta x = x_i - x_{i-1}$. Also, note that $x_0 = a$ and $x_n = b$.

Furthermore, within each interval $[x_{i-1}, x_i]$, select some value, and call it w_i. Now draw each of the n rectangles with a width of Δx and a height of w_i. Figure 10.27 shown below illustrates $f(x)$ and the construction of the rectangles.

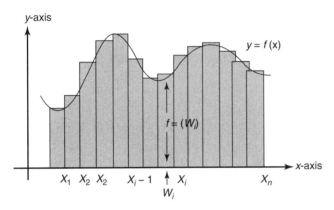

Figure 10.27

The **definite integral** of $f(x)$ on $[a, b]$, written as $\int_a^b f(x)dx$, is defined as $\lim_{n\to\infty} \sum_{i=1}^n f(w_i)(\Delta x)$. This implies that $\int_a^b f(x)dx$ represents the actual area enclosed by the x-axis, the vertical lines $x = a$ and $x = b$, and $f(x)$. Notice that in Figure 10.27, $f(x)$ lies entirely above the x-axis.

If any part of $f(x)$ ever lies below the x-axis on a specific interval [c, d], then $\int_c^d f(x)dx$ would be negative. To find its area, the quantity $-\int_c^d f(x)dx$, which is $F(c) - F(d)$, would be calculated. The reason is that area is always a non-negative quantity. Look at Figure 10.28 shown below, in which $f(x)$ assumes negative values in [c, d].

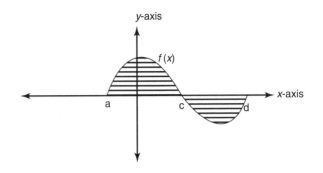

Figure 10.28

The total *shaded area* becomes $\int_a^c f(x)dx$
$$- \int_c^d f(x)dx = F(c) - F(a) - F(d) + F(c).$$

The value of the *integral*, however, would be
$$\int_a^d f(x)dx = F(d) - F(a).$$

Fundamental Theorem of Calculus

One part of the **Fundamental Theorem of Calculus** states that if $F(x)$ is any antiderivative of $f(x)$, where $f(x)$ is continuous on the closed interval $[a, b]$, then $\int_a^b f(x)dx = F(b) - F(a)$. For practical purposes, we use the specific antiderivative in which the constant is zero. For example, if $f(x) = x^2$, then $F(x) = \frac{1}{3}x^3$.

EXAMPLE 60

What is the value of $\int_0^4 (x^2 + 3)dx$?

SOLUTION

Here is the associated diagram.

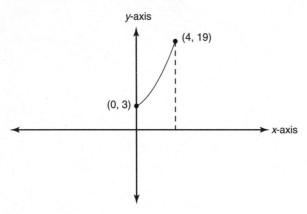

$$\int_0^4 (x^2+3)dx = \left(\frac{1}{3}x^3+3x\right)\Big|_0^4$$

$$= \left(\frac{64}{3}+12\right)-(0+0)=\frac{100}{3}.$$

NOTE:

> This is also the area bounded by the function, x-axis, y-axis, and $x=4$.

EXAMPLE 61

> What is the value of $\int_{\pi/2}^{2\pi} \sin x\, dx$?

SOLUTION

This is the associated diagram.

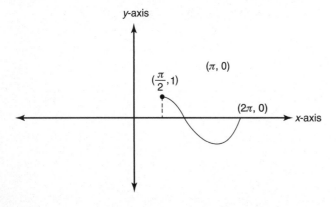

$$\int_{\pi/2}^{2\pi} \sin x\, dx = -\cos x \Big|_{\pi/2}^{2\pi}$$

$$= -\cos(2\pi)-\left(-\cos\frac{\pi}{2}\right)=-1.$$

NOTE:

> This is <u>not</u> the total area between the function and the x-axis.

EXAMPLE 62

> What is the area of the region bounded by the function $f(x)=\frac{5}{x}$, the x-axis, the line $x=1$, and the line $x=6$?

SOLUTION

This is the associated diagram, with the region shaded.

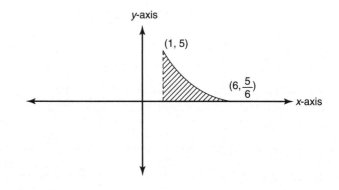

NOTE:

> $f(x)>0$ for the interval $[1,6]$. So, we are looking for the value of $\int_1^6 \frac{5}{x}\,dx$, which becomes $(5)(\ln x)\Big|_1^6 = (5)(\ln 6)-5(\ln 1)\approx 8.96$.

EXAMPLE 63

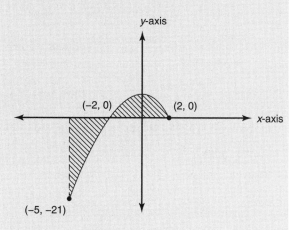

The diagram below describes the function $f(x) = -x^2 + 4$.

What is the combined area of the shaded regions?

NOTE:

If the problem had simply asked for the value of the definite integral $\int\limits_{-5}^{2} (-x^2 + 4)dx$, our answer would have been quite different. The computation would appear as $\left[-\frac{1}{3}x^3 + 4x \right] \Bigg|_{-5}^{2}$

$= \left[-\frac{8}{3} + 8 \right] - \left[\frac{125}{3} - 20 \right] = -16\frac{1}{3}$.

SOLUTION

The region bounded by the function, the x-axis, and the line $x = -5$ lies below the x-axis, so

its area is $-\int\limits_{-5}^{-2} (-x^2 + 4)dx = -\left(-\frac{1}{3}x^3 + 4x \right) \Bigg|_{-5}^{-2}$

$= -\left[\left(\frac{8}{3} - 8 \right) - \left(\frac{125}{3} - 20 \right) \right] = 27$. The area of the

region bounded by the function and the x-axis that lies between $x = -2$ and $x = 2$ is found by evaluat-

ing $\int\limits_{-2}^{2} (-x^2 + 4)dx$, which becomes $\left(-\frac{1}{3}x^3 + 4x \right) \Bigg|_{-2}^{2} =$

$\left[-\frac{8}{3} + 8 \right] - \left[\frac{8}{3} - 8 \right] = \frac{32}{3} = 10\frac{2}{3}$. Thus, the final answer

is $37\frac{2}{3}$.

Quiz for Chapter 10

1. What is the value of $\lim_{x \to 3} \dfrac{4x - 12}{x^3 - 27}$?

(A) $\dfrac{8}{27}$ (C) $\dfrac{3}{27}$

(B) $\dfrac{4}{27}$ (D) 0

2. Consider the following graph of $g(x)$.

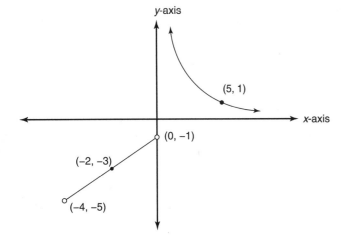

Which one of the following statements is <u>completely</u> correct?

(A) $\lim_{x \to 0^-} g(x)$ exists and $\lim_{x \to 0^+} g(x)$ does not exist.

(B) $\lim_{x \to -4} g(x)$ exists and $g(x)$ is continuous at $x = 5$.

(C) $\lim_{x \to -2} g(x) = -3$ and $g(x)$ is continuous at $x = 0$.

(D) $\lim_{x \to 0^+} g(x) = -1$ and the domain of $g(x)$ is all real numbers greater than -4.

3. If $\dfrac{6x^8 - 2x^2 + 3}{2x^n - 5x + 2}$ is in reduced form and $\lim_{x \to \infty} \dfrac{6x^8 - 2x^2 + 3}{2x^n - 5x + 2} = \infty$, then which one of the following is true concerning the value of n?

(A) $n > 8$ (C) $n > 3$

(B) $n < 8$ (D) $n < 3$

4. Consider the following graph of $h(x)$.

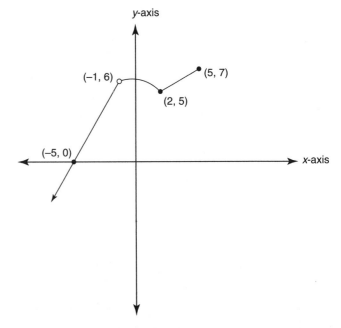

At which point(s) is $h(x)$ <u>not</u> continuous?

(A) Only at $(-1, 6)$

(B) Only at $(5, 7)$

(C) At both $(-1, 6)$ and $(5, 7)$

(D) At both $(-5, 0)$ and $(2, 5)$

5. Which one of the following must have discontinuities at $x = -2$, $x = 1$, and $x = -3$?

    (A) $f(x) = \dfrac{2x - 3}{(x - 2)(x + 1)(x - 3)}$

    (B) $g(x) = \dfrac{(x + 2)(x - 1)(x + 3)}{x + 4}$

    (C) $h(x) = \dfrac{3x + 5}{(x + 2)(x - 1)(x + 3)}$

    (D) $k(x) = \dfrac{(x - 2)(x + 1)(x - 3)}{x - 5}$

6. Let $f(x) = x^3 - x^2 + 1$. Consider the closed interval $[2, 4]$. The Intermediate Value Theorem would guarantee which of the following?

    (A) There is at least one c value, where $2 < c < 4$ such that $f(c) < 5$ or $f(c) > 49$.

    (B) There is no c value, where $2 < c < 4$, such that $f(c) > 49$ or $f(c) < 5$.

    (C) There is at least one c value, where $5 < c < 49$, such that $2 < f(c) < 4$.

    (D) There is at least one c value, where $2 < c < 4$, such that $5 < f(c) < 49$.

7. What is the average rate of change for $k(x) = x^3 + x - 2$ over the interval $[-1, 4]$?

    (A) 14   (C) $23\dfrac{1}{3}$

    (B) 18   (D) $27\dfrac{2}{3}$

8. For the function $g(x) = -4x^2 + 3$, what is the equation of the tangent line at $x = 2$?

    (A) $y = -16x + 45$ (C) $y = -16x + 19$

    (B) $y = -8x + 3$ (D) $y = -8x + 29$

9. If $y = x^5 - 6x^3 + 4$, what is the value of $\dfrac{dy}{dx}$ at $x = -1$?

    (A) -19 (C) -9

    (B) -13 (D) -3

10. If $y = \dfrac{x - 2}{3x^2 + 2x + 1}$, which of the following is the simplified expression for $\dfrac{dy}{dx}$?

    (A) $\dfrac{-3x^2 + 12x + 5}{3x^2 + 2x + 1}$

    (B) $\dfrac{-3x^2 - 8x - 3}{(3x^2 + 2x + 1)^2}$

    (C) $\dfrac{-3x^2 - 8x - 3}{6x + 2}$

    (D) $\dfrac{-3x^2 + 12x + 5}{(3x^2 + 2x + 1)^2}$

11. If $y = (4 \sec x)(3^x)$, what is the simplified expression for $\dfrac{dy}{dx}$?

    (A) $[(3^x)(4 \sec x)][\ln 3 + \tan x]$

    (B) $[(3^x)(4 \tan x)][\ln 3 + \sec x]$

    (C) $[(3^x)(\tan x \sec x)][4 \ln 3 + \sec x]$

    (D) $[(3^x)(\tan x \sec x)][4 \ln 3 + \tan x]$

12. If $f(x) = e^{2 - 3x}$, what is the simplified expression for $f''(x)$?

    (A) $9e^{2 - 3x}$ (C) $-3e^{2 - 3x}$

    (B) $2e^{2 - 3x}$ (D) $-6e^{2 - 3x}$

13. Suppose that $h(x)$ is a continuous function with a domain of all reals and that $(6, -1)$ is its only critical point. Which one of the following sets of conditions implies that $(6, -1)$ represents a local minimum point?

    (A) $h'(-2) < 0$ and $h'(0) > 0$

    (B) $h'(5) > 0$ and $h'(7) < 0$

    (C) $h'(-2) > 0$ and $h'(0) < 0$

    (D) $h'(5) < 0$ and $h'(7) > 0$

14. In the interval [4, 9], the function $f(x)$ is concave downward. If $4 < c < 9$, which one of the following must be true?

(A) $f'(c) < 0$ (C) $f'(c) > 0$

(B) $f''(c) < 0$ (D) $f''(c) > 0$

15. For which value of c in the open interval (3, 5) does $g'(c)$ equal the average rate of change for $g(x) = 4x^3 - 2x + 5$ over the closed interval [3, 5]?

(A) 4.24   (C) 4.04

(B) 4.14   (D) 3.94

16. In the XYZ company, the cost to manufacture x tables each day is given by $C = x^3 - 39x^2 + 480x + 50$. How many tables each day should this company manufacture in order to minimize its cost?

(A) 16   (C) 10

(B) 13   (D) 8

17. The area inside a circle is being expanded at the rate of 10 square inches per minute. At what rate, in inches per minute, is the radius changing at the instant that the radius is 3 inches? (The area of a circle is given by $A = \pi r^2$)

(A) $\dfrac{10}{9\pi}$ (C) $\dfrac{5}{3\pi}$

(B) $\dfrac{5}{9\pi}$ (D) $\dfrac{10}{3\pi}$

18. $\int \left(\dfrac{12}{x} - \tan x \right) dx$ is equivalent to which of the following functions?

(A) $12(\ln x) - \ln(\cos x)$

(B) $-6x^2 - \ln(\sin x)$

(C) $-6x^2 + \ln(\sin x)$

(D) $12(\ln x) + \ln(\cos x)$

19. What is the value of $\int_1^4 (2x^2 + 5)dx$?

(A) 59   (C) $57\dfrac{2}{3}$

(B) $58\dfrac{1}{3}$ (D) 57

20. The diagram below describes the function $f(x) = -x^2 + 9$.

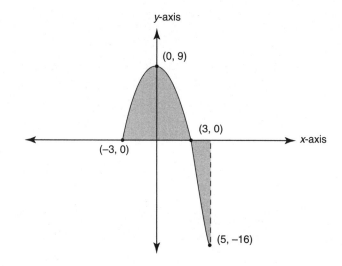

What is the combined area of the shaded regions?

(A) $62\dfrac{1}{3}$ (C) $34\dfrac{2}{3}$

(B) $50\dfrac{2}{3}$ (D) $21\dfrac{1}{3}$

Quiz for Chapter 10
SOLUTIONS

1. (B)

Rewrite the fraction as $\dfrac{4(x-3)}{(x-3)(x^2+3x+9)}$

$= \dfrac{4}{x^2+3x+9}$, provided that $x \neq 3$. By substitution,

$\dfrac{4}{3^2+(3)(3)+9} = \dfrac{4}{27}$.

2. (A)

$\lim_{x \to 0^-} g(x) = -1$, but the part of the graph of $g(x)$ that lies in the first quadrant shows that $\lim_{x \to 0^+} g(x)$ does not exist. In answer choice (B), the first part is wrong and the second part is correct. In answer choice (C), the first part is correct and the second part is wrong. In answer choice (D), both parts are wrong.

3. (B)

Given that $\dfrac{p(x)}{q(x)}$ is in reduced form, if the degree of $q(x)$ is less than the degree of $p(x)$, then $\lim_{x \to \infty} \dfrac{p(x)}{q(x)} = \infty$.

4. (C)

Since $h(x)$ is not defined at $(-1, 6)$, it is not continuous at that point. Also, the domain of $h(x)$ does not extend to any value greater than 5, so it is not continuous at $(5, 7)$.

5. (C)

For rational functions, the discontinuities occur at their vertical asymptote(s). For $h(x)$, these asymptotes are $x = -2$, $x = 1$, and $x = -3$.

6. (D)

$f(2) = 5$ and $f(4) = 49$. Since $f(x)$ is continuous over the closed interval $[2, 4]$, the Intermediate Value Theorem guarantees that there is at least one c value between 2 and 4 such that $f(c)$ lies between 5 and 49.

7. (A)

$k(-1) = -4$ and $k(4) = 66$. The average rate of change is $\dfrac{66-(-4)}{4-(-1)} = 14$.

8. (C)

$g'(x) = -8x$, so $g'(2) = -16$. Also, $g(2) = -4(2)^2 + 3 = -13$. Then $y - (-13) = -16(x-2)$, which simplifies to $y = -16x + 19$.

9. (B)

$\dfrac{dy}{dx} = 5x^4 - 18x^2$. Then for $x = -1, \dfrac{dy}{dx} 5(-1)^4 - 18(-1)^2 = -13$.

10. (D)

$\dfrac{dy}{dx} = \dfrac{(3x^2+2x+1)(1) - (x-2)(6x+2)}{(3x^2+2x+1)^2}$

$= \dfrac{3x^2+2x+1 - 6x^2+10x+4}{(3x^2+2x+1)^2}$

$= \dfrac{-3x^2+12x+5}{(3x^2+2x+1)^2}$.

11. (A)

Using the rule for the multiplication of two functions,

$$\frac{dy}{dx} = (4\sec x)(3^x)(\ln 3) + (3^x)(4\sec x)(\tan x)$$

$$= [(3^x)(4\sec x)][\ln 3 + \tan x].$$

12. (A)

$$f'(x) = (e^{2-3x})(-3) = -3e^{2-3x}, \text{so } f''(x) = (-3e^{2-3x})(-3) = 9e^{2-3x}.$$

13. (D)

Since $(6, -1)$ is the only critical point, it is a local minimum point if the first derivative changes from negative to positive. This means that if $x_1 < 6$, then $h'(x_1) < 0$. Also, if $x_2 > 6$, then $h'(x_2) > 0$.

14. (B)

If $f(x)$ is concave downward on a specific interval, then for any c value in that interval, $f''(c)$ must be negative. However, $f'(c)$ may be positive or negative, depending on whether $f(x)$ is increasing or decreasing, respectively.

15. (C)

The average rate of change over the interval [3, 5] is $\frac{g(5) - g(3)}{5 - 3} = \frac{495 - 107}{5 - 3} = 194$. By the Mean Value Theorem, there exists c, where $3 < c < 5$, such that $g'(c) = 194$. Then $12c^2 - 2 = 194$, so $c^2 = 16.3$. Thus, using only the positive square root value, $c \approx 4.04$.

16. (A)

$$\frac{dC}{dx} = 3x^2 - 78x + 480 = 0 \text{ to find the mini-}$$

mum (or maximum) points. Dividing by 3 and factoring leads to $(x - 16)(x - 10) = 0$. The two possible

answers are 16 and 10. Note that $\frac{d^2C}{dx^2} = 6x - 78$, so that when $x = 16$, $\frac{d^2C}{dx^2} = 18$; when $x = 10$, $\frac{d^2C}{dx^2} = -18$. Since we want the minimum cost, we choose $x = 16$ because $\frac{d^2C}{dx^2}$ is positive.

17. (C)

Use the formula $\frac{dA}{dt} = \left(\frac{dA}{dr}\right)\left(\frac{dr}{dt}\right)$. It is given that $\frac{dA}{dt} = 10$. Since $A = \pi r^2, \frac{dA}{dr} = 2\pi r$. When $r = 3$, $\frac{dA}{dr} = 6\pi$. Finally, $10 = (6\pi)\left(\frac{dr}{dt}\right)$, so $\frac{dr}{dt} = \frac{5}{3\pi}$.

18. (D)

$$\int \left(\frac{12}{x} - \tan x\right)dx = \int \frac{12}{x}dx - \int \tan x dx =$$

$$(12)(\ln x) - (-\ln(\cos x)) = (12)(\ln x) + \ln(\cos x).$$

19. (D)

$$\int_1^4 (2x^2 + 5)dx = \frac{2}{3}x^3 + 5x \Big|_1^4$$

$$= \left(\frac{128}{3} + 20\right) - \left(\frac{2}{3} + 5\right) = 57.$$

20. (B)

The combined area is

$$\int_{-3}^3 (-x^2 + 9)dx - \int_3^5 (-x^2 + 9)dx$$

$$= -\left(-\frac{1}{3}x^3 + 9x\right)\Big|_{-3}^3 \qquad -\left(-\frac{1}{3}x^3 + 9x\right)\Big|_3^5$$

$$= (-9 + 27) - (9 - 27) - \left[\left(-\frac{125}{3} + 45\right) - (-9 + 27)\right]$$

$$= 18 + 18 - \frac{10}{3} + 18 = 50\frac{2}{3}.$$

Measurement in Geometry

Welcome to Chapter 11. In this chapter, we will review the following topics:

(a) Perimeters and areas of two-dimensional figures

(b) Surface areas and volumes of three-dimensional figures

(c) Areas between curves and arc length, using calculus

Perimeters and Areas of Two-dimensional Figures

A **polygon** is a closed geometric figure that has line segments as its sides. **Triangles** are three-sided figures and **quadrilaterals** are four-sided figures.

Categories of Quadrilaterals

Parallelograms have two pairs of parallel sides. Opposite sides and opposite angles are congruent.

Rectangles are parallelograms with four right angles.

Rhombi (singular: **rhombus**) are parallelograms with all sides congruent.

Squares are parallelograms with all sides congruent and four right angles.

Trapezoids have exactly one pair of parallel sides.

Kites have two pairs of adjacent congruent sides.

Figures 11.1 – 11.6 illustrate these special quadrilaterals.

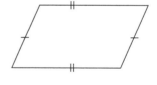

**Figure 11.1
Parallelogram**

**Figure 11.2
Rectangle**

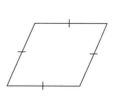

**Figure 11.3
Rhombus**

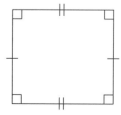

**Figure 11.4
Square**

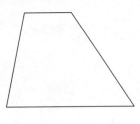

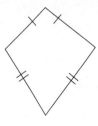

Figure 11.5
Trapezoid

Figure 11.6
Kite

NOTE:

> Slash marks are used to indicate congruence with sides of polygons. Thus, if a single slash mark appears on two different sides, these sides are congruent. Likewise for double slash marks.

CAUTION:

> A side with a double slash mark is not necessarily larger than a side with a single slash mark.

Perimeters

The **perimeter** for any polygon is simply the sum of the sides. In particular, if a triangle has a right angle, then given the lengths of any two sides, we can determine the length of the missing side by using the **Pythagorean** Theorem. This theorem states that the sum of the squares of the two shorter sides equals the square of the longest side, known as the hypotenuse. ($a^2 + b^2 = c^2$)

In Figure 11.7 shown below, $a^2 + b^2 = c^2$. The symbol ⌐ indicates that $\angle C$ is a right angle.

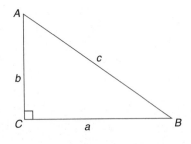

Figure 11.7

Be aware that either of sides a or b may be the shortest side. They may also be congruent. Also, by convention, any time a side of a triangle is labeled as "b," for example, the opposite angle will be $\angle B$.

EXAMPLE 1

Using Figure 11.7, if $a = 4$ and $b = 6$, then what is the value of c, to the nearest hundredth?

SOLUTION

Since we have a right triangle, we use the Pythagorean Theorem. $4^2 + 6^2 = 52 = c^2$. Thus, $c = \sqrt{52} \approx 7.21$.

EXAMPLE 2

One side of a triangle is 10 units. The second side is 3 units longer than the third side. If the perimeter is 55 units, what is the length of the longest side?

SOLUTION

Let x represent the length of the third side and let $x + 3$ represent the length of the second side. Then, $10 + (x + 3) + x = 55$. This equation simplifies to $2x + 13 = 55$, so $x = 21$. Thus, the longest side is 24 units.

*For **squares** and **rhombi**, the perimeter is four times the length of any side.*

*For **parallelograms** and **rectangles**, the perimeter is twice the length added to twice the width.*

*For **kites**, the perimeter is twice the sum of any two unequal sides.*

EXAMPLE 3

If the length of a rectangle is 19 and the perimeter is 56, what is the width?

SOLUTION

Let w represent the width. Then $(2)(19) + 2w = 56$, which simplifies to $2w = 18$. Thus, the width is 9.

EXAMPLE 4

The length of a parallelogram is 5 units more than three times its width. If the perimeter is 110, what is the length?

SOLUTION

Let w and $3w + 5$ represent the width and length, respectively. Then $(2)(w) + 2(3w + 5) = 110$. This equation simplifies to $8w + 10 = 110$, so $w = 12.5$. Thus, the length is $(3)(12.5) + 5 = 42.5$.

Areas

The **area of a polygon** is the number of square units enclosed by its sides. For triangles, there are three area formulas that can be used.

- If the length of any side (also called the base) and the length of the altitude (also called the height) drawn to this side are known, then the area is one-half the product of these two numbers. In symbols, the formula is $A = \dfrac{1}{2}bh$.

- If the lengths of the three sides are known, then **Heron's** formula can be used. Let a, b, and c represent the lengths of the sides. Define s as half the perimeter so that $s = \dfrac{1}{2}(a + b + c)$. Then the area can be found by $A = \sqrt{(s)(s - a)(s - b)(s - c)}$.

- A third method can be used if the lengths of two sides and the measure of the included angle are known. Look at Figure 11.8 shown below:

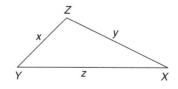

Figure 11.8

If we know the lengths of x, y and the measure of $\angle Z$, then the area of $\triangle XYZ$ is $\left[\dfrac{1}{2}\right](x)(y)(\sin \angle Z)$.

EXAMPLE 5

Consider the following $\triangle DEF$, with altitude $\overline{DG}$.

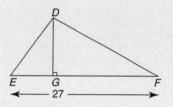

If the area is 216, what is the value of DG?

SOLUTION

Let x represent the value of DG. Then $216 = \left[\dfrac{1}{2}\right](27)(x)$. Thus, $x = \dfrac{216}{13.5} = 16$.

EXAMPLE 6

If the three sides of a triangle are 4, 5, and 7, what is its area, to the nearest hundredth?

SOLUTION

The value of $s = \left[\dfrac{1}{2}\right](4 + 5 + 7) = 8$. Then $A = \sqrt{(8)(8 - 4)(8 - 5)(8 - 7)} = \sqrt{96} \approx 9.80$.

EXAMPLE 7

In a right triangle, one of the legs is 7 and the hypotenuse is 25. What is the area of the triangle?

SOLUTION

Using the Pythagorean theorem, we determine that the length of the other leg is $\sqrt{25^2 - 7^2} = \sqrt{576} = 24$. If one leg represents the base, the other leg represents the height. Then the area is $\left[\dfrac{1}{2}\right](7)(24) = 84$.

EXAMPLE 8

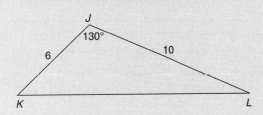

Consider the following $\triangle JKL$.

To the nearest hundredth, what is the area of the triangle?

SOLUTION

The area is $\left[\dfrac{1}{2}\right](6)(10)(\sin 130°) \approx 22.98$.

NOTE:

The formula used in Example 8 can also be used if we have a right triangle. The two legs would be the base and height and the included angle would be $90°$. The formula for the area would appear as $A = \left[\dfrac{1}{2}\right](b)(h)(\sin 90°)$, but since $\sin 90° = 1$, the formula would simplify to a more familiar $A = \left[\dfrac{1}{2}\right](b)(h)$.

For **squares**, the area is the square of any side. The formula is $A = s^2$, in which s represents one side.

For **rectangles**, the area is the product of the length and width. The formula is $A = (l)(w)$, in which l and w represent the length and width, respectively.

For **parallelograms** and **rhombi**, the area is the product of the base and height. The height is the vertical distance between any two parallel sides. The formula is $A = (b)(h)$, in which b and h represent the base and height, respectively.

Another formula for area that can be quite useful for squares and for rhombi is $A = \left[\dfrac{1}{2}\right](d_1)(d_2)$, in which d_1 and d_2 represent the diagonals. For a square, $d_1 = d_2$.

For **trapezoids**, the area is one half the product of the height and the sum of the bases. The formula is $A = \left[\dfrac{1}{2}\right](h)(b_1 + b_2)$, in which h is the height and b_1 and b_2 represent the (parallel) bases.

EXAMPLE 9

A square and a rectangle have equal areas. The length and width of the rectangle are 22 and 8, respectively. To the nearest hundredth, what is the side of the square?

SOLUTION

The area of the rectangle, which is $(22)(8) = 176$, must also be the area of the square. Thus, the side of the square is $\sqrt{176} \approx 13.27$.

EXAMPLE 10

A rhombus and a parallelogram have equal areas. The diagonals of the rhombus are 8 and 10. If the base of the parallelogram is twice its height, what are the dimensions of the base and height, to the nearest hundredth?

SOLUTION

The area of the rhombus is $\left[\dfrac{1}{2}\right](8)(10) = 40$. Using $2x$ and x to represent the base and height of the parallelogram, respectively, $40 = (2x)(x)$. Thus, $x = $ height $= \sqrt{20} \approx 4.47$. The base is approximately 8.94.

EXAMPLE 11

> The area of a trapezoid is 264 square inches. If the height is 11 inches and one of the bases is 18 inches, what is the length of the other base?

SOLUTION

Let x represent the unknown base. Then $264 = \left[\dfrac{1}{2}\right](11)(18 + x)$, which simplifies to $264 = 99 + 5.5x$. Thus, $x = \dfrac{165}{5.5} = 30$ inches.

Three-dimensional Figures

Surface Area of Three-dimensional Figures

We will now focus on the surface areas and volumes of specific three-dimensional figures. **Surface area** refers to the sum of the areas of all the faces. **Volume** refers to the region enclosed within the faces.

A **prism** is any three-dimensional figure that contains two congruent polygon faces in parallel planes and all its other faces are rectangles. Our study on prisms will be limited to **rectangular prisms**. For these prisms all six faces must be rectangles.

Figure 11.9 illustrates a rectangular prism.

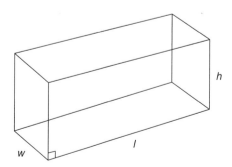

Figure 11.9

The surface area of this figure is given by the formula $SA = 2lw + 2lh + 2wh$, in which $l = $ length, $w = $ width, and $h = $ height. The volume is given by the formula $V = lwh$.

A **cube** is a special type of rectangular prism in which length = width = height.

Figure 11.10 illustrates a cube.

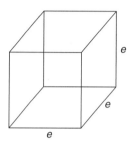

Figure 11.10

The surface area of a cube is given by the formula $SA = 6e^2$ and the volume is given by the formula $V = e^3$. The letter e, called an **edge**, represents each segment of each face.

EXAMPLE 12

> The volume of a cube is 500 cubic inches. To the nearest hundredth, what is its surface area?

SOLUTION

Since $500 = e^3$, each edge is $\sqrt[3]{500} \approx 7.937$ inches. Thus, the surface area is $(6)(7.937)^2 \approx 377.98$ square inches.

(Do not be too concerned if your answer was approximately 378.26, which would result from using 7.94 as the approximate length of each edge.)

EXAMPLE 13

> The volume of a rectangular prism is twice that of a cube whose edge is 5. If the length and width of the rectangular prism are 10 and 4, respectively, what is its height?

SOLUTION

Since the volume of the cube is $5^3 = 125$, the volume of the rectangular prism must be 250. Letting h represent the height, $250 = (10)(4)(h)$. Thus, $h = 6.25$.

EXAMPLE 14

What is the surface area, in square inches, of a rectangular prism whose dimensions are 9 inches by 2 feet by 1 yard?

SOLUTION

Change 2 feet to 24 inches and change 1 yard to 36 inches. Then the surface area is $(2)(9)(24) + (2)(9)(36) + (2)(24)(36) = 2808$ square inches.

A **pyramid** is a three-dimensional figure that has a polygon as its base and triangular faces that meet at a common point, called the vertex. A **regular pyramid** is one in which the base is a regular polygon. Our discussion will be limited to a regular pyramid with a square base. Figure 11.11 illustrates a regular pyramid.

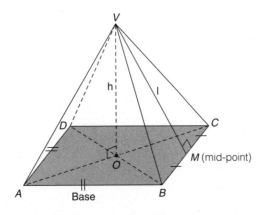

Figure 11.11

The line segment $\overline{OV}$, labeled as h, is called the **perpendicular height** of the pyramid. The point O is the center of the square base. The line segment $\overline{VM}$ is called a **lateral height**. The point M is the midpoint of $\overline{BC}$. Since each lateral height is the height of one of the triangular faces, there are four (congruent) segments that represent lateral heights.

NOTE:

$OM = \left[\dfrac{1}{2}\right](AB)$ and that any triangle that consists of points O, V, and any point on the segments that comprise square $ABCD$ would form a right triangle. As examples, $\triangle VOM$ and $\triangle VOB$ are right triangles, with a right angle at O.

The **total surface area** is the area of all the faces plus the area of the base. For the regular pyramid in Figure 11.1, this area is represented by $(4)\left[\dfrac{1}{2}\right](BC)(l) + (BC)^2$ $= (2)(BC)(l) + (BC)^2$.

Volume of a Three-dimensional Figure

Pyramid

The volume of a **regular pyramid** is given by the formula $V = \left[\dfrac{1}{3}\right](B)(h)$, in which B represents the area of the base and h is the perpendicular height of the pyramid. In Figure 11.1, the area of the base can be represented as $(BC)^2$, so the volume would be $\left[\dfrac{1}{3}\right](BC)^2(h)$.

EXAMPLE 15

Using Figure 11.1, what is the total surface area if the lateral height is 7 and the area of the base is 64?

SOLUTION

Each side of the base must be $\sqrt{64} = 8$. Then the total surface area is $(2)(8)(7) + 64 = 176$.

EXAMPLE 16

A regular pyramid with a square base has a volume of 250 cubic meters. Each side of the base is 9 meters. What is the perpendicular height, to the nearest hundredth?

SOLUTION

The area of the base is 81 square meters. Then $250 = \left[\dfrac{1}{3}\right](81)(h)$. Thus, $h \approx 9.26$ meters.

Cylinder

A **right circular cylinder** is a three-dimensional figure that has two congruent circular bases that lie in parallel planes. It is formed as follows: Draw a line segment that joins the centers of the two bases and a second congruent line segment that is parallel to the first and has endpoints on the two circles that form the bases. Then rotate the second segment about the first. Figure 11.12 illustrates a cylinder.

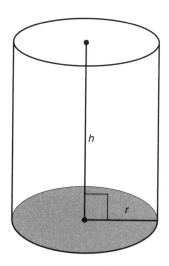

Figure 11.12

The total surface area (SA) of a cylinder is given by the formula $SA = 2\pi r^2 + 2\pi rh$.

Note that this includes the area of each circular base.

The volume of a cylinder is given by the formula $V = \pi r^2 h$.

In both formulas for the cylinder, r = radius of either circular base and h = height.

EXAMPLE 17

Using Figure 11.12, what is the total surface area, to the nearest hundredth, if $r = 10$ and $h = 18$?

SOLUTION

The total surface area is $(2)(\pi)(10)^2 + (2)(\pi)(10)(18) = 560\pi \approx 1759.29$.

EXAMPLE 18

The volume of a cylinder is 600 cubic inches. If the height is three times the radius, then to the nearest hundredth, what is the length of the radius?

SOLUTION

Let r represent the radius and let $3r$ represent the height. Then $600 = (\pi)(r^2)(3r) = 3\pi r^3$. This means that $r^3 = \dfrac{200}{\pi}$. Thus, $r = \sqrt[3]{\dfrac{200}{\pi}} \approx 3.99$ inches.

Cone

A **cone** is a three-dimensional figure that has a circular base. It can be constructed as follows: Begin with a right triangle in which one of the legs (l_1) lies in plane P and the other leg (l_2) is perpendicular to P. Then rotate the hypotenuse about l_2.

Figure 11.13 illustrates a cone.

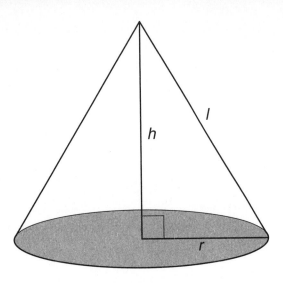

Figure 11.13

NOTE:

The shape of the cone is closely related to the shape of a pyramid. The main difference in appearance is that whereas the pyramid has triangular faces, the cone has no faces. As with the pyramid, l represents the lateral height. (Some math books use the term "slant" instead of "lateral.")

The total surace area of a cone is given by the formula $SA = \pi r^2 + \pi r l$.

Similar to a pyramid, the volume of a cone is given by the formula $V = \dfrac{1}{3}Bh$. But, since the base is a circle, we can write the volume formula more explicitly as $V = \dfrac{1}{3}\pi r^2 h$.

Since h represents the perpendicular height to the base, we have the relationship $r^2 + h^2 = l^2$.

EXAMPLE 19

Using Figure 11.13, what is the total surface area, to the nearest hundredth, if $r = 8$ inches and $h = 15$ inches?

SOLUTION

We first find that $l = \sqrt{8^2 + 15^2} = \sqrt{289} = 17$ inches. Then the total surface area is $(\pi)(8^2) + (\pi)(8)(17) = 200\pi \approx 628.32$ square inches.

EXAMPLE 20

The volume of a cone is 2400 cubic centimeters. If the radius is 12 centimeters, how large is the perpendicular height?

SOLUTION

$$2400 = \left(\frac{1}{3}\right)(\pi)(12^2)(h) = 48\pi h.$$

Thus, $h = \dfrac{50}{\pi} \approx 15.92$ centimeters.

Sphere

A **sphere** is a three-dimensional figure that represents the set of all points in space that are a fixed distance from a given point P. A tennis ball, bowling ball, and balloon are a few common objects that are shaped like a sphere. Figure 11.14 illustrates a sphere.

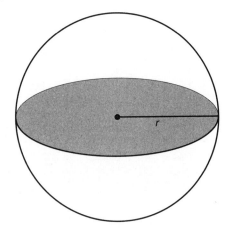

Figure 11.14

The **surface area of a sphere** is given by the formula $SA = 4\pi r^2$.

The **volume of a sphere** is given by the formula $V = \frac{4}{3}\pi r^3$. Of course, r is the radius.

Do you see a relationship between these two formulas? In Chapter 10, one of the concepts we discussed was the first derivative of a function. Note that if $f(x) = \frac{4}{3}\pi x^3$, then $f'(x) = 4\pi x^2$. This means that the expression for the surface area is the first derivative of the expression for the volume.

EXAMPLE 21

If the radius of a sphere is 15 inches, what is its volume, to the nearest hundredth, in cubic feet?

SOLUTION

Change 15 inches to 1.25 feet. Then the volume is $\left(\frac{4}{3}\right)(\pi)(1.25)^3 \approx 2.604\pi \approx 8.18$ cubic feet.

NOTE:

We could have first found the volume in cubic inches, then divided by $12^3 = 1728$ in order to convert the answer to cubic feet.

EXAMPLE 22

For a certain sphere, the numerical value of the volume is five times the numerical value of the surface area. What is the size of the radius?

SOLUTION

Let r represent the radius. Then $\frac{4}{3}\pi r^3 = (5)(4\pi r^2) = 20\pi r^2$. The fastest way to solve this equation is to divide by πr^2, which yields $\frac{4}{3}r = 20$. Thus, $r = 15$.

NOTE:

Normally we would have factored the equation $\frac{4}{3}\pi r^3 - 20\pi r^2 = 0$ to solve for r. However, the only other value for r would have been zero, which cannot happen.

Using Calculus for Areas between Curves and Arc Length

We will now use some information we discussed in Chapter 10 in order to determine

(a) the area between two curves and (b) the length of an arc of a curve.

You recall that we defined the definite integral of the function $f(x)$ on the closed interval $[a, b]$, where $f(x) \geq 0$ and $\Delta x = \frac{b-a}{n}$, as $\lim_{n\to\infty}\sum_{i=1}^{n} f(w_i)(\Delta x)$.

Riemann Sum

This limit is called a **Riemann Sum,** and we mentioned that this limit can also be written as $\int_a^b f(x)dx$.

Furthermore, this integral (provided that $f(x) \geq 0$) also represents the area bounded by $f(x)$, the x-axis, the vertical line $x = a$, and the vertical line $x = b$.

This is also commonly called the area under the curve $f(x)$ between $x = a$ and $x = b$.

Area between Curves

We can extend the meaning of $\int_a^b f(x)dx$ to include the determination of the area between any two functions $f(x)$ and $g(x)$, and bounded by $x = a$ and $x = b$. In all examples, each of $f(x)$ and $g(x)$ is continuous on $[a, b]$.

There are two specific cases that we will consider.

1. $f(x) \geq g(x)$ over the entire interval [a, b].
2. $f(x) \geq g(x)$ over part of [a, b], and $g(x) > f(x)$ over the remaining portion of [a, b].

EXAMPLE 23

> What is the area between the graphs of $y = x + 3$ and $y = 2x - 2$ over the interval [0, 3] ?

SOLUTION

Here is a sketch of the area we are seeking.

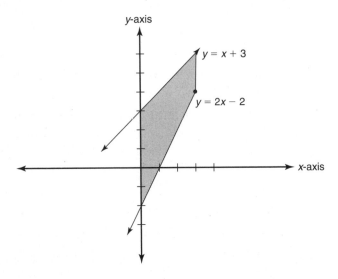

The area will be $\int_{a}^{b} (f(x) - g(x))dx$ over the interval [a, b], provided that $f(x) \geq g(x)$. In this case, choose $f(x) = x + 3$ and $g(x) = 2x - 2$. Since we know that $a = 0$ and $b = 3$, we need to evaluate $\int_{0}^{3} [(x + 3) - (2x - 2)]dx = \int_{0}^{3} (-x + 5)dx$. The next step is $\left(-\dfrac{x^2}{2} + 5x \right)\Big|_{0}^{3} = -\dfrac{9}{2} + 15 - 0 = 10\dfrac{1}{2}$.

NOTE:

> This figure is a trapezoid, with vertical segments as its bases. This answer can be verified by observing that the two bases are 5 and 2, and that the height is 3.

EXAMPLE 24

> What is the area between the graphs of $y = -x + 10$ and $y = x^2 + 4$ over the interval [–3, 2]?

SOLUTION

A sketch of the area we are seeking is shown below.

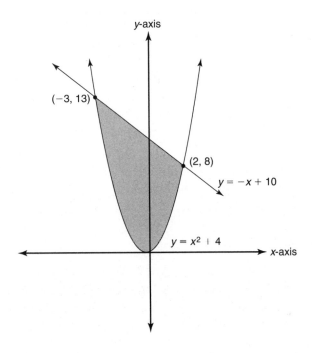

Since the graph of $y = -x + 10$ lies above the graph of $y = x^2 + 4$ over the entire interval [–3, 2], let $f(x) = -x + 10$ and let $g(x) = x^2 + 4$.

The desired area is $\int_{-3}^{2}[(-x+10)-(x^2+4)]dx =$

$\int_{-3}^{2}(-x-x^2+6)dx$. Then we get $\left[-\frac{x^2}{2}-\frac{x^3}{3}+6x\right]\Big|_{-3}^{2}$

$=\left[-2-\frac{8}{3}+12\right]-\left[-\frac{9}{2}+9-18\right]=20\frac{5}{6}$.

In Example 24, you will notice that the points $(-3,13)$ and $(2, 8)$ belong to both graphs.

Thus, we have actually found the area of the region bounded by the graphs of $f(x) = -x + 10$ and $g(x) = x^2 + 4$.

EXAMPLE 25

What is the area between the graphs of $y = -x^2 + 9$ and $y = 2x - 6$ over the interval $[0, 5]$?

SOLUTION

Let's look at the sketch that describes the regions.

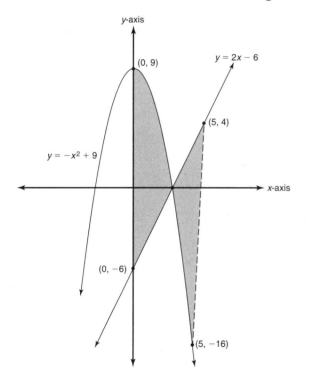

Notice that between $x = 0$ and $x = 3$, the graph of $y = -x^2 + 9$ lies above the graph of $y = 2x - 6$. However, between $x = 3$ and $x = 5$, the graph of $y = 2x - 6$ lies above that of $y = -x^2 + 9$. This means that we must

perform two separate integral calculations. In each one, we need to be sure that when using $\int_{a}^{b}(f(x)-g(x))dx$, the graph of $f(x)$ lies above that of $g(x)$. Our initial set-up should appear as follows:

Total area $= \int_{0}^{3}[(-x^2+9)-(2x-6)]dx +$

$\int_{3}^{5}[(2x-6)-(-x^2+9)]dx$

$= \int_{0}^{3}(-x^2-2x+15)dx + \int_{3}^{5}(x^2+2x-15)dx$.

We'll do each integral separately, then combine their answers.

$\int_{0}^{3}(-x^2-2x+15)dx = \left[-\frac{x^3}{3}-x^2+15x\right]\Big|_{0}^{3}$

$(-9-9+45)-0 = 27$

$\int_{3}^{5}(x^2+2x-15)dx = \left[\frac{x^3}{3}+x^2-15x\right]\Big|_{0}^{5}\Big|_{3}$

$= \left[\frac{125}{3}+25-75\right]-(9+9-45)=18\frac{2}{3}$.

Thus, the final answer is $45\frac{2}{3}$.

EXAMPLE 26

Look at the following graph.

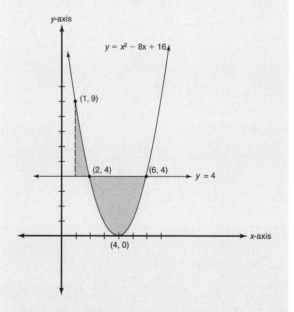

What is the total area of the shaded regions?

SOLUTION

On the interval [1, 2], the graph of $y = x^2 - 8x + 16$ lies above that of $y = 4$. On the interval [2, 6], the graph of $y = 4$ lies above that of $y = x^2 - 8x + 16$. Then the total area is

$$\int_1^2 [(x^2 - 8x + 16) - 4]dx + \int_2^6 [4 - (x^2 - 8x + 16)]dx$$

$$= \int_1^2 [(x^2 - 8x + 12)dx + \int_2^6 (-12 - x^2 + 8x)dx .$$

Let's calculate each integral separately, then combine the results.

$$\int_1^2 [(x^2 - 8x + 12)dx \quad = \quad \left[\frac{x^3}{3} - 4x^2 + 12x\right]\Big|_1^2$$

$$= \left[\frac{8}{3} - 16 + 24\right] - \left[\frac{1}{3} - 4 + 12\right] = 2\frac{1}{3}.$$

$$\int_2^6 (-12 - x^2 + 8x)dx = \left[-12x - \frac{x^3}{3} + 4x^2\right]\Big|_2^6$$

$$= (-72 - 72 + 144) - \left[-24 - \frac{8}{3} + 16\right] = 10\frac{2}{3}$$

Thus, the final answer is 13.

Arc Length

Our last topic for this chapter deals with the length of an arc of a curve. As expected, the **curve** will be a well-defined continuous and differentiable function over a closed interval. Let $f(x)$ be such a function over the interval $[a, b]$. If L represents the length of the curve of $f(x)$ from $x = a$ to $x = b$, then

$$L = \int_a^b \sqrt{1 + (f'(x))^2}\, dx .$$

EXAMPLE 27

What is the length of the curve of $f(x) = 3 - x^2$ on the closed interval [0, 1]?

SOLUTION

We determine that $f'(x) = -2x$, so $(f'(x))^2 = 4x^2$. Then $L = \int_0^1 \sqrt{1 + 4x^2}\, dx$. Unfortunately, the evaluation of this integral requires a technique that involves trigonometric substitution. This is not a method that we have covered in the chapter on Calculus.

However, if you are using a TI-83 calculator, you can use the CALC button to complete this example. First, be sure that you have already used the graphing feature to display the function $y = \sqrt{1 + 4x^2}$.

CAUTION:

> Be sure you don't display the original function $f(x) = 3 - x^2$.

Then press the 2nd CALC button, followed by item number 7, which reads $\int f(x)dx$. The calculator will prompt you for the lower limit and upper limit. Press 0 and 1, respectively. Now the screen will show the shaded region of the function $y = \sqrt{1 + 4x^2}$ between $x = 0$ and $x = 1$, as well as the approximate answer of 1.48 This number represents the area of the region bounded by $y = \sqrt{1 + 4x^2}$, the x-axis, the line $x = 0$, and the line $x = 1$. But, this number is <u>also</u> the answer to the length of the curve of $f(x) = 3 - x^2$ on the interval [0, 1]. Our final answer is 1.48.

EXAMPLE 28

What is the length of the curve $f(x) = x^3 + x - 1$ on the closed interval [1, 3]?

SOLUTION

$f'(x) = 3x^2 + 1$, so that $(f'(x))^2 = 9x^4 + 6x^2 + 1$. So, $1 + (f'(x))^2 = 9x^4 + 6x^2 + 2$. Then the length of the curve is found by evaluating $\int_1^3 \sqrt{9x^4 + 6x^2 + 2}\,dx$. Using the CALC feature, after graphing the function $y = \sqrt{9x^4 + 6x^2 + 2}$, the answer is approximately 28.10.

As with Example 27, we cannot find the required antiderivative of the function $y = \sqrt{9x^4 + 6x^2 + 2}$ with the techniques we have mastered in Chapter 10.

TABLE 1 – PERIMETERS AND AREAS OF TWO-DIMENSIONAL FIGURES

FIGURE	PERIMETER	AREA
Triangle	$a + b + c$	$\frac{1}{2}bh$, $\frac{1}{2}(ab)(\sin\angle C)$, or $\sqrt{(s)(s-a)(s-b)(s-c)}$
Square	$4s$	s^2
Rectangle	$2l + 2w$	lw
Rhombus	$4s$	bh or $\frac{1}{2}d_1d_2$
Parallelogram	$2l + 2w$	bh
Trapezoid	$a + b + c + d$	$\frac{1}{2}h(b_1 + b_2)$

TABLE 2 – SURFACE AREAS AND VOLUMES OF THREE-DIMENSIONAL FIGURES

FIGURE	SURFACE AREA	VOLUME
Cube	$6s^2$	s^3
Rectangular Prism	$2lw + 2lh + 2wh$	lwh
Pyramid with Square Base	$2sl + s^2$	$\frac{1}{3}s^2h$
Cylinder	$2\pi r^2 + 2\pi rh$	$\pi r^2 h$
Cone	$\pi r^2 + \pi rl$	$\frac{1}{3}\pi r^2 h$
Sphere	$4\pi r^2$	$\frac{4}{3}\pi r^3$

Quiz for Chapter 11

1. In a right triangle, the length of the hypotenuse is twice that of the smallest leg. If the other leg is 15 inches, how many inches, to the nearest hundredth, is the hypotenuse?

   (A) 8.66   (C) 13.42

   (B) 10.86   (D) 17.32

2. A parallelogram and a rhombus have equal perimeters. Each side of the rhombus is 16 units. If the length of the parallelogram is 21 units, what is its width?

   (A) 17 units   (C) 13 units

   (B) 15 units   (D) 11 units

3. To the nearest hundredth, what is the area of a triangle with sides of lengths 7, 14, and 17?

   (A) 59.98   (C) 35.52

   (B) 47.75   (D) 23.29

4. In $\triangle JKL$, $JK = 8$, $KL = 18$, and the measure of $\angle K$ is $40°$. To the nearest hundredth, what is the area of $\triangle JKL$?

   (A) 55.16   (C) 49.24

   (B) 52.20   (D) 46.28

5. The area of a rhombus is twice the area of a rectangle. The diagonals of the rhombus are 10 centimeters and 16 centimeters. If the width of the rectangle is 3.2 centimeters, what is the rectangle's length?

   (A) 12.5 centimeters   (C) 25 centimeters

   (B) 14.5 centimeters   (D) 29 centimeters

6. In a given trapezoid, one base is 7 units larger than the other base. If the height is 14 units and the area is 315 square units, what is the length, in units, of the shorter base?

   (A) 12   (C) 26

   (B) 19   (D) 33

7. The surface area of a cube is 337.5 square inches. In cubic inches, what is its volume, to the nearest hundredth?

   (A) 506.25   (C) 421.88

   (B) 464.07   (D) 379.70

8. The total surface area of a regular pyramid with a square base is 2100 square centimeters. If the lateral height is 20 centimeters, how many centimeters is the length of one side of the base?

   (A) 15   (C) 25

   (B) 20   (D) 30

9. The volume of a cylinder is 2400 cubic inches. If the height is twice the radius, then to the nearest hundredth, what is the height in inches?

   (A) 7.26   (C) 19.54

   (B) 14.51   (D) 24.57

10. The area of each circular base of a cylinder is 100π square units. If the height is 13 units, what is the total surface area in square units?

    (A) 460π (C) 360π

    (B) 400π (D) 300π

11. The area of the base of a cone is 225π square inches and the volume is 1875π cubic inches. To the nearest hundredth, what is the lateral height?

    (A) 32.15 inches   (C) 29.15 inches

    (B) 30.65 inches   (D) 27.65 inches

12. If the surface area of a sphere is 25π square units, what is the volume in cubic units?

    (A) 4.5π (C) $20.8\overline{3}\pi$

    (B) 12.9π (D) $18.1\overline{6}\pi$

13. What is the area between the graphs of $y = 3$ and $y = -x^2 + 10x - 13$ over the closed interval $[2, 8]$?

(A) 15.25

(C) 30.5

(B) 18

(D) 36

14. Which one of the following is the correct representation of the combined area between the graphs of $y = 9x$ and $y = x^3$ on the closed interval $[0, 5]$?

(A) $\int_0^3 (9x - x^3)dx + \int_3^5 (x^3 - 9x)dx$

(B) $\int_0^{2.5} (9x - x^3)dx + \int_{2.5}^5 (x^3 - 9x)dx$

(C) $\int_0^3 (x^3 - 9x)dx + \int_3^5 (9x - x^3)dx$

(D) $\int_0^{2.5} (x^3 - 9x)dx + \int_{2.5}^5 (9x - x^3)dx$

15. Using your CALC button, what is the approximate length of the curve of $y = x^{3/2}$ on the closed interval $[2, 4]$?

(A) 5.55

(C) 8.86

(B) 7.21

(D) 10.54

Quiz for Chapter 11
SOLUTIONS

1. (D)

Let x and $2x$ represent the shorter leg and hypotenuse, respectively. Then $x^2 + 15^2 = (2x)^2$. This equation simplifies to $3x^2 = 225$. This means that $x = \sqrt{75} \approx 8.66$ is the shorter leg. Thus, the hypotenuse is approximately 17.32.

2. (D)

The perimeter of the rhombus is $(4)(16) = 64$ units, which is also the perimeter of the parallelogram. Let x represent the width of the parallelogram. Then $2x + (2)(21) = 64$. Thus, $x = \dfrac{22}{2} = 11$ units.

3. (B)

Using Heron's formula, with $s = 19$, the area is $\sqrt{(19)(12)(5)(2)} = \sqrt{2280} \approx 47.75$.

4. (D)

If two sides and the included angle of a triangle are known, then the formula for the triangle's area is one half the product of the two sides and the sine of the included angle. Thus, the area is $\left(\dfrac{1}{2}\right)(8)(18)(\sin 40°) \approx 46.28$.

5. (A)

The area of the rhombus is $\left(\dfrac{1}{2}\right)(10)(16) = 80$ square centimeters. Then the rectangle's area must be 40 square centimeters. Thus, the rectangle's length is $\dfrac{40}{3.2} = 12.5$ centimeters.

6. (B)

Let x and $x + 7$ represent the two bases. Then $315 = \left(\dfrac{1}{2}\right)(14)(x + x + 7)$. This equation simplifies to $45 = 2x + 7$. Thus, $x = 19$.

7. (C)

Let e represent the length of an edge. Then $6e^2 = 337.5$, which leads to $e = \sqrt{56.25} = 7.5$. Thus, the volume is $(7.5)^3 \approx 421.88$.

8. (D)

Let x represent the length of one side of the square base. Then $(2)(x)(20) + x^2 = 2100$. This equation factors as $(x + 70)(x - 30) = 0$. Thus, $x = 30$.

9. (B)

Let r represent the radius and let $2r$ represent the height. Then $2400 = (\pi)(r^2)(2r) = 2\pi r^3$. So, $r^3 = \dfrac{1200}{\pi} \approx 381.97$. This means that $r \approx 7.256$. Thus, the height is approximately 14.51.

10. (A)

The total surface area is $100\pi + 100\pi + (2\pi)(r)(13) = 200\pi + 26\pi r$. But we know that $100\pi = \pi r^2$, so $r = 10$. Thus, $200\pi + 26\pi r = 460\pi$.

11. (C)

Since $225\pi = \pi r^2$, $r = 15$. Also, $1875\pi = \dfrac{1}{3}\pi r^2 h = 75\pi h$. Then $h = 25$. Finally, r, h, and l form a right triangle, with l as the hypotenuse. So, $15^2 + 25^2 = 850 = l^2$, Thus, $l = \sqrt{850} \approx 29.15$.

12. (C)

Since $4\pi r^2 = 25\pi$, $r = \sqrt{\dfrac{25}{4}} = 2.5$. Then the volume is $\left(\dfrac{4}{3}\right)(\pi)(2.5^3) = 20.8\overline{3}\pi$.

13. (D)

Since the graph of $y = -x^2 + 10x - 13$ lies completely above the graph of $y = 3$, the area is given by

$$\int_2^8 [(-x^2 + 10x - 13) - 3]dx = \int_2^8 (-x^2 + 10x - 16)dx$$

This integral becomes $\left[\dfrac{-x^3}{3} + 5x^2 - 16x\right]\Bigg|_2^8 =$

$$\left[-\dfrac{512}{3} + 320 - 128\right] - \left[-\dfrac{8}{3} + 20 - 32\right] = 36.$$

14. (A)

The graphs of $y = x^3$ and $y = 9x$ intersect at $x = 0$ and $x = 3$. In the closed interval $[0, 3]$, the graph of $y = 9x$ lies above that of $y = x^3$, so the corresponding area between these curves is given by $\int_0^3 (9x - x^3)dx$. However, on the closed interval $[3, 5]$, the graph of $y = x^3$ lies above that of $y = 9x$; thus the corresponding area is given by $\int_3^5 (x^3 - 9x)dx$. The total area is represented by the sum of these two integrals. (The actual area is 84.25).

15. (A)

Since $f(x) = x^{3/2}$, $(f'(x))^2 = \left(\dfrac{3}{2}x^{1/2}\right)^2 = \dfrac{9}{4}x$.

Then the length of the curve is given by $\int_2^4 \sqrt{1 + \dfrac{9}{4}x}\,dx$.

Using the CALC feature, the value of this integral is approximately 5.55.

Axioms, Properties, and Theorems of Euclidean Geometry

Welcome to Chapter 12. In this chapter, we will review the following topics:

(a) Properties of points, line segments, rays, angles, planes, and distances
(b) Categories of triangles
(c) Properties of sides and angles of triangles
(d) Theorems concerning congruent and similar triangles
(e) Properties of quadrilaterals
(f) Similarity for three-dimensional figures
(g) Geometric constructions using a compass and straightedge

Properties of Points, Line Segments, Rays, Angles, Planes, and Distances

Points

A **point** is a figure with no dimensions; it only has a location and is named with a capital letter. Figure 12.1 shows a point P.

• P

Figure 12.1

Lines

A **line** has length, but no other dimension; its length is infinite. A line is named using any two of its points, with the line symbol above these points. For example, a line that includes points A and B is named as $\overleftrightarrow{AB}$ (or $\overleftrightarrow{BA}$). Lines may also be named using a single lower case letter, usually with a subscript. This is shown in Figure 12.2.

Figure 12.2

Line Segments

A **line segment** is a finite portion of a line; it has a finite length. A line segment is named using its two endpoints, with a line segment symbol above these points. For example, a line segment for which its endpoints are C and D is named as $\overline{CD}$ (or $\overline{DC}$). This is shown in Figure 12.3.

C
O

Figure 12.3

Rays

A **ray** is a part of a line that contains an endpoint and extends in just one direction; its length is infinite. A ray is named by using its endpoint, followed by any other point that lies on it. A corresponding ray symbol lies over the two letters that are used. Figure 12.4 shows a ray $\overrightarrow{FG}$. Note that this ray <u>cannot</u> be written as $\overrightarrow{GF}$.

Figure 12.4

Angles

An **angle** is a union of two rays with a common endpoint. It is measured by the space between its rays. **Acute** angles measure less than 90°; **right** angles measure 90°; **obtuse** angles measure more than 90°, but less than 180°; **straight** angles measure 180°; **reflex** angles measure more than 180°; but less than 360°. An angle is named by using the symbol $\angle$, followed by three letters, a single letter, or a number. When named with three letters, we use one point from one ray, the common point of both rays (vertex), and then one point from the other ray. Figure 12.5 shows an acute angle that may be named as $\angle XYZ$, $\angle Y$, or $\angle 1$.

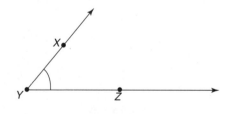

Figure 12.5

Planes

A **plane** is a flat surface that extends indefinitely in all directions; a plane has length and width, but no depth. We can imagine a plain piece of paper that has an infinite length and width. A plane is named with a single capital letter and is shown as a parallelogram. Figure 12.6 shows plane Q.

Figure 12.6

Distances

The **distance between two points**, J and K, is measured by the length of the line segment that contains points J and K as endpoints.

The distance between a point P and a line $\overleftrightarrow{RT}$ not containing P is measured by the length of the perpendicular segment from P to $\overleftrightarrow{RT}$. (Perpendicular means forming a right angle). In Figure 12.7, the length of $\overline{PQ}$, which is commonly written as simply PQ, is the distance between P and $\overleftrightarrow{RT}$.

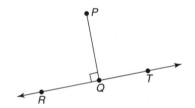

Figure 12.7

Two lines are **parallel** if they lie in one plane, but never intersect. **The distance between parallel lines** is the length of any perpendicular line segment whose endpoints lie on these lines. In Figure 12.8, MN represents the distance between point line l_1 and line. The box symbols used at points M and N indicate a 90-degree angle.

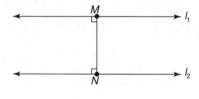

Figure 12.8

The distance between a point H and a plane P that does not contain H is the length of the perpendicular segment from H to P. This is shown is Figure 12.9 as HJ.

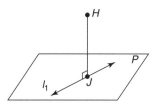

Figure 12.9

In Figure 12.9, line l_1 is one of an infinite number of lines that lie in plane *P* and which contain point *J*. Suppose that a line l_1 is parallel to a plane P. Then the **distance between a line and a plane** is the length of the perpendicular segment from any point on the line to the plane. In Figure 12.10, YZ represents the distance between line l_1 and plane *P*.

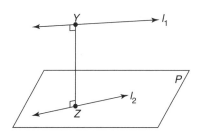

Figure 12.10

NOTE:

> Line l_2 is <u>any</u> line in plane P that contains point Z. Technically, it is not a requirement that the lines l_1 and l_2 be parallel to each other.

The symbol for parallelism is given by ‖. This symbol can be used between any two parallel figures. Thus, in Figure 12.8, we can write $l_1 \parallel l_2$. Likewise, in Figure 12.10, we can write $l_1 \parallel P$.

Two planes are **parallel** if they never intersect. **The distance between parallel planes** is the length of a segment (a) with endpoints in each plane and (b) that is perpendicular to each plane. In Figure 12.11, planes *P* and *Q* are parallel to each other. This can be written as $P \parallel Q$. Also, RS represents the distance between these planes.

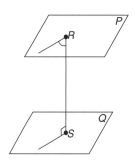

Figure 12.11

Categories of Triangles

Triangles are simply three line segments, each of which is connected to the other two segments. Each triangle must have three vertices and three angles. There are several important categories of triangles.

A **scalene** triangle is one in which no two sides (or two angles) are congruent.

An **isosceles** triangle has at least two congruent sides. Opposite these congruent sides are congruent angles.

An **equilateral** triangle has three congruent sides (and angles). Since the sum of the angle measures of any triangle is 180°, each angle of an equilateral triangle must have a measure of 60°.

A **right** triangle must have one right angle. If a right triangle has two 45-degree angles, then it is called an **isosceles right** triangle.

An **acute** triangle is one in which the measure of each angle is less than 90°.

An **obtuse** triangle is one in which the measure of one angle is greater than 90°.

Figures 12.12 thru 12.18 illustrate each of these types of triangles.

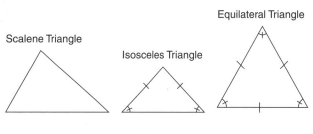

| **Figure 12.12** | **Figure 12.13** | **Figure 12.14** |

Right Triangle

Figure 12.15

Right Isosceles Triangle

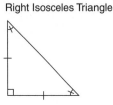

Figure 12.16

Acute Triangle

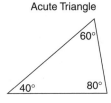

Figure 12.17

Obtuse Triangle

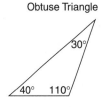

Figure 12.18

NOTE:

> A triangle can often be classified in more than one way. For example, an equilateral triangle is also an acute triangle. Likewise, if the angles of a triangle are 20°, 20°, and 140°, then this is both an obtuse triangle and an isosceles triangle.

NOTE:

> Congruent sides are indicated by the same number of slash marks. In a similar way, congruent angles are also shown with the same number of slash marks.

Properties of Sides and Angles of Triangles

1. The **largest side** of a triangle is opposite the largest angle. The same situation exists for the smallest side and the smallest angle. Consider ΔABC, as shown in Figure 12.19.

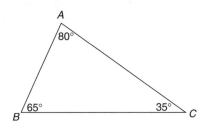

Figure 12.19

The correct inequality for the sides is $BC > AC > AB$.

2. The **sum of any two sides** of a triangle must exceed the length of the third side. Consider ΔDEF, for which it is known that $DE = 6$ and $EF = 9$. Without seeing the actual triangle, we know that DF must satisfy the following inequality: $3 < DF < 15$.

3. A **midsegment** joins the midpoints of two sides of a triangle. It is parallel to and one-half the length of the third side. In Figure 12.20, we can conclude that $KL = 5$ and $\overline{KL} \parallel \overline{HJ}$.

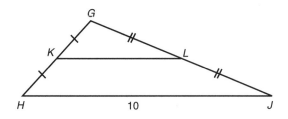

Figure 12.20

4. An **altitude** is a segment that originates at a vertex and is perpendicular to the opposite side of a triangle. In some cases, the opposite side must be extended. In particular, given an obtuse triangle, an altitude that is drawn from a vertex at which the angle measure is greater than 90° will meet the extension of the opposite side. Figures 12.21 and 12.22 show the appearance of an altitude in both an acute triangle and in an obtuse triangle.

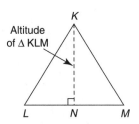

Figure 12.21

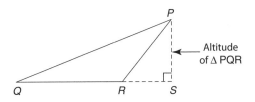

Figure 12.22

5. A **median** is a segment whose endpoints are a vertex and the midpoint of the opposite side. In drawing any median, the triangle is split into two smaller triangles of equal area. This results from the fact that each base of these two smaller triangles are congruent and their altitudes are also congruent.

In Figure 12.23, $\overline{MQ}$ is a median of $\triangle MNP$. Also, the areas of $\triangle MNQ$ and $\triangle MPQ$ are equal.

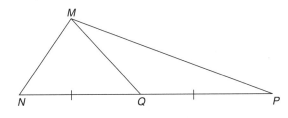

Figure 12.23

6. An **angle bisector** is a segment in which the endpoints are a vertex and a point on the opposite side such that the vertex angle is divided in half. In addition, the lengths of the two sides that comprise the angle that is bisected are in the same ratio as the two segments of the opposite side.

In Figure 12.24, $\overline{TV}$ is the angle bisector of $\angle UTW$. This implies that $\dfrac{TU}{TW} = \dfrac{UV}{VW}$.

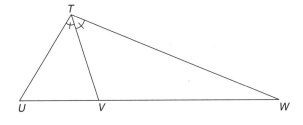

Figure 12.24

7. The **geometric mean** of any two numbers is the square root of their product. For example, given the numbers 4 and 9, the positive geometric mean is $\sqrt{(4)(9)} = \sqrt{36} = 6$. Another way to view this is as follows: If x is the geometric mean of 4 and 9, then $\dfrac{4}{x} = \dfrac{x}{9}$.

In a right triangle, the length of the altitude drawn to the hypotenuse is the geometric mean between the two legs of the triangle.

In Figure 12.25, $\overline{ZB}$ is the altitude drawn to the hypotenuse of right triangle *AYZ*. Then $\dfrac{YB}{ZB} = \dfrac{ZB}{AB}$.

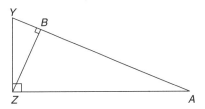

Figure 12.25

EXAMPLE 1

In $\triangle BCD$, $\angle B = 42°$ and $\angle C = 75°$. Which side is the largest?

SOLUTION

$\angle D = 180° - 42° - 75° = 63°$. Since the largest side lies opposite the largest angle, $\overline{BD}$ is the largest side.

EXAMPLE 2

All the sides of a triangle are integers. If two sides have lengths of 7 inches and 16 inches, what is the shortest possible length of the third side?

SOLUTION

Let x represent the length of the third side. The triangle inequality for the lengths of sides states that $7 + x > 16$. Since x is an integer and $x > 9$, the lowest value of x is 10 inches.

EXAMPLE 3

> In $\triangle BCD$, $\overline{BE}$ is the median to $\overline{CD}$. If the area of $\triangle BCE$ is represented by $13 - x$, and the area of $\triangle BCD$ is represented by $x + 5$, what is the value of x?

SOLUTION

The area of $\triangle BCD$ must be twice the area of $\triangle BCE$. Then $x + 5 = 2(13 - x)$. This equation simplifies to $3x = 21$, so $x = 7$.

EXAMPLE 4

> Consider $\triangle XYZ$, as shown below, in which $\overline{WZ}$ is the angle bisector of $\angle Z$.
>
>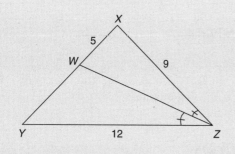
>
> What is the value of WY?

SOLUTION

Since $\overline{WZ}$ is an angle bisector, we have the proportion $\dfrac{XZ}{YZ} = \dfrac{WX}{WY}$. Using x to represent WY and making all substitutions, we get $\dfrac{9}{12} = \dfrac{5}{x}$. Then $9x = 60$, so $x = 6.\overline{6}$.

EXAMPLE 5

> Consider right triangle *GHJ*, as shown below, in which $\overline{HK}$ is the altitude to the hypotenuse.
>
>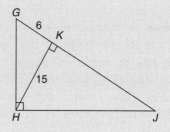
>
> What is the value of *JK*?

SOLUTION

HK is the geometric mean for *GK* and *JK*. Let x represent JK, so that $\dfrac{6}{15} = \dfrac{15}{x}$. Thus, $x = \dfrac{225}{6} = 37.5$.

Theorems Concerning Congruent and Similar Triangles

Congruent Triangles

We will now investigate the requirements for two triangles to be exactly the same size. Two triangles are **congruent** if each of the three sides and angles of one triangle are equal in measure to each of the three sides and angles of a second triangle. The symbol for "congruent" is "$\cong$". By stating that $\triangle ABC \cong \triangle DEF$, we are confirming that: $\overline{AB} \cong \overline{DE}$, $\overline{AC} \cong \overline{DF}$, $\overline{BC} \cong \overline{EF}$, $\angle A \cong \angle D$, $\angle B \cong \angle E$, and $\angle C \cong \angle F$.

The order of the sets of congruencies must match the order in which the letters are presented for the triangles. Other congruencies are possible, but not required. For example, if we can determine that $AB = AC$, then it must be true that *DE* = *DF*. *Two triangles can be proved congruent with just a minimum of three sets of congruencies.*

Proving Congruence between Two Triangles

Here is a list of the minimum number of congruencies of triangle parts in order to prove congruence between two triangles. In each case, we are trying to establish that $\triangle ABC \cong \triangle DEF$.

1. **Side-Angle-Side (SAS)** - Two sides of one triangle are congruent respectively to two sides of a second triangle. In addition the included angles are congruent. For example, $\overline{AB} \cong \overline{DE}$, $\overline{AC} \cong \overline{DF}$, and $\angle A \cong \angle D$, as shown in Figure 12.26.

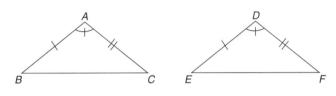

Figure 12.26

2. **Angle-Side-Angle (ASA)** – Two angles of one triangle are congruent respectively to two angles of a second triangle. In addition, the included sides are congruent. For example, $\angle B \cong \angle E$, $\angle C \cong \angle F$, and $\overline{BC} \cong \overline{EF}$, as shown in Figure 12.27.

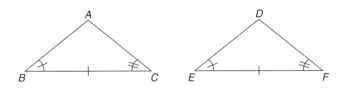

Figure 12.27

3. **Side-Angle-Angle (SAA)** – Two angles of one triangle are congruent respectively to two angles of a second triangle. In addition, a pair of non-included sides are congruent. For example $\angle B \cong \angle E$, $\angle C \cong \angle F$, and $\overline{AC} \cong \overline{DF}$, as shown in Figure 12.28.

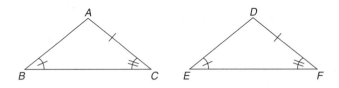

Figure 12.28

NOTE:

When two pairs of angles are congruent, we just require <u>any</u> pair of corresponding sides to be congruent. This set of conditions will then guarantee that the triangles are congruent.

4. **Side-Side-Side (SSS)** - All three pairs of sides of one triangle are congruent respectively to all three pairs of sides of a second triangle. This means that $\overline{AB} \cong \overline{DE}$, $\overline{AC} \cong \overline{DF}$, and $\overline{BC} \cong \overline{EF}$, as shown in Figure 12.29.

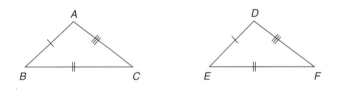

Figure 12.29

CAUTION:

It is important to recognize why certain combinations of congruencies between the parts of triangles do <u>not</u> imply that the triangles are congruent. We'll label these as fallacies. The figures illustrate that the triangles are not congruent.

1. **Side-Side-Angle Fallacy (SSA)**- Figure 12.30

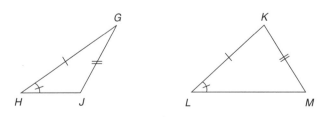

Figure 12.30

For this example, $\overline{GH} \cong \overline{KL}$, $\overline{GJ} \cong \overline{KM}$, and $\angle H \cong \angle L$. However, the triangles are not congruent.

2. **Angle- Angle-Angle Fallacy (AAA)-Figure 12.31**

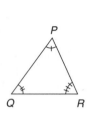 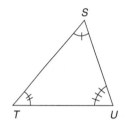

Figure 12.31

For this example, $\angle P \cong \angle S$, $\angle Q \cong \angle T$, and $\angle R \cong \angle U$. Although the triangles are not congruent, there is a relationship that does exist. This relationship will be discussed in our next topic.

Congruent Right Triangles

For some special triangles, there are even fewer stated requirements needed for a congruence. For example, two right triangles are congruent if any two pairs of corresponding sides are congruent. The reason is that the Pythagorean Theorem can be applied to show that the third pair of corresponding sides will also be congruent.

CAUTION:

Be certain that corresponding sides and angles match up when identifying a congruence between two triangles. Consider the two triangles shown below in Figure 12.32.

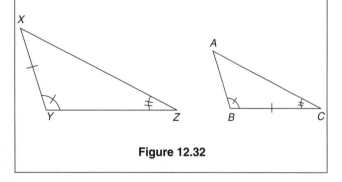

Figure 12.32

NOTE:

Even though $\angle Y \cong \angle B$ and $\angle Z \cong \angle C$, the corresponding sides of $\overline{YZ}$ and $\overline{BC}$ are not congruent. The fact that we also have $\overline{XY} \cong \overline{BC}$ is not sufficient to establish a congruence between these two triangles.

Similar Triangles

As we look back at Figure 12.31 in which all three pairs of angles are congruent, we can make an assertion about these triangles. Two triangles are **similar** if the corresponding pairs of angles are congruent. Technically, we just need two pairs of congruent angles; the third pair must then be congruent because the sum of the angles of any triangle is 180°. The symbol for similarity between any two geometric figures is " $\sim$ ". Thus, using Figure 12.31, we can write $\Delta PQR \sim \Delta STU$.

There is also a strong relationship concerning the sides of similar triangles, namely that the ratio of any two corresponding sides must be constant. This means that in Figure 12.31, $\frac{PQ}{ST} = \frac{PR}{SU} = \frac{QR}{TU}$. Furthermore, the ratio of corresponding medians, altitudes, midsegments, and angle bisectors of similar triangles must be the same as the ratio of any two corresponding sides. Let's consider Figure 12.33, which is a re-creation of Figure 12.31, plus the altitudes $\overline{RB}$ and $\overline{UC}$.

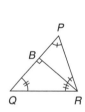 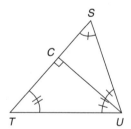

Figure 12.33

We can now state that the ratio of RB to UC must be equal to the ratio of any two corresponding sides. Thus, $\frac{PQ}{ST} = \frac{PR}{SU} = \frac{QR}{TU} = \frac{RB}{UC}$. A similar argument can be made for any pair of corresponding medians, midsegments, or angle bisectors.

Relationships between Perimeters and Areas of Similar Triangles

We know that any two congruent triangles ought to have the same perimeter and the same area. *The ratio of the perimeters of similar triangles is the same as the ratio of any two corresponding sides.* Suppose the first triangle has sides of lengths 4, 7, and 9. The second triangle has lengths of 8, 14, and 18. Their perimeters are 20 and 40, respectively. Notice that the ratio of a pair of corresponding sides is 1 : 2, and so is the ratio of the perimeters.

In order to establish the relationship between the areas of two similar triangles, let's consider Figure 12.34, in which triangles *DEF* and *HJK* are similar, as shown by the angle markings.

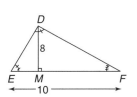
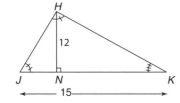

Figure 12.34

The ratio of corresponding sides is 10 : 15, which reduces to 2 : 3. Notice that the ratio of the altitudes $\overline{DM}$ and $\overline{HN}$ is also 2 : 3. The area of ΔDEF is $\left(\frac{1}{2}\right)(10)(8) = 40$, whereas the area of ΔHJK is $\left(\frac{1}{2}\right)(15)(12) = 90$. So the ratio of the areas is 40 : 90, which reduces to 4 : 9. Even though 2 : 3 is not equal to 4 : 9, we do observe that $\left(\frac{2}{3}\right)^2 = \frac{4}{9}$.

NOTE:

Although not formally proven, we conclude that the ratio of the areas of similar triangles is equal to the square of the ratio of the corresponding sides. This statement is reversible in the sense that the ratio of the sides is the square root of the ratio of the areas.

EXAMPLE 6

If $\Delta BCF \sim \Delta GLM$ and $\frac{BC}{GL} = \frac{3}{5}$, which other ratio has a value of $\frac{3}{5}$?

SOLUTION

There are many answers that would be correct. For examples, any two corresponding altitudes or corresponding angle bisectors would have the same ratio $\frac{3}{5}$. In terms of the sides of the two triangles, we could use ratio $\frac{CF}{LM}$.

EXAMPLE 7

Referring back to Example 6, suppose the perimeter of ΔBCF is 36. What is the perimeter of ΔGLM?

SOLUTION

The perimeters are in the same ratio as a pair of corresponding sides. Letting x represent the perimeter of ΔGLM, $\frac{3}{5} = \frac{36}{x}$. Thus, $x = 60$.

EXAMPLE 8

Referring back to Example 6, suppose the area of ΔGLM is 65. What is the area of ΔBCF?

SOLUTION

The ratio of the area of ΔBCF to the area of ΔGLM is $\left(\frac{3}{5}\right)^2 = \frac{9}{25}$. Letting x represent the area of ΔBCF, $\frac{9}{25} = \frac{x}{65}$. Thus, $x = 23.4$.

EXAMPLE 9

> The ratio of the perimeter of Triangle I to the perimeter of Triangle II is $\frac{8}{3}$. The altitude to the base of Triangle I is five units more than twice the corresponding altitude to the base of Triangle II. How many units is the altitude to the base of Triangle I?

SOLUTION

The ratio of the altitudes matches the ratio of the perimeters. Let $2x + 5$ and x represent the corresponding altitudes of Triangles I and II, respectively. Then $\frac{8}{3} = \frac{2x + 5}{x}$, which simplifies to $8x = 6x + 15$, so $x = 7.5$. Thus, the corresponding altitude to the base of Triangle I is 20 units.

EXAMPLE 10

> The ratio of the areas for two similar triangles is $\frac{4}{5}$. If the perimeter of the smaller triangle is 30 inches, what is the perimeter of the larger triangle to the nearest hundredth?

SOLUTION

The ratio of the perimeters is $\sqrt{\frac{4}{5}} = \frac{2}{\sqrt{5}}$. Let x represent the perimeter of the larger triangle. Then $\frac{2}{\sqrt{5}} = \frac{30}{x}$. Thus, $x = 15\sqrt{5} \approx 33.54$ inches.

Properties of Quadrilaterals

In Chapter 11, we discussed the basic definitions of quadrilaterals, including specific ones such as the square and rectangle. Each quadrilateral has two diagonals.

Our objectives now will be to examine the properties of the diagonals for specific quadrilaterals and to do a similar comparison of perimeter and area as we did for triangles. If necessary, refer to Figures 11.2 – 11.7.

For squares:	The diagonals are congruent and are perpendicular bisectors of each other. They also bisect the angles from which they originate.
For rectangles:	The diagonals are congruent and bisect each other, but they are not perpendicular to each other, nor do they bisect the angles from which they originate.
For rhombi:	The diagonals are perpendicular bisectors of each other. They also bisect the angles from which they originate. They are not congruent.
For parallelograms:	The diagonals bisect each other.
For trapezoids:	The diagonals show no special properties, except for isosceles trapezoids; in that case, the diagonals are congruent.
For kites:	The diagonals are perpendicular to each other. Only the longer diagonal bisects both the angles from which it originates and the short diagonal.

The concepts of congruence and similarity that we explored for triangles are very close to the ones needed for quadrilaterals.

Congruent and Similar Quadrilaterals

- Two quadrilaterals are congruent if each pair of angles and each pair of sides can be matched.

- Two quadrilaterals are similar if each pair of angles can be matched and each pair of corresponding sides are in the same ratio.

- The ratio of the corresponding diagonals and the ratio of the perimeters is the same as the ratio of corresponding sides.

- The ratio of corresponding altitudes is also the same as the ratio of the perimeters.

- The ratio of the areas is the square of the ratio of corresponding sides.

NOTE:

> Any two squares are automatically similar. This statement cannot be made regarding other quadrilaterals.

EXAMPLE 11

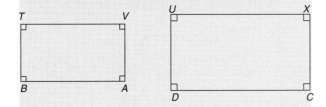

Rectangles TVAB and UXCD, shown below, are similar.

The ratio of the perimeter of *TVAB* to that of *UXCD* is $\dfrac{7}{10}$. If *CD* is 9 units larger than *AB*, what is the value of *CD*?

SOLUTION

Let x and $x + 9$ represent *AB* and *CD*, respectively. Then $\dfrac{7}{10} = \dfrac{x}{x + 9}$. Then $7x + 63 = 10x$, so $x = 21$. Thus, $CD = 30$ units.

EXAMPLE 12

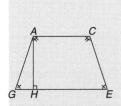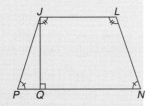

Trapezoids *ACEG* and *JNLP*, shown below, are similar.

The area of *ACEG* is 64 and the area of *JNLP* is 110. If *JQ* is five units larger than *AH*, what is the value of *AH*? (Nearest hundredth)

SOLUTION

The ratio of corresponding altitudes is $\sqrt{\dfrac{64}{110}}$ $= \dfrac{8}{\sqrt{110}}$. Let x represent AH and $x + 5$ represent JQ. Then $\dfrac{8}{\sqrt{110}} = \dfrac{x}{x + 5}$. Since $\sqrt{110} \approx 10.49$, we have. Thus $10.49x = 8x + 40$, $x \approx 16.06$ units.

EXAMPLE 13

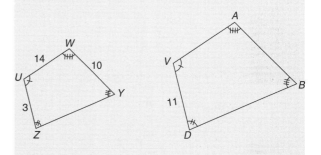

Quadrilaterals *UWYZ* and *VABD* are similar, as shown below.

If the perimeter of *UWYZ* is 51, what is the value of *DB*?

SOLUTION

$ZY = 51 - 3 - 14 - 10 = 24$. Let x represent *DB*. Then $\dfrac{3}{11} = \dfrac{24}{x}$, so $x = 88$.

EXAMPLE 14

Consider the following two similar rhombi, as shown below.

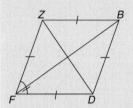 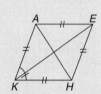

The area of *ZBDF* is 35 square inches larger than the area of *AEHK*. $\frac{FD}{KH} = \frac{4}{3}$. What is the product of the diagonals in *ZBDF*?

SOLUTION

Let $x + 35$ and x represent the areas of *ZBDF* and *AEHK,* respectively. Then $\frac{x+35}{x} = \left(\frac{4}{3}\right)^2 = \frac{16}{9}$, which leads to $16x = 9x + 315$. Then $x = 45$, so the area of *ZBDF* is 80 square inches. The area of a rhombus is one half the product of its diagonals. Thus, the product of the diagonals in *ZBDF* is 160.

Similarity for Three-dimensional Figures

In Chapter 11, we explored the surface areas and volumes of several specific types of three-dimensional solids. Now we'll consider the relationship between similarity of three-dimensional figures as compared to surface areas and volumes.

For three-dimensional figures, similarity means that pairs of congruent angles and the corresponding linear measurements must be in the same ratio. Many of the linear measurements refer to edges. (*Edges* in three dimensions

is equivalent to *sides* in two dimensions.) If necessary, you can refer to Figures 11.9 – 11.14 of Chapter 11.

Similar Prisms

Let's consider a rectangular prism with length, width and height of 10, 6, and 5, respectively. Its surface area is $(2)(10)(6) + (2)(10)(5) + (2)(6)(5) = 280$, and its volume is $(10)(6)(5) = 300$. Suppose a second rectangular prism has length, width, and height of 30, 18, and 15, respectively. We note that these rectangular prisms are similar. For this second rectangular prism, the surface area is $(2)(30)(18) + (2)(30)(15) + (2)(18)(15) = 2520$. Its volume is $(30)(18)(15) = 8100$.

The ratio of the corresponding edges is $\frac{1}{3}$. We note that the ratio of the surface areas is $\frac{280}{2520} = \frac{1}{9}$ and the ratio of the volumes is $\frac{300}{8100} = \frac{1}{27}$. We note that $\frac{1}{9} = \left(\frac{1}{3}\right)^2$ and $\frac{1}{27} = \left(\frac{1}{3}\right)^3$. It appears that the ratio of the surface areas is the square of the ratio of the linear dimensions. Also, the ratio of the volumes is the cube of the ratio of the linear dimensions.

Similar Cones

Let's consider two similar cones and explore whether we arrive at the same conclusions. The first cone has a radius of 3 and a (perpendicular) height of 4. This means that its lateral height is $\sqrt{3^2 + 4^2} = 5$. The surface area of this cone is $(\pi)(3^2) + (\pi)(3)(5) = 24\pi$, and its volume is $\left(\frac{1}{3}\right)(\pi)(3^2)(4) = 12\pi$.

Suppose a second cone has a radius of 15 and a height of 20. The lateral height is $\sqrt{15^2 + 20^2} = 25$, and the two cones must be similar, since each linear dimension has been multiplied by 5.

For this second cone, the surface area is $(\pi)(15^2) + (\pi)(15)(25) = 600\pi$ and its volume is $\left(\frac{1}{3}\right)(\pi)(15^2)(20) = 1500\pi$. We note that the ratio of the surface areas is $\dfrac{24\pi}{600\pi} = \dfrac{1}{25}$ and the ratio of the volumes

is $\dfrac{12\pi}{1500\pi} = \dfrac{1}{125}$. Noting that $\dfrac{1}{25} = \left(\dfrac{1}{5}\right)^2$ and $\dfrac{1}{125} = \left(\dfrac{1}{5}\right)^3$,

the ratio of the surface areas is the square of the ratio of the linear dimensions. Also, the ratio of the volumes is the cube of the ratio of the linear dimensions.

NOTE:

Without a formal proof, we declare that given two similar three-dimensional figures, the ratio of their surface areas will be the square of the ratio of their linear dimensions. Also, the ratio of their volumes will be the cube of the ratio of their linear dimensions.

EXAMPLE 15

The ratio of the volumes of two similar rectangular prisms is $\dfrac{8}{27}$. If the surface area of the smaller figure is 48 square inches, what is the surface area of the larger figure?

SOLUTION

The ratio of the linear dimensions is $\sqrt[3]{\dfrac{8}{27}} = \dfrac{2}{3}$, so

the ratio of their surface areas is $\left(\dfrac{2}{3}\right)^2 = \dfrac{4}{9}$. Let x repre-

sent the surface area of the larger figure. Then $\dfrac{4}{9} = \dfrac{48}{x}$,

so $x = 108$ square inches.

Similar Spheres

EXAMPLE 16

The ratio of the radii of two similar spheres is $\dfrac{6}{1}$. If the volume of the larger sphere is 1620, what is the volume of the smaller sphere?

SOLUTION

The ratio of their volumes is $\left(\dfrac{6}{1}\right)^3 = \dfrac{216}{1}$. Using

x to represent the volume of the smaller sphere, we

can write $\dfrac{216}{1} = \dfrac{1620}{x}$. Thus, $x = 7.5$.

Similar Cylinders

EXAMPLE 17

The height of the larger of two similar cylinders is 20 inches more than the height of the smaller cylinder. If the ratio of their surface areas is $\dfrac{9}{49}$, what is the height of the larger cylinder?

SOLUTION

The ratio of their heights is $\sqrt{\dfrac{9}{49}} = \dfrac{3}{7}$. Let x and

$x + 20$ represent the heights of the two cylinders. Then

$\dfrac{3}{7} = \dfrac{x}{x+20}$, which simplifies to $7x = 3x + 60$. So

$x = 15$, which means that the height of the larger cylinder is 35 inches.

Geometric Constructions Using a Compass and a Straightedge

FIRST CONSTRUCTION

Given a line l_1 and a point P on l_1, construct a line l_2 that is perpendicular to l_1 and contains P.

SOLUTION

With your compass, use *P* as the center of a circle and draw a semicircle so that *AB* is a diameter, where *A* and *B* lie on l_1. Figure 12.35 illustrates this construction.

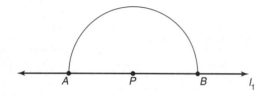

Figure 12.35

Second, use your compass, with each of A and B as a center, and make two intersecting arcs directly above P. Call this intersection point Q. This is shown in Figure 12.36.

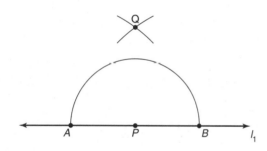

Figure 12.36

Third, draw a line that contains the point of intersection, Q, of the two arcs and point P. This is line l_2 and the construction is complete. Figure 12.37 shows this final step.

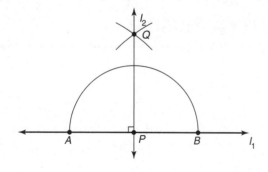

Figure 12.37

SECOND CONSTRUCTION

Given a line l_1 and a point *P* not on l_1, construct a line l_2 that is perpendicular to l_1 and contains *P*.

SOLUTION

From point P, use your compass to swing an arc large enough to intersect l_1 in two points *A* and *B*. Figure 12.38 shows this construction.

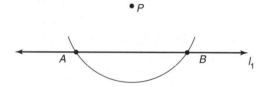

Figure 12.38

Second, use your compass, with each of *A* and *B* as a center, and make two intersecting arcs directly below *P*. Call this intersection point *Q*. This is shown in Figure 12.39.

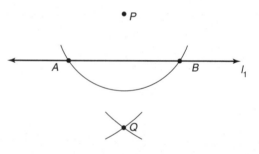

Figure 12.39

Third, draw a line that contains the point of intersection, Q, of the two arcs and point P. This is line l_2 and the construction is complete. Figure 12.40 illustrates this final step.

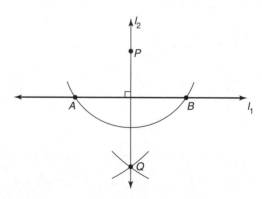

Figure 12.40

THIRD CONSTRUCTION

> Given a line segment $\overline{AB}$, construct a line l that is the perpendicular bisector of $\overline{AB}$.

SOLUTION

From each of points A and B, use your compass to swing an arc both above and below $\overline{AB}$, such that there are two intersecting points, P and Q. The length of the arcs should be the same. Figure 12.41 shows this construction.

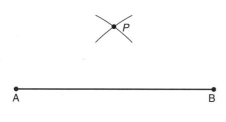

Figure 12.41

Second, draw line l that contains points P and Q. This is the perpendicular bisector of $\overline{AB}$. Figure 12.42 shows the final step.

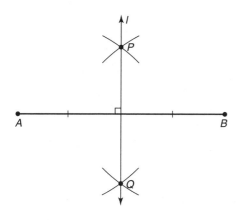

Figure 12.42

FOURTH CONSTRUCTION

> Given an angle $\angle ABC$ and any point E not on this angle, construct an angle $\angle DEF$ such that $\angle ABC$ is congruent to $\angle DEF$.

SOLUTION

Use your compass at point B and swing an arc so that it intersects both rays of the angle at points A and C. Figure 12.43 shows this construction.

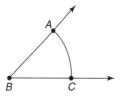

Figure 12.43

Second, draw any ray $\overrightarrow{EF}$, where neither E nor F are points of $\angle ABC$. Swing the same size arc at point E that was used at point B. This is shown in Figure 12.44.

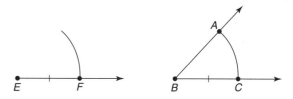

Figure 12.44

Third, using your compass to measure the opening between A and C, place the compass at point F and duplicate this opening on the arc formed at F. Call this point G on this arc. Figure 12.45 shows the location of point G.

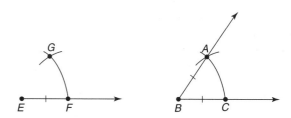

Figure 12.45

Fourth, draw ray $\overrightarrow{EG}$. Then $\angle GEF$ is congruent to $\angle ABC$. Figure 12.46 shows the final step.

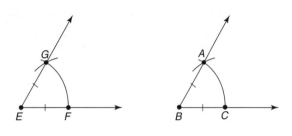

Figure 12.46

FIFTH CONSTRUCTION

Given any line l_1 and a point P not on l_1, construct a line l_2 that contains P and is parallel to l_1.

SOLUTION

Draw any line m that contains point P and intersects line l_1 at point A. Figure 12.47 shows line m.

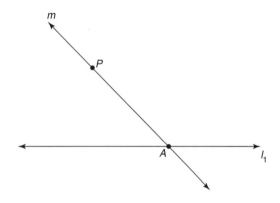

Figure 12.47

Second, using another point B on line l_1 and a point C on line m, use the techniques of the fourth construction to duplicate $\angle BAC$ at point P. Figure 12.48 shows all steps up to here.

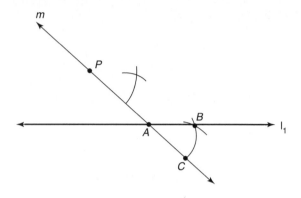

Figure 12.48

Third, complete the construction of the duplicated angle at P to form ray $\overrightarrow{PD}$. Then draw line $\overleftrightarrow{PD}$ and call it line l_2. This is the required line that is parallel to l_1, as shown in Figure 12.49. Note that $\angle DPE \cong \angle BAC$.

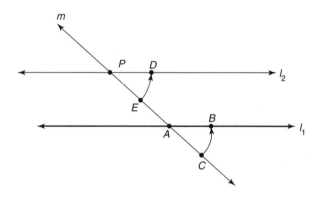

Figure 12.49

SIXTH CONSTRUCTION

Given any $\angle ABC$, construct a ray $\overrightarrow{BD}$ that bisects $\angle ABC$.

SOLUTION

Position your compass at point B and swing an arc to extend from $\overrightarrow{BC}$ to $\overrightarrow{BA}$, as shown in Figure 12.50.

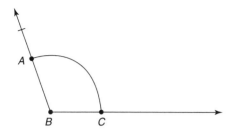

Figure 12.50

SOLUTION

Using the techniques of the first construction, select any point P on line l_2 and construct line m perpendicular to l_2. The line should be continued so that it intersects line l_1 at point Q. This is shown in Figure 12.53.

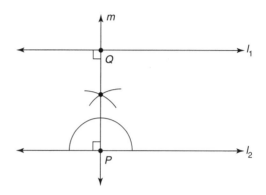

Figure 12.53

Second, construct two arcs of equal size from points A and C so that they intersect at a point D. This is illustrated in Figure 12.51.

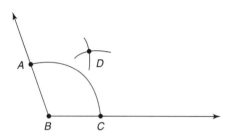

Figure 12.51

Second, follow the techniques of the third construction. This will produce the perpendicular bisector of $\overline{PQ}$, which can be labeled as line l_3.

This is the required line, as shown in Figure 12.54.

Third, draw $\overrightarrow{BD}$, which will be the angle bisector of $\angle ABC$, as shown in Figure 12.52.

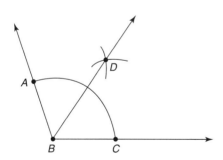

Figure 12.52

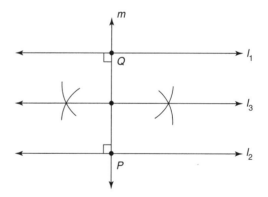

Figure 12.54

SEVENTH CONSTRUCTION

Given two parallel lines l_1 and l_2, construct a line l_3 that is parallel to and equidistant from both lines.

Quiz for Chapter 12

1. Consider the following definition: "An angle consists of two rays." This definition is faulty. Which one of the following should be added to the end of this definition so that it is a complete description of an angle?

    (A) going in opposite directions

    (B) with a common endpoint

    (C) that are congruent

    (D) with different endpoints

2. Given parallel lines l_1 and l_2, suppose that AB represents the distance between these lines. Point A lies on l_1, whereas points B and C lie on l_2. Which one of the following <u>must</u> be true?

    (A) $AB = BC = AC$

    (B) $AB < BC$

    (C) $AB < AC$

    (D) $\overline{AC}$ is perpendicular to l_2.

3. Which one of the following could represent two angles of a triangle that is both acute and isosceles?

    (A) 58° and 64°   (C) 56° and 60°

    (b) 41° and 41°   (D) 35° and 55°

4. In $\triangle XYZ$, $XY = 8$ and $XZ = 13$. Which one of the following is <u>not</u> possible?

    (A) $YZ > 19$ (C) YZ is the smallest side

    (B) $\angle Y < \angle Z$ (D) $\triangle XYZ$ is isosceles

5. Which one of the following <u>always</u> divides a triangle into two smaller triangles of equal area?

    (A) An altitude   (C) A midsegment

    (B) A median   (D) An angle bisector

6. Consider $\triangle JKL$, as shown below, in which $\overline{JM}$ is the angle bisector of $\angle J$.

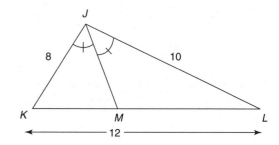

What is the length of $\overline{KM}$?

(A) $4\dfrac{1}{3}$ (C) $5\dfrac{1}{3}$

(B) $4\dfrac{2}{3}$ (D) $5\dfrac{2}{3}$

7. Consider right triangle PQR, as shown below, in which $\overline{QS}$ is the altitude to the hypotenuse.

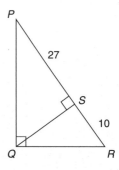

What is the best approximation of QS?

(A) 13.43   (C) 16.43

(B) 15.5   (D) 18.5

8. Each of triangles ACE and BDF have angle measures of 13° and 40°. Which one of the following is a valid conclusion?

    (A) The triangles are acute.

    (B) The triangles are isosceles.

(C) The triangles are congruent.

(D) The triangles are similar.

9. Triangles *GHJ* and *LMN* are similar. If ΔGHJ has sides of 14, 18, and 30, and the largest side of ΔLMN is 75, what is the <u>difference</u> of the perimeters of these triangles?

(A) 31   (C) 135

(B) 93   (D) 155

10. Triangles I and II are similar and the ratio of their areas is $\dfrac{25}{36}$. An altitude of triangle II is three units less than twice the corresponding altitude of triangle I. How many units is the altitude of triangle I?

(A) $\dfrac{10}{9}$ (C) $\dfrac{19}{6}$

(B) $\dfrac{8}{3}$ (D) $\dfrac{15}{4}$

11. Quadrilateral *ABCD* is a kite, in which $\overline{AC}$ is the longer diagonal. The diagonals intersect at point *E*. Which one of the following is <u>false</u>?

(A) $\angle ABD \cong \angle DBC$

(B) $\overline{AC} \perp \overline{BD}$

(C) $\angle DAC \cong \angle BAC$

(D) $\overline{DE} \cong \overline{BE}$

12. The ratio of the sides of two rhombi is $\dfrac{2}{5}$. The area of the larger rhombus is 300 square inches. Which one of the following pairs of numbers could represent the lengths of the diagonals of the smaller rhombus?

(A) 8 inches and 6 inches

(B) 10 inches and 16 inches

(C) 10 inches and 32 inches

(D) 16 inches and 6 inches

13. The ratio of the surface areas of two spheres is $\dfrac{9}{100}$. The radius of the smaller sphere is 12. What is the surface area of the larger sphere?

(A) 6400π (C) 3200π

(B) 4800π (D) 2400π

14. The height of the larger of two similar cylinders is 10 inches less than twice the height of the smaller cylinder and the ratio of their surface areas is $\dfrac{16}{25}$. The radius of the smaller cylinder is 6 inches. What is the volume of the smaller cylinder, in cubic inches?

(A) 512π (C) 360π

(B) 480π (D) 232π

15. Which one of the following shows all the correct markings for the construction of the perpendicular bisector of $\overline{RT}$?

(A)
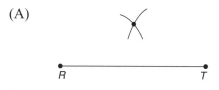

(B)

(C)
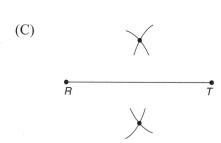

(D)
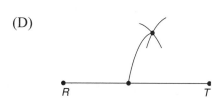

16. Look at the following markings for an unfinished construction.

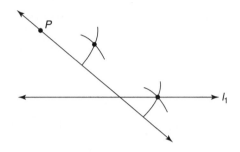

What type of construction is being represented?

(A) A line perpendicular to a given line through a given point

(B) A ray that bisects a given angle

(C) A line parallel to a given line through a given point

(D) A line parallel to and equidistant from two given parallel lines

Quiz for Chapter 12
SOLUTIONS

1. (B)

The definition of an angle specifically requires a common endpoint for its two rays.

2. (C)

Since *AB* represents the distance between these two parallel lines, it must be one of the legs of the triangle *ABC*. Thus, *AB* < *AC*.

3. (A)

If two of the angles are 58° and 64°, then the third angle is $180° - 58° - 64° = 58°$. A triangle with these angle measurements is acute and isosceles.

4. (B)

The order of the angle measurements in a triangle must be exactly the same as the order of their respective

opposite sides. Since $XY < XZ$, it follows that $\angle Z < \angle Y$. Answer choices (A) and (C) are possible because the restriction on *YZ* is 5 < *YZ* < 21. Answer choice (D) is a correct statement if *YZ* = 8 or *YZ* = 13.

5. (B)

A median joins a vertex with the midpoint of the opposite side. Two smaller triangles of equal area are formed.

6. (C)

Let *x* represent *KM* and let $12 - x$ represent *LM*. Then $\dfrac{8}{x} = \dfrac{10}{12 - x}$, which simplifies to $10x = 96 - 8x$. Thus, $x = 5\dfrac{1}{3}$.

7. (C)

QS is the geometric mean between PS and SR. Then $\dfrac{27}{QS} = \dfrac{QS}{10}$. Thus, $QS = \sqrt{270} \approx 16.43$.

8. (D)

The third angle of each triangle must be 127°, so these triangles are similar and obtuse.

9. (B)

The ratio of the perimeters is $\dfrac{30}{75} = \dfrac{2}{5}$, which also means that each side of the larger triangle is 2.5 times the corresponding side of the smaller triangle. Besides 75, the other two sides of ΔLMN are $(2.5)(14) = 35$ and $(2.5)(18) = 45$. So, the perimeter of ΔLMN is 155. Thus, since the perimeter of ΔGHJ is 62, the difference of perimeters is 93.

10. (D)

The ratio of the altitudes of these triangles is $\sqrt{\dfrac{25}{36}} = \dfrac{5}{6}$. Let x and $2x - 3$ represent the corresponding altitudes of Triangles I and II, respectively. Then $\dfrac{5}{6} = \dfrac{x}{2x - 3}$, which simplifies to $6x = 10x - 15$. Thus, $x = \dfrac{15}{4}$ units.

11. (A)

The shorter diagonal does not bisect the angles from which it originates.

12. (D)

The ratio of their areas is $\left(\dfrac{2}{5}\right)^2 = \dfrac{4}{25}$. Let x represent the area of the smaller rhombus. Then $\dfrac{4}{25} = \dfrac{x}{300}$,

so $x = 48$. Since the area of a rhombus is one half the product of the diagonals, the product of the diagonals of the smaller rhombus is 96. Only answer choice (D) has two numbers whose product is 96.

13. (A)

The ratio of their radii is $\sqrt{\dfrac{9}{100}} = \dfrac{3}{10}$. Let r represent the radius of the larger sphere. Then $\dfrac{3}{10} = \dfrac{12}{r}$, so $r = 40$. Thus, the surface area of the larger sphere is $(4)(\pi)(40^2) = 6400\pi$.

14. (B)

Let x and $2x - 10$ represent the two heights. Then $\dfrac{x}{2x - 10} = \sqrt{\dfrac{16}{25}} = \dfrac{4}{5}$. This equation becomes $5x = 8x - 40$, so $x = \dfrac{40}{3}$. Thus, the volume of the smaller cylinder is $(\pi)(6^2)\left(\dfrac{40}{3}\right) = 480\pi$ cubic inches.

15. (C)

In order to construct the perpendicular bisector of a line segment, a set of congruent arcs must be made above and below the line segment.

16. (C)

The markings shown are for the construction of a line through point P that is parallel to line l_1.

Chapter 13

Applications of Euclidean Geometry to Circles and Composite Figures

Welcome to Chapter 13. In this chapter, we will review the following topics:

(a) Properties of lines and angles related to circles
(b) Areas of circles and portions of circles
(c) Properties of regular polygons
(d) Perimeters and areas of composite figures
(e) Cross-sections and nets of three-dimensional figures
(f) Geometric constructions related to circles

Properties of Lines and Angles Related to Circles

Figure 13.1, in which point P is the center, shows the major lines and segments related to a circle.

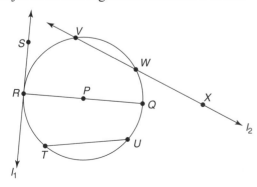

Figure 13.1

A circle is named by its center point. In Figure 13.1, this is **circle P**.

A **radius** is a line segment whose endpoints are the center and a point on the circle. Each of $\overline{PR}$ and $\overline{PQ}$ is a radius. (Plural: radii).

A **diameter** is a line segment whose endpoints are points of the circle and whose midpoint is the center. $\overline{QR}$ is a diameter.

A **chord** is a line segment whose endpoints are any two points of the circle. $\overline{UT}$ is a chord. Note that any diameter is also a chord.

A **tangent** is a line that intersects a circle at exactly one point, which is called the **point of tangency**. Line l_1 is a tangent for which R is the point of tangency.

A **tangent segment** is the portion of a tangent for which one endpoint is the point of tangency. $\overline{RS}$ is a tangent segment.

A **secant** is a line that intersects a circle at exactly two points. Line l_2 is a secant line.

A **secant segment** is the portion of a secant whose endpoints are a point of the secant line outside the circle and the furthest intersection point of the circle. $\overline{VX}$ is a secant segment.

An **external part of a secant segment** is the portion of a secant whose endpoints are a point of the secant line outside the circle and the closest intersection point of the circle. $\overline{WX}$ is an external part of the secant segment $\overline{VX}$.

The **circumference** is the length of the closed curve that constitutes the circle.

A **semicircle** describes the part of the circle whose length is one half the circumference. It is denoted with an arc symbol and three letters such that the first and last letters are the endpoints of a diameter. Each of $\overset{\frown}{RVQ}$ and $\overset{\frown}{QTR}$ is a semicircle.

A **minor arc** describes a part of the circle that is less than a semicircle. It is denoted by an arc symbol and its two endpoints. Each of $\overset{\frown}{RT}$ and $\overset{\frown}{VW}$ is a minor arc.

A **major arc** describes a part of the circle that is greater than a semicircle. It is denoted by an arc symbol and three letters such that the first and last letters are the endpoints. Each of $\overset{\frown}{RVU}$ and $\overset{\frown}{TUV}$ is a major arc.

Arcs of a circle can be measured in angular units or in linear units. If angular units are used, the two most popular choices are degrees and radians. A full circle represents 360° or 2π radians. Thus, a semicircle represents 180° or π radians. A minor arc has a measure of less than 180°. A major arc has a measure of more than 180° but less than 360°.

Major Angles

Figure 13.2, in which point P is the center, shows the major angles formed by lines and arcs of a circle.

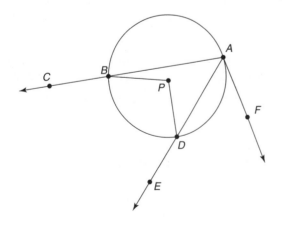

Figure 13.2

$\overrightarrow{AF}$ is a **tangent ray** (part of a tangent line) and each of $\overrightarrow{AC}$ and $\overrightarrow{AE}$ is a **secant ray** (part of a secant line).

An **inscribed angle** is an angle formed by two rays whose vertex lies on the circle. Each of $\angle CAE$ and $\angle FAD$ are examples of inscribed angles.

A **central angle** is an angle formed by two radii. $\angle BPD$ is a central angle.

Theorems Associated with Line Segments, Rays and Angles of a Circle

The proofs of the following theorems can be found in most geometry books. In each of these theorems, point P is the center of the circle.

FIRST THEOREM

Any two tangent segments drawn to a circle from a common external point are congruent. In Figure 13.3, $AB = AC$.

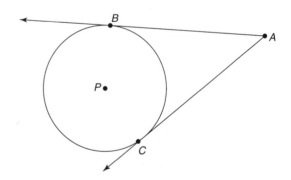

Figure 13.3

SECOND THEOREM

If two secants are drawn to a circle from a point outside the circle, the product of the lengths of one secant segment and its external part is equal to the product of the other secant segment and its external part. In Figure 13.4, $(DF)(DE) = (DH)(DG)$.

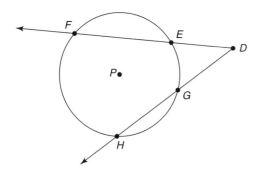

Figure 13.4

THIRD THEOREM

If a secant and a tangent are drawn to a circle from a point outside the circle, the product of the length of the secant segment and its external part equals the square of the tangent segment. In Figure 13.5, $(JL)(JK) = (JM)^2$.

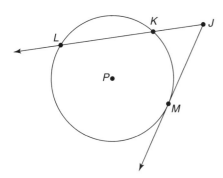

Figure 13.5

FOURTH THEOREM

If two chords intersect in the interior of a circle, the product of the of the lengths of the segments of one chord equals the product of the lengths of the segments of the other chord. In Figure 13.6, $(NT)(RT) = (QT)(ST)$.

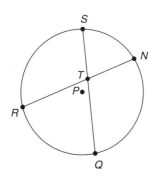

Figure 13.6

EXAMPLE 1

Using Figure 13.4, if $DE = 4$, $EF = 6$, and $DH = 8$, what is the value of DG?

SOLUTION

Noting that $DF = 10$, the equation becomes $(10)(4) = (8)(DG)$. Thus, $DG = 5$.

EXAMPLE 2

Using Figure 13.5, if $JL = 20$ and $JK = 7$, what is the value of JM to the nearest hundredth?

SOLUTION

$(20)(7) = 140 = (JM)^2$. Thus, $JM = \sqrt{140} \approx 11.83$.

EXAMPLE 3

Using Figure 13.6, if $NT = 5$, $RT = 7$, and $QT = 9$, what is the value of QS?

SOLUTION

$(5)(7) = (9)(ST)$, so $ST = 3\dfrac{8}{9}$. Thus, $QS = QT + ST = 12\dfrac{8}{9}$.

Theorems Related to the Angles Formed by Secants, Tangents, and Chords of Circles

FIFTH THEOREM

A radius drawn to a point of tangency is perpendicular to the tangent . In Figure 13.7, $\overleftrightarrow{UV} \perp \overline{PV}$.

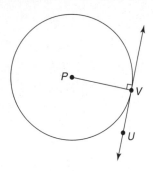

Figure 13.7

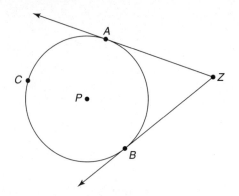

Figure 13.9

SIXTH THEOREM

If an angle consists of a tangent ray and a chord drawn to the point of tangency, the measure of the angle is one half the measure of the intercepted arc. In Figure 13.8,

$$\angle WXY = \left(\frac{1}{2}\right)(\overarc{WX}).$$

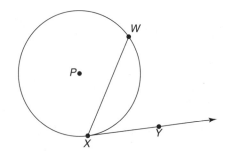

Figure 13.8

NOTE:

If $\angle WXY$ is an obtuse angle, then the intercepted arc will be a major arc, which must be named using three letters.

SEVENTH THEOREM

If an angle is formed by two tangents from a common external point, its measure is one half the difference of the measures of the intercepted arcs. In Figure 13.9,

$$\angle Z = \left(\frac{1}{2}\right)(\overarc{ACB} - \overarc{AB}).$$

EIGHTH THEOREM

If an angle is formed by either two secants or a secant and a tangent from an external point, its measure is one half the difference of the measures of the intercepted arcs. In Figure 13.10, $\angle D = \left(\frac{1}{2}\right)(\overarc{FH} - \overarc{EG})$.

In Figure 13.11, $\angle J = \left(\frac{1}{2}\right)(\overarc{LM} - \overarc{KM})$.

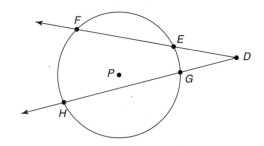

Figure 13.10

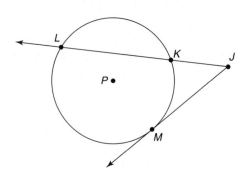

Figure 13.11

NINTH THEOREM

The measure of a central angle equals the measure of the intercepted arc. In Figure 13.12, $\angle NPQ = \angle 1 = \overset{\frown}{NQ}$.

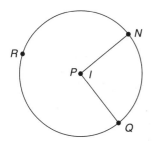

Figure 13.12

NOTE:

The measure of the reflex angle NPQ is also equal to its intercepted arc, which is $\overset{\frown}{NRQ}$.

TENTH THEOREM

The measure of an inscribed angle is one half the measure of its intercepted arc. In Figure 13.13, $\angle U = \left(\dfrac{1}{2}\right)(\overset{\frown}{ST})$.

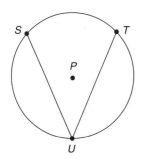

Figure 13.13

ELEVENTH THEOREM

If two chords intersect in the interior of a circle, the measure of each angle formed is one half the sum of its intercepted arc and the intercepted arc of its vertical angle. In Figure 13.14, $\angle 1 = \left(\dfrac{1}{2}\right)(\overset{\frown}{VW} + \overset{\frown}{XAY})$.

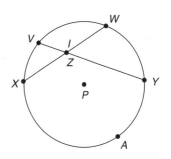

Figure 13.14

EXAMPLE 4

Using Figure 13.9, if $\overset{\frown}{ACB} = 238°$, what is the measure of $\angle Z$?

SOLUTION

We first determine that $\overset{\frown}{AB} = 360° - 238° = 122°$. Then $\angle Z = \left(\dfrac{1}{2}\right)(238° - 122°) = 58°$.

EXAMPLE 5

Using Figure 13.10, if $\angle D = 24°$ and $\overset{\frown}{EG} = 30°$, what is the measure of $\overset{\frown}{FH}$?

SOLUTION

Let x represent $\overset{\frown}{FH}$. Then $24° = \left(\dfrac{1}{2}\right)(x - 30°)$, which can be simplified to $48° = x - 30°$. Thus, $x = 78°$.

EXAMPLE 6

Using Figure 13.11, if $\angle J = 45°$ and $\overset{\frown}{KM} = 70°$, what is the measure of $\overset{\frown}{KL}$?

SOLUTION

Let x represent $\overset{\frown}{LM}$. Then $45° = \left(\dfrac{1}{2}\right)(x - 70°)$, which can be simplified to $90° = x - 70°$. So $x = 160°$, which means that $\overset{\frown}{KL} = 360° - 160° - 70° = 130°$.

NOTE:

Since $\overset{\frown}{KL} = 130°$, we can determine that $\overset{\frown}{LKM} = 200°$. This implies that $\overset{\frown}{LKM}$ really is a major arc. It is important to remember that major arcs <u>must</u> be identified with three letters. For minor arcs, two letters are sufficient; however, it is acceptable (though not common) to use three letters.

EXAMPLE 7

Look at the following diagram.

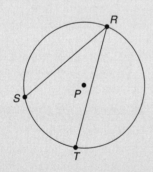

If $\overset{\frown}{RS} = 128°$ and $\overset{\frown}{RT} = 144°$, what is the measure of $\angle R$?

SOLUTION

$\overset{\frown}{ST} = 360° - \overset{\frown}{RS} - \overset{\frown}{RT} = 88°$. Thus, $\angle R = \left(\dfrac{1}{2}\right)(88°)$ $= 44°$.

EXAMPLE 8

Using Figure 13.14, if $\overset{\frown}{VW} = 76°$ and $\angle 1 = 124°$, what is the measure of $\overset{\frown}{XAY}$?

SOLUTION

Let x represent the measure of $\overset{\frown}{XAY}$. Then $124° = \left(\dfrac{1}{2}\right)(76° + x)$, which simplifies to $248° = 76° + x$. Thus, $x = 172°$.

Areas of Circles and Portions of Circles

A **sector** of a circle is a region bounded by two radii and the minor arc between them.

A **segment** of a circle is a region bounded by a chord and the minor arc that contains the same endpoints.

In Figure 13.15, sector *BPC* is shaded. In Figure 13.16, segment *DE* is shaded.

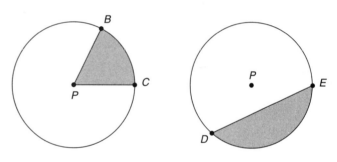

Figure 13.15   **Figure 13.16**

NOTE:

It is unfortunate that some mathematical terms are used in more than one context. You have already seen more than one interpretation of *tangent* and *secant*. The word *segment* can refer to either a portion of a line or to a region bounded by a chord and a minor arc. If we need to refer to the line segment in Figure 13.16, we will use the notation $\overline{DE}$.

We already know that $C = 2\pi r$ and $A = \pi r^2$ refer to the circumference and the area of a circle, respectively. Following are the formulas for the length of the minor arc of a sector and the area of a sector.

Let L_S represent the arc length of a sector, let A_S represent the area of a sector, let θ represent the central angle (in degrees), let C represent the circumference, and let A_C represent the area of the circle. Then $\dfrac{L_S}{C} = \dfrac{\theta}{360°}$. Also, $\dfrac{A_S}{A_C} = \dfrac{\theta}{360°}$.

NOTE:

> For either formula, if θ is measured in radians, replace 360° with 2π.

EXAMPLE 9

> The radius of a circle is 4 units. What is the length of an arc of a sector for which the central angle is 60°?

SOLUTION

The circumference is 8π. Let x represent the length of the arc. Then $\dfrac{x}{8\pi} = \dfrac{60°}{360°} = \dfrac{1}{6}$. Thus, $x = \dfrac{4\pi}{3}$ units.

EXAMPLE 10

> The radius of a circle is 10 inches. If the area of a sector is 35π square inches, what is the measure of the central angle (in degrees)?

SOLUTION

Let x represent the measure of the central angle. We determine that the area of the circle is 100π. Then $\dfrac{35\pi}{100\pi} = \dfrac{7}{20} = \dfrac{x}{360°}$. Thus, $x = 126°$.

EXAMPLE 11

> The length of an arc of a circle is 15π and the central angle is $\dfrac{5\pi}{6}$ radians. What is the area of the circle?

SOLUTION

Let x represent the circumference. Then $\dfrac{15\pi}{x} = \dfrac{\frac{5\pi}{6}}{2\pi} = \dfrac{5}{12}$, so $x = 36\pi$. A circumference of 36π means that the radius is 18. Finally, the area of the circle must be 324π.

In order to determine the area of a segment of a circle, we must find the area of the sector that contains the segment, then subtract the area of the triangle formed with the associated line segment and the radii with endpoints matching this line segment. Let's return to Figure 13.16. If you draw the radii $\overline{PD}$ and $\overline{PE}$, then the area of the shaded region described by the segment DE is the difference in the areas of the sector DPE and $\triangle DPE$. You recall that we identified three different ways to calculate the area of a triangle, namely

a) $A = \left(\dfrac{1}{2}\right)(b)(h)$,   b) $A = \sqrt{(s)(s-a)(s-b)(s-c)}$,

and c) $A = \left(\dfrac{1}{2}\right)(a)(b)(\sin\angle C)$.

EXAMPLE 12

> Consider the following diagram:
>
>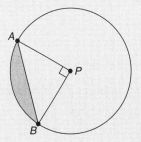
>
> If $AB = 10$, what is the area of the (shaded) segment AB? (Nearest hundredth)

SOLUTION

Since we have an isosceles right triangle, each of AP and BP has a value of $\dfrac{10}{\sqrt{2}} = 5\sqrt{2}$. Then the area of the circle is $(\pi)(5\sqrt{2})^2 = 50\pi$. This means that we can find the area of this sector (A_S) using the proportion $\frac{A_S}{50\pi} = \frac{90°}{360°}$. So, $A_S = 12.5\pi$. The area of ΔPAB is $\left(\frac{1}{2}\right)(5\sqrt{2})(5\sqrt{2}) = 25$. Thus, the area of segment AB is $12.5\pi - 25 \approx 14.27$.

EXAMPLE 13

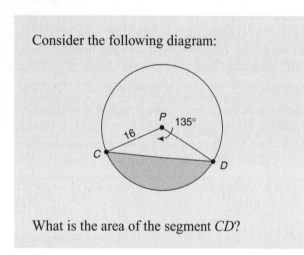

Consider the following diagram:

What is the area of the segment *CD*?

SOLUTION

We know that $PD = 16$, since it is a radius. Then the area of ΔPCD is $\left(\frac{1}{2}\right)(16)(16)(\sin 135°) \approx 90.51$. The area of the circle is 256π, so the area of the sector PCD (A_S) is found by the proportion $\frac{A_S}{256\pi} = \frac{135°}{360°}$. This leads to $A_S = 96\pi$. Thus, the area of segment *CD* is $96\pi - 90.51 \approx 211.08$

Properties of Regular Polygons

A **regular polygon** is one in which all sides are congruent and all angles are congruent. The formula for determining the measure of each angle of a regular polygon of n sides is $\frac{(180°)(n-2)}{n}$. For example, in a regular octagon (8-sided polygon), the measure of each angle is $\frac{(180°)(6)}{8} = 135°$.

The **center** of a regular polygon is the point that is equidistant from all vertices.

An **apothem** of a regular polygon is a line segment whose endpoints are the center and the midpoint of one of the sides.

A **radius** of a regular polygon is a line segment whose endpoints are the center and one of the vertices.

Figure 13.17 illustrates a regular pentagon (5-sided polygon) with center P, apothem $\overline{PK}$, and radius $\overline{PG}$.

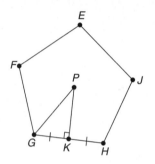

Figure 13.17

NOTE:

There are five apothems and five radii for this pentagon. Also, each apothem is perpendicular to the side to which it is drawn.

Inscribed and Circumscribed Circles

An **inscribed** circle of a polygon is a circle for which each side is a tangent segment.

A **circumscribed** circle of a polygon is a circle that contains each vertex. Figures 13.18 and 13.19 illustrate an inscribed circle and a circumscribed circle respectively for the pentagon shown in Figure 13.17.

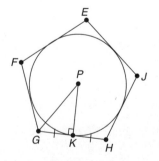

Figure 13.18

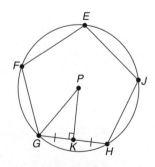

Figure 13.19

NOTE:

> The radius of the inscribed circle is the length of an apothem of the pentagon. The radius of the circumscribed circle is the radius of the pentagon.

Given a regular polygon of n sides, in which the length of each side is s and the length of the apothem is a, then the perimeter is ns and the area is $\left(\frac{1}{2}\right)(a)(n)(s)$. If the perimeter is known, you can substitute that value for ns in the area formula. In many textbooks, the area formula is shown as $A = \frac{1}{2}ap$, where p is the perimeter. Be aware that these formulas apply <u>only</u> to regular polygons.

From our earlier discussion concerning the measure of each angle of a regular polygon, we note that since $EFGHJ$ is a pentagon, $\angle FGK = \frac{(180°)(3)}{5} = 108°$. As you would probably guess, $\angle FGK = (2)(\angle PGK)$. Thus $\angle PGK = 54°$. This angle measure will be needed for the next few examples.

EXAMPLE 14

> Using Figure 13.17, if the radius is 15 inches, what is the perimeter of the pentagon, to the nearest hundredth of an inch?

SOLUTION

From our knowledge of trigonometry, $\cos 54° = \frac{GK}{15}$. Then $GK = (15)(\cos 54°) \approx 8.817$. This means that $GH \approx 17.634$. Thus, the perimeter is approximately $(5)(17.634) \approx 88.17$ inches.

EXAMPLE 15

> Using the information of Example 14, what is the area of $EFGHJ$, to the nearest hundredth?

SOLUTION

We use the relationship $\sin 54° = \frac{PK}{15}$. Then $PK = (15)(\sin 54°) \approx 12.135$ Since $\overline{PK}$ represents the apothem, the area of the pentagon is $\left(\frac{1}{2}\right)(12.135)$ $(88.17) \approx 534.97$ square inches.

EXAMPLE 16

> Using Figure 13.18, if the area of the circle is 25π, what is the perimeter of the pentagon? (Nearest hundredth)

SOLUTION

The radius of the circle, which is also the value of PK, is 5. Now we note that $\tan 54° = \frac{5}{GK}$. So $GK = \frac{5}{\tan 54°} \approx 3.633$, which means that $GH \approx 7.266$. Thus, the perimeter is approximately $(5)(7.266) = 36.33$.

EXAMPLE 17

> Using Figure 13.19, if the perimeter of $EFGHJ$ is 80 inches, what is the area of the circumscribed circle, to the nearest hundredth?

SOLUTION

Each side of the pentagon must be 16 inches, which means that $GK = 8$ inches. Then $\cos 54° = \frac{8}{PG}$, so that $PG = \frac{8}{\cos 54°} \approx 13.61$. Since $\overline{PG}$ is the radius, the area of the circle is $(\pi)(13.61)^2 \approx 581.92$ square inches.

Regular Hexagon

Figures 13.20 and 13.21 show a regular hexagon with its inscribed circle and circumscribed circle, respectively.

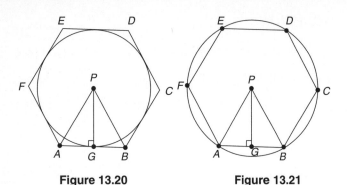

| Figure 13.20 | Figure 13.21 |

Each angle of a regular hexagon must be $\frac{(180°)(4)}{6} = 120°$. This means that for each of Figures 13.20 and 13.21, $\angle PAG = 60°$. As an added bonus, since $\angle PBG = 60°$, ΔPAB must be equilateral. Furthermore, each of ΔPAG and ΔPBG is a 30°-60°-90° right triangle. This implies that the ratio of AG : PG : AP $= 1 : \sqrt{3} : 2$. These phenomena make our computations concerning perimeter and area much simpler.

EXAMPLE 18

Using Figure 13.20, if the radius of the circle is $4\sqrt{3}$, what is the perimeter of the hexagon *ABCDEF*?

SOLUTION

Using the ratio of sides of a 30°-60°-90° right triangle, since $PG = 4\sqrt{3}$, $AG = 4$. Then $AB = 8$, so the perimeter of *ABCDEF* is $(8)(6) = 48$.

EXAMPLE 19

Using Figure 13.21, if the area of the circle is 144π, what is the length of the apothem of *ABCDEF*, to the nearest hundredth ?

SOLUTION

The radius of the circle, which is also the radius of the hexagon (AP), is 12. Since *AP* is the hypotenuse of the 30°-60°-90° right triangle *PAG*, we can use

the basic ratio of sides, which is $1 : \sqrt{3} : 2$. The value of *AP* corresponds to the number 2 in this ratio, so $PG = 6\sqrt{3} \approx 10.39$.

EXAMPLE 20

If each side of a regular hexagon is 3 centimeters, what is its area, to the nearest hundredth of a centimeter?

SOLUTION

Even without a diagram, we can consider the apothem as the altitude of an equilateral triangle in which each side is 3 centimeters. From our knowledge of geometry, if x represents the side of an equilateral triangle, then $\left(\frac{x}{2}\right)(\sqrt{3})$ represents the length of the altitude (height). In this example, the apothem must be $\left(\frac{3}{2}\right)(\sqrt{3})$. The perimeter of the hexagon is 18, so its area is $\left(\frac{1}{2}\right)\left(\frac{3}{2}\right)(\sqrt{3})(18) \approx 23.38$ square centimeters.

NOTE:

There is another method to calculating this answer. The formula $A = \left(\frac{x^2}{4}\right)(\sqrt{3})$ can be applied to find the area of any equilateral triangle with a side of x. In Example 20, this area becomes $\left(\frac{9}{4}\right)(\sqrt{3})$. This answer represents the area of ΔPAG. The hexagon contains a total of five other triangles that are congruent to ΔPAG. Each of these triangles would have two consecutive vertices and the point P. Thus, the area of the hexagon is $(6)\left(\frac{9}{4}\right)(\sqrt{3}) \approx 23.38$ square centimeters.

Perimeters and Areas of Composite Figures

Composite figures are combinations of two or more figures, but each of our examples will contain only two figures. In each case, the two figures will be connected with a common side or one figure will lie entirely within the other figure.

EXAMPLE 21

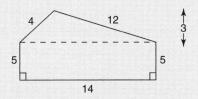

Consider the following composite figure.

What is its perimeter and area?

SOLUTION

The perimeter is 5 + 14 + 5 + 4 + 12 = 40. The total area (A) is the area of the rectangle added to the area of the triangle. Thus, $A = (14)(5) + \left(\frac{1}{2}\right)(14)(3) = 91$.

EXAMPLE 22

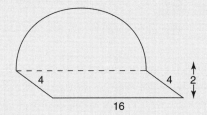

The following composite figure consists of a semicircle on top of a parallelogram.

What is the perimeter and area, to the nearest hundredth?

SOLUTION

The three sides of the parallelogram add up to 24. The length of the semicircle is equivalent to half the circumference of a circle with a radius of 8. This value is 8π, so the perimeter for the entire figure is $24 + 8\pi \approx 49.13$. The area of the parallelogram portion is $(16)(2) = 32$. The area of the semicircle is $\left(\frac{1}{2}\right)(\pi)(8^2) \approx 100.53$. Thus, the area for the entire figure is approximately 132.53.

EXAMPLE 23

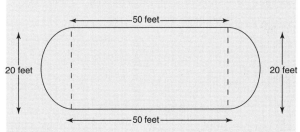

The following figure is a small track consisting of two semicircles that are attached to the widths of a rectangle.

What is the perimeter and area, to the nearest hundredth?

SOLUTION

The perimeter is composed of two lengths of the rectangle and the equivalent of the circumference of a circle. The circumference of a circle with a diameter of 20 feet is 20π feet. Thus, the perimeter for the entire figure is $50 + 50 + 20\pi \approx 162.83$ feet. The area for the entire figure is $(50)(20) + (\pi)(10^2) \approx 1314.16$ square feet.

We now look at areas of shaded regions in which one geometric figure *lies completely inside* another figure.

EXAMPLE 24

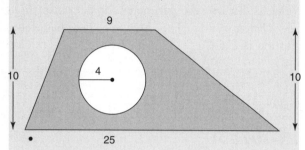

In the following diagram, a circle lies inside a trapezoid.

What is the area of the shaded region, to the nearest hundredth?

SOLUTION

The area of the trapezoid is $\left(\dfrac{1}{2}\right)(10)(25 + 9) = 170$

and the area of the circle is 16π. Thus, the area of the shaded region is $170 - 16\pi \approx 119.73$.

EXAMPLE 25

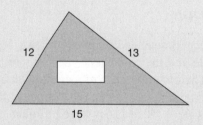

In the following diagram, a rectangle lies inside a triangle.

If the length and width of the rectangle are 7 and 3, respectively, what is the area of the shaded region, to the nearest hundredth?

SOLUTION

Using Heron's formula, the area of the triangle is $\sqrt{(20)(8)(7)(5)} \approx 74.83$. Since the area of the rectangle

is 21, the area of the shaded region is approximately $74.83 - 21 = 53.83$.

EXAMPLE 26

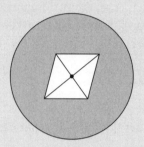

In the following diagram, a rhombus lies inside a circle.

The diameter of the circle is 14 inches and the diagonals of the rhombus are 8 inches and 5 inches.

What is the area of the shaded region, to the nearest hundredth?

SOLUTION

The radius of the circle is 7 inches, so the circle's area is 49π square inches. The area of the rhombus is $\left(\dfrac{1}{2}\right)(8)(5) = 20$ square inches. Thus, the area of the shaded region is $49\pi - 20 \approx 133.94$ square inches.

Cross-sections and Nets of Three-dimensional Figures

A **net** is a two-dimensional unfolded representation of the pieces of a three-dimensional figure. Figures 13.22 – 13.26 are the five most common nets you will encounter. For each net, the three-dimensional figure is named.

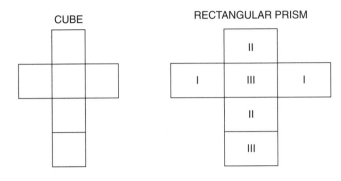

CUBE

Figure 13.22

RECTANGULAR PRISM

Figure 13.23

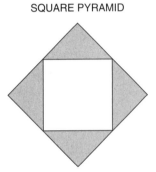

SQUARE PYRAMID

Figure 13.24

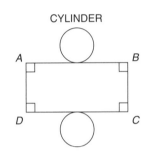

CYLINDER

Figure 13.25

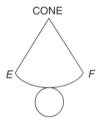

CONE

Figure 13.26

Figure 13.22 consists of six squares.

Figure 13.23 consists of three pairs of congruent rectangles.

Figure 13.24 consists of a square and four triangles that are either isosceles or equilateral.

Figure 13.25 consists of two circles and one square or rectangle. In addition, AB must equal the length of the circumference.

Figure 13.26 consists of one circle and a sector of a larger circle. In addition, the length of $\overset{\frown}{EF}$ must equal the length of the circumference of the small circle.

Geometric Constructions Related to Circles

As with the constructions in Chapter 12, only a straightedge or a compass may be used.

FIRST CONSTRUCTION

Given a circle, locate its center.

SOLUTION

Draw any two chords $\overline{AB}$ and $\overline{CD}$, as shown in Figure 13.27.

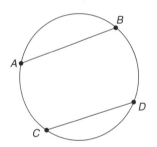

Figure 13.27

Second, use the third construction of Chapter 12 to create the perpendicular bisectors of $\overline{AB}$ and $\overline{CD}$. This is shown in Figure 13.28.

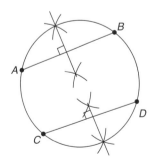

Figure 13.28

Third, extend these perpendicular bisectors until they intersect at point P. Then P is the center of this circle, as shown in Figure 13.29.

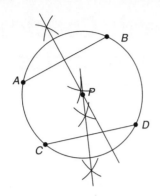

Figure 13.29

SECOND CONSTRUCTION

Given a point *A* on circle *P*, draw a tangent line at *A*.

SOLUTION

Draw ray $\overrightarrow{PA}$, as shown in Figure 13.30.

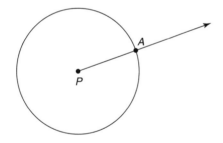

Figure 13.30

Second, use the first construction of Chapter 12 to create a line l_1 perpendicular to $\overrightarrow{PA}$. The line l_1 is the required tangent line, as shown in Figure 13.31.

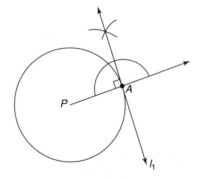

Figure 13.31

THIRD CONSTRUCTION

Given a point *E* not on circle *P*, draw a tangent to the circle.

SOLUTION

Draw the line segment $\overline{EP}$, then locate its midpoint *F* by using the third construction of Chapter 12. (This construction actually yields the perpendicular bisector, but we only need the midpoint.) Figure 13.32 shows this construction.

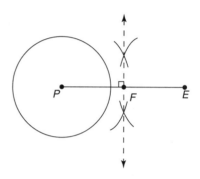

Figure 13.32

Second, using F as the center, draw the circle with either $\overline{FP}$ or $\overline{FE}$ as the radius. Label the intersection points of the two circles as *C* and *D*. Figure 13.33 illustrates this new circle with the intersection points.

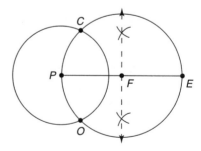

Figure 13.33

Third, draw either $\overrightarrow{EC}$ or $\overrightarrow{ED}$. These are the tangent rays to circle *P* from point *E*. This is shown in Figure 13.34.

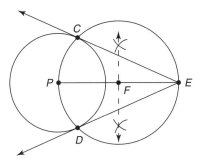

Figure 13.34

FOURTH CONSTRUCTION

> Draw a circle that contains three given non-collinear points X, Y, and Z.

SOLUTION

Draw any two line segments joining two of these three points, as shown in Figure 13.35.

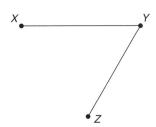

Figure 13.35

Second, construct the perpendicular bisector of each of $\overline{XY}$ and $\overline{YZ}$. Extend them until they intersect at a point P, as shown in Figure 13.36.

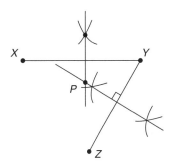

Figure 13.36

Third, using P as the center and the distance PX as the length of the radius, draw the circle that will now contain each of X, Y, and Z. This is shown in Figure 13.37.

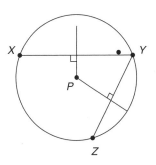

Figure 13.37

Quiz for Chapter 13

1. Consider the following diagram, in which point *P* is the center of the circle.

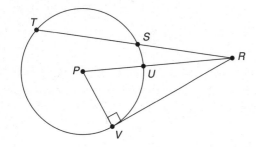

   Which one of the following is a secant segment?

   (A) $\overline{RT}$ (C) $\overline{RU}$

   (B) $\overline{RS}$ (D) $\overline{RV}$

2. In the following diagram, each of $\overline{LM}$ and $\overline{LN}$ is a tangent to circle *P*.

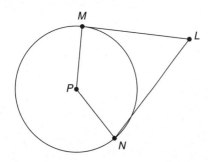

   Which one of the following is <u>not necessarily</u> <u>true</u>?

   (A) $LM = LN$

   (B) $LM = PM$

   (C) $LM + PM$ is one half the perimeter of *LMPN*.

   (D) $\overline{LM} \perp \overline{PM}$

3. In the following diagram, $\overrightarrow{QT}$ is tangent to circle *P* at point *T*.

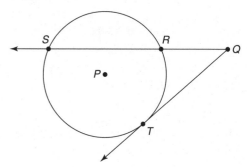

   If $RS = 8$ and $QR = 6.24$, what is the best approximation of *QT*?

   (A) 9.43   (C) 7.68

   (B) 8.28   (D) 7.07

4. Consider the following diagram, in which point *P* is the center of the circle.

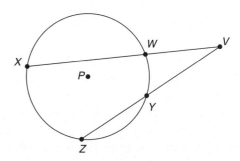

   If $VW = 9$, $WX = 12$, and $VZ = 18$, what is the value of *YZ*?

   (A) 13.5   (C) 7.5

   (B) 10.5   (D) 6.5

5. In the following diagram, in which P is the center, chords $\overline{AC}$ and $\overline{BD}$ intersect at point E.

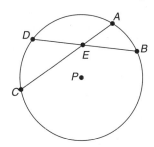

$DE = 2$ and $EB = 5$. If CE is twice as large as AE, what is the value of AE?

(A) 2.24   (C) 3.74

(B) 2.98   (D) 4.48

6. In the following diagram, in which P is the center, $\overset{\frown}{JF} = 28°$, $\angle FGH = 52°$, and $\overrightarrow{GH}$ is a tangent ray.

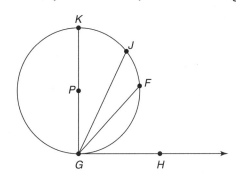

What is the measure of $\overset{\frown}{JK}$?

(A) 54°   (C) 50°

(B) 52°   (D) 48°

7. Consider the following diagram, in which P is the center. Each of $\overline{LM}$ and $\overline{LQ}$ is a tangent segment.

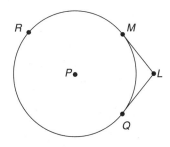

If the measure of $\overset{\frown}{MRQ}$ is four times the measure of $\overset{\frown}{MQ}$, what is the measure of $\angle L$?

(A) 102°   (C) 114°

(B) 108°   (D) 120°

8. For the following diagram, in which P is the center, $\overrightarrow{TV}$ is a secant ray and $\overrightarrow{TW}$ is a tangent ray.

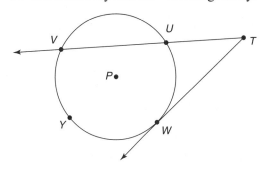

If $\overset{\frown}{UW} = 86°$ and $\angle T = 42°$, what is the measure of $\overset{\frown}{UV}$?

(A) 120°   (C) 104°

(B) 112°   (D) 96°

9. Use the following diagram, in which P is the center.

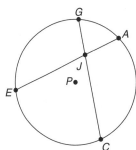

If $\overset{\frown}{EG} + \overset{\frown}{AC} = 210°$, what is the measure of $\angle GJA$?

(A) 60°   (C) 70°

(B) 65°   (D) 75°

10. The radius of a circle is 15 units. If the area of a sector is 100π square units, what is the measure of the central angle?

(A) 145°   (C) 155°

(B) 150°   (D) 160°

11. The central angle of a sector of a circle is 130°. If the associated arc length is 2.6π feet, what is the area of this sector in square feet?

    (A) 4.68π (C) 10.08π

    (B) 7.2π (D) 12.96π

12. Consider the following diagram, in which *P* is the center.

    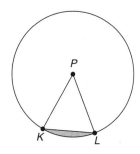

    If $PK = 12$ and $\angle KPL = 30°$, what is the area of the segment *KL* to the nearest hundredth?

    (A) 1.50   (C) 2.05

    (B) 1.70   (D) 2.15

13. A regular polygon is inscribed in a circle. Which one of the following must be congruent to the radius of the circle?

    (A) The radius of the polygon

    (B) The apothem of the polygon

    (C) The diameter of the polygon

    (D) The perimeter of the polygon

14. The following diagram shows a regular hexagon and its inscribed circle.

    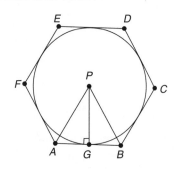

If the radius of the circle is $8\sqrt{3}$, what is the area of hexagon *ABCDEF*?

(A) $96\sqrt{3}$ (C) $288\sqrt{3}$

(B) $192\sqrt{3}$ (D) $384\sqrt{3}$

15. The following composite figure consists of a semi-circle on top of an equilateral triangle.

    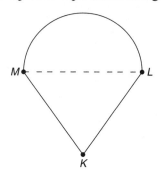

    If $KM = 10$, which one of the following lists the correct perimeter <u>and</u> area of the entire figure?

    (A) Perimeter $= 30 + 5\pi$ and area $= 12.5\pi + 25\sqrt{3}$

    (B) Perimeter $= 30 + 5\pi$ and area $= 25\pi + 12.5\sqrt{3}$

    (C) Perimeter $= 20 + 5\pi$ and area $= 12.5\pi + 25\sqrt{3}$

    (D) Perimeter $= 20 + 5\pi$ and area $= 25\pi + 12.5\sqrt{3}$

16. In the following diagram, a rhombus lies inside a trapezoid.

    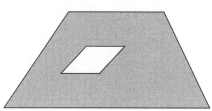

    The sum of the bases of the trapezoid is 36 and its height is 9. If the diagonals of the rhombus are 5 and 3, what is the shaded area?

    (A) 140.5   (C) 154.5

    (B) 147.5   (D) 161.5

17. Look at the following diagram.

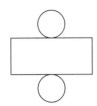

This represents the net of which geometric figure?

(A) Cone   (C) Cube

(B) Cylinder   (D) Pyramid

18. The net of a rectangular prism consists of six rectangles. Which one of the following is the correct description of these rectangles?

(A) They are all congruent.

(B) None of them are congruent.

(C) Four of them must be congruent.

(D) They are congruent in pairs.

19. The diagram below shows a regular pentagon *TUVWX* with its circumscribed circle. Point *P* is the center.

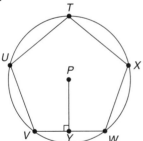

If the perimeter of this pentagon is 120 inches, what is the length of *PY* to the nearest hundredth? (<u>HINT</u>: Draw triangle *PVY* and use the measure of *PVY*).

(A) 9.71 inches   (C) 16.52 inches

(B) 13.11 inches   (D) 19.92 inches

20. Look at the following completed geometric construction, in which *P* is the center of the circle.

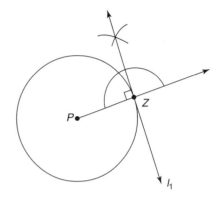

Which construction does this represent?

(A) Given a point Z on a circle, draw a tangent line l_1 at Z.

(B) Given a line l_1 containing a point Z, draw a perpendicular line at Z.

(C) Given a tangent line l_1 to a circle, find a radius $\overline{PZ}$.

(D) Given a radius $\overline{PZ}$, draw its perpendicular bisector l_1.

Quiz for Chapter 13
SOLUTIONS

1. (A)

A secant segment is that part of the secant for which one endpoint lies outside the circle and the other endpoint lies at the furthest intersection point of the secant and the circle.

2. (B)

There is no specific relationship between the length of a tangent to a circle and the length of the radius.

3. (A)

$QS = 14.24$, so $(QT)^2 = (14.24)(6.24) \approx 88.86$. Thus, $QT = \sqrt{88.86} \approx 9.43$.

4. (C)

$VX = 21$, so $(21)(9) = (18)(VY)$. Then $VY = 10.5$. Thus, $YZ = 21 - 10.5 = 7.5$.

5. (A)

Let x and $2x$ represent AE and CE, respectively. Then $(x)(2x) = 10$. So $x^2 = 5$, which means that $x = \sqrt{5} \approx 2.24$.

6. (D)

$\overset{\frown}{FG} = (2)(\angle FGH) = 104°$. Since $\overset{\frown}{KJG}$ is a semicircle, $\overset{\frown}{JK} = 180° - 28° - 104° = 48°$.

7. (B)

Let x and $4x$ represent the measures of $\overset{\frown}{MQ}$ and $\overset{\frown}{MRQ}$, respectively. Then, $x + 4x = 360°$ which means that $x = 72°$ and $4x = 288°$. Thus, $\angle L = \left(\frac{1}{2}\right)(288° - 72°) = 108°$.

8. (C)

Let x represent the measure of $\overset{\frown}{UYW}$. (We use three letters because we do not know in advance whether this arc is minor or major.) Then $42° = \left(\frac{1}{2}\right)(x - 86°)$, which simplifies to $84° = x - 86°$. So $x = 170°$. Thus, $\overset{\frown}{UV} = 360° - 170° - 86° = 104°$.

9. (D)

$\overset{\frown}{AG} + \overset{\frown}{EC} = 360° - 210° = 150°$.

Thus, $\angle GJA = \left(\frac{1}{2}\right)(150°) = 75°$.

10. (D)

The area of the circle is 225π. Let x represent the central angle of the sector. Then $\frac{100\pi}{225\pi} = \frac{4}{9} = \frac{x}{360°}$, so $x = 160°$.

11. (A)

Let C represent the circumference. Then $\frac{130°}{360°} = \frac{2.6\pi}{C}$, which leads to $C = 7.2\pi$. This means that the radius must be 3.6, so that the area of the circle is 12.96π. Letting x represent the area of the sector, we can write $\dfrac{130°}{360°} = \dfrac{x}{12.96\pi}$. Thus, $x = 4.68\pi$ square feet.

12. (B)

The area of ΔPKL is $\left(\dfrac{1}{2}\right)(12)(12)(\sin 30°) = 36$. Since the area of the circle is 144π, we can find the area of the sector, denoted as A_S by using the proportion $\dfrac{A_S}{144\pi} = \dfrac{30°}{360°}$. So $A_S = 12\pi$. Thus, the area of the segment is $12\pi - 36 \approx 1.70$.

13. (A)

A radius of a polygon is the segment joining its center and any vertex. When a regular polygon is inscribed in a circle, the radius of the circle must be congruent to the radius of the polygon.

14. (D)

An apothem of $ABCDEF$, which is PG, has a value of $8\sqrt{3}$. In the equilateral triangle APB, the hypotenuse must be 16. Each side of a regular hexagon is also 16, so that its perimeter is 96. Finally, the area of the hexagon is $\left(\dfrac{1}{2}\right)(8\sqrt{3})(96) = 384\sqrt{3}$.

15. (C)

The perimeter consists of two sides of the triangle and one half the circumference. The radius of the top figure is 5, so one half the circumference is 5π. The perimeter is $10 + 10 + 5\pi = 20 + 5\pi$. The area of a half circle is $\left(\dfrac{1}{2}\right)(\pi)(5^2) = 12.5\pi$. The area of the equi-

lateral triangle is $\dfrac{10^2}{4}\sqrt{3} = 25\sqrt{3}$. Thus, the total area is $12.5\pi + 25\sqrt{3}$.

16. (C)

The shaded area is the difference between the area of the trapezoid and the area of the rhombus, which is $\left(\dfrac{1}{2}\right)(9)(36) - \left(\dfrac{1}{2}\right)(5)(3) = 154.5$.

17. (B)

The net of a cylinder consists of a rectangle and two circles.

18. (D)

There are three pairs of congruent rectangles for the net of a rectangular prism.

19. (C)

Draw triangle PVY. Then since $VW = \left(\dfrac{1}{5}\right)(120) = 24$ and $\overline{PY}$ is the perpendicular bisector of $\overline{VW}$, we know that $VY = 12$. Now $\angle UVY = \dfrac{(180°)(3)}{5} = 108°$, so $\angle PVY = 54°$. Finally, $PY = (12)(\tan 54°) \approx 16.52$.

20. (A)

This construction shows a perpendicular line drawn at a point Z of a circle. The resulting line l_1 is the tangent to the circle at point Z.

Coordinate, Transformational, and Vector Geometry

Welcome to Chapter 14. In this chapter, we will review the following topics:

(a) Transformations and their properties
(b) Concepts and properties of slope, midpoint, and distance in the coordinate plane
(c) Equations and properties of conic sections
(d) Geometric properties of matrices and vectors

Transformations and Their Properties

Types of Transformations

A **transformation** is motion applied to a geometric figure that causes it to change size, location, or orientation. Theoretically, it is possible to apply more than one transformation to a given figure; however, our discussion will be limited to just one transformation per figure. All transformations will take place in a *plane*.

Translation

Our first transformation is called a translation. A **translation** is a motion in which the figure changes its location, but not its size or orientation. This motion is accomplished by sliding the figure along a stationary vector. Each point of the figure will move the same distance and in the same direction. Figures 14.1 and 14.2 show a translation of a triangle and a circle. In each case, the vector that determines the translation is shown.

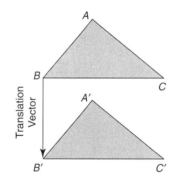

Figure 14.1

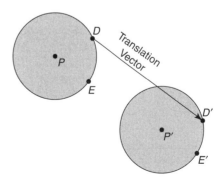

Figure 14.2

Each point of the new location of the figure is called an **image**. Thus, in Figure 14.1, the image of point B is point B'. In Figure 14.2, the image of point D is point D'. Also, in Figure 2, point E is called the **pre-image** of point E'.

From chapter 2, you recall that equivalent vectors have the same magnitude and the same direction. This means that for Figure 14.1, we could have used the translation vector $\overrightarrow{AA'}$. Likewise, for Figure 14.2, we could have used the translation vector $\overrightarrow{EE'}$.

In the *xy*-coordinate plane, a translation can be shown by the change in *x* coordinates, *y* coordinates, or both. Let's consider a line segment $\overline{AB}$, for which the coordinates of A and B are $(-2,4)$ and $(3,1)$, respectively. If the translation vector $\overrightarrow{AA'}$ is $3\mathbf{i} - \mathbf{j}$, then we will move each point of $\overline{AB}$ 3 units to the right and 1 unit down. Then the location of A' must be $(1,3)$ and the location of B' becomes $(6,0)$. Each point of $\overline{AB}$ will be translated in exactly the same way, so that this segment does not change size or orientation. Figure 14.3 shows this translation.

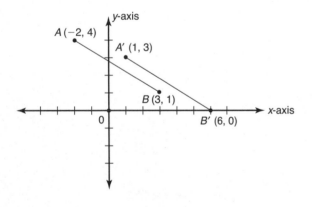

Figure 14.3

EXAMPLE 1

Using the translation vector $3\mathbf{i} - \mathbf{j}$, if point C lies on $\overline{AB}$ and the coordinates of C are $\left(0, \dfrac{14}{5}\right)$ what is the location of point C'?

SOLUTION

We just add 3 units to the *x* coordinate of C and subtract 1 unit from the *y* coordinate of C. The coordinates of C' are $\left(3, \dfrac{9}{5}\right)$.

EXAMPLE 2

Point D also lies on $\overline{AB}$ and the coordinates of its image D' are $\left(2, \dfrac{12}{5}\right)$. Using the same translation vector in Example 1, what are the coordinates of D?

SOLUTION

In a sense, we are going "backwards," since we have the image point D' and we need to find D. The procedure to follow will be to subtract 3 units from the *x* coordinate and add 1 unit to the *y* coordinate. Thus, the coordinates of D are $\left(-1, \dfrac{17}{5}\right)$.

Just Some Notes

1. The translation vector has been omitted in Figure 14.3 solely for the reason that it would clutter the diagram. This is a common practice when using the *xy*-coordinate plane, since one can see the change in coordinates from the original figure to the image figure.

2. Notice that the points chosen for Examples 1 and 2 are not completely random. The points must actually lie on $\overline{AB}$, since the translation applies to this entire segment. One way in which these points can be found is to first establish the equation of the line segment. Then, assign any *x* value between -2 and 3, followed by the corresponding *y* value.

Now consider ΔGHJ with coordinates as follows: $G: (-2,-3)$, $H: (4,-3)$, and $J: (6,5)$.

Use the translation vector is $5\mathbf{i} + 2\mathbf{j}$ for Examples 3, 4, and 5.

EXAMPLE 3

> What are the coordinates of G' ?

SOLUTION

The translation vector is telling us to move each point 5 units to the right and 2 units up. Thus, the coordinates of G' are $(3, -1)$.

EXAMPLE 4

> What are the coordinates of the image of the midpoint of $\overline{HJ}$?

SOLUTION

Let K represent the midpoint of $\overline{HJ}$. The coordinates of K are $\left(\dfrac{4+6}{2}, \dfrac{-3+5}{2}\right) = (5,1)$. Then the coordinates of K' are $(10, 3)$.

EXAMPLE 5

> Point L' is the image of point L, which lies on $\triangle GHJ$. If the coordinates of L' are $\left(5\dfrac{1}{2}, 1\dfrac{1}{2}\right)$, what are the coordinates of L?

SOLUTION

In order to <u>reverse</u> the translation vector, subtract 5 units from the x coordinate and subtract 2 units from the y coordinate. Thus, the coordinates of L are $\left(\dfrac{1}{2}, -\dfrac{1}{2}\right)$.

Figure 14.4, though not required to find the solutions to Examples 3, 4, and 5, does show the actual translation.

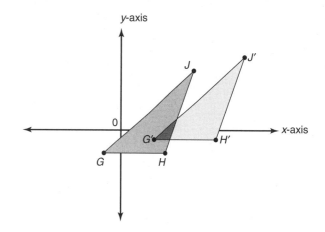

Figure 14.4

To avoid any congestion on the graph for Figure 14.4, the coordinate values were omitted. Note that $\triangle G'H'J'$ overlaps $\triangle GHJ$.

Reflection

The transformation called **reflection** is a motion in which a figure is presented as a mirror image about a given line, which is called the **axis of reflection**. Figures 14.5, 14.6, and 14.7 illustrate a reflection of a line, a triangle, and a quadrilateral, respectively. The individual axis of reflection is shown for each figure as l_1, l_2, or l_3.

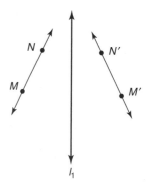

Figure 14.5

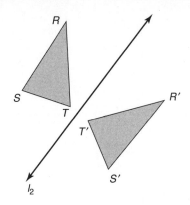

Figure 14.6

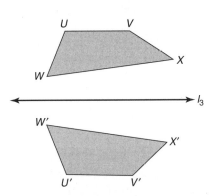

Figure 14.7

As with translations, each point of the new location of the figure is called an *image*. The mathematical procedure used to find any image point P' for a given point P and a given axis of reflection l_1 is as follows:

(a) Construct the ray $\overrightarrow{PQ}$ that is perpendicular to l at point Q. This is shown in Figure 14.8.

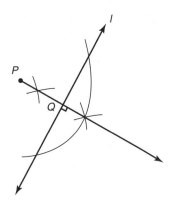

Figure 14.8

(b) Using your compass, determine point P' on $\overrightarrow{PQ}$ such that $PQ = QP'$. Point P' is the location of the image of P, with l as the axis of reflection. This step is shown in Figure 14.9.

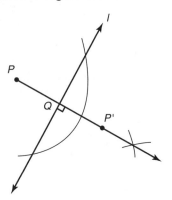

Figure 14.9

In the *xy*-coordinate plane, a reflection about an axis of reflection is identified by a specific change in coordinates. The only four axes of reflection for our discussion will be

(a) the *x*-axis, (b) the *y*-axis, (c) the line $y = x$, and (d) the line $y = -x$

For a given point P with coordinates (x, y), let P' represent its reflection across the *x*-axis. Then the coordinates of P' will be $(x, -y)$. For example, if the coordinates of P are $(8, 3)$, the coordinates of P' will be $(8, -3)$.

For a given point Q with coordinates (x, y), let Q' represent its reflection across the *y*-axis. Then the coordinates of Q' will be $(-x, y)$. For example, if the coordinates of Q are $(9, -4)$, the coordinates of Q' will be $(-9, -4)$.

For a given point R with coordinates (x, y), let R' represent its reflection across the line $y = x$. Then the coordinates of R' will be (y, x). For example, if the coordinates of R are $(-7, 5)$, the coordinates of R' will be $(5, -7)$.

For a given point S with coordinates (x, y), let S' represent its reflection across the line $y = -x$. Then the coordinates of S' will be $(-y, -x)$. For example, if the coordinates of S are $(-4, 6)$, the coordinates of S' will be $(-6, 4)$.

The first two reflections are normally easy to remember because the graphing aspect will practically reveal the correct answer. The last reflection is usually the most difficult to remember. A suggestion would be to think of a reflection across $y = x$ as a "switch" and a reflection across $y = -x$ as a "switch with a twist." Figures 14.10, 14.11, 14.12, and 14.13 illustrate these reflections.

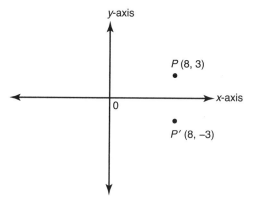

Figure 14.10

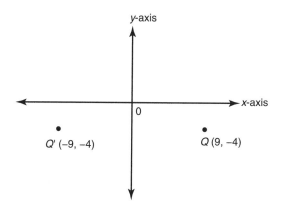

Figure 14.11

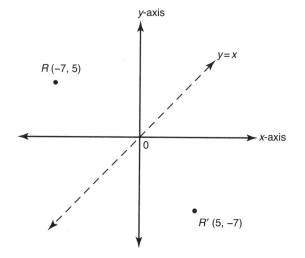

Figure 14.12

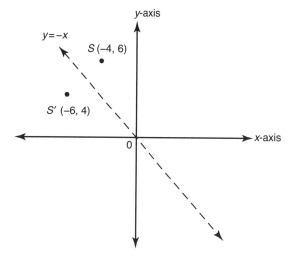

Figure 14.13

Glide Reflections

A **glide reflection** is a combination of a translation and a reflection. A clever way to remember this type of transformation is to imagine a dancer gliding across the dance floor, then changing positions with his/her partner. Since this requires two separate steps, a point A will be labeled as A' following the translation. Then the point will be labeled as A'' following the reflection. Figures 14.10 and 14.11 combined show a glide reflection of $\triangle ABC$.

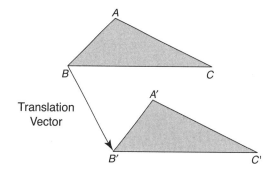

Figure 14.10

Axis of
Reflection

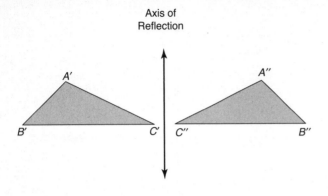

Figure 14.11

A glide reflection of a point in the xy-coordinate plane will affect the change in coordinates by following the guidelines for both translations and reflections.

We'll show two examples.

EXAMPLE 6

A glide reflection is done for the point T, located at $(-1, 3)$, as follows: It will be translated using the translation vector $2\mathbf{i} + \mathbf{j}$, then reflected across the x-axis. What are the coordinates of T'', which is the result of this transformation?

SOLUTION

The translation vector tells us to move T two units to the right and one unit up. Thus, the location of T' is $(1, 4)$, as shown below. Next, we need to reflect T' across the x-axis. This means that we just change the sign of the y coordinate of T'. Thus, the location of T'' is $(1, -4)$. The points T, T', and T'' are shown below.

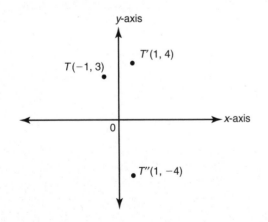

EXAMPLE 7

A glide reflection for the point V, located at $(-3, -4)$, is done as follows: It will be translated using the translation vector $-2\mathbf{i} + 3\mathbf{j}$, then reflected across the line $y = x$. What are the coordinates of V'', which is the result of this transformation?

SOLUTION

First, move V two units to the left and three units up. Thus, the location of V' is $(-5, -1)$. Next, by reflecting V' across the line $y = x$, we simply interchange the x and y coordinates of V'. Thus, the coordinates of V'' are $(-1, -5)$. The points V, V', and V'' are shown below.

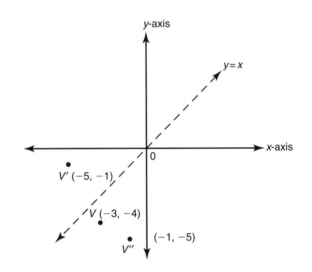

A Rotation

Given two rays $\overrightarrow{PQ}$ and $\overrightarrow{PR}$, a rotation about P is a motion created as follows: We start with a point W on $\overrightarrow{PQ}$. Then the point W' on $\overrightarrow{PR}$ is the result of a rotation corresponding to the measure of $\angle QPR$ if $PW = PW'$. Figures 14.12 and 14.13 illustrate this concept of rotation. Notice that the rotation in Figure 14.12 is clockwise, whereas the rotation in Figure 14.13 is counterclockwise.

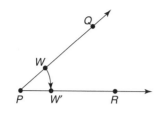

Figure 14.12

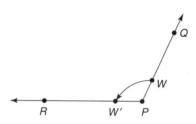

Figure 14.13

In the *xy*-coordinate plane, we will be concerned with just three different rotations of points, each of which will be about the origin. They are (a) 90°-clockwise, (b) 90°-counterclockwise, and (c) 180°.

NOTE:

The concept of rotation could be extended to other fixed points and that other geometric figures can be used for rotation. In a 90°-clockwise rotation about the origin, a point K with coordinates (x, y) will become the point K' with the coordinates $(y, -x)$. For example, if K is located at $(3, 2)$, then K' is located at $(2, -3)$.

NOTE:

The slope of $\overline{OK}$ is $\frac{2}{3}$ and the slope of $\overline{OK'}$ is $-\frac{3}{2}$. This result is what we expect because the slopes of two perpendicular lines (or line segments) must be negative reciprocals of each other. Figure 14.14 shows this rotation.

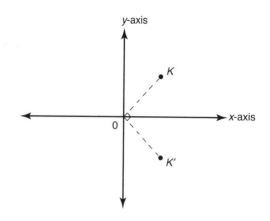

Figure 14.14

In a 90°-counterclockwise rotation about the origin, a point M with coordinates (x, y) will become the point M' with the coordinates $(-y, x)$. For example, if M is located at $(-1, 3)$, then M' is located at $(-3, -1)$. Just as with a clockwise rotation, the slope of $\overline{OM}$ is -3 and the slope of $\overline{OM'}$ is $\frac{1}{3}$. This means that $\overline{OM}$ must be perpendicular to $\overline{OM'}$. Figure 14.15 shows this counterclockwise rotation.

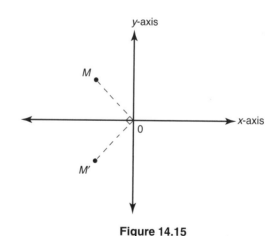

Figure 14.15

The last of our rotations for consideration is the 180°-rotation. In this case, it is not important whether the rotation is clockwise or counterclockwise; the result is the same. Imagine that initially you are facing east. Whether you turn 180° clockwise or counterclockwise, the result is that you are then facing west.

In a 180°-rotation about the origin, a point N with the coordinates (x, y) will become the point N' with the coordinates $(-x, -y)$. For example, if N is located at $(6, -2)$, then N' is located at $(-6, 2)$. Note that the points $(6, -2), (0, 0)$, and $(-6, 2)$ are collinear and that $ON = ON'$. Figure 14.16 shows this 180°-rotation.

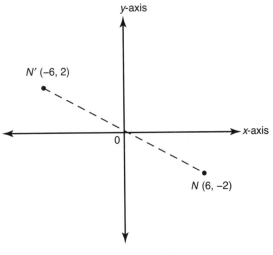

Figure 14.16

EXAMPLE 8

If the point W is located at $(5, -9)$ and is rotated 90°-counterclockwise about the origin to the point W', what are the coordinates of W'?

SOLUTION

Switch the original x and y values and change the sign of the new x value. The coordinates of W' are $(9, 5)$.

EXAMPLE 9

If the point V is located at $(-8, 10)$ and is rotated 180° about the origin to the point V', what are the coordinates of V'?

SOLUTION

Change the signs of the original x and y values. The coordinates of V' are $(8, -10)$.

EXAMPLE 10

The point Z', which is located at $(-5, -7)$, is the result of a 90°-clockwise rotation of point Z about the origin. What are the coordinates of Z?

SOLUTION

Caution, this is a curve ball! In order to find the coordinates of Z, we are looking for a 90°-counterclockwise rotation of Z'. Following the procedure used in Example 8, the answer is $(7, -5)$.

DILATIONS

Our fifth transformation is called a **dilation**. This type of transformation, which is most often applied to a closed geometric figure, changes the size proportionately. Essentially, if two figures are similar, then either is a dilation of the other. The ratio of the corresponding sides is called the **scale factor**. This number represents the ratio of a side from the second figure to its corresponding side of the first figure. A scale factor greater than 1 means that the second figure is larger than the first figure.

EXAMPLE 11

$\triangle ABC$ is similar to $\triangle DEF$. If $AB = 10$ and $DE = 40$, what is the scale factor.

SOLUTION

Here is a quick diagram (although it is not needed).

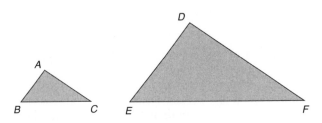

The answer is $\dfrac{40}{10} = \dfrac{4}{1}$ or 4.

EXAMPLE 12

Quadrilateral *GHJK* is similar to quadrilateral *LMNP*. The perimeter of *GHJK* is 36 and the scale factor is 5:6. What is the perimeter of quadrilateral *LMNP*?

SOLUTION

Another quick diagram, but it is not needed either. Let x represent the perimeter of *LMNP*. The ratio of the perimeters equals the ratio of the corresponding sides. Then $\frac{5}{6} = \frac{x}{36}$, so $x = 30$.

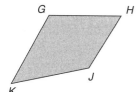
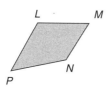

EXAMPLE 13

In $\triangle ABC$, the coordinates of point A are $(1,3)$ and the coordinates of point B are $(13,11)$. If $\angle A$ is a right angle, what is the slope of $\overline{AC}$?

SOLUTION

The slope of $\overline{AB}$ is $\frac{11-3}{13-1} = \frac{2}{3}$. Since the slope of $\overline{AC}$ must be the negative reciprocal of the slope of $\overline{AB}$, our answer is $-\frac{3}{2}$.

EXAMPLE 14

In isosceles $\triangle DEF$, $DE = DF$. If the coordinates of point E are $(3, -7)$ and the coordinates of point F are $(23, -3)$, what is the slope of the altitude from D?

SOLUTION

The slope of $\overline{EF}$ is $\frac{-3+7}{23-3} = \frac{1}{5}$. Thus, the slope of the altitude is -5.

EXAMPLE 15

Referring to the information in Example 14, if $\overline{DH}$ is the altitude from point D, what are the coordinates of point H?

SOLUTION

The quickest way to find the coordinates of H is to recognize that H must be the midpoint of $\overline{EF}$, since the altitude and the median from the vertex angle of an isosceles triangle are the same. Thus, the coordinates of H are $(13, -5)$.

Concepts and Properties of Slope, Midpoint, and Distance in the Coordinate Plane

In Chapter 6, we discussed the concepts of slope, perpendicularity, and parallelism of lines. In Chapters 11 and 12, we explored the properties of the sides of various types of triangles and quadrilaterals. In these two chapters, we also applied the concepts of parallel and perpendicular line segments.

Our current objective is to utilize the material from Chapters 6, 11, and 12 in order to verify the properties of specific triangles and quadrilaterals in the coordinate plane.

EXAMPLE 16

> In right triangle JKL, $\angle K = 90°$. The coordinates of J are $(-9, -3)$ and the coordinates of L are $(-7, -10)$. If $JK = 6$, what is the value of KL? (Nearest hundredth.)

SOLUTION

The length of the hypotenuse JL is $\sqrt{(-9+7)^2 + (-3+10)^2} = \sqrt{53}$. By the Pythagorean theorem, $KL^2 = JL^2 - JK^2 = 53 - 36 = 17$. Thus, $KL = \sqrt{17} \approx 4.12$.

EXAMPLE 17

> For the square $MNPQ$, the coordinates of M are $(1, 4)$. If the coordinates of N are given as $(5, y)$ and the area of the square is 64, what is the value of y? (Nearest hundredth).

SOLUTION

Since the area is equivalent to a side squared, $(5-1)^2 + (y-4)^2 = 64$. This equation simplifies to $(y-4)^2 = 48$, which leads to $y = 4 \pm \sqrt{48}$. Thus, the two answers for y are approximately -2.93 and 10.93.

EXAMPLE 18

> In rhombus $RSTU$, the coordinates of R are $(6, 7)$ and the coordinates of T are $(14, 2)$. If $SU = 16$, what is the area of the rhombus? (Nearest hundredth.)

SOLUTION

The area of $RSTU$ is one half the product of the diagonals. $\overline{RT}$ is one of the diagonals, and has a length of $\sqrt{(14-6)^2 + (2-7)^2} = \sqrt{89}$. Thus, the area is $\left(\dfrac{1}{2}\right)(16)\left(\sqrt{89}\right) \approx 75.47$.

EXAMPLE 19

> In parallelogram $WXYZ$, the diagonals intersect at point V. The coordinates of W are $(-2, 4)$, the coordinates of X are $(12, 4)$, and the coordinates of V are $(4, 1)$. What are the coordinates of Y?

SOLUTION

Let (x, y) represent the coordinates of Y. Since the diagonals of a parallelogram bisect each other, V must be the midpoint of $\overline{WY}$. Then $4 = \dfrac{x-2}{2}$ and $1 = \dfrac{y+4}{2}$. Thus, the coordinates of Y are $(10, -2)$.

EXAMPLE 20

> Using the information in Example 19, what is the area of $WXYZ$?

SOLUTION

Since $WX = 14$, we can easily determine that the coordinates of Z are $(-4, -2)$. If $\overline{WX}$ (or $\overline{YZ}$) represents a base, then the height of $WXYZ$ is the distance between $\overline{WX}$ and $\overline{YZ}$. So, the height can be determined by the difference in y coordinates between these parallel segments, which is $4 - (-2) = 6$. Finally, the area is $(14)(6) = 84$.

Equations and Properties of Conic Sections

At this point, we plan to describe various conic sections in the area of coordinate geometry. These conic sections consist of circles, ellipses, parabolas, and hyperbolas.

Circles

A **circle** is the set of all points at a given distance from a given point. Suppose the given point P is located at $(7, 3)$, and the given distance is 5. Figure 14.17 illustrates the given information.

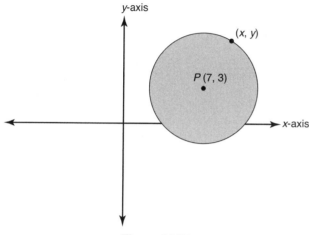

Figure 14.17

Then each point (x, y) must satisfy the condition that $\sqrt{(x-7)^2 + (y-3)^2} = 5$, which can also be written as $(x-7)^2 + (y-3)^2 = 25$. In general, if (h, k) is the center of a circle with radius r, then the equation can be written as $(x-h)^2 + (y-k)^2 = r^2$.

Ellipses

Given any two fixed points F and F' in the xy-coordinate plane, an **ellipse** is the set of all points P such that the sum of FP and $F'P$ is a constant. The points F and F' are called the **foci**. (The singular is "focus".) Suppose the given foci are $F(4, 3)$ and $F'(-4, 3)$, and the constant sum is 10. Figure 14.18 illustrates the given information, with additional points to be referenced later.

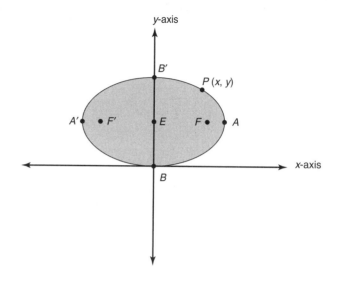

Figure 14.18

Then point P must satisfy the condition $FP' + FP = 10$, which translates to $\sqrt{(x+4)^2 + (y-3)^2} + \sqrt{(x-4)^2 + (y-3)^2} = 10$. The algebra needed to simplify this equation can be torturous, but when this equation is simplified, it can be written as $9x^2 + 25y^2 - 150y = 0$. By cleverly rewriting this equation as $9(x-0)^2 + 25(y^2 - 6y + 9) = 225$, and then dividing by 225, we get the equation $\dfrac{(x-0)^2}{25} + \dfrac{(y-3)^2}{9} = 1$. This last equation can also be expressed as $\dfrac{(x-0)^2}{5^2} + \dfrac{(y-3)^2}{3^2} = 1$.

Figure 14.19 is an enlarged redrawing of Figure 14.18 with the coordinates shown for each point that is referenced. We now make a few important observations about the relationship between this equation and the corresponding graph.

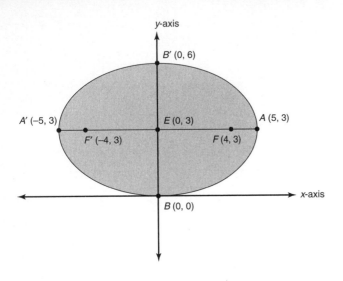

Figure 14.19

(a) The center of the ellipse E is located at $(0, 3)$, which corresponds to the numerators of the fractions containing x and y.

(b) The points $A(5, 3)$ and $A'(-5, 3)$ represent the endpoints of a segment called the **major axis.** Notice that $AE = A'E = 5$, which is the value of the number being squared in the denominator of the first fraction of the equation. AA' represents the original fixed distance.

(c) The points $B(0, 0)$ and $B'(0, 6)$ represent the endpoints of a segment called the **minor axis.** Notice that $BE = B'E = 3$, which is the value of the number being squared in the denominator of the second fraction of the equation.

(d) Each of the original fixed points F and F' is located 4 units from the center of the ellipse. Note that 4 and each of the numbers being squared in the denominators of the two fractions form a Pythagorean triple. Since ΔBEF is a right triangle,
$BF = \sqrt{(EF)^2 + (EB)^2} = \sqrt{4^2 + 3^2} = 5$. Likewise, we can show that $BF' = 5$. This means that
$BF = BF' = AE = A'E$.

(e) Given any equation in the form
$\dfrac{(x-h)^2}{a^2} + \dfrac{(y-k)^2}{b^2} = 1$, where $a > b$, the graph
is an ellipse for which its center is (h, k), its major axis has a length of $2a$, and its minor axis has a length of $2b$. In addition, the foci lie on the major

axis (horizontal), and the distance between the center and each focus is $\sqrt{a^2 - b^2}$.

(f) Given any equation in the form
$\dfrac{(x-h)^2}{b^2} + \dfrac{(y-k)^2}{a^2} = 1$, where $a > b$, the major
axis on which the foci will lie, will be <u>vertical</u>. The major axis will still have a length of $2a$ and the minor axis will still have a length of $2b$.

EXAMPLE 21

What is the circumference of a circle whose graph is given by the equation $(x-4)^2 + (y+5)^2 = 49$?

SOLUTION

The radius is $\sqrt{49} = 7$, so the circumference is 14π.

EXAMPLE 22

What is the equation of a circle whose area is 144π and whose center is located at $(-8, 2)$?

SOLUTION

The radius of this circle is 12, so the equation is $(x+8)^2 + (y-2)^2 = 144$.

EXAMPLE 23

What are the coordinates of the center of the circle whose equation is given as $x^2 + 6x + y^2 + 20y = 30$?

SOLUTION

Rewrite this equation as $(x^2 + 6x + \_) + (y^2 + 20y + \_) = 30$, where we intend to complete each set of parentheses to make a perfect trinomial square. The required numbers are 9 and 100, respectively. Then we get $(x^2 + 6x + 9) + (y^2 + 20y + 100)$

$= 30 + 9 + 100$, which becomes $(x + 3)^2 + (y + 10)^2$
$= 139$. The center has the coordinates $(-3, -10)$.
Incidentally, the radius is $\sqrt{139} \approx 11.79$.

EXAMPLE 24

What is the equation of an ellipse with its center located at $(6, 0)$, a horizontal major axis of length 14, and a minor axis of length 8?

SOLUTION

In the equation $\dfrac{(x - h)^2}{a^2} + \dfrac{(y - k)^2}{b^2} = 1$, $a = 7$, $b = 4$, $h = 6$, and $k = 0$. Thus, the required equation is $\dfrac{(x - 6)^2}{49} + \dfrac{y^2}{16} = 1$.

EXAMPLE 25

Given that the equation of an ellipse is $\dfrac{(x + 1)^2}{25} + \dfrac{(y + 7)^2}{81} = 1$, what is the distance between the center and one of the foci? (Nearest hundredth)

SOLUTION

This ellipse has a vertical major axis, but the value of c, the distance between the center and either focus, is still $\sqrt{a^2 - b^2} = \sqrt{81 - 25} \approx 7.48$.

EXAMPLE 26

Using the information in Example 25, what are the coordinates of each focus?

SOLUTION

The center of the ellipse is $(-1, -7)$. Since the major axis is vertical, each focus lies 7.48 units directly above and directly below $(-1, -7)$. Thus, the foci lie at $(-1, 0.48)$ and $(-1, -14.48)$.

EXAMPLE 27

Given that the equation of an ellipse is $\dfrac{(x - 3)^2}{100} + \dfrac{(y + 2)^2}{4} = 1$, what are the coordinates of the endpoints of the major axis?

SOLUTION

Since $100 > 4$, the major axis must be horizontal. The center is located at $(3, -2)$, $a = 10$, and $b = 2$. We need to count 10 units to the left and 10 units to the right of $(3, -2)$. Thus, the endpoints of the major are located at $(-7, -2)$ and $(13, -2)$.

Note that if $a = b$, the ellipse "collapses" into a circle. This phenomenon can be seen algebraically. For example, suppose we are given the equation $\dfrac{(x - 1)^2}{4} + \dfrac{(y - 2)^2}{4} = 1$. This equation can be written as $(x - 1)^2 + (y - 2)^2 = 4$, which is the equation of a circle centered at $(1, 2)$ with a radius of 2.

The Parabola

In Chapter 6, we studied quadratic functions of the form $y = a(x - h)^2 + k$. These functions are actually parabolas, whose definition we now provide. Given a fixed point F and a fixed line l in the xy-coordinate plane that does not contain F, a **parabola** is the set of all points P such that FP equals the distance from P to l. The point F is called the **focus** and the line l is called the **directrix** Technically, a directrix may be horizontal, vertical, or slanted. For our purposes, each directrix will be either horizontal or vertical. The point V is the **vertex**, which represents the point on the parabola that is closest to the directrix.

Suppose the directrix is the line $x = 2$ and the focus is located at $(4, 1)$. Figure 14.20 illustrates the given information.

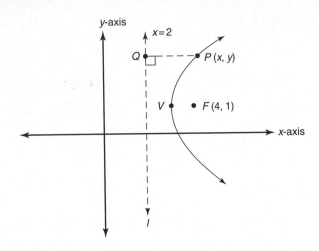

Figure 14.20

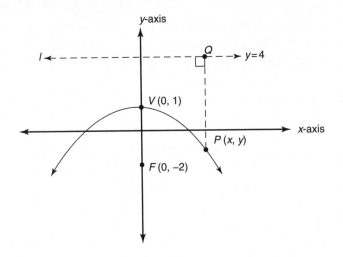

Figure 14.21

Then point P must satisfy the condition $PF = PQ$, where Q is the point on l such that $PQ \perp l$. Note that the coordinates of Q are $(2, y)$. This leads to the equation $\sqrt{(x-4)^2 + (y-1)^2} = x - 2$. In simplifying, this equation becomes $(y-1)^2 = 4(x-3)$.

NOTE:

> The vertex is located at (3, 1). The meaning of the number 4 is less evident. The distance between the vertex and either the focus or directrix is 1 unit.

Without a formal proof, we state the following for any parabola in the form $(y-k)^2 = 4p(x-h)$.

(a) The vertex is located at (h, k).

(b) p represents the distance between the vertex and either the focus or the directrix.

(c) If $p > 0$, the parabola opens to the right; if $p < 0$, the parabola opens to the left.

(d) If $p > 0$, the focus is located at $(h+p, k)$; if $p < 0$, the focus is located at $(h-p, k)$.

Let's consider a parabola with a horizontal directrix. Suppose the directrix is the line $y = 4$ and the focus is located at $(0, -2)$. Figure 14.21 illustrates this situation.

We must still have the condition $PF = PQ$, where Q is the point on l such that $PQ \perp l$.

The coordinates of Q are $(x, 4)$, and the appropriate equation becomes $\sqrt{(x-0)^2 + (y+2)^2} = 4 - y$. In simplifying, this equation becomes $(x-0)^2 = -12(y-1)$. The vertex is located at $(0,1)$. By equating -12 with the expression $4p$, we find that $p = -3$. The distance between the vertex and either the focus or the directrix is 3 units and the parabola faces downward. Without a formal proof, we state the following for any parabola in the form $(x-h)^2 = 4p(y-k)$.

(a) The vertex is located at (h, k).

(b) p represents the distance between the vertex and either the focus or the directrix.

(c) If $p > 0$, the parabola opens upward; if $p < 0$, the parabola opens downward.

(d) If $p > 0$, the focus is located at $(h, k+p)$; if $p < 0$, the focus is located at $(h, k-p)$.

EXAMPLE 28

> What are the coordinates of the vertex for the graph of $(y+8)^2 = -1(x+9)$?

SOLUTION

The vertex is located at $(-9, -8)$.

EXAMPLE 29

What is the equation of a parabola whose focus is located at $(3, 2)$, and whose directrix is the line $x = 11$?

SOLUTION

The equation must be of the form $(y - k)^2 = 4p(x - h)$. In addition, the parabola opens to the left, so $p < 0$. The vertex is located halfway between the line $x = 11$ and the point $(3, 2)$, which means that its location is $(7, 2)$. Now we know that $p = -4$, so the equation for this parabola becomes $(y - 2)^2 = -16(x - 7)$.

EXAMPLE 30

What is the equation of the directrix for the graph of $(x + 5)^2 = -24(y - 1)$?

SOLUTION

The vertex is located at $(-5, 1)$. Since $4p = -24$, $p = -6$, which means that the parabola opens downward. The directrix must be a horizontal line that lies 6 units above the vertex. Thus, the equation of the directrix is $y = 7$.

EXAMPLE 31

What are the coordinates of the focus for the graph of $y^2 + 8y - 8x + 8 = 0$?

SOLUTION

We first need to rewrite this equation in the form $(y - k)^2 = 4p(x - h)$. The first step is to write the equation as $(y^2 + 8y + \_) = 8x - 8$. The missing term to create a perfect trinomial is 16, so the equation becomes $(y^2 + 8y + 16) = 8x - 8 + 16$. In factored form this equation is $(y + 4)^2 = 8(x + 1)$. This form of the equation reveals that the vertex is located at $(-1, -4)$, the value of p is 2, and the parabola opens to the right. To find the coordinates of the focus, simply

add 2 units to the x coordinate of the vertex. Thus, the focus is located at $(1, -4)$.

Hyperbolas

Given two fixed points F and F' in the xy-coordinate plane, a **hyperbola** is the set of all points P such that the difference between FP and $F'P$ is a constant. This definition sounds extremely close to the one given for an ellipse, since the word *difference* has replaced the word *sum*. Just as with the ellipse, each of F and F' is called a *focus*. Suppose the given foci are $F(10, 0)$ and $F'(-10, 0)$, and that the common difference is 12. Figure 14.22 illustrates this situation.

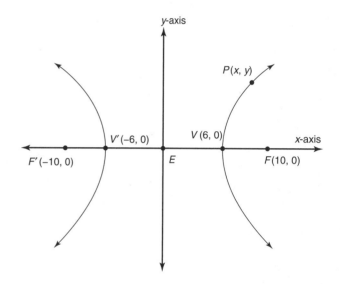

Figure 14.22

Notice that P is located on the "branch" of the hyperbola associated with F. Then point P must satisfy the condition $PF' - PF = 12$. This leads to the following equation: $\sqrt{(x + 10)^2 + y^2} - \sqrt{(x - 10)^2 + y^2} = 12$. As with the ellipse, we will skip many of the intermediate steps by stating that this equation simplifies to $(3)\left(\sqrt{(x - 10)^2 + y^2}\right) = 18 - 5x$. This last equation will further simplify to $16x^2 - 9y^2 = 576$. The last step is to divide by 576 to get the equation, in simplified fraction form, as $\dfrac{x^2}{36} - \dfrac{y^2}{64} = 1$. Let's rewrite this as $\dfrac{(x - 0)^2}{6^2} - \dfrac{(y - 0)^2}{8^2} = 1$. Figure 14.23 is a replay of

Figure 14.22, along with the associated coordinates of each point to be referenced.

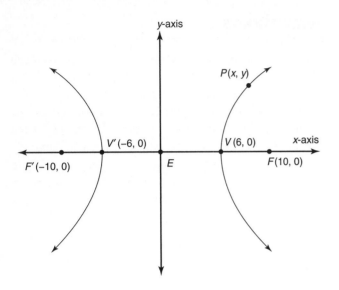

Figure 14.23

The point V and V' are the vertices and point E is called the center of this hyperbola. The coordinates of V and V', and E have been identified as $(6, 0)$, $(-6, 0)$, and $(0, 0)$, respectively. E lies midway between V and V'. Without a formal proof, we state that in the equation $\dfrac{(x-0)^2}{6^2} - \dfrac{(y-0)^2}{8^2} = 1$, the number 6 corresponds to the value of both EV and EV'. Also, without a formal proof, we state that the number 8 corresponds to $\sqrt{10^2 - 6^2}$. The line segment $\overline{VV'}$ is called the **transverse axis.**

Asymptotes

In order to understand the geometric meaning of the number 8 in the equation $\dfrac{(x-0)^2}{6^2} - \dfrac{(y-0)^2}{8^2} = 1$, we consider the asymptotes to the graph in Figure 14.23. These can be found by solving $\dfrac{x^2}{6^2} - \dfrac{y^2}{8^2} = 1$ for y. Clearing this equation of denominators leads to

$16x^2 - 9y^2 = 576$. Let's rewrite this last equation as $y^2 = \dfrac{16}{9}x^2 - 64 = \left(\dfrac{16}{9}x^2\right)\left(1 - \dfrac{36}{x^2}\right)$.

Then $y = \left(\pm\dfrac{4}{3}x\right)\left(\sqrt{1 - \dfrac{36}{x^2}}\right)$. As $|x|$ increases, the value of $\left(\sqrt{1 - \dfrac{36}{x^2}}\right)$ approaches 1; this means that the value of y approaches. $\pm\dfrac{4}{3}x$. The lines $y = \pm\dfrac{4}{3}x$ are called the **asymptotes** for the graph of $\dfrac{x^2}{6^2} - \dfrac{y^2}{8^2} = 1$.

We will now draw the **asymptotic rectangle**, which has its center at $(0, 0)$, a horizontal length of $(2)(6) = 12$, and a vertical length of $(2)(8) = 16$. Figure 14.24 is a replica of Figure 14.23, with the addition of the two asymptotes and the asymptotic rectangle.

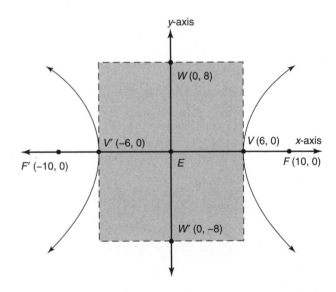

Figure 14.24

We already know that $\overline{VV'}$ is called the transverse axis, whose length is 12. The segment $\overline{WW'}$ is called the **conjugate axis**, which is always perpendicular to the transverse axis. We observe that the length of $\overline{WW'}$ is 16.

We now take a sizeable leap to our next claim. In general, if we are given the equation $\dfrac{(x-h)^2}{a^2} - \dfrac{(y-k)^2}{b^2} = 1$, its graph is a hyperbola with the following properties:

(a) The center is located at (h, k).

(b) Its vertices are located at $(h \pm a, k)$.

(c) Its foci are located at $(h \pm c, k)$, where $c^2 = a^2 + b^2$.

(d) Its transverse axis has length $2a$.

(e) Its conjugate axis has length $2b$.

(f) Its asymptotes are $y - k = \pm \dfrac{b}{a}(x - h)$.

Now we consider a hyperbola for which the center is at $(0, 0)$ and whose vertices are on the y-axis. Suppose that the given foci are $F(0, 13)$ and $F'(0, -13)$, and that the common difference is 10. Recall that this common difference, which has a value of VV', is represented algebraically as $PF' - PF$ for any point P on the branch nearest F.

Figure 14.25 illustrates this situation.

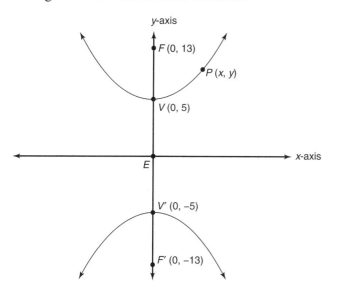

Figure 14.25

For Figure 14.25, point P must satisfy the condition $PF' - PF = 10$, which translates to $\sqrt{x^2 + (y+13)^2} - \sqrt{x^2 + (y-13)^2} = 10$. In solving this equation, move $\sqrt{x^2 + (y-13)^2}$ to the right side of the equation, then square both sides. This leads to the equation $x^2 + y^2 + 26y + 169 = 100 + 20\sqrt{x^2 + y^2 - 26y + 169} + x^2 + y^2 - 26y + 169$.

Now simplify this equation to $52y - 100 = 20\sqrt{x^2 + y^2 - 26y + 169}$, which becomes $13y - 25 = (5)\sqrt{x^2 + y^2 - 26y + 169}$. Squaring both sides leads to $169y^2 - 650y + 625 = 25x^2 + 25y^2 - 650y + 4225$. This last equation will simplify to $144y^2 - 25x^2 = 3600$. In dividing by 3600, the fractional form of the equation becomes $\dfrac{y^2}{25} - \dfrac{x^2}{144} = 1$. By rewriting this equation as $\dfrac{(y-0)^2}{5^2} - \dfrac{(x-0)^2}{12^2} = 1$, we recognize some similarities to the graph of a hyperbola centered at $(0, 0)$ whose foci lie on the x-axis. In particular, the number 5 corresponds to the distance between either vertex and the center. Also, the distance between either focus and the center, which is 13, is connected to 5 and 12 by the Pythagorean identity $13^2 = 5^2 + 12^2$.

Furthermore, the **transverse axis**, which is the line segment connecting the vertices, has a length of twice the value of the number being squared in the denominator of $\dfrac{(y-0)^2}{5^2}$.

By drawing the asymptotic rectangle, we can create the conjugate axis, whose length is 24. Figure 14.26 is a re-creation of Figure 14.25, with the addition of the asymptotic rectangle.

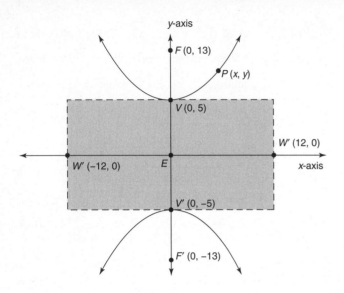

Figure 14.26

As with Figure 14.24, $\overline{VV'}$ is the transverse axis and $\overline{WW'}$ is the conjugate axis.

In order to find the equations of the asymptotes, we'll rewrite the equation $\dfrac{y^2}{25} - \dfrac{x^2}{144} = 1$ as

$$y^2 = \frac{25}{144}x^2 + 25 = \left(\frac{25}{144}x^2\right)\left(1 + \frac{144}{x^2}\right).$$ Then

$y = \left(\pm\dfrac{5}{12}x\right)\left(\sqrt{1 + \dfrac{144}{x^2}}\right)$. As $|x|$ increases, the value of

$\sqrt{1 + \dfrac{144}{x^2}}$ approaches 1; so the value of y approaches

$\pm\dfrac{5}{12}x$. Thus, the asymptotes are $y = \pm\dfrac{5}{12}x$. Following is the claim about the properties concerning the

graph of $\dfrac{(y - k)^2}{a^2} - \dfrac{(x - h)^2}{b^2} = 1$.

(a) The center is located at (h, k).

(b) Its vertices are located at $(h, k \pm a)$.

(c) Its foci are located at $(h, k \pm c)$, where $c^2 = a^2 + b^2$.

(d) Its transverse axis has length $2a$.

(e) Its conjugate axis has length $2b$.

(f) Its asymptotes are $y - k = \pm\dfrac{a}{b}(x - h)$.

We need to make a few comments concerning ellipses and hyperbolas. By the nature of the similarity of their equations, they appear to be distant cousins. With the graph of an ellipse, the location of the larger denominator determines the direction of the major axis and the minor axis. With the graph of a hyperbola, the size comparison of a and b does not determine the direction of the transverse axis and the conjugate axis; this is determined by which one of x^2 or y^2 has a positive sign. Remember that with an ellipse, $c^2 = a^2 - b^2$. In the case of a hyperbola, $c^2 = a^2 + b^2$.

EXAMPLE 32

What is the equation of a hyperbola for which the center is located at $(0, 0)$, the horizontal transverse axis length is 18, and the conjugate axis length is 8 ?

SOLUTION

The general equation must be of the form $\dfrac{x^2}{a^2} - \dfrac{y^2}{b^2} = 1$, since the transverse axis is horizontal. Since $2a = 18$ and $2b = 8$, we know that $a = 9$ and $b = 4$. Thus, the equation is $\dfrac{x^2}{81} - \dfrac{y^2}{16} = 1$.

EXAMPLE 33

What is the equation of a hyperbola for which the center is located at $(-1, 2)$, one vertex is located at $(-1, 6)$, and the distance between the center and either focus is 7?

SOLUTION

Given the locations of a vertex and the center, the transverse axis must be vertical. Using the location of the center, we can write the equation as $\dfrac{(y - 2)^2}{a^2} - \dfrac{(x + 1)^2}{b^2} = 1$. The value of a is 4, since it corresponds to the distance between $(-1, 2)$ and

$(-1, 6)$. Finally, $b^2 = c^2 - a^2 = 7^2 - 4^2 = 33$. Thus, the equation is $\dfrac{(y-2)^2}{16} - \dfrac{(x+1)^2}{33} = 1$.

EXAMPLE 34

If the equation of a hyperbola is $\dfrac{(y+6)^2}{16} - \dfrac{x^2}{49} = 1$, what are the coordinates of the foci? (Nearest hundredth)

SOLUTION

The center is located at $(0, -6)$ and since $a = 4$, the vertices are located at $(0, -2)$ and $(0, -10)$. We know that $b = 7$, so $c = \sqrt{16 + 49} \approx 8.06$. This number must be added to the y-coordinate of $(0, -6)$ and subtracted from the y-coordinate of $(0, -6)$. Thus, the foci are located at $(0, 2.06)$ and $(0, -14.06)$.

EXAMPLE 35

If the equation of a hyperbola is $\dfrac{(x-5)^2}{81} - \dfrac{(y+1)^2}{64} = 1$, what are the equations of the asymptotes?

SOLUTION

The center is located at $(5, -1)$, a = 9, and b = 8. Thus the equations of the asymptotes are $y + 1 = \pm\dfrac{8}{9}(x - 5)$.

EXAMPLE 36

The equations of the asymptotes of a hyperbola are $y = \pm\dfrac{1}{3}x$. If the endpoints of the transverse axis are $(0, 1)$ and $(0, -1)$, what is the equation of the hyperbola?

SOLUTION

The center is located at $(0, 0)$, and since the transverse axis is vertical, the general equation is $\dfrac{y^2}{a^2} - \dfrac{x^2}{b^2} = 1$. In this form, the equations of the asymptotes are $y = \pm\dfrac{a}{b}x$. Then $a = 1$ and $b = 3$, so the equation of the hyperbola is $\dfrac{y^2}{1} - \dfrac{x^2}{9} = 1$.

Geometric Properties of Matrices and Vectors

In Chapter 2 and 3, we discussed the basic rules for arithmetic operations on matrices and vectors. In addition, we investigated the properties of associativity, commutativity, and distributivity for matrices and vectors. Furthermore, we identified the existence of an inverse for certain matrices.

Earlier in this chapter, we explored the geometric and algebraic meanings of several different types of transformations. These included translations, reflections, glide reflections, rotations, and dilations. We want to show a connection between each of the transformations and both matrices and vectors.

Translation Matrices

Consider the point $(7, -1)$ in the xy-coordinate plane. We could express this point in matrix form as $\begin{bmatrix} 7 \\ -1 \end{bmatrix}$. Next, suppose that we are to perform the following matrix addition: $\begin{bmatrix} 7 \\ -1 \end{bmatrix} + \begin{bmatrix} 20 \\ 3 \end{bmatrix} = \begin{bmatrix} 27 \\ 2 \end{bmatrix}$. We can interpret the matrix $\begin{bmatrix} 20 \\ 3 \end{bmatrix}$ as a translation of the point $(7, -1)$ to the point $(27, 2)$ using the translation vector $20\mathbf{i} + 3\mathbf{j}$ In words, we have moved the point $(7, -1)$ twenty units to the right and 3 units up in the xy-coordinate plane.

We can also represent this transformation algebraically for any point $(2, 3)$. If this point is moved a units horizontally and b units vertically, (where a, b may be positive, negative, or zero), then the point's new location (x', y') can be expressed as $\begin{bmatrix} x \\ y \end{bmatrix} + \begin{bmatrix} a \\ b \end{bmatrix}$

The matrix $\begin{bmatrix} a \\ b \end{bmatrix}$ is called the **translation matrix**. The translation vector is $a\mathbf{i} + b\mathbf{j}$.

EXAMPLE 37

If the point $\begin{bmatrix} -3 \\ 5 \end{bmatrix}$ is translated to the point $\begin{bmatrix} -8 \\ 7 \end{bmatrix}$, what is the translation matrix?

SOLUTION

$-8 - (-3) = -5$ and $7 - 5 = 2$. The translation matrix is $\begin{bmatrix} -5 \\ 2 \end{bmatrix}$

Reflection Matrices

Another transformation that we had previously considered is a reflection. Our reflections involved four possibilities, namely (a) over the x-axis, (b) over the y-axis, (c) over the line $y = x$, and (d) over the line $y = -x$. As a review, suppose that P is the original point that is located at (x,y). (In terms of vectors, this is the vector $x\mathbf{i} + y\mathbf{j}$.) For the reflections mentioned in (a), (b), (c), and (d), the coordinates of P' are $(x, -y)$, $(-x, y)$, (y, x), and $(-y, -x)$, respectively. Let (x', y') represent the reflection of (x, y) for these four different types of reflections.

Without a formal proof, we claim that
$$\begin{bmatrix} x' \\ y' \end{bmatrix} = \begin{bmatrix} \cos 2\theta & \sin 2\theta \\ \sin 2\theta & -\cos 2\theta \end{bmatrix} \times \begin{bmatrix} x \\ y \end{bmatrix}$$

This is called the **reflection matrix.** In equation form, we have $x' = x\cos 2\theta + y\sin 2\theta$ and $y' = x\sin 2\theta - y\cos 2\theta$. As you would guess, θ is the angle between the axis of reflection and positive position of the x-axis. For our four different reflections, the only values of θ we are using are 0°, 45°, 90, and 135°.

EXAMPLE 38

If the point $(8, 2)$ is reflected across the y-axis, what is the reflection matrix?

SOLUTION

Since $\theta = 90°$, the reflection matrix is $\begin{bmatrix} \cos 180° & \sin 180° \\ \sin 180° & -\cos 180° \end{bmatrix} = \begin{bmatrix} -1 & 0 \\ 0 & 1 \end{bmatrix}$

The solution to Example 38 is quite easy to check, since $\begin{bmatrix} -1 & 0 \\ 0 & 1 \end{bmatrix} \times \begin{bmatrix} 8 \\ 2 \end{bmatrix} = \begin{bmatrix} -8 \\ 2 \end{bmatrix}$

EXAMPLE 39

If the point $(-3, -6)$ is reflected across the line $y = -x$, what is the reflection matrix?

SOLUTION

The line $y = -x$ forms an angle of 135° with the positive x-axis. Since $\theta = 135°$, the reflection matrix is
$\begin{bmatrix} \cos 270° & \sin 270° \\ \sin 270° & -\cos 270° \end{bmatrix} = \begin{bmatrix} 0 & -1 \\ -1 & 0 \end{bmatrix}$

Glide Reflection Matrices

You recall that a glide reflection is simply a combination of a translation and a reflection. We'll use the information given in Example 6 of this chapter. The last matrix we will be seeking will be the reflection matrix.

EXAMPLE 40

What is the glide reflection matrix of the point $(-1, 3)$ that is translated by the vector $2\mathbf{i} + \mathbf{j}$, then reflected across the x-axis?

SOLUTION

In matrix form, following the given translation, the point becomes $\begin{bmatrix} 1 \\ 4 \end{bmatrix}$. For the reflection, $\theta = 0°$. Thus, the reflection matrix is $\begin{bmatrix} \cos 0° & \sin 0° \\ \sin 0° & -\cos 0° \end{bmatrix} = \begin{bmatrix} 1 & 0 \\ 0 & -1 \end{bmatrix}$.

Rotation Matrices

The three rotations that we have studied in this chapter are (a) 90° clockwise, (b) 90° counterclockwise, and (c) 180°-rotation.

Remember that we are only considering rotations about the origin.

Let (x', y') represent a clockwise rotation of θ degrees about the origin for the point (x, y). Without a formal proof, we claim that

$$\begin{bmatrix} x' \\ y' \end{bmatrix} = \begin{bmatrix} \cos\theta & \sin\theta \\ -\sin\theta & \cos\theta \end{bmatrix} \times \begin{bmatrix} x \\ y \end{bmatrix}$$

This is called a **rotation matrix**. We really do not need a separate formula for a counterclockwise rotation, since a counterclockwise rotation of θ degrees leads to the same point as a clockwise rotation of $(360° - \theta)$ degrees. Furthermore, a 180-degree rotation is also included in the above-mentioned formula.

EXAMPLE 41

If a point is rotated 90° clockwise about the origin, what is the rotation matrix?

SOLUTION

By substituting $(\theta = 90°)$, the matrix becomes $\begin{bmatrix} \cos 90° & \sin 90° \\ -\sin 90° & \cos 90° \end{bmatrix} = \begin{bmatrix} 0 & 1 \\ -1 & 0 \end{bmatrix}$.

EXAMPLE 42

If the point $(7, -5)$ is rotated 90° counterclockwise about the origin, what is the rotation matrix?

SOLUTION

To change this to a clockwise rotation, we substitute $\theta = 270°$ in the rotation matrix. Thus, the answer is

$\begin{bmatrix} \cos 270° & \sin 270° \\ -\sin 270° & \cos 270° \end{bmatrix} = \begin{bmatrix} 0 & 1 \\ 1 & 0 \end{bmatrix}$

To ensure that our matrix is correct, let's check it for the point $(7, -5)$. Note that $\begin{bmatrix} 0 & -1 \\ 1 & 0 \end{bmatrix} \times \begin{bmatrix} 7 \\ -5 \end{bmatrix} = \begin{bmatrix} 5 \\ 7 \end{bmatrix}$, which corresponds to the point $(5, 7)$.

Quiz for Chapter 14

1. Point A is located at $(-1, 6)$ and point B is located at $(5, 0)$. Using the translation vector $-3\mathbf{i} + 4\mathbf{j}$, what are the coordinates of the image of the midpoint of $\overline{AB}$?

(A) $(2, 3)$ (C) $(-1, 3)$

(B) $(2, 7)$ (D) $(-1, 7)$

2. Which one of the following diagrams illustrates a reflection of $\triangle ABC$ to its image $\triangle A'B'C'$ over the line l_1?

(A)

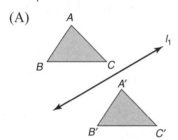

(B)

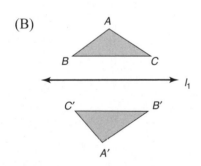

(C)

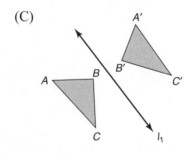

(D)

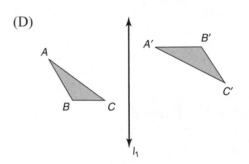

3. A glide reflection is done from the point V, which is located at $(3, 7)$, to the point V'' as follows: The translation vector to get to the point V' is $8\mathbf{i} - \mathbf{j}$, then V' is reflected across the line $y = -x$ to get to the point V''. What are the coordinates of V''?

(A) $(-6, -11)$ (C) $(11, 6)$

(B) $(6, 11)$ (D) $(-11, -6)$

4. The point R', which is located at $(4, 2)$, is the result of a $90°$-counterclockwise rotation of the point R about the origin. What are the coordinates of R?

(A) $(2, -4)$ (C) $(2, 4)$

(B) $(-2, 4)$ (D) $(-2, -4)$

5. Pentagon $ABCDE$ is similar to pentagon $FGHJK$. The scale factor is $\dfrac{3}{4}$. If $JK = 48$, what is the value of DE?

(A) 27   (C) 56

(B) 36   (D) 64

6. In $\triangle MNQ$, the coordinates of M, N, and Q are $(5, 3)$, $(1, -4)$, and $(9, -3)$, respectively. What is the slope of the altitude from M to NQ?

(A) 8   (C) $-\dfrac{1}{8}$

(B) $\dfrac{1}{8}$ (D) -8

7. In rhombus *EFGH*, the coordinates of *E* are $(-4, -3)$ and the coordinates of *G* are $(3, 6)$. If the area of *EFGH* is 90, what is the length of the diagonal *FH* ? (Nearest hundredth)

(A) 15.79   (C) 31.58

(B) 17.74   (D) 35.48

8. Which one of the following equations represents the graph of a circle whose center is located at $(6, -5)$ and whose radius is 4?

(A) $(x + 6)^2 + (y - 5)^2 = 16$

(B) $(x - 6)^2 + (y + 5)^2 = 16$

(C) $(x - 6)^2 + (y + 5)^2 = 2$

(D) $(x + 6)^2 + (y - 5)^2 = 2$

9. The equation of an ellipse is given as $\dfrac{(x - 3)^2}{9} + \dfrac{(y + 1)^2}{a^2} = 1$. If one of the foci is located at $(3, 11)$, which one of the following represents the coordinates of an endpoint of the vertical major axis?

(A) $(3, 16)$ (C) $(-3, -15)$

(B) $(3, 15)$ (D) $(-3, -16)$

10. The sum of the distances from any point on an ellipse to the two foci is 24 and the length of vertical minor axis is 10. If the center is located at $(0, 0)$, what is the equation of this ellipse?

(A) $\dfrac{x^2}{169} + \dfrac{y^2}{25} = 1$ (C) $\dfrac{x^2}{144} + \dfrac{y^2}{25} = 1$

(B) $\dfrac{x^2}{25} + \dfrac{y^2}{169} = 1$ (D) $\dfrac{x^2}{25} + \dfrac{y^2}{144} = 1$

11. What is the distance between the vertex and the directrix for the graph of the parabola $x^2 - 20y + 100 = 0$?

(A) 4   (C) 10

(B) 5   (D) 20

12. What is the equation of a parabola whose focus is located at $(0, 8)$ and whose vertex is located at $(0, 2)$?

(A) $x^2 = 8(y - 2)$ (C) $x^2 = -8(y - 2)$

(B) $x^2 = 24(y - 2)$ (D) $x^2 = -24(y - 2)$

13. A hyperbola has a center at $(1, 0)$, the length of its conjugate axis is 12, and one of its foci is located at $(10, 0)$. What is the equation of this hyperbola?

(A) $\dfrac{(x - 1)^2}{36} - \dfrac{y^2}{45} = 1$

(B) $\dfrac{(x - 0)^2}{36} - \dfrac{y^2}{64} = 1$

(C) $\dfrac{(x - 1)^2}{45} - \dfrac{y^2}{36} = 1$

(D) $\dfrac{(x - 0)^2}{64} - \dfrac{y^2}{36} = 1$

14. The equation of one of the asymptotes of a hyperbola with its center at $(-8, k)$ is $y = \dfrac{5}{4}x + 13$. Its transverse axis is parallel to the *x*-axis. What is the value of *k*?

(A) 3   (C) -3

(B) 5   (D) -5

15. What are the coordinates of the glide reflection of the point $(7, 2)$ that is translated by the vector $-\mathbf{i} + 5\mathbf{j}$, then reflected across the *y*-axis?

(A) $(-7, 6)$ (C) $(7, -6)$

(B) $(-6, 7)$ (D) $(6, -7)$

16. What is the rotation matrix for any point that is rotated 180° about the origin?

(A) $\begin{bmatrix} -1 & 0 \\ 0 & -1 \end{bmatrix}$ (C) $\begin{bmatrix} 0 & -1 \\ -1 & 0 \end{bmatrix}$

(B) $\begin{bmatrix} 1 & 0 \\ 0 & -1 \end{bmatrix}$ (D) $\begin{bmatrix} 0 & 1 \\ -1 & 0 \end{bmatrix}$

Quiz for Chapter 14
SOLUTIONS

1. (D)

The midpoint of $\overline{AB}$ is $(2, 3)$. Using the translation vector $-3\mathbf{i} + 4\mathbf{j}$, we subtract 3 from the x-coordinate and add 4 to the y-coordinate. Thus, the image point is located at $(-1, 7)$.

2. (C)

In a reflection over l_1, it must be true that l_1 is the perpendicular bisector of any segment PP', where P' is the image of P.

3. (A)

Using the translation vector $8\mathbf{i} - \mathbf{j}$ leads to the point $(11, 6)$. Then reflecting $(11, 6)$ over the line $y = -x$ leads to the answer of $(-6, -11)$.

4. (A)

Since we already have the coordinates of R', we require a 90°-clockwise rotation to find the coordinates of R. Thus, the coordinates of R are $(2, -4)$.

5. (D)

Let x represent the length of $\overline{DE}$. Then $\dfrac{3}{4} = \dfrac{48}{x}$, so $x = 64$.

6. (D)

The slope of $\overline{NQ}$ is $\dfrac{-3 + 4}{9 - 1} = \dfrac{1}{8}$. Thus, the slope of the altitude from M to $\overline{NQ}$ is the negative reciprocal of $\dfrac{1}{8}$, which is -8.

7. (A)

$EG = \sqrt{(3 + 4)^2 + (6 + 3)^2} \approx 11.40$. Then $90 = \left(\dfrac{1}{2}\right)(11.40)(FH)$. Thus, $FH \approx 15.79$.

8. (B)

We are given $h = 6$, $k = -5$, and $r = 4$. The correct equation of the circle is $(x - 6)^2 + (y + 5)^2 = 16$.

9. (D)

Since the center is located at $(3, -1)$, the distance between the center and each focus is 12. Then $a^2 = 9^2 + 12^2$, which means that $a = \pm 15$. Thus, the endpoints of the major axis are $(3, 14)$ and $(3, -16)$.

10. (C)

Since the minor axis is vertical, the general equation must be $\dfrac{x^2}{a^2} + \dfrac{y^2}{b^2} = 1$. We also know that $2a = 24$ and $2b = 10$. Thus, $a = 12$ and $b = 5$, which means that the equation is $\dfrac{x^2}{144} + \dfrac{y^2}{25} = 1$.

11. (B)

Rewrite the equation as $(x-0)^2 = 20(y-5)$. Then $20 = 4p$, which means that $p = 5$. This is the distance between the vertex and the directrix.

12. (B)

Since the vertex is located at $(0, 2)$ and the focus is on the y-axis, the equation of the parabola must be in the form $(x-0)^2 = 4p(y-2)$.

Also, p represents the distance between the vertex and the focus, which is 6. Since the parabola opens upward, $p > 0$. Thus, the equation must be $x^2 = 24(y-2)$.

13. (C)

Since the center is located at $(1, 0)$ and one focus is located at $(10, 0)$, the general equation must be $\frac{(x-0)^2}{a^2} - \frac{y^2}{b^2} = 1$. In addition, we know that $c = 9$ and $b = (0.5)(12) = 6$. Then $a^2 = 9^2 - 6^2 = 45$. Thus, the equation becomes $\frac{(x-1)^2}{45} - \frac{y^2}{36} = 1$.

14. (A)

Since its center is at $(-8, k)$, let's rewrite the equation $y = \frac{5}{4}x + 13$ as $y - k = \frac{5}{4}(x+8)$. Then $y - k = \frac{5}{4}x + 10$, which can be written as $y = \frac{5}{4}x + 10 + k$. This means that $k = 3$.

15. (B)

Using the translation vector $-\mathbf{i} + 5\mathbf{j}$, the point $(7, 2)$ becomes $(6, 7)$. By reflecting this point across the y-axis, the new point becomes $(-6, 7)$.

16. (A)

The $180°$ - rotation matrix is given by
$$\begin{bmatrix} \cos 180° & \sin 180° \\ -\sin 180° & \cos 180° \end{bmatrix} = \begin{bmatrix} 1 & 0 \\ 0 & 1 \end{bmatrix}.$$

Graphical and Numerical Techniques to Analyze Data

Welcome to Chapter 15. In this chapter, we will review the following topics:

(a) Measurement scales for data
(b) Various displays to represent data
(c) Measures of central tendency and dispersion
(d) Linear transformations of data
(e) Summary of Formulas

Measurement Scales for Data

The four major categories for the classification of data are identified as **nominal**, **ordinal**, **interval**, and **ratio**.

Nominal Level of Measurement

For non-numerical data, the category that is used is commonly called a **nominal level of measurement**. Here are some examples of data that would use this measurement technique:

1. subjects offered at a university
2. marital status
3. religious affiliation
4. gender
5. name of a street.

For each of these five categories, we cannot assign a truly meaningful numerical value.

Ordinal Level of Measurement

For numerical data, there are three categories to be considered. The first of these is called an **ordinal level of measurement**. With this category, data may be ranked; however, the differences between data in adjacent ranks is inexact. Here are some examples that would use this technique of measurement:

1. letter grades in school

2. rankings of first, second, third, …for an event

3. ratings of customer service such as excellent, good, fair, and poor

For each of these examples, there is a definite order in the ranking. Thus, for customer service, "excellent" ranks higher than "good," and "fair" ranks higher than "poor." However, we cannot put a numerical value on the difference between any two such categories.

Interval Level of Measurement

With the **interval level of measurement** we can identify differences between the assigned numerical values. However, there is no meaningful value of absolute zero. Here are some examples to illustrate this category:

1. scores on a standardized test

2. temperature in Fahrenheit degrees.

We cannot claim that a person who scores zero on a standardized test has no intelligence. Similarly, a temperature of zero degrees does not mean that there is no temperature.

Ratio Level of Measurement

The highest category for numerical data is the **ratio level of measurement**. With this category, there are measurable differences between data, zero has meaning, and data can be compared using multiples. By far, this is the most common and useful form for comparing numerical data. Here are a few examples:

1. scores on an exam for which the scores are in the range $0 - 100$

2. weights of people in a room

3. number of cats in a specific animal shelter

4. time in minutes spent doing math homework

A mnemonic way to remember these categories is to think of the French word *noir*, (which means *black*). N = nominal, O = ordinal, I = interval, and R = ratio.

The ratio level of measurement a little further can be subdivided into two types, namely discrete and continuous.

Discrete Data

Discrete data is an exact number with no accompanying approximation. In almost every instance, discrete data refers to a numerical count. Examples are:

1. number of people in a classroom

2. number of buildings in Philadelphia

3. number of marbles on the top of a table

Continuous Data

Continuous data does not contain the same standard of exactness. If a person claims that he is 6 feet 3 inches tall, his actual height might be 6 feet 2.6 inches or even 6 feet 3.2 inches. Similarly, if the lightest person in an exercise class claims that she weighs 105 pounds, she would be truthful if her weight were 104.5 pounds or even 105.1 pounds. As a third illustration, suppose you were running a race of 100 meters and your time were listed as 12.45 seconds. The stopwatch that was used to record your time would be accurate to the nearest hundredth of a second. Your actual time could have been numbers such as 12.453 seconds or perhaps 12.449 seconds.

Various Displays to Represent Data

Scatter Plots

In displaying data, there are many tools at our disposal. A **scatter plot** is a method of showing the relationship of two different numerical quantities by using an *xy*-coordinate plane.

EXAMPLE 1

In a small class of 9 students, the teacher was interested in comparing the number of absences during the school year with each student's final numerical grade. Here are the results in tabular form:

Number of Absences:	0	5	3	9	1	7	3	2	6
Final Grade:	98	80	90	60	93	55	85	90	75

Draw a scatter plot of these results.

SOLUTION

The positive *x*-axis will be labeled "Number of Absences" and the positive *y*-axis will be labeled "Final Grade."

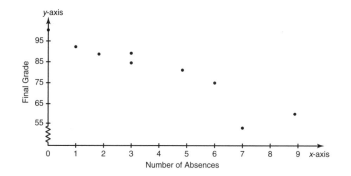

Since the grades range from 55 to 98, a squiggle line is shown between 0 and 55. This indicates that there are no values between 0 and 55. The teacher could draw the conclusion that absences negatively affect students' final grade.

Frequency Distributions

A **frequency distribution** is a method by which the given data is classified by a type or label. For each label, its frequency in the distribution is recorded. We'll show three examples.

EXAMPLE 2

At a gathering of 30 people, each person was asked to write his/her eye color. Here are the data:

brown	amber	amber	blue	blue
hazel	hazel	blue	amber	hazel
brown	blue	amber	brown	amber
hazel	brown	hazel	amber	amber
hazel	amber	blue	blue	blue
amber	blue	amber	hazel	amber

Write a frequency distribution for these four eye colors.

SOLUTION

We'll create two columns, namely eye color and frequency.

Eye Color	Frequency
Amber	11
Blue	8
Brown	4
Hazel	7

In this next example, we will use numerical data that is grouped into classes. Each class of numbers contains a minimum and a maximum value. With this method, two or more numbers may be placed into the same class. For example if a class is listed as $60 - 80$, then each of 61 and 75 would be placed into this class. No two classes may overlap.

EXAMPLE 3

Employees at the XYZ watch company were requested to state their heights, to the nearest inch. The shortest person listed her height as 58 inches, and the tallest person listed his height as 86 inches. Here is the list of the heights, in inches, of all 36 employees: 73, 86, 66, 82, 73, 66, 80, 76, 75, 70, 79, 69, 62, 68, 63, 77, 76, 64, 68, 71, 71, 60, 68, 71, 58, 72, 59, 65, 59, 71, 68, 65, 64, 65, 59, and 64. Construct a grouped frequency distribution, using the following six classes of data:

$58 - 62, 63 - 67, 68 - 72, 73 - 77, 78 - 82,$ and $83 - 87$.

SOLUTION

Use your TI-83 calculator to sort the list of 36 numbers in ascending order. The list of numbers will read as follows: 58, 59, 59, 59, 60, 62, 63, 64, 64, 64, 65, 65, 65, 66, 66, 68, 68, 68, 68, 69, 70, 71, 71, 71, 71, 72, 73, 73, 75, 76, 76, 77, 79, 80, 82, and 86. Now we list each class and count its corresponding frequency. The grouped frequency distribution will appear as follows:

Class	Frequency
58 − 62	6
63 − 67	9
68 − 72	11
73 − 77	6
78 − 82	3
83 − 87	1

Each class identifies the same number of potential entries; that is the first class contains the five entries 58, 59, 60, 61, 62; the second class contains the five entries 63, 64, 65, 66, 67; etc. This pattern of five entries per class is used for each class. The frequency column corresponds to the actual number of data that belong to the entries of the particular class. For a class such as 58 − 62, the number 58 is called the **lower limit** and the number 62 is called the **upper limit**. For each class, the difference between the upper and lower limits <u>must</u> be the same. Furthermore, there is no overlap of assigned entry numbers from one class to the next.

EXAMPLE 4

On a four-question quiz given to her class of 20 students, a student's possible grade is 0, 25, 50, 75, or 100. The results of this quiz for the whole class were as follows: 50, 0, 100, 25, 75, 75, 100, 50, 75, 0, 75, 75, 100, 100, 75, 75, 75, 50, 100, and 50. Create a vertical table of the five possible grades and show their respective frequencies.

SOLUTION

Using the sorting feature of the TI − 83 calculator, this list becomes: 0, 0, 25, 50, 50, 50, 50, 75, 75, 75, 75, 75, 75, 75, 75, 100, 100, 100, 100, and 100. Here is this list in vertical table form, with the corresponding frequencies.

Grade	Frequency
0	2
25	1
50	4
75	8
100	5

Stem-and-Leaf Plot

Another method in which individual data may be tabulated is called a **stem-and-leaf plot.** This method requires that the data be arranged in ascending order. It should be used only when all the data are integers that contain the same number of placeholders. The data are arranged into two groups in which a vertical bar is used. The stem consists of all digits, except the units digit. The leaf contains the units digit of each number that is associated with that stem. Thus, if each of the data is between 100 and 999, the stem would consist of the hundreds digit and the tens digit; the leaf would consist of the units digit of each of the data. For example, the number 235 would appearas 23 | 5. The stems are shown in ascending order in a vertical column and the leaves for each stem are written horizontally in ascending order.

EXAMPLE 5

Using the individual data in Example 3, create a stem-and-leaf plot.

SOLUTION

Using the solution to Example 3, which contains the data sorted in ascending order, the stem-and-leaf plot would be as follows:

5 | 8 9 9 9

6 | 0 2 3 4 4 4 5 5 5 6 6 8 8 8 8 9

7 | 0 1 1 1 1 2 3 3 5 6 6 7 9

8 | 0 2 6

EXAMPLE 6

Ken is an avid bowler. He has kept track of his bowling scores for the 30 most recent games. As a tribute to his consistency, his lowest score was 160 and his highest score was 219. (He hopes to bowl 300 some day!) His results were as follows: 189, 209, 195, 162, 175, 189, 202, 218, 213, 210, 192, 178, 176, 163, 196, 160, 188, 182, 195, 212, 168, 197, 219, 210, 210, 184, 198, 161, 169, and 192. Construct a stem-and-leaf plot.

SOLUTION

Since each number has three digits, the first two digits appear on the left side of the vertical bar. The right side of the vertical bar (i.e., the "leaf" part) must only contain single digits.

Arranged in ascending order, the data appears as follows: 160, 161, 162, 163, 168, 169, 175, 176, 178, 182, 184, 188, 189, 189, 192, 192, 195, 195, 196, 197, 198, 202, 209, 210, 210, 210, 212, 213, 218, and 219. The completed stem-and-leaf plot is as follows:

16 | 0 1 2 3 8 9

17 | 5 6 8

18 | 2 4 8 9 9

19 | 2 2 5 5 6 7 8

20 | 2 9

21 | 0 0 0 2 3 8 9

Histograms

In addition to the preceding examples of organizing and interpreting data, there are several pictorial methods that are available. One of these is called a **histogram,** which is a graph that contains vertical connected rectangular bars in the first quadrant of the xy-coordinate plane. The given data is grouped into classes and each bar shows the frequency of these classes.

EXAMPLE 7

The record low temperatures of last year for twenty-five cities were collected. The results were displayed in a grouped frequency distribution, which appeared as follows:

Class	Frequency
3° – 9°	3
10° – 16°	5
17° – 23°	9
24° – 30°	6
31° – 37°	2

Construct an appropriate histogram.

SOLUTION

Following Example 3, we use the words **lower limit** and **upper limit** in referring to the two extreme numbers of each class. Thus, for the first class, 3° represents the lower limit and 9° represents the upper limit. In order to create connected rectangular bars, we use lower and upper boundaries for each class. Each temperature represents a continuous number. For example, 3° could represent any number between 2.5° and 3.5°, not including 3.5°. Similarly, 9° could represent any number between 8.5° and 9.5°, not including 9.5°. The numbers 2.5 and 3.5 are called the **lower** and **upper boundaries** for 3. In creating the connected bars for each class, we use the lower boundary of the lower limit and the upper boundary of the upper limit. The classes would then appear as 2.5° − 9.5°, 9.5° − 16.5°, 16.5° − 23.5°, 23.5° − 30.5°, and 30.5° − 37.5°.They will be shown on the x-axis. The frequencies will be listed on the y-axis. The completed histogram appears below.

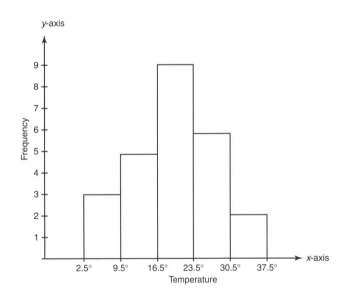

Pie Graphs

Another popular pictorial method for showing data is a **pie graph**. This type of graph is best used to show the percent (or fractional) contribution of the component parts of one category. In a pie graph, each component is assigned to a percent, which then becomes a sector of the circle containing all the component parts.

EXAMPLE 8

The mayor of the town of Peoplefine has mailed a survey to each adult resident, who was asked to rate the quality of the mayor's ability to govern the town. The five ratings given were (a) excellent, (b) very good, (c) average, (d) below average, and (e) poor.

The results showed that $\frac{2}{5}$ of the population ranked the mayor as "excellent," $\frac{1}{3}$ ranked him as "very good," $\frac{1}{10}$ ranked him as "average," $\frac{1}{12}$ ranked him as "below average," and $\frac{1}{12}$ ranked him as "poor." Create an appropriate pie graph.

SOLUTION

You recall that a circle contains 360°, so we need to convert each fraction into degrees. For example, $\frac{2}{5}$ corresponds to $\left(\frac{2}{5}\right)(360°) = 144°$. Following this procedure, here are the conversions for the other given fractions: $\frac{1}{3}$ corresponds to 120°, $\frac{1}{10}$ corresponds to 36°, and $\frac{1}{12}$ corresponds to 30°. The last step is to partition a circle into sectors with the appropriate central angles. Each sector is labeled with a category. Here is the completed pie graph.

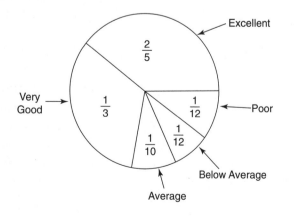

Time Series Line Graphs

Our final pictorial method for showing data will be a **time series line graph**. This type of graph is extremely useful when we wish to show trends of a single quantity over a period of time.

EXAMPLE 9

During the first six months of this year, Amanda kept track of how many different projects to which she was assigned at work. Here are her results: January, 28; February, 22; March, 52; April, 8; May, 12; June, 40. Construct a time series graph.

SOLUTION

The months are placed on the horizontal axis, in order from January through June. Dots are placed that correspond to the respective values for each month. Finally, line segments are drawn to connect the monthly values. We will use a scaling unit of 4. Notice that all but one of the numbers divides evenly by 4. The number 22 will be measured by approximating one-half the distance between 20 and 24. Here is how the time series graph should appear:

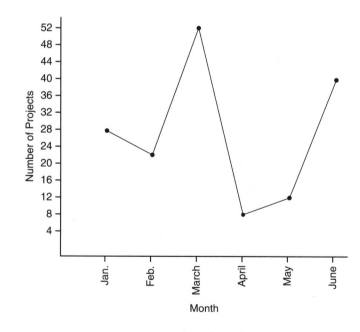

Measures of Central Tendency and Dispersion

There are instances in which we need only a summary of the information for a data set. One such statistic is called the **range**, which is simply the difference between the highest and lowest numbers. For example, if the highest grade on a test is 90 and the lowest grade is 60, the range is 30. This number has limited value because it tells us nothing about the nature of the individual data.

The following quantities are often called measures of **central tendency**, since they reveal how the data are distributed. We will discuss the three most popular measures of central tendency, identified as the **mean**, **median**, and **mode**. Each of these concepts will be applied both to individual data and to grouped data.

Mean for Individual Data

The **mean** of a list of individual data is found by adding the numbers, then dividing by the total frequency. The commonly used symbol for a mean is $\overline{X}$.

EXAMPLE 10

What is the mean for the numbers 24, 18, 50, 22, and 18?

SOLUTION

The sum of these five numbers is 132, so that $\overline{X} = \dfrac{132}{5} = 26.4$.

CAUTION:

You must count all frequencies of a number. The easiest way to do this is to multiply each different number by its frequency, as shown in Examples 11 and 12.

EXAMPLE 11

In a room of ten people, six people each weigh 150 pounds. Of the remaining four people, one weighs 200 pounds and two others each weigh 140 pounds. If the mean weight for all ten people is 154.5 pounds, what is the weight of the tenth person?

SOLUTION

Let x represent the weight of the tenth person. Then we can write $[(6)(150) + (1)(200) + (2)(140) + x] \div 10 = 154.5$. This equation simplifies to $(1380 + x) \div 10 = 154.5$. Multiplying this equation by 10, then subtracting 1380 yields the answer of $x = 165$ pounds.

EXAMPLE 12

The mean weight of the 34 cats and dogs at the We-Love-Pets Animal Shelter is 38 pounds. If two of the dogs that weigh 40 pounds and 60 pounds, respectively, are adopted, what is the mean weight of the remaining cats and dogs?

SOLUTION

We can avoid the use of algebra for this example. The total weight of 34 dogs and cats is $(34)(38) = 1292$ pounds. When two of the dogs are adopted, the total weight of the remaining cats and dogs is $1292 - 100 = 1192$ pounds. Since there are now 32 cats and dogs, the mean weight becomes $1192 \div 32 = 37.25$ pounds.

Median for Individual Data

The **median** of a list of individual data is the middle number of all the data. First, the data must be arranged in ascending order. (Arrangement in descending order, though less common, would also be acceptable.)

There are actually two distinct situations, namely, if there is an odd number of data or an even number of data. Let n represent the number of data values, where *n* is an odd number. Then the position of the median is given as $(n + 1) \div 2$.

If *n* represents the number of data, where *n* is even, then the median is defined as the mean of the two middle numbers. The position of the median is still given as $(n + 1) \div 2$.

EXAMPLE 13

What is the median for the numbers 26, 22, 16, 11, 27, 26, 20, 20, and 15?

SOLUTION

In order, the numbers appear as 11, 15, 16, 20, 20, 22, 26, 26, and 27. In this case, *n* is 9, so the position of the median is given by $(9 + 1) \div 2 = 5$. The fifth number is 20.

EXAMPLE 14

A list of numbers consists of five 13s, two 21s, one 32, and seven 40s. What is the median?

SOLUTION

There are $5 + 2 + 1 + 7 = 15$ numbers in this list of data, which is already arranged in ascending order. Since $n = 15$, the position of the median is given by $(15 + 1) \div 2 = 8$. Since the first five numbers are 13 and the next two numbers are 21, the eighth number (median) is 32. (The solution could have been obtained by listing all 15 numbers.)

EXAMPLE 15

What is the median for the numbers 44, 38, 19, 6, 31, and 37?

SOLUTION

In order, the numbers appear as 6, 19, 31, 37, 38, and 44. Since $n = 6$, the position of the median is $(6 + 1) \div 2 = 3.5$. There really is no such position as 3.5, so the number corresponding to this position is defined

as the arithmetic average (mean) of the third and fourth numbers. Thus, the median is $(31 + 37) \div 2 = 34$.

EXAMPLE 16

The median for a list of numbers, arranged in ascending order occurs midway between the 29th and 30th numbers. How many data are there?

SOLUTION

Let *n* represent the number of data. Then $(n + 1) \div 2$ = 29.5. Solving this equation by multiplying by 2 and subtracting 1 yields the answer $n = 58$.

Mode for Individual Data

The **mode**, when it exists, is the number(s) that occur(s) most frequently. The only situation for which a mode does not exist is when each of the given data has a frequency of 1. Thus, the set of data 3, 8, 19, 20, and 90 has no mode.

Here are three sets of data that have a single mode:

Group A: 15, 16, 18, 5, 5, 12.

Group B: 1, 5, 1, 3, 5, 1, 4, 9

Group C: 7, 7, 7, 7, 2, 2, 2, 10, 10, 10

In group A, the mode is 5; in group B, the mode is 1; and in group C, the mode is 7.

Here are three sets of data that have two modes:

Group D: 2, 4, 2, 4, 2, 4

Group E: 14, 30, 30, 25, 19, 14, 11, 20, 40

Group F: 1, 1, 1, 1, 5, 5, 3, 8, 8, 8, 8

In group D, the modes are 2 and 4; in group E, the modes are 14 and 30; and in group F, the modes are 1 and 8.

NOTE:

The data need not be arranged in ascending order to determine the mode(s). Theoretically, there may be many modes for a particular list of data. However, the importance of the mode is limited in situations with many modes.

Now we will explore the meaning of the mean, median, and mode in the context of grouped data. In order to calculate the mean for grouped data, the midpoint of each class will be used. Then each midpoint will be multiplied by the class frequency. After adding up these products, the sum will be divided by the total frequency.

Mean for Grouped Data

EXAMPLE 17

What is the mean for the following grouped frequency distribution?

Class	Frequency
58 – 62	6
63 – 67	9
68 – 72	11
73 – 77	6
78 – 82	3
83 – 87	1

SOLUTION

This is Example 3 of this chapter, in grouped frequency distribution form. In order to calculate the mean, we need to find the midpoint of each class, which are 60, 65, 70, 75, 80, and 85. Each of these midpoints, called **class marks**, is really the mean of the lower and upper limits. Then, we calculate $[(60)(6) + (65)(9) + (70)(11) + (75)(6) + (80)(3) +$

$(85)(1)] \div 36 = 2490 \div 36 \approx 69.17$.

Incidentally, you may recall that initially we were given the individual data. If we had just used these individual numbers, the mean would be 68.94, which is remarkably close to our answer of 69.17.

EXAMPLE 18

What is the mean for the following grouped frequency distribution?

Class	Frequency
3° – 9°	3
10° – 16°	5
17° – 23°	9
24° – 30°	6
31° – 37°	2

SOLUTION

This is a replica of Example 7 of this chapter. The class marks (midpoints of each class) are 6°, 13°, 20°, 27°, and 34°. Thus, the mean is $[(6)(3) + (13)(5) + (20)(9) + (27)(6) + (34)(2)] \div 25$ $= 493 \div 25 = 19.72$.

Median for Grouped Data

We are about to explore the technique for calculating the median for grouped data. Let's first mention that with grouped data, the position of the median for n data is always $n \div 2$, regardless of whether the number of data is odd or even. Since this process is rather involved, we will illustrate it in conjunction with the data of Example 17.

EXAMPLE 19

What is the median for the following grouped data distribution?

Class	Frequency
58 – 62	6
63 – 67	9
68 – 72	11
73 – 77	6
78 – 82	3
83 – 87	1

SOLUTION

We know that there are a total of 36 numbers, and that the position of the median is $36 \div 2 = 18$. Here are the steps to follow:

1. Starting with the frequency of the first class, determine in which class the 18th number will appear. Notice that the total frequency for the first two classes is $6 + 9 = 15$. The next 11 numbers will appear in the third class, so this class will include the 18th number.

2. $18 - 15 = 3$, so we are looking for the third number, out of 11, that is in this third class. Write the fraction $\frac{3}{11}$.

3. Identify the lower and upper boundaries for this class, which are 67.5 and 72.5, respectively. The width of this class is the difference in these boundaries, which is $72.5 - 67.5 = 5$.

4. Multiply $\frac{3}{11}$ by 5, which is approximately 1.36.

5. Finally, add 1.36 to the lower boundary of 67.5 to get the answer of 68.86.

The actual individual data for this example, arranged in ascending order, can be found in Example 3 of this chapter. You will notice that the median, which is located midway between the 18th and 19th numbers, is 68. The closeness of this answer to our answer for grouped data is certainly reassuring.

As with most procedures in mathematics, there is really a formula that can be used to determine the median for a grouped frequency distribution.

Let N = total number of data, F = frequency of the class containing the median, C = cumulative frequency up through the class immediately preceding the class containing the median, L = lower boundary, and W = width of each class. Then we can write, Median =

$$L + \left(\frac{\frac{N}{2} - C}{F} \right)(W).$$

A good way to remember this formula is to associate it with the mnemonic: **L**et's **N**ot **C**onsider **F**eeding **W**olves. However, you must remember that N is divided

by 2. Also, you must be able to locate the class that contains the median. As applied to Example 19, Median =

$$67.5 + \left(\frac{\frac{36}{2} - 15}{11} \right)(5) \approx 68.86.$$

EXAMPLE 20

What is the median for the following grouped data distribution?

Class	Frequency
3° – 9°	3
10° – 16°	5
17° – 23°	9
24° – 30°	6
31° – 37°	2

SOLUTION

This is the same distribution we saw in Examples 7 and 18. Since the total frequency is 25, the position of the median is 12.5. The cumulative frequency for the first two classes is 8 and the cumulative frequency for the first three classes is 17. This means that the median is located in the class $17° - 23°$, for which the lower boundary is 16.5°. For the formula Median

$$= L + \left(\frac{\frac{N}{2} - C}{F} \right)(W), \text{ we know that: } L = 16.5°, N = 25,$$

$C = 3 + 5 = 8$, F = frequency of the class containing the median = 9, and W = width of the class containing the median = $23.5° - 16.5° = 7°$. Thus, the median =

$$16.5° + \left(\frac{\frac{25}{2} - 8}{9} \right)(7°) = 20°.$$

NOTE:

> In Example 20, the median is located exactly in the middle of the third class. This result occurred because of the symmetry of the data, i.e.: 8 of the data lie in lower classes and 8 of the data lie in higher classes than the third class.

Class	Frequency
17 − 22	2
23 − 28	4
29 − 34	9
35 − 40	13
41 − 46	20

Mode for Grouped Data

When we talk about the mode with respect to grouped data, we use the term **modal class.** This refers to the class (or classes) that contain the highest frequency. In Example 19, the modal class is 68 − 72; in Example 20, the modal class is 17° − 23°. The following grouped distribution would be an example that contains two modal classes.

Class	Frequency
10 − 19	8
20 − 29	4
30 − 39	5
40 − 49	8
50 − 59	3

The two modal classes are 10 − 19 and 40 − 49, since each of them contains the highest frequency. Unlike individual data, grouped data must have at least one modal class.

Skewness for Grouped Data

We continue our discussion of grouped frequency distributions with the concept of **skewness**, which refers to a lack of symmetry concerning the frequencies for the classes of the data.

Negative Skewness

For a **negatively skewed** distribution of data, the frequencies for the classes that contain the larger numbers tend to be greater than the frequencies for the classes that contain the smaller numbers. Another term for "negatively skewed" is "skewed left."

The following grouped data distribution is an example of a negatively skewed distribution.

Let's calculate the mean, median, and modal class for this grouped distribution of data. The mean ($\overline{X}$) = $[(19.5)(2) + (25.5)(4) + (31.5)(9) + (37.5)(13) + (43.5)(20)] \div 48 = 37.125$

The median $= 34.5 + \left(\dfrac{\frac{48}{2} - 15}{13} \right)(6) \approx 38.65$.

The modal class is 41 − 46.

Observe that the mean is less than the median, which is less than the mode (although the exact value of the mode is not known). This is the key to what constitutes a negatively skewed distribution. Here is a representative histogram for this grouped data distribution.

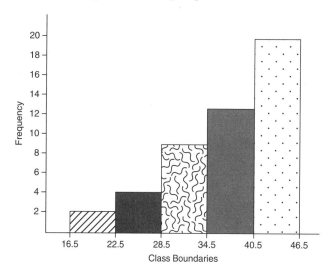

Figure 15.1

Positive Skewness

For a **positively skewed** distribution of data, the frequencies for the classes that contain the larger numbers tend to be lower than the frequencies for the classes that contain the smaller numbers. Another term for *positively skewed* is *skewed right*. The following grouped data distribution is an example of a positively skewed distribution.

Class	Frequency
75−87	23
88−100	19
101−113	16
114−126	10
127−139	6
140−152	1

Let's calculate the mean, median, and modal class for this grouped distribution of data.

The mean ($\overline{X}$) = [(81)(23) + (94)(19) + (107)(16) + (120)(10) + (133)(6) + (146)(1)] ÷ 75 ≈ 100.07 .

The median $= 87.5 + \left(\dfrac{\dfrac{75}{2} - 23}{19} \right)(13) \approx 97.42$. The modal class is 75 − 87.

Observe that the mean is greater than the median, which is greater than the mode (although the exact value of the mode is not known). This is the key to what constitutes a positively skewed distribution. Here is a representative histogram for this grouped data distribution.

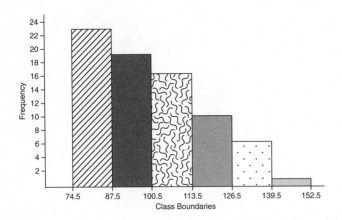

Figure 15.2

Symmetric Distribution

For a **symmetric** distribution of data, the middle class(es) tends to have the largest frequency. The further away a particular class is from the middle class(es), the lower the frequency. In addition, two classes that are equally "distant" from the middle class(es) will tend to have the same frequency. This implies that the classes with the smallest frequencies will be the first and last classes. There is one "middle" class for a distribution containing an odd number of classes, whereas there are two "middle" classes for a distribution with an even number of classes.

The following grouped data distribution is an example of a symmetric distribution.

Class	Frequency
31 − 35	3
36 − 40	6
41 − 45	13
46 − 50	18
51 − 55	13
56 − 60	5
61 − 65	2

Let's calculate the mean, median, and modal class for this grouped distribution of data.

The mean ($\overline{X}$) = [(33)(3) + (38)(6) + (43)(13) + (48)(18) + (53)(13) + (58)(5) + (63)(2)] ÷ 60 ≈ 47.58.

The median $= 45.5 + \left(\dfrac{\dfrac{60}{2} - 22}{18} \right)(5) \approx 47.72$. The modal class is 46 − 50.

Observe that the values of the mean, median, and modal class are extremely close, which is the key to a symmetrical distribution. In a perfectly symmetrical distribution, which is nearly impossible, these three values would be identical.

Here is a representative histogram for this grouped data distribution.

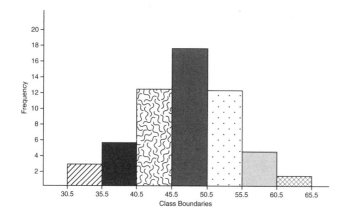

Figure 15.3

The mean, median, and mode are measures that describe data with respect to the "middle" of a particular individual or grouped data distribution.

We will now explore the meaning of terms that illustrate the position of specific data with respect to all the other data in the given distribution.

Percentile

Each number in a given distribution of data corresponds to a **percentile**, which indicates how high (or low) its value is when compared to all other numbers. For example, if you scored 90 on an exam, your percentile would be dependent on the scores of the rest of the class. If the class mean were only 70, then a score of 90 would correspond to a relatively high percentile. However, if the class mean were 95, then a score of 90 would correspond to a relatively low percentile.

The actual percentile assigned to an individual score indicates the approximate percent of scores that lie at or below it. Thus, if your score of 90 were ranked as the 80th percentile, it means that approximately 80% of the other scores were at or below 90.

First Quartile

The **first quartile,** abbreviated as Q_1, represents the value for a distribution of data for which 25% of all the data lies at or below Q_1 and 75% of the all the data lies above Q_1.

Another name for Q_1 is the **25th percentile.** Q_1 is actually the median of the lower half of all the data.

Second Quartile

The **second quartile**, abbreviated as Q_2, represents the value for a distribution of data for which 50% of all the data lies at or below Q_2 and 50% of all the data lies above Q_2.

Two other names for Q_2 are the **50th percentile** and the **median**.

Third Quartile

The **third quartile**, abbreviated as Q_3, represents the value for a distribution of data for which 75% of all the data lies at or below Q_3 and 25% of all the data lies above Q_3.

Another name for Q_3 is the **75th percentile**. Q_3 is actually the median of the upper half of all the data.

Before we express the formulas used to locate the values of $Q_1, Q_2,$ and Q_3, we will look at various situations regarding the number of data in the distribution. Our current focus will be for individual data, listed in ascending order. Since we already know how to find Q_2, we'll look specifically at the positions of Q_1 and Q_3. Let's consider two distributions for which there are an even number of data.

EXAMPLE 21

What are the values of Q_1 and Q_3 for the following distribution?

2, 5, 6, 9, 10, 16, 17, 20, 23, 27, 30, and 32.

SOLUTION

The lower half of this distribution of 12 numbers is represented by the first six numbers: 2, 5, 6, 9, 10, and 16. Then Q_1 is the mean of 6 and 9, which is 7.5.

Likewise, since the upper half of this distribution is represented by 17, 20, 23, 27, 30, and 32, Q_3 is the mean of 23 and 27, which is 25. Notice that the positions of Q_1 and Q_3 are 3.5th and 9.5th, respectively. Of course, the value of the median is 16.5.

EXAMPLE 22

What are the values of Q_1 and Q_3 for the following distribution?

11, 11, 16, 19, 24, 28, 33, 40, 55, and 60.

SOLUTION

The lower half of this distribution of 10 numbers consists of the five numbers 11, 11, 16, 19, and 24. Then Q_1 is the third number, which is 16. In a similar way, the upper half of this distribution consists of the numbers 28, 33, 40, 55, and 60. Then Q_3 is the middle number of this quintet, which is 40. Notice that the positions of Q_1 and Q_3 are 3rd and 8th, respectively.

Rules for Positions of Q_1 and Q_3 - Even Number of Data

Let n represent an even number of data. The position of Q_1 is given by $\dfrac{n+2}{4}$, and the position of Q_3 is given by $\dfrac{3n+2}{4}$. This rule is <u>not</u> influenced by the repetition of data. This rule can be easily verified for both Examples 21 and 22.

Thus, if a distribution of individual data had 72 numbers, Q_1 would be the 18.5th number and Q_3 would be the 54.5th number. The actual value of Q_1 would be the mean of the 18th and 19th numbers. Likewise, the actual value of Q_3 would be the mean of the 54th and 55th numbers.

EXAMPLE 23

Suppose Q_3 is the 23rd number in a distribution of an even number of data (arranged in ascending order). How many data are in this distribution?

SOLUTION

We can use the formula $Q_3 = \dfrac{3n+2}{4}$. Then $23 = \dfrac{3n+2}{4}$. Multiplying both sides of the equation by 4, we get $92 = 3n + 2$. Solving, we get $n = 30$.

We now explore how to determine Q_1 and Q_3 for an odd number of data. Let's look at two specific distributions.

EXAMPLE 24

What are the values of Q_1 and Q_3 for the following distribution?

20, 24, 26, 28, 30, 31, 36, 40, and 48.

SOLUTION

The median is the fifth number, which is 30. Since there are four numbers in the lower half, Q_1 equals the mean of the second and third numbers, which is 25.

Likewise, the upper half consists of the four numbers 31, 36, 40, and 48. Then Q_3 equals the mean of the seventh and eighth numbers, which is 38. The positions of Q_1 and Q_3 are 2.5 and 7.5, respectively.

EXAMPLE 25

What are the values of Q_1 and Q_3 for the following distribution?

1, 5, 6, 8, 10, 14, and 19.

SOLUTION

The median is 8, the fourth number. For the three numbers that comprise the lower half, namely, 1, 5, and 6, Q_1 equals the middle number 5. The numbers 10, 14, and 19 comprise the upper half. Thus, Q_3 equals the middle of these numbers, which is 14.

Rules for Positions of Q_1 and Q_3 - Odd Number of Data

Let n represent an odd number of data. The position of Q_1 is given by $\dfrac{n+1}{4}$, and the position of Q_3 is given by $\dfrac{3n+3}{4} = (3)\left(\dfrac{n+1}{4}\right)$. Notice that the position of Q_3 is three times the position of Q_1. This rule can be easily verified for Examples 24 and 25.

Thus, if a distribution of individual data has 37 numbers, Q_1 would be the mean of the 9th and 10th numbers. The value of Q_3 would be the mean of the 28th and 29th numbers and the median would be the 19th number.

EXAMPLE 26

Suppose that Q_1 is the 11th number in a distribution of an odd number of data (arranged in ascending order). How many data are in this distribution?

SOLUTION

We use the formula $Q_1 = \dfrac{n+1}{4}$, so that $11 = \dfrac{n+1}{4}$. After multiplying both sides by 4, we get $n + 1 = 44$. Thus, $n = 43$.

Values of Q_1 and Q_3 For Grouped Data

Given n data, regardless of whether n is odd or even, the position of Q_1 is $\dfrac{n}{4}$ and the position of Q_3 is $\dfrac{3n}{4}$. In order to determine the values of Q_1 and Q_3, these are the formulas we use: $Q_1 = L + \left(\dfrac{\dfrac{N}{4} - C}{F}\right)(W)$ and

$Q_3 = L + \left(\dfrac{\dfrac{3N}{4} - C}{F}\right)(W)$. As a quick review, $L =$ lower boundary of the desired class (of Q_1 or Q_3), $N =$ total number of data, $C =$ cumulative frequency up through the class immediately preceding the desired class (of Q_1 or Q_3), $F =$ frequency of the desired class (of Q_1 or Q_3), and $W =$ the common width of each class.

EXAMPLE 27

What are the values of Q_1 and Q_3 in the following grouped frequency distribution?

Class	Frequency
58−62	6
63−67	9
68−72	11
73−77	6
78−82	3
83−87	1

This is a replica of Example 19, for which we have already found the mean and the median. There are a total of 36 data, so the position of Q_1 is $(0.25)(36) = 9$. Since 6 numbers are found in the first class and 15 numbers are found in the first two classes, the desired class is the second class, namely, 63−67.

For this second class, $L = 62.5$, $C = 6$, $F = 9$, and $W = 5$. By substitution, $Q_1 = 62.5 + \left(\dfrac{\dfrac{36}{4} - 6}{9}\right)(5)$

$\approx 62.5 + 1.67 = 64.17$.

Similarly, the position of Q_3 is $(0.75)(36) = 27$. There are a total of 26 numbers in the first three classes and a total of 32 numbers in the first four classes. Therefore, Q_3 must lie in the fourth class, which is 73 − 77. For this fourth class, $L = 72.5$, $C = 26$, $F = 6$, and $W = 5$. By substitution, $Q_3 =$

$72.5 + \left(\dfrac{\dfrac{(3)(36)}{4} - 26}{6}\right)(5) = 72.5 + \left(\dfrac{1}{6}\right)(5) \approx 73.33$.

EXAMPLE 28

What are the values of Q_1 and Q_3 in the following grouped frequency distribution?

Class	Frequency
3° - 9°	3
10° - 16°	5
17° - 23°	9
24° - 30°	6
31° - 37°	2

SOLUTION

This is a replica of Example 20, for which we have already found the mean and the median. There are a total of 25 data, so the position of Q_1 is $(0.25)(25) = 6.25$. There are 3 numbers in the first class and a combined total of 8 numbers in the first two classes; so Q_1 must lie in the class $10° - 16°$. For this class, $L = 9.5°$, $C = 3$, $F = 5$,

and $W = 7°$. Thus, $Q_1 = 9.5° + \left(\dfrac{\frac{25}{4} - 3}{5} \right)(7°) = 14.05°$.

The position for Q_3 is $(0.75)(25) = 18.75$. There are a total of 17 numbers in the first three class, and a total of 23 numbers in the first four classes. Then Q_3 must lie in the fourth class, for which $L = 23.5°$, $C = 17$, $F = 6$, and

$W = 7°$. Thus, $Q_3 = 23.5° + \left(\dfrac{\frac{(3)(25)}{4} - 17}{6} \right)(7°) \approx 25.54°$.

Boxplots

A very useful graphical way to summarize key elements of either individual data or grouped data is a **boxplot**. In particular, a boxplot shows the lowest value, the first quartile, the median, the third quartile, and the highest value. Incidentally, another name for *boxplot* is *box-and-whisker diagram*.

EXAMPLE 29

Construct a boxplot for the following set of twelve individual data.

2, 5, 6, 9, 10, 16, 17, 20, 23, 27, 30, and 32.

SOLUTION

The lowest value is 2, $Q_1 = 7.5$, $Q_2 = 16.5$, $Q_3 = 25$, and the highest value is 32. The next step is to draw a horizontal scale (line segment) so that these five values are found between the endpoints. One possible choice is as follows:

This scale begins at 0 and ends at 35. The scale is subdivided into equal parts, so that the numbers on the scale are 5 units apart. Another equally good choice would be to begin the scale at 2, end it at 32, and subdivide the scale into equal parts so that the numbers on the scale are 2 units apart. Above the scale, draw a segment connecting the lowest point and Q_1.

Also, draw a segment connecting Q_3 and the highest point. These two segments should be drawn at the same distance above the scale. Since the scale is marked off in units of 5, you will have to estimate the locations of these four points. Your diagram should now appear as follows:

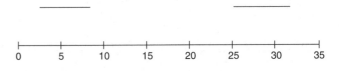

Now draw a rectangular box between Q_1 and Q_3 so that the vertical sides of this box contain Q_1 and Q_3. Then draw a vertical bar inside the box that best estimates the value of the median (Q_2). At this point, here is how your diagram should appear:

The last step can be viewed as a courtesy to the reader. You want to be 100% sure that a person looking at this boxplot can easily determine these five critical values. The lowest and highest values are placed directly above their corresponding points. The values of each of Q_1, Q_2, and Q_3 are placed on the upper horizontal segment of the box. Here is the final picture of the boxplot:

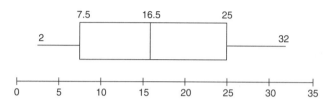

EXAMPLE 30

Construct a boxplot for the following grouped frequency distribution:

Class	Frequency
70 − 74	2
75 − 79	3
80 − 84	6
85 − 89	4
90 − 94	5
95 − 99	25

SOLUTION

The construction of a boxplot requires the lowest and highest numbers. However, these values are not usually known in a grouped frequency distribution. We can safely assume that the lowest value is 70, since the conventional way to create the distribution is to use the lowest number as the lower limit of the first class. It is not as likely that the highest number is 99, so we'll just assume that the highest value is actually 98. In reality, the highest value may be any of the numbers 95, 96, 97, 98, or 99. Recall that in constructing the grouped frequency distribution, the difference between the limits of each class must be equal. Thus, 99 should represent the upper limit of the last class. Here is the summary of our five key statistics, with the computations shown for review purposes:

The lowest value is 70,

$$Q_1 = 84.5 + \left(\frac{\frac{45}{4} - 11}{4}\right)(5) \approx 84.81,$$

$$Q_2 = 94.5 + \left(\frac{\frac{45}{2} - 20}{25}\right)(5) = 95,$$

$$Q_3 = 94.5 + \left(\frac{\frac{(3)(45)}{4} - 20}{25}\right)(5) = 97.25,$$ and the highest

(assumed) number is 98.

We will use a scale that begins at 70 and ends at 98. The scale will be subdivided into equal parts, so that the numbers on the scale are 4 units apart; thus, the numbers on the scale will be 70, 74, 78, 82, …, 98. Here is the picture of the boxplot:

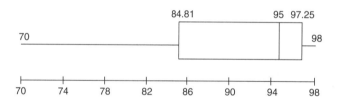

As you recall the concept of skewness that was discussed earlier in this chapter, you can conclude that Example 29 illustrates a symmetric distribution and Example 30 illustrates a negatively skewed distribution. Notice that the "tails" of a symmetric distribution seem to be about equal; in a negatively skewed distribution, the left tail of the box is longer than the right tail. For completeness, we'll now show the boxplot of a positively skewed distribution, for which the right tail of the box will be longer than the left tail.

EXAMPLE 31

Construct a boxplot for the following grouped frequency distribution of the highest recorded temperatures (Fahrenheit) on a specific day for a sample of 60 cities.

Class	Frequency
$20° - 33°$	19
$34° - 47°$	14
$48° - 61°$	9
$62° - 75°$	7
$76° - 89°$	5
$90° - 103°$	4
$104° - 116°$	2

SOLUTION

We can safely assume that the lowest temperature is 20°, but we need to make a random assumption about the highest temperature. Let's suppose that the highest temperature is 110°. The lowest and highest temperatures are 20° and 110°, respectively. As such, we can create a scale that begins at 20°, ends at 110°, and is subdivided into equal parts so that the numbers on the scale are 10 units apart. Then the scale will read 20°, 30°, 40°, 50°, ..., 110°. Q_1 is the 15th number, so its value is

$$19.5 + \frac{15 - 0}{19}(14) \approx 19.5 + 11.05 = 30.55°.$$ Q_2 is the

30th number, so its value is $33.5 + \left(\frac{30 - 19}{14}\right)(14) =$

$33.5 + 11 = 44.5°$. Q_3 is the 45th number, so its value

is $61.5 + \left(\frac{45 - 42}{7}\right)(14) = 61.5 + 6 = 67.5°$.

The five key statistics are 20°, 30.55°, 44.5°, 67.5°, and 110°. The boxplot should appear as follows:

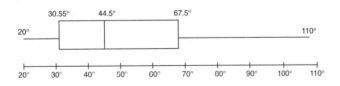

Interquartile Range

Related to the five key statistics of the boxplot is the definition of the **interquartile range**. This concept is sometimes abbreviated as the IQR, and is simply the numerical difference between the third quartile and the first quartile. In a boxplot, it represents the width of

the box, which is approximately the middle 50% of the data. The IQR's for Examples 29, 30, and 31 are 17.5°, 12.44°, and 36.95°, respectively.

Standard Deviation and Variance

When we are interested in learning more about the variability of the data in any distribution (individual or grouped) with respect to the mean, the **standard deviation** is the most commonly used statistic. The (nonnegative) number associated with the standard deviation reveals the extent to which the data are dispersed about the mean. The higher this value, the more "spread out" are the actual data. For lower values, the data tend to lie closer to the mean. A standard deviation of zero can only occur if all the data are equal.

We will consider each distribution of data as a sample, for reasons to be explained in Chapter 17. For a distribution of individual data, the sample standard deviation, denoted as s, is defined as $\sqrt{\dfrac{\sum(X - \overline{X})^2}{n - 1}}$.

In this formula, X represents each individual data value, $\overline{X}$ represents the mean, and n represents the number of data. Other variations of this formula are:

a) $\sqrt{\dfrac{\sum f(X - \overline{X})^2}{n - 1}}$, for which f represents the frequency of each <u>different</u> value in the data and X represents each <u>different</u> data value. If each number in the distribution occurs only once, then this formula and the one identified with the definition are virtually identical. We'll use this formula for our computations.

b) $\sqrt{\dfrac{\sum X^2 - [(\sum X)^2 / n]}{n - 1}}$, for which each X is accounted for. Note that $\sum X^2$ means to square each X first, then sum up these squared values. However, $(\sum X)^2$ means to sum up all X values first, then square this sum.

The square of the sample standard deviation is called the **sample variance**, denoted as s^2. Thus, the sample variance can be calculated as $\dfrac{(X - \overline{X})^2}{n - 1}$, as

$$\frac{\sum X^2 - \left[\dfrac{\left(\sum X\right)^2}{n}\right]}{n-1}, \text{ or as } \frac{\sum f(X - \overline{X})^2}{n-1}. \text{ The data}$$

need not be arranged in order.

EXAMPLE 32

What are the sample variance and standard deviation for the following data?

12, 3, 8, 6, 16, and 15

SOLUTION

The sum of these six numbers is 60, so the mean is 10. Then the variance is

$$\frac{(12-10)^2 + (3-10)^2 + (8-10)^2 + (6-10)^2}{5}$$
$$\frac{+ (16-10)^2 + (15-10)^2}{}$$

$$= \frac{4 + 49 + 4 + 16 + 36 + 25}{5} = 26.8. \text{ Thus, the stan-}$$

dard deviation is $\sqrt{26.8}$, which is approximately 5.18.

EXAMPLE 33

What are the sample variance and standard deviation for the following data?

24, 18, 50, 22, and 18

SOLUTION

These are the numbers we saw in Example 10. We had already calculated the mean as 26.4. We'll combine the two 18's together so that the sample variance (s^2)

$$= \frac{(24-26.4)^2 + (2)(18-26.4)^2 + (50-26.4)^2}{4}$$
$$\frac{+ (22-26.4)^2}{} = \frac{5.76 + 141.12 + 556.96 + 19.36}{4}$$

$$= 180.8. \text{ Thus, the standard deviation } (s) = \sqrt{180.8}$$

$$\approx 13.45.$$

EXAMPLE 34

What are the sample variance and standard deviation for the following data?

Five 13's, two 21's, one 33, and seven 40's

SOLUTION

These are almost the same numbers found in Example 14, (32 was changed to 33). We must first determine the value of the mean, which

is $\dfrac{(5)(13) + (2)(21) + 33 + (7)(40)}{15} = 28$.

Then the variance is computed as

$$\frac{(5)(13-28)^2 + (2)(21-28)^2 + (33-28)^2 +}{14} =$$

$$\frac{(7)(40-28)^2}{14} \quad \frac{1125 + 98 + 25 + 1008}{14} \approx 161.14.$$

Thus, the standard deviation is $\sqrt{161.14} \approx 12.69$.

If we have a grouped frequency distribution, the formulas for variance and standard deviation are very similar. The key difference is that we need to compute the class marks for each class. Let X_m represent each class mark. Then the sample variance

$$s^2 = \frac{\sum f(X_m - \overline{X})^2}{n-1}, \text{ and the sample standard devia-}$$

tion $s = \sqrt{\dfrac{\sum f(X_m - \overline{X})^2}{n-1}}$.

EXAMPLE 35

What are the sample variance and standard deviation for the following data?

Class	Frequency
58−62	6
63−67	9
68−72	11
73−77	7
78−82	5
83−87	2

SOLUTION

This example is very similar to Example 27. We first calculate X, which is

$$\frac{(60)(6) + (65)(9) + (70)(11) + (75)(7) + (80)(5) +}{40}$$

$$\frac{+ (85)(2)}{} = \frac{2810}{40} = 70.25.$$ Now, using the class

marks for each class, we calculate each of $(X_m - \overline{X})^2$ for each class. For example, in the first class, this value is $(60 - 70.25)^2 \approx 105.06$. To avoid an unnecessary number of decimal places, we'll round off the values of $(X_m - \overline{X})^2$ to the nearest hundredth. In a similar fashion, the values of $(X_m - \overline{X})^2$ for the other classes are approximately 27.56, 0.06, 22.56, 95.06, and 217.5625, respectively. Then the sample variance is approximately

$$\frac{(6)(105.06) + (9)(27.56) + (11)(0.06) + (7)(22.56) +}{}$$

$$\frac{(5)(95.06) + (2)(217.56)}{39} = \frac{1947.4}{39} \approx 49.93.$$ Thus,

the standard deviation is $\sqrt{49.93} \approx 7.07$.

EXAMPLE 36

What are the sample variance and standard deviation for the following data?

Class	Frequency
3 – 7	1
8 – 12	3
13 – 17	9
18 – 22	5
23 – 27	2

SOLUTION

Using the class marks of 5, 10, 15, 20, and 25, the

mean is $\dfrac{(1)(5) + (3)(10) + (9)(15) + (5)(20) + (2)(25)}{20}$

$= \dfrac{320}{20} = 16$. Then $s^2 = \dfrac{(1)(5 - 16)^2 + (3)(10 - 16)^2}{}$

$$\frac{+ (9)(15 - 16)^2 + (5)(20 - 16)^2 + (2)(25 - 16)^2}{19}$$

$$= \frac{121 + 108 + 9 + 80 + 162}{19} \approx 25.26.$$ Thus,

$$s = \sqrt{25.26} \approx 5.03.$$

Use of TI-83 Calculator

As you can readily observe, the calculation of s^2 and s requires extreme care. One misstep is all that is needed to yield a wrong answer. Luckily, your friendly TI-83 calculator does have a built-in feature that will compute the sample variance and standard deviation. (It also has the features necessary to compute a mean and a median for data.) Let's use the data in Example 32 to illustrate the procedure for finding s^2 on the TI-83 calculator.

Press "2nd," "List," scroll to "Math," press "8," and then the word "variance" along with a left parenthesis. Now insert the left brace, which is denoted as {. At this point, enter each number, separated by a comma. When you have completed entering the last number, insert a right brace followed by a right parenthesis. Your screen should appear as follows: variance ({12,3,8,6,16,15}). When you press "enter," the answer of 26.8 should appear. If you get an "error" message, you probably omitted a parenthesis or brace. The procedure for finding the standard deviation (s) is identical, except that instead of selecting "8" when you scroll to "Math," select "7." Of course, you can find the standard deviation by simply taking the square root of the variance.

As with many of our examples, many individual numbers have frequencies higher than 1. Of course, we do not want to spend an undue amount of time inputting these numbers. Our TI-83 calculator has this base covered also. Here is the procedure for finding the variance in Example 34.

In this example, most of the numbers have a frequency higher than 1. Follow the procedure discussed above up to the point where the word "variance" appears along with the left parenthesis and the left brace. Now, just enter each different number, separated by a comma. When you have entered each of 13, 21, 33, and 40, insert a right brace, followed by a comma. Do not insert a right parenthesis yet. Now you must insert the corresponding frequency for each number you have already entered. Start by inserting a left brace, followed by the numbers 5, 2, 1, and 7. Each of these numbers corresponds to the frequency of the entered numbers, in the correct order. Now, finish inputting by inserting a right brace, then a right parenthesis. This is how your screen should appear before you press the "enter" button: variance({13,21,33,40},{5,2,1,7})

Now press "enter" and the answer of approximately 161.14 should appear on your screen. Be aware that any number of miscues can occur. If you get a different answer, check to see that your frequencies match exactly the data you entered initially. The pesky "error" message means that you either omitted a brace (or parenthesis), or that you switched the correct order of the brace and parenthesis. The human eye makes allowances for these oversights, but not the calculator.

Linear Transformation of Data

The last topic of this chapter will deal with the effect of a linear transformation on the values of the mean, median, variance, and standard deviation of a list of individual numbers. A **linear transformation** on a number X is the creation of a number Y such that $Y = aX + b$, where a and b are real numbers.

For each of the next six examples, we will use the numbers 12, 3, 8, 6, 16, and 15. The mean is 10, the variance is 26.8, and the standard deviation is approximately 5.18.

EXAMPLE 37

If each number is increased by 3, how does this affect the value of the mean?

SOLUTION

For this example $a = 1$ and $b = 3$ in the formula $Y = aX + b$. The new numbers become 15, 6, 11, 9, 19, and 18. The new mean is 78/6 = 13, so our conclusion is that the mean increased by the same amount as did each number in the original list.

EXAMPLE 38

If each number is increased by 3, how does this affect the variance and the standard deviation?

SOLUTION

We calculate the variance for the new numbers, which is

$$\frac{(15-13)^2 + (6-13)^2 + (11-13)^2 + (9-13)^2}{5}$$
$$\frac{+ (19-13)^2 + (18-13)^2}{} = 26.8$$

Of course, this implies that the standard deviation is about 5.18. Our conclusion is that adding (or subtracting) a constant does not influence the values of the variance or the standard deviation.

Based on the meanings of the variance and the standard deviation, this result should not be surprising. Remember that these two terms refer to the variability of the data with respect to the mean. Adding (or subtracting) a constant will retain the degree of variability.

EXAMPLE 39

If each number is multiplied by 4, how does this affect the value of the mean?

SOLUTION

For this example $a = 4$ and $b = 0$ in the formula $Y = aX + b$. The new numbers become 48, 12, 32, 24, 64, and 60. The new mean becomes 240 / 6 = 40, which is four times as large as the mean of the original data.

EXAMPLE 40

If each number is multiplied by 4, how does this affect the value of the variance and the standard deviation?

SOLUTION

We calculate the variance for the new numbers, as shown in Example 39.

Then the value of s^2 is
$$\frac{(48-40)^2 + (12-40)^2 + (32-40)^2 + (24-40)^2 + (64-40)^2 + (60-40)^2}{5}$$
$= 2144/5 = 428.8$. This number is $16 = 4^2$ times as large as the variance of the original numbers, which was 26.8. This implies that the new standard deviation is $\sqrt{428.8} \approx 20.71$, which is practically the same as $(4)(5.18)$. In fact, the "error" is due to rounding off.

In multiplying a group of numbers by a constant, the standard deviation is also multiplied by that same constant. However, the variance is multiplied by the square of that constant.

EXAMPLE 41

> If each number is multiplied by $\frac{1}{2}$ and subtracted by 8, how does this affect the value of the mean?

SOLUTION

For this example $a = \frac{1}{2}$ and $b = -8$ in the formula $Y = aX + b$. Based on the conclusions for Examples 37 and 39, we should be able to make a very educated guess! The new numbers are -2, -6.5, -4, -5, 0, and -0.5; the new mean is $-18/6 = -3$. Recall that the original mean was 10. Sure enough, $(10)\left(\frac{1}{2}\right) - 8 = -3$.

This means that as we change each number with a linear transformation, the mean changes in exactly the same way.

EXAMPLE 42

> If each number is multiplied by $\frac{1}{2}$ and subtracted by 8, how does this affect the variance and the standard deviation?

SOLUTION

Let's save some time. Using your TI-83 calculator, follow the procedure that was shown following Example 36. Then, for the numbers -2, -6.5, -4, -5, 0, and -0.5, we find that $s^2 = 6.7$. This implies that $s \approx 2.59$. Recall that the variance of the original data was 26.8. The new variance is 6.7, which is $\left(\frac{1}{4}\right)(26.8)$. Note that $\frac{1}{4} = \left(\frac{1}{2}\right)^2$, which tells us that the variance has been multiplied by the square of the value of a. The new standard deviation of approximately 2.59 is one-half the standard deviation of the original data.

Without presenting a formal proof, we can assert the following:

Let each number of an original group of individual data be identified as the variable X, and each number of a second group of data be identified as the variable Y, where $Y = aX + b$. In addition, $\overline{X}$, s_X^2, and s_X represent the mean, variance, and standard deviation, respectively, of the original group; $\overline{Y}$, s_Y^2, and s_Y represent the mean, variance, and standard deviation, respectively of the second (new) group. Then $\overline{Y} = a\overline{X} + b$, $s_Y^2 = a^2 s_X^2$, and $s_Y = a s_X$. This result is also true for grouped data.

EXAMPLE 43

> The mean of a group of individual data is 16, and its variance is 5. A new group of data is formed by multiplying each number by 3 and subtracting 11. What are the mean and variance of this new group?

SOLUTION

The mean of the new group is $(16)(3) - 11 = 37$. The variance becomes $(3^2)(5) = 45$.

Summary of Formulas

1. For n individual numbers, the mean $(\overline{X}) = \dfrac{\sum X_i}{n}$

2. For n individual numbers, the median is the $\dfrac{n+1}{2}$ th number. If n is odd, this position corresponds to one of the numbers. If n is even, the median is the arithmetic average of the numbers in positions $\dfrac{n}{2}$ and $\dfrac{n}{2}+1$.

3. For n individual numbers, the mode is (are) the number(s) that occur most frequently.

4. If n represents an odd number of individual data, the position of Q_1 is given by $\dfrac{n+1}{4}$ and the position of Q_3 is given by $\dfrac{3n+3}{4}$.

5. If n represents an even number of individual data, the position of Q_1 is given by $\dfrac{n+2}{4}$ and the position of Q_3 is given by $\dfrac{3n+2}{4}$.

6. For n individual numbers, the variance $(s^2) = \dfrac{\sum f(X-\overline{X})^2}{n-1}$. The standard deviation (s) is the square root of the variance.

7. If n represents the number of data in a grouped frequency distribution, the mean $= \dfrac{\sum(x_{m_i})(f_{m_i})}{n}$,

where each x_{m_i} represents a class mark and each f_{m_i} represents the frequency of the class to which the class mark belongs.

8. If n represents the number of data in a grouped frequency distribution, then $Q_1 = L + \left(\dfrac{\dfrac{N}{4}-C}{F}\right)(W)$,

Q_2 (median) $= L + \left(\dfrac{\dfrac{N}{2}-C}{F}\right)(W)$, and $Q_3 = L + \left(\dfrac{\dfrac{3N}{4}-C}{F}\right)(W)$. In each formula, $N =$ number of data, $C =$ cumulative frequency up through the class containing Q_1, Q_2, or Q_3, $F =$ frequency of the class containing Q_1, Q_2, or Q_3, and $W =$ class width.

9. If n represents the number of data in a grouped frequency distribution, then the variance is given by $s^2 = \dfrac{\sum f(X_m-\overline{X})^2}{n-1}$. The standard deviation (s) is the square root of the variance.

10. For both individual and grouped data, the interquartile range $(IQR) = Q_3 - Q_1$.

11. A linear transformation from X to Y is given by the formula $Y = aX + b$

Quiz for Chapter 15

1. Which one of the following would be considered as ordinal data?

   (A) Performance appraisal rated as excellent, good, or average

   (B) A numerical exam score, based on a scale of 0 to 150

   (C) A color of a crayon in a box for which the colors are white, black, and red

   (D) The number of people at a concert

2. A person's weight was measured to be 175.12 pounds. What is the lower boundary of this number?

   (A) 175.115   (C) 175.125

   (B) 175.123   (D) 175.13

3. In a grouped frequency distribution, the lower and upper limits of the first class are 19 and 27, respectively. What is the lower limit of the third class?

   (A) 23   (C) 37

   (B) 28   (D) 45

4. Suppose that a stem-and-leaf plot is constructed for integers, each of which lies between 1000 and 9000. For each number, how many digits lie to the right of the vertical bar?

   (A) 4   (C) 2

   (B) 3   (D) 1

5. Ms. Trigley teaches a statistics course. She asked her students to list their heights in inches, after which she developed a histogram. The lower and upper boundaries of the first class are 59.5 and 63.5, respectively. If there were a total of five classes, what is the upper limit of the fifth class?

   (A) 80   (C) 76

   (B) 79   (D) 75

6. Sherry is an executive at the Top Drawer Financial Corporation. She has been asked to identify the percent of investors in different age brackets. Here are her results: 15% are in the age bracket 20−34; 36% are in the age bracket 35−49; 31% are in the age bracket 50−64; the remaining percent are in the age bracket 65−79. (No investor is over the age of 79.) If a pie graph is constructed, how many degrees is the central angle for the investors in the 65−69 age bracket (to the nearest degree)?

   (A) 18°   (C) 65°

   (B) 36°   (D) 82°

7. In which one of the following groups of data is the mode less than the median?

   (A) 6, 9, 10, 10, 11, 19, 20

   (B) 6, 9, 9, 9, 12, 12, 16, 21

   (C) 6, 10, 11, 13, 13, 13

   (D) 6, 6, 11, 14, 17, 17, 17

8. In a room of 16 people, the mean height of 6 people is 64 inches, and the mean height of 9 of the remaining people is 74 inches. If the mean height for all 16 people is 70.125 inches, what is the height of the 16th person?

   (A) 67 inches

   (B) 68 inches

   (C) 72 inches

   (D) 73 inches

9. A list of numbers has no mode. Which one of the following could represent this list?

   (A) 8, 8, 8, 8, 8, 8   (C) 6, 6, 7, 7, 9, 9

   (B) 7, 8, 9, 10, 11, 12   (D) 5, 5, 6, 6, 6, 7, 7

10. What is the value of the median for the following grouped data distribution?

Class	Frequency
15−23	12
24−32	7
33−41	8
42−50	21

    (A) 38.125   (C) 34.375

    (B) 37.625   (D) 32.875

11. If a grouped frequency distribution is negatively skewed, which one of the following inequalities is correct?

    (A) mean < mode < median

    (B) mean < median < mode

    (C) median < mode < mean

    (D) median < mean < mode

12. A list of individual data consists of three 7s, two 12s, five 20s, two 28s, and one 30. What is the value of the third quartile?

    (A) 16   (C) 24

    (B) 20   (D) 28

13. What is the value of the first quartile for the following grouped frequency distribution?

Class	Frequency
10−16	4
17−23	10
24−30	8
31−37	12
38−44	9
45−51	11
52−58	6

(A) 25.625   (C) 24.875

(B) 25.125   (D) 24.375

14. Which one of the following does not correspond to one of the five key elements used in constructing a boxplot?

(A) mean   (C) lowest value

(B) median   (D) third quartile

15. What is the sample standard deviation for the following data? (nearest hundredth)

8, 9, 16, 20, 31, and 42

(A) 9.79   (C) 12.11

(B) 10.95   (D) 13.27

16. What is the sample variance for the following grouped data distribution? (Nearest integer)

Class	Frequency
12 − 16	6
17 − 21	7
22 − 26	4
27 − 31	3

(A) 24   (C) 28

(B) 26   (D) 30

17. In a given group of individual numbers, the mean is 9 and the variance is 5. Each number is multiplied by 6 and subtracted by 2. Which one of the following is correct concerning the new group of numbers created by this linear transformation?

(A) $\overline{X} = 52$ and $s^2 = 30$

(B) $\overline{X} = 52$ and $s^2 = 180$

(C) $\overline{X} = 54$ and $s^2 = 28$

(D) $\overline{X} = 54$ and $s^2 = 178$

Quiz for Chapter 15

SOLUTIONS

1. (A)

Ordinal data can be ranked, but their differences cannot be measured numerically. Ratings of excellent, good, and average would qualify as ordinal.

2. (A)

Since this weight is given to the nearest hundredth, the lower limit is found by subtracting 0.005 from 175.12, which is 175.115 .

3. (C)

The first three classes are $19 - 27$, $28 - 36$, and $37 - 45$; thus, 37 is the lower limit of the third class.

4. (D)

Regardless of the number of digits, only one digit lies to the right of the vertical bar in a stem-and-leaf plot.

5. (B)

The limits of the first class are 60 and 63. Since the limits of the second class are 64 and 67, we can just add consecutive 5's to find any limit of the remaining classes. So, the upper limits of the third, fourth, and fifth classes are 71, 75, and 79, respectively.

6. (C)

The percent of investors in the age bracket $65 - 79$ is $(100 - 15 - 36 - 31)\% = 18\%$. The number of degrees in the central angle of the corresponding sector is $(0.18)(360°) \approx 65°$.

7. (B)

The mode is 9 and the median is $(9 + 12) \div 2 = 10.5$.

8. (C)

The height of the sixteenth person is $(16)(70.125) - (6)(64) - (9)(74) = 72$ inches.

9. (B)

A list of numbers, in which no number appears more than once, has no mode.

10. (A)

The median is the 24th number, which is $32.5 + \left(\dfrac{5}{8}\right)(9) = 38.125$.

11. (B)

In a negatively skewed distribution, the frequencies of the higher numbers tend to be larger than those of the lower numbers. This implies that the mean is less than the median, which is less than the mode.

12. (C)

For a list of 13 numbers, the third quartile is located in position $\dfrac{(3)(13) + 3}{4} = 10.5$. Thus, its value is $\dfrac{20 + 28}{2} = 24$.

13. (D)

The first quartile is the 15th number, which is $23.5 + \left(\dfrac{1}{8}\right)(7) = 24.375$.

14. (A)

The five key elements are the lowest value, first quartile, median, third quartile, and the highest number. The mean is not included among these.

15. (D)

$$s = \sqrt{\frac{(8-21)^2 + (9-21)^2 + (16-21)^2 + (20-21)^2 + (31-21)^2 + (42-21)^2}{5}} = \sqrt{\frac{880}{5}} \approx 13.27.$$

16. (C)

$$s^2 = \frac{(6)(14-20)^2 + (7)(19-20)^2 + (4)(24-20)^2 + (3)(29-20)^2}{19} \approx 28.$$

17. (B)

The linear transformation is $Y = 6X - 2$. Thus, the mean becomes $(9)(6) - 2 = 52$ and the variance becomes $(6^2)(5) = 180$.

Probability Concepts and Applications

Welcome to Chapter 16. In this chapter, we will review the following topics:

(a) Sample spaces

(b) Categories of probability

(c) Permutations and combinations

(d) Application of probability to permutations and combinations

(e) Application of probability to geometric regions

Sample Spaces

A **probability experiment** is simply a series of actions from which we can ascertain the likelihood of a particular action to occur. For example when we toss a penny twice, there are four different results, known formally as **outcomes**, that may occur. Letting H = heads and T = tails, the four outcomes are HH, HT, TH, and TT. There are two parts to each outcome. Also, the outcome HT is different from the outcome TH.

A **sample space,** usually denoted as *S,* is the set of all possible outcomes of a probability experiment. In the example mentioned above, we can write $S = $ {HH, HT, TH, TT}.

EXAMPLE 1

A probability experiment consists of rolling an ordinary die once. What is the complete sample space?

SOLUTION

Since the only possible outcomes are 1, 2, 3, 4, 5, and 6, the sample space is {1, 2, 3, 4, 5, 6}.

EXAMPLE 2

A five-sided solid figure is numbered 1, 2, 3, 4, and 5 on each of its faces. If this figure is rolled twice, how many outcomes are in its sample space?

SOLUTION

Any of the numbers 1, 2, 3, 4, or 5 may appear on either the first roll or the second roll. Thus, there are $(5)(5) = 25$ different outcomes that can occur. As examples, (2,4), (5,5), and (3,2) are three of these outcomes.

In this example, (2,4) means "2" is the number on the first roll and "4" is the number on the second roll.

The outcome (2,4) is <u>not</u> equivalent to the outcome (4,2), since (4,2) means "4" is the result of the first roll and "2" is the result of the second roll.

EXAMPLE 3

An experiment consists of drawing three cards in succession from a deck of 52 cards. Each of the second and third cards are drawn without replacement. How many outcomes are there in the sample space?

SOLUTION

Each outcome consists of three parts. For the first draw, there are 52 possibilities; however, since each of the remaining two cards are drawn without any replacement, there are 51 and 50 possibilities respectively for these two draws. Thus, there are $(52)(51)(50) = 132,600$ outcomes. One of the outcomes might appear as $A_S 2_D Q_H$, where A_S means ace of spades, 2_D means two of diamonds, and Q_H means queen of hearts.

In Example 3, <u>if</u> the selections were made <u>with</u> replacement, then we could have the same card appear twice or even three times. For this experiment, there would be $(52)^3 = 140,608$ outcomes.

Any collection of outcomes is called an **event**, usually denoted by a capital letter. However, an event may consist of just one outcome. In Example 1, if event A consists of outcomes that are even numbers, then $A = \{2, 4, 6\}$. In Example 2, if event B consists of outcomes in which the same number appears twice, then $B = \{(1,1), (2,2), (3,3), (4,4), (5,5)\}$.

In Example 3, if event C consists of outcomes in which the first draw is the jack of diamonds, the second draw is the ace of clubs, and the third draw is the 5 of hearts, then $C = \{ J_D A_C 5_H \}$.

Categories of Probability

Probability is defined as the chance of an event occurring. If A represents an event, then P(A) represents the probability of A occurring. If an event is certain to occur, then P(A) = 1. As you can imagine, very few events contain absolute certainty. As an example, if A represents the event that it is raining today somewhere, then we can be sure that P(A) = 1.

If an event cannot possibly occur, then its probability is zero. Let B represent the event that a person can run a mile in one minute. Even the fastest of horses cannot approach this speed, so we can state that no human can run this fast. Thus, P(B) = 0.

Most of the probability questions you will face will have values between 0 and 1. Be aware that we cannot have a probability value of less than zero or greater than 1.

Classical Probability

Classical probability refers to the determination of probability values based on a sample space. The most common sample spaces involve a) coins b) dice, and c) cards. In each sample space, all outcomes are assumed to be equally likely to occur. The next few examples involve classical probability.

EXAMPLE 4

A penny and a nickel are each tossed once. What is the probability that both land on heads?

SOLUTION

Let the penny be tossed first. The sample space is {HH, HT, TH, TT}. Out of the four possible outcomes, only the outcome HH shows both heads. Therefore the required probability is $\frac{1}{4}$. (We assume that each outcome is equally likely.)

EXAMPLE 5

Using the experiment of Example 1, let D represent the event of all outcomes in which the number is greater than 2. What is the value of P(D)?

SOLUTION

Since $D = \{3, 4, 5, 6\}$, $P(D) = \dfrac{4}{6} = \dfrac{2}{3}$.

EXAMPLE 6

Using the experiment in Example 2, let E represent the event of all outcomes in which the first number is odd and the second number is even. What is P(E)?

SOLUTION

$E = \{(1,2), (1,4), (3,2),(3,4), (5,2), (5,4)\}$. Recalling that there are 25 outcomes in this sample space, we conclude that P(E) = $\dfrac{6}{25}$.

EXAMPLE 7

A penny, a nickel, and a dime are tossed once, in that order. What is the probability that the coins all land on heads or they all land on tails?

SOLUTION

There are eight outcomes in this sample space, namely HHH, HHT, HTH, HTT, THH, THT, TTH, and TTT. Of these, there are only two outcomes in which the coins all land the same, namely HHH and TTT. Thus, the required probability is $\dfrac{2}{8} = \dfrac{1}{4}$.

The words *successful outcomes* can be used in place of *events*. In this way, probability can be interpreted as the ratio of successful outcomes to total outcomes. Here are a few more examples involving coins, dice, and cards.

EXAMPLE 8

A dime is tossed four times. What is the probability that it will land on tails all four times?

SOLUTION

Each time the dime is tossed, the only possibilities are heads (H) or tails (T). This means that the sample space consists of $2^4 = 16$ outcomes. The only "successful" outcome is TTTT, so the required probability is $\dfrac{1}{16}$.

EXAMPLE 9

An ordinary die is rolled twice. What is the probability that the sum of the two rolls is 4?

SOLUTION

We first recognize that there are (6)(6) = 36 outcomes. Since the lowest number possible for either roll of the die is 1, we only need to examine the outcomes in which each roll shows a number less than 4. If the first roll shows 1, then the only result for the second roll is 3. This leads to (1,3). Continuing in this fashion, the other two possibilities are (2,2) and (3,1). Thus, the required probability is $\dfrac{3}{36}$, which reduces to $\dfrac{1}{12}$.

EXAMPLE 10

An ordinary die is rolled twice. What is the probability that the first roll will land on an even number and the second roll will land on a number greater than 4?

SOLUTION

We need to examine each roll separately. The first roll must be a 2, 4, or 6. In addition, the second roll must be a 5 or a 6. Each of the three "successful" possibilities of the first roll must be paired with one of two "successful" possibilities of the second roll. There are 6 successful outcomes, namely (2,5),(2,6), (4,5), (4,6), (6,5), and (6,6). Thus, the required probability is $\dfrac{6}{36}$, which reduces to $\dfrac{1}{6}$.

Let's do a quick review of the 52 cards in an ordinary deck. There are 13 cards of each suit, which are clubs, diamonds, hearts, and spades. The clubs and spades are black, whereas the diamonds and hearts are red. The cards of each suit are identified as ace, 2, 3, 4, …, 10, jack, queen, king. The jacks, queens, and kings are considered picture cards.

EXAMPLE 11

In drawing one card from a deck of cards, what is the probability of getting a red jack?

SOLUTION

The two red jacks are the jack of diamonds and the jack of hearts. Thus, the required probability is $\frac{2}{52}$, which reduces to $\frac{1}{26}$.

EXAMPLE 12

In drawing one card from a deck of cards, what is the probability of getting any nonpicture diamond card?

SOLUTION

The nonpicture diamond cards are the ace, 2, 3, …, 10. So, there are 10 such cards. Thus, the required probability is $\frac{10}{52}$, which reduces to $\frac{5}{26}$

EXAMPLE 13

In drawing two cards from a deck of cards, one card at a time, with the replacement of the first card prior to drawing the second card, what is the probability that the first card is an ace and the second card is a black picture card?

SOLUTION

In this probability experiment, there are $(52)(52)$ = 2704 outcomes. We know that there are four aces

and six black picture cards (jack of clubs, jack of spades, queen of clubs, queen of spades, king of clubs, king of spades). This means that there are $(4)(6) = 24$ "successful" outcomes. The required probability is $\frac{24}{2704} = \frac{3}{338}$.

EXAMPLE 14

In drawing two cards from a deck of cards, one at a time, with no replacement, what is the probability that the first card is red and the second card is a black 10?

SOLUTION

Since the first card is not replaced when we draw the second card, there are $(52)(51) = 2652$ outcomes. There are 26 red cards and two black 10s, which means that there are $(26)(2) = 52$ "successful" outcomes. Thus, the required probability is $\frac{52}{2652} = \frac{1}{51}$.

Empirical Probability

Empirical probability refers to the determination of probability values based on observations or historical data. If A represents an event, its empirical probability is simply the ratio of its frequency and the total frequency of all observations (or data).

EXAMPLE 15

A particular die is rolled 1800 times and the results of the frequency of each outcome is as follows:

Outcome	Frequency
1	120
2	140
3	250
4	450
5	300
6	540

Based on this chart, what is the probability that in rolling this die, it will land on a 3 or a 4?

SOLUTION

The number of times in which this die has landed on 3 or 4 is 250 + 450 = 700. Since this die was rolled 1800 times, the required probability is $\frac{700}{1800} = \frac{7}{18}$.

EXAMPLE 16

A particular dime is tossed 3 times, and the experiment is repeated 4000 times. Here are the results:

Outcome	Frequency
HHH	2050
HHT	510
HTH	430
HTT	240
THH	500
THT	100
TTH	120
TTT	50

Based on this chart, what is the probability that when this dime is tossed three times, the result will be all exactly two tails?

SOLUTION

The "successful" outcomes are HTT, THT, and TTH, for which the combined frequency is 240 + 100 + 120 = 460. Thus, the required probability is $\frac{460}{4000}$, which reduces to $\frac{23}{200}$.

EXAMPLE 17

A random group of 90 people was asked to select their favorite ice cream flavor. The choice of flavors was limited to vanilla, chocolate, strawberry, butter pecan, and cherry. Here are the results:

Flavor	Frequency
Vanilla	32
Chocolate	24
Strawberry	16
Butter Pecan	10
Cherry	8

Based on this chart, what is the probability that a person selected from this group had chosen either vanilla or chocolate as his/her favorite flavor?

SOLUTION

A total of 32 + 24 = 56 people chose one of these two flavors. Thus, the required probability is $\frac{56}{90}$, which reduces to $\frac{28}{45}$.

Compound Events

An event that consists of two or more "actions" is called a **compound event**. Examples are a) rolling a die twice, b) tossing a coin three times, c) drawing two cards from a deck of cards, one at a time, with replacement, and d) selecting two different people from a group of 20 people. Most of the examples presented thus far in this chapter are compound events.

Independent Events

Two events are **independent** if the probability for one event to occur has no effect on the probability of the other event to occur. Further, the probability that both occur is the product of the probability for each event to occur. In symbols, the probability for both events A and B to occur is denoted as $P(A \cap B)$. So, if A and B are independent events, we can write $P(A \cap B) = P(A) \bullet P(B)$.

EXAMPLE 18

> A five-sided solid figure is numbered 1, 2, 3, 4, and 5 on each of its faces. If this figure is rolled twice, what is the probability that the first number is odd and the second number is even?

SOLUTION

This example should look familiar! It is a repeat of Example 6. Let A represent the event of getting an odd number on the first roll and B represent the event of getting an even number on the second roll. Then $P(A) = \dfrac{3}{5}$ and $P(B) = \dfrac{2}{5}$. Clearly, these events are independent, so $P(A \cap B) = \dfrac{3}{5} \bullet \dfrac{2}{5} = \dfrac{6}{25}$. Our answer matches the answer from Example 6.

EXAMPLE 19

> An ordinary die is rolled twice. What is the probability that the first roll will land on an even number and the second roll will land on a number greater than 4?

SOLUTION

Another familiar example, namely Example 10. Let A represent the event of getting an even number on the first roll and let B represent the event of getting a number greater than 4 on the second roll. By just using the sample space for a single roll of the die, we can see that $P(A) = \dfrac{3}{6} = \dfrac{1}{2}$ and $P(B) = \dfrac{2}{6} = \dfrac{1}{3}$. These events are independent, so $P(A \cap B) = \dfrac{1}{2} \bullet \dfrac{1}{3} = \dfrac{1}{6}$. (This matches our answer in Example 10.)

EXAMPLE 20

> In drawing two cards from a deck of cards, one card at a time, with the replacement of the first card prior to drawing the second card, what is the probability that the first card is an ace and the second card is a black picture card?

SOLUTION

Familiarity rides again! This is Example 13. We just use the sample space of 52 outcomes that represent the 52 cards. Let A represent the event of getting an ace on the first draw and let B represent the event of getting a black picture card on the second draw. Since the first card is replaced before the second one is drawn, these events are independent. $P(A) = \dfrac{4}{52} = \dfrac{1}{13}$ and $P(B) = \dfrac{6}{52} = \dfrac{3}{26}$. Thus, $P(A \cap B) = \dfrac{1}{13} \bullet \dfrac{3}{26} = \dfrac{3}{338}$.

Dependent Events

Events A and B are called **dependent** if the occurrence of one event will affect the probability of the occurrence of another event. There are many examples in real life that illustrate dependence of events. As an example, reading this book will definitely affect the probability that you will do well on your Math Teacher Certification Exam. As a second example, leaving on time for work will affect the probability that you will arrive at work on time.

We now introduce the symbol $P(A \mid B)$. This notation means the probability that event A occurs, given that event B has occurred. This is generally <u>not</u> equivalent in meaning to $P(B \mid A)$, which means the probability that event B occurs, given that event A has occurred. Note that if $P(A \mid B) = 0$, then event A <u>cannot</u> occur if event B has already occurred. Similarly, if $P(A \mid B) = 1$, then event A <u>must</u> occur if event B has occurred. Based on the examples we have shown thus far, when two (or more) cards are drawn from a deck <u>without</u> replacement, the events are dependent. When A and B are dependent events, the formula to use for $P(A \cap B)$ is as follows: $P(A \cap B) = P(A) \bullet P(B \mid A)$ or $P(A \cap B) = P(B) \bullet P(A \mid B)$.

EXAMPLE 21

In drawing two cards from a deck of cards, one at a time, with no replacement, what is the probability that the first card is red and the second card is a black 10?

SOLUTION

You already discovered the answer, since this is Example 14. Let A represent the event of drawing a red card. Let $B \mid A$ represent the event of drawing a black 10, given that a red card has already been drawn. Then $P(A) = \dfrac{26}{52} = \dfrac{1}{2}$ and $P(B \mid A) = \dfrac{2}{51}$. Thus, $P(A \cap B) = \dfrac{1}{2} \cdot \dfrac{2}{51} = \dfrac{1}{51}$, which matches the answer to Example 14.

EXAMPLE 22

In a bag of jellybeans, there are 6 red, 8 yellow, 4 black, and 7 green ones. Two jellybeans will be randomly selected, one at a time, with no replacement. What is the probability of drawing a red jellybean, followed by a green jellybean?

SOLUTION

We need not always use the letters A and B to represent events. Let R represent the event of selecting a red jellybean. Let G represent the event of selecting a green jellybean. Then $P(R) = \dfrac{6}{25}$ and since only 24 jellybeans remain, $P(G \mid R) = \dfrac{7}{24}$. Thus, $P(R \cap G) = \left(\dfrac{6}{25}\right)\left(\dfrac{7}{24}\right) = \dfrac{7}{100}$.

EXAMPLE 23

The probability that it will rain today is 0.24. The probability that it will rain today and rain tomorrow is 0.15. What is the probability that it will rain tomorrow, given that it rains today? (Assume that these events are dependent.)

SOLUTION

Let T represent the event that it rains today, and let M represent the event that it rains tomorrow. Then $T \cap M$ represents the event that it rains today and tomorrow, and $M \mid T$ represents the event that it will rain tomorrow, given that it rains today. Substituting into the formula $P(T \cap M) = P(T) \bullet P(M \mid T)$, we get $0.15 = 0.24 \bullet P(M \mid T)$. Thus, $P(M \backslash T) = \dfrac{0.15}{0.24} = 0.625$.

NOTE:

In Example 23 we used decimals and we solved for the conditional probability value. We don't have enough information to calculate P(*M*), which is just the probability that it will rain tomorrow. Fortunately, that value is not needed to complete the solution.

EXAMPLE 24

The probability that Laura will go to work today is 0.85. The probability that she will go to work today and finish all her projects is 0.68. What is the probability that she will finish all her projects, given that she goes to work today?

SOLUTION

Let C represent the event that Laura will go to work today, and let $(C \cap D)$ represent the event that Laura will go to work today and finish all her projects. Then $(D \mid C)$ represents the event that she will finish all her projects, given that she goes to work today. Substituting into the formula $P(C \cap D) = P(C) \bullet P(D \mid C)$, we get $0.68 = 0.85 \bullet P(D \mid C)$. Thus, $P(D \mid C) = 0.80$.

Mutually Exclusive Events

Two events A and B are called **mutually exclusive** if they cannot both occur at the same time. Here are a few examples of mutually exclusive events.

(a) In drawing one card from a deck, event C represents getting an ace, and event D represents getting a queen.

(b) In rolling a die once, event E represents getting an even number, and event F represents getting a 3.

(c) In tossing a penny twice, event G represents getting two tails, and event H represents getting two heads.

If A and B are any two mutually exclusive events, then $P(A \cap B) = 0$. This is a natural conclusion because the two events cannot both occur at the same time. It is also possible that <u>neither</u> event actually occurs. Using example (a) shown above, it is possible to draw a card that is neither an ace nor a queen.

Furthermore, each of $P(A \mid B)$ and $P(B \mid A)$ must equal zero, because the occurrence of one of these events automatically prevents the occurrence of the other event. For this reason, mutually exclusive events must also be dependent events.

Suppose we have any two events M and N. The symbol $P(M \cup N)$ means the probability that event M occurs, or event N occurs, or both M and N occur. Another interpretation for $P(M \cup N)$ is the probability that at least one of M and N occurs. The general formula for calculating the value of $P(M \cup N)$ is as follows: $P(M \cup N) = P(M) + P(N) - P(M \cap N)$.

The justification for this formula is more readily understood with the use of a Venn diagram. Consider Figure 16.1 shown below:

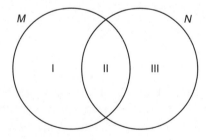

Figure 16.1

In this diagram, M and N represent subsets that overlap. Each Roman numeral indicates elements that belong to that region. So, set M consists of regions I and II; set N consists of regions II and III; set $M \cap N$ consists of region II. By substitution, Regions (I + II + III) = Regions (I + II) + Regions (II + III) – Region II.

In using this formula, let's begin with two mutually exclusive events. In this situation, remember that $P(M \cap N) = 0$, so the formula contracts to $P(M \cup N) = P(M) + P(N)$.

EXAMPLE 25

> A die is rolled twice. What is the probability of getting a sum of 3 or a sum of 8?

SOLUTION

Let C represent the event of getting a sum of 3, and let D represent the event of getting a sum of 8. You recall that there are a total of 36 outcomes. The only outcomes for which a sum of 3 is possible are $(1,2)$ and $(2,1)$, so $P(C) = \dfrac{2}{36} = \dfrac{1}{18}$. The outcomes for which a sum of 8 is possible are $(2,6)$, $(3,5)$, $(4,4)$, $(5,3)$, and $(6,2)$. So $P(D) = \dfrac{5}{36}$. Thus, $P(C \cup D) = \dfrac{1}{18} + \dfrac{5}{36} = \dfrac{7}{36}$.

EXAMPLE 26

> One card is drawn from a deck of cards. What is the probability of drawing a picture card or a 2?

SOLUTION

Let G represent the event of drawing a picture card, and let H represent the event of drawing a 2. There are 12 picture cards and four 2s, so $P(G) = \dfrac{12}{52} = \dfrac{3}{13}$ and $P(H) = \dfrac{4}{52} = \dfrac{1}{13}$. Thus, $P(G \cup H) = \dfrac{4}{13}$.

When two events X and Y are not mutually exclusive, they may both occur. For this situation, $P(X \cap Y) \neq 0$. The calculation of $P(X \cap Y)$ is either $P(X) \bullet P(Y)$

or $P(X) \bullet P(Y \mid X)$. This determination is based on whether X and Y are independent or dependent events.

EXAMPLE 27

A nickel is tossed 3 times. What is the probability of getting exactly 2 tails or getting a heads on the third toss?

SOLUTION

Let K represent the event of getting exactly 2 tails, and let L represent the event of getting a heads on the third toss. There are a total of 8 outcomes in the sample space. $K = \{TTH, THT, HTT\}$, so $P(K) = \frac{3}{8}$. $L = \{HHH, HTH, THH, TTH\}$, so $P(L) = \frac{4}{8} = \frac{1}{2}$. The only outcome that belongs to the event $K \cap L$ is TTH, so $P(K \cap L) = \frac{1}{8}$. Thus, $P(K \cup L) = \frac{3}{8} + \frac{1}{2} - \frac{1}{8} = \frac{6}{8} = \frac{3}{4}$.

EXAMPLE 28

In Ms. Green's class, there are 36 students. One day, Ms. Green decided to create a chart that divides the students into categories of hair color and gender. Here are the results:

	Brunette	Auburn	Blond (e)
Female	8	4	3
Male	5	12	4

Ms. Green selects a student from her class and tosses an ordinary dime twice. What is the probability that she selects a student with auburn hair or gets tails both times when tossing the dime twice?

SOLUTION

Let C represent the event of selecting a student with auburn hair, and let D represent getting two tails when tossing the dime twice. Since there are 16 students

with auburn hair, $P(C) = \frac{16}{36} = \frac{4}{9}$. In tossing the dime twice, only one of the four possible outcomes shows TT, so $P(D) = \frac{1}{4}$. Then $P(C \cap D) = \frac{4}{9} \times \frac{1}{4} = \frac{1}{9}$. Thus, $P(C \cup D) = \frac{4}{9} + \frac{1}{4} - \frac{1}{9} = \frac{21}{36} = \frac{7}{12}$.

EXAMPLE 29

In a bag of 40 marbles, 15 are white, 20 are yellow, and the rest are purple. Two marbles will be randomly drawn, one at a time, with replacement. What is the probability that at least one of these is white?

SOLUTION

Let V represent the event that the first marble is white, and let W represent the event that the second marble is white. Then $P(V) = P(W) = \frac{15}{40} = \frac{3}{8}$. Also, $P(V \cap W) = \left(\frac{3}{8}\right)\left(\frac{3}{8}\right) = \frac{9}{64}$. Thus, $P(V \cup W) = \frac{3}{8} + \frac{3}{8} - \frac{9}{64} = \frac{39}{64}$.

EXAMPLE 30

Two cards will be randomly drawn from a deck, one at a time, without replacement. What is the probability that at least one of them is a picture card?

SOLUTION

Let X represent the event that the first card drawn is a picture card and let Y represent the event that the second card drawn is a picture card. Since these events are dependent, $P(X \cap Y) = P(X) \bullet P(Y \mid X) = \left(\frac{12}{52}\right)\left(\frac{11}{51}\right) = \frac{11}{221}$. $P(X) = P(Y) = \frac{12}{52} = \frac{3}{13}$, so $P(X \cup Y) = \frac{3}{13} + \frac{3}{13} - \frac{11}{221} = \frac{91}{221} = \frac{7}{17}$.

In Example 30, we had two <u>dependent</u> events. Be careful that you understood the difference between the meaning of $P(Y)$ and $P(Y \mid X)$. Another (longer) approach to the solution would be to note that the sample space for drawing two cards, without replacement consists of $(52)(51) = 2652$ elements. Of these, the number of elements that do <u>not</u> contain at least one picture card is $(40)(39) = 1560$. So, there are $2652 - 1560 = 1092$ elements that do contain at least one picture card. Thus the required probability is $\dfrac{1092}{2652} = \dfrac{7}{17}$.

By the way, if these two cards had been drawn <u>with</u> replacement, your answer would have been $\dfrac{69}{169}$.

Permutations and Combinations

Permutations and combinations deal with counting techniques. These techniques are used in conjunction with probability.

Fundamental Counting Principle

The **Fundamental Counting Principle** states that given a sequence of events, the total number of possibilities is the product of the possibilities of each event.

EXAMPLE 31

In a room of 9 Republicans, 7 Democrats, and 4 Independents, an advisory committee of three people must be chosen. The committee must consist of one person from each of the three different political groups. How many different committees are possible?

SOLUTION

For each of the 9 Republicans, one of 7 Democrats can be selected. Thus far, there are $9 \times 7 = 63$ different possibilities for just the first two political groups. Finally, each of these 63 possibilities can be combined

with any one of 4 Independents. Thus, we have a total of $63 \times 4 = 252$ different committees.

EXAMPLE 32

Charlene is selecting her college courses for next term. She must take one class in each of the following subjects: English, math, science, history, and education. The college offers 3 different English courses, 5 different math courses, 4 different science courses, only 1 history course, and 7 different education courses. If she is eligible to take any of these courses, how many different schedules are possible?

SOLUTION

The choice of any particular course does not affect any of Charlene's other choices. By the Fundamental Counting Principle, the answer is $3 \times 5 \times 4 \times 1 \times 7 = 420$.

When a sequence of events includes ones that are dependent, we can still use the Fundamental Counting Principle. Just be aware of the actual number of choices for each event.

EXAMPLE 33

Six people are to be assigned to six different seats. In how many ways can this be done?

SOLUTION

The first person has a choice of any one of six seats. Since one seat is then taken, the second person has a choice of any one of five seats. Continuing in this manner, the third person would have any one of four seats. This means that the number of ways of seating all six people is $(6)(5)(4)(3)(2)(1) = 720$.

EXAMPLE 34

Ten people wish to line up for a photograph. How many different arrangements are possible?

SOLUTION

The first person has a choice of any one of 10 places in the line, the second person has any one of 9 places to choose from, the third person has any one of 8 places to choose from, and so forth. Each following person has a choice of 1 less position in the line. For the tenth person, there will only be 1 available position in line. The answer is $(10)(9)(8)(\cdots)(2)(1) = 3,628,800$.

EXAMPLE 35

A high school bowling club consists of 8 members. A president, vice president and a treasurer are to be chosen. If 3 different people will be selected, in how many ways can this be done?

SOLUTION

Any one of 8 people may be chosen for president. Then any one of 7 people may be chosen for vice president. Finally, any one of 6 people is eligible for the position of treasurer. The answer is $8 \times 7 \times 6 = 336$.

EXAMPLE 36

The Jackson family has won 11 trophies in tennis. They would like to display all of them on a shelf in the living room. Unfortunately, there is only room for 5 of them on the shelf. In how many ways can they select and arrange any 5 of these 11 trophies?

SOLUTION

From left to right, any one of the 11 trophies can be placed first, any one of 10 trophies can be placed second, any one of 9 trophies can be placed third, and so forth. You can see that by the time the Jackson family reaches the fifth (last) open place on the shelf, the selection narrows down to one of 7 trophies. The answer is $11 \times 10 \times 9 \times 8 \times 7 = 55,440$.

Factorial Numbers

Special products of numbers, such as those found in Examples 33 and 34, lead us to our next definition. The symbol $n!$, read as "n factorial," is the following product: $(n)(n-1)(n-2)(\cdots)(2)(1)$. Thus, we could have used 6! and 10! in computing the answers to Examples 33 and 34, respectively. This definition only applies to nonnegative integers, so that expressions such as $(-2)!$ and $\left(\frac{1}{3}\right)!$ have no meaning.

It is easy to see that $1! = 1$ and $2! = 2$, but what about $0!$? Most books will state that $0! = 1$ by definition, but there is really a logical explanation. We can verify the following identities: $4! \div 4 = 3!$, $3! \div 3 = 2!$, and $2! \div 2 = 1!$. Based on this pattern, $1! \div 1$ should be $0!$ But $1! \div 1 = 1$, so this implies that $0! = 1$. Your TI-83 calculator has a factorial button. In order to calculate $19!$, press in sequence: "19," "Math," scroll to "PRB," and press 4. Your screen should display $19!$. Press enter to get the result of approximately 1.216... E 17. This is interpreted as the number 1.216×10^{17}.

Permutations

Another instance of special products is illustrated by Examples 35 and 36. A **permutation** is an arrangement of a set of objects. The number of permutations of n objects taken r at a time is given by the symbol $_nP_r$. Its value is $\frac{n!}{(n-r)!}$

$$= \frac{(n)(n-1)(n-2)(\cdots)(n-r)(n-r-1)(\cdots)(1)}{(n-r)(n-r-1)(\cdots)(1)}$$

$= (n)(n-1)(n-2)(\cdots)(n-r+1)$. Note that if $n = r$, then $_nP_n = \frac{n!}{(n-n)!} = \frac{n!}{0!} = n!$ So, Example 35 could have been solved with the value of the expression $_8P_3$. Likewise, Example 36 could have been solved with the value of the expression $_{11}P_5$.

Your TI-83 calculator does have a feature for permutations. In order to calculate $_8P_3$, press in sequence: the number 8, the "Math" button, scroll to "PRB, the item number 2, and then the number 3. At this point your calculator screen should display the following: 8 nPr 3. Now press "Enter" and the number 336 should appear.

We could have even solved Example 33 in this fashion. (But all we needed is the factorial button). The answer to Example 33 could have been expressed as $_6P_6$, for which the answer is 720.

Examples 31 and 32 could not be solved by factorials or permutations. They were solved by multiplying a succession of numbers, not arranged in any particular numerical order.

Identical Elements

There also exist permutation problems in which there are identical (also called indistinguishable) elements. In such instances, an adjustment must be made in order to determine the number of different arrangements.

EXAMPLE 37

In how many different ways can all the letters of the word *BROOM* be arranged to form a sequence of 5 letters?

SOLUTION

The five letters in the word *BROOM* are not all different. Thus, the answer will <u>not</u> be 5! = 120. The reason is that the two Os cannot be distinguished from each other. If we labeled these Os as O_1 and O_2, the sequence BRO_1O_2M would appear the same as the sequence BRO_2O_1M. Likewise, the sequence BO_1R O_2M would appear the same as the sequence BO_2RO_1 M. The way to handle this situation is to pretend that the word "BROOM" has 5 different letters and then divide by 2!. Thus, the answer is $\frac{5!}{2!} = \frac{120}{2} = 60$.

EXAMPLE 38

In how many different ways can all the letters of the word *COLORADO* be arranged to form a sequence of 8 letters?

SOLUTION

We cannot treat this as an ordinary eight-letter word, in which the answer would be 8! = 40,320. Let's label the Os as O_1, O_2, and O_3. Then the sequence CO_1LO_2 RADO_3 would appear the same as CO_2LO_3RADO_1 or even the same as CO_3LO_1RADO_2. In fact, there are 3! = 6 ways that the sequence COLORADO could appear in which just the Os are switched. We solve this type of problem by pretending that the word *COLORADO* has 8 different letters and then dividing by 3! The answer is $\frac{8!}{3!} = \frac{40,320}{6} = 6720$.

EXAMPLE 39

In how many different ways can all the letters of the word *BANANA* be arranged?

SOLUTION

Now we have more than one letter that repeats. There are a total of 6 letters, with 3 As and 2 Ns. Then the answer is $\frac{6!}{3! \times 2!} = \frac{720}{6 \times 2} = \frac{720}{12} = 60$.

EXAMPLE 40

In how many different ways can all the letters of the word *REPETITION* be arranged?

SOLUTION

An easy way to be sure that you have counted all letters that repeat is to line them up as you read the word from left to right. Here is how this would look:

```
R E P T I O N
  E     T I
```

Now it is easier to see that out of a total of 10 letters, there are 2 Es, 2 Ts, and 2 Is. As in Example 39, the answer is found by using the total number of letters in the numerator and the number of repetitions (factorial) in the denominator for each letter that repeats. So, we get

$$\frac{10!}{2! \times 2! \times 2!} = \frac{3,628,800}{2 \times 2 \times 2} = \frac{3,628,800}{8} = 453,600.$$

Examples 33, 34, 35, and 36 are permutations because the order in which the objects are arranged is vital in determining the answers.

Combinations

A **combination** is an arrangement of objects <u>without</u> regard to their order. Commonly used synonyms for *combination* are *group*, *team*, and *committee*. The number of combinations of n objects taken r at a time is given by the symbol $_nC_r$. Its value is $\frac{n!}{(n-r)! \times r!} = \frac{_nP_r}{r!}$. This fraction is also equivalent to $\frac{(n)(n-1)(n-2)(\cdots)(n-r+1)}{r!}$.

Note the following identities:

(a) $_nC_n = \frac{_nP_n}{n!} = \frac{n!}{n!} = 1$, and (b) $_nC_r = {_nC_{n-r}}$.

Your TI-83 calculator does have a feature for combinations. Follow the same procedure as for permutations, with one exception. After scrolling to "PRB", select item 3 instead of item 2. After you press "Enter," your calculator screen will contain "$_nC_r$" in place of "$_nP_r$".

EXAMPLE 41

From a group of 15 children, how many different groups of 10 children are possible?

SOLUTION

The answer is $_{15}C_{10} = {_{15}C_5} = \frac{(15)(14)(13)(12)(11)}{5!}$ = 3003. Of course, we can simply enter $_{15}C_{10}$ and let the TI-83 display the answer.

EXAMPLE 42

Given a conference of 11 women and 7 men, a committee of three people is selected. How many different committees are possible?

SOLUTION

There are a total of 18 people, from which a committee of three is to be selected. The answer is $_{18}C_3 = 816$.

EXAMPLE 43

Mr. Fields coaches a high school baseball team. He wishes to select a team of 9 players. There are a total of 25 available players. Assuming that any of these players can play any position, how many different teams are possible?

SOLUTION

The order in which the 9 players are selected is not important. Thus, the answer is $_{25}C_9 = \frac{25!}{16! \times 9!} = 2,042,975$. Note that the answer can be found without using the fraction in this equation.

Application of Probability to Permutations and Combinations

EXAMPLE 44

A restaurant has 2 different soups, 3 different main courses, and 5 different beverages. A meal consists of one item from each category. Let's suppose that chicken noodle soup is one of the soups, and that coffee is one of the beverages. If Randy randomly orders 1 soup, 1 main course, and 1 beverage, what is the probability that his meal will consist of chicken noodle soup and coffee?

SOLUTION

The number of "successful" outcomes is found by determining the number of meals that are available to

Randy when he chooses chicken noodle soup and coffee. This means that he has only 1 option for soup, 3 options for a main course, and 1 option for a beverage, which becomes $(1)(3)(1) = 3$. With no restrictions, the total number of available meals is $(2)(3)(5) = 30$. Thus, the required probability is $\dfrac{3}{30} = \dfrac{1}{10}$.

EXAMPLE 45

> Six people are assigned to six different seats. Let's suppose that these six seats are arranged in a row, and that the assignment of seats is random. If Danny and Danielle are two of the people to be seated, what is the probability that one of them will be assigned to the first seat and the other will be assigned to the sixth seat?

SOLUTION

We need to determine in how many ways Danny can occupy one of these two seats and Danielle can occupy the other. There are 2 ways that Danny can be assigned to either the first or sixth seat. Once Danny is assigned to a seat, there is only 1 seat available for Danielle. The other 4 people can be assigned to their seats in 4! ways. Then, the number of "successful" arrangements is $(2)(1)(4!) = 48$. The total number of ways to seat 6 people with no restrictions is $6! = 720$. Thus, the required probability is $\dfrac{48}{720} = \dfrac{1}{15}$.

EXAMPLE 46

> Consider the letters in the word *SPEAKING*. Each letter will be placed on a piece of paper and then put in a jar. Each of the 8 letters will be drawn, one at a time, with no replacement, and then placed in a row from left to right. What is the probability that all 3 vowels will appear as the first 3 letters?

SOLUTION

We need to determine the number of ways that all 3 vowels (E, A, I) can appear in the first 3 slots. This is really a permutation of 3 letters, which is $3! = 6$. Now, we must figure out in how many ways the remaining 5 letters can appear in the fourth, fifth, sixth, seventh, and eighth slots. This is a permutation of 5 letters, which is $5! = 120$. Since any of the 6 arrangements of the vowels can be matched up with any of the 120 arrangements of the other 5 letters, the number of "successful" arrangements is $(6)(120) = 720$. The total number of ways of arranging all the letters of *SPEAKING* (with no restrictions) is $8! = 40{,}320$. Thus, the required probability is $\dfrac{720}{40{,}320} = \dfrac{1}{56}$.

Probability Problems that Involve Combinations

A **hypergeometric probability** distribution is one that has the following properties: A sample of N items consists of x items of one group, and $N - x$ items of a second group. A random sample of n items are drawn, where $n < N$. The formula for the probability of getting k items of the first group and $n - k$ items of the second group, where $k \leq x$ and $n - k \leq N - x$ is given by the expression $\dfrac{(_xC_k)(_{N-x}C_{n-k})}{_NC_n}$. This expression looks formidable, but let's see how relatively easy it is to apply.

EXAMPLE 47

> There are 7 men and 9 women in a room. The names of five of these people will be randomly selected. What is the probability that the selection consists of 3 men and 2 women?

SOLUTION

In this example, $N = 16$, $n = 5$, $x = 7$, $N - x = 9$, $k = 3$, and $n - k = 2$. The required probability is $\dfrac{(_7C_3)(_9C_2)}{_{16}C_5} = \dfrac{(35)(36)}{4368} = \dfrac{15}{52}$.

Due to the size of the numerators and denominators, this is probably an ideal time to illustrate another feature of your TI-83 calculator. The reducible fraction in the solution to Example 47 is $\frac{1260}{4368}$. Enter on your calculator the number 1260, the division sign, and the number 4368. Your screen should read as "1260 / 4368. At this point, do not press "Enter." Instead, press in sequence: "Math," "1," and then "Enter." Your screen will read as "1260 / 4368 ▷ Frac 15/52." This is the fraction reduced to lowest terms.

EXAMPLE 48

In a certain card game, a player is dealt four cards. What is the probability that all four cards are clubs?

SOLUTION

$N = 52$, $n = 4$, $x = 13$, $N - x = 39$, $k = 4$, and $n - k = 0$. Then the required probability is
$$\frac{(_{13}C_4)(_{39}C_0)}{_{52}C_4} = \frac{(715)(1)}{270,725} = \frac{11}{4165}.$$

In Example 48, notice that the first group of cards are the clubs and the second group of cards are the non-clubs. Also, you saw a rather unusual combination, namely $_{39}C_0$. For any n, $_nC_0$ is defined to be 1. The logic for this definition can be explained as follows: By definition, $_nC_0 = \frac{n!}{(n-0)! \times 0!} = \frac{n!}{n! \times 1} = 1$. Remember that $0! = 1$.

EXAMPLE 49

In a game of poker, a player is dealt five cards. What is the probability that three of the cards are aces?

SOLUTION

In most instances, this is certainly a winning hand! We divide the cards into two groups, namely aces and non-aces. Then $N = 52$, $n = 5$, $x = 4$, $N - x$

$= 48$, $k = 3$, and $n - k = 2$. The required probability is
$$\frac{(_4C_3)(_{48}C_2)}{_{52}C_5} = \frac{(4)(1128)}{2,598,960} = \frac{94}{54,145}.$$

EXAMPLE 50

Wally wants to randomly select six friends to come to his bungalow by the seashore. He has a list of ten friends, among whom are Amy, Chet, and Robin. He puts each person's name on a piece of paper in a jar, then draws out six of them. What is the probability that exactly two of Amy, Chet, and Robin will be selected?

SOLUTION

Amy, Chet, and Robin form one sub list of three people and the other seven people form a separate sub list. Then $N = 10$, $n = 6$, $x = 3$. $N - x = 7$, $k = 2$, and $n - k = 4$. The required probability is
$$\frac{(_3C_2)(_7C_4)}{_{10}C_6} = \frac{(3)(35)}{210} = \frac{1}{2}.$$

Application of Probability to Geometric Figures

In this application we are given one region inside a larger region and asked to determine the probability that a randomly selected point of the larger region also lies in the inner region.

EXAMPLE 51

A circle with a radius of 3 inches lies completely within a rectangle whose length is 20 inches and whose width is 15 inches. What is the probability that a randomly selected point that lies inside the rectangle also lies inside the circle? (nearest hundredth)

SOLUTION

The area of the circle is $\pi(3)^2 = 9\pi$. The area of the rectangle is $(20)(15) = 300$. The required probability is simply the ratio of these two numbers, which is $\frac{9\pi}{300} \approx 0.09$.

EXAMPLE 52

An equilateral triangle with a side of 6 lies completely inside a square with a perimeter of 40. What is the probability that a randomly selected point that lies inside the square also lies inside the triangle? (nearest hundredth)

SOLUTION

The area of the triangle is $\frac{6^2}{4}\sqrt{3} = 9\sqrt{3}$. Since the perimeter of the square is 40, each side must be 10. So, the area of the square is 100. The required probability is $\frac{9\sqrt{3}}{100} \approx 0.16$.

EXAMPLE 53

A rhombus with diagonals of 12 and 8 lies completely inside a parallelogram with a base of 20. The probability is 0.18 that a point lying inside the parallelogram also lies inside the rhombus. To the nearest hundredth, what is the height of the parallelogram?

SOLUTION

Let h represent the height of the parallelogram, so its area is $20h$. The area of the rhombus is $\left[\frac{1}{2}\right](12)(8) = 48$. Then $\frac{48}{20h} = 0.18$, which simplifies to $3.6h = 48$. Thus, $h \approx 13.33$.

Quiz for Chapter 16

1. A seven-sided die is rolled three times. How many outcomes are in the sample space?

    (A) 2187   (C) 210

    (B) 343   (D) 21

2. Which one of the following experiments has the least number of outcomes in its sample space?

    (A) Drawing two cards from a deck, one at a time, with replacement

    (B) Drawing two cards from a deck, one at a time, without replacement

    (C) Tossing an ordinary coin 13 times

    (D) Rolling a six-sided die five times

3. A penny, a nickel, and a dime are each tossed once. Let F represent the event of all outcomes in which the penny and the nickel land on tails. How many outcomes does F contain?

    (A) 8   (C) 2

    (B) 4   (D) 1

4. An ordinary die is rolled twice. What is the probability that the first roll will land on a number less than 3 and the second roll will land on a number greater than 4?

    (A) $\frac{1}{4}$ (C) $\frac{1}{9}$

    (B) $\frac{1}{6}$ (D) $\frac{1}{12}$

5. In drawing two cards from a deck, one at a time, with the replacement of the first card prior to drawing the second card, what is the probability that the first card is a black queen and the second card is any 10?

(A) $\dfrac{1}{2704}$ (C) $\dfrac{2}{663}$

(B) $\dfrac{1}{338}$ (D) $\dfrac{1}{104}$

6. A particular die is rolled 200 times. Following are the results.

Outcome	Frequency
1	45
2	60
3	10
4	15
5	20
6	50

If this die is rolled twice, what is the probability that it will land on an odd number on the first roll and on the number 6 on the second roll?

(A) $\dfrac{3}{32}$ (C) $\dfrac{7}{16}$

(B) $\dfrac{3}{16}$ (D) $\dfrac{7}{8}$

7. The probability that Nancy will go shopping today is $\dfrac{3}{4}$. The probability that she will go shopping today and that she will buy at least one pair of shoes is $\dfrac{5}{8}$. What is the probability that she will buy at least one pair of shoes, given that she does go shopping?

(A) $\dfrac{5}{6}$ (C) $\dfrac{15}{32}$

(B) $\dfrac{9}{11}$ (D) $\dfrac{1}{8}$

8. Which one of the following implies that events X and Y <u>must</u> be mutually exclusive?

(A) $P(X) = P(Y)$ (C) $P(X \mid Y) = P(X)$

(B) $P(X) + P(Y) = 1$ (D) $P(Y \mid X) = 0$

9. A bag of 24 blocks contains 2 that are square, 4 that are round, and the rest are triangular. Bob will select two blocks, one at a time, with replacement. What is the probability that at least one of his selections is a triangular block?

(A) $\dfrac{5}{8}$ (C) $\dfrac{7}{8}$

(B) $\dfrac{13}{16}$ (D) $\dfrac{15}{16}$

10. A major television network is planning a lineup for 3 consecutive time slots. The network producers have a list of 20 different shows that they will consider using for these time slots. In how many ways can the producers select and arrange a lineup for these time slots?

(A) 8000   (C) 1140

(B) 6840   (D) 1000

11. In how many different ways can all the letters of the word ARRANGED be arranged to form a sequence of 8 letters?

(A) 10,080   (C) 40,320

(B) 20,520   (D) 41,040

12. Which one of the following is equivalent to $_{2000}C_{500}$?

(A) $2000! + 500!$ (C) $_{2000}P_{500}$

(B) $_{2000}C_{1500}$ (D) $(2000!)(500!)$

13. Miniscule College offers only seven different math courses, five different English courses, three different science courses, and three different history courses. One of the math courses is calculus and one of the English courses is poetry. A student's schedule must consist of one course in each of these disciplines. If Melinda decides to use the college computer to select her schedule, what is the probability that her schedule will consist of calculus and poetry?

(A) $\dfrac{12}{35}$ (C) $\dfrac{1}{12}$

(B) $\dfrac{47}{420}$ (D) $\dfrac{1}{35}$

14. Each letter of the word *MARKET* is placed on a piece of paper, which are then placed in a jar. Each of the letters will be drawn, one at a time, and then placed in a row from left to right. What is the probability that both vowels will appear as the first 2 letters?

    (A) $\dfrac{1}{6}$ (C) $\dfrac{1}{15}$

    (B) $\dfrac{1}{8}$ (D) $\dfrac{1}{16}$

15. From a deck of 52 cards, Mary Jo is dealt three cards. What is the probability that she has three picture cards?

    (A) $\dfrac{11}{1105}$ (C) $\dfrac{11}{221}$

    (B) $\dfrac{3}{221}$ (D) $\dfrac{3}{52}$

16. The personnel director of a large company plans to send five people on a business trip. From the list of 12 eligible employees, four particular employees are Roberta, Tony, Steve, and Donna. If the five people are selected randomly, what is the probability that exactly three of the four people Roberta, Tony, Steve, and Donna will be selected?

    (A) $\dfrac{1}{99}$ (C) $\dfrac{7}{99}$

    (B) $\dfrac{7}{198}$ (D) $\dfrac{14}{99}$

17. Ten people are to be seated in a straight line at a table. Alex and Debra, who are two of these people, cannot be seated at either end. In how many different ways can these ten people be seated at this table?

    (A) 3,628,800   (C) 2,257,920

    (B) 2,580,480   (D) 1,290,240

18. A trapezoid lies completely within a circle with a diameter of 20. The bases of the trapezoid are 8 and 4, and its height is 6. What is the probability that a randomly selected point that lies inside the circle also lies inside the trapezoid? (nearest hundredth)

    (Λ) 0.11   (C) 0.05

    (B) 0.08   (D) 0.03

Quiz for Chapter 16

SOLUTIONS

1. **(B)**

    There are seven different possibilities for each of the three rolls. Thus, the sample space consists of $7^3 = 343$ outcomes.

2. **(B)**

    The number of outcomes in the sample space for drawing two cards from a deck, one at a time, without replacement, is $(52)(51) = 2652$. The number of outcomes in the sample space for answer choices (A), (C), and (D) are 2704, 8192, and 7776, respectively.

3. **(C)**

    There are a total of eight outcomes, of which TTT and TTH represent the outcomes where the penny and nickel show tails.

4. (C)

There are 36 outcomes in the sample space. The four "successful" outcomes are (1,5), (1,6), (2,5), and (2,6). Thus, the probability is $\dfrac{4}{36} = \dfrac{1}{9}$

Another explanation is to use the multiplication principle for independent events. Using one die, the probability of either rolling a number less that 3 or greater than 4 is $\dfrac{1}{3}$. Then the answer becomes $\left(\dfrac{1}{3}\right)\left(\dfrac{1}{3}\right) = \dfrac{1}{9}$.

5. (B)

The probability of drawing a black queen is $\dfrac{2}{52} = \dfrac{1}{26}$. The probability of drawing any 10, after replacing the first card, is $\dfrac{4}{52} = \dfrac{1}{13}$. Thus, the required probability is $\left(\dfrac{1}{26}\right)\left(\dfrac{1}{13}\right) = \dfrac{1}{338}$.

6. (A)

The required probability is $\left(\dfrac{45 + 10 + 20}{200}\right)\left(\dfrac{50}{200}\right)$ $= \dfrac{3}{32}$.

7. (A)

Let S = shopping and T = buying shoes. Then $P(S) = \dfrac{3}{4}$ and $P(S \cap T) = \dfrac{5}{8}$. Thus, $\dfrac{5}{8} = \left(\dfrac{3}{4}\right) \times P(T \mid S)$, which means that $P(T \mid S) = \dfrac{5}{8} \div \dfrac{3}{4} = \dfrac{5}{6}$.

8. (D)

Any one of the statements $P(X \mid Y) = 0$, $P(Y \mid X) = 0$, or $P(X \cap Y) = 0$ implies that events X and Y cannot both occur, and thus are mutually exclusive.

9. (D)

There are 18 triangular blocks, so the probability of selecting a triangular block is $\dfrac{18}{24} = \dfrac{3}{4}$. Thus, the required probability is $\dfrac{3}{4} + \dfrac{3}{4} - \left(\dfrac{3}{4}\right)^2 = \dfrac{15}{16}$.

10. (B)

This is a permutation of 3 objects taken from 20 objects. The answer is $_{20}P_3 = 6840$.

11. (A)

There are 2 A's and 2 R's, so the answer is given by $\dfrac{8!}{(2!)(2!)} = 10,080$.

12. (B)

Use the identity $_nC_r = {}_nC_{n-r}$, with $n = 2000$ and $r = 500$.

13. (D)

With no restrictions, the number of allowable schedules is $(7)(5)(3)(3) = 315$. Since Melinda must choose a specific math course and a specific English course, she has a total of $(1)(1)(3)(3) = 9$ different schedules. The required probability is $\dfrac{9}{315} = \dfrac{1}{35}$.

14. (C)

For the vowels, there are just two ways that they can appear first and second. There are $4! = 24$ different ways of placing the other four letters. Since the number of ways of placing any six distinct letters is $6! = 120$, the required probability is $\dfrac{(2)(4!)}{6!} = \dfrac{1}{15}$.

15. (A)

There are 12 picture cards, so using the hypergeometric distribution, the required probability is

$$\frac{(_{12}C_3)(_{40}C_0)}{_{52}C_3} = \frac{11}{1105}.$$

16. (D)

Using the hypergeometric distribution, the required probability is $\dfrac{(_4C_3)(_8C_2)}{_{12}C_5} = \dfrac{14}{99}.$

17. (C)

There are only eight people who are eligible to sit at either end of this table. So, there are eight selections for one end, and only seven left for the other end. After the two end seats have been filled, there are eight people left (including Alex and Debra) to fill the other eight seats. Thus, the answer is $(8)(7)(8!) = 2,257,920$.

18. (A)

Since the radius of the circle is 10, its area is $100\pi \approx 314.16$. The area of the trapezoid is $\left(\dfrac{1}{2}\right)(6)(8 + 4) = 36$. The required probability is

$$\frac{36}{314.16} \approx 0.11$$

Probability Distributions, Sampling, and Statistical Inference

Welcome to Chapter 17. In this chapter, we will review the following topics:

(a) General probability distributions
(b) Binomial, geometric, and normal distributions
(c) Inferences based on random samples
(d) Hypothesis testing
(e) Regression analysis for linear and nonlinear data

Probability Distribution

A **probability distribution** is a chart of values for a specific set of values along with their corresponding probabilities. These probabilities may be either classical or empirical. Although the data values may be either discrete or continuous, our discussion will be confined to only discrete data. Recall that discrete data, such as the number of students in a class, can be counted. Continuous data, such as temperatures, represent a band of numbers.

EXAMPLE 1

An experiment consists of tossing an ordinary coin twice. Construct a probability distribution to represent the number of tails.

SOLUTION

First we assign a variable X to represent the number of tails. The only possible values for X are 0, 1, or 2, since we cannot possibly get more than two tails when tossing the coin twice. We remember that the sample space is {HH, HT, TH, TT}, so here are the associated probabilities: P(no tails) $= \frac{1}{4}$, P(1 tail) $= \frac{1}{2}$, and P (2 tails) $= \frac{1}{4}$.

This is how the chart should appear:

X	0	1	2
P(X)	$\frac{1}{4}$	$\frac{1}{2}$	$\frac{1}{4}$

It should be noted that if X represented the number of heads, the table values would have been identical.

EXAMPLE 2

An experiment consists of rolling an ordinary die once. Construct a probability distribution for which X represents the number shown on the die.

SOLUTION

We know that there are only six different numbers possible, so X = 1, 2, 3, 4, 5, or 6. The probability for any of these numbers is $\frac{1}{6}$. The chart will appear as follows:

X	1	2	3	4	5	6
P(X)	$\frac{1}{6}$	$\frac{1}{6}$	$\frac{1}{6}$	$\frac{1}{6}$	$\frac{1}{6}$	$\frac{1}{6}$

EXAMPLE 3

A jar of 20 marbles has the following mix. Three of them are labeled 1, five of them are labeled 2, four of them are labeled 3, and eight of them are labeled 4. An experiment consists of drawing one marble. Construct a probability distribution in which X represents the number on the drawn marble.

SOLUTION

The probability of drawing a marble with the number 1, represented as P(1), is $\frac{3}{20}$. Similarly, we can determine that P(2) = $\frac{5}{20} = \frac{1}{4}$, P(3) = $\frac{4}{20} = \frac{1}{5}$, and P(4) = $\frac{8}{20} = \frac{2}{5}$. The chart should appear as follows:

X	1	2	3	4
P(X)	$\frac{3}{20}$	$\frac{1}{4}$	$\frac{1}{5}$	$\frac{2}{5}$

EXAMPLE 4

A popular magazine conducted a survey among its readers. The survey asked how many long vacations, on average, did the subscriber take each year. (A long vacation was defined as one that lasted at least two weeks.) Let X represent the number of long vacations, where X = 0, 1, 2, 3, 4. We'll assume that no subscriber would choose 5 or higher. A total of 1000 people responded as follows: 100 people said they took no long vacation; 280 said they took one long vacation; 350 said they took two long vacations; 220 said they took three long vacations; and 50 said they took four long vacations. One person is randomly selected. Construct a probability distribution.

SOLUTION

Each of the numbers 100, 280, 350, 220, and 50 are divided by 1000 to yield the following decimals: 0.10, 0.28, 0.35, 0.22, and 0.05, respectively. Here is the appropriate chart:

X	0	1	2	3	4
P(X)	0.10	0.28	0.35	0.22	0.05

Similar to our discussion with samples, a probability distribution has an associated mean, variance, and standard deviation. The mean is commonly called the **expected value**. Let $X_1, X_2, X_3, ..., X_n$ represent the possible values of X, and let $P(X_1), P(X_2), P(X_3), ..., P(X_n)$ represent their respective probabilities. Then the mean (expected value) for the probability distribution, denoted as μ or E(X), is computed as $(X_1) \bullet P(X_1) + (X_2) \bullet P(X_2) + (X_3) \bullet P(X_3) + ... + (X_n) \bullet P(X_n)$. Using the summation notation, we can also write this expression as $\sum_{i=1}^{n}[(X_i) \bullet P(X_i)]$.

We recall that with samples, the variance measures the degree of the dispersion of the data. This concept can be extended to probability distributions, for which the symbol used is σ^2. Its value is calculated as $(X_1^2) \bullet P(X_1) + (X_2^2) \bullet P(X_2) + (X_3^2) \bullet P(X_3) + ...$ $+ (X_n^2) \bullet P(X_n) - \mu^2$. Using the summation notation, this expression becomes $\displaystyle\sum_{i=1}^{n}[(X_i^2) \bullet P(X_i)] - \mu^2$. The standard deviation, denoted as σ, is simply $\sqrt{\sigma^2}$.

EXAMPLE 5

> What are the values of the mean and the variance for Example 1?

SOLUTION

The mean $= \mu = (0)\left(\dfrac{1}{4}\right) + (1)\left(\dfrac{1}{2}\right) + (2)\left(\dfrac{1}{4}\right) = 1$.

The variance $= \sigma^2 = (0^2)\left(\dfrac{1}{4}\right) + (1^2)\left(\dfrac{1}{2}\right) + (2^2)\left(\dfrac{1}{4}\right) - 1^2$

$= \dfrac{1}{2}$.

An instructive way to appreciate the similarity between these statistics and the ones used for samples is to toss a coin twice and record the number of tails. Repeat this experiment of tossing the coin twice 100 times, so that you have 100 numbers each of which is 0, 1, or 2. Treat this group of 100 numbers as a sample. Using the formulas from Chapter 15, you can then calculate the mean and variance of these numbers. You should find that the mean is very close to 1 and the variance is very close to $\dfrac{1}{2}$.

EXAMPLE 6

> What are the mean and the standard deviation for Example 4:

SOLUTION

$\mu = (0)(0.10) + (1)(0.28) + (2)(0.35) + (3)(0.22)$
$\qquad + (4)(0.05) = 1.84$

$\sigma = \sqrt{(0^2)(0.10) + (1^2)(0.28) + (2^2)(0.35)}$

$\overline{(3^2)(0.22) + (4^2)(0.05) - (1.84)^2}$

$= \sqrt{1.0744} \approx 1.0365$

For completeness, you should practice using these formulas for Examples 2 and 3. You will find that in Example 2, $\mu = 3.5$, $\sigma^2 = 2.916$, and $\sigma \approx 1.7078$. In Example 3, $\mu = 2.85$, $\sigma^2 = 1.2275$, and $\sigma \approx 1.1079$.

We will now investigate three popular probability distributions, namely the binomial distribution, the geometric distribution, and normal distribution.

A **binomial experiment** is one in which the following conditions must be met:

(a) Each of the fixed number of trials must be reducible to two outcomes, labeled as "success" or "failure."

(b) The outcomes of each trial must be independent of each other.

(c) The probability for "success" (and for "failure") must remain the same for each trial.

Examples of binomial experiments would include the following:

(a) Tossing a coin three times, in which landing on tails is a "success" and landing on heads is a "failure."

(b) Rolling a die twice, in which landing on a 1 is a "success" and landing on any other number is a "failure."

(c) Drawing four cards from a deck of cards, one at a time, with replacement after each card is drawn, in which drawing a picture card is a "success" and drawing a nonpicture card is a "failure."

An important principle to bear in mind is that each outcome must be classifiable as either "success" or "failure". For example, in rolling a die twice, if we designate landing on 1 as a "success", we cannot designate landing on just 2 as a "failure." Each of the six different outcomes (1, 2, 3, ..., 6) must be identified as either "success" or "failure."

Binomial Distribution

A **binomial distribution** is a list of the outcomes of a binomial experiment and their associated probabilities. Given a binomial experiment in which there are n trials, X successes (where $X \leq n$), and $p =$ probability of a success on a single trial, then the probability of exactly X successes is $P(X) = ({}_nC_X)(p)^X(1 - p)^{n-X}$.

A binomial distribution has specific formulas for the mean, variance, and standard deviation of its variable X. The value of the mean (μ) is given by np, the value of the variance (σ^2) is given by $(n)(p)(1-p)$, and the value of the standard deviation (σ) is given by $\sqrt{(n)(p)(1-p)}$. (The proofs of these formulas are beyond the scope of this book.)

EXAMPLE 7

An ordinary coin is tossed 12 times. What is the probability of getting tails exactly 6 times?

SOLUTION

Let X represent the variable for the number of tails. Then $n = 12$, $X = 6$, and $p = \dfrac{1}{2}$. Thus,
$$P(X = 6) = (_{12}C_6)\left(\frac{1}{2}\right)^6 \left(\frac{1}{2}\right)^6 \approx (924)(0.00024414) \approx 0.2256.$$

EXAMPLE 8

What are the values of the mean and variance of the variable X in Example 7?

SOLUTION

$$\mu = (12)\left(\frac{1}{2}\right) = 6 \text{ and } \sigma^2 = (12)\left(\frac{1}{2}\right)\left(\frac{1}{2}\right) = 3.$$

EXAMPLE 9

An ordinary die is rolled seven times. What is the probability that a number greater than 4 will show exactly once?

SOLUTION

The phrase "greater than 4" means "5 or 6." Let X represent the variable for the number of times that a 5 or a 6 is showing on the die. Then $n = 7$, $X = 1$, and $p = \dfrac{1}{3}$. Thus, $P(X = 1) = (_7C_1)\left(\frac{1}{3}\right)^1 \left(\frac{2}{3}\right)^6 \approx (7)(0.\overline{3})$ $(0.0878) \approx 0.2048$.

EXAMPLE 10

What are the values of the mean and standard deviation of the variable X in Example 9?

SOLUTION

$$\mu = (7)\left(\frac{1}{3}\right) = 2.\overline{3} \text{ and } \sigma = \sqrt{(7)\left(\frac{1}{3}\right)\left(\frac{2}{3}\right)} = \sqrt{1.\overline{5}}$$
≈ 1.2472.

EXAMPLE 11

Three cards are drawn from a deck, one at a time, with replacement. What is the probability that none of the cards are clubs?

SOLUTION

On any one draw, the probability of getting a club is $\dfrac{1}{4}$. Let X represent the variable for the number of times that a club is drawn. Then, $n = 3$, $X = 0$, and $p = \dfrac{1}{4}$.

Thus, $P(X = 0) = (_3C_0)\left(\frac{1}{4}\right)^0 \left(\frac{3}{4}\right)^3 = \left(\frac{3}{4}\right)^3 \approx 0.4219$.

EXAMPLE 12

In a jar of 10 jellybeans, eight are yellow, one is red, and one is green. Six jellybeans are drawn, one at a time, with replacement. What is the probability that exactly two of them are yellow?

SOLUTION

On any one draw, the probability of getting a yellow jellybean is 0.8. Using X to represent the number of yellow jellybeans, we have $n = 6$, $X = 2$, and $p = 0.8$. Thus $P(X = 2) = (_6C_2)(0.8)^2(0.2)^4 = (15)(0.64)(0.0016) \approx 0.0154$.

Your TI-83 calculator has a feature that will automatically display probabilities for a binomial distribution. We'll show this feature for Examples 9 and 11. In Example 9, $n = 7$, $p = \dfrac{1}{3}$, and $X = 1$. On your calculator press in sequence "2nd," "Distr," and the number 0 on your screen will appear "binompdf(" . Fill in the values 7, $\dfrac{1}{3}$, 1, and a right parenthesis. Be sure you have a comma between each number. Press "Enter" and your screen should show .2048468221, which we have rounded off to 0.2048.

By following these instructions for Example 11, you would use the values 3, $\dfrac{1}{4}$, and 0 when your screen shows "binompdf(" . After filling in a right parenthesis, press "Enter" to reveal the answer of .421875, which we have rounded off to 0.4219.

Remember that the sequence of numbers to enter in the parentheses corresponds to n, p, x (alphabetically). It is recommended that you return to Examples 7 and 12 and solve them by using this calculator feature.

EXAMPLE 13

An ordinary coin is tossed 20 times. What is the probability of getting tails fewer than five times?

SOLUTION

The phrase "fewer than five" translates to the sum of zero times, one time, twice, three times, and four times. This would mean that we would need to use the formula $P(X) = (_nC_X)(p)^X(1 - p)^{n-X}$ five times, or use the calculator shortcut shown above five times. However, there is good news on the horizon, because the inventor of your TI-83 has this issue covered. First locate the green "alpha" button and the green letters on the keyboard. On your calculator, press in sequence "2nd," "Distr," "Alpha," "A." Your screen will show "binomcdf(." Now fill in the numbers 20, $\dfrac{1}{2}$, 4, and a right parenthesis. Be certain that you have supplied a comma between each number. Press "Enter" and your

screen should show .0059089661, which we will round off to 0.0059.

Incidentally, the abbreviation "binomcdf" means "binomial cumulative distribution function."

EXAMPLE 14

An ordinary die is rolled ten times. What is the probability that the number 2 will show at most seven times?

SOLUTION

The phrase "at most seven" includes zero times through seven times. We know that $n = 20$, $p = \dfrac{1}{6}$, and $x = 7$. Following the instructions from Example 13, press "2nd," "Distr," "Alpha," "A," the values of n, p, x, a right parenthesis, and finally "Enter." Rounded off to four places, your screen should show 0.9887.

EXAMPLE 15

A five-sided solid figure has the letters A, B, C, D, and E on each of its faces. If this figure is rolled 16 times, what is the probability that a vowel appears more than six times?

SOLUTION

The probability that a vowel appears on any roll is $\dfrac{2}{5} = 0.4$. We certainly do not want to sum up individually the probability that a vowel appears seven times, eight times, …, 16 times. Our plan will be to find the cumulative probability that the figure shows a vowel up to and including six times. Since we are looking for the event in which this does <u>not</u> occur, we just subtract this answer from 1. In effect, we are using the fact that the sum of the probabilities that the figure shows a vowel zero times, once, twice, …., up to 16 times must be a certainty (that is 1). Now, use the numbers 16, 0.4, 6, in conjunction with the "binomcdf" feature on your calculator to get the (temporary) answer of approximately

0.5272. Thus, the required answer is $1 - 0.5272 = 0.4728$.

EXAMPLE 16

In a jar of 25 jellybeans, 14 of them are red and the rest are brown. Ten jellybeans will be taken out of the jar, one at a time, with replacement. What is the probability that a red jellybean will be selected at least four times?

SOLUTION

The probability of selecting a red jellybean is $\frac{14}{25} = 0.56$. We will first find the cumulative probability that at most three of the drawn jellybeans are red. Using the numbers 10, 0.56, 3 in conjunction with the "binomcdf" feature on the calculator, we get the (temporary) answer of approximately 0.0908. In symbols, we can write $P(X \leq 3) \approx 0.0908$. Thus, the required probability, which can be written as $P(X \geq 4)$, is $1 - 0.0908 = 0.9092$.

EXAMPLE 17

Six cards are drawn from a deck, one at a time, with replacement. What is the probability that a diamond is drawn at least five times?

SOLUTION

This example is short enough that we can return to the "binompdf" feature on the calculator. The probability of drawing a diamond is $\frac{1}{4} = 0.25$. In symbols, we are looking for the value of $P(X = 5) + P(X = 6)$. The value of $P(X = 5)$ is found from the calculator screen display of "binompdf(6,0.25,5)," which is approximately 0.0044. Similarly, the value of $P(X = 6)$ is determined by displaying "binompdf(6, 0.25,6)," which is approximately 0.0002. Thus, the required answer is 0.0046.

An interesting special case of the binomial distribution is the **geometric distribution**, which is the probability of getting the first success in a binomial distribution experiment. The probability that the first success will occur on the xth trial is given by the expression $p(1 - p)^{x-1}$. This expression automatically includes the probability that the first $x - 1$ trials result in failures.

EXAMPLE 18

An ordinary coin is tossed. What is the probability that the first time tails appears is on the sixth toss?

SOLUTION

$p = 0.5$ and $x = 6$. The required probability is $(0.5)(0.5)^5 \approx 0.0156$.

EXAMPLE 19

A card is drawn from a deck, then replaced before a second card is drawn. What is the probability that the first time a picture card is drawn is on the fourth draw?

SOLUTION

$p = \frac{12}{52} = \frac{3}{13}$, so the required probability is $\left(\frac{3}{13}\right)\left(\frac{10}{13}\right)^3 \approx 0.1050$.

EXAMPLE 20

Christine is a star basketball player. In free throw shooting, she averages 17 baskets for every 20 shots she takes. She is about to do some free throw shooting. What is the probability that her first successful free throw is on her third shot?

SOLUTION

$p = \dfrac{17}{20} = 0.85$, so the required probability is

$(0.85)(0.15)^2 \approx 0.0191$.

As with the binomial distribution, your TI-83 calculator does have a feature designed for the geometric distribution. Press in sequence "2nd," "Distr," "Alpha," "D." At this point, your screen should read "geometpdf(". Just insert the values of p and x, separated by a comma, then a right parenthesis. Finally, press "Enter." Following these instructions for Example 20, the calculator screen would appear as "geometpdf(.85,3)." When you press "Enter," the number that appears is .019125, which agrees with our answer for this example. Due to the relative simplicity of using the formula, you will not often use the TI-83 feature for a geometric distribution.

By far, the statistical distribution that is most widely used is the **normal distribution**. Some continuous variables that resemble a normal distribution are:

(a) heights of all adult women, (b) weights of all adult men, (c) highest daily temperatures in a given city over a period of time, and (d) the diameters of cylinders manufactured in a factory in which the machines produce them. When graphed, a set of data that is normally distributed will resemble a histogram that is symmetric.

Here are the basic properties that govern a normal distribution:

(a) The mean, median, and mode are equal.

(b) The curve is symmetric about the mean.

(c) The curve is continuous and assumes all values of the independent variable (x).

(d) The curve never intersects the x-axis and all dependent variable values (y) are positive.

The main ingredients that drive the shape of a normal distribution are its mean (μ) and its standard deviation (σ). The symbol σ is used, rather than s, to represent the standard deviation. There is a very good reason for this notation. A normal distribution is theoretical because all x values are permitted. However, the meaning of standard deviation, which is a measure of the spread of the data, is still applicable.

Figure 17.1 shows two normal distributions for which the means are the same, but the standard deviations differ. Note the use of subscripts to describe the mean and standard deviation of each curve.

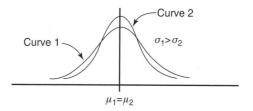

Figure 17.1

Figure 17.2 shows two normal distributions for which the means differ ($\mu_2 > \mu_1$), but the standard deviations are the same.

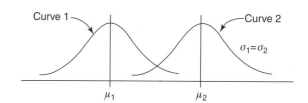

Figure 17.2

In Figure 17.3, neither the means nor the standard deviations are the same.

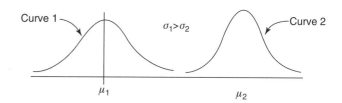

Figure 17.3

In order to apply the normal distribution to practical problems, the **standard normal distribution** is used. This distribution has all the properties of a normal distribution but adjusted as follows: (a) the mean is zero, (b) the standard deviation is 1, and (c) the area under the curve above the x-axis is 1.

The values of x of a normal distribution are called **raw scores**. For a standard normal distribution, the independent values become z scores, which are called **standard scores**.

Just as x scores can assume any value (that is, between $-\infty$ to $+\infty$), z scores can also assume all values. But, we will discover that a negligible amount of the area of the curve lies greater than 3 or less than -3. For this reason, our z values will be confined to the closed interval [-3, 3]. The actual formula for converting x scores to z scores is $z = \dfrac{x - \mu}{\sigma}$.

Figure 17.4 shows a standard normal distribution.

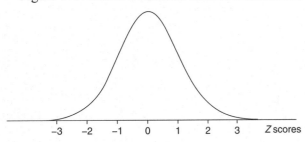

Figures 17.4

Statistics books will provide a table of areas under a standard normal distribution, given as decimals rounded off to four decimal places. In some books, the table values represent an area between a specific z value and the mean ($z = 0$). In other books, the table values represent an area to the left of the specific z value. Your TI-83 calculator will calculate the area between any two z values. If we want the area to the left of a specific z value, we can use -1×10^{99} as the lower bound. Likewise, if we want any area to the right of a specific z value, we can use 1×10^{99} as the upper bound. The calculator interprets -1×10^{99} as $-\infty$ and interprets 1×10^{99} as $+\infty$. For the next few examples, a diagram will be shown. Each of these examples refer to a standard normal distribution.

EXAMPLE 21

What is the area to the left of $z = 2$?

SOLUTION

The diagram appears as follows:

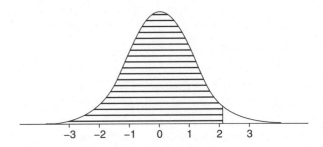

Press "2nd," "Distr" and "2" in sequence so that your TI-83 reads as "normalcdf(" . Following the left parenthesis, enter -1×10^{99} , 2, 0, 1, followed by a right parenthesis. Your screen will now appear as "normalcdf $(-1 \times 10^{99}, 2, 0, 1)$." Press "Enter" and the result shows the answer of approximately 0.9772 .

A few comments are in order. The answer of 0.9772 means that over 97% of the entire graph under the curve lies to the left of $z = 2$. The four numbers to input after your calculator shows "normalcdf(" are the lower bound, the upper bound, 0, and 1). The entry of 0 represents the mean and the entry of 1 represents the standard deviation. Incidentally, if you do not enter the 0 and 1, your calculator just assumes that those were the intended mean and standard deviation. Thus, if your screen shows "normalcdf(-1×10^{99} , 2)," press "Enter," and you will still get the answer of 0.9772 .

Note that "normalcdf" means "normal cumulative distribution function."

EXAMPLE 22

What is the area to the right of $z = 0.8$?

SOLUTION

The diagram appears as follows:

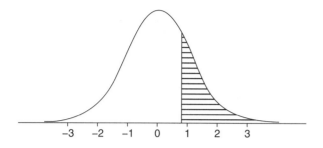

Follow the instructions of Example 21, so that your calculator reads as "normalcdf (" . Now enter 0.8, 1×10^{99} , 0, 1, followed by a right parenthesis. Press "Enter" and your result is approximately 0.2119, which is slightly more that 21%.

EXAMPLE 23

What is the area between $z = -1.5$ and $z = -0.5$?

SOLUTION

The diagram appears as follows:

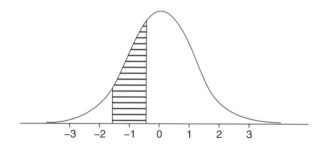

When your calculator reads as "normalcdf (" , enter -1.5, -0.5, 0, 1, then a right parenthesis. Now press "Enter" to get the answer of approximately 0.2417 .

EXAMPLE 24

What is the area for the region that lies within one standard deviation of the mean?

SOLUTION

One standard deviation from the mean of a standard normal distribution are the numbers -1 and 1. Here is the appropriate diagram:

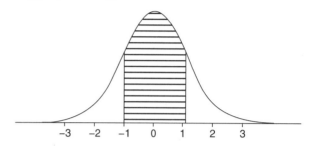

So, we need to find the area between $z = -1$ and $z = 1$. This value is found by pressing the following sequence: "2nd", "Distr," "2," "-1," "1," "0," "1," "right parenthesis," "Enter." Your answer will be approximately 0.6827.

EXAMPLE 25

What is the area of the regions that lie greater than z = 2.5 or less than $z = -1.2$.

SOLUTION

The diagram appears as follows:

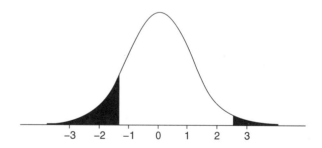

One practical way to solve this example is to first find the area between $z = -1.2$. and z = 2.5. Then, subtract this answer from 1, which represents the total area under the standard normal curve. When your calculator screen reads "normalcdf(", input "-1.2 ," "2.5," "0," "1," right parenthesis, "Enter," your answer will be approximately 0.8787. Thus, the required area is $1 - 0.8787 = 0.1213$.

Now we will look at everyday applications of the normal distribution. In each case, we assume that the variable in question is approximately normally distributed and that the population is very large. Before the arrival of calculators such as the TI-83, it would have been necessary to first convert raw scores to standard scores. Then, a written chart of values for a standard normal distribution would be used. The magic of the TI-83 has eliminated much of the work involved. Simply follow the procedures for Examples 21 − 25, and insert the given mean and standard deviation.

EXAMPLE 26

The Time is Tight company makes watches. The mean lifetime of these watches is 38 months, with a standard deviation of 4 months. What percent of this company's watches will last longer than 35 months?

SOLUTION

In order to use our TI-83 calculator, the phrase "longer than 35" must be changed to "between 35 and 1×10^{99}." After pressing "2nd," "Distr," "2," press in sequence "35," "1×10^{99}," "38," "4," a right parenthesis, and "Enter," your answer should be approximately 0.7734, which is 77.34%.

EXAMPLE 27

The amount of coffee dispensed in the paper cups of an automatic machine has a mean of 5.5 ounces and a standard deviation of 0.3 ounces. What percent of all the paper cups will have between 5.2 and 5.6 ounces of coffee?

SOLUTION

By this time, you probably know the sequence of steps by heart! When the calculator screen shows "normalcdf (5.2, 5.6, 5.5, 0.3)," press "Enter" to display approximately 0.4719, which is 47.19%.

EXAMPLE 28

The ages of the Chief Operating Officers (COOs) in the United States are 54 years old, with a standard deviation of 5 years. What percent of these COOs are younger than 47 years old?

SOLUTION

The phrase "younger than 47" must be changed to "between -1×10^{99} and 47." The calculator screen should show the following: "normalcdf (-1×10^{99}, 47, 54, 5)." Press "Enter" to reveal the approximate answer of 0.0808, which is 8.08%.

EXAMPLE 29

On a certain national standardized test, the mean of the scores is 150 and the standard deviation is 10. What percent of all the test takers score above 144?

SOLUTION

The data that was used in Examples 26, 27, and 28 were continuous. However, data scores on a test are discrete numbers. Since the normal distribution is composed of continuous data, we must make a slight adjustment. The phrase "above 144" is changed to "above 144.5". This adjustment is called the **continuity correction factor**. It is used when the value(s) of a discrete distribution needs to be adapted to value(s) of a continuous distribution. Then, we follow the procedure used in Examples 22 and 26. This means that "above 144.5" is changed to "between 144.5 and 1×10^{99}. The calculator screen should show the following: "normalcdf (144.5, 1×10^{99}, 150, 10)." Press "Enter" to reveal the approximate answer of 0.7088, which is 70.88%.

EXAMPLE 30

In thousands of dollars, a consumers report study revealed that the mean value for all homes in Delaware is 175, with a standard deviation of 40. What percent of all Delaware homes are priced between $180,000 and $220,000?

SOLUTION

Using the numbers in thousands of dollars, we are looking for the percent of data between 180 and 220. Since prices are discrete data, we should adjust these numbers to 179.5 and 220.5. In this way, we are including all values that are between these two numbers, as well as integer values that round off to these two numbers. Your calculator screen should read as follows: "normalcdf (179.5, 220.5, 175, 40)." The result of pressing the "Enter" key is approximately 32.75%.

If an example uses discrete data containing the phrase "less than" or "below," use the value that is 0.5 units below the given number. For example, "below 15" is changed to "below 14.5." Remember to make this adjustment only when the data is discrete. You may be curious as to the "error" incurred if you fail to use the continuity correction factor in Examples 29 and 30. The answer to Example 29 would have been 72.57% and the answer to Example 30 would have been 32.00%. Most statistics books encourage the usage of this "correction" factor when the data is discrete. For situations in which the standard deviation is only a very small fraction of the mean, omitting the correction factor has a minimal effect. Thus, if the mean for a population of discrete data were 200,000 and the standard deviation were 10, the difference between using and not using the correction factor would be negligible.

In some instances, we are interested in **drawing conclusions concerning a sample taken from a population of normally distributed data.** Let's return to Example 26, which involves the Time is Tight company. Suppose this company made 100,000 watches in a year. If you were to consider all samples of 20 watches, there would be a total of $_{100,000}C_2 \approx 4.10 \times 10^{81}$ different samples. Each one of these 4.10×10^{81} samples would have a

sample mean. This group of 4.10×10^{81} means is called the **distribution of sample means**. If you could then determine the mean this distribution of sample means, you would find that it equals the mean of 38 months. This number matches exactly the mean of all watches made by this company. (Please do not try to perform this experiment, for it would take more years than a lifetime!) In addition, this huge sample of 4.10×10^{81} numbers would also have a standard deviation. Statisticians have proven that this value would equal $\frac{4}{\sqrt{20}} \approx 0.89$ months.

You recall that 4 months is the standard deviation of the population of all the watches this company makes.

Without any formal proof, let's generalize the information in the last paragraph. Given a population that is normally distributed, with a mean of μ and a standard deviation of σ, consider the set of sample means of all samples of size n. This distribution of sample means is itself a normal distribution, whose mean equals the mean of the population. In addition, the standard deviation of this distribution is equal to the standard deviation of the population divided by the square root of the size of each sample.

Note that each of the samples must be the same size. The notation for the mean and standard deviation of this distribution of sample means is denoted as $\mu_{\overline{X}}$ and $\sigma_{\overline{X}}$, respectively. Thus, we can write $\mu_{\overline{X}} = \mu$ and $\sigma_{\overline{X}} = \frac{\sigma}{\sqrt{n}}$. Also, the standard deviation of the distribution of sample means is commonly called the **standard error of the mean.**

The **Central Limit Theorem** states that for any distribution, as the sample size increases, the distribution of sample means will approach a normal distribution. Additionally, its mean will equal the mean of the original population and its standard deviation will equal the quotient of the original population divided by the square root of the sample size. Thus, in symbols, $\mu_{\overline{X}} = \mu$ and $\sigma_{\overline{X}} = \frac{\sigma}{\sqrt{n}}$. Statisticians have agreed that for sample sizes greater than or equal to 30, the distribution of sample means can be considered to resemble a normal distribution.

As an example, suppose that the population under consideration are the salaries of all current baseball players. Let's further assume that this population of data is not normally distributed, and that its mean is $100,000 with a standard deviation of $15,000. Consider all possible samples of size 40. The group of data that consists of the mean of each of these samples would constitute a normal distribution. Furthermore this group of data would have a mean of $100,000 and a standard deviation of $\frac{\$15,000}{\sqrt{40}} \approx \$2372$.

EXAMPLE 31

A popular magazine surveyed its readers to indicate the number of hours of sleep needed per night. The results showed a mean of six hours, with a standard deviation of 1.5 hours. A random group of 100 entries are selected. What is the probability that the sample mean will be less than 5.8 hours? (Assume that the population of hours of sleep needed is normally distributed.)

SOLUTION

Since the population is normally distributed, the distribution of sample means must also be normally distributed. For this distribution of sample means, $\mu_{\bar{X}} = \mu = 6$ and $\sigma_{\bar{X}} = \frac{\sigma}{\sqrt{n}} = \frac{1.5}{\sqrt{100}} = 0.15$. We want to find the probability that a value of this distribution is less than 5.8. Following the procedure shown in Example 28, your calculator should display the following: "normalcdf(-1×10^{99}, 5.8, 6, 0.15)". Press "Enter" to get the approximate answer of 0.0912.

EXAMPLE 32

The town of Whisper Pines has been keeping statistics on its highest temperature each day for more than 200 years. For that period of time, its mean high temperature has been 47.3 degrees with a standard deviation of 3.6 degrees. A random sample of 64 days are chosen. What is the probability that the sample mean will exceed 48 degrees?

SOLUTION

We are not told whether the population of temperatures is normally distributed. Luckily, this is not a necessity. For our distribution of sample means, $n \geq 30$. This implies that the distribution of sample means can be treated as a normal distribution. We first determine that $\mu = \mu_{\bar{X}} = 47.3$ and $\sigma_{\bar{X}} = \frac{\sigma}{\sqrt{n}} = \frac{3.6}{\sqrt{64}} = 0.45$.

Thus, we find that normalcdf($48, 1 \times 10^{99}, 47.3, 0.45$) ≈ 0.0599.

EXAMPLE 33

The mean score of a nationally given high school math test is 530, with a standard deviation of 80. Assume that this is a normal distribution. If a sample of 20 scores are selected, what is the probability that the mean score of this sample is between 520 and 550?

SOLUTION

Since $n < 30$, the distribution of sample means must be normally distributed. Then $\mu = \mu_{\bar{X}} = 530$ and $\sigma_{\bar{X}} = \frac{\sigma}{\sqrt{n}} = \frac{80}{\sqrt{20}} \approx 17.89$. At this point, we remind ourselves that scores on a test are discrete data. Therefore, "between 520 and 550" becomes "between 519.5 and 550.5." Thus, the required probability is found by the calculator display of normalcdf($519.5, 550.5, 530, 17.89$) ≈ 0.5955.

In this last example, the stipulation of a normal distribution for the population was mandatory, since the sample size was less than 30. The Central Limit Theorem <u>cannot</u> be used when the original population is not normally distributed and the sample size is under 30.

EXAMPLE 34

In a survey conducted with animal shelters, it was found that the mean number of cats per shelter is 65, with a standard deviation of 9.6. A random sample of 40 shelters is selected. What is the probability that the mean number of cats in this sample is less than 67?

SOLUTION

Since $n \geq 30$, the distribution of sample means must be normally distributed. We discover that $\mu = \mu_{\overline{X}} = 65$

and $\sigma_{\overline{X}} = \dfrac{\sigma}{\sqrt{n}} = \dfrac{9.6}{\sqrt{40}} \approx 1.52$.

As in Example 33, these data are discrete numbers. The phrase "less than 67" becomes "less than 66.5". Thus, we find the value of the calculator display of normalcdf$(-1 \times 10^{99}, 66.5, 65, 1.52) \approx 0.8381$.

At this time, we would like to return to the hypergeometric distribution that was discussed in Chapter 16. Consider the following two examples.

EXAMPLE 35

Suppose we have a jar of 100 marbles of which seven of them are red and the rest are brown. Ten marbles are randomly selected, one at a time, with no replacement. What is the probability that exactly two of them are red?

SOLUTION

The exact answer is given by the expression $\dfrac{(_{7}C_{2})(_{93}C_{8})}{_{100}C_{10}} \approx 0.1235$.

EXAMPLE 36

Using the information of Example 35, except that each of the ten marbles was replaced before the next one was drawn. What is the probability that exactly two of them are red?

SOLUTION

We now have a binomial distribution, in which $p = 0.07$. The answer is given by $(_{10}C_{2})(0.07)^{2}(0.93)^{8} \approx 0.1234$, which is remarkably close to the solution for Example 35.

In situations where the number of items in a population is fairly large (100 or more), the probabilities for a specific result will be extremely close, whether the selection is made with (binomial distribution) or without (hypergeometric distribution) replacement. Furthermore, statisticians have shown that for certain conditions, the normal distribution can be used as an excellent approximation to the binomial distribution. Let n represent the size of a sample and let p represent the probability of a success on any one trial. If we are given a large population (100 or more), with the conditions $np \geq 5$ and $(n)(1 - p) \geq 5$, then the normal distribution may be used as an approximation to the binomial distribution. As such, the mean $(\mu) = np$, and the standard deviation $(\sigma) = \sqrt{(n)(p)(1 - p)}$.

EXAMPLE 37

Among the 8000 licensed drivers in the town of Greenlawn, it has been estimated that 32% of them listen to the radio while they are driving. A random sample of 50 drivers is selected. Using the normal distribution, what is the probability that exactly 18 of them listen to the radio while driving?

SOLUTION

We have $n = 50$, $p = 0.32$, and $1 - p = 0.68$. First check to be sure that each of np and $(n)(1 - p)$ is at least 5. In this example, $np = 16$ and $(n)(1 - p) = 34$, so we can use the normal distribution. The mean is $np = 16$ and a standard deviation is $\sqrt{(n)(p)(1 - p)} = \sqrt{10.88} \approx 3.30$. Since the binomial distribution consists of discrete data, we must use the continuity correction factor. The phrase "exactly 18" is changed to "between 17.5 and 18.5." Using your TI-83 calculator we want to calculate the value of the display normalcdf (17.5, 18.5, 16, 3.30), which is approximately 0.1004. (Note that the number 8000 is not used in any of the calculations.)

EXAMPLE 38

> Using the information in Example 37, what is the probability that at least 20 drivers are listening to the radio?

SOLUTION

The phrase "at least 20" becomes "at least 19.5." Then the value of normalcdf (19.5, 1×10^{99}, 16, 3.30) ≈ 0.1444.

EXAMPLE 39

> Among all married women in the United States, studies have shown that 65% of them have jobs outside the home. A random sample of 300 married women is selected. What is the probability that fewer than 220 of them have jobs outside the home?

SOLUTION

We verify that each of $np = (300)(0.65) = 195$ and $(n)(1 - p) = (300)(0.35) = 105$ is at least 5. Then we use the normal approximation with $\mu = 195$ and $\sigma = \sqrt{(300)(0.65)(0.35)} \approx 8.26$. Next, change "fewer than 220" to "fewer than 219.5." Now we calculate the value of the display normalcdf (-1×10^{99}, 219.5, 195, 8.26), which is approximately 0.9985.

EXAMPLE 40

> Among all married men in the United States, studies have shown that 22% of them enjoy playing tennis. A random sample of 150 men is selected. What is the probability that between 30 and 40 of them enjoy playing tennis?

SOLUTION

We first confirm that each of (150)(0.22) and (150)(0.78) is at least 5. Use the normal distribution with $\mu = (150)(0.22) = 33$ and

$\sigma = \sqrt{(150)(0.22)(0.78)} \approx 5.07$. The phrase "between 30 and 40" is then changed to "between 29.5 and 40.5." Then, our calculator display should read as normalcdf (29.5, 40.5, 33, 5.07), which is approximately 0.6855.

EXAMPLE 41

> A restaurant owner estimates that 85% of his patrons order complete meals. A sample of 120 patrons is selected. What is the probability that exactly 100 of them order complete meals?

SOLUTION

Each of (120)(0.85) and (120)(0.15) is at least 5. As a normal distribution, we use $\mu = (120)(0.85) = 102$ and $\sigma = \sqrt{(120)(0.85)(0.15)} \approx 3.91$. The phrase "exactly 100" is changed to "between 99.5 and 100.5." Thus, our answer is the result of normalcdf (99.5, 100.5, 102, 3.91) ≈ 0.0893.

In Examples 31 through 41, we assumed knowledge of population statistics, and then determined the value of sample statistics. More often, we have better information about sample data and wish to extend this information to draw conclusions about population data. For example, we can usually determine the value of a sample mean, $\bar{x}$. Based on this value, we would like to project a good estimate of the mean of the population, μ, from which this sample was extracted.

For the following discussion, we will assume that at least one of the following two conditions holds:

(a) the sample size n is at least 30.

(b) the population standard deviation, σ, is known and the population is normally distributed.

If we do not know the value of σ, but condition (a) is met, we can substitute the sample standard deviation, s.

A **confidence interval** for the mean of a population is an open inequality that corresponds to the percent of samples of that population whose mean satisfies that inequality. This confidence interval is given by the expression $\bar{x} \pm (z_c)(\frac{\sigma}{\sqrt{n}})$, when σ is known. This expression changes to $\bar{x} \pm (z_c)\left(\dfrac{s}{\sqrt{n}}\right)$, when σ is not known. The term z_c refers to a critical z value of the standard normal distribution. It will be easier to understand these terms, once we show some examples.

EXAMPLE 42

A survey of 60 homeowners in Maryland was conducted, during which time it was discovered that the average age of their homes was 25 years, with a sample standard deviation of 4 years. What is the 95% confidence interval for the age of all homeowners in Maryland?

SOLUTION

Since $n = 60$, we know that the distribution of all samples of size 60, from the population of Maryland homeowners, is normally distributed. It is highly unlikely that the unknown population mean is equal to this sample mean of 60. However, we want to create an inequality for which 95% of all possible sample means (from samples of size 60) contain the actual population mean. Here are the known quantities thus far: $\bar{x} = 25$, $s = 4$, and $n = 60$. The critical z value, known as z_c, is computed as the z value for which $\left(\dfrac{100 - 95}{2}\right)\% =$ 2.5% of all z values are larger than z_c, and 2.5% of all z values are smaller than $-z_c$. An equivalent interpretation is that we are looking for a z value of the standard normal such that 97.5% of all z scores lie below this z_c value. The diagram below shows the middle 95% of a standard normal distribution.

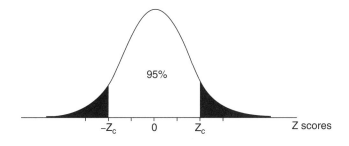

Using a table of standard normal values, to the nearest hundredth, $z_c = 1.96$. You can actually verify this z value by calculating normalcdf(-1×10^{99}, 1.96, 0, 1), which rounds off to 0.975. Each shaded region of Figure 17.5 represents 2.5% of the area under the graph. Thus, the unshaded region represents the middle 95% of the area.

The required interval for the population mean becomes $25 \pm (1.96)\left(\dfrac{4}{\sqrt{60}}\right) \approx 25 \pm 1.01$. Another acceptable way to write this interval is $23.99 < \mu < 26.01$.

A few comments concerning this confidence interval are in order. First, we indicate that the width of the interval $23.99 < \mu < 26.01$ is $26.01 - 23.99 = 2.02$, Second, we cannot state that there is a 95% probability that the interval $23.99 < \mu < 26.01$ contains the actual value of μ, since μ is already a fixed number (although we may not know its value). Technically, either μ is in this interval or it is not. But, we <u>can</u> declare that if all possible sample means were considered and each one were constructed with the same width as the one in our solution to Example 42, then 95% of these intervals would contain the actual value of μ.

Thus, suppose another sample mean was 27, instead of 25, with all other quantities remaining the same. Then the appropriate 95% confidence interval would be 27 ± 1.01, or equivalently $25.99 < \mu < 28.01$.

For Example 42, the number 1.01 is also known as the **maximum error of estimate**. In general, the expression $(z_c)\left(\dfrac{s}{\sqrt{n}}\right)$ is the maximum error of estimate when determining a confidence interval for the population mean, given a particular sample mean.

Now, the really good news that you have been waiting for! Your ever-friendly TI-83 calculator is programmed to provide confidence intervals for the population mean. All that is required is the sample mean, sample standard deviation, number of data in the sample, and the desired confidence level.

We will use this information in finding the solution to the following example.

EXAMPLE 43

Ninety English professors at various universities were asked how many minutes they required to grade a student's term paper. The responses showed that the mean time was 18.6 minutes, with a (sample) standard deviation of 3.5 minutes. What is the 99% confidence interval for the mean number of minutes required by all English professors to grade a student's term paper?

SOLUTION

Here is a diagram of the middle 99% of a standard normal distribution.

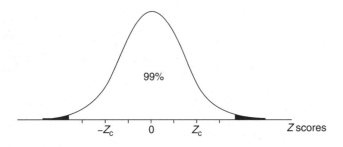

Although we will not need its value, $z_c \approx 2.575$ in this diagram. We know that $\bar{x} = 18.6$, $s = 3.5$, and $n = 90$. On your calculator press "Stat," scroll to "Tests," then press "7." At this point your screen will show "Zinterval" at the top. On the second line, scroll to "Stats," then follow these steps: For σ, enter the value of s, which is 3.5. For $\bar{x}$, enter "18.6"; for n, enter "90;" for C-level, enter ".99." Now , press "Calculate" and you screen should show on the second line "(17.65, 19.55)." Another acceptable answer is $17.65 < \mu < 19.55$.

Here are some additional notes about this solution to Example 43.

If we wanted the value of the maximum error of estimate, just determine the (positive) difference between the sample mean (18.6) and either end value of the interval. Thus, the maximum error of estimate is $18.6 - 17.65 = 0.95$. We could have just as easily computed $19.55 - 18.6$.

Suppose you just wanted the corresponding critical z value (z_c) for the diagram of Example 43. Since the maximum error of estimate equals $(z_c)\left(\dfrac{s}{\sqrt{n}}\right)$, you would just solve the equation $0.95 = (z_c)\left(\dfrac{3.5}{\sqrt{90}}\right)$ for z_c. Your answer is approximately 2.575.

EXAMPLE 44

The noise level for hospitals is a normal distribution for which the standard deviation is accepted as 4.5 decibels. A health care official is tasked with creating a 90% confidence interval for the noise levels for all hospitals. He uses a sample of 20 hospitals whose mean noise level is 52 decibels. What is the 90% confidence interval for the mean noise level (in decibels) for all hospitals?

SOLUTION

The middle 90% of a standard normal distribution is shown below.

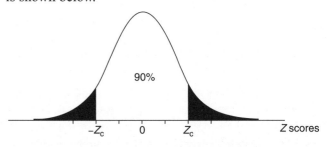

Although the sample size is below 30, we do know the value of σ and the population is normally distributed. This information is sufficient to warrant the construction of the confidence interval in the same manner as we did for Examples 42 and 43. Press "Stat," scroll to "Tests," and press "7." Now enter the values for σ, $\bar{x}$, n, and C-level as 4.5, 52, 20, and .90, respectively. Press "Calculate" to reveal the answer of (50.345, 53.655). This answer may be written as $50.345 < \mu < 53.655$.

Now we need to consider the technique for the construction of a confidence interval when the sample size is less than 30, the population is normally distributed, and the value of σ is not known. In such a situation, a *t*-distribution of scores is used in place of *z* scores. A *t*-distribution is really a family of curves that approaches the shape of a standard normal distribution, as *n* approaches 30. Comparable to the standard normal distribution with critical *z* values, the *t*-distribution contains critical *t* values.

EXAMPLE 45

In a small city in Michigan, a survey of 16 schools was conducted to determine the number of teachers in each school. The results showed a mean of 35 with a sample standard deviation of 5. Assuming that the population of the number of teachers in each Michigan school is normally distributed, what is the 90% confidence interval for the mean number of teachers in all Michigan schools?

SOLUTION

The formula to use is $\bar{x} \pm (t_c)\left(\dfrac{s}{\sqrt{n}}\right)$. We already know that $\bar{x} = 35$, $s = 5$, and $n = 16$. Tables for critical *t* values are provided in textbooks, but our trusty TI-83 calculator already has these table values. In sequence, press "Stats," scroll to "Tests," press "8" (for Tinterval), highlight "Stats," then input 35, 5,16, and .90 for $\bar{x}$, *s*, *n*, and C-Level, respectively. Then press "Calculate" to reveal the interval (32.809, 37.191), which can be written as $32.809 < \mu < 37.191$. (The maximum error of estimate would be found by $35 - 32.809 = 2.191$. As expected, this answer can also be found by calculating $37.191 - 35$.)

EXAMPLE 46

The Texas State Police recorded the speed for each of twenty-four randomly selected automobiles on a busy road. Their mean speed was 43 miles per hour, with a standard deviation of 5.5 miles per hour. Assuming that the speeds of all automobiles on this road are normally distributed, what is the 98% confidence interval for the mean speed of all automobiles on this road?

SOLUTION

After pressing "Stats," scroll to "Tests," then press "8." Now enter 43, 5.5, 24, and .98 for $\bar{x}$, *s*, *n*, and C-Level, respectively. By pressing "Calculate," your answer should be (40.193, 45.807). The answer may be written as $40.193 < \mu < 45.807$.

EXAMPLE 47

Using the information in Example 46, what is the 80% confidence level for the mean speed of all automobiles on this road?

SOLUTION

Just replace .98 with .80 for the C-level value. Your answer will appear as (41.519, 44.481) or alternatively as $41.519 < \mu < 44.481$.

The purpose of Example 47 was to highlight the fact that as the level of confidence (percent) decreases, so does the confidence interval. Similarly, as the level of confidence increases, so too does the confidence interval. As an example, let's return to Example 45 and change 90% to 95%. Leave all the other quantities as is, and you should find that the confidence interval is (32.336, 37.664), which is slightly wider than the answer to Example 45.

A common difficulty is knowing when to use the Z interval feature and when to use the T interval feature. The following Flow Chart should help you.

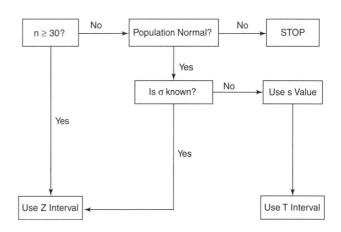

If $n \geq 30$ and σ is not known, use the value of *s*.

Hypothesis Testing

Statistical hypothesis testing is a process by which decisions are made concerning claims about population values. In particular, we will be interested in testing claims about a population mean, based on the results of a sample mean and sample standard deviation. This discussion is very closely aligned with our study of confidence intervals.

A **null hypothesis**, symbolized as H_0, is one that states that there is no statistical difference between observed data (in a sample) and expected data (in a population).

An **alternative hypothesis**, symbolized as H_1, is one that states that there is a statistical difference between observed and expected data.

Let μ_0 represent a specific value for the population mean. There are three different types of hypothesis testing to consider:

<u>Type 1:</u> $H_1 : \mu = \mu_0$ and $H_1 : \mu \neq \mu_0$

<u>Type 2:</u> $H_0 : \mu \leq \mu_0$ and $H_1 : \mu > \mu_0$

<u>Type 3:</u> $H_0 : \mu \geq \mu_0$ and $H_1 : \mu < \mu_0$

Type 1 is called a **two-tailed test,** whereas types 2 and 3 are called **one-tailed tests**.

In each of our examples, a claim will be made about the value of the population mean. A sample will be considered, in which the sample mean and standard deviation are determined. Based on this information, we will either reject the claim or fail to reject the claim concerning the value of the population mean. When a claim cannot be rejected, statisticians hesitate to use the phrase "accept the claim" because only a single sample is being used. **The level of significance** is defined as the maximum probability of rejecting a null hypothesis when it is actually true.

In order to help illustrate how these tests are applied, we will use examples very similar to Examples $42 - 47$.

EXAMPLE 48

Among all the homeowners of Dallas County, a noted researcher has claimed that the average age of their homes is 19 years. A current study of 50 homes reveals an average age of 21 years, with a sample standard deviation of 2 years. At the 10% level of significance, what decision should be made concerning the researcher's claim?

SOLUTION

In this example, our null hypothesis is $H_0 : \mu = 19$ and our alternative hypothesis is $H_1 : \mu \neq 19$. So, this is a two-tailed test. Since $n \geq 30$, we will use the Z-test on our TI-83 calculator. The procedure is as follows: Press "Stat," scroll to "Tests," press "1." At this point, your screen should read "Z-Test." On the first line below "Z-Test." highlight "Stats." For the values of μ_0, σ, $\bar{x}$, and n, input the values 19, 2, 21, and 50, respectively. For the line beginning "μ:", be sure to highlight "$\neq \mu_0$". Now press "Calculate." Note that the p value is about 1.54×10^{-12}, which means that the probability of obtaining a sample mean value of 21 if the actual population mean were really 19 is only about 1.54×10^{-12}. Thus, since $1.54 \times 10^{-12} < 0.10$, the researcher's claim is rejected. (Note that since σ is unknown, the value of s is used.)

EXAMPLE 49

It has been already established that the time required for math professors to grade a student's final exam is normally distributed. A well-known educator claims that the mean time for this distribution is 10.5 minutes. A current study involving 15 mathematics professors at a local college showed that the mean time was 10.1 minutes, with a standard deviation of 0.7 minutes. At the 2% level of significance, what decision should be made concerning the educator's claim?

SOLUTION

Our null hypothesis is $H_0 : \mu = 10.5$ and our alternative hypothesis is $H_1 : \mu \neq 10.5$. This is another two-tailed test; the 2% level of significance implies a 100% − 2% = 98 % confidence interval. Since $n < 30$, we will need to apply the T-test on the calculator. Press "Stat," scroll to "Tests," and press "2," At this point, your screen should show "T-Test." The values of μ_0, x, s_x, and n become 10.5, 10.1, 0.7, and 15, respectively. Leave highlighted "$\mu : \neq \mu_0$", and press "Calculate." The p value is about 0.044, which is larger than our given significance level of 0.02. Therefore, the educator's claim cannot be rejected.

EXAMPLE 50

Among all hospitals in Oklahoma, a state health official has claimed that the average noise level is at least equal to 60 decibels. A recent study of 40 hospitals shows a mean noise level of 59 decibels, with a standard deviation of 4 decibels. At the 5% level of significance, what decision should be made concerning the health official's claim?

SOLUTION

Based on the wording of the state health official, our null hypothesis is $H_0 : \mu \geq 60$ and our alternative hypothesis is $H_1 : \mu < 60$. In essence, we are seeking to determine if the sample noise level of 59 decibels is **significantly** less than 60 decibels. On your calculator, follow the procedure for Example 48 in using the Z-Test. The key numbers to input are as follows: 60, 4, 59, and 40 for the values of μ_0, σ, $\bar{x}$, and n, respectively. Now on the line beginning "$\mu :$", you must highlight "$< \mu_0$". After you press "Calculate," the p value is approximately 0.057. Since 0.057 is greater than our level of significance (5%), we cannot reject the state health official's claim.

We need to emphasize an important concept, regarding the solution to Example 50. While it is true that the value of 59 is not greater than or equal to 60, it is <u>not</u> <u>significantly</u> lower than 60 either.

EXAMPLE 51

Along Interstate 81, many motorists seem to obey the posted speed limit. A Department of Transportation official has claimed that the average speed is no greater than 62 miles per hour. A recent study of a random sample of 25 vehicles that use this interstate revealed that their average speed was actually 65 miles per hour, with a standard deviation of 2.5 miles per hour. At the 1% level of significance, what decision should be made concerning the Department of Transportation official's claim? Assume that the average speed is normally distributed.

SOLUTION

Based on the wording of the statement that the average speed is "no greater than 62" miles per hour, our null hypothesis is $H_0 : \mu \leq 62$. Then the alternative hypothesis is $H_1 : \mu > 62$. Since $n < 30$, σ is unknown, and the distribution is normal, we will use the T-Test. Following the procedure in Example 49, the numbers to enter when you reach the screen with T-Test on the top line are 62, 65, 2.5, and 25. These numbers correspond to μ_0, $\bar{x}$, s_x, and n, respectively. Then be sure to highlight $\mu > \mu_0$ before pressing "Calculate." The result yields a p value of about 1.70×10^{-6}. Since this number is less than our level of significance (1%), we must reject the official's claim. The speed of 65 miles per hour is significantly larger than 62 miles per hour.

Hypothesis testing exists for other statistics besides the population mean, but this material would be beyond the scope of our book. However, in every instance, the use of the null hypothesis (H_0) involves an equal sign or an inequality that includes an equal sign. The alternative hypothesis (H_1) involves a strict inequality.

The last topic of this chapter deals with the study of two variables in which a relationship may exist. One of these variables, usually labeled as x, is the independent variable. The other variable, usually labeled as y, is the dependent variable. Throughout this discussion, keep in mind that a relationship between the two variables is not necessarily a result of "cause and effect."

Statisticians use the word **correlation** to describe the method used to determine whether a relationship exists. In particular, we will be interested in a linear relationship between the variables. The term **correlation coefficient,** denoted as *r,* is used to describe mathematically the strength of the relationship between the variables. The value of r lies between -1 and 1, inclusive. When two variables both increase or decrease at the same time, the value of r will be positive. The closer to -1 or to 1 the value of r lies, the stronger the relationship between the variables. The actual value of r is given by the following formula:

$$r = \frac{n\left(\sum xy\right) - \left(\sum x\right)\left(\sum y\right)}{\sqrt{\left[n\left(\sum x^2\right) - \left(\sum x\right)^2\right]\left[n\left(\sum y^2\right) - \left(\sum y^2\right)\right]}} .$$

The kind people who designed your TI-83 calculator did not want you to struggle with this formula, so they developed a program to do this intense computation. This procedure will be shown in the following example.

EXAMPLE 52

Ms. Jones was interested in trying to determine whether a correlation existed between students' final exam grades and the number of hours they claimed they studied for this exam. Her class consisted of eight students, for which the results are as follows: The independent variable x represents the number of hours of study, and the dependent variable y represents the exam grade. For ease of reading, Ms. Jones arranged the number of hours of study in ascending order:

x	1	1.5	2	2.5	3.5	4	5	6.5
y	70	78	75	82	80	85	83	90

What is the value of r?

SOLUTION

We'll do this calculation with the TI-83. Press "Stat," then highlight "Edit" and press "1." You will see three columns, labeled L_1, L_2, and L_3. Next, fill in the column L_1 with x values and the column L_2 with the corresponding y

values. After all data has been entered, press "Stat," scroll to "Calc," then press "4" (Linear Regression). Your screen will now show "LinReg($ax + b$)." Press "Enter" and one of the entries on the screen will show that r is approximately 0.895. This number indicates a strong positive correlation.

NOTE:

If you have a TI-83+ calculator, use the following sequence of buttons after you have filled in the L_1 and L_2 lists. Press "Stat," scroll to "Tests," then press "Alpha E." The first line on your screen should be "LinRegTTest." Scroll down to and press "Calculate." One of the entries on your screen will show the value of r to be approximately 0.895.

Regression Analysis

Let's further explore the data showing on your screen. The variable r^2 is called the **coefficient of determination.** Its value is simply the square of the correlation coefficient, but its true application to statistics is beyond the scope of this book. You will also notice the line $y = ax + b$, followed by $a \approx 2.95$ and $b \approx 70.79$. Then the equation $y = 2.95x + 70.79$ is called the **line of best fit.** This line is the best approximation of all the ordered pairs. A **scatterplot**, which can be conveniently used to show the graph of these ordered pairs is shown below in Figure 17.5.

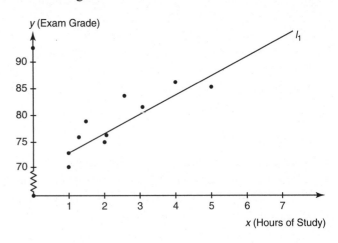

Figure 17.5

The line of best fit l_1 has also been included. In order to create this line, substitute the given x values into $y = 2.95x + 70.79$. For example, when $x = 1$, $y = 73.74$. You should expect that the y values you obtain will differ from the given y values. However, they will be reasonably close.

EXAMPLE 53

A research scientist was interested in determining whether a relationship exists between an individual's age (x) and number of hours of walking each week (y). A sample of seven people was used, with the following results:

x	30	34	40	45	50	66	70
y	5	4	4.2	3.2	3.5	2.5	2

What is the value of r and what is the equation of the line of best fit?

SOLUTION

Begin by pressing "Stat," then "Edit." Fill in L_1 with the x values and fill in L_2 with the corresponding

y values. (Be certain that you did not leave in any data from the previous example.) Now press "Stat," scroll to "Calc," then press "4." Press "Enter" to show that $r \approx -0.95$. Using the nearest hundredth for the a and b values, the line of best fit (l_2) is $y = -0.06x + 6.54$. For Example 53, a scatterplot and the line of best fit is shown in below in Figure 17.6.

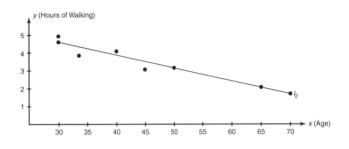

Figure 17.6

Notice that this line has a negative slope. There is a strong negative correlation between x and y. As with Example 52, the line of best fit is constructed by substituting the actual x values. For example, when $x = 30$, $y = (-0.06)(30) + 6.54 = 4.74$.

Quiz for Chapter 17

1. Consider the following probability distribution:

X	0	2	4	6
P(X)	0.5	0.2	0.25	0.05

What is the mean of this distribution?

(A) 1.7 (C) 5.8

(B) 2.2 (D) 6.3

2. Consider the following probability distribution:

X	1	2	3	4	5
P(X)	$\frac{1}{12}$	$\frac{1}{3}$	$\frac{1}{6}$	$\frac{1}{4}$	$\frac{1}{6}$

What is the variance of this distribution?

(A) $3\frac{1}{12}$ (C) $11\frac{1}{12}$

(B) $7\frac{1}{6}$ (D) $15\frac{1}{6}$

3. Which one of the following is <u>not</u> a requirement for a binomial experiment?

   (A) Each trial is either labeled as success or failure.

   (B) The probability for success is the same for each trial.

   (C) The probability for success equals the probability for failure on each trial.

   (D) Each trial is independent of the other trials.

4. An ordinary die is rolled five times. What is the probability that the number 3 will show exactly once? (nearest hundredth)

   (A) 0.50   (C) 0.30

   (B) 0.40   (D) 0.20

5. In a jar of 15 marbles, nine are white, five are black, and one is yellow. Eight marbles are drawn, one at a time, with replacement. What is the probability that fewer than four of them are white? (nearest hundredth)

   (A) 0.10   (C) 0.27

   (B) 0.17   (D) 0.40

6. Twelve cards are drawn from a deck, one at a time, with replacement. What is the probability that a non-picture card is drawn more than seven times? (nearest hundredth)

   (A) 0.71   (C) 0.82

   (B) 0.77   (D) 0.88

7. A bowl contains 40 slips of paper. Eight of these slips are labeled as A, fifteen are labeled as B, and the rest are labeled as C. Slips of paper are drawn, one at a time, with replacement. What is the probability that the first time that a slip of paper with the letter A is drawn is on the fifth draw? (nearest thousandth)

   (A) 0.90   (C) 0.74

   (B) 0.82   (D) 0.66

8. Which one of the following statements is <u>not</u> <u>necessarily</u> <u>true</u>?

   (A) Two normal curves with the same mean have the same standard deviation.

   (B) The mean, median, and mode of a normal distribution are equal.

   (C) The area under a standard normal curve is 1.

   (D) The normal curve does not intersect the x-axis.

9. For a standard normal curve, what is the area to the right of $z = 1.3$? (nearest thousandth)

   (A) 0.171   (C) 0.097

   (B) 0.134   (D) 0.062

10. The amount of soda dispensed in a paper cup of an automatic machine has a mean of 6.2 ounces and a standard deviation of 0.4 ounces. What percent of all paper cups will have between 5.7 and 6.0 ounces of soda? (nearest tenth of one percent)

    (A) 26.5%   (C) 22.7%

    (B) 24.8%   (D) 20.3%

11. In thousands of dollars, the mean salary for all high school teachers in Texas is 52, with a standard deviation of 3. What percent of these teachers earn more than $49,000? (nearest tenth of one percent)

    (A) 82.3%   (C) 77.3%

    (B) 79.8%   (D) 74.8%

12. In a normally distributed population, the mean is 24 and the standard deviation is 4.8. Which one of the following is completely correct with reference to the distribution of sample means of all samples of size 64?

    (A) Its mean is 24 and its standard deviation is 4.8.

    (B) Its mean is 3 and its standard deviation is 4.8.

    (C) Its mean is 24 and its standard deviation is 0.6.

    (D) Its mean is 3 and its standard deviation is 0.6.

13. A popular national newspaper asked its readers to indicate the number of minutes per day that they did "leisurely" reading. The results from thousands of readers showed a mean of 32 minutes and a standard deviation of 4.2 minutes. A random group of 36 of these readers is selected. What is the probability that the sample mean will be less than 31 minutes? (nearest hundredth)

    (A) 0.41   (C) 0.19

    (B) 0.30   (D) 0.08

14. Among the thousands of banks in the United States, it is estimated that 60% of them charge a service fee for customers who maintain a checking account. In a random sample of 100 banks, what is the probability that more than 70 of them charge this fee? (nearest thousandth)

    (A) 0.026   (C) 0.016

    (B) 0.021   (D) 0.011

15. Two hundred owners of food stores were asked how many customers they have per day. The results showed a mean of 75 and a standard deviation of 6. What is the 98% confidence interval for the number of customers per day in food stores?

    (A) (72.741, 77.259)   (C) (73.907, 76.093)

    (B) (73.801, 76.199)   (D) (74.013, 75.987)

16. The manager of an auto body shop timed ten of his employees on the time it took them to rotate and balance four tires on a car. Their average time was 28 minutes, with a standard deviation of 3.3 minutes. What is the 95% confidence interval for the true average time for changing and balancing four tires on a car? (Assume that the population is normally distributed.)

    (A) (26.277, 29.729)   (C) (25.639, 30.361)

    (B) (25.905, 30.095)   (D) (25.311, 30.689)

17. A state official claims that the mean age of all freshmen in Pennsylvania schools is 14.6 years. A current study of 45 freshmen at several Pennsylvania schools reveals that the mean age is 14.9 years, with a standard deviation of 1.2 years. At the 5% level of significance, what decision should be made?

    (A) The value of p is approximately 0.09 and the claim must be rejected.

    (B) The value of p is approximately 0.09 and the claim cannot be rejected.

    (C) The value of p is approximately 0.55 and the claim must be rejected.

    (D) The p value is approximately 0.55 and the claim cannot be rejected.

18. A report in a noted journal claims that people sneeze at least 20 times per day. Assume that the number of times people sneeze per day is a normal distribution. A well-known doctor conducts her own study, using a sample of thirteen patients. She finds that $\bar{x} = 18$ and that $s = 2.5$. At the 1% level of significance, which one of the following is completely correct?

    (A) The p value is approximately 0.007 and the claim must be rejected.

    (B) The p value is approximately 0.007 and the claim cannot be rejected.

    (C) The p value is approximately 0.002 and the claim must be rejected.

    (D) The p value is approximately 0.002 and the claim cannot be rejected.

19. Consider the following table of x and y values:

x	3	5	7	9
y	10	13	15	20

    What is the value of the correlation coefficient? (nearest hundredth)

    (A) 0.98   (C) 0.94

    (B) 0.96   (D) 0.92

20. Using the results of #19, which one of the following points lies on the line of best fit?

    (A) (3, 9.5)   (C) (7, 16.9)

    (B) (5, 12.7)   (D) (9, 19.3)

Quiz for Chapter 17 Solutions

1. (A)

The value of the mean is $(0)(0.5) + (2)(0.2) + (4)(0.25) + (6)(0.05) = 1.7$.

2. (C)

The value of the variance is calculated as

$$(1)^2\left(\frac{1}{12}\right) + (2)^2\left(\frac{1}{3}\right) + (3)^2\left(\frac{1}{6}\right) + (4)^2\left(\frac{1}{4}\right) + (5)^2\left(\frac{1}{6}\right) = 11\frac{1}{12}.$$

3. (C)

For a binomial experiment, it is not a requirement that the probability of success equals the probability of failure. For example, in tossing a die once, let landing on a "1" represent a success. Then the probability of success is $\frac{1}{6}$, whereas the probability of failure is $\frac{5}{6}$.

4. (B)

The required probability is $({}_5C_1)\left(\frac{1}{6}\right)^1\left(\frac{5}{6}\right)^4 \approx 0.40$.

5. (B)

Using the cumulative binomial probability distribution feature on the TI-83 calculator, the answer is binomcdf$(8, 0.6, 3) \approx 0.17$.

6. (D)

The probability of drawing a non-picture card is $\frac{40}{52} \approx 0.77$. Then the cumulative probability of drawing at most seven non-picture cards is binomcdf$(12, 0.77, 7) \approx 0.12$. Thus, the probability of drawing more than seven non-picture cards is $1 - 0.12 = 0.88$.

7. (B)

This is a geometric distribution, for which $p = \frac{8}{40} = 0.20$ and $x = 5$. The required probability is $(0.20)(0.80)^4 \approx 0.082$.

8. (A)

Two normal curves need not have either the same mean or the same standard deviation. A standard normal curve must have a mean of zero and a standard deviation of 1.

9. (C)

The calculator screen should read as "normalcdf $(1.3, 1 \times 10^{99}, 0, 1)$", which is approximately 0.097.

10. (D)

The solution is given by normalcdf $(5.7, 6.0, 6.2, 0.4) \approx 20.3\%$.

11. (B)

The use of the continuity correction factor changes 49 to 49.5. Then we calculate normalcdf $(49.5, 1 \times 10^{99}, 52, 3) \approx 79.8\%$.

12. (C)

The distribution of sample means has the same mean as the original population. Its standard deviation is equal to the standard deviation of the population divided by the square root of the sample size. Thus,

$$\mu_{\overline{X}} = 24 \text{ and } \sigma_{\overline{X}} = \frac{4.8}{\sqrt{64}} = 0.6.$$

13. (D)

The distribution of sample means has a mean of 32 and a standard deviation of $\frac{4.2}{\sqrt{36}} = 0.7$. Then normalcdf $(-1 \times 10^{99}, 31, 32, 0.7) \approx 0.08$.

14. (C)

This is a binomial distribution for which each of np and $np(1-p)$) is at least 5. The mean is $(100)(0.60) = 60$ and the standard deviation is $\sqrt{(100)(0.60)(0.40)} \approx 4.9$. Change "more than 70" to "at least 70.5." Then normalcdf $(70.5, 1 \times 10^{99}, 60, 4.9) \approx 0.016$.

15. (D)

Using "Stats," "Tests," and "Z Interval," enter the values 6, 75, 200, and 0.98. Then, by pressing "Calculate," the interval becomes (74.013, 75.987).

16. (C)

Using "Stat," "Tests," and "T Interval," enter the values 28, 3.3, 10, and 0.95. Upon pressing "Calculate," the interval becomes (25.639, 30.361). Note that the T Interval was required because $n < 30$.

17. (B)

Using "Stat," "Tests," and "Z-Test," enter the values 14.9, 1.2, 14.6, 45, and highlight "$\mu \neq \mu_0$". Then the results show a p value of approximately 0.09. Since $0.09 > 0.05$, the claim cannot be rejected.

18. (A)

Using "Stat," "Tests," and "T-Test," enter the values 20, 18, 2.5, 13, and highlight "$\mu < \mu_0$". The results show a p value of approximately 0.007. Since $0.007 < 0.01$, the claim must be rejected.

19. (A)

Using the TI-83 "Stat," "Edit" features and filling the lists L_1 and L_2, then "Stat," "Calc," and "LinReg(ax+b)," $r \approx 0.98$.

20. (D)

The line of best fit is $y = 1.6x + 4.9$. Using the x values of 3, 5, 7, and 9, the corresponding y values are 9.7, 12.9, 16.1, and 19.3, respectively. Thus, the point (9, 19.3) lies on the line of best fit.

Mathematical Reasoning and Problem solving

Welcome to Chapter 18. In this chapter, we will review the following topics:

(a) Indirect proof
(b) Deductive reasoning
(c) Inductive reasoning
(d) Counterexamples
(e) Evaluating mathematical models in real-world situations

Indirect Proof

Indirect proof is a method by which a statement is proven to be true by using the contradiction approach. Any mathematical statement must be either true or false. We assume that the original statement is false. Then, through a series of logical mathematical steps, we arrive at a contradiction of a known fact. Our conclusion is that the original statement must be true. Although indirect proof can apply to any branch of mathematics, it is most commonly used in geometry. For this reason, we will confine our examples to this area.

EXAMPLE 1

In the following diagram, $\angle 1$ is supplementary to $\angle 2$.

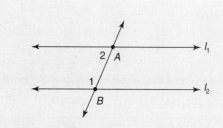

Prove that l_1 and l_2 cannot intersect.

SOLUTION

Let's redraw the diagram and assume that lines l_1 and l_2 intersect at point C.

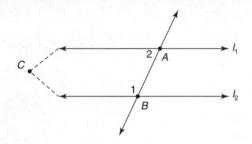

We are given that $m\angle 1 + m\angle 2 = 180°$, since the angles are supplementary.

However, in $\triangle ABC$, the sum of the measures of the three angles is also 180º. This would imply that $m\angle C = 0°$. This is a contradiction, since each angle of a triangle must be positive.

EXAMPLE 2

In the following diagram, $\overrightarrow{EG}$ is perpendicular to $\overrightarrow{DF}$.

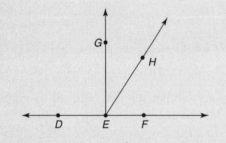

Prove that $m\angle DEH > 90°$.

SOLUTION

Assume that the measure of $\angle DEH$ is less than or equal to 90º. By the addition rule of adjacent angles, $m\angle DEH = m\angle DEG + m\angle GEH$. Since $\overrightarrow{EG}$ is perpendicular to $\overleftrightarrow{DF}$, $m\angle DEG = 90°$. Then $m\angle DEH = 90° + m\angle GEH$, which implies that $m\angle GEH = m\angle DEH - 90°$.

If the measure of $\angle DEH$ were less than or equal to 90º, this would imply that the measure of $\angle GEH$ would be less than or equal to zero degrees. This is a contradiction, since an angle must have positive measure.

EXAMPLE 3

In the following diagram, $\triangle JKM$ is scalene and $\overline{JL}$ is perpendicular to $\overline{KM}$.

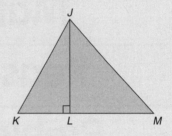

Prove that $KL \neq LM$.

SOLUTION

Assume that $KL = LM$. Since $\overline{JL}$ is perpendicular to KM, $m\angle JLK = m\angle JLM = 90°$. JL = JL by the identity postulate. Then, $\triangle JLK$ would be congruent to $\triangle JLM$ by the side-angle-side correspondence. This would lead to JK = JM, since corresponding parts of congruent triangles are congruent. This is a contradiction because $\triangle JKM$ has been given as scalene, for which no two sides are congruent.

EXAMPLE 4

In the following diagram, $\overline{QR}$ is a chord of circle P, but it does not contain the center of the circle.

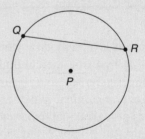

Prove that QR is less than the length of the diameter of the circle.

SOLUTION

We'll redraw the diagram, adding diameter $\overline{RS}$, which contains the center point P. Also, we'll connect points Q and S.

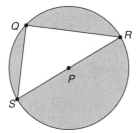

Assume that $\overline{QR}$ is at least equal to the length of $\overline{RS}$. Within one triangle, the order of the sizes of the angles is exactly the same as the order of the sides opposite these angles. This would imply that $m\angle S \geq m\angle Q$. Since the measure of an inscribed angle is one half the measure of its intercepted arc, the statement $m\angle S \geq m\angle Q$ implies that $\overset{\frown}{RQ} > \overset{\frown}{RS}$. However, $\overset{\frown}{RS}$ represents a semicircle, which is the largest arc in a circle. Thus, $\overset{\frown}{RQ} > \overset{\frown}{RS}$ is impossible, which means $QR < RS$.

Deductive Reasoning

Deductive reasoning involves the application of a generally accepted or proven theory to a specific example. Usually, we are given a set of premises, from which a valid conclusion can be drawn. We'll look at some examples in the areas of geometry, algebra, and logic.

In geometry, we may be given a theorem involving numerical values or a list of statements that lead to a conclusion.

EXAMPLE 5

The Pythagorean Theorem states that $a^2 + b^2 = c^2$, whenever a and b are the legs of a right triangle and c is the hypotenuse. If $a = 3$ and $b = 4$ in a right triangle, then the hypotenuse must equal 5, since $3^2 + 4^2 = 5^2$.

EXAMPLE 6

In an equilateral triangle with sides s, the area is given by the expression $\frac{s^2}{4}\sqrt{3}$. Thus, if we are given an equilateral triangle whose side is 6, the area must be $\frac{6^2}{4}\sqrt{3} = 9\sqrt{3}$.

EXAMPLE 7

In any triangle, the three medians must meet at a common interior point. In triangle XYZ, shown below, the three medians are drawn.

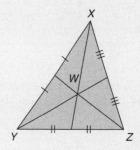

Therefore, the medians meet at a common interior point (point W).

EXAMPLE 8

Two sides of one triangle are congruent to two sides of a second triangle. In addition, the included angle of one triangle is congruent to the included angle of a second triangle. Then, the triangles are congruent. Thus, given $\triangle ABC$ and $\triangle DEF$, for which $AB = DE$, $BC = EF$, and $\angle B \cong \angle E$, our conclusion is that $\triangle ABC \cong \triangle DEF$.

Let's look at a few examples that use algebraic properties.

EXAMPLE 9

Whenever equals are added to equals, the results are equal.
Given that $m = n$, then $m + 5 = n + 5$.

EXAMPLE 10

> The product of two odd integers is an odd integer. Specifically, if we are given the numbers 7 and 9, their product must be odd.

EXAMPLE 11

> The square root of the sum of two positive numbers is less than the sum of the square roots of these two numbers. Thus, if 5 and 6 are the given numbers, $\sqrt{5+6} < \sqrt{5} + \sqrt{6}$.
>
> (This can be verified by noting that the value of the left side is approximately 3.32, whereas the value of the right side is approximately 4.69.)

Here are a few examples that can be classified as logic. In each case, we assume that the given statements are true.

EXAMPLE 12

> The two given statements are: *All pets are friendly. Casper is a pet.* Our conclusion is that *Casper is friendly.*

EXAMPLE 13

> The two given statements are: *All teachers are underpaid. Marcella is a teacher.* Our conclusion is that *Marcella is underpaid.*
>
> There is a major caution that must be taken when drawing a conclusion using deductive reasoning. Be sure that you are not switching a premise with the conclusion.

EXAMPLE 14

> The two statements are: *All lions eat meat. Lenny eats meat.* We <u>cannot</u> draw the conclusion that *Lenny is a lion.* He might be a lion, but he could just as easily be your next-door neighbor!

Referring to Example 14, we could have created two statements for which there would be a valid conclusion as follows: The two statements are: *All lions eat meat. Lenny is a lion.* The conclusion that *Lenny eats meat* is valid.

Inductive Reasoning

Inductive reasoning uses specific examples in order to make valid generalizations. This process is the reverse of deductive reasoning. As with deductive reasoning, our premises must be valid. Let's look at a few examples from the areas of geometry and algebra.

EXAMPLE 15

> In a given triangle ABC, $m\angle C = 90°$, $m\angle A = 44°$, and $m\angle B = 46°$. In a given triangle DEF, $m\angle F = 90°$, $m\angle D = 30°$, and $m\angle E = 60°$.
>
> Inductive reasoning would lead to the following statement: *The sum of the acute angles of any right triangle must be 90°.*

EXAMPLE 16

> Given circle P, where P is the center and points A and B are on the circle, if $m\angle APB = 60°$, then $\overarc{AB}$ represents one-sixth the circumference. Given circle Q, where Q is the center and points D and E are on the circle, if $m\angle DQE = 60°$, then $\overarc{DE}$ represents one-sixth the circumference. Inductive reasoning would lead to the following statement: Given any circle, if the angle formed by the center and two points on the circle is 60°, then the minor arc formed by the two points on the circle is one-sixth the circumference.

EXAMPLE 17

> Given the three equations $(5)(8) = 40$, $(10)(3) = 30$, and $(11)(12) = 132$, it would be nearly impossible to determine which statement would represent the conclusion. One possibility is that the product of an odd integer and an even integer is always an even integer.

EXAMPLE 18

Consider the following three statements:
$$1 + 2 + 3 = \left(\frac{3}{2}\right)(1 + 3), \quad 4 + 5 + 6 + 7 + 8$$
$$= \left(\frac{5}{2}\right)(4 + 8), \text{ and } 10 + 11 + 12 + 13 + 14$$
$$+ 15 = \left(\frac{6}{2}\right)(10 + 15).$$ By inductive reasoning, the following statement seems plausible:

The sum of a number of consecutive integers equals the product of one-half the number of integers and the sum of the first and last integers.

There is a formal process (beyond the scope of our book) for proving a general statement by induction. In some cases, the truth of a few examples is insufficient for claiming that the general case is also true.

EXAMPLE 19

Consider the following sequence of numbers: 1, 2, 3, ... If we were asked for the next number, our natural guess would be 4. We would assume that the sequence is 1, 2, 3, 4, 5, ...But, consider that the sequence could be as follows: 1, 2, 3, 5, 8, 13, ..., in which each term is the sum of the previous two terms. Another less likely possibility for the fourth number is −1. This would be true if the sequence were as follows: 1, 2, 3, −1, −2, −3, 1, 2, 3, −1, −2, −3,....

Counterexamples

Counterexamples are examples used to disprove the truth of a claim. Mathematically, only one counterexample is needed to disprove a claim. Usually, a claim is made by using the process inductive reasoning.

EXAMPLE 20

Consider the following three statements:

The number 16 is divisible by 4. The number 36 is divisible by 4. The number 96 is divisible by 4. A claim is made that any two-digit number with a units digit of 6 is divisible by 4. Provide a counterexample.

SOLUTION

There would be several counterexamples, one of which is 46.

EXAMPLE 21

Consider the following three statements:
$$30° + 10° + 15° < 90°$$
$$35° + 12° + 28° < 90°$$
$$39° + 11° + 20° < 90°.$$ A claim is made that *the sum of the measures of three acute angles is less than 90°.* Provide a counterexample.

SOLUTION

Many counterexamples exist, including the following: 40°, 35°, 27°, since $40° + 35° + 27° > 90°$.

EXAMPLE 22

Consider the following three statements.

A rectangle with length 12 and width 3 has a perimeter of 30 and an area of 36.

A rectangle with length 15 and width 5 has a perimeter of 40 and an area of 75.

A rectangle with length 32 and width 8 has a perimeter of 80 and an area of 256.

A claim is made that *for any rectangle, the numerical value of the perimeter is less than the numerical value of the area.* Provide a counterexample.

SOLUTION

If x and y represent the length and width of a rectangle, then $2x + 2y$ is the perimeter and xy is the area. Let $x = 10$. The perimeter is $20 + 2y$ and the area is $10y$. For a counterexample, we just need to solve $20 + 2y > 10y$. Thus, any solution to $y < 2.5$ would be correct. So, if $x = 10$ and $y = 2$, the perimeter is 24 and the area is 20.

Our last topic for this chapter deals with linear mathematical models, as applied to real-world situations. In each case, we will be given three data points. A linear model will then be computed for two of these points. Our objective will be to test the level of accuracy when this linear model is applied to the third set of data points. When the "fit" is not exact, we will determine the level of accuracy.

EXAMPLE 23

Student A had a final exam grade of 80 and received a course grade of 85. Student B had a final exam grade of 75 and received a course grade of 82.

Based on this data, an educational statistician is constructing a linear model for predicting a student's course grade based on his/her final exam grade. If student C had a final exam score of 92 and received a course grade of 93, what percent of error exists based on the linear model?

SOLUTION

Let x represent the final exam grade and let y represent the course grade. Then the two points for which a linear model equation will be constructed are $(80, 85)$ and $(75, 82)$. The slope of the line joining these points is $\dfrac{82 - 85}{75 - 80} = 0.6$. Then the slope-intercept form of the equation is $y = 0.6x + b$. Substituting the point $(80, 85)$, we get $85 = (0.6)(80) + b$. Then $b = 37$, so the equation becomes $y = 0.6x + 37$. Based on this equation, if a student receives a final exam grade of 92, the predicted course grade would be $(0.6)(92) + 37 = 92.2$.

The actual course grade assigned is 93, so the error is $\left|\dfrac{93 - 92.2}{92.2}\right|(100) \approx 0.87\%$. This is remarkable accuracy. (Less than 1% error!)

EXAMPLE 24

The temperature at which a person perspires is a function of his/her weight. Sharon weighs 120 pounds and she perspires at a temperature of 83°. Howie weighs 200 pounds and he perspires at a temperature of 76°. Based on this data, a health official will construct a linear model to predict the temperature at which a person perspires, based on weight.

If Chantel weighs 105 pounds and perspires at a temperature of 88°, what percent of error exists based on the linear model?

SOLUTION

Let x represent weight and let y represent temperature. Then the two points under consideration for a linear model are $(120, 83)$ and $(200, 76)$. The slope of the line containing these points is $\dfrac{76 - 83}{200 - 120} = -0.0875$. So, the slope-intercept form of the linear equation is $y = -0.0875x + b$. Either point may be substituted, so let's use the point $(200, 76)$. Then $76 = (-0.0875)(200) + b$, which means that $b = 93.5$.

The linear model equation becomes $y = -0.0875x + 93.5$. Now, for a weight of 105 pounds, the predicted temperature for perspiring is $-0.0875(105) + 93.5 = 84.3125°$. The actual temperature at which Chantel perspires is 88°, so the error is $\left|\dfrac{88 - 84.3125}{84.3125}\right|(100) \approx 4.37\%$.

A special note about error should be acknowledged. If you had used –0.088 in place of –0.0875 for the slope, the predicted temperature would have been 84.26 and the error would have been about 4.44%.

Quiz for Chapter 18

1. In establishing an indirect proof, which one of the following is necessary?

    (A) a statement that verifies the given assumption

    (B) a statement that contradicts the given assumption

    (C) a geometric drawing

    (D) an algebraic explanation

2. In the figure below, $CB = 8$ and $AC = 10$.

    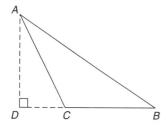

    Which one of the following statements should be used to prove indirectly that the area of ΔABC is less than 40?

    (A) Determine the measure of $\angle ACD$.

    (B) Determine the measure of $\angle B$.

    (C) Determine the restriction for the value of AD.

    (D) Determine the restriction for the value of AB.

3. Which one of the following is an example of deductive reasoning?

    (A) The first term of a sequence of numbers is 1, the second term is 3, and the third term is 5. Thus, the nth term is $2n - 1$.

    (B) The sum of the angles is ΔXYZ and in ΔTUV is 180°. Therefore, the sum of the angles in any triangle is 180°.

    (C) All rectangles have four right angles. Since $ABCD$ is a rectangle, it must have four right angles.

    (D) Line l_2 has a slope of 5 and line l_1 has a slope of 4. Line l_2 is closer to the appearance of a vertical line than line l_1. Thus, the larger the slope of a line, the more vertical the line will appear.

4. One of two given statements is "All books in this library are for sale." Suppose the conclusion, using deductive reasoning, is "The book *Oliver Twist* is for sale." Which one of the following would represent the second given statement?

    (A) *Oliver Twist* is a book in this library.

    (B) *Oliver Twist* is not a book in this library.

    (C) All books for sale are in this library.

    (D) Some books for sale are not in this library.

5. A claim is made that the product of two positive numbers is at least as large as either number. Which one of the following provides a counter example?

    (A) $(8)(1) = 8$ (C) $(\sqrt{10})(\sqrt{40}) = 20$

    (B) $(6)(0.5) = 3$ (D) $(3)(\pi) < 10$

6. What is the primary purpose of a mathematical counterexample?

    (A) to justify a general claim based on a given set of statements

    (B) to provide new examples that do not resemble a given set of statements

    (C) to provide a different approach to solving a given equation

    (D) to negate a general claim based on a given set of statements

7. Consider the following three statements:

    (a) $1 + 3 = 2^2$,   (b) $1 + 3 + 5 = 3^2$,

    (c) $1 + 3 + 5 + 7 = 4^2$.

    Using inductive reasoning, which one of the following statements would apply?

    (A) The sum of the first n consecutive positive odd integers equals n^2.

    (B) The sum of any consecutive n odd integers equals n^2.

    (C) The sum of the squares of the first n positive odd integers equals n.

    (D) The sum of the squares of any n consecutive odd integers equals $(n + 1)^2$.

8. A study has shown that the measure of a person's reaction time is a function of the average number of hours of sleep per night. Marc averages four hours of sleep per night and his reaction time is 2.5 seconds. Natalie averages nine hours of sleep per night and her reaction time is 1.8 seconds. Based on this data and using y to represent reaction time in seconds and x to represent sleep in hours, which one of the following is the appropriate linear model?

    (A) $y = -0.14x + 1.94$

    (B) $y = -0.14x + 3.06$

    (C) $y = 0.14x + 1.94$

    (D) $y = 0.14x + 3.06$

9. Referring to the information in #8, suppose that Brianna averages seven hours of sleep and her reaction time is 2.2 seconds. What is the percent of error, based on the linear model? (nearest hundredth of one percent)

    (A) 14.66%   (C) 8.74%

    (B) 11.71%   (D) 5.77%

Quiz for Chapter 18
Solutions

1. **(B)**

    In establishing an indirect proof, a statement showing a contradiction is required.

2. **(C)**

    The area of $\triangle ABC$ is $\left(\dfrac{1}{2}\right)(BC)(AD) = (4)(AD)$.

    Use the fact that the hypotenuse of a right triangle is the largest side, so $AD < 10$.

3. **(C)**

    In deductive reasoning, the validity of a general statement is applied to a specific case.

4. **(A)**

    "*Oliver Twist* is a book in this library" should be the second statement.

5. **(B)**

    A counterexample must show that the product is less than one of the given numbers. This is shown in answer choice (B), since $3 < 6$.

6. (D)

By its definition, the purpose of a counterexample is to provide evidence that contradicts a general claim that is based on a given set of statements.

7. (A)

"The sum of the first n consecutive positive odd integers equals n^2" expresses the relationship that exists in each of the three examples.

8. (B)

The points are (4, 2.5) and (9, 1.8). The slope of the linear function is $\dfrac{1.8 - 2.5}{9 - 4} = -0.14$. Then $y = -0.14x + b$. Substituting the point (4, 2.5), we get $2.5 = (-0.14)(4) + b$. Thus $b = 3.06$ and the equation becomes $y = -0.14x + 3.06$.

9. (D)

Substituting $x = 7$ into the equation $y = -0.14x + 3.06$ yields a y value of 2.08. The percent of error is $\left(\dfrac{2.2 - 2.08}{2.08}\right)(100) \approx 5.77\%$.

Communicating Mathematical Concepts

Welcome to Chapter 19. In this section we will review:

(a) Mathematical connections both inside and outside of mathematics.

(b) Communication of mathematical ideas and concepts

In addition to being a mainstay of every student's course load, mathematics is intricately connected to all aspects of our lives. Our credit reports, medical tests and even our bowling scores depend on mathematical models. Although mathematical connections to our modern society are nearly endless, we will focus on mathematical connections to:

a) Biology

b) Engineering

c) Business and finance

d) Leisure and entertainment activities.

Application to Biology

Biologists use exponential growth models to predict future results.

EXAMPLE 1

A bacterial culture doubles in size every 24 minutes. How many minutes are needed for a culture of 4.8×10^5 bacteria to grow to 7.2×10^5 ?

SOLUTION

Use the formula $N = N_0 b^{\frac{t}{k}}$ where N_0 is the original amount, N is the amount at time t and b is a growth (or decay) factor. Let k equal a predetermined period for growth (or decay) to occur. Then $7.2 \times 10^5 = 4.8 \times 10^5 (2)^{\frac{t}{24}}$, which simplifies to $1.5 = 2^{\frac{t}{24}}$. Taking logarithms of both sides leads to $\log 1.5 = \frac{t}{24} \log 2$. Then $0.585 = \frac{t}{24}$, so $14.03 \approx t$. The culture will take approximately 14.03 minutes to grow to 7.2×10^5.

Application to Engineering

Engineers devise mathematical models to test data.

EXAMPLE 2

A group of civil engineers were designing a tunnel below a freeway. The tunnel, a parabolic arch, is 36 feet wide and 16 feet tall. The engineers calculate the maximum width of a truck going through the tunnel is 7'9". Furthermore, they assume trucks will travel 1 foot from the center line. If 1 foot is allowed between the truck and the roof, what is the maximum height of a truck passing through the tunnel?

SOLUTION

Graph the parabola.

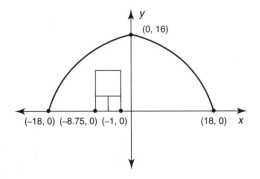

Figure 19.1

Find the equation of the parabola by substituting both (18, 0) and (0, 16) into the equation $y = a(x - h)^2 + k$ Since (0, 16) lies on the parabola, $h = 0$ and $k = 16$. Then $y = ax^2 + 16$. Now substituting (18, 0), we have $0 = (a)(18^2) + 16$. Thus $a = -\frac{16}{18^2} = -\frac{4}{81}$. So, the equation for the parabola is $y = \frac{-4}{81}x^2 + 16$.

The height of the tunnel, 8'9" from the center, is given by $y = \frac{-4}{81}(8.75)^2 + 16$. Then, $y \approx 12.22$. Allowing a 1 foot space for the truck's passage, the maximum height of a truck passing through the tunnel is approximately 11.22 feet.

Business and Finance

Mathematical models are useful for making sound business decisions.

EXAMPLE 3

Jake's software firm is being purchased by a larger company. The buyer has offered Jake $50,000 per year for 20 years or a lump sum of $400,000. Jake makes the following assumptions:

a) He can invest the lump sum offer in a risk-free certificate growing 4.6 % per year.

b) The compounding will be continuous.

   Excluding tax considerations, should Jake accept the lump sum offer?

SOLUTION

The growth of 4.6 % is continuous, so use the formula $A = Pe^{rt}$ where:

A is the dollar amount accrued after 20 years

P is the principal, $400,000

r is the rate of growth, .046 (4.6 %)

t is time in years, 20.

e is a constant, (approximately 2.718)

Then $A = 400,000e^{(.046 \times 20)}$, so $A \approx 1,003,716.2$. If Jake takes $50,000 for 20 years, he will have $1,000,000. The lump sum is a more profitable deal, since Jake will earn $1,003,716.20 - 1,000,000 = \$3,716.20$ more money.

Leisure and Entertainment

Our leisure time activities have connections to mathematics.

EXAMPLE 4

In the diagram of a target shown below, each of the concentric rings numbered 10, 20, 30 or 40 has a radius that is 1" larger than the next smallest ring. The bull's eye, worth 50 points, has a 1" radius.

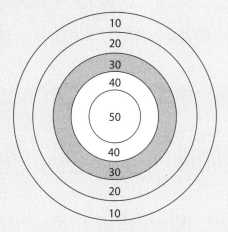

Figure 19.2

Marcia is a skillful dart player. What is the probability that her dart will land in the 30-ring?

SOLUTION

First, we'll find the area of the 30-ring. The radius of the circle, from the center of the bull's eye to the edge of the 30 ring, is 3 inches. Therefore, its area is 9π. The inner circle containing the bull's eye and the 40 ring has a radius of 2 inches. So, its area is 4π. Then the area of the 30- ring is $9\pi - 4\pi = 5\pi$. The target has a radius of 5", so its area is 25π. Thus, the required probability is $\dfrac{5\pi}{25\pi} = \dfrac{1}{5}$ or 0.20.

Connections to Mathematics

Mathematics has connections to itself.

EXAMPLE 5

Jorge is teaching his first year Algebra students how to factor quadratic equations. How could he show the class a quick way to multiply $(61)(59)$ by using the difference of squares?

SOLUTION

$a^2 - b^2 = (a + b)(a - b)$. Then $(61)(59) = (60-1)$ $(60 + 1) = 3600 - 1 = 3599$.

Communicating Mathematical Concepts

The advent of the internet and personal computers have facilitated and enriched the communication of mathematical concepts. A math teacher in California peruses a Texas state educational website and locates the exact regimen of practice exercises she has been looking for. Students needing supplementary explanations of challenging mathematical concepts often have to go no further than the PC on their desks. Clearly, students can access vast amounts of information via the internet and a good math teacher will harness this invaluable tool.

There are other avenues available to educators to help students visualize sophisticated math topics. One of these techniques is to use algebra tiles. These inexpensive, easy-to-use tiles use simple geometry to help students visualize the factorization of polynomials.

EXAMPLE 6

James asked his students to use algebra tiles to demonstrate that $(2x + 3)(x + 4)$ is the correct way to factor $2x^2 + 11x + 12$.

SOLUTION

Algebra tiles use the areas of squares and rectangles to illustrate the correct factoring of the polynomial $2x^2 + 11x + 12$, as shown in the diagram below.

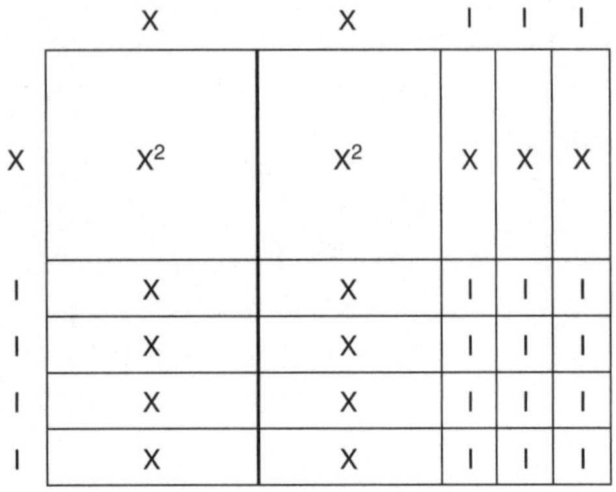

Figure 19.3

Notice that squared numbers are represented with squares, while all other quantities are portrayed with rectangles. The length of the largest rectangle is $x + x + x + 1 + 1 - 3x + 2$. Its width is $x + 1 + 1 + 1 + 1 = x + 4$. The combined area of the two squares, each with an area of x^2, is $2x^2$. The combined area of the twelve squares, each with an area of 1, is 12. There are eleven boxes, each with an area of x, so their combined area is $11x$. Thus, the combined area of the 25 boxes is $2x^2 + 11x + 12$.

Graphing Calculators

Graphing calculators are another resource a math teacher can use to communicate mathematical concepts. In addition to graphing equations, the graphing calculator can help students quickly solve problems dealing with topics such as matrices, trigonometry, statistics, probability, and calculus.

In the following example, a teacher demonstrates how the graphing calculator has become a boon to mathematics.

EXAMPLE 7

Imelda, a 1980 graduate of Bonita Vista High School, is now an Algebra 2 teacher at the same school. She wants to show her students how a graphing calculator not only drastically reduces the time needed to solve complicated problems, but also how it integrates graphs with polynomials. She explains the steps necessary to solve the problem $x^3 + 3x^2 + 10x + 16 = 0$ when she was an Algebra 2 student. We'll call this Solution A.

SOLUTION A

<u>Step 1</u>: Test to see if the equation has any rational roots in the form $\frac{p}{q}$, where p is an integral factor of 16 and q is an integral factor of 1, which is the coefficient of x^3. This means writing all possibilities of $\frac{p}{q}$, which are $\pm 1, \pm 2, \pm 4, \pm 8, \pm 16$.

<u>Step 2</u>: Using the pool of 10 possible rational factors, use synthetic division to determine that -2 is the sole rational root of the equation.

Figure 19.4

<u>Step 3</u>: Note that when the original equation is divided by $x + 2$, the quotient is $x^2 + x + 8$. Quick inspection suggests that the quotient is not factorable, so determine the remaining roots using the quadratic equation. $\frac{-b \pm \sqrt{b^2 - 4ac}}{2a}$, where $a = 1$, $b = 1$ and $c = 8$.

The final roots of the equation are $\dfrac{-1 \pm i\sqrt{31}}{2}$.

Today, Imelda suggests, the task of performing the same problem is much simpler and quicker. Let's call this Solution B.

SOLUTION B

Step 1: Input the equation into the graphing function of the calculator. The graph is shown below.

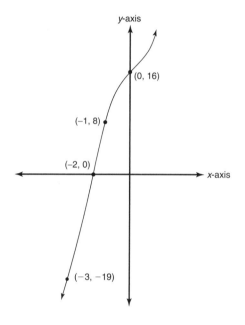

Figure 19.5

Step 2: The student can observe at a glance that -2 is the sole rational root of this equation. Given that the graph does not intersect the x-axis at any other points, the remaining roots must be imaginary or complex.

NOTE:

The student could find the rational roots using an equally quick alternative in Step 2. After graphing the equation, immediately input the possible rational roots into the table function. The table yields the following results:

x	y
1	30
-1	8
2	56
-2	0
4	168
-4	-40
8	800
-8	-384
16	5040
-16	-3472

The students will observe that only -2 yields a y-value of 0. Thus, -2 is a zero of the function. Clearly, the simple application of the graphing or table function reduces the time needed for discerning rational roots to mere seconds. The time needed for tedious synthetic division (itself a short-cut) has all been eliminated.

At this point, Imelda suggests the students return to steps 2 and 3 of Solution A above, to find the remaining roots of the equation. She indicates, however, that slightly more powerful graphing calculators can find the remaining complex roots in seconds.

Quiz for Chapter 19

1. What is the value of $7,500 invested for 42 months at 16.4% if the interest is compounded monthly? (Nearest cent.)

   (A) $8,642.51

   (B) $9,000.87

   (C) $11,263.51

   (D) $13,263.50

2. A ceramic artist uses 259 in^3 of clay to create a cylindrical planter, as shown below.

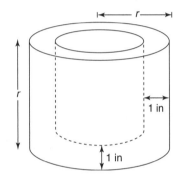

   The walls of the planter are 1" wide and the artist wants the height and outside radius to be the same. To the nearest hundredth of an inch, what is the value *r*?

   (A) 4.87

   (B) 5.73

   (C) 6.68

   (D) 9.54

3. Investigators for the Texas State Police are investigating a statewide series of bank robberies. Although investigators know the suspect has a late model blue sedan, they have only a partial identification of the license plate: the second space contains the number *7* and the sixth space contains the letter *R*. There are seven spaces in any Texas license plate, with the following restrictions:

   First space: Must be a digit, but *0* and *1* are excluded

   Second space: Any digit except *0*

   Third space: Any digit

   Fourth Space: Any letter from *A* to *F*, inclusive

   Fifth space: Any letter from *M* to *P*, inclusive

   Sixth space: Any letter or digit, excluding *0,1,O* and *I*

   Seventh space: Any letter except *X* or *Y*

   How many license plates must the investigators consider?

   (A) 13,742,113

   (B) 987,633

   (C) 46,080

   (D) 720

4. Two pool cleaners, working together, must clean an Olympic-sized pool. One worker can clean the pool in 5 hours while the other can clean the pool in 4 hours. To the nearest minute, how long will it take both cleaners to clean the pool?

   (A) 2 hours 13 minutes

   (B) 2 hours 14 minutes

   (C) 2 hours 47 minutes

   (D) 3 hours 1 minute

5. Look at the following diagram.

	X	X	X	I
X	X^2	X^2	X^2	X
I	X	X	X	I
I	X	X	X	I
I	X	X	X	I

   This is an example of the usage of algebraic tiles to represent the factoring of which polynomial?

   (A) $4x^2 + 9x + 3$ (C) $3x^2 + 10x + 3$

   (B) $3x^2 + 3x + 10$ (D) $4x^2 + 12x + 7$

6. A group of 6 college students was surveyed about the number of hours the students had studied for a recent mathematics exam. The following table was constructed:

Hours spent studying	Grade (%)
2.5	60
2	75
3	80
3.5	85
3	90
4	95

To the nearest hundredth, what is the correlation coefficient, r?

(A) −0.92   (C) 0.74

(B) 0.13   (D) 0.87

7. Two boats head toward a sandbar as indicated in the figure below.

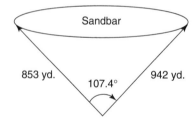

Which formula should be used to calculate the distance between the two boats when they land and how far apart will the boats be when they land? (Nearest yard).

(A) Pythagorean Theorem; 985 yards

(B) Distance Formula; 842 yards

(C) Law of Sines; 694 yards

(D) Law of Cosines; 1,448 yards

8. A once bustling metropolis has seen its population decline by 6.8% per year. By January 1, 2000, the government census reported the population to be 975,000. On that same day, the city council resolved to sell off public lands to private developers once the population had declined to 700,000. However, the city planners need 15 months in advance to begin negotiations. When should the city planners begin negotiations?

(A) December, 2002

(B) February, 2003

(C) May, 2003

(D) August, 2003

9. Shelby has been offered a sales position with a pharmaceutical company. There are two different three-year compensation packages for her to consider.

Package A: Annual salary of $100,000, plus an increase based on an annual inflation rate of 2.1% .

Package B: Annual salary of $60,000, plus a commission of 5% based on sales.

Sales are projected to be $1,200,000 during her first year, but will decrease by 1.5% per year for the following two years.

Which of the following is the best approximation of the difference in total compensation for these two packages?

(A) $51,000   (C) $55,000

(B) $53,000   (D) $57,000

10. In the diagram of a target shown below, each of the concentric rings numbered 10, 20, 30, or 40 is 3" wider than the next smallest ring. The bull's eye, worth 50 points, has a 4" diameter.

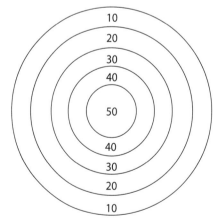

Hank is competing in the last round of an archery contest. If he scores a bull's-eye, he wins the contest. If he scores a 20, then he will place fourth in the contest. Assuming that he hits the target on his next shot, what is the probability that he wins the contest or places fourth?

(A) 0.256   (C) 0.294

(B) 0.279   (D) 0.311

Quiz for Chapter 19
SOLUTIONS

1. (D)

Use the formula $A = P(1 + \frac{r}{n})^{nt}$, where A = dollar amount at time t, P = principal, the initial amount deposited, r = annual rate, expressed as a decimal, n = number of compounding periods annually, and t = time expressed in years. Thus, $A = 7500(1 + \frac{.164}{12})^{(12 \times 3.5)} \approx$ $13,263.50. (Note that t, 42 months, was expressed as 3.5 years.)

2. (B)

Our objective is to find the volume of the cylinder less the volume of the empty, cylindrical space. Use the formula $V = \pi r^2 h$. Let πr^3 = the volume of the cylinder and let $\pi(r - 1)^3$ = volume of the empty, cylindrical space. Then $\pi r^3 - \pi(r - 1)^3 = 259$. This equation simplifies to $(\pi)(3r^2 - 3r + 1) = 259$, which can be approximated by $3r^2 - 3r - 81.44 = 0$.

Using the quadratic formula, the positive value is approximately 5.73.

3. (C)

We can express the restrictions of numbers and letters with the following multiplication array.

$\underline{8} \times \underline{1} \times \underline{10} \times \underline{6} \times \underline{4} \times \underline{1} \times \underline{24} = 46,080$

4. (A)

Let p be the number of hours needed to fill the pool.

Since the first worker can clean the pool in 5 hours, his share of the job will be $\frac{p}{5}$ hours. The faster worker will clean the pool in $\frac{p}{4}$ hours. Therefore, the time needed to clean the pool can be expressed as $\frac{p}{5} + \frac{p}{4} = 1$. The 1 expressed at the right of the equal sign represents one whole pool that has been cleaned. Solving for p, we arrive at $p = \frac{20}{9}$ hours, which rounds to 2 hours 13 minutes.

5. (C)

There are three boxes labeled as "x^2," ten boxes labeled as "x," and three boxes labeled as "1." Thus, the represented polynomial is $3x^2 + 10x + 3$. The actual factors are shown by the horizontal and vertical representations that lie outside the boxes. They are $3x + 1$ and $x + 3$, respectively. Note that $3x^2 + 10x + 3 = (3x + 1)(x + 3)$.

6. (C)

Press the "Stats" button on your calculator. Next press "Edit" to input the data. Let l_1 be a list of the hours studied and l_2 be the grades each student earned. After inputting the data, press "Calc" and scroll down to LinReg $(ax + b)$ and press "Enter." You should see, at the bottom of the list, the value $r \approx 0.74$.

7. (D)

When the lengths of two sides of the triangle are known, along with their included angle, use the Law of Cosines to determine the length of the third side. $a^2 = b^2 + c^2 - 2bc\cos A$.

Then $a^2 = 942^2 + 853^2 - 2(942)(853)(\cos 107.4°)$.

So $a^2 = 2,095,547.103$, which means $a \approx 1,448$.

8. (C)

Use the formula $y = ab^x$ and note that a 6.8% annual decline is the same as a 93.2% retention rate. $700,000 = 975,000(.932)^x$, which means that $.718 = .932^x$ Dividing the log of .718 by the log of .932, we get $x = 4.70$ years. Adding 4.70 years to January 1, 2000 we arrive at August 15, 2004. Subtract 15 months for the beginning phase of negotiations to start in May 2003.

9. (A)

Shelby's total compensation for Package A will be $100,000 + (\$100,000)(1.021) + (\$100,000)(1.021)^2 \approx \$306,344$. For Package B, her total salary will be $(3)(\$60,000) = \$180,000$. Her sales will be $1,200,000 for the first year, $(\$1,200,000)(0.985) = \$1,182,000$ for the second year, and $(\$1,182,000)(0.985) = \$1,164,270$ for the third year. The total projected sales are $3,546,270, so her total commission will be $(0.05)(\$3,546,270) \approx \$177,314$. Thus, her total compensation from Package B is $180,000 + $177,314 = $357,314. The difference of the two packages is approximately $51,000.

10. (D)

Since the radius of the bull's eye is 2 inches, its area is 4π square inches. The radius of the ring labeled 20 must be $2 + 3 + 3 + 3 = 11$ inches. Then the area of the four rings labeled 20, 30, 40, and 50 is 121π square inches. The radius of the 30 ring is $2 + 3 + 3 = 8$ inches, which means that the total area of the three rings labeled 30, 40, and 50 is 64π square inches. The area of the 20 ring is $121\pi - 64\pi = 57\pi$ square inches. The combined area of the bull's eye and the 20 ring is 61π. The radius of the 10 ring is 14 inches, which means that its area is 196π. Finally, the required probability is $\dfrac{61\pi}{196\pi} \approx 0.311$.

Instruction and Assessment

Welcome to Chapter 20. In this chapter, we will review the following topics:

(a) Effective teaching methods

(b) Different student learning styles

(c) Strategies for solving various types of math problems

(d) Challenges for students for whom English is not their native language

(e) Connecting mathematical concepts to real-world situations

(f) Assessment instruments to measure students' learning

Mathematics Instruction: Then and Now

The days are long past when teaching and management of math classrooms relied solely on teachers' personal experience and intuition. Nowadays, state-of-the-art pedagogical and instructional styles and procedures are developed to guide you toward a quality math classroom and highly accomplished career.

In this chapter, we will cover all the basic aspects of such procedures and notions developed for instruction and assessment in math classrooms.

What Makes a Good Math Teacher?

Teaching mathematics is a challenging task. It requires hard work and self-discipline to be an effective math teacher. You must be well-versed in the subject matter and be able to present the subject in accordance with the learning capacity of the students. You need to recognize your students' learning limitations and be equipped with the communication skills suitable for youngsters of all abilities. Critical thinking, problem solving and decision-making need to be central to the instructional strategy that you use at all levels.

EXAMPLE 1

John has just arrived in your Algebra I classroom. He has transferred from another state and thinks his knowledge and skills are far ahead of your course objectives. In the midst of your lecture on the coordinate plane he objects to your notation $A(a, b)$ and claims that it must be in the form $A = (a, b)$, because his previous teacher taught him this way. How do you handle this controversial discourse in a professional manner?

SOLUTION

First of all, in order to handle the discourse in a professional manner, the "*previous teacher*" must be taken out of the picture. Do not allow John to signify his point by quoting an absent source. Then, you can discuss the difference between $A = (a, b)$ and $A(a, b)$ by distinguishing (a, b) from A as two different entities which cannot be equal. The symbol $A(a, b)$ is used to show that the coordinates of part A are (a, b). The statement $A = (a.b)$ would mean that a point is equal to the numerical value of its coordinates, which is <u>not</u> true.

How Children Learn Mathematics

Being active in their own world, children begin from their early lives to develop the basic quantitative and spatial concepts. As they grow up, each child assumes his or her own way of absorbing quantitative skills, which are the cornerstone of mathematical skills.

Types of Learners

1. Visual learners: Students that tend to use images to absorb math concepts are visual learners. Seeing and visualizing math concepts is a way of learning for this group of learners.

EXAMPLE 2

Which is a good instructional tool to use with visual learners?

SOLUTION

Manipulatives work well with both visual and tactile learners.

2. Auditory Learners: Such learners think in a linear way and tend to learn through hearing rather than writing or reading. they benefit most from well-planned lectures.

3. Read-Write Learners: For this group of learners writing and reading play significant role in their learning process. Organizing and listing the instructed information in their own way is vital to their learning. They learn better by repeating and practicing math concepts on their own rather than by listening to instructions.

EXAMPLE 3

To teach the quadratic formula to a read-write learner, what approach is the best to be taken as the first step?

SOLUTION

Give the learner a paper that asks him to compare the coefficients of a quadratic equation with the quadratic formula. His assignment would be to write down their values.

4. Kinesthetic Learners: This group of learners absorbs math concepts and skills slowly.

They are slow in decision-making and adopting a solid strategy. Using the method of trial and error is common among this group of learners. They are more interested in real-life applications of mathematics rather than the abstract concepts.

EXAMPLE 4

To teach the Pythagorean theorem to a kinesthetic learner, how do you prepare the learner's mind for adopting the Pythagorean relationship among the sides of all right triangle?

SOLUTION

Draw right triangles with side-lengths listed below:

3, 4, 5

6, 8, 10

9, 12, 15

12, 16, 20

15, 20, 25

Calculate the square of each side and then by adding the squares of the two shorter sides show that in each triangle, it is equal to the square of the hypotenuse.

These examples prepare the learner to engage actively when he or she is exposed to the theorem and learn it as a general and abstract notion.

Connect Past to the Present

To be a successful math teacher you must build every new concept on the previous skills and knowledge of the students. In this way, the students are not overwhelmed by a pile of new tedious procedures. They also are able to solidify their logical competency and reasoning skills.

EXAMPLE 5

How do you build the solving process of the following system of equations on the concept of a linear equation in one variable?
$$\begin{cases} 3x + 2y = 11 \\ 2x - 5y = 1 \end{cases}$$

SOLUTION

First, explain that in a linear equation you can consider one variable as a constant quantity and solve the equation for the other variable. So, take x as the variable and assume that everything else in the equation is a constant. Solve the first equation for x. Its solution will include the variable y. Then using the properties of real numbers, where you can replace any quantity with its equivalent, replace x in the second equation with the expression you found in the first equation. From here on, the result is one equation in one variable, namely y. Now, everything is based on prior knowledge. Solve this equation for y, then substitute this value in either equation in order to solve for x.

An Effective Instructional Plan

Problem solving can be a challenging task for many of your students. It can be especially and frustrating if the solution is not immediately obvious. Guide your students through some practical examples to help them to recognize that they should take time to explore, reflect, and think when they face non-routine math problems. They can use tactics such as rewriting the problem in their own words, talk to themselves to analyze the structure of the problem, and ask as many questions before beginning the solution process.

EXAMPLE 6

List some hints you can give to your students to use as tactics and strategies for solving all math problems.

SOLUTION

The best approach is the Polya's universal plan for dealing with all types of math problems:

Step 1.

Understanding the Problem: Comprehension of a math problem is the primary phase to process the solution. At this stage, after reading the statement of the problem, students must be able to paraphrase the problem using the main and necessary components of the problem. Are all necessary facts given or are there some unknowns that must be determined? Then students brainstorm on what tasks are asked for in the problem. Are these tasks able to be accomplished by the given facts and previously learned techniques and strategies or are further information or skills are needed?

Step 2.

Devising a Plan: After understanding the givens, identifying unknowns, and determining the inquiries of the problem, the next step is to devise a blueprint to proceed to the answer. To do so, students can look for a pattern, examine an earlier solved problem that is similar to the given problem, explore simpler problems, and generalize their solutions. Students can also use tables, graphs, develop equations or functions, use trial and error methods, and apply other mathematical tools.

Step 3.

Carrying Out the Plan: Upon developing a strategy for solving the problem, students carry out the designated strategy step-by-step. They need to check each step to be sure that all the operations and computations are free of any errors.

Step 4.

Checking and Looking Back: Upon completing Step 3 which results in the final solution(s), students should check the solution(s) in the original problem and be sure they satisfy the conditions of the problem. It is possible that a "solution" will not satisfy the original conditions. This "solution" must be disregarded.

EXAMPLE 7

> (Step 1 of Polya Method) Read the following problem carefully and determine whether it contains all necessary and sufficient conditions to be solved.

"The difference between two adjacent sides of a parallelogram is 8 in. and their sum is 24 in. The height of the parallelogram is 12 in. Find the area of the parallelogram."

SOLUTION

At first glance, we notice that the problem does not specify which side is longer than the other side. That is, it does not indicate that the difference of two sides is whether

$$AD - CD \text{ or } GH - EH.$$

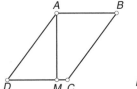 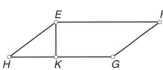

But we can check to see which option should be chosen. If we choose the parallelogram *EFGH*, then we can generate the following system of equations:

$$GH + EH = 24$$

$$GH - EH = 8$$

Solving this system results in $GH = 16$ and $EH = 8$. On the other hand, the height EK is given as 12 in. In the right triangle *EHK*, such side lengths are not possible. So, the problem includes unique facts for a unique inquiry. We can choose the parallelogram *ABCD* and establish the system of equations based on the conditions (where the horizontal sides are shorter than the lateral sides) of this figure. For the parallelogram *ABCD*,

$$AD + DC = 24$$

$$AD - DC = 8$$

Solving this system, we get $AD = 16$ and $DC = 8$

Then, in right triangle *ADM*, $AD = 16$, and $AM = 12$. This is an acceptable situation, since *AD* must be greater than *AM*. Thus the area of the parallelogram *ABCD* is $(DC)(AM) = (8)(12) = 96$.

EXAMPLE 8

> (Step 2 of Polya Method) The following expression is given to be factored. What strategy could you use to factor the expression?
> $$(x^2 - 4)^2 + 7(x^2 - 4) + 10$$

SOLUTION

We can expand both parentheses, and after simplifying the result, try to factor the final polynomial. But this is a lengthy and tedious way. Using a dummy variable such as $m = (x^2 - 4)$ converts the given expression to the following expression.

$$m^2 + 7m + 10$$

This is factored as $(m + 2)(m + 5)$. Replacing the equivalent of *m* in this product gives the final answer.

$$(x^2 - 4 + 2)(x^2 - 4 + 5) = (x^2 - 2)(x^2 + 1)$$

EXAMPLE 9

> (Step 4 of Polya's Method) The following equation is given. Find the solutions and process as per Step 4 of Polya's Method.
> $$(x - 6)^2 - 9 = 0$$

SOLUTION

Add 9 to each side and simplify.

$$(x - 6)^2 - 9 + 9 = 9$$

$$(x - 6)^2 = 9$$

Take square root of both sides.

$$x - 6 = \pm 3$$

$$x = 3 \text{ or } x = 9$$

Replacing both answers in the original equation leads to two valid equations.

EXAMPLE 10

> Sometimes, direct proof is not possible using the principles and rules of basic mathematics. In such cases, finding a pattern among all the typical cases and generalizing this pattern as a universal conclusion is a productive method. Using a pattern method, find a formula for the measure of an interior angle of *n*-gon.

SOLUTION

Establish a table as follows and discuss the trend that leads to a universal formula for an *n*-gon.

Polygon	Total Interior Angle Measures	Measure of Interior Angle
Triangle (3-gon)	$180(3-2)$	$\frac{180}{3}(3-2)$
Quadrilateral (4-gon)	$180(4-2)$	$\frac{180}{4}(4-2)$
Pentagon (5-gon)	$180(5-2)$	$\frac{180}{5}(5-2)$
Hexagon (6-gon)	$180(6-2)$	$\frac{180}{6}(6-2)$
Heptagon (7-gon)	$180(7-2)$	$\frac{180}{7}(7-2)$
Octagon (8-gon)	$180(8-2)$	$\frac{180}{8}(8-2)$
Nonagon (9-gon)	$180(9-2)$	$\frac{180}{9}(9-2)$
Decagon (10-gon)	$180(10-2)$	$\frac{180}{10}(10-2)$
......	.....	......
......	.....	......
......	.....	......
n-gon	$180(n-2)$	$\frac{180}{n}(n-2)$

Encouraging the Use of Mathematical Tactics

Often students will convert the reasoning problems to routine computational problems, and avoid validating their arguments based on math principles and rules. Use your teaching skills to encourage them to focus using various mathematical tactics.

EXAMPLE 11

> How do you deal with students who answer the following equation using mental math: $x + 6 = 12$?

SOLUTION

Help students to advance their mathematical abilities by applying the properties of real numbers to isolate x on the left side instead of finding a number using mental math such that adding it to 6 gives 12.

From Empirical Examples to Concrete and Abstract Notions

Most higher-level pre-college math concepts can be challenging for students. To overcome such barriers, it is common sense to expose the same theoretical notion in the context of practical examples and then tackle the concept in an abstract manner. In this way, students can absorb the notion with less confusion and resistance.

EXAMPLE 12

> Some students have difficulty in absorbing the concept of the Pythagorean relationship and cannot relate the sides of a right triangle to the formula $c^2 = a^2 + b^2$. How do you help them with their dilemma?

SOLUTION

To help your students to grasp the concept of the Pythagorean relationship, use a right triangle such as the one below and assign Pythagorean numbers to a, b, and c.

Then show the computational process so student can see how the relationship works empirically. As an example, let $a = 3$, $b = 4$, and $c = 5$. Then $3^2 + 4^2 = 9 + 16 = 25 = 5^2$.

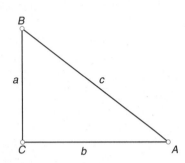

More than One Choice

Expose the diversity of mathematical approaches and tactics. Your students need to gradually learn that there can be more than one unique approach to a single math problem. Showing these characteristics of math problems through instructional plans prepares your students to understand that there could be many approaches to one problem. They can be encouraged to explore some of these approaches on their own.

EXAMPLE 13

All the side-lengths and an interior angle are given in the following triangle. Find its area.

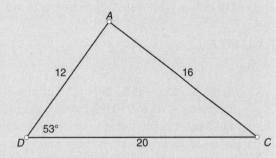

Note: The measure of $\angle D$ has been rounded off to the nearest degree.

SOLUTION

Students may use Heron's formula and replace the side-lengths to reach the area. In this approach there is no need of the given angle.

Students may draw the altitude AB and then, using the definition of the tangent in the right triangle, find the length of AB. Then having both the height and the base allows them to find the area.

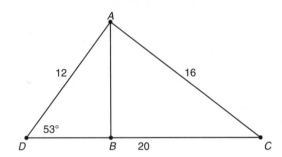

Students may use the area formula $A = \frac{1}{2}ab\sin C$ and replace the given measures to calculate the area.

A fourth method, and the quickest, is to recognize that $\angle A$ is a right angle, since $12^2 + 16^2 = 20^2$. Then the area of $\triangle ADC = \left(\frac{1}{2}\right)(12)(16) = 96$.

English Language Learners in Math Classrooms

Often, math classes include students for whom English is their second language. Even if some of these students have a higher desire for learning mathematics and lack "math phobia," vetting them to a mathematics classroom could be extremely cumbersome and challenging. In such cases, you might need to prescreen ELL students for language proficiency and be sure these students are not floundering in the instructional environment. If you notice that some of your ELL students are struggling with the language, you can consult their English teachers or the foreign students' advisor in your school to design a team plan to enhance the language proficiency of your ELL students.

EXAMPLE 14

ELL students can often have difficulty with mathematical terms. Their limited English vocabulary and experience with English grammar puts them at a disadvantage. How can you help them to improve their language capability?

SOLUTION

(Answer may vary.) You may have them submit their math assignments with written explanations. In this way they have additional practice in the specific aspects of working in English while doing math work. Assignments might have to be smaller to allow for the additional time needed.

Learning Environment

To best utilize the learning environment of your math class, you can engage your students in the instructional process using all types of strategies and tactics. The more students are engaged in mathematical discourse, the more they can learn and retain their learning. Integrate some questions into every step of your instructions. This can help your students to stay awake through the teaching process and become proactive for the entire instructional period.

EXAMPLE 15

Assume that the exploring the following pattern is a component of your instruction:

$1 = 2^1 - 1$

$1 + 2 = 2^2 - 1$

$1 + 2 + 2^2 = 2^3 - 1$

$1 + 2 + 2^2 + 2^3 = 2^4 - 1$

$1 + 2 + 2^2 + 2^3 + 2^4 = 2^5 - 1$

When presenting these equations how do you engage your students in the discourse?

SOLUTION

You can verify the first few equations and then ask students to work out the remaining equations. Also try to show how to write an equivalent expression for $1 + 2^1 + 2^2 + 2^3 + ... + 2^n$. (The answer is $2^{n+1} - 1$.)

Disconnect from Math

Sometimes, students who are not well-connected to the core nature of mathematics consider mathematical concepts to be useless in their present and future life.

They feel that the purpose of learning mathematics is only to fulfill the requirements for their high school program and that math will not have any impact or use in their later life and career. Exposing students to some interesting applications of math in real-life situations can reverse the mindset of such students.

EXAMPLE 16

Modeling many real-life phenomena using mathematical procedures and principles is very common in various fields of science, industry, and so forth. Which of the following cases using mathematical concepts would make more sense to high school students and draw their attention?

1. Modeling deer population in a wildlife area for the past 5 years

2. Modeling toxic concentration in a river for 3 years

3. Modeling the number of musicians inducted each year into the rock and roll hall of fame within the last 30 years

4. Modeling lung cancer cases in the last 10 years

SOLUTION

Case (3) seems to be more appealing to high school students and provides them with a mathematical curve to see how the numbers within different time intervals changed.

EXAMPLE 17

(*Connect Algebra to Geometry*) Illustrating a concept from one math subject through tools of another math subject can be productive as well. For example, exploring algebraic skills and concepts by employing geometric tools can sharpen students' strategic potential. How can you verify the identity $(a + b)^2 = a^2 + 2ab + b^2$ using geometric illustrations and formulas?

SOLUTION

Draw a square with side-length $(a + b)$.

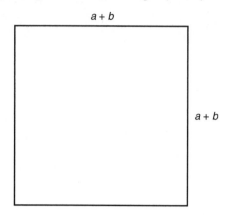

Divide each side into two segments with lengths a and b. Then connect the points on each pair of parallel sides. Label the squares and rectangles generated inside the square by A, B, C, and D.

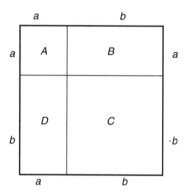

The area of the square is equal to $(a + b)^2$. On the other hand, the area is equal to the sum of the areas of A, B, C, and D. These areas are as follows:

$A = a^2$

$B = ab$

$C = b^2$

$D = ab$

Thus these two methods for the area of the square are the same. That is,

$(a + b)^2 = a^2 + ab + b^2 + ab = a^2 + 2ab + b^2$

EXAMPLE 18

(*Connect Geometry to Algebra*) The difference between angles a and b is 25 degrees and the difference between angles b and c is 25 degrees. Find the measures of each interior angle.

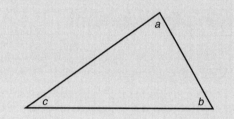

SOLUTION

By the given data,

$a - b = 25$

$b - c = 25$

$a + b + c = 180$

Add the first and the second equations.

$a - c = 50$

Add this equation to the third equation.

$2a + b = 230$

Add this equation to the first equation, and solve for a.

$2a + a = 230 + 25$

$3a = 255$

$a = 85$ degrees

Replace a in the first equation and solve for b.

$85 - b = 25$

$b = 60$ degrees

Replace $b = 60$ in the second equation and solve for c.

$60 - c = 25$

$c = 35$ degrees

Assessment

Scoring Rubrics

Rubrics are used to present students' performance and assessment in a quantitative manner. As a scoring tool, a rubric is a list of points allocated to pieces of a mathematical work. This work could be a homework assignment, a quiz, a project, or an exam. Allocating points to each segment of a math problem must be proportional to its level of complexity and the time required for its solution.

EXAMPLE 19

If you allocate 10 points to the solution of each of the following problems, the final numerical answer of which problem should have fewer points than the others? Why?

1. Find the perimeter of a rectangle with dimensions 12 and 23.

2. Find the area of a square with a side length of 19.

3. Find the area of a rectangle whose perimeter is 20 and its length is 2 units longer than its width.

4. Find the area of a trapezoid with bases 12 and 18 units long and a height of 23 units.

SOLUTION

The solution of problem 3 involves many steps. So, the final answer is a smaller proportion of the steps of the solution. Therefore, it should have fewer points so that you can allocate some points to other steps of the problem.

Fair Assessment

In an effective instructional environment, you must have a direct connection between the content of your course and the assessment items. Assessments are not for tricking or challenging the learners. Rather, they are tools to give them feedback on their learning process and performance.

EXAMPLE 20

Which problem is <u>not</u> an appropriate stem for a multiple-choice question?

(1) Solve the equation $6x - 12 = 45x + 11$.

(2) Graph the equation $4x - 6 = 12x$.

(3) Find the answers of $x^2 + 24x + 144 = 0$ and replace the answer in the expression $(x + 4)^2 + (x - 4)$.

(4) Solve the following system:

$$4x - 11y = 56$$
$$4x + y = 21$$

(5) Find the area of a circle whose diameter is 12 in.

SOLUTION

Problem (3) is not a good choice for a multiple-choice question because there are two objectives integrated in the problem. Having two objectives in one item leads to an imbalance among the test questions.

EXAMPLE 21

Which question is an appropriate item for an open-ended question?

(1) Find the area of a rectangle whose dimensions are 23 and 34.

(2) Find the perimeter of a square whose sides is 33.

(3) Find the interior angle of an equilateral triangle.

(4) Find the interior angles of an isosceles triangle in which the difference of the vertex angle and a base angle is 34 degrees.

SOLUTION

Problem (4) is an appropriate item for open-end assessment. This problem involves a series of mathematical steps.

Summative Assessment

Summative assessment is a way to evaluate and monitor the overall learning of your students as well as the effectiveness of your instructional plans on a cumulative basis over a long period of instruction. This type of assessment is used to determine whether both students and you could meet your course objectives and the mandated standards and benchmarks at the midpoint or at the end of the course.

EXAMPLE 22

List a few types of summative tests.

SOLUTION

SAT or ACT Tests

State assessments

District assessments

End-of-unit or tests

End-of-chapter tests

End-of-semester exams

EXAMPLE 23

List types of assessment tests that can be used as summative test items.

SOLUTION

Fill-in-the-blank

Extended written response

Multiple-choice

Multi-selection items

True/false

Matching

Short-answer

Formative Assessments

To keep a continual track of learning and instructional progress, you should plan to give assessment tests to your students to monitor their performance after each segment of a chapter or a section. In this way, both you and your students can remedy any deficiencies before moving to the next topic. Using formative assessments, you and your students can explore where they are and where they want to head at any particular point of the instructional process. Assessments ensure that the path from "now" to the next phase is smooth and all can connect the present situation in the learning environment to the next immediate stage.

EXAMPLE 24

List some types of formative assessments.

SOLUTION

quiz, essay, lab or workshop report

EXAMPLE 25

Give an assessment item by which you can be assured that your students have achieved all necessary objectives with regard to the properties of midlines in both triangles and trapezoids.

SOLUTION

(Answer may vary.) For example, you can consider the following figure in which the segments on AB are proportional to the segments on AC. Then you can explore the properties of DF (as a midline in the triangle AEG) and of EG (as the midline in the trapezoid $DFCB$).

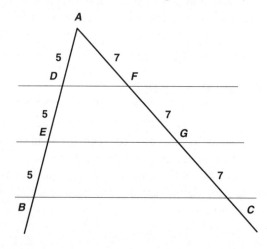

Quiz for Chapter 20

1. When assessing students' knowledge of linear functions, which of the following notions should be the core point?

   (A) The concept of a coordinate plane

   (B) The concept of graphing functions

   (C) The concept of solving a system of linear equations

   (D) The concept of modeling paired data

2. Which of the following inequalities can be used to assess students' knowledge on solving linear inequalities in order to ensure that they learn necessary skills beyond those used to solve linear equations?

   (A) $3x > -5$ (C) $-3x < 5$

   (B) $4x < 0.11$ (D) $9x > 0.11$

3. Which problem can be best used to evaluate students' understanding of the domain of a function?

   (A) Find the domain of the function $f(x) = 3x + 4$.

   (B) Find the domain of the function $f(x) = \dfrac{1}{x+1} + \dfrac{1}{x^2+1}$.

   (C) Find the domain of the function $f(x) = \dfrac{x+1}{3} + \dfrac{1}{6}$.

   (D) Find the domain of the function $f(x) = \dfrac{1}{6}\left(\dfrac{x+1}{3}\right)$.

4. Which equation can be used as a summative quiz problem to evaluate students' knowledge on solving all common types of linear equations?

   (A) $3x + 11 = -4x$

   (B) $3(x - 11) = 4x - 19$

   (C) $3x + 4x - x = 3 + 11 - 2$

   (D) $-4x + 4 - 9x = -7x + 11 - 8x$

5. Which problem can be used as an informative quiz problem?

   (A) Solve the equation $x^2 - 5x + 3 = 0$.

   (B) What are the solutions of the equation $x^2 + 9x - 32 = 0$?

   (C) Solve the equation $3x - 29 = 4x$.

   (D) Given $ax^2 + bx + c = 0$, what are the values of a, b, and c in the equation $x^2 - 9x + 44 = 0$?

6. Using a scoring rubric, fewer points must be allocated to the final answer of which problem?

   (A) Find the area of a rectangle whose dimensions are 12 inches and 32 inches.

   (B) Find the area of a square whose side is 33 inches.

   (C) Find the area of a circle in square inches whose circumference is 56π feet.

   (D) Find the perimeter of a parallelogram whose sides are 22 inches and 45 inches.

7. Which skills must be acquired in a problem-solving assessment?

   (A) Organizing and selecting data, using necessary principles, and applying complex procedures

   (B) Solving the problem numerically and then verifying it theoretically.

   (C) Solving the problem backwards.

   (D) Using the problem in the context of real-life situations.

8. In order to simplify the polynomial $x^6 - 4x^4 + 3x^6 - 4x^3 + 11 + 21x^3 + 9$, which of the following options is NOT a plausible distracter?

    (A) $x^6 - 4x^4 + 21x^2 + 20$

    (B) $x^6 - 4x^4 + 21x^3 + 2$

    (C) $4x^6 - 4x^4 + 19x^3 - 2$

    (D) $-3x^6 + 4x^4 + 2x^3 - 20$

9. After grading your students' exams, you notice that many of your students draw the conclusion $3x = 11y$ from the series of equations "$3x(5 - 5) = 11y(9 - 9)$ and $3x(0) = 11y(0)$". This error among your students is an indication of what type of mathematical misconception?

    (A) Multiplication property for inequalities

    (B) Distribution property for real numbers

    (C) Division by zero

    (D) Inverse property for nonzero numbers

10. A student finds the expression $(x^2 - 4)(x^2 - 4)$ as the common denominator of the expression below:

    $$\frac{5}{x^2 - 4} - \frac{1}{x + 2} + \frac{3}{x - 2}$$

    What algebraic concept is not well established in the mind of the student?

    (A) The greatest common factor of two equivalent expressions

    (B) The least common multiple of two equivalent expressions

    (C) Binomial product

    (D) Conjugate identity

Quiz for Chapter 20
SOLUTIONS

1. **(D)**

    A linear function, in essence, is a basic tool for modeling a set of paired data. Other answer options may be the secondary characteristics of linear functions.

2. **(C)**

    When solving a linear equation, dividing both sides by a number does not affect the equality sign. But in this case, despite the other inequalities in the problem, the direction of the sign must be changed upon dividing both sides by this negative coefficient.

3. **(B)**

    In order to find the domain of the function $f(x) = \frac{1}{x + 1} + \frac{1}{x^2 + 1}$, students must investigate the values of the denominators, where one of them is not nonzero for all real numbers while the other is nonzero for all real numbers.

4. **(B)**

    Solving $3(x - 11) = 4x - 19$ requires applying all the real number properties plus the distribution property.

5. (D)

In this problem, only some information needs to be extracted from the equation to determine the answers.

6. (C)

This problem—unlike the others, which involve only a one-step solution—requires a series of steps each with its own calculations. A student may carry out all steps of the problem correctly but make an error at the end. So, to evaluate his or her work fairly, the final solution should not be allocated the majority of points.

7. (A)

Problem-solving assessment requires a broad range of skills, from organizing the given information as the first step to applying complex procedures.

8. (A)

In this expression, one of the exponents of x's is 2 while there is no x to the power of 2 in the original polynomial.

9. (C)

Students must understand that they cannot divide both sides of an equation by zero.

10. (B)

The common denominator of the last two fractions is $x^2 - 4$, which is the same as the first denominator. Student should know that the least common multiple of two equivalent expressions is just one of them. Thus, $x^2 - 4$ is the common denominator.

TExES

Mathematics (135)

Practice Test I

Summary of Formulas for TExES 135 Mathematics

ALGEBRA

The imaginary number $i = \sqrt{-1}$ and $i^2 = -1$.

The inverse of matrix A is denoted as A^{-1}.

$A = P\left(1 + \dfrac{r}{n}\right)^{nt}$ is used for compound interest, where A = final value, P = principal, r = interest rate, t = term, and n = number of divisions within the term.

$[x] = n$ is called the greatest integer function, where n is the integer such that $n \leq x < n + 1$.

TRIGONOMETRY

Formulas refer to the triangle shown in Figure I.

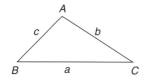

Figure I

Law of Sines:

$$\frac{\sin A}{a} = \frac{\sin B}{b} = \frac{\sin C}{c}$$

Law of Cosines:

$$c^2 = a^2 + b^2 - (2ab)(\cos C)$$
$$b^2 = a^2 + c^2 - (2ac)(\cos B)$$
$$a^2 = b^2 + c^2 - (2bc)(\cos A)$$

PROBABILITY

$$p(A \text{ or } B) = p(A) + p(B) - p(A \& B)$$
$$p(A \& B) = p(A) \cdot p(B|A) = p(B) \cdot (A|B)$$

CALCULUS

The first derivative of $f(x)$ is denoted as $f'(x)$ or $\dfrac{dy}{dx}$.

The second derivative of $f(x)$ is denoted as $f''(x)$ or $\dfrac{d^2y}{dx^2}$.

GEOMETRY

Congruent angles or congruent sides are denoted by an identical number of slash marks, as shown in Figures II and III.

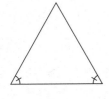

Figure II

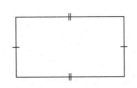

Figure III

Parallel sides are denoted by an identical number of arrowheads, as shown in Figure IV.

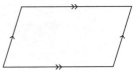

Figure IV

Circumference of a circle $= 2\pi r$.

Formulas

Description	Formula
Areas	
Circle	πr^2
Triangle	$\left(\dfrac{1}{2}\right)(\text{base})(\text{height})$
Rhombus	$\left(\dfrac{1}{2}\right)(\text{diagonal 1})\,(\text{diagonal 2})$
Trapezoid	$\left(\dfrac{1}{2}\right)(\text{height})(\text{base 1} + \text{base 2})$
Surface Areas	
Cylinder (lateral)	$2\pi rh$
Sphere	$(4\pi)(\text{radius squared})$
Volume	
Cylinder	$(\text{area of base})(\text{height})$
Sphere	$\left(\dfrac{4}{3}\pi\right)(\text{radius cubed})$
Cone	$\left(\dfrac{1}{3}\right)(\text{area of base})(\text{height})$
Prism	$(\text{area of base})(\text{height})$

Answer Sheet

1. Ⓐ Ⓑ Ⓒ Ⓓ	22. Ⓐ Ⓑ Ⓒ Ⓓ	43. Ⓐ Ⓑ Ⓒ Ⓓ	64. Ⓐ Ⓑ Ⓒ Ⓓ	85. Ⓐ Ⓑ Ⓒ Ⓓ
2. Ⓐ Ⓑ Ⓒ Ⓓ	23. Ⓐ Ⓑ Ⓒ Ⓓ	44. Ⓐ Ⓑ Ⓒ Ⓓ	65. Ⓐ Ⓑ Ⓒ Ⓓ	86. Ⓐ Ⓑ Ⓒ Ⓓ
3. Ⓐ Ⓑ Ⓒ Ⓓ	24. Ⓐ Ⓑ Ⓒ Ⓓ	45. Ⓐ Ⓑ Ⓒ Ⓓ	66. Ⓐ Ⓑ Ⓒ Ⓓ	87. Ⓐ Ⓑ Ⓒ Ⓓ
4. Ⓐ Ⓑ Ⓒ Ⓓ	25. Ⓐ Ⓑ Ⓒ Ⓓ	46. Ⓐ Ⓑ Ⓒ Ⓓ	67. Ⓐ Ⓑ Ⓒ Ⓓ	88. Ⓐ Ⓑ Ⓒ Ⓓ
5. Ⓐ Ⓑ Ⓒ Ⓓ	26. Ⓐ Ⓑ Ⓒ Ⓓ	47. Ⓐ Ⓑ Ⓒ Ⓓ	68. Ⓐ Ⓑ Ⓒ Ⓓ	89. Ⓐ Ⓑ Ⓒ Ⓓ
6. Ⓐ Ⓑ Ⓒ Ⓓ	27. Ⓐ Ⓑ Ⓒ Ⓓ	48. Ⓐ Ⓑ Ⓒ Ⓓ	69. Ⓐ Ⓑ Ⓒ Ⓓ	90. Ⓐ Ⓑ Ⓒ Ⓓ
7. Ⓐ Ⓑ Ⓒ Ⓓ	28. Ⓐ Ⓑ Ⓒ Ⓓ	49. Ⓐ Ⓑ Ⓒ Ⓓ	70. Ⓐ Ⓑ Ⓒ Ⓓ	
8. Ⓐ Ⓑ Ⓒ Ⓓ	29. Ⓐ Ⓑ Ⓒ Ⓓ	50. Ⓐ Ⓑ Ⓒ Ⓓ	71. Ⓐ Ⓑ Ⓒ Ⓓ	
9. Ⓐ Ⓑ Ⓒ Ⓓ	30. Ⓐ Ⓑ Ⓒ Ⓓ	51. Ⓐ Ⓑ Ⓒ Ⓓ	72. Ⓐ Ⓑ Ⓒ Ⓓ	
10. Ⓐ Ⓑ Ⓒ Ⓓ	31. Ⓐ Ⓑ Ⓒ Ⓓ	52. Ⓐ Ⓑ Ⓒ Ⓓ	73. Ⓐ Ⓑ Ⓒ Ⓓ	
11. Ⓐ Ⓑ Ⓒ Ⓓ	32. Ⓐ Ⓑ Ⓒ Ⓓ	53. Ⓐ Ⓑ Ⓒ Ⓓ	74. Ⓐ Ⓑ Ⓒ Ⓓ	
12. Ⓐ Ⓑ Ⓒ Ⓓ	33. Ⓐ Ⓑ Ⓒ Ⓓ	54. Ⓐ Ⓑ Ⓒ Ⓓ	75. Ⓐ Ⓑ Ⓒ Ⓓ	
13. Ⓐ Ⓑ Ⓒ Ⓓ	34. Ⓐ Ⓑ Ⓒ Ⓓ	55. Ⓐ Ⓑ Ⓒ Ⓓ	76. Ⓐ Ⓑ Ⓒ Ⓓ	
14. Ⓐ Ⓑ Ⓒ Ⓓ	35. Ⓐ Ⓑ Ⓒ Ⓓ	56. Ⓐ Ⓑ Ⓒ Ⓓ	77. Ⓐ Ⓑ Ⓒ Ⓓ	
15. Ⓐ Ⓑ Ⓒ Ⓓ	36. Ⓐ Ⓑ Ⓒ Ⓓ	57. Ⓐ Ⓑ Ⓒ Ⓓ	78. Ⓐ Ⓑ Ⓒ Ⓓ	
16. Ⓐ Ⓑ Ⓒ Ⓓ	37. Ⓐ Ⓑ Ⓒ Ⓓ	58. Ⓐ Ⓑ Ⓒ Ⓓ	79. Ⓐ Ⓑ Ⓒ Ⓓ	
17. Ⓐ Ⓑ Ⓒ Ⓓ	38. Ⓐ Ⓑ Ⓒ Ⓓ	59. Ⓐ Ⓑ Ⓒ Ⓓ	80. Ⓐ Ⓑ Ⓒ Ⓓ	
18. Ⓐ Ⓑ Ⓒ Ⓓ	39. Ⓐ Ⓑ Ⓒ Ⓓ	60. Ⓐ Ⓑ Ⓒ Ⓓ	81. Ⓐ Ⓑ Ⓒ Ⓓ	
19. Ⓐ Ⓑ Ⓒ Ⓓ	40. Ⓐ Ⓑ Ⓒ Ⓓ	61. Ⓐ Ⓑ Ⓒ Ⓓ	82. Ⓐ Ⓑ Ⓒ Ⓓ	
20. Ⓐ Ⓑ Ⓒ Ⓓ	41. Ⓐ Ⓑ Ⓒ Ⓓ	62. Ⓐ Ⓑ Ⓒ Ⓓ	83. Ⓐ Ⓑ Ⓒ Ⓓ	
21. Ⓐ Ⓑ Ⓒ Ⓓ	42. Ⓐ Ⓑ Ⓒ Ⓓ	63. Ⓐ Ⓑ Ⓒ Ⓓ	84. Ⓐ Ⓑ Ⓒ Ⓓ	

TExES Mathematics 135
Practice Test 1

TIME: 5 hours
90 questions

<u>Directions</u>: Read each item and select the best response.

1. Which one of the following functions has the same domain as the function? $f(x) = \dfrac{x+4}{2x^2 - 2}$?

   (A) $g(x) = \dfrac{x-4}{(x-1)(x+1)}$

   (B) $g(x) = \dfrac{x+4}{(2)(x^2 - 2)}$

   (C) $g(x) = \dfrac{x-4}{(x-2)(x+1)}$

   (D) $g(x) = \dfrac{x+4}{(2x)(x-1)}$

2. The area of the base of a cone is 169π and its lateral height is 16. To the nearest hundredth, what is its perpendicular height?

   (A) 20.62 (C) 9.33

   (B) 14.98 (D) 5.27

3. For a system of linear equations in the form $ax + by = c$ and $dx + ey = f$, where each of $a, b, c, d, e,$ and f are constants, suppose the final augmented matrix is $\begin{bmatrix} 3 & 2 & | & 4 \\ 0 & 0 & | & 0 \end{bmatrix}$. What is the solution for x and y?

   (A) An infinite number of paired answers

   (B) $x = 3$ and $y = 2$

   (C) No solution

   (D) $x = 2$ and $y = 4$

4. In a game of Poker, each player is dealt five cards. What is the probability to the nearest thousandth that a player's hand consists of exactly four diamonds?

   (A) 0.011 (C) 0.006

   (B) 0.009 (D) 0.004

5. Point R is located in a quadrant in which the sine ratio is negative and the tangent ratio is positive. Which one of the following could represent the coordinates of R?

   (A) $(-4, 0)$ (C) $(4, -5)$

   (B) $(-5, 4)$ (D) $(-5, -4)$

6. Each face of a cube is sliced along dotted lines to produce a number of smaller cubes, as shown below.

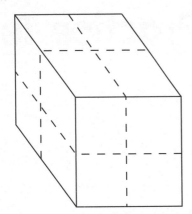

If the total surface area of all the smaller cubes is 300 square inches, what is the volume, to the nearest tenth, of one of the smaller cubes, in cubic inches?

(A) 10.4   (C) 29.7

(B) 15.6   (D) 42.9

7. In the diagram below, *TUXY* is a rectangle and *UVWX* is a square.

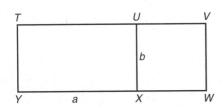

Which expression represents the area of rectangle *TVWY*?

(A) $(a + b)^2$ (C) $ab + b^2$

(B) $a^2 + b^2$ (D) $ab + a^2$

8. Which one of the following numbers is irrational and has a value between 5 and 5.5?

(A) $\sqrt{28}$ (C) $\sqrt{29.16}$

(B) 5.35   (D) 2π

9. One of two statements is "All items on the shelf are expensive." Suppose that the conclusion, using deductive reasoning, is "This vase is expensive."

Which one of the following could represent the second statement?

(A) This vase is not on the shelf.

(B) This vase is on the shelf.

(C) All expensive items are on the shelf.

(D) The shelf contains items other than vases.

10. The volume of a gas varies inversely with its pressure and directly with its Kelvin temperature. If a particular gas has a volume of 288 m^3 under a pressure of 180 kPa (kilopascals) at a temperature of 320° K, what will be the volume if the temperature is increased by 40° K but the pressure is decreased by 20 kPa?

(A) 238.4   (C) 364.5

(B) 279.6   (D) 421.6

11. What is the value of $lim_{x \to 1} \dfrac{2x^2 - 2x}{x^3 - 1}$?

(A) $\dfrac{3}{2}$ (C) $\dfrac{2}{3}$

(B) 1   (D) 0

12. If the translation vector $-4\mathbf{i} + 5\mathbf{j}$ is applied to the point *C* with coordinates $(2, -1)$, what are the coordinates of the image of *C*?

(A) $(-2, -6)$ (C) $(-2, 4)$

(B) $(2, -6)$ (D) $(2, 4)$

13. Which one of the following sets of angles describes an isosceles triangle that is obtuse?

(A) 35°, 35°, and 130°

(B) 45°, 45°, and 90°

(C) 30°, 75°, and 75°

(D) 15°, 15°, and 150°

14. Which one of the following equations represents the graph of a parabola whose vertex is its highest point and whose axis of symmetry is $x = 6$?

(A) $y = -2(x + 6)^2 + 3$

(B) $y = 2(x - 6)^2 + 3$

(C) $y = -2(x-6)^2 - 3$

(D) $y = 2(x+6)^2 - 3$

15. Which one of the following is an example of a function that has three elements in its domain and two elements in its range?

(A) {(3, 5), (2, 8), (4, 3)}

(B) {(1,1), (3, 1), (6, 1)}

(C) {(2, 5), (5, 2), (2, 9)}

(D) {(4, 0), (6, 4), (8, 4)}

16. Samantha deposits \$3250 into a bank in which the interest rate is 3% compounded monthly. To what amount, to the nearest dollar, will this money grow after six years?

(A) \$3900   (C) \$3880

(B) \$3890   (D) \$3870

17. The greatest common factor of M and N is g. Which of the following represents the least common multiple of M and N?

(A) $MN - g$ (C) $\dfrac{MN}{g}$

(B) $M + N + g$ (D) $\left(\dfrac{M}{N}\right)(g)$

18. What is the equation for the slant asymptote for

$$h(x) = \frac{-6x^3 + 4x^2 - 1}{2x^2 + 1}?$$

(A) $y = -3x + 1$ (C) $y = -3x - 2$

(B) $y = -3x - 1$ (D) $y = -3x + 2$

19. Look at the construction markings in the following diagram.

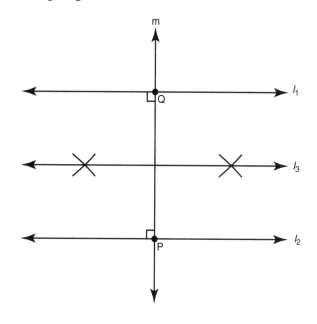

This is the final phrase of which construction?

(A) Given two parallel lines l_1 and l_2, construct a third line that is perpendicular to and equidistant from l_1 and l_2.

(B) Given three parallel lines l_1, l_2, and l_3, construct a transversal that forms a right angle with exactly two of them.

(C) Given two parallel lines l_1 and l_2, construct a third line that is parallel to and equidistant from l_1 and l_2.

(D) Given three parallel lines l_1, l_2, and l_3, construct a transversal across these lines that does not form right angles.

20. A recent census indicates the global population is 6.3 billion. A projected growth rate of 3.7% annually has been forecast for each of the next 25 years. What will be the projected global population at that time?

(A) 9.2 billion   (C) 13.7 billion

(B) 11.3 billion   (D) 15.6 billion

21. In a certain arithmetic sequence, the tenth term is -2 and the 30th term is 26. What is the fourth term?

   (A) -10.4 (C) -3.8

   (B) -7.2 (D) -0.6

22. What is the conjugate of $(3+i)(-4+2i)$?

   (A) $-10-10i$ (C) $-14+10i$

   (B) $-10-2i$ (D) $-14-2i$

23. How is the expression "the quotient of y and the difference between x and w" written algebraically?

   (A) $\dfrac{y}{x}-w$ (C) $\dfrac{y-x}{w}$

   (B) $\dfrac{y}{x-w}$ (D) $y-\dfrac{x}{w}$

24. A circle of radius 4 lies completely inside an equilateral triangle with a side of 20. What is the probability to the nearest hundredth that a randomly selected point inside the triangle also lies inside the circle?

   (A) 0.36   (C) 0.22

   (B) 0.29   (D) 0.15

25. In the following diagram, P is the center of the circle.

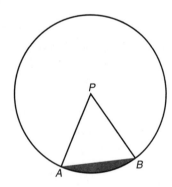

   If $\angle APB = 72°$ and $AP = 8$, what is the area of the segment AB, to the nearest tenth?

   (A) 11.2   (C) 9.8

   (B) 10.6   (D) 8.4

26. A scale factor of $\dfrac{3}{5}$ is applied to $\triangle TUV$ in creating $\triangle XYZ$. The area of $\triangle TUV$ is 30. What is the area of $\triangle XYZ$?

   (A) 10.8   (C) 50

   (B) 18   (D) $83.\overline{3}$

27. What is the sum of the values of x that satisfy the equation $\sqrt{5x-21}=x-3$?

   (A) 9   (C) 13

   (B) 11   (D) 15

28. Look at the following diagram.

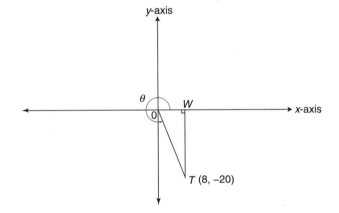

   What is the value of $\sin\theta$ to the nearest hundredth?

   (A) -0.93 (C) -0.57

   (B) -0.75 (D) -0.39

29. Point A is reflected across the line $y=-x$ so that the coordinates of its image point are $(-3, 7)$. What are the coordinates of A?

   (A) $(7, 3)$ (C) $(-7, -3)$

   (B) $(7, -3)$ (D) $(-7, 3)$

30. In using algebra tiles to demonstrate the factoring of the expression $2x^2+13x+15$, which of the following could represent the composition of one of the thirty rows of tiles?

   (A) Three tiles labeled as x^2 and two tiles labeled as x.

   (B) Two tiles labeled as x^2 and three tiles labeled as x.

(C) Two tiles labeled as x^2, one tile labeled as x, and two tiles labeled as 1.

(D) One tile labeled as $2x^2$ and four tiles labeled as 1.

31. If $\log_4 P = \log_8 Q = x$, which of the following expressions is equivalent to $\dfrac{Q}{P}$?

(A) $2x$ (C) x^2

(B) 2^x (D) $\dfrac{x}{2}$

32. Which one of the following is a requirement for the graph of an even function?

(A) It intersects the x-axis.

(B) It intersects the y-axis.

(C) It is symmetric about the x-axis.

(D) It is symmetric about the y-axis.

33. Consider $\triangle DEG$, with angle bisector $\overline{DF}$, as shown below.

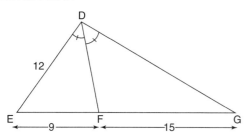

What is the perimeter of $\triangle DEG$?

(A) 58.4   (C) 54

(B) 56   (D) 52.6

34. What is the sum of all the terms of the following infinite sequence?

12, 9.6, 7.68, 6.144, ….

(A) 60   (C) 56

(B) 58   (D) 54

35. Given the complex number $Z = 6 - 3i$, what are its polar coordinates?

(A) $\left(3\sqrt{5}, 153°\right)$ (C) $\left(3\sqrt{3}, 153°\right)$

(B) $\left(3\sqrt{5}, 333°\right)$ (D) $\left(3\sqrt{3}, 333°\right)$

36. For which one of the following set of conditions must the T-Test be used in creating a confidence interval for an unknown population mean?

(A) The sample size is greater than 30 and the population standard deviation is unknown.

(B) The sample size is greater than 30, the population is normally distributed and the population standard deviation is known.

(C) The sample size is less than 30, the population is normally distributed, and the population standard deviation is unknown.

(D) The sample size is less than 30 and the population is not normally distributed.

37. $\triangle ABC$ is <u>not</u> congruent to $\triangle DEF$. Which one of the following situations is possible?

(A) $AB = DE$, $AC = DF$, and $BC = EF$

(B) $AB = DE$, $AC = DF$, and $\angle B \cong \angle E$

(C) $AC = DF$, $\angle C \cong \angle F$, and $BC = EF$

(D) $AC = DF$, $\angle C \cong \angle F$, and $\angle A \cong \angle D$

38. The mean weight of 36 apples and oranges is 5.9 ounces. If the mean weight of the 20 apples is 5.5 ounces, what is the mean weight of the oranges?

(A) 6.6 ounces   (C) 6.4 ounces

(B) 6.5 ounces   (D) 6.3 ounces

39. In the following diagram, P is the center of the circle.

If $EC = 15$, $AC = 12$, and $EG = (2)(GK)$, what is the value of GK to the nearest tenth?

(A) 7.5   (C) 10.7

(B) 8.2   (D) 11.6

40. Six friends are seated in a booth at a local diner. In how many ways can the friends be seated?

(A) 120   (C) 480

(B) 240   (D) 720

41. What is the sum of the zeros for the function $y = 40x^2 + 32x - 90$?

(A) 2.25   (C) −0.8

(B) 0.8   (D) −2.25

42. In how many different ways can all the letters of the word "SCHOOLS" be arranged to form a sequence of seven letters?

(A) 1260   (C) 3780

(B) 2520   (D) 5040

43. Among all auto shops in Nebraska, a claim has been made that the mean time needed to rotate the tires on a car is 16 minutes. Recently, a study of 20 auto shops revealed a mean time of 17 minutes, with a sample standard deviation of 1.5 minutes. At the 1% level of confidence, which one of the following conclusions is correct?

(A) The p value is 0.003 and the claim of $\mu_0 = 16$ is rejected.

(B) The p value is 0.003 and the claim of $\mu_0 = 16$ cannot be rejected.

(C) The p value is 0.008 and the claim of $\mu_0 = 16$ is rejected.

(D) The p value is 0.008 and the claim of $\mu_0 = 16$ cannot be rejected.

44. Given that $x \equiv 4 \pmod 7$, which one of the following could represent the value of $2x$?

(A) 120   (C) 80

(B) 100   (D) 60

45. Given a sequence in which $a_1 = -4$, $a_2 = 3$, and $a_n = a_{n-1} - 5a_{n-2}$ for $n > 2$, what is the sum of the third and fourth terms?

(A) 15   (C) 31

(B) 23   (D) 39

46. A polynomial function is of degree 8. Which one of the following situations <u>cannot</u> exist regarding the nature of the zeros of this function?

(A) Eight distinct real zeros

(B) Five distinct real zeros and three distinct complex zeros

(C) Four distinct real zeros, a double zero, and two distinct complex zeros

(D) Eight distinct complex zeros

47. What is the value of the third quartile for the following grouped frequency distribution?

Class	Frequency
9 − 12	3
13 − 16	4
17 − 20	1
21 − 24	12

(A) $23.\overline{83}$ (C) $22.\overline{83}$

(B) $23.\overline{16}$ (D) $22.\overline{16}$

48. Which one of the following is the equation of a function that is <u>not</u> one-to-one?

(A) $f(x) = x^2 + 5x + 4$

(B) $f(x) = x^3 - 1$

(C) $f(x) = 2x^2 - 4x + 2$

(D) $f(x) = 7x + 5$

49. If $f(x) = (x + 1)(2x - 1)^3(x - 6)$, for which values of x is $f(x) > 0$?

(A) All numbers between -1 and $\dfrac{1}{2}$, or all numbers greater than 6

(B) All numbers between -1 and $\dfrac{1}{2}$

(C) All numbers less than −1, or all numbers greater than 6

(D) All numbers between $\frac{1}{2}$ and 6

50. A national toy distributor uses the mathematical model $f(x) = -.064x^2 + x + 12$ to gauge advertising costs versus units sold (in millions) for a new doll. Using this model, what is the maximum sales volume for this doll?

(A) 9.2 million   (C) 15.9 million

(B) 10.2 million   (D) 17.2 million

51. Which one of the following is a sixth root of $8i$?

(A) $(\sqrt[6]{8})(\cos 45° + i \sin 45°)$

(B) $(\sqrt[6]{8})(\cos 105° + i \sin 105°)$

(C) $(\sqrt[6]{8})(\cos 235° + i \sin 235°)$

(D) $(\sqrt[6]{8})(\cos 315° + i \sin 315°)$

52. An amount of money had been placed into an account for five years, where it was compounded quarterly at an annual interest rate of 9%. If the current value of the money is $12,000, what was its value to the nearest dollar five years ago?

(A) $7780   (C) $7690

(B) $7735   (D) $7645

53. Look at the following graph of $f(x)$.

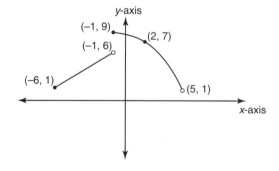

Which one of the following statements is correct?

(A) $Lim_{x \to -1^-} = 6$ and $lim_{x \to -1^+} = 9$.

(B) $Lim_{x \to -1^-}$ does not exist and $lim_{x \to -1^+} = 9$.

(C) $Lim_{x \to -1^-} = 6$ and $lim_{x \to -1^+}$ does not exist.

(D) Each of $lim_{x \to -1^-}$ and $lim_{x \to -1^+}$ does not exist.

54. The amount of hot chocolate dispensed in the paper cups of a vending machine is normally distributed, with a mean of 4.5 ounces and a standard deviation of 0.2 ounces. What percent of all the paper cups will have more than 4.8 ounces of hot chocolate? Figure to the nearest tenth of one percent.

(A) 6.1%   (C) 7.3%

(B) 6.7%   (D) 7.9%

55. Look at the following boxplot.

Which one of the following statements concerning this distribution must be true?

(A) It is positively skewed.

(B) It is negatively skewed.

(C) Its mean is 32.

(D) Its interquartile range is 37.

56. A radioactive substance has a half-life of 12 hours. Initially, there are 60 grams of this substance. How many grams (to the nearest gram) have decayed after nine hours?

(A) 36   (C) 24

(B) 30   (D) 18

57. Look at the diagram shown below.

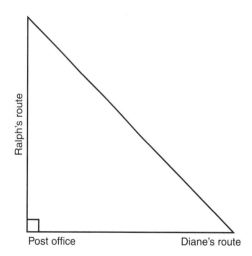

From the Post Office, Diane walks east at a constant speed. At the same time, Ralph walks north at a constant speed. After two hours, they are 14 miles apart.

If Ralph's speed is one mile per hour faster than Diane's speed, what is Diane's distance to the nearest tenth of a mile?

(A) 10.8 miles   (C) 6.8 miles

(B) 8.8 miles   (D) 4.8 miles

58. Let $g(x)$ represent a continuous function on the closed interval $[-2,2]$. If $g(2) = 11$ and the average rate of change of $g(x)$ over the interval $[-2,2]$ is 5, what is the value of $g(-2)$?

(A) -3 (C) -7

(B) -5 (D) -9

59. Phil and Jill are processing payroll checks for a company. Working alone, Jill could complete this task in 24 minutes. Working together, they complete the task in 16 minutes. How many minutes would Phil require if he were working alone?

(A) 40   (C) 48

(B) 44   (D) 52

60. In a geometry class, a teacher may need to have a set of Pythagorean triples handy in order to present examples and exercises on the Pythagorean theorem. Knowing that 3, 4, and 5 represent the smallest group of Pythagorean triples, how do you generate other related Pythagorean triples?

(A) Multiply these numbers by any positive integer greater than 1.

(B) Square each of these numbers.

(C) Add a fixed number to each of these numbers.

(D) Multiply these numbers by squared numbers only.

61. Triangle PQR is similar to triangle STU and $\dfrac{PQ}{ST} = \dfrac{4}{3}$. If the area of $\triangle STU$ is 72, what is the area of $\triangle PQR$?

(A) 48   (C) 96

(B) 54   (D) 128

62. Which one of the following describes the graph of $h(x) = -2x^6 + x^5 - 7x^2 + 10$?

(A) As $x \to \infty$, $h(x) \to \infty$. Also, as $x \to -\infty$, $h(x) \to \infty$.

(B) As $x \to \infty$, $h(x) \to -\infty$. Also, as $x \to -\infty$, $h(x) \to -\infty$.

(C) As $x \to \infty$, $h(x) \to -\infty$. Also, as $x \to -\infty$, $h(x) \to \infty$.

(D) As $x \to \infty$, $h(x) \to \infty$. Also, as $x \to -\infty$, $h(x) \to -\infty$.

63. Given that **A**, **B**, and **C** are square matrices, which one of the following is <u>not necessarily</u> true?

(A) $\mathbf{A} + (\mathbf{B} + \mathbf{C}) = (\mathbf{A} + \mathbf{B}) + \mathbf{C}$

(B) $\mathbf{A} \times \mathbf{B} = \mathbf{B} \times \mathbf{A}$

(C) $\mathbf{A} \times (\mathbf{B} + \mathbf{C}) = \mathbf{A} \times \mathbf{B} + \mathbf{A} \times \mathbf{C}$

(D) $\mathbf{A} \times (\mathbf{B} \times \mathbf{C}) = (\mathbf{A} \times \mathbf{B}) \times \mathbf{C}$

64. Given the function $f(x) = -2x^3 + 3x$, what is the y-intercept of the tangent line to the graph of $f(x)$ at $x = 2$?

(A) 21   (C) 32

(B) 26   (D) 37

65. For inequalities such as $-11x < 44$, the solution is given as $x > -4$. Which rule for reversing the order of inequalities is being used?

(A) Division of a smaller coefficient

(B) Division of a larger coefficient

(C) Division in which the constant term is negative

(D) Division in which the variable term is negative

66. To the nearest tenth, what is the area of a triangle with sides of 4, 8, and 10?

    (A) 14.1   (C) 16.3

    (B) 15.2   (D) 17.4

67. If the matrix $\begin{bmatrix} -3 & 6 \\ 2 & n \end{bmatrix}$ has no inverse, what is the value of n?

    (A) −4   (C) 3

    (B) 0   (D) 4

68. A group of 20 individual numbers has a mean of 50 and a standard deviation of 5. Which one of the following correctly describes the new group of 20 numbers that results from subtracting 3 from each individual number?

    (A) The mean is 50 and the standard deviation is 2.

    (B) The mean is 50 and the variance is 25.

    (C) The mean is 47 and the variance is 25.

    (D) The mean is 47 and the standard deviation is 2.

69. Consider the following diagram.

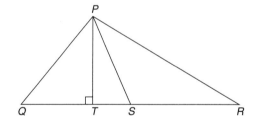

    Points Q, T, S, and R are collinear. $PS = 6$ and $QR = 14$. If we want to use an indirect proof in order to show that the area of $\triangle PQR$ is less than 42, which one of the following procedures would be best?

    (A) Demonstrate that $TS < QT$.

    (B) Determine the values of QT, TS, and SR.

    (C) Determine that the measure of $\angle QPR$ is greater than 90°.

    (D) Demonstrate that $PT < PS$.

70. When teaching measures of central tendencies, which type of data set would be used to best illustrate the application of the standard deviation value?

    (A) Data for which there is a large range value

    (B) Data for which there is a small range value

    (C) Data for which the difference between consecutive numbers varies

    (D) Data for which the median is greater than the mean

71. Let [3] represent all numbers congruent to 3 modulo 5. Which one of the following numbers is a member of [3] ?

    (A) −6   (C) −10

    (B) −8   (D) −12

72. Consider the following probability distribution.

X	2	4	6	8
P(X)	0.62	0.21	0.05	0.12

    What is the value of the variance to the nearest hundredth?

    (A) 11.98   (C) 4.16

    (B) 7.32   (D) 2.04

73. A ladder is leaning against the vertical side of a building. The angle of elevation is 33° and the bottom of the ladder is 16 feet from the bottom of the building. To the nearest tenth of a foot, what is the length of the ladder?

    (A) 19.1   (C) 29.4

    (B) 24.6   (D) 32.9

74. Assuming that the annual rate of interest is compounded continuously, at what interest rate to the nearest percent will $600 grow to $1800 in a period of five years?

    (A) 26%   (C) 22%

    (B) 24%   (D) 20%

75. Which of the following mutual processes does NOT fit in the "do-undo" mathematical operations?

(A) Addition-subtraction

(B) Multiplication-division

(C) Function-variable

(D) Exponentiation-logarithmic

76. Consider the following three statements.

The greatest common factor of 9 and 10 is 1. The greatest common factor of 16 and 17 is 1. The greatest common factor of 102 and 103 is 1. Which of the following conclusions would be valid by using the process of induction ?

(A) The product of any two consecutive numbers is an integer.

(B) The greatest common factor of any two integers is 1.

(C) The difference of any two integers is less than either integer.

(D) The greatest common factor of any two consecutive integers is 1.

77. Which quadrilateral(s) has (have) two pairs of congruent sides, such that each pair shares a common point?

(A) Only a trapezoid

(B) Only a kite

(C) Only a kite and a parallelogram

(D) Only a trapezoid and a parallelogram

78. In the following diagram, a regular pentagon is inscribed in a circle with center P. $\overline{PT}$ is an apothem.

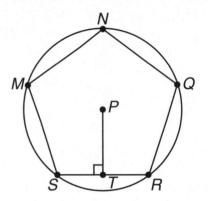

If $PT = 6$, what is the area of the circle to the nearest tenth?

(A) 141.4   (C) 164.2

(B) 153.6   (D) 172.8

79. A claim is made that given any two-digit integer whose units digit is 4, the number must be divisible by 3, 7, or 8. How many counterexamples are there to disprove this claim?

(A) 4   (C) 2

(B) 3   (D) 1

80. What is the main reason that most students do not gain deep reasoning skills on a long-division procedure?

(A) Because it is just a procedure rather than a theorem

(B) Because teachers present the concept in a procedural manner

(C) Because it is just an illustration of a mathematical concept

(F) Because students cannot understand the reasoning aspect of this procedure

81. What is the value of x in the equation $9^{x-3} = 0.4$?

(A) −1.92   (C) 1.08

(B) −0.42   (D) 2.58

82. Which one of the following statements is sufficient to prove that events M and N are dependent?

   (A) $P(M \mid N) = 1$

   (B) $P(M) + P(N) = 1$

   (C) $P(M) + P(N) < 1$

   (D) $P(M \mid N) = P(M)$

83. For which one of the following functions is the amplitude equal to 4 and the period equal to 3π?

   (A) $f(x) = -4 \sin\left(\dfrac{2}{3}x\right)$

   (B) $f(x) = 4 \sin\left(\dfrac{3}{2}x\right)$

   (C) $f(x) = \dfrac{1}{4} \sin\left(\dfrac{2}{3}x\right)$

   (D) $f(x) = -\dfrac{1}{4} \sin\left(\dfrac{3}{2}x\right)$

84. Given $\overrightarrow{AB} = 9\mathbf{i} + 4\mathbf{j}$, which one of the following vectors is parallel to $\overrightarrow{AB}$ and faces in the opposite direction?

   (A) $-4\mathbf{i} - 9\mathbf{j}$

   (B) $-22.5\mathbf{i} - 10\mathbf{j}$

   (C) $-18\mathbf{i} + 13\mathbf{j}$

   (D) $-13.5\mathbf{i} + 6\mathbf{j}$

85. In a jar of 12 marbles, three are red and nine are blue. Six marbles are drawn, one at a time, with replacement. What is the probability to the nearest hundredth that fewer than three of them are red?

   (A) 0.96   (C) 0.83

   (B) 0.89   (D) 0.76

86. If $y = \dfrac{2x - 7}{x + 4}$, what is the expression for dy/dx?

   (A) $\dfrac{1}{(x+4)^2}$ (C) $\dfrac{1}{x^2 + 16}$

   (B) $\dfrac{15}{(x+4)^2}$ (D) $\dfrac{15}{x^2 + 16}$

87. A study has shown that the measure of a person's reaction time is a function of his or her age. Carmine's age is 35 and his reaction time is 2.3 seconds. Carol's age is 30 and her reaction time is 1.9 seconds. Based on this data, a linear model is constructed. If Julia's age is 48 and her reaction time is 3.2 seconds, what is the percent error to the nearest tenth of one percent for her reaction time, based on the linear model?

   (A) 2.7%   (C) 3.7%

   (B) 3.2%   (D) 4.2%

88. The area of a rhombus is 240 square inches. The length of one diagonal is three times the length of the other diagonal. To the nearest tenth, what is the sum of the lengths of the diagonals?

   (A) 36.8   (C) 50.6

   (B) 43.7   (D) 57.5

89. What are the equations of the asymptotes for the curve whose equation is $\dfrac{(x-3)^2}{16} - \dfrac{y^2}{25} = 1$?

   (A) $y - 3 = \pm\dfrac{4}{5}x$ (C) $y - 3 = \pm\dfrac{5}{4}x$

   (B) $y = \pm\dfrac{4}{5}(x-3)$ (D) $y = \pm\dfrac{5}{4}(x-3)$

90. $\overrightarrow{EF} = 3\mathbf{i} - \mathbf{j}$ and $\overrightarrow{GH} = \mathbf{i} + 5\mathbf{j}$. To the nearest degree, what is the measure of the angle between $\overrightarrow{EF}$ and $\overrightarrow{GH}$?

   (A) 97°   (C) 87°

   (B) 93°   (D) 83°

Answer Key Practice Test 1

Number	Answer	Chapter	Competency
1	A	5	Functions
2	C	11	Measurement in Geometry
3	A	6	Linear and Quadratic Functions
4	A	16	Probability Concepts and Applications
5	D	9	Trigonometric and Circular Functions
6	B	11	Measurement in Geometry
7	C	13	Applications of Euclidean Geometry to Circles and Composite Figures
8	A	1	Real Number System
9	B	18	Mathematical Reasoning and Problem Solving
10	C	19	Mathematical Connections
11	C	10	Differential and Integral Calculus
12	C	14	Coordinate, Transformational, and Vector Geometry
13	D	12	Axioms, Properties, and Theorems of Euclidean Geometry
14	C	6	Linear and Quadratic Functions
15	D	5	Functions
16	B	4	Sequences and Series
17	C	3	Number Theory
18	D	7	Rational and Radical Functions
19	C	12	Axioms, Properties, and Theorems of Euclidean Geometry
20	D	19	Mathematical Connections
21	A	4	Sequences and Series
22	D	2	Complex Number System
23	B	1	Real Number System
24	B	16	Probability Concepts and Applications
25	C	13	Applications of Euclidean Geometry to Circles and Composite Figures
26	A	14	Coordinate, Transformational, and Vector Geometry
27	B	7	Rational and Radical Functions
28	A	9	Trigonometric and Circular Functions
29	D	14	Coordinate, Transformational, and Vector Geometry
30	B	19	Mathematical Connections

Number	Answer	Chapter	Competency
31	B	8	Exponential and Logarithmic Functions
32	D	5	Functions
33	B	12	Axioms, Properties, and Theorems of Euclidean Geometry
34	A	4	Sequences and Series
35	B	2	Complex Number System
36	C	17	Probability Distributions, Sampling, and Statistical Inference
37	B	12	Axioms, Properties, and Theorems of Euclidean Geometry
38	C	15	Graphical and Numerical Techniques to Analyze Data
39	B	13	Applications of Euclidean Geometry to Circles and Composite Figures
40	D	19	Mathematical Connections
41	C	6	Linear and Quadratic Functions
42	A	16	Probability Concepts and Applications
43	C	17	Probability Distributions, Sampling, and Statistical Inference
44	A	3	Number Theory
45	C	4	Sequences and Series
46	B	7	Rational and Radical Functions
47	C	15	Graphical and Numerical Techniques to Analyze Data
48	A	5	Functions
49	A	7	Rational and Radical Functions
50	C	19	Mathematical Connections
51	D	2	Complex Number System
52	C	8	Exponential and Logarithmic Functions
53	A	10	Differential and Integral Calculus
54	B	17	Probability Distributions, Sampling, and Statistical Inference
55	B	15	Graphical and Numerical Techniques to Analyze Data
56	C	8	Exponential and Logarithmic Functions
57	B	6	Linear and Quadratic Functions
58	D	10	Differential and Integral Calculus
59	C	6	Linear and Quadratic Functions
60	A	20	Mathematical Learning, Instruction, and Assessment
61	D	12	Axioms, Properties, and Theorems of Euclidean Geometry
62	B	7	Rational and Radical Functions
63	B	3	Number Theory
64	C	10	Differential and Integral Calculus
65	D	20	Mathematical Learning, Instruction, and Assessment
66	B	11	Measurement in Geometry

67	A	3	Number Theory
68	C	15	Graphical and Numerical Techniques to Analyze Data
69	D	18	Mathematical Reasoning and Problem Solving
70	C	20	Mathematical Learning, Instruction, and Assessment
71	D	3	Number Theory
72	C	17	Probability Distributions, Sampling, and Statistical Inference
73	A	9	Trigonometric and Circular Functions
74	C	4	Sequences and Series
75	C	20	Mathematical Learning, Instruction, and Assessment
76	D	18	Mathematical Reasoning and Problem Solving
77	B	11	Measurement in Geometry
78	D	13	Applications of Euclidean Geometry to Circles and Composite Figures
79	A	18	Mathematical Reasoning and Problem Solving
80	B	20	Mathematical Learning, Instruction, and Assessment
81	D	8	Exponential and Logarithmic Functions
82	A	16	Probability Concepts and Applications
83	A	9	Trigonometric and Circular Functions
84	B	2	Complex Number System
85	C	17	Probability Distributions, Sampling, and Statistical Inference
86	B	10	Differential and Integral Calculus
87	D	18	Mathematical Reasoning and Problem Solving
88	C	11	Measurement in Geometry
89	D	14	Coordinate, Transformational, and Vector Geometry
90	A	2	Complex Number System

Practice Test 1 Progress Chart

Real Number System

8	23

__/2

Complex Number System

22	35	51	84	90

__/5

Number Theory

17	44	63	67	71

__/5

Sequences and Series

16	21	34	45	74

__/5

Functions

1	15	32	48

__/4

Linear and Quadratic Functions

3	14	41	57	59

__/5

Rational and Radical Functions

18	27	46	49	62

__/5

Exponential and Logarithmic Functions

31	52	56	81

__/4

Trigonometric and Circular Functions

5	28	73	83

___/4

Differential and Integral Calculus

11	53	58	64	86

___/5

Measurement in Geometry

2	6	66	77	88

___/5

Axioms, Properties, and Theorems of Euclidean Geometry

13	19	33	37	61

___/5

Applications of Euclidean Geometry to Circles and Composite Figures

7	25	39	78

___/4

Coordinate, Transformational, and Vector Geometry

12	26	29	89

___/4

Graphical and Numerical Techniques to Analyze Data

38	47	55	68

___/4

Probability Concepts and Applications

4	24	42	82

___/4

Probability Distributions, Sampling, and Statistical Inference

36	43	54	72	85

___/5

Mathematical Reasoning and Problem Solving

9	69	76	79	87

___/5

Mathematical Connections

10	20	30	40	50

___/5

Mathematical Learning, Instruction, and Assessment

60	65	70	75	80

___5

Total

___/90

Detailed Solutions

1. (A)

$f(x)$ has a domain of all numbers that satisfy the inequality $2x^2 - 2 \neq 0$. Since $2x^2 - 2 = (2)(x-1)(x+1)$, the domain is all real numbers except 1 and -1. The domain of $g(x) = \dfrac{x-4}{(x-1)(x+1)}$ is also all real numbers except 1 and -1.

2. (C)

Since the area of the base is 169π, the radius is $\sqrt{169} = 13$. The radius, perpendicular height (h), and lateral height form a right triangle, so that $h^2 = 16^2 - 13^2 = 87$. Thus, $h = \sqrt{87} \approx 9.33$.

3. (A)

If an augmented matrix has a row of zeros, there are an infinite number of paired answers. One such example is the system $3x + 2y = 4$ and $6x + 4y = 8$. The initial augmented matrix is $\begin{bmatrix} 3 & 2 & | & 4 \\ 6 & 4 & | & 8 \end{bmatrix}$. Change the second row as follows: multiply the first row by -2 and add this number to the second row. The resulting augmented matrix is $\begin{bmatrix} 3 & 2 & | & 4 \\ 0 & 0 & | & 0 \end{bmatrix}$

4. (A)

There are 13 diamonds in a deck of cards, so the required probability is $\dfrac{(_{13}C_4)(_{39}C_1)}{_{52}C_5} \approx 0.011$.

5. (D)

In quadrant III, the sine ratio is negative and the tangent ratio is positive. With the given answer choices, only $(-5, -4)$ lies in the third quadrant.

6. (B)

When the large cube is sliced, there will be a total of 8 smaller cubes. Let s represent the length of one side of a smaller cube. Since the total surface area is 300, $(8)(6s^2) = 300$. Then $s^2 = 6.25$, so $s = 2.5$. Thus, the volume is $2.5^3 \approx 15.6$.

7. (C)

Since $UX = b$, the area of $TUXY$ is ab and the area of $UVWX$ is b^2. Thus, the area of $TVWY$ is the sum of these two pieces, which is $ab + b^2$.

8. (A)

The number $\sqrt{28}$ cannot be written as the quotient of two integers, and its value is approximately 5.29.

9. (B)

The second statement must be "This vase is on the shelf." Combined with the first statement, we can conclude that "This vase is expensive."

10. (C)

Use the formula $v = \dfrac{kt}{p}$, where v = volume, k = constant of variation, t = temperature (Kelvin), and p = pressure (kPa). Then $288 = \dfrac{k320}{180}$, so $k = 162$.

Thus, the new equation becomes $v = \dfrac{162(360)}{160}$, so $v = 364.5$

11. (C)

Rewrite the fraction as $\dfrac{(2x)(x-1)}{(x-1)(x^2+x+1)}$

$= \dfrac{2x}{x^2+x+1}$. Substitute $x=1$ to get the answer of $\dfrac{2}{3}$.

12. (C)

The vector $-4\mathbf{i} + 5\mathbf{j}$ means that we subtract 4 units in the x direction and add 5 units in the y direction. The point $(2,-1)$ becomes $(-2,4)$.

13. (D)

The triangle must contain two congruent acute (less than 90°) angles and one obtuse (greater than 90°) angle. Note that answer choice (A) is wrong because the sum of the angles exceeds 180°.

14. (C)

In the form $y = a(x-h)^2 + k$, the axis of symmetry is $x = h$. If $a < 0$, the parabola has a highest point.

15. (D)

The domain is {4, 6, 8} and the range is {0, 4}.

16. (B)

The amount after six years is $(\$3250)(1+\dfrac{0.03}{12})^{72}$ $\approx \$3890$.

17. (C)

The product of any two numbers equals the product of their greatest common factor and least common multiple. Let x represent the least common multiple. Then $(M)(N) = (g)(x)$, so $x = \dfrac{MN}{g}$.

18. (D)

By long division,

$$\dfrac{-6x^3 + 4x^2 - 1}{2x^2 + 1} = -3x + 2 + \dfrac{3x-3}{2x^2+1}.$$

The remainder is not used. Thus, the equation of the slant asymptote is $y = -3x + 2$.

19. (C)

Lines l_1 and l_2 are given as parallel and line l_3 is constructed so that it is parallel to and equidistant from lines l_1 and l_2. Line m serves as a transversal that is perpendicular to $l_1, l_2,$ and l_3.

20. (D)

$6.3(1.037)^{25} \approx 15.6$ billion

21. (A)

Let a represent the first term and d represent the common difference. Then $-2 = a + 9d$ and $26 = a + 29d$. Subtracting the first equation from the second equation leads to $28 = 20d$, so $d = 1.4$. By substitution, $-2 = a + (9)(1.4)$, which means that $a = -14.6$. Thus, the fourth term is $-14.6 + (3)(1.4) = -10.4$.

22. (D)

$(3+i)(-4+2i) = -12 + 2i + 2i^2 = -14 + 2i$, for which the conjugate is $-14 - 2i$.

23. (B)

The difference of x and w is written as $x - w$. Then a quotient involving y and $x - w$ means that a division operation is required. Thus, the answer is $\dfrac{y}{x - w}$.

24. (B)

The area of the circle is 16π and the area of the equilateral triangle is $\dfrac{20^2}{4}\sqrt{3} \approx 173.2$. The required probability is about $\dfrac{16\pi}{173.2} \approx 0.29$.

25. (C)

The area of the circle is 64π. Let A_s represent the area of sector PAB. Then $\dfrac{A_s}{64\pi} = \dfrac{72°}{360°} = \dfrac{1}{5}$.

So, $A_s = \dfrac{64\pi}{5} \approx 40.2$. The area of $\triangle PAB = \left[\dfrac{1}{2}\right](8)(8)(\sin 72°) \approx 30.4$. Thus, the area of the segment AB is approximately $40.2 - 30.4 = 9.8$.

26. (A)

The ratio of the areas from $\triangle XYZ$ to $\triangle TUV$ is $\left[\dfrac{3}{5}\right]^2 = \dfrac{9}{25}$. Let x represent the area of $\triangle XYZ$. Then $\dfrac{x}{30} = \dfrac{9}{25}$, so $x = 10.8$.

27. (B)

Squaring each side leads to $5x - 21 = x^2 - 6x + 9$, which simplifies to $x^2 - 11x + 30 = 0$. Then $(x - 5)(x - 6) = 0$, so the solutions are 5 and 6. Since both of these numbers satisfy the original equation, the sum of the solutions is 11.

28. (A)

$WT = 20$ and $OT = \sqrt{8^2 + 20^2} = \sqrt{464} \approx 21.54$.

Thus, $\sin\theta = \dfrac{-20}{21.54} \approx -0.93$.

29. (D)

When a point (x, y) is reflected across the line $y = -x$, the coordinates of its image become $(-y, -x)$. Thus, the pre-image of $(-3, 7)$ is $(-7, 3)$.

30. (B)

Here is how the tiles should appear.

	X	X	I	I	I
X	X²	X²	X	X	X
I	X	X	I	I	I
I	X	X	I	I	I
I	X	X	I	I	I
I	X	X	I	I	I
I	X	X	I	I	I

In this formation, the tiles in the row appear as either two labeled x^2 and three labeled x, or as two labeled x and three labeled as 1. If the rows and columns are switched, then the rows are labeled as follows: one labeled as x^2 and five labeled as x, or one labeled as x and five labeled as 1.

31. (B)

$\mathrm{Log}_4 P = x$ can be written as $4^x = 2^{2x} = P$, and $\log_8 Q = x$ can be written as $8^x = 2^{3x} = Q$. Thus, $\dfrac{Q}{P} = \dfrac{2^{3x}}{2^{2x}} = 2^x$.

32. (D)

The graph of an even function must be symmetric about the y-axis. Note that answer choice (B) is wrong, since the function may not be continuous at $x = 0$.

33. (B)

Since $\overline{DF}$ is an angle bisector, $\dfrac{12}{9} = \dfrac{DG}{15}$. Then $DG = \dfrac{180}{9} = 20$. Thus, the perimeter of $\triangle DEG$ is $12 + 9 + 15 + 20 = 56$.

34. (A)

The first term is 12 and the common ratio is 0.8. Thus, the sum of this infinite geometric sequence is $\dfrac{12}{1 - 0.8} = 60$.

35. (B)

The point $6 - 3i$ is located in the fourth quadrant in the complex number plane. The value of r is $\sqrt{6^2 + (-3)^2} = \sqrt{45} = 3\sqrt{5}$. The value of θ is $\tan^{-1}\left|-\dfrac{3}{6}\right| \approx 333°$.

36. (C)

The conditions for using the T-Test are the following: a) sample size under 30, b) normal distribution for the population, and c) the value of σ unknown. Note that answer choice (D) would not allow the use of either the T-Test or the Z-Test.

37. (B)

If two sides and a non-included angle of one triangle are congruent respectively to two sides and a non-included angle of a second triangle, the triangles need not be congruent.

38. (C)

The total weight of the oranges is $(36)(5.9) - (20)(5.5) = 102.4$ ounces. Thus, the mean weight of the oranges is $\dfrac{102.4}{16} = 6.4$ ounces.

39. (B)

$EA = 27$ and letting $x = GK$ and $2x = EG$, we can represent EK by $3x$. Then $(27)(15) = (3x)(2x) = 6x^2$. Then $x^2 = 67.5$, so $x \approx 8.2$.

40. (D)

The seating arrangements can be counted as follows: $6 \times 5 \times 4 \times 3 \times 2 \times 1 = 720$. Any one of the six people can be seated in a particular seat. However, when that seat is filled, only five people can be seated in the second seat and so on. Another way to solve this problem is $6! = 720$.

41. (C)

The sum of the zeros is given by $-\dfrac{32}{40} = -0.8$.

42. (A)

There are seven letters, including two s's and two o's. The total number of arrangements is $\dfrac{7!}{(2!)(2!)} = 1260$.

43. (C)

Press "Stat," scroll to "Tests," press 2, then enter 16 for μ_0, enter 17 for $\bar{x}$, enter 1.5 for $s_{\bar{x}}$, enter 20 for n, highlight $\mu \neq \mu_0$, then press "Calculate." The p value will be approximately 0.008, and since $0.008 < 0.01$, the claim is rejected.

44. (A)

The quantity $x - 4$ must be divisible by 7. If $2x = 120$, then $x = 60$. Thus, we note that $60 - 4 = 56$, which is divisible by 7.

45. (C)

$a_3 = 3 - (5)(-4) = 23$ and $a_4 = 23 - (5)(3) = 8$. Thus, $a_3 + a_4 = 31$.

46. (B)

Complex zeros of a polynomial function must appear in pairs.

47. (C)

The third quartile is the 15th number, so its value is $20.5 + \left(\dfrac{15 - 8}{12}\right)(4) = 22.8\overline{3}$.

48. (A)

In a one-to-one function, each y value corresponds to only one x value. The function $f(x) = x^2 + 5x + 4$ contains, as an example, both $(-1, 0)$ and $(-4, 0)$.

49. (A)

The three zeros of $f(x)$ are -1, $\dfrac{1}{2}$, and 6. When $x < -1$, each of the three factors of $f(x)$ are negative, so their product is negative. When $-1 < x < \dfrac{1}{2}$, the first factor is positive and the other two factors are negative, so their product is positive. When $\dfrac{1}{2} < x < 6$, the first two factors are positive and the third factor is negative, so their product is negative. Finally, when $x > 6$, each of the three factors are positive, so their product is positive. Thus, the regions for which $f(x) > 0$ are $-1 < x < \dfrac{1}{2}$ and $x > 6$.

50. (C)

Find the vertex using the expression $\dfrac{-b}{2a}$.

$\dfrac{-b}{2a} = \dfrac{1}{2(-.064)} \approx 7.8$ million. Place 7.8 (million)

into the formula to find the units sold. $F(x) = -.064(7.8)^2 + 7.8 + 12 = 15.9$ The toy company will spend \$7.8 million in advertising to reach a peak sales volume of 15.9 million dolls.

51. (D)

The angle associated with $8i$ is $90°$, so the sixth roots are of the form

$(\sqrt[6]{8})\left[\cos\left(\dfrac{90°}{6} + \dfrac{360°k}{6}\right) + i\sin\left(\dfrac{90°}{6} + \dfrac{360°k}{6}\right)\right]$, where

$k = 0, 1, 2, 3, 4,$ and 5. For $k = 5$, $\left(\dfrac{90°}{6} + \dfrac{360°k}{6}\right)$ has a value of $315°$.

52. (C)

Let P represent the initial amount five years ago.

Then $\$12,000 = (P)\left(1 + \dfrac{0.09}{4}\right)^{(5)(4)} = (P)(1.0225)^{20}$.

Thus, $P = \dfrac{\$12,000}{(1.0225)^{20}} \approx \$7690$.

53. (A)

As x approaches -1 from the left, the limit of $f(x)$ is 6. As x approaches -1 from the right, the limit of $f(x)$ is 9. Note that a function need not be defined at a particular point in order for the limit to exist.

54. (B)

Your TI−83 calculator screen should read as follows. "normalcdf (4.8, 1×10^{99}, 4.5, 0.2)." By pressing "Enter," the result is approximately 6.7%.

55. (B)

When the left tail of a boxplot is longer than its right tail, the distribution is negatively skewed.

56. (C)

The amount of grams that remain after nine hours is given by the expression $(60)\left(\dfrac{1}{2}\right)^{9/12} \approx 36$. Thus, the number of grams that had decayed is $60 - 36 = 24$.

57. (B)

Let x represent Diane's speed in miles per hour and let $x + 1$ represent Ralph's speed in miles per hour. Then $(2x)^2 + (2x+2)^2 = 14^2$. This equation simplifies to $8x^2 + 8x - 192 = 0$ or $x^2 + x - 24 = 0$. Using the quadratic formula, the positive value for x is approximately 4.4. Thus, Diane's distance in two hours is about 8.8 miles.

58. (D)

Using the definition of the average rate of change, $\dfrac{11 - g(-2)}{2 - (-2)} = 5$. This equation simplifies to $11 - g(-2) = 20$. Thus, $g(-2) = -9$.

59. (C)

Let x represent Phil's time, if he were working alone. Then $\dfrac{16}{24} + \dfrac{16}{x} = 1$. After reducing $\dfrac{16}{24}$ to $\dfrac{2}{3}$, this equation can be simplified to $2x + 48 = 3x$. Thus, $x = 48$ minutes.

60. (A)

Let m be an arbitrary positive integer. Then multiplying the numbers 3, 4, and 5 by m results in $3m$, $4m$, and $5m$. Applying the Pythagorean Theorem to these numbers gives $(5m)^2 = (3m)^2 + (4m)^2$, which leads to $25m^2 = 9m^2 + 16m^2$, or more simply, $25 = 9 + 16$. The result indicates that the generated numbers satisfy the Pythagorean theorem.

61. (D)

The ratio of the areas equals the square of the ratio of any pair of corresponding sides, which equals $\left(\dfrac{4}{3}\right)^2 = \dfrac{16}{9}$. Let x represent the area of $\triangle PQR$. Then $\dfrac{x}{72} = \dfrac{16}{9}$, so $x = 128$.

62. (B)

The leading coefficient of the function is negative and the degree of the function is even. Thus, as x approaches either infinity or negative infinity, $h(x)$ approaches negative infinity.

63. (B)

The commutative property of multiplication does not necessarily apply to matrices. For example, let
$$\mathbf{A} = \begin{bmatrix} 3 & 1 \\ 2 & 5 \end{bmatrix} \text{ and } \mathbf{B} = \begin{bmatrix} 1 & 0 \\ 4 & 2 \end{bmatrix}$$

Then $\mathbf{A} \times \mathbf{B} =$
$$\begin{bmatrix} (3)(1) + (1)(4) & (3)(0) + (1)(2) \\ (2)(1) + (5)(4) & (2)(0) + (5)(2) \end{bmatrix} = \begin{bmatrix} 7 & 2 \\ 22 & 10 \end{bmatrix}$$

But $\mathbf{B} \times \mathbf{A} =$
$$\begin{bmatrix} (1)(3) + (0)(2) & (1)(1) + (0)(5) \\ (4)(3) + (2)(2) & (4)(1) + (2)(5) \end{bmatrix} = \begin{bmatrix} 3 & 1 \\ 16 & 14 \end{bmatrix}$$

64. (C)

When $x = 2$, $f(x) = (-2)(2^3) + (3)(2) = -10$. So the point $(2, -10)$ lies on the tangent line. The slope of the tangent line is given by the expression for the first derivative, namely $-6x^2 + 3$. When $x = 2$, this slope is -21; so the equation of the tangent line is in the form $y = -21x + b$. Substituting $(2, -10)$ into $y = -21x + b$, we get $-10 = -42 + b$. Then $b = 32$. The equation of the tangent line is $y = -21x + 32$, which means that the y-intercept is 32.

65. (D)

Whenever an inequality contains a variable term that is negative, the operations of multiplication or division requires that the order of inequality be reversed.

66. (B)

Using Heron's formula, the area is $\sqrt{(11)(7)(3)(1)} \approx 15.2$.

67. (A)

The matrix will have no inverse if $-3n - (6)(2) = 0$. Thus, $n = -4$.

68. (C)

If a constant is added to or subtracted from a group of individual numbers, the mean is affected in the same way. However, the standard deviation and the variance remain unchanged.

69. (D)

The area of $\triangle PQR$ is one-half the product of PT and QR. By showing that $PT < PS$, the area of $\triangle PQR$ must be less than $\left(\dfrac{1}{2}\right)(6)(14) = 42$.

70. (C)

When the variation of a set of data is inconsistent, then the application of the standard deviation can be best illustrated.

71. (D)

A member of [3] modulo 5 must be of the form $5n + 3$, where n is an integer. The equation $5n + 3 = -12$ does have an integer solution of -3, whereas the other answer choices do not have an integer solution.

72. (C)

The expected value of X is $(2)(0.62) + (4)(0.21) + (6)(0.05) + (8)(0.12) = 3.34$. Then the variance of $X = (4)(0.62) + (16)(0.21) + (36)(0.05) + (64)(0.12) - (3.34)^2 \approx 4.16$.

73. (A)

Let x represent the length of the ladder. Then $\cos 33° = \dfrac{16}{x}$. Thus, $x = \dfrac{16}{\cos 33°} \approx 19.1$.

74. (C)

Let r represent the rate. Then $\$1800 = (\$600)(e^{5r})$ which simplifies to $3 = e^{5r}$. Then $\ln 3 \approx 1.0986 = 5r$, so $r \approx 22\%$.

75. (C)

The relationship between a function and a variable is a "dependent – independent" association rather than a math operation.

76. (D)

The three given statements demonstrate that the greatest common factor of any two consecutive integers is 1.

77. (B)

Only the kite has two pairs of congruent sides, for which each pair shares a common point.

78. (D)

Connect points P and S to form triangle PST, with a right angle at T. The measure of $\angle SPT = (0.1)(360°) = 36°$. Then $\cos 36° = \dfrac{6}{PS}$, so $PS \approx 7.416$. Thus, the area of the circle is about $(\pi)(7.416^2) \approx 172.8$.

79. (A)

The four counterexamples are 34, 44, 74, and 94.

80. (B)

Most teachers avoid tackling this method in a reasoning way. Students do have sufficient prior knowledge needed to analyze the procedure in the context of math rules and principles.

81. (D)

Rewrite by using log base 10. Then the equation becomes $(x-3)(\log_{10} 9) = \log_{10} 0.4$. So, $x - 3 = \dfrac{\log_{10} 0.4}{\log_{10} 9} \approx -0.42$. Thus, $x = 2.58$.

82. (A)

If $P(M \mid N) = 1$, then the probability of M occurring is a certainty, given that N has occurred. This implies that the two events are dependent.

83. (A)

For the function $f(x) = A \sin Bx$, the amplitude equals $|A|$ and the period equals $\dfrac{2\pi}{B}$. In answer choice (A), $|-4| = 4$ and $\dfrac{2\pi}{2/3} = 3\pi$.

84. (B)

A vector that is parallel to and faces in the opposite direction of $9\mathbf{i} + 4\mathbf{j}$ must be of the form (k) $(9\mathbf{i} + 4\mathbf{j})$, where $k < 0$. If $k = -2.5$, then $(k)(9\mathbf{i} + 4\mathbf{j}) = -22.5i - 10j$.

85. (C)

The phrase "fewer than three" means "at most two." Your TI-83 calculator screen should read as binomcdf $(6, 0.25, 2) \approx 0.83$.

86. (B)

$$dy/dx = \frac{(x+4)(2) - (2x-7)(1)}{(x+4)^2} =$$

$$\frac{2x+8-2x+7}{(x+4)^2} = \frac{15}{(x+4)^2}.$$

87. (D)

Letting x represent age (in years) and y represent reaction time (in seconds), the two given points are (35, 2.3) and (30, 1.9). The slope of the linear model is $\dfrac{2.3 - 1.9}{35 - 30} = 0.08$. Substituting (30, 1.9) into $y = 0.08x + b$, we find that $b = -0.5$. The linear model is $y = 0.08x - 0.5$. Julia's age is 48, so her predicted reaction time is $(0.08)(48) - 0.5 = 3.34$ seconds. Since her actual reaction time is 3.2 seconds, the error is $\left| \dfrac{3.2 - 3.34}{3.34} \right| \times 100\% \approx 4.2\%$.

88. (C)

Let x and $3x$ represent the lengths of the diagonals. Then, $\left(\dfrac{1}{2}\right)(x)(3x) = 240$. This equation simplifies to $x^2 = 160$, so $x \approx 12.65$ and $3x \approx 37.95$. Thus, their sum is approximately 50.6.

89. (D)

For the general hyperbola $\dfrac{(x-h)^2}{a^2} - \dfrac{(y-k)^2}{b^2} = 1$, the equations of the asymptotes are $y - k = \pm\dfrac{b}{a}(x-h)$. In this example, $k = 0$, $h = 3$, $a = 4$, and $b = 5$. Thus, the equations of the asymptotes are $y = \pm\dfrac{5}{4}(x-3)$.

90. (A)

$(3\mathbf{i} - \mathbf{j}) \bullet (\mathbf{i} + 5\mathbf{j}) = (3)(1) + (-1)(5) = -2$.

Also, $(|3\mathbf{i} - \mathbf{j}|)(|\mathbf{i} + 5\mathbf{j}|) = (\sqrt{10})(\sqrt{26}) = \sqrt{260}$.

Then $\theta = \cos^{-1}\left(\dfrac{-2}{\sqrt{260}}\right) \approx 97°$.

TExES

Mathematics (135)

Practice Test 2

Summary of Formulas for TExES 135 Mathematics

ALGEBRA

The imaginary number $i = \sqrt{-1}$ and $i^2 = -1$.

The inverse of matrix A is denoted as A^{-1}.

$A = P\left(1 + \dfrac{r}{n}\right)^{nt}$ is used for compound interest, where A = final value, P = principal, r = interest rate, t = term, and n = number of divisions within the term.

$[x] = n$ is called the greatest integer function, where n is the integer such that $n \leq x < n + 1$.

TRIGONOMETRY

Formulas refer to the triangle shown in Figure I.

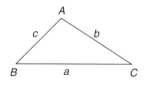

Figure I

Law of Sines: $\dfrac{\sin A}{a} = \dfrac{\sin B}{b} = \dfrac{\sin C}{c}$

Law of Cosines: $c^2 = a^2 + b^2 - (2ab)(\cos C)$

$b^2 = a^2 + c^2 - (2ac)(\cos B)$

$a^2 = b^2 + c^2 - (2bc)(\cos A)$

PROBABILITY

$p(A \text{ or } B) = p(A) + p(B) - p(A \& B)$

$p(A \& B) = p(A) \cdot p(B|A) = p(B) \cdot (A|B)$

CALCULUS

The first derivative of $f(x)$ is denoted as $f'(x)$ or $\dfrac{dy}{dx}$.

The second derivative of $f(x)$ is denoted as $f''(x)$ or $\dfrac{d^2 y}{dx^2}$.

GEOMETRY

Congruent angles or congruent sides are denoted by an identical number of slash marks, as shown in Figures II and III.

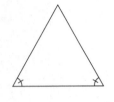

Figure II

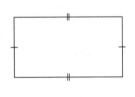

Figure III

Parallel sides are denoted by an identical number of arrowheads, as shown in Figure IV.

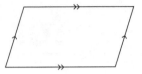

Figure IV

Circumference of a circle $= 2\pi r$.

Formulas

Description	Formula
Areas	
Circle	πr^2
Triangle	$\left(\dfrac{1}{2}\right)(\text{base})(\text{height})$
Rhombus	$\left(\dfrac{1}{2}\right)(\text{diagonal 1})(\text{diagonal 2})$
Trapezoid	$\left(\dfrac{1}{2}\right)(\text{height})(\text{base 1} + \text{base 2})$
Surface Areas	
Cylinder (lateral)	$2\pi rh$
Sphere	$(4\pi)(\text{radius squared})$
Volume	
Cylinder	$(\text{area of base})(\text{height})$
Sphere	$\left(\dfrac{4}{3}\pi\right)(\text{radius cubed})$
Cone	$\left(\dfrac{1}{3}\right)(\text{area of base})(\text{height})$
Prism	$(\text{area of base})(\text{height})$

Answer Sheet

1. Ⓐ Ⓑ Ⓒ Ⓓ   22. Ⓐ Ⓑ Ⓒ Ⓓ   43. Ⓐ Ⓑ Ⓒ Ⓓ   64. Ⓐ Ⓑ Ⓒ Ⓓ   85. Ⓐ Ⓑ Ⓒ Ⓓ
2. Ⓐ Ⓑ Ⓒ Ⓓ   23. Ⓐ Ⓑ Ⓒ Ⓓ   44. Ⓐ Ⓑ Ⓒ Ⓓ   65. Ⓐ Ⓑ Ⓒ Ⓓ   86. Ⓐ Ⓑ Ⓒ Ⓓ
3. Ⓐ Ⓑ Ⓒ Ⓓ   24. Ⓐ Ⓑ Ⓒ Ⓓ   45. Ⓐ Ⓑ Ⓒ Ⓓ   66. Ⓐ Ⓑ Ⓒ Ⓓ   87. Ⓐ Ⓑ Ⓒ Ⓓ
4. Ⓐ Ⓑ Ⓒ Ⓓ   25. Ⓐ Ⓑ Ⓒ Ⓓ   46. Ⓐ Ⓑ Ⓒ Ⓓ   67. Ⓐ Ⓑ Ⓒ Ⓓ   88. Ⓐ Ⓑ Ⓒ Ⓓ
5. Ⓐ Ⓑ Ⓒ Ⓓ   26. Ⓐ Ⓑ Ⓒ Ⓓ   47. Ⓐ Ⓑ Ⓒ Ⓓ   68. Ⓐ Ⓑ Ⓒ Ⓓ   89. Ⓐ Ⓑ Ⓒ Ⓓ
6. Ⓐ Ⓑ Ⓒ Ⓓ   27. Ⓐ Ⓑ Ⓒ Ⓓ   48. Ⓐ Ⓑ Ⓒ Ⓓ   69. Ⓐ Ⓑ Ⓒ Ⓓ   90. Ⓐ Ⓑ Ⓒ Ⓓ
7. Ⓐ Ⓑ Ⓒ Ⓓ   28. Ⓐ Ⓑ Ⓒ Ⓓ   49. Ⓐ Ⓑ Ⓒ Ⓓ   70. Ⓐ Ⓑ Ⓒ Ⓓ
8. Ⓐ Ⓑ Ⓒ Ⓓ   29. Ⓐ Ⓑ Ⓒ Ⓓ   50. Ⓐ Ⓑ Ⓒ Ⓓ   71. Ⓐ Ⓑ Ⓒ Ⓓ
9. Ⓐ Ⓑ Ⓒ Ⓓ   30. Ⓐ Ⓑ Ⓒ Ⓓ   51. Ⓐ Ⓑ Ⓒ Ⓓ   72. Ⓐ Ⓑ Ⓒ Ⓓ
10. Ⓐ Ⓑ Ⓒ Ⓓ   31. Ⓐ Ⓑ Ⓒ Ⓓ   52. Ⓐ Ⓑ Ⓒ Ⓓ   73. Ⓐ Ⓑ Ⓒ Ⓓ
11. Ⓐ Ⓑ Ⓒ Ⓓ   32. Ⓐ Ⓑ Ⓒ Ⓓ   53. Ⓐ Ⓑ Ⓒ Ⓓ   74. Ⓐ Ⓑ Ⓒ Ⓓ
12. Ⓐ Ⓑ Ⓒ Ⓓ   33. Ⓐ Ⓑ Ⓒ Ⓓ   54. Ⓐ Ⓑ Ⓒ Ⓓ   75. Ⓐ Ⓑ Ⓒ Ⓓ
13. Ⓐ Ⓑ Ⓒ Ⓓ   34. Ⓐ Ⓑ Ⓒ Ⓓ   55. Ⓐ Ⓑ Ⓒ Ⓓ   76. Ⓐ Ⓑ Ⓒ Ⓓ
14. Ⓐ Ⓑ Ⓒ Ⓓ   35. Ⓐ Ⓑ Ⓒ Ⓓ   56. Ⓐ Ⓑ Ⓒ Ⓓ   77. Ⓐ Ⓑ Ⓒ Ⓓ
15. Ⓐ Ⓑ Ⓒ Ⓓ   36. Ⓐ Ⓑ Ⓒ Ⓓ   57. Ⓐ Ⓑ Ⓒ Ⓓ   78. Ⓐ Ⓑ Ⓒ Ⓓ
16. Ⓐ Ⓑ Ⓒ Ⓓ   37. Ⓐ Ⓑ Ⓒ Ⓓ   58. Ⓐ Ⓑ Ⓒ Ⓓ   79. Ⓐ Ⓑ Ⓒ Ⓓ
17. Ⓐ Ⓑ Ⓒ Ⓓ   38. Ⓐ Ⓑ Ⓒ Ⓓ   59. Ⓐ Ⓑ Ⓒ Ⓓ   80. Ⓐ Ⓑ Ⓒ Ⓓ
18. Ⓐ Ⓑ Ⓒ Ⓓ   39. Ⓐ Ⓑ Ⓒ Ⓓ   60. Ⓐ Ⓑ Ⓒ Ⓓ   81. Ⓐ Ⓑ Ⓒ Ⓓ
19. Ⓐ Ⓑ Ⓒ Ⓓ   40. Ⓐ Ⓑ Ⓒ Ⓓ   61. Ⓐ Ⓑ Ⓒ Ⓓ   82. Ⓐ Ⓑ Ⓒ Ⓓ
20. Ⓐ Ⓑ Ⓒ Ⓓ   41. Ⓐ Ⓑ Ⓒ Ⓓ   62. Ⓐ Ⓑ Ⓒ Ⓓ   83. Ⓐ Ⓑ Ⓒ Ⓓ
21. Ⓐ Ⓑ Ⓒ Ⓓ   42. Ⓐ Ⓑ Ⓒ Ⓓ   63. Ⓐ Ⓑ Ⓒ Ⓓ   84. Ⓐ Ⓑ Ⓒ Ⓓ

TExES Mathematics 135
Practice Test 2

TIME: 5 hours
90 questions

> **Directions: Read each item and select the best response.**

1. Suppose $f(x)$ is a one-to-one function that is neither even nor odd. Which one of the following could represent $f(x)$?

    (A) $x^2 - 8$

    (B) $10 - 3x$

    (C) $2x^4 + x^2 + 1$

    (D) $x^3 - 2x^2 + x$

2. An experiment consists of rolling a seven-sided die twice. The faces of the die are numbered 1, 2, 3, 4, 5, 6, 7. The event of getting an odd number on both rolls contains how many different outcomes?

    (A) 49

    (B) 16

    (C) 14

    (D) 8

3. The figure below shows two intersecting chords in circle P.

    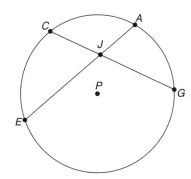

    $AJ = 5$, $JE = 18$, and $AJ < CJ < JG$. If each of CJ and JG is an integer, which one of the following could represent the length of $\overline{CJ}$?

    (A) 6

    (B) 8

    (C) 10

    (D) 15

4. The polar coordinates of the complex number Z are $(8, 120°)$. Which one of the following represents Z in rectangular coordinate form?

    (A) $4 - 4i\sqrt{3}$

    (B) $4\sqrt{3} + 4i$

    (C) $-4\sqrt{3} - 4i$

    (D) $-4 + 4i\sqrt{3}$

5. Which equation represents the graph of an ellipse that has a vertical major axis of length 12?

    (A) $\dfrac{x^2}{16} + \dfrac{y^2}{36} = 1$

    (B) $\dfrac{x^2}{36} + \dfrac{y^2}{16} = 1$

    (C) $\dfrac{x^2}{144} + \dfrac{y^2}{64} = 1$

    (D) $\dfrac{x^2}{64} + \dfrac{y^2}{144} = 1$

6. Rectangle $CDEF$ is similar to rectangle $GHJK$, as shown below.

    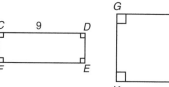

    If $\dfrac{GH}{CD} = \dfrac{10}{3}$, what is the area of rectangle $GHJK$?

    (A) 360

    (B) 300

    (C) 270

    (D) 240

7. Look at the following four diagrams consisting of unit squares.

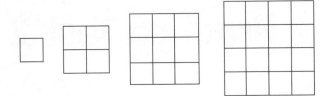

If this pattern continues, how many more unit squares will there be in the 20th diagram than in the tenth diagram?

(A) 100

(C) 200

(B) 150

(D) 300

8. Seven cards are drawn from a deck, one at a time, with replacement. What is the probability to the nearest hundredth of drawing at most three hearts?

(A) 0.76

(C) 0.93

(B) 0.85

(D) 0.98

9. Mrs. Robertson teaches a class of ten girls and five boys. She puts each child's name on a piece of paper before placing them in a jar. If she randomly selects four of these, one at a time with no replacement, what is the probability that she selects the names of three girls and one boy?

(A) $\dfrac{3}{50}$

(C) $\dfrac{24}{85}$

(B) $\dfrac{8}{81}$

(D) $\dfrac{40}{91}$

10. Which shortcut could a student use to multiply 48 by 52 using mental math?

(A) the sum of cubes

(B) the difference of cubes

(C) the sum of squares

(D) the difference of squares

11. On a certain national standardized test, the mean score is 200 and the standard deviation is 15. Assuming a normal distribution, and using the continuity correction factor, what percent of the test takers score between 182 and 209, inclusive? Figure to the nearest tenth of one percent.

(A) 0.63

(C) 0.55

(B) 0.59

(D) 0.51

12. What is the polar form for the value of $(4 - i)^4$?

(A) $(289)(\cos 236° + i\sin 236°)$

(B) $(\sqrt[4]{17})(\cos 236° + i\sin 236°)$

(C) $(\sqrt[4]{17})(\cos 304° + i\sin 304°)$

(D) $(289)(\cos 304° + i\sin 304°)$

13. The figure below shows a part of the graph of $f(x) = -x^2 + 16$ and triangle ABC.

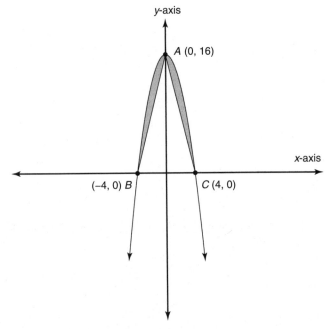

What is the area of the shaded region?

(A) $8.\overline{6}$

(C) $17.\overline{3}$

(B) $10.\overline{6}$

(D) $21.\overline{3}$

14. In the town of Branchville, the population has been growing at an exponential rate. Ten years ago, the population was 1200. Today, the population is 9000. What is the annual rate of growth figured to the nearest tenth of one percent?

(A) 12.8%   (C) 20.1%

(B) 16.4%   (D) 23.7%

15. A function $g(x)$ is created by using these four steps.

Step 1: Multiply 2 by a number x. Step 2: Subtract five. Step 3: Take the square root. Step 4: Add one half. Which one of the following numbers belongs to the range of $g(x)$?

(A) $\dfrac{3}{4}$ (C) $-\dfrac{1}{3}$

(B) $\dfrac{2}{5}$ (D) -1

16. Which geometric sequence has a sum of 18.75?

(A) 15, 3, 0.6, 0.12,….

(B) 16, 2, $\dfrac{1}{4}$, $\dfrac{1}{32}$,….

(C) 17, 1.7, 0.17, 0.017, ….

(D) 17, $\dfrac{1}{17}$, $\dfrac{1}{289}$, $\dfrac{1}{4913}$,….

17. A polynomial function of degree six has a triple real zero and a complex zero of $5 + i$. Which statement is true?

(A) There are no other complex zeros.

(B) The only other complex zero is $5 - i$.

(C) There are two other complex zeros, including $5 - i$.

(D) The only other complex zero is $-5 - i$.

18. What is the median for the following distribution?

Class	Frequency
30 − 34	5
35 − 39	4
40 − 44	10
45 − 49	6

(A) 42.75   (C) 41.5

(B) 42.5   (D) 41.25

19. If $18 \equiv x \pmod 4$, then which one of the following could represent the value of $x + 1$?

(A) 4   (C) -1

(B) 2   (D) -3

20. Two local banks advertise their respective compounding interest rates. One compounds interest monthly while the other compounds interest continuously. If $1000 is invested in each bank at 4.3%, what will be the difference in investments after one year?

(A) $0.08   (C) $8.00

(B) $0.80   (D) $80.00

21. An ordinary six-sided die is rolled. What is the probability to the nearest hundredth that the first time that a "2" appears is on the fifth roll?

(A) 0.14   (C) 0.10

(B) 0.12   (D) 0.08

22. With respect to $f(x) = \sin x$, the graph of $y = \sin(Bx - C)$ represents a phase shift of π units to the right. If the period of $y = \sin(Bx - C)$ is 4π, what is the value of C?

(A) 2π (C) $\dfrac{\pi}{2}$

(B) π (D) $\dfrac{\pi}{4}$

23. Suppose X represents a set of ten individual numbers. Each number is then multiplied by four then subtracted by two. This new set of ten individual numbers is represented by Y. The variance of set Y is 9. What is the variance of set X?

(A) $\dfrac{1}{16}$ (C) $\dfrac{4}{9}$

(B) $\dfrac{1}{4}$ (D) $\dfrac{9}{16}$

24. For which one of the following would the normal distribution <u>not</u> be a good approximation to the binomial distribution?

    (A) $n = 200, p = 0.90$

    (B) $n = 300, p = 0.99$

    (C) $n = 400, p = 0.40$

    (D) $n = 500, p = 0.15$

25. Triangle TUV is acute and isosceles. If the measure of $\angle T$ is 42°, what conclusion can be reached about the measure of $\angle U$?

    (A) It must be 42°

    (B) It may be either 42° or 69°

    (C) It must be 69°

    (D) It must be more than 90°

26. What is the value of $\lim_{x \to -2} \dfrac{4x^2 + 3x - 10}{x + 2}$?

    (A) 4   (C) -13

    (B) 0   (D) -16

27. If $h(x) = \sqrt{\dfrac{3x - 2}{5}}$, which one of the following represents $h^{-1}(x)$?

    (A) $\dfrac{5x^2 - 3}{2}$ (C) $\dfrac{2x^2 - 5}{3}$

    (B) $\dfrac{5x^2 + 2}{3}$ (D) $\dfrac{2x^2 + 3}{5}$

28. Which statement shows <u>both</u> the Commutative Law and Associative Law of Multiplication?

    (A) $(6 + 4) \times 2 = 6 \times 2 + 4 \times 2$

    (B) $(6 \times 4) \times 2 = 6 \times (2 \times 4)$

    (C) $(6 + 4) + 2 = 6 + (2 + 4)$

    (D) $(6 \times 4) \div 2 = 6 \times (4 \div 2)$

29. Two cones are similar and the volume of the smaller cone is 54 cubic meters. If the ratio of their areas is $\dfrac{9}{25}$, what is the volume of the larger cone?

    (A) 100 cubic meters

    (B) 150 cubic meters

    (C) 200 cubic meters

    (D) 250 cubic meters

30. The Texas General Land Office was trying to assess the relationship between temperature and beach attendance. The office compiled a table showing attendance during a ten-day period at a Galveston beach and a recording of the 2:00 PM temperature each day.

Attendance (in 000's)	Temperature (F°)
42	81
54	89
33	71
69	91
72	93
59	84
54	79
60	85
38	71
43	77

    There were no holidays during this period that would skew data. What is r, the correlation coefficient, for this data?

    (A) 0.96   (C) 0.87

    (B) 0.91   (D) 0.79

31. Consider the following diagram.

What is the value of QR to the nearest tenth?

(A) 37.6   (C) 35.4

(B) 36.5   (D) 34.3

32. Given that $\begin{pmatrix} 0 & 4 \\ 5 & 0 \end{pmatrix} \times \begin{pmatrix} a & b \\ c & d \end{pmatrix} = \begin{pmatrix} 8 & 12 \\ 40 & 20 \end{pmatrix}$, what is the value of $a+b-c-d$?

(A) 5   (C) 13

(B) 7   (D) 17

33. The graph of $g(x) = \begin{cases} \dfrac{1}{x-1}, & \text{if } 1 < x \le 5 \\ -x-1, & \text{if } x < -1 \end{cases}$ is shown below.

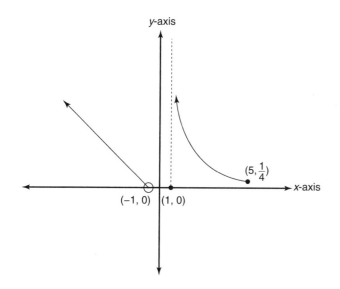

At which x value(s) does $\lim g(x)$ <u>not</u> exist?

(A) Only at -1 (C) Only at 1

(B) Only at -2 (D) Only at 1 and -1

34. Tonya claims that any decimal number that shows a pattern must be rational. Which one of the following numbers illustrates an exception to her claim?

(A) π (C) $0.\overline{65}$

(B) $2.13\overline{8}$ (D) $0.13113111311113....$

35. What is the simplest form of a unit vector in the <u>opposite</u> direction of $-3\mathbf{i} + 4\mathbf{j}$?

(A) $-\dfrac{3}{7}\mathbf{i} + \dfrac{4}{7}\mathbf{j}$ (C) $\dfrac{3}{7}\mathbf{i} - \dfrac{4}{7}\mathbf{j}$

(B) $-\dfrac{3}{5}\mathbf{i} + \dfrac{4}{5}\mathbf{j}$ (D) $\dfrac{3}{5}\mathbf{i} - \dfrac{4}{5}\mathbf{j}$

36. Look at the following boxplot:

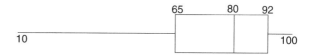

Which statement is completely correct?

(A) The distribution is positively skewed and the range is 90.

(B) The distribution is negatively skewed and the third quartile is 92.

(C) The distribution is positively skewed and the first quartile is 10.

(D) The distribution is negatively skewed and the mean is 80.

37. A radioactive substance decays exponentially with time. After a period of eight hours, 50% of the initial amount has decayed. If 20 grams of this substance remains after ten hours, how many grams of this substance were there initially? (Nearest tenth)

(A) 34.8   (C) 47.6

(B) 41.2   (D) 53.4

38. Which function has a single discontinuity at $x = 4$?

(A) $f(x) = \dfrac{x^2 + x + 4}{x - 4}$

(B) $g(x) = \dfrac{x^2 + x + 2}{(x)(x-4)}$

(C) $h(x) = \dfrac{(x-4)(x+4)}{x+2}$

(D) $k(x) = \dfrac{(x-4)}{(x+2)(x+4)}$

39. A report in a national journal claims that people travel, on average, no more than 200 miles per week An independent study of 100 people revealed that the mean number of miles of travel per week was 206 miles, with a standard deviation of 30 miles. At the 1% level of significance, which of the following is completely correct?

(A) The p value is approximately 0.023 and the claim cannot be rejected.

(B) The p value is approximately 0.023 and the claim must be rejected.

(C) The p value is approximately 0.033 and the claim cannot be rejected.

(D) The p value is approximately 0.033 and the claim must be rejected.

40. Skeeball is a game that combines bowling and shooting skills. The player rolls a ball that lands into one of several concentric circular gutters that resemble an archery target, as shown below.

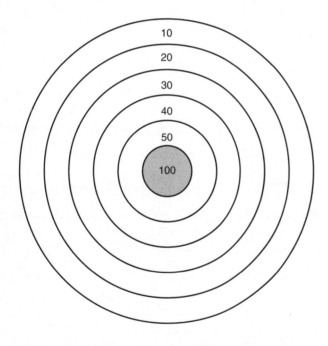

The radius of each ring of the target is 4" larger than the next smallest ring and the bull's eye is 6" across. What is the probability, to the nearest hundredth, of rolling a bull's eye?

(A) 0.16   (C) 0.02

(B) 0.05   (D) 0.01

41. The expression $(-0.8)^{-5}$ is equivalent to which one of the following?

(A) -0.8 raised to the power of 5

(B) -0.8 raised to the reciprocal of -5

(C) the reciprocal of -0.8 raised to the power of 5

(D) the reciprocal of -0.8 raised to the power of -5

42. If $f(x) = -x^2 + x$ and $g(x) = x^3$, what is the value of $g[f(-2)]$?

(A) -216 (C) 8

(B) -56 (D) 48

43. If $C = \log_b X$ and $D = \log_b Y$, which expression is equivalent to $\log_b\left(\dfrac{X^2}{Y^3}\right)$?

(A) $2C + 3D$ (C) $C^2 - D^3$

(B) $C^2 D^3$ (D) $2C - 3D$

44. Consider the following three statements: One pax is worth five pexes. One pex is worth two pyxes. One pix is worth four pyxes. Which of the following shows the correct order of the value of each of these, from lowest to highest?

(A) pyx, pex, pax, pix

(B) pyx, pix, pax, pex

(C) pyx, pix, pex, pax

(D) pyx, pex, pix, pax

45. What is the measure to the nearest degree of the acute angle between the vectors $2\mathbf{i} + \mathbf{j}$ and $2\mathbf{i} + 5\mathbf{j}$?

(A) 42°   (C) 50°

(B) 46°   (D) 54°

46. In $\triangle PQR$, $PQ = 5$, $PR = 6$, and the area of the triangle is 14. Given that $\angle P$ is an obtuse angle, what is the measure to the nearest degree of $\angle P$?

(A) 121°   (C) 111°

(B) 116°   (D) 106°

47. Which rational function has only one real zero and a domain of all numbers except zero?

(A) $f(x) = \dfrac{3x^2 + 12}{x^2 + x}$

(B) $g(x) = \dfrac{3x^2 + 12x + 12}{x^2}$

(C) $h(x) = \dfrac{3x^2 - 12}{x^2 + x}$

(D) $k(x) = \dfrac{3x^2 + 12x - 12}{x^2}$

48. The circumference of a cylinder is 16π. If the height is 12, what is the volume?

(A) 768π (C) 384π

(B) 576π (D) 192π

49. For a standard normal curve, the area to the right of $z = 0.7$ is exactly the same as which one of the following?

(A) Area to the left of $z = 0.3$

(B) Area to the left of $z = -0.3$

(C) Area to the right of $z = -0.7$

(D) Area to the left of $z = -0.7$

50. Sylvia wishes to show her class a quick way, using a graphing calculator, to find the possible rational roots of the equation $x^3 - x^2 - 34x - 56 = 0$. Let p represent the coefficient of x^3 and let q represent the constant term. Then she should tell her students to do which of the following?

(A) Compose a list of factors in which $\dfrac{p}{q} = \dfrac{-56}{1}$

and input those factors into the Table function of the graphing calculator.

(B) Compose a list of factors in which $\dfrac{p}{q} = \dfrac{1}{-56}$

and input those factors into the Table function of the graphing calculator.

(C) Compose a list of factors in which $\dfrac{p}{q} = \dfrac{-56}{1}$

and use synthetic division to assess the rational roots of the equation. Calculations should be double-checked in the calculator.

(D) Compose a list of factors in which $\dfrac{p}{q} = \dfrac{1}{-56}$

and use synthetic division to assess the rational roots of the equation. Calculations should be double-checked in the calculator.

51. What is the average rate of change for $p(x) = x^2 - x - 7$ over the closed interval $[2,6]$?

(A) 4.5   (C) 6.5

(B) 5   (D) 7

52. Martina considers the following four statements.

a) There are four prime numbers between 1 and 10.

b) There are four prime numbers between 10 and 20.

c) There are two prime numbers between 20 and 30.

d) There are two prime numbers between 30 and 40.

Based on these statements, she concludes that there is always an even number of prime numbers between any two consecutive multiples of 10. Which of the following groups of numbers would offer a counterexample?

(A) Integers between 80 and 90

(B) Integers between 70 and 80

(C) Integers between 60 and 70

(D) Integers between 50 and 60

53. What is the length to the nearest tenth of the curve $f(x) = \dfrac{3}{2}x^2 - 2x$ on the closed interval $[2,5]$?

(A) 40.5   (C) 30.8

(B) 35.6   (D) 25.7

54. The line segment with endpoints $(2,7)$ and $(-6,1)$ is rotated $90°$ clockwise. If M is the midpoint of the original line segment, what are the coordinates of M'?

    (A) $(-4,-2)$ (C) $(2,-4)$

    (B) $(4,2)$ (D) $(-2,4)$

55. What is the nature of the angles that represent the solutions for the equation $2\cos x + 3\sin 2x = 0$?

    (A) Two quadrantal, one in the second quadrant, and one in the third quadrant

    (B) One quadrantal, one in the first quadrant, and one in the second quadrant

    (C) Two quadrantal, one in the third quadrant, and one in the fourth quadrant

    (D) One quadrantal, one in the first quadrant, and one in the fourth quadrant

56. For the function $h(x) = x^3 + 2x^2 - 1$, what is the equation of the tangent line at $x = -2$?

    (A) $y = 4x + 7$ (C) $y = -4x + 9$

    (B) $y = 4x + 5$ (D) $y = -4x + 3$

57. The probability that event M will occur is 0.24 and the probability that event N will occur is 0.42. If the probability that at least one of M and N will occur is 0.57, what is the probability that both M and N will occur?

    (A) 0.04   (C) 0.30

    (B) 0.09   (D) 0.39

58. A pyramid with a square base has a total surface area of 144 square inches. If the lateral height is 9 inches, what is the perimeter of the base in inches?

    (A) 6   (C) 24

    (B) 12   (D) 48

59. What is the equation of the slant asymptote of $g(x) = \dfrac{5x^3 - 4x^2 + 3x + 2}{x^2 + x - 2}$?

    (A) $y = 5x - 1$ (C) $y = 5x - 9$

    (B) $y = 5x + 1$ (D) $y = 5x + 9$

60. You are given the information that for a non-zero integer x, $\dfrac{3x + 6}{x}$ is a positive integer. Which one of the following approaches would be best in order to find the value of x?

    (A) $\dfrac{3x + 6}{x} = m$, where m is an integer.

    (B) $\dfrac{3x + 6}{x} = \dfrac{m}{n}$, where m is divisible by n.

    (C) $\dfrac{3x + 6}{x} = \dfrac{3x}{x} + \dfrac{6}{x}$

    (D) $\dfrac{3x + 6}{x} = \dfrac{3(x + 2)}{x}$

61. In the diagram shown below, $ABCD$ is an isosceles trapezoid. If $DE = 50$, which one of the following represents the area of $ABCD$?

    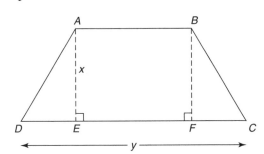

    (A) $(x)(y - 50)$ (C) $\left(\dfrac{1}{2}\right)(x + y + 100)$

    (B) $(x)(y + 50)$ (D) $\left(\dfrac{1}{2}\right)(x)(y - 100)$

62. From a room of 22 people with a mean weight of 125 pounds, Sam and Lisa leave. The mean weight of the remaining people is 121 pounds. If Lisa weighs two-thirds as much as Sam, what is Lisa's weight?

    (A) 134 pounds   (C) 130 pounds

    (B) 132 pounds   (D) 128 pounds

63. The lowest range value of the graph of $y = A\sin 3x + B$ is 9. Given that $A > 0$, which one of the following must be true?

    (A) $B - A = 9$ (C) $A - B = 6$

    (B) $B + A = -9$ (D) $A + B = 6$

64. The point $(-5,1)$ belongs to the graph of the function $y = k(x)$. Which point must belong to the graph of the function $y = 4[k(x-1)]$?

(A) $(-6,4)$ (C) $(-20,2)$

(B) $(-4,4)$ (D) $(-20,0)$

65. Which statement concerning an isosceles triangle can be solved for a unique solution?

(A) One of the angles is 45 degrees. Find the measures of the other two interior angles.

(B) One of the two acute angles is 60 degrees, find the measure of the other two angles.

(C) One of the angles is 120 degrees, find the measures of the other two angles.

(D) The difference of two interior angles is 20 degrees. Find the measures of all three angles.

66. The area of a parallelogram is 28. Which group of coordinates could represent the locations of the vertices?

(A) (0,0), (28,0), (29,4), (1,4)

(B) (0,0), (4,0), (5,14), (1,14)

(C) (1,4), (8,4), (11,8), (4,8)

(D) (1,4), (15,4), (3,8), (17, 8)

67. Rochelle ran a race in which her time was recorded as 51.27 seconds. Ray ran this same race and his time was recorded as 51.83 seconds. Both of their times were actually measured with a stopwatch that shows time in thousandths of a second. What would be the <u>maximum</u> difference between their running times if the results of the stopwatch were used?

(A) 0.575 seconds   (C) 0.565 seconds

(B) 0.569 seconds   (D) 0.551 seconds

68. Which equation has only one real answer?

(A) $\sqrt{1-5x} = x-3$

(B) $\sqrt{5x+34} = x+2$

(C) $\sqrt{x^2+4x+1} = x+3$

(D) $\sqrt{2x^2-10x+44} = x+2$

69. What is the multiplicative inverse of $\begin{pmatrix} 9 & 3 \\ 2 & 1 \end{pmatrix}$?

(A) $\begin{pmatrix} \dfrac{1}{3} & -\dfrac{2}{3} \\ -1 & 3 \end{pmatrix}$ (C) $\begin{pmatrix} -1 & 3 \\ \dfrac{1}{3} & -\dfrac{2}{3} \end{pmatrix}$

(B) $\begin{pmatrix} -1 & \dfrac{1}{3} \\ 3 & -\dfrac{2}{3} \end{pmatrix}$ (D) $\begin{pmatrix} \dfrac{1}{3} & -1 \\ -\dfrac{2}{3} & 3 \end{pmatrix}$

70. If $\left(x^2 + \dfrac{4}{x^2}\right) = 20$, which expression has a value of 16?

(A) $\left(x - \dfrac{2}{x}\right)$ (C) $\left(x - \dfrac{2}{x}\right)^2$

(B) $\left(x + \dfrac{2}{x}\right)$ (D) $\left(x + \dfrac{2}{x}\right)^2$

71. Look at the diagram below, in which $\overline{LM} \perp \overline{MN}$ and $\overline{MK} \perp \overline{LN}$.

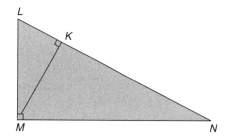

$LN = 75$ and $\overline{KN}$ is four times the length of $\overline{LK}$. What is the area of $\triangle LMN$?

(A) 937.5   (C) 1345

(B) 1125   (D) 1406.25

72. In the figure below, P is the center of the circle and $\overline{RS}$ is a diameter.

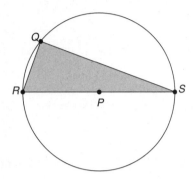

If the circumference of the circle is 20π and the length of $\overline{QS}$ is three times the length of $\overline{QR}$, what is the value to the nearest hundredth of QS?

(A) 18.96   (C) 12.64

(B) 15.48   (D) 10.16

73. In how many different ways can all the letters of the word RESERVED be arranged in a sequence of eight letters?

(A) 40,320   (C) 6720

(B) 10,080   (D) 3360

74. How much larger is each angle of a regular octagon than each angle of a regular 20-sided figure?

(A) 12°   (C) 22°

(B) 17°   (D) 27°

75. Which is the best approach to teaching how to solve a literal equation that contains two or more variables?

(A) Treat all but one of the variables as constants

(B) Discuss that such equations have infinite solutions.

(C) Try to cancel one of the variables using the algebraic principles.

(D) Assign all but one variable a value of 1.

76. The diagram shown below consists of a triangle inside a trapezoid.

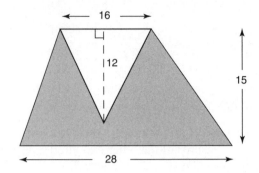

What is the area of the shaded region?

(A) 246   (C) 222

(B) 234   (D) 210

77. The graph of the circle $(x-3)^2 + (y-5)^2 = r^2$ intersects each of the x and y axes twice. Which of the following is a valid conclusion?

(A) $r^2 > 25$ (C) $9 < r^2 < 16$

(B) $16 < r^2 < 25$ (D) $r^2 < 9$

78. A triangle with an area of 27 lies completely inside a rectangle. The probability is 0.20 that a randomly selected point inside the rectangle also lies inside the triangle. If the width of the rectangle is 10, what is the perimeter of the rectangle?

(A) 135   (C) 47

(B) 54   (D) 13.5

79. Working alone, Amy can paint a room in five hours. Working with Matt, the two of them can paint this room in three hours. Suppose Matt decides to paint this room by himself. If he starts painting at 2:00PM, at what time will he finish?

(A) 6:00PM   (C) 8:30PM

(B) 7:00PM   (D) 9:30PM

80. Scientific calculators are becoming an inevitable tool in all math calculations due to their accuracy and speed. Which problem can be used to convince students that mastering algebraic principles and doing calculations manually can be just as effective as using a calculator?

    (A) $2001^2 + 2000^2$ (C) $2001 + 2000^2$

    (B) $2001^2 - 2000^2$ (D) $2001^2 + 2000$

81. Given the equation of a parabola in the form $(x - h)^2 = 4p(y - k)$, what is the distance between the focus and the directrix?

    (A) $8p$ (C) $2p$

    (B) $4p$ (D) p

82. In the diagram below, $\overrightarrow{QT}$ and $\overrightarrow{QV}$ are secants to circle P. If the measure of each of $\angle Q$ and $\overset{\frown}{RS}$ is x degrees, what is the measure of $\overset{\frown}{TV}$?

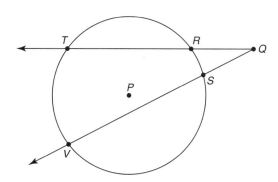

    (A) $360 - x$ degrees (C) $2x$ degrees

    (B) $3x$ degrees   (D) $180 - x$ degrees

83. A list of individual data consists of four 9s, seven 13s, and five 20s. What is the value of the first quartile?

    (A) 9   (C) 10.5

    (B) 9.5   (D) 11

84. *BDFHKL* is a regular hexagon circumscribed about circle P, as shown below. $\overline{PG}$ is an apothem. Each of $\overline{PK}$ and $\overline{PH}$ is a radius of the hexagon.

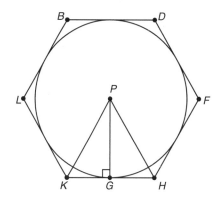

    If the perimeter of the hexagon is 60, what is the area of the circle?

    (A) 75π (C) 125π

    (B) 100π (D) 180π

85. A recursive sequence is given in which $a_1 = 0.5$, $a_2 = 2.5$, and $a_n = a_{n-1} + 2a_{n-2}$ for $n > 2$. What is the sum of the first four terms?

    (A) 13   (C) 15

    (B) 14   (D) 16

86. A glide reflection is performed on point Q, which has coordinates $(0, 5)$. First the translation vector $6\mathbf{i} - 3\mathbf{j}$ is applied to create the point Q', then Q' is reflected across the y-axis. The final point is called Q''. What are the coordinates of Q''?

    (A) $(-6, 2)$ (C) $(6, -2)$

    (B) $(6, 2)$ (D) $(-6, -2)$

87. If $\cos\theta = 0.25$ and θ is <u>not</u> in the first quadrant, what is the value of $\sin\theta$?

    (A) $\dfrac{\sqrt{15}}{4}$ (C) $-\dfrac{\sqrt{15}}{4}$

    (B) $\dfrac{\sqrt{17}}{4}$ (D) $-\dfrac{\sqrt{17}}{4}$

88. One cube root of Z is $(\sqrt[3]{2})(\cos 290° + i \sin 290°)$. Which one of the following represents another cube root of Z?

    (A) $(\sqrt[3]{2})(\cos 250° + i \sin 250°)$

    (B) $(\sqrt[3]{2})(\cos 170° + i \sin 170°)$

    (C) $(\sqrt[3]{2})(\cos 130° + i \sin 130°)$

    (D) $(\sqrt[3]{2})(\cos 80° + i \sin 80°)$

89. Helium is entering a spherical balloon at a constant rate of 2 cubic inches per minute. At what rate is the radius changing instantaneously when the radius is 5 inches?

    (A) $\dfrac{1}{100\pi}$

    (C) $\dfrac{4\pi}{25}$

    (B) $\dfrac{1}{50\pi}$

    (D) $\dfrac{8\pi}{25}$

90. Which triple has the <u>largest</u> greatest common factor?

    (A) 16, 30, 36

    (C) 8, 20, 28

    (B) 12, 21, 33

    (D) 6, 42, 49

Answer Key Practice Test 2

Number	Answer	Chapter	Competency
1	B	5	Functions
2	B	16	Probability Concepts and Applications
3	A	13	Applications of Euclidean Geometry to Circles and Composite Figures
4	D	2	Complex Number System
5	A	14	Coordinate, Transformational, and Vector Geometry
6	B	12	Axioms, Properties, and Theorems of Euclidean Geometry
7	D	4	Sequences and Series
8	C	17	Probability Distributions, Sampling, and Statistical Inference
9	D	16	Probability Concepts and Applications
10	D	19	Mathematical Connections
11	A	17	Probability Distributions, Sampling, and Statistical Inference
12	D	2	Complex Number System
13	D	10	Differential and Integral Calculus
14	C	8	Exponential and Logarithmic Functions
15	A	5	Functions
16	A	4	Sequences and Series
17	B	7	Rational and Radical Functions
18	D	15	Graphical and Numerical Techniques to Analyze Data
19	C	3	Number Theory
20	A	19	Mathematical Connections
21	D	17	Probability Distributions, Sampling, and Statistical Inference
22	C	9	Trigonometric and Circular Functions
23	D	15	Graphical and Numerical Techniques to Analyze Data
24	B	17	Probability Distributions, Sampling, and Statistical Inference
25	C	12	Axioms, Properties, and Theorems of Euclidean Geometry
26	C	10	Differential and Integral Calculus
27	B	5	Functions
28	B	1	Real Number System
29	D	12	Axioms, Properties, and Theorems of Euclidean Geometry
30	B	19	Mathematical Connections
31	D	9	Trigonometric and Circular Functions

Number	Answer	Chapter	Competency
32	B	3	Number Theory
33	C	10	Differential and Integral Calculus
34	D	1	Real Number System
35	D	2	Complex Number System
36	B	15	Graphical and Numerical Techniques to Analyze Data
37	C	8	Exponential and Logarithmic Functions
38	A	10	Differential and Integral Calculus
39	A	17	Probability Distributions, Sampling, and Statistical Inference
40	C	19	Mathematical Connections
41	C	1	Real Number System
42	A	5	Functions
43	D	8	Exponential and Logarithmic Functions
44	D	18	Mathematical Reasoning and Problem Solving
45	A	2	Complex Number System
46	C	11	Measurement in Geometry
47	B	7	Rational and Radical Functions
48	A	11	Measurement in Geometry
49	D	17	Probability Distributions, Sampling, and Statistical Inference
50	B	19	Mathematical Connections
51	D	10	Differential and Integral Calculus
52	B	18	Mathematical Reasoning and Problem Solving
53	D	11	Measurement in Geometry
54	B	14	Coordinate, Transformational, and Vector Geometry
55	C	9	Trigonometric and Circular Functions
56	A	10	Differential and Integral Calculus
57	B	16	Probability Concepts and Applications
58	C	11	Measurement in Geometry
59	C	7	Rational and Radical Functions
60	C	20	Mathematical Learning, Instruction, and Assessment
61	A	6	Linear and Quadratic Functions
62	B	15	Graphical and Numerical Techniques to Analyze Data
63	A	9	Trigonometric and Circular Functions
64	B	5	Functions
65	C	20	Mathematical Learning, Instruction, & Assessment
66	C	14	Coordinate, Transformational, and Vector Geometry
67	B	15	Graphical and Numerical Techniques to Analyze Data
68	B	7	Rational and Radical Functions

69	D	3	Number Theory
70	C	20	Mathematical Learning, Instruction, and Assessment
71	B	12	Axioms, Properties, and Theorems of Euclidean Geometry
72	A	6	Linear and Quadratic Functions
73	D	16	Probability Concepts and Applications
74	D	13	Applications of Euclidean Geometry to Circles and Composite Figures
75	A	20	Mathematical Learning, Instruction, and Assessment
76	B	13	Applications of Euclidean Geometry to Circles and Composite Figures
77	A	14	Coordinate, Transformational, and Vector Geometry
78	C	16	Probability Concepts and Applications
79	D	6	Linear and Quadratic Functions
80	B	20	Mathematical Learning, Instruction, and Assessment
81	C	14	Coordinate, Transformational, and Vector Geometry
82	B	13	Applications of Euclidean Geometry to Circles and Composite Figures
83	D	15	Graphical and Numerical Techniques to Analyze Data
84	A	13	Applications of Euclidean Geometry to Circles and Composite Figures
85	C	4	Sequences and Series
86	A	14	Coordinate, Transformational, and Vector Geometry
87	C	9	Trigonometric and Circular Functions
88	B	2	Complex Number System
89	B	10	Differential and Integral Calculus
90	C	3	Number Theory

Practice Test 2 Progress Chart

Real Number System

28	34	41

___/3

Complex Number System

4	12	35	45	88

___/5

Number Theory

19	32	69	90

___/4

Sequences and Series

7	16	85

___/3

Functions

1	15	27	42	64

___/5

Linear and Quadratic Functions

61	72	79

___/3

Rational and Radical Functions

17	47	59	68

___/4

Exponential and Logarithmic Functions

14	37	43

___/3

Trigonometric and Circular Functions

22	31	55	63	87

__/5

Differential and Integral Calculus

13	26	33	38	51	56	89

__/7

Measurement in Geometry

46	48	53	58

__/4

Axioms, Properties, and Theorems of Euclidean Geometry

6	25	29	71

__/4

Applications of Euclidean Geometry to Circles and Composite Figures

3	74	76	82	84

__/5

Coordinate, Transformational, and Vector Geometry

5	54	66	77	81	86

__/6

Graphical and Numerical Techniques to Analyze Data

18	23	36	62	67	83

__/6

Probability Concepts and Applications

2	9	57	73	78

__/5

Probability Distributions, Sampling, and Statistical Inference

8	11	21	24	39	49

__/6

Mathematical Reasoning and Problem Solving

44   52   __/2

Mathematical Connections

10   20   30   40   50   __/5

Mathematical Learning, Instruction, and Assessment

60   65   70   75   80   __/5

Total   __/90

Detailed Solutions

1. (B)

$f(x) = 10 - 3x$ does not satisfy the conditions of being either even or odd. In addition, it is one-to-one since each x value corresponds to only one $f(x)$ value and vice versa. Answer choices (A) and (C) are even functions. Answer choice (D) is not one-to-one; for example $(0, 0)$ and $(1, 0)$ belong to the graph of $f(x) = x^3 - 2x^2 + x$.

2. (B)

Any one of the four odd numbers may appear on each roll, so the number of outcomes is $(4)(4) = 16$.

3. (A)

$90 = (AJ)(JE) = (CJ)(JG)$. Since $CJ > AJ$, the possible sets of values of CJ and JG are: a) 6 and 15, and b) 9 and 10. Finally, since $CJ < JG$, the only allowable values of CJ are 6 and 9.

4. (D)

An angle of $120°$ forms a $30°-60°-90°$ triangle in quadrant II, so the x-coordinate is negative and the y-coordinate is positive. The horizontal length is $\frac{8}{2} = 4$ and the vertical length is $\frac{8}{2}\sqrt{3} = 4\sqrt{3}$. Thus, the rectangular coordinates are $-4 + 4i\sqrt{3}$.

5. (A)

If $a > b$, then $\frac{x^2}{b^2} + \frac{y^2}{a^2} = 1$ represents the equation of an ellipse with a vertical major axis with a length of $2a$. Given that $2a = 12$, it follows that $a^2 = 36$. Only answer choice (A) has both 36 as the value of a^2 and has a value lower than 36 for b^2.

6. (B)

$\frac{GH}{9} = \frac{10}{3}$ and $\frac{GK}{3} = \frac{10}{3}$. So, $GH = 30$ and $GK = 10$. Thus, the area of $GHJK$ is 300.

7. (D)

The number of squares in the 20th diagram is $20^2 = 400$ and the number of squares in the tenth diagram is $10^2 = 100$. The difference is 300.

8. (C)

The probability of drawing a heart is 0.25. Thus, the TI − 83 calculator display should be binomcdf (7, 0.25,3), which is approximately 0.93.

9. (D)

Using the hypergeometric distribution, the required probability is $\frac{(_{10}C_3)(_5C_1)}{_{15}C_4} = \frac{(120)(600)}{1365} = \frac{40}{91}$.

10. (D)

The difference of squares, $a^2 - b^2$, can be used to calculate $(48)(52)$. $(50 - 2)(50 + 2) = 2500 - 4 = 2496$.

11. (A)

Since the desired scores lie between 182 and 209 inclusive, we want the percent of scores between the values of 181.5 and 209.5. Thus, your TI −83 display should be normalcdf (181.5, 209.5, 200, 15) ≈ 0.63.

12. (D)

The number $4 - i$ forms a triangle in quadrant IV in which $r = \sqrt{4^2 + 1^2} = \sqrt{17}$. Also, $\theta = \tan^{-1}\left(-\dfrac{1}{4}\right) \approx 346°$. Then $\left[\sqrt{17}(\cos 346° + i\sin 346°)\right]^4 = (289)(\cos 1384° + i\sin 1384°)$. But $1384°$ is equivalent to $(1384 - 360k)°$ for any integer k. In particular, if $k = 3$, then $(289)(\cos 1384° + i\sin 1384°)$ is equivalent to $(289)(\cos 304° + i\sin 304°)$.

13. (D)

The area under the parabola $f(x) = -x^2 + 16$ that is bounded by the x-axis is $\displaystyle\int_{-4}^{4}(-x^2 + 16)dx = \left(-\dfrac{x^3}{3} + 16x\right) = \left(-\dfrac{64}{3} + 64\right) - \left(\dfrac{64}{3} - 64\right) = 85.\overline{3}$.

The area of $\triangle ABC$ is $\left(\dfrac{1}{2}\right)(8)(16) = 64$.

Thus, the shaded area is $85.\overline{3} - 64 = 21.\overline{3}$.

14. (C)

$9000 = 1200e^{10r}$. Then $\ln 9000 = \ln 1200 + 10r$. Thus, $r = \dfrac{\ln 9000 - \ln 1200}{10} \approx 20.1\%$.

15. (A)

After following the four steps, $g(x) = \sqrt{2x - 5} + \dfrac{1}{2}$. Since the square root of any real number quantity must be nonnegative, $g(x) \geq \dfrac{1}{2}$. Only answer choice (A) has a value of at least $\dfrac{1}{2}$.

16. (A)

The sum of the terms of 15, 3, 0.6, 0.12,…. is $\dfrac{15}{1 - 0.2} = 18.75$.

17. (B)

There are two remaining unknown zeros. The conjugate of $5 + i$, which is $5 - i$, must be one of these zeros. The other zero must be a real number since conjugate zeros must come in pairs.

18. (D)

The mean of 25 numbers in a grouped distribution is the 12.5th number. Thus, the median is $39.5 + \left(\dfrac{3.5}{10}\right)(5) = 41.25$

19. (C)

If $x + 1 = -1$, then $x = -2$. Note that $18 - (-2)$ is divisible by 4.

20. (A)

For the bank that compounds monthly, the amount is given by the formula $A = P\left(1 + \dfrac{r}{n}\right)^{nt}$. Then $A = 1000\left(1 + \dfrac{.043}{12}\right)^{12 \cdot 1} \approx \$1043.86$. For the bank that compounds continuously, the amount is given by the formula $A = Pe^{rt}$. Then $A = 1000e^{.043 \times 1} \approx \$1043.94$. Thus, the difference is $\$1,043.94 - \$1,043.86 = \$0.08$.

21. (D)

This is a geometric distribution in which $p = \dfrac{1}{6}$. Thus, the required probability is $\left(\dfrac{1}{6}\right)\left(\dfrac{5}{6}\right)^4 \approx 0.08$.

22. (C)

The phase shift to the right of π units means that $\dfrac{C}{B} = \pi$. The period of this function is 4π, so $\dfrac{2\pi}{B} = 4\pi$. Solving this equation, we get $B = \dfrac{1}{2}$. Thus, $\dfrac{C}{1/2} = \pi$, so $C = \dfrac{\pi}{2}$.

23. (D)

$Y = 4X - 2$. Then the variance of Y is $4^2 = 16$ times the variance of X. Thus, the variance of X is $\left(\dfrac{1}{16}\right)$ (the variance of Y) $= \dfrac{9}{16}$.

24. (B)

If either np or $(n)(1-p)$ is less than 5, than the normal distribution is not a good approximation for the binomial distribution. In answer choice (B), $(300)(1 - 0.99) < 5$.

25. (C)

If the measure of $\angle U$ is 69°, then the measure of $\angle V$ is $180° - 69° - 42° = 69°$. So triangle TUV would be isosceles and scalene. Note that $\angle U$ cannot be 42°, since this would mean that $\angle V$ would be $180° - 42° - 42° = 96°$, an obtuse angle.

26. (C)

$4x^2 + 3x - 10 = (4x - 5)(x + 2)$. After canceling the factor $x + 2$ from the numerator and denominator, we can write $\lim_{x \to -2} \dfrac{4x^2 + 3x - 10}{x + 2} = \lim_{x \to -2}(4x - 5) = -13$.

27. (B)

Replace $h(x)$ by x and replace x by y. Then $x = \sqrt{\dfrac{3y - 2}{5}}$, which becomes $x^2 = \dfrac{3y - 2}{5}$. Multiplying both sides by 5 leads to $5x^2 = 3y - 2$, which simplifies to $y = \dfrac{5x^2 + 2}{3}$. The last step is to replace y by $h^{-1}(x)$.

28. (B)

By the Associative Law of Multiplication, $(6 \times 4) \times 2 = 6 \times (4 \times 2)$. Then, by the Commutative Law of Multiplication, $4 \times 2 = 2 \times 4$.

29. (D)

The ratio of their corresponding linear dimensions is $\sqrt{\dfrac{9}{25}} = \dfrac{3}{5}$, so the ratio of their volumes must be $\left(\dfrac{3}{5}\right)^3 = \dfrac{27}{125}$. Let v represent the volume of the larger cone. Then $\dfrac{27}{125} = \dfrac{54}{v}$, so $v = 250$.

30. (B)

Go to L_1 and L_2 in your graphing calculator and enter attendance and temperature data, respectively. Proceed to the STAT menu and select CALC, then scroll down to LinReg $(ax + b)$ and press ENTER. The correlation coefficient, r, is 0.91.

31. (D)

$$PR = (18)(\sin 44°) \approx 12.5.$$

Thus, $QR = \dfrac{12.5}{\tan 20°} \approx 34.3$.

32. (B)

From the left side of the equation, we determine that $4c = 8$, $4d = 12$, $5a = 40$, and $5b = 20$. Thus, $a + b - c - d = 8 + 4 - 2 - 3 = 7$.

33. (C)

The limit of $g(x)$ does not exist at $x = 1$, since there exists a vertical asymptote. Even though $g(x)$ is not defined at $x = -1$, the limit of $g(x)$ as x approaches -1 is zero.

34. (D)

The number 0.13113111311113…. shows a pattern of an incremental increasing number of 1's between 3's, but this pattern does not repeat. Note that answer choice (A), written as a decimal, has no pattern.

35 (D)

Since $\sqrt{(-3)^2 + (4)^2} = 5$, $-\dfrac{3}{5}\mathbf{i} + \dfrac{4}{5}\mathbf{j}$ represents the unit vector in the same direction as $-3\mathbf{i} + 4\mathbf{j}$. Thus, the unit vector in the opposite direction is $\dfrac{3}{5}\mathbf{i} - \dfrac{4}{5}\mathbf{j}$.

36. (B)

The boxplot of a negatively skewed distribution shows a longer tail on left than on the right. The third quartile is illustrated by the number furthest to the right in the box, which is 92. Note that answer choice (D) is wrong because the number 80 represents the median, not the mean.

37. (C)

Let A_0 represent the initial amount. The substance's half-life is eight hours, so $20 = (A_0)\left(\dfrac{1}{2}\right)^{10/8} \approx 0.42A_0$. Thus, $A_0 \approx 47.6$ grams.

38. (A)

A discontinuity of a rational function is determined by values of x for which the denominator is zero. In answer choice (A), a denominator of $x - 4$ becomes zero when $x = 4$. Note that the discontinuities for answer choice (B) are 0 and 4.

39. (A)

Press "Stat," scroll to "Tests," press $\underline{1}$, then enter 200 for μ_0, enter 30 for σ, enter 206 for x, enter 100 for n, highlight $\mu > \mu_0$, then press "Calculate." The p value will be approximately 0.023, and since $0.023 > 0.01$, the claim cannot be rejected.

40. (C)

Divide the area of the bull's-eye by the area of the entire target. The area of bull's-eye is 9π. The radius of the entire target is 23, so its area is 529π. Thus, $\dfrac{9\pi}{529\pi} \approx .02$.

41. (C)

$(-0.8)^{-5} = \dfrac{1}{(-0.8)^5}$, which translates as "the reciprocal of -0.8 raised to the power of 5."

42. (A)

$f(-2) = -(-2)^2 + (-2) = -6$, so $g[f(-2)] = g(-6) = (-6)^3 = -216$.

43. (D)

$$\log_b\left(\frac{X^2}{Y^3}\right) =$$

$$\log_b X^2 - \log_b Y^3 = 2\log_b X - 3\log_b Y = 2C - 3D.$$

44. (D)

Suppose a pyx were worth one cent. Then one pex would be worth two cents and one pix would be worth four cents. In addition, one pax would be worth ten cents. Thus, the correct order of their values from lowest to highest are: pyx, pex, pix, pax.

45. (A)

$(2\mathbf{i} + \mathbf{j}) \bullet (2\mathbf{i} + 5\mathbf{j}) = (2)(2) + (1)(5) = 9.$ Also,

$(|2\mathbf{i} + \mathbf{j}|)(|2\mathbf{i} + 5\mathbf{j}|) = \left(\sqrt{5}\right)\left(\sqrt{29}\right) = \sqrt{145}$. Thus,

$\theta = \cos^{-1}\left(\dfrac{9}{\sqrt{145}}\right) \approx 42°.$

46. (C)

$14 = \left(\dfrac{1}{2}\right)(5)(6)(\sin\angle P).$ Then $\sin\angle P = \dfrac{14}{15}$,

which means that $\angle P = \sin^{-1}\left(\dfrac{14}{15}\right) \approx 111°.$ Note that

$\sin 69° \approx \dfrac{14}{15}$, but 69° is not an obtuse angle.

47. (B)

The function $g(x) = \dfrac{3x^2 + 12x + 12}{x^2}$ has a

domain of all numbers except zero. Its zeros are found by solving $3x^2 + 12x + 12 = (3)(x + 2)^2 = 0.$ The only zero is -2.

48. (A)

The radius must be 8, so the volume is $(\pi)(8^2)(12) = 768\pi$.

49. (D)

The area to the right of $z = 0.7$ is found by normalcdf $(0.7,\ 1 \times 10^{99},\ 0,\ 1) \approx 0.242$. This is the same answer as the area to the left of $z = -0.7$, which is found by normalcdf $(-1 \times 10^{99},\ -0.7,\ 0,\ 1)$.

50. (B)

$\dfrac{p}{q} = \dfrac{1}{-56}$ is equivalent to $\dfrac{q}{p} = \dfrac{-56}{1}$. By input-

ting the factors of $\dfrac{-56}{1}$ into the Table function of the

graphing calculator, the students will quickly discover the rational roots of the equation are $-2, -4$ and 7.

51. (D)

$p(2) = -5$ and $p(6) = 23$. The average rate of

change is $\dfrac{23 - (-5)}{6 - 2} = 7$.

52. (B)

Between 70 and 80, there are three prime numbers, namely 71, 73, and 79. For each of the other answer choices, there are two prime numbers.

53. (D)

$f'(x) = 3x - 2,$ so $1 + (f'(x))^2 = 9x^2 - 12x + 5$. Then using the CALC feature on the TI-83 calculator, we determine $\displaystyle\int_2^5 \sqrt{9x^2 - 12x + 5}\,dx \approx 25.7$.

54. (B)

The coordinates of M are $(-2, 4)$. A 90°- clockwise rotation changes a point with coordinates of (x, y) to its image with coordinates of $(y, -x)$. Thus, the image of $(-2, 4)$ is $(4, 2)$.

55. (C)

Substitute with the identity $\sin 2x = 2\sin x \cos x$. Then $2\cos x + (3)(2\sin x \cos x) = 0$. This leads to $(2\cos x)(1 + 3\sin x) = 0$. If $2\cos x = 0$, then $x = \cos^{-1}(0) = 90°$ and $270°$. If $1 + 3\sin x = 0$, then $x = \sin^{-1}\left(-\dfrac{1}{3}\right) \approx 199°$ and $341°$. Thus, there are two quadrantal angles, one angle in the third quadrant, and one angle in the fourth quadrant.

56. (A)

When $x = -2$, $h(x) = (-2)^3 + 2(-2)^2 - 1 = -1$. So, $(-2, -1)$ lies on the graph of $h(x)$. $dy/dx = 3x^2 + 4x$. At $x = -2$, $dy/dx = 3(-2)^2 + 4(-2) = 4$. Then $y = 4x + b$. By substituting $(-2, -1)$, $-1 = (4)(-2) + b$, so $b = 7$. Thus, the equation of the tangent line is $y = 4x + 7$.

57. (B)

The probability that both events will occur is $0.24 + 0.42 - 0.57 = 0.09$.

58. (C)

Using the total surface area formula for a pyramid with a square base, $144 = (2)(s)(9) + s^2$, where s is the length of a side of the base. This equation simplifies to $s^2 + 18s - 144 = 0$, which factors as $(s + 24)(s - 6) = 0$. Then $s = 6$, so the perimeter of the base is 24.

59. (C)

By long division, $\dfrac{5x^3 - 4x^2 + 3x + 2}{x^2 + x - 2} = 5x - 9 + \dfrac{22x - 16}{x^2 + x - 2}$. Thus, the slant asymptote is $y = 5x - 9$.

60. (C)

Using the decomposition method, we get $\dfrac{3x + 6}{x} = \dfrac{3x}{x} + \dfrac{6}{x}$. This yields $3 + \dfrac{6}{x}$. Then, x must be 1, 2, 3, or 6 in order for $3 + \dfrac{6}{x}$ to be a positive integer.

61. (A)

$FC = DE = 50$ and $AB = FE = y - 50 - 50 = y - 100$.

The area of trapezoid $ABCD = \left(\dfrac{1}{2}\right)(AE)(AB + DC)$ $= \left(\dfrac{1}{2}\right)(x)(y - 100 + y) = (x)(y - 50)$.

62. (B)

The total weight of all 22 people is $(22)(125) = 2750$ pounds. Since the mean weight of 20 people is 121 pounds, the combined weight of Lisa and Sam is $2750 - (20)(121) = 330$ pounds. Let $2x$ represent Lisa's weight and let $3x$ represent Sam's weight. Then $5x = 330$, so $x = 66$. Thus, Lisa's weight is 132 pounds.

63. (A)

If $A > 0$, then the lowest point on the graph of $y = A\sin 3x + B$ is represented by $B - A$. Thus, $B - A = 9$.

64. (B)

The point $(-5 + 1, 1) = (-4, 1)$ must lie on the graph of the function $y = k(x - 1)$. Thus, for the function $y = 4[k(x - 1)]$, a point which must lie on its graph is given by $(-4, 4)$.

65. (C)

If one of the angles equal to 120 degrees, then this must represent the vertex angle. Thus, each of the other two angles has a measure of $\dfrac{180 - 120}{2} = 30°$.

66. (C)

In answer choice (C), the length is $8 - 1 = 7$ and the height is $8 - 4 = 4$. The area is $(7)(4) = 28$.

67. (B)

In order to maximize the difference in their running times, we note that the actual fastest time for Rochelle would be 51.265 seconds, while the actual slowest time for Ray would be 51.834 seconds. Then $51.834 - 51.265 = 0.569$ seconds.

68. (B)

For the equation $\sqrt{5x + 34} = x + 2$, the only real answer is 6. (The number -5 does not check.) For answer choices (A) and (C), there are no real answers. For answer choice (D), the two real answers are 4 and 10.

69. (D)

The determinant of $\begin{pmatrix} 9 & 3 \\ 2 & 1 \end{pmatrix}$ is $(9)(1) - (3)(2) = 3$,

so the inverse matrix is $\left(\dfrac{1}{3}\right) \times \begin{pmatrix} 1 & -3 \\ -2 & 9 \end{pmatrix} = \begin{pmatrix} \dfrac{1}{3} & -1 \\ -\dfrac{2}{3} & 3 \end{pmatrix}$.

70. (C)

Rewrite $\left(x^2 + \dfrac{4}{x^2}\right) = 20$ as follows:

$\left(x^2 - 4 + \dfrac{4}{x^2}\right) = 20 - 4$. Factoring the left side, we get

$\left(x - \dfrac{2}{x}\right)^2 = 16$.

71. (B)

Let x represent LK and let $4x$ represent KN. Then $x + 4x = 75$, so $LK = 15$ and $KN = 60$. Also, $\dfrac{15}{MK} = \dfrac{MK}{60}$,

so $MK = \sqrt{900} = 30$. Thus, the area of $\triangle LMN$ is

$\left(\dfrac{1}{2}\right)(75)(30) = 1125$.

72. (A)

Let x represent QR and let $3x$ represent QS. Since QRS is a right triangle, $x^2 + (3x)^2 = 20^2$. This equation simplifies to $10x^2 = 400$, so that $x = \sqrt{40} \approx 6.32$. Thus, $QS \approx 18.96$.

73. (D)

There are a total of eight letters, including two R's and three E's. The number of different arrangements is

$\dfrac{8!}{(2!)(3!)} = 3360$.

74. (D)

Each angle of a regular 20-sided figure is $\left(\dfrac{18}{20}\right)(180)° = 162°$ and each angle of a regular octagon

is $\left(\dfrac{6}{8}\right)(180)° = 135°$. Their difference is 27°.

75. (A)

The best approach is to treat all but one variable as constants. Then there will be only one "variable" in the problem, which should be isolated on one side of the equation.

76. (B)

The shaded area is $\left(\dfrac{1}{2}\right)(15)(16 + 28)$

$-\left(\dfrac{1}{2}\right)(16)(12) = 234$.

77. (A)

The center of the circle is located at (3,5). In order for the circle to intersect both axes twice, r must be greater than 5. Thus $r^2 > 25$.

78. (C)

0.20 is the ratio of the area of the triangle to the area of the rectangle, so the area of the rectangle is 135. Since the width is 10, the length must be 13.5. Thus, the perimeter of the rectangle is $(2)(13.5) + (2)(10) = 47$.

79. (D)

Let x represent the number of hours that Matt would need working alone. Then $\dfrac{3}{x} + \dfrac{3}{5} = 1$. This equation simplifies to $15 + 3x = 5x$. So, $x = 7.5$ hours. Thus, the time Matt will finish is 9:30PM.

80. (B)

Using the principle of the difference of two squares factoring, students can write $2001^2 - 2000^2$ as $(2001 - 2000)(2001 + 2000) = 1(4001) = 4001$.

81. (C)

Given $(x - h)^2 = 4p(y - k)$, the value of p represents the distance between the vertex and the focus or between the vertex and the directrix. Therefore, the distance between the focus and the directrix is twice p.

82. (B)

$\angle Q = \left(\dfrac{1}{2}\right)\left(\overset{\frown}{TV} - \overset{\frown}{RS}\right).$ By substitution,

$x = \left(\dfrac{1}{2}\right)\left(\overset{\frown}{TV} - x\right).$ Then $2x = \overset{\frown}{TV} - x$, so the measure

of $\overset{\frown}{TV}$ is $3x$ degrees.

83. (D)

There are 16 individual numbers, so the position of the first quartile is $\dfrac{16 + 2}{4} = 4.5$. Thus, the value of the first quartile is $\dfrac{9 + 13}{2} = 11$.

84. (A)

Each side of the hexagon must be 10. This is also the value of PH and PK, since $\triangle PKH$ is equilateral. Triangle PGK is a 30°-60°-90° right triangle in which $PG = 5\sqrt{3}$. Thus, the area of the circle is $\pi\left(5\sqrt{3}\right)^2 = 75\pi$.

85. (C)

$a_3 = 2.5 + (2)(0.5) = 3.5$ and $a_4 = 3.5 + (2)(2.5) = 8.5$. Thus, the sum of the first four terms is $0.5 + 2.5 + 3.5 + 8.5 = 15$.

86. (A)

The coordinates of Q' become $(6, 2)$. Upon reflecting across the y-axis, the coordinates of Q'' become $(-6, 2)$.

87. (C)

Since θ is not in the first quadrant and $\cos\theta > 0$, θ must be in the fourth quadrant. The reference triangle has a horizontal side of 1, a hypotenuse of 4, and a vertical side whose length is $\sqrt{4^2 - 1^2} = \sqrt{15}$. Thus, $\sin\theta = -\dfrac{\sqrt{15}}{4}$.

88. (B)

If $Z = r(\cos\theta + i\sin\theta)$, then its cube roots are

$Z = \sqrt[3]{r}\left[\cos\left(\dfrac{\theta}{3} + \dfrac{360k}{3}\right) + i\sin\left(\dfrac{\theta}{3} + \dfrac{360k}{3}\right)\right]$, with $k = 0$,

1, and 2. Since $\dfrac{\theta}{3} = 290°$, the other two angles must be $290° + 120° = 410°$ and $290° + 240° = 530°$. Furthermore, $410°$ is equivalent to $50°$ and $530°$ is $170°$.

89. (B)

$\dfrac{dV}{dt} = \left(\dfrac{dV}{dr}\right)\left(\dfrac{dr}{dt}\right)$. We are given that $\dfrac{dV}{dt} = 2$.

Since $V = \dfrac{4}{3}\pi r^3$, $\dfrac{dV}{dr} = 4\pi r^2$. When $r = 5$,

$\dfrac{dV}{dr} = 100\pi$. Then $2 = (100\pi)\left(\dfrac{dr}{dt}\right)$. Thus, $\dfrac{dr}{dt} = \dfrac{1}{50\pi}$.

90. (C)

For answer choice (C), the greatest common factor is 4. For each of answer choices (A), (B), and (D), the greatest common factor is 2, 3, and 1, respectively.

Index